Antisocial Behavior in School: Strategies and Best Practices

Antisocial Behavior in School: Strategies and Best Practices

Hill M. Walker
UNIVERSITY OF OREGON

Geoff Colvin
UNIVERSITY OF OREGON

Elizabeth Ramsey

Brooks/Cole Publishing Company
I(T)P™ An International Thomson Publishing Company

Pacific Grove • Albany • Bonn • Boston • Cincinnati • Detroit • London • Madrid • Melbourne
Mexico City • New York • Paris • San Francisco • Singapore • Tokyo • Toronto • Washington

Sponsoring Editor: *Vicki Knight*
Marketing Team: *Carolyn Crockett, Roxane Buck Ezcurra, and Margaret Parks*
Marketing Representative: *Tamy Stenquist*
Editorial Associate: *Lauri Banks Ataide*
Production Editor: *Laurel Jackson*
Production Assistant: *Tessa McGlasson*
Manuscript Editor: *Eve Lehmann*
Permissions Editor: *Elaine Jones*
Credits continue on page 479.
Interior Design: *Rick Chafian*
Interior Illustration: *Suffolk Technical Illustrators, Inc.*
Cover Design: *Roy R. Neuhaus and Robert J. Western*
Cover Photo: *David M. Grossman*
Art Coordinator: *Lisa Torri*
Photo Editor: *Kathleen Olson*
Indexer: *James Minkin*
Typesetting: *Weimer Graphics, Inc.*
Printing and Binding: *Malloy Lithographing, Inc.*

For more information, contact:

BROOKS/COLE PUBLISHING COMPANY
511 Forest Lodge Road
Pacific Grove, CA 93950
USA

International Thomson Publishing Europe
Berkshire House 168-173
High Holborn
London WC1V 7AA
England

Thomas Nelson Australia
102 Dodds Street
South Melbourne, 3205
Victoria, Australia

Nelson Canada
1120 Birchmount Road
Scarborough, Ontario
Canada M1K 5G4

International Thomson Editores
Campos Eliseos 385, Piso 7
Col. Polanco
11560 México D. F. México

International Thomson Publishing Gmbh
Königswinterer Strasse 418
53227 Bonn
Germany

International Thomson Publishing Asia
221 Henderson Road
#05-10 Henderson Building
Singapore 0315

International Thomson Publishing Japan
Hirakawacho Kyowa Building, 3F
2-2-1 Hirakawacho
Chiyoda-ku, Tokyo 102
Japan

Printed in the United States of America

10 9 8 7 6 5 4 3

Library of Congress Cataloging-in-Publication Data

Walker, Hill M.
Antisocial behavior in school: strategies and best practices / Hill M. Walker, Geoff Colvin, and Elizabeth Ramsey.
p. cm.
Includes bibliographical references and index.
ISBN 0-534-25644-9
1. School discipline—United States. 2. Problem children—Education—United States. 3. Conduct disorders in children—United States. 4. School violence—United States. I. Colvin, Geoffrey, [date]. II. Ramsey, Elizabeth, [date]. III. Title.
LB3012.W335 1994
371.5′8—dc20 94-24744
CIP

This book is dedicated to the pioneering efforts and world-class work of Jerry Patterson, John Reid, and their colleagues at the Oregon Social Learning Center in furthering our understanding of antisocial behavior patterns among children, youth, and families.

ABOUT THE AUTHORS

Collectively, the authors of this volume have over 50 years of experience in dealing with antisocial, aggressive students within school settings. In addition, each author has had varied experiences as researcher, teacher, and consultant in this area.

Hill M. Walker, Ph.D., has had an extensive research career in the area of school-related behavior disorders. His professional interests include the study of aggressive, acting-out behavior patterns in school; social skills assessment; training and curricular development; mainstreaming and social integration; and the development of comprehensive behavior-management packages for use in regular classroom and playground settings. Since 1984, he has been the principal investigator of a longitudinal follow-up study of antisocial and at-risk boys, in collaboration with Jerry Patterson and his associates of the Oregon Social Learning Center. Dr. Walker is also the author of *The Acting Out Child* and *The Walker Problem Behavior Identification Checklist.*

Geoff Colvin, Ph.D., is a nationally recognized behavioral consultant to school districts on best practices to use in working with acting-out students who exhibit severe levels of involvement. He has worked directly with educators in developing behavioral and academic intervention plans for such students for approximately 20 years. For five years, he was director of the Lane School for severely disturbed children and youth, an exemplary day-treatment school program serving 16 county school districts. In addition, Dr. Colvin is the author of *Managing Acting Out Behavior,* a video-based, staff inservice module for enhancing educators' skills in dealing with this population.

Elizabeth Ramsey, Ph.D., until recently, was a project coordinator at the Oregon Social Learning Center for the Linking the Interests of Families and Teachers (LIFT) project, a national center on preventing conduct disorders funded by the National Institute of Mental Health. Dr. Ramsey is currently developing a family-based program to complement *Second-Step: A Violence Prevention Curriculum* by the Committee for Children in Seattle, Washington. She holds a School Counseling Certificate and continues to consult with families and teachers who must deal with aggressive and acting-out children daily.

BRIEF CONTENTS

1 Antisocial Behavior Patterns in Children and Youth: Characteristics, Causes, and Outcomes *1*

2 Issues and Procedural Recommendations Regarding Effective Interventions for Antisocial Behavior in School *30*

3 The Acting-Out Behavior Cycle of Antisocial Students in the Classroom: A Conceptual Model *72*

4 Strategies for Managing the Phases of Acting-Out Behavior *96*

5 Establishing a Schoolwide Discipline Plan *120*

6 Instructing and Managing the Classroom Environment *152*

7 An Instructional Approach to Teaching Adaptive Behavior Patterns *170*

8 Instructing and Managing the Antisocial Student on the Playground *184*

9 Social Skills: Importance and Assessment *216*

10 Social Skills: Implementation and Generalization *238*

11 Parent Involvement in the Schooling of Antisocial Students *266*

12 Case-Study Applications of Best Practices with Antisocial Students *306*

13 School Violence, Gangs, and Safety: Toward Proactive Strategies *356*

Epilogue 386

Appendix A Empirical Foundations in Discriminating, Predicting, and Changing Aggressive, Antisocial Behavior in School and at Home *387*

Appendix B The Case of Judge Hargreaves: Society Is Failing Its Children, Forsaking Its Future *429*

Appendix C Generals in the War on School Violence *436*

CONTENTS

1 Antisocial Behavior Patterns in Children and Youth: Characteristics, Causes, and Outcomes *1*

Antisocial Behavior Defined *2*
The Prevalence of Antisocial Behavior and Conduct Disorder *3*
Diagnostic Classification of Conduct Disorder *4*
The Responsiveness of Conduct Disorder and Antisocial Behavior Patterns to Intervention *4*
The Stability of Antisocial Behavior and Conduct Disorder *5*
Conduct Disorder and Juvenile Delinquency *5*
School Adjustment, Conduct Disorder, and Antisocial Behavior *7*
Behavioral Characteristics and Correlates of Antisocial Behavior Patterns *9*
Classroom Behavior *13*
Playground Behavior *14*
Affective Status *16*
Long-Term Outcomes for Antisocial and At-Risk Boys *17*
Gender, Conduct Disorder, and Antisocial Behavior *17*
The Causes and Origins of Antisocial Behavior Patterns *18*
Pathways to Acquiring Antisocial Behavior Patterns and Conduct Disorder *19*
Antisocial Behavior and Violence *22*
A Perspective on Violence *23*
The Costs of Antisocial Behavior *23*
A Look to the Future *24*
Recommended Sources on Violence *29*
Study Questions *29*
Key Terms *29*

2 Issues and Procedural Recommendations Regarding Effective Interventions for Antisocial Behavior in School *30*

The School's Role in the Prevention and Remediation of Antisocial Behavior Patterns *33*
The Broader Societal Context and Influence Factors Affecting the Development of Antisocial Behavior *37*
Factors Affecting the Magnitude of Outcomes Achievable by School-Based Interventions *42*
Developmental Continuum of Service Delivery and Expected Outcomes for Antisocial Behavior Patterns *44*
Design and Application of Comprehensive, Coordinated Interventions Applied Early in a Child's School Career *46*
Early Screening and Identification of Antisocial Behavior Patterns *47*
Achenbach Case 49
Drummond Case 50
Walker, Severson, and Feil Case 53
Key Target Areas That Antisocial Interventions Should Address *55*
Universal and Selected Interventions for Addressing Antisocial Behavior Patterns in School *57*
Recommended Intervention Techniques for Use in Designing Interventions for Antisocial Behavior *59*
Guidelines for Implementing Best-Practice Intervention Procedures *61*
Generic Strategies 61
Implementation Recommendations 64
Program-Environment Fit or Match Considerations *67*
The NCTV Ten-Point Plan to Sweep Violence off TV and off Our Streets *68*
Conclusion *69*
Study Questions *70*
Key Terms *71*

3 The Acting-Out Behavior Cycle of Antisocial Students in the Classroom: A Conceptual Model *72*

Example of an Acting-Out Behavior Pattern Sequence *74*
Indicators of Agitation 78
Presence of an Escalating Behavioral Chain 78
Presence of Successive Interactions 80
Seven Phases in an Acting-Out Behavior Cycle *80*
Phase One: Calm 81
Phase Two: Triggers 82
Phase Three: Agitation 84
Phase Four: Acceleration 85

Phase Five: Peak 87
Phase Six: De-Escalation 87
Phase Seven: Recovery 88
Summary of Phases in the Acting-Out Cycle *89*
Illustration and Application *89*
Conclusion *89*
Study Questions *92*
Key Terms *94*

4 Strategies for Managing the Phases of Acting-Out Behavior *96*

Strategies for Each Phase of the Acting-Out Cycle *98*
Phase One: Calm 98
Phase Two: Triggers 103
Phase Three: Agitation 105
Phase Four: Acceleration 107
Phase Five: Peak 111
Phase Six: De-Escalation 113
Phase Seven: Recovery 114
Summary Form and Case Study *115*
Conclusion *115*
Study Questions *119*
Key Terms *119*

5 Establishing a Schoolwide Discipline Plan *120*

Research Findings and Best Practices for Schoolwide Discipline *123*
Discipline Is an Instrument 123
Proactive Approaches 123
Visible, Supportive Leadership from the Principal 123
Collegial Commitment 124
Staff Development and Effective Teacher-Training Practices 124
Setting High Expectations 124
Clear Communication between Administration and Staff 124
Strong, Positive School Climate 125
Interdisciplinary Cooperation and Collaboration 125
Clear, Functional Rules and Expectations 125
Data Management and Evaluation 125
Foundational Phases in the Design of an Effective Schoolwide Discipline Plan *126*
Phase 1: Formulate a Basic Direction for Establishing Expected Behavior and Managing Problem Behavior 126
Phase 2: Specify Schoolwide Expected Behaviors 128

Phase 3: Develop Procedures for Teaching Schoolwide Behavioral Expectations 129
Phase 4: Develop Procedures for Correcting Problem Behavior 134
Phase 5: Develop Procedures for Record Keeping, Evaluation, and Dissemination 146
Implementation Steps for a Schoolwide Discipline Plan 147
Step 1: Establish a Commitment from All Staff to Work Together to Improve the Schoolwide Discipline Plan 147
Step 2: Establish a Building Team and Operating Procedures 147
Step 3: Develop or Revise a School Discipline Manual 148
Step 4: Design and Implement a Staff Development Plan 148
Step 5: Develop a Data Management, Feedback, and Review System 149
Conclusion 149
Additional Resources on Schoolwide Discipline 150
Study Questions 150
Key Terms 151

6 Instructing and Managing the Classroom Environment 152

Classroom Structure 155
Designing the Physical Arrangement of the Classroom 155
Developing a Checklist of Operating Procedures 156
Planning Teacher Expectations 157
Delivering Instruction 158
Schedule 159
Instructional Objectives 159
Teaching to Mastery 159
Continuous Monitoring of Student Performance 159
Rates of Success 160
Pacing 160
Planned Variation of Instruction 160
Establishing Independent Routines 161
Teacher-Student Interactions 161
Academic Engagement 161
Managing Student Errors 163
Shaping Student Responses 163
Intervening during Instruction 163
Implement Classroom Expectations or Rules 163
Frequently Acknowledge Cooperative Students 164
Establish Consequences for Students Who Do Not Comply with Rules 164
Establish a Classroom Entry Activity 165

Keep Initial Explanations Brief *165*
Secure the Attention of All Students before Beginning Explanations *166*
Catch Problems Early *166*
Plan for Difficult Transitions *167*
Use Direct Speech *167*
Avoid Dead Time *167*
Settle Students Down near the End of Each Period *168*
Conclusion *168*
Study Questions *168*
Key Terms *169*

7 An Instructional Approach to Teaching Adaptive Behavior Patterns *170*

Teaching Adaptive Behavior *172*
Instructional Steps for Teaching Adaptive Behavior *172*
Application of a Behavior-Instruction Plan *176*
Pre-Correction: Anticipating Problem Behavior *176*
Pre-Correction Procedures *176*
Application of Pre-Correction Procedures *181*
Conclusion *181*
Study Questions *182*
Key Terms *183*

8 Instructing and Managing the Antisocial Student on the Playground *184*

Bullying by Antisocial Students and Resulting Peer Reactions *189*
Playground Situations That Are Particularly Difficult for Antisocial Students *194*
Generic Strategies and Procedures for Preventing and Remediating Negative-Aggressive Behavior and Rule Infractions on the Playground *199*
Teaching Normative Standards *199*
Teaching Adaptive Strategies for Specific Social Situations *200*
Teaching Generic Social Skills *202*
Teaching Anger Management and Conflict-Resolution Strategies *203*
RECESS: A Comprehensive Intervention for Aggressive Behavior *205*
Conclusion *212*
Recommended Resources for Use in Addressing Teasing, Bullying, and Negative-Aggressive Forms of Student Behavior *214*
Study Questions *215*
Key Terms *215*

9 Social Skills: Importance and Assessment *216*

The Social Status, Social Skills, and Social Adjustment of Antisocial Children and Youth *218*
Methods for Identifying Students in Need of Social-Skills Training *224*
Definition and Conceptualization of Social Skills *227*
Criteria and Procedures for Targeting Specific Skills for Training *228*
Ascertaining Specific Skill Deficits 228
Social Validity 228
Assessment 230
Recommendations and Best Practices for Evaluating Social-Skills Interventions *235*
Documenting Skill Acquisition 236
Evaluating Outcomes of Social-Skills Interventions 236
Conclusion *236*
Study Questions *237*
Key Terms *237*

10 Social Skills: Implementation and Generalization *238*

Approaches to Teaching Social Skills *240*
Contextual Factors Mediating the Teaching of Social Skills *241*
A Universal Approach to Teaching Social Skills: Example and Guidelines *245*
The Playground Behavior Game 248
Getting a Universal Social-Skills Program Going in Your Classroom 252
Example of a Selected Approach to Teaching Social Skills *253*
Use of Opportunistic Teaching Methods to Facilitate the Display of Previously Taught Social Skills *255*
Recommendations and Guidelines Governing Best Practices in Social-Skills Interventions in School *260*
Resources for Evaluating Curricula and Conducting Social-Skills Training *261*
Conclusion *264*
Study Questions *264*
Key Terms *265*

11 Parent Involvement in the Schooling of Antisocial Students *266*

The Role of Parents *269*
Improving Ongoing Interactions with Parents *273*
Developing a Positive Attitude toward Parents 273

Regular Communication *274*
A Problem-Solving Approach *279*
Home–School Interventions *282*
Encouragement at Home *284*
Discipline at Home *293*
Coping with Noncompliance *296*
Preventing Abuse *302*
Conclusion *303*
Recommended Resources on Parent Practices *304*
Study Questions *304*
Key Terms *305*

12 Case-Study Applications of Best Practices with Antisocial Students *306*

Jamie: Reducing High-Risk Life-Style Factors *308*
Background *308*
Intervention *309*
Results *313*
Discussion *313*
Bobby and Greg: Increasing Positive Peer Interactions *314*
Background *314*
Intervention *315*
Results *318*
Discussion *318*
Charlotte: Encouraging Positive Behavior at Home and School *319*
Background *319*
Intervention *320*
Discussion *321*
Second Step: Implementing Classwide Social Skills *322*
Background *322*
Intervention *323*
Results *324*
Discussion *325*
Project PREPARE: Establishing a Schoolwide and Classroom-Level Management System—A Building-Team Approach *325*
Project PREPARE *325*
Background *328*
Intervention *328*
Results *339*
Discussion *343*
Jimmy: Early Intervention for the Prevention of Antisocial Behavior among Kindergartners—The First Steps Program *344*
The First Steps Program *344*

Background *347*
Intervention *349*
Results *350*
Discussion *351*
Billy: Victim of Circumstances and Victimizer of Others *352*
Background *352*
Discussion *354*
Conclusion *354*

13 School Violence, Gangs, and Safety: Toward Proactive Strategies *356*

Violence: Causes, Trends, Societal Factors, and Recommendations *359*
Dimensions of Violence *359*
Causal Factors *361*
Trends *361*
Societal Changes Associated with Increases in Violent Behavior *362*
Recommended Methods for Reducing Violence *362*
Gangs and Gang Activity *374*
School Safety *379*
Conclusion *382*
Resources on Violence, Gangs, and School Safety *383*
Additional Resources *383*
Study Questions *384*
Key Terms *385*

Epilogue *386*

Appendix A Empirical Foundations in Discriminating, Predicting, and Changing Aggressive, Antisocial Behavior in School and at Home *387*

Appendix B The Case of Judge Hargreaves: Society Is Failing Its Children, Forsaking Its Future *429*

Appendix C Generals in the War on School Violence *436*

References *440*

Name Index *459*

Subject Index *463*

EXHIBITS IN APPENDIX A

Exhibit 1 The Influence of Arrest Status and Special Education Certification on Adjustment Status for At-Risk Students: Markers for Negative Developmental Outcomes

Exhibit 2 Regular Classroom Behavioral Profiles of Negative-Aggressive versus Acting Out/Disruptive Students in the Primary Grades

Exhibit 3 Comparisons of the School Adjustment Status of Middle School At-Risk Boys Who Are Deviant in Two or More Settings, Deviant in Only One Setting, or Deviant in No Settings

Exhibit 4 Adjustment Profiles of Antisocial and At-Risk Middle School Boys

Exhibit 5 Positive versus Negative Social Behavior in Discriminating Antisocial and At-Risk Students in Playground and Classroom Settings

Exhibit 6 Differential Parenting Profiles That Discriminate Antisocial and At-Risk Students

Exhibit 7 The Path from Failed Parenting to Antisocial Behavior in School to Delinquency in Adolescence

Exhibit 8 Generalization of Antisocial Behavior Patterns from Home to School

Exhibit 9 The Efficacy of Praise, Token Reinforcement, and Cost Contingency in Reducing Negative-Aggressive Social Interactions among Antisocial Boys

Exhibit 10 Application of Reinforcement and Response Cost in Reducing Negative-Aggressive Social Interactions in Regular Classrooms

Exhibit 11 The Efficacy of a Response Cost Intervention in Increasing Positive Social Interactions in Free-Play Settings

Exhibit 12 Response Cost and Its Required Frequency of Use in Maintaining Behavioral Levels of Students

Exhibit 13 External Replications of the RECESS Program for Aggressive Students

PREFACE

During the past two decades, our society has undergone a profound series of social, demographic, economic, and cultural changes that have radically altered the way in which we relate to one another and view ourselves. Unfortunately, many of these changes are negative; their occurrence places both families and identifiable clusters of individuals at serious risk. The enormous problems with drugs, violence, domestic abuse and neglect, and social conflict experienced by our society are examples of these changes; collectively, they have greatly diminished our overall quality of life.

These unfortunate results are partially accounted for by three factors that add up to an enormous public burden and are associated with pervasive social conflict: *high rates of juvenile crime, school failure and dropout,* and *adolescent childbearing* (see Schorr, 1988). The impact of criminal and violent acts committed by adolescents who leave school illiterate and unemployable and who become parents far too soon are registered in life paths characterized by dependency, lack of productivity, and pain. These factors, which Lisbeth Schorr refers to in her seminal work *Within Our Reach* as *rotten outcomes,* threaten to overwhelm our society.

The U.S. Centers for Disease Control have declared violence the most pressing health issue facing our society. The American Psychological Association's Commission on Violence and Youth (APA, 1993) recently published an important study on youth, antisocial-aggressive behavior, and violence. This extensive study is psychology's response to the dramatic escalation in violence that we have witnessed in our society in the past decade. The Commission found that children and youth are becoming involved in violent behavior at ever-younger ages, and the report states that parenting failure, school factors, and academic achievement are important causal influences. Further, the Commission cites empirical evidence that points to four individual social factors that play a major role in the development of violent behavior patterns among our children and youth: (1) easy access to firearms, (2) involvement with drugs and alcohol; (3) affiliation with gangs and antisocial groups, and (4) exposure to violence depicted in the mass media.

The spillover into the schooling process of these social conditions, with their negative effects upon students, is extensive and destructive. Children and youth are bringing complex needs and severe deficits in their school readiness to the schoolhouse door.

Schools are not adequately set up to cope with these enormous problems, but they are charged with educating all children who come to them. These social pressures are prompting substantial changes in the structure and nature of schooling. It is likely that the school of the 21st century will be a delivery site for integrated, school-linked services needed to meet the full spectrum of complex needs that these children present.

This book is written for the educator-practitioner who must cope with students who either already have or are at high risk for developing antisocial behavior patterns. Traditionally, schools have used such strategies as control, containment, punishment, and exclusion to deal with students who have behavior problems. Aside from the ineffectiveness of these techniques, the sheer number of antisocial students now populating our schools makes this approach untenable. The material in this book is designed to enhance educators' understanding of the nature, origins, and causes of antisocial behavior. This book also includes information on the best available practices, interventions, and model programs for preventing and remediating this most destructive of behavior disorders occurring in school. Whenever possible, schools must become partners with families and social agencies in providing for the needs of antisocial students and in coping with the complex problems they present. We hope the content of this book will aid educators in this regard.

This book is based upon principles of social learning that govern how diverse forms of behavior are acquired, maintained, and reduced or eliminated. These principles are derived from a solid empirical knowledge base developed through objective, rigorous scientific methods. However, we acknowledge the existence of many different ways of knowing and the diversity of avenues that lead to truth. Gerald Patterson, an eminent social learning theorist and scientist, once observed that one's observation coding system is simply one's "window on the world." In a very real sense, the coding systems, methodologies, and beliefs about human behavior in which we invest are powerful determinants of what we see and how we see it.

We perceive the world from a broad, ecological social-learning perspective. Understanding social contingencies and their influence on the behavior of individuals and interactions is extremely important to using this approach effectively. The intervention procedures and strategies described in this book are derived from this perspective and are highly effective if carried out according to best-practice standards.

This book contains thirteen chapters that address the issue of antisocial behavior in school and its prevention and remediation. The book does not contain any magical cures, but we attempt to apprise the reader of what is needed to ameliorate this unfortunate and often tragic behavior pattern. Finally, Appendix A of this book contains 13 exhibits that illustrate the research upon which many of the best practices in this book are based. This is a "Read More About It" feature in which technical information on aggressive, antisocial behavior, information that involves scientific research, is presented, described, and interpreted for the reader. The senior author and his colleagues have conducted most of this research, and several studies described here are replications of their work by independent investigators. We present this material for the reader who has a technical interest in understanding antisocial behavior patterns and in finding procedures for changing them in school settings.

ACKNOWLEDGMENTS

First, we would like to thank those who reviewed earlier drafts of this book for their many helpful comments and suggestions. These reviewers include Margaret Coleman, University of Texas at Austin; Karna Nelson, Western Washington University; Robert B. Rutherford, Jr., Arizona State University; Edward J. Sabornie, North Carolina State University; and K. Richard Young, Utah State University.

We also want to acknowledge Ann Thurber, as well as the rest of the office staff at the Center on Human Development of the University of Oregon, for their valuable assistance in the preparation of this book.

Finally, we wish to thank our families, including Jan and Seth Walker; Nola and Kylee Colvin; and John Woodward, Lauren Woodward, and Alex Elizabeth Woodward, for their support and encouragement.

Hill M. Walker

Geoff Colvin

Elizabeth Ramsey

1 Antisocial Behavior Patterns in Children and Youth: Characteristics, Causes, and Outcomes

Antisocial Behavior Defined

The Prevalence of Antisocial Behavior and Conduct Disorder

Diagnostic Classification of Conduct Disorder

The Responsiveness of Conduct Disorder and Antisocial Behavior Patterns to Intervention

The Stability of Antisocial Behavior and Conduct Disorder

Conduct Disorder and Juvenile Delinquency

School Adjustment, Conduct Disorder, and Antisocial Behavior

Behavioral Characteristics and Correlates of Antisocial Behavior Patterns

- Classroom Behavior
- Playground Behavior
- Affective Status

Long-Term Outcomes for Antisocial and At-Risk Boys

Gender, Conduct Disorder, and Antisocial Behavior

The Causes and Origins of Antisocial Behavior Patterns

Pathways to Acquiring Antisocial Behavior Patterns and Conduct Disorder

Antisocial Behavior and Violence

A Perspective on Violence

The Costs of Antisocial Behavior

A Look to the Future

Recommended Sources on Violence

Antisocial behavior is felt pervasively and profoundly in literally all school districts in this country. This book is about antisocial behavior in school—its manifestations and its impact. Student aggression, antisocial behavior, delinquency, and violence are strongly linked dimensions of an unfortunate behavior pattern that students in our schools are adopting in droves (American Psychological Association, 1993; Reid, 1993; Schorr, 1988). The pressures and social effects resulting from these behavioral manifestations are threatening to overwhelm the process of schooling for *all* of our students. School safety, for staff and students alike, has risen to a level of great importance and excruciating national concern.

Educators, as a rule, are not trained to deal with moderate to severe levels of antisocial behavior occurring among the school-age population of children and youth. Furthermore, school personnel generally lack an understanding of the origins and developmental course of this disorder. However, in the past two decades, enormous strides have been made in understanding and treating antisocial behavior patterns. Through longitudinal and retrospective studies, we also know a great deal about the long-term outcomes that result from the adoption of this behavior pattern by at-risk students, especially those who bring it to school or adopt it as they begin their school careers (see Kazdin, 1987; Parker & Asher, 1987).

The field of psychology, in particular, has developed a very powerful empirical literature around antisocial behavior that can assist school personnel in coping with this most difficult of behavior disorders. This knowledge base has been infused into the educational information and decision-making system only in a very limited fashion. A major goal of this book is to communicate and adapt this knowledge base for effective use by educators in coping with the increasing tide of antisocial students who are populating our schools.

ANTISOCIAL BEHAVIOR DEFINED

Antisocial behavior is defined as "recurrent violations of socially prescribed patterns of behavior" (Simcha-Fagan, Langner, Gersten, & Eisenberg, 1975, p. 7). *Antisocial* is the opposite of *prosocial*, which is composed of cooperative, positive, and mutually reciprocal social behavior. Antisocial behavior suggests hostility to others, aggression, a willingness to commit rule infractions, defiance of adult authority, and violation of the social norms and mores of society. The dictionary definition of *antisocial* is "hostile to the well-being of society and aversive to others." This behavior pattern involves deviation from accepted rules and expected standards governing appropriate behavior across a range of settings (for example, home, school, and community). Antisocial behavior is one of the most common forms of psychopathology among children and youth and is *the* most frequently cited reason for referral to mental health services (see Achenbach, 1985; Quay, 1986; Reid, 1993).

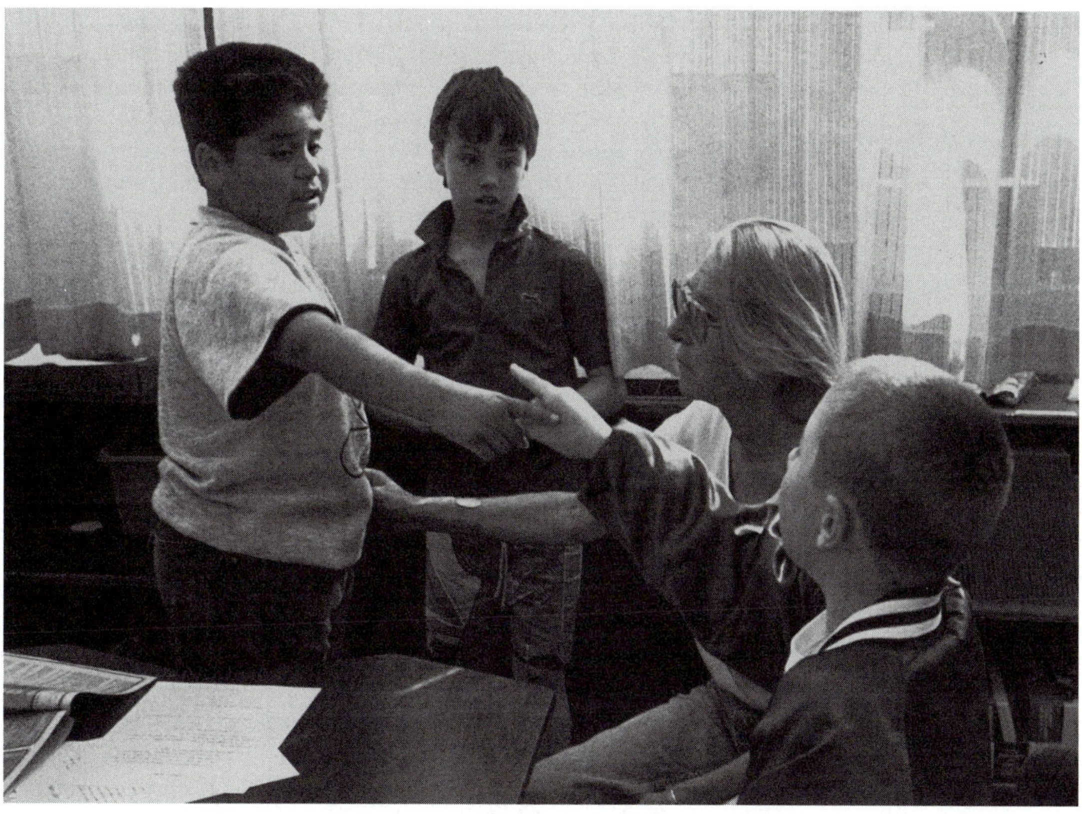

Hostile, aggressive behavior with peers. *Elizabeth Crews*

THE PREVALENCE OF ANTISOCIAL BEHAVIOR AND CONDUCT DISORDER

The prevalence of conduct disorder among children and youth is substantial. Formal surveys indicate that conduct disorder varies between 2 and 6% of the general population of youth in this country; this translates into a figure ranging from 1.3 to 3.8 million cases (Institute of Medicine, 1989; Kazdin, 1993). Half of these youth will maintain the disorder into adulthood; the remainder will suffer significant adjustment problems during their adult lives (Kazdin, 1993; Robins, 1978).

The pool of students with serious conduct disorders needing comprehensive services is many times the size of the currently certified severely emotionally disturbed (SED) school-age population (which is less than 1% of the school-age population or approximately 356,000 students). Conduct-disordered behavior patterns appear to be increasing dramatically, and their presence severely constrains the ability of school systems to educate all students effectively (Horne & Sayger, 1990; Kauffman, 1989; Reid, 1990). In addition, our deteriorating societal conditions are producing a much larger class of children who are designated as "at-risk" or as "special needs" populations—many of whom will ultimately develop severe conduct disorders and antisocial behavior patterns leading to such negative outcomes as delinquency, school dropout, vocational adjustment problems, interpersonal adjustment problems, and appearance on community psychiatric registers in adulthood (Forness, 1992; Kazdin, 1987; Parker & Asher, 1987). Approximately 50% of hyperactive children and youth either have or will develop conduct disorder during their school careers (Fowler, 1992).

DIAGNOSTIC CLASSIFICATION OF CONDUCT DISORDER

According to the third revised edition of the *Diagnostic and Statistical Manual of Mental Disorders* (DSM-III-R) of the American Psychiatric Association, antisocial behavior forms the clinical content and foundation for the syndrome classified as *conduct disorder* (see American Psychiatric Association, 1987). Examples of antisocial behaviors that are used to diagnose conduct disorder include "is frequently truant," "frequently initiates physical fights," "has been physically cruel to other people," "cheats with others in games or in schoolwork," and "has deliberately destroyed property of others." (See Kazdin, 1987, for a complete listing of symptoms.) Children and youth exhibiting this behavior pattern also frequently steal and lie about their activities in order to attain goals or rewards at others' expense, break rules, and avoid accountability for their actions.

If three or more of these antisocial behaviors are exhibited consistently at higher than normal levels over a six-month period, then a diagnosis of conduct disorder is indicated (Richters & Cicchetti, 1993). This syndrome, or diagnostic category, is defined as "clinically severe antisocial behavior(s) in which the everyday functioning of the individual is impaired, as defined by parents, teachers and others" (Kazdin, 1987, p. 22). In schools, antisocial behavior and conduct disorder are commonly referred to by educators as *social maladjustment.* Children and youth with these behavioral characteristics and patterns historically have been excluded from special education eligibility as defined by P.L. 94-142 and its reauthorization, the Individuals with Disabilities Education Act (IDEA).

THE RESPONSIVENESS OF CONDUCT DISORDER AND ANTISOCIAL BEHAVIOR PATTERNS TO INTERVENTION

Conduct disorder is regarded by most experts as a chronic, lifelong disorder that is highly resistant to intervention and is generally unresponsive to adult-controlled tactics of social influence (Coie & Jacobs, 1993; Kazdin, 1985). To date, no intervention has been developed that permanently alters this condition and that successfully diverts children and youth from a trajectory leading to a host of long-term, negative developmental outcomes. In fact, Kazdin (1987) argues persuasively that after about age 8, antisocial behavior and conduct disorder should be viewed as a chronic disorder (like diabetes) for which there is no cure but that can be controlled and managed with a sensible regimen of supports and appropriate interventions. However, in recent reviews, Dodge (1993) and Reid (1993) have both described promising interventions for the treatment and possible prevention of this disorder in family and school contexts. It should be noted that no intervention reported to date has produced results that last longer than one year (see Dodge, 1993; Kazdin, 1993). Thus, it is safe to say that, so far, no cure has been found and reported for conduct disorder and severe antisocial behavior patterns among children and youth.

THE STABILITY OF ANTISOCIAL BEHAVIOR AND CONDUCT DISORDER

If a pattern of antisocial behavior persists into adulthood (that is, to age 18 and beyond), it is then referred to as *antisocial personality disorder*, as opposed to conduct disorder. Given what we know about the developmental course of conduct disorder, if a child brings an antisocial behavior pattern to school and if this pattern ultimately leads to a diagnosis of conduct disorder, it will very likely persist into adulthood. Very often, this behavior disorder is exacerbated severely by adoption of a delinquent lifestyle in adolescence.

As previously noted, a tremendous amount has been learned about conduct disorder and its expression through antisocial behavior among children and youth (see Cicchetti & Nurcombe, 1993; Patterson, Reid, & Dishion, 1992). We have considerable information about the causal factors that contribute to its origins and its behavioral expression among children and youth (Kazdin, 1985, 1987; Parker & Asher, 1987; Patterson et al., 1992). This knowledge (1) helps us to understand and predict the path and likely outcomes of antisocial behavior, (2) allows us to recognize and identify its early behavioral signs, and (3) provides a road map of sorts for the development of strategies for its remediation and prevention. Box 1.1 presents some empirically derived facts that provide a summary of some of the most important findings to date on antisocial behavior patterns.

These findings indicate that antisocial behavior is an extremely destructive and difficult-to-manage disorder. Given its stability and its relatively strong association with delinquency in adolescence, most experts agree that antisocial behavior requires the earliest possible intervention that targets three primary settings and the key social agents within them: (1) the home setting and parents, (2) the classroom and teachers, and (3) the playground and peers (see Dodge, 1993; Reid, 1993).

CONDUCT DISORDER AND JUVENILE DELINQUENCY

A well-developed pattern of antisocial behavior during the early school years, culminating in conduct disorder, is perhaps the single best predictor of adolescent *delinquency* which, in turn, is the best predictor of adult criminality (Wahler & Dumas, 1986). Some experts have argued that conduct disorder and delinquency are synonymous and are differentiated only on the basis of age or developmental status; that is, children displaying antisocial behavior who are too young to be arrested are conduct disordered, while antisocial youth of adolescent age and older are delinquent. However, Kazdin (1987)

Box 1.1 Facts on Antisocial Behavior

- The vast majority of antisocial children are boys; antisocial behavior in girls is less evident and expressed differently than in boys (that is, antisocial behavior among girls is more often self-directed than outer-directed).
- There are two types of antisocial behavior (overt and covert). Overt involves acts against people; covert involves acts against property and/or self-abuse. By adolescence, many at-risk children display both forms, which escalates their risk status substantially.
- Antisocial behavior early in a child's school career is the single best predictor of delinquency in adolescence.
- Three years after leaving school, 70% of antisocial youth have been arrested at least once.
- The stability of aggressive behavior over a decade is approximately equal to that for intelligence. The correlation for IQ over ten years is .70; for aggressive behavior, it approximates .80.
- Antisocial children can be identified very accurately at age 3 or 4.
- The more severe the antisocial behavior pattern, the more stable it is over the long term and across settings (for example, home to school); severity is also associated with higher risk for negative developmental outcomes and for police contacts/arrest.
- If an antisocial behavior pattern is not changed by the end of grade 3, it should be treated as a chronic condition, much like diabetes. That is, it cannot be cured but can be managed with the appropriate supports and continuing interventions.
- Early intervention in home, school, and community is the single best hope we have of diverting children from this path.
- Children who grow up antisocial are at severe risk for a host of long-term, negative developmental outcomes, including school dropout, vocational adjustment problems, drug and alcohol abuse, relationship problems, and higher hospitalization and mortality rates.
- Using three measures of school-related adjustment in grade 5, the arrest status of a high-risk sample can be correctly predicted in 80% of cases five years later. These measures are (1) a 5-minute teacher rating of social skills, (2) two 20-minute observations of negative-aggressive behavior on the playground involving peers, and (3) the number of discipline contacts with the principal's office that are written up and placed in the child's permanent school record.

makes the case that they are not the same thing. He argues that conduct disorder refers to clinically severe forms of antisocial behavior, whereas delinquency involves a legal designation and usually includes police or court contacts. Approximately half of children and youth having conduct disorder also are delinquent (Patterson, in press). However, there is substantial overlap in the behavioral characteristics of students who are conduct disordered without being delinquent and those who are delinquent. Most of this overlap is in the realm of antisocial behavior.

SCHOOL ADJUSTMENT, CONDUCT DISORDER, AND ANTISOCIAL BEHAVIOR

When children enter school, they are required to negotiate two extremely important social-behavioral adjustments: teacher-related and peer-related (see Walker, McConnell, & Clarke, 1985). *Teacher-related* adjustment refers to the process of students meeting the minimal behavioral demands and expectations that the great majority of teachers require in order to teach and manage instructional environments (Hersh & Walker, 1983; Walker, 1986). *Peer-related* adjustment refers to the ability to forge satisfactory relationships with peers, to develop friendships, and to recruit and maintain social support networks (Dodge, 1993; Hollinger, 1987; Patterson et al., 1992). Satisfactory adjustment in these two critically important domains is essential to gaining teacher and peer acceptance. During middle school, a third form of adjustment, self-related, comes into play. *Self-related* adjustment includes managing emotions, being organized, asserting one self, and protecting one's reputation. This form of adjustment has great relevance to adolescent development (Williams, Walker, Holmes, Todis, & Fabre, 1989).

If children and youth fail to satisfactorily negotiate either teacher-related *or* peer-related adjustment relatively early in their school careers, they are at a substantially elevated risk for later school failure. If they fail in *both* adjustment areas, they are at risk for a host of negative developmental outcomes that play out over the long term (Strain, Guralnick, & Walker, 1986). Figure 1.1 presents a model of teacher- and peer-related adjustment along with associated outcomes for each. Enhancers (student adaptive behaviors) and impairers (student maladaptive behaviors) of each form of adjustment are listed.

Long-term positive and negative outcomes, predicted by the enhancers and impairers, respectively, are also listed in Figure 1.1. Empirical evidence exists that documents the association between the success or failure of teacher and peer adjustment and the listed enhancers and impairers in Figure 1.1 (Parker & Asher, 1987; Robins, 1978).

Students with conduct disorder and antisocial behavior patterns are at substantial risk for failure in both of these adjustment areas. Because of their high rates of aggressive behavior, antisocial students are especially vulnerable to social rejection by their non-antisocial peers. If they are also noncompliant with teacher directives or engage in oppositional-defiant behavior, then rejection by teachers is also a real possibility. In such cases, failure in both teacher- and peer-related adjustment areas is virtually assured with all of the associated negative outcomes.

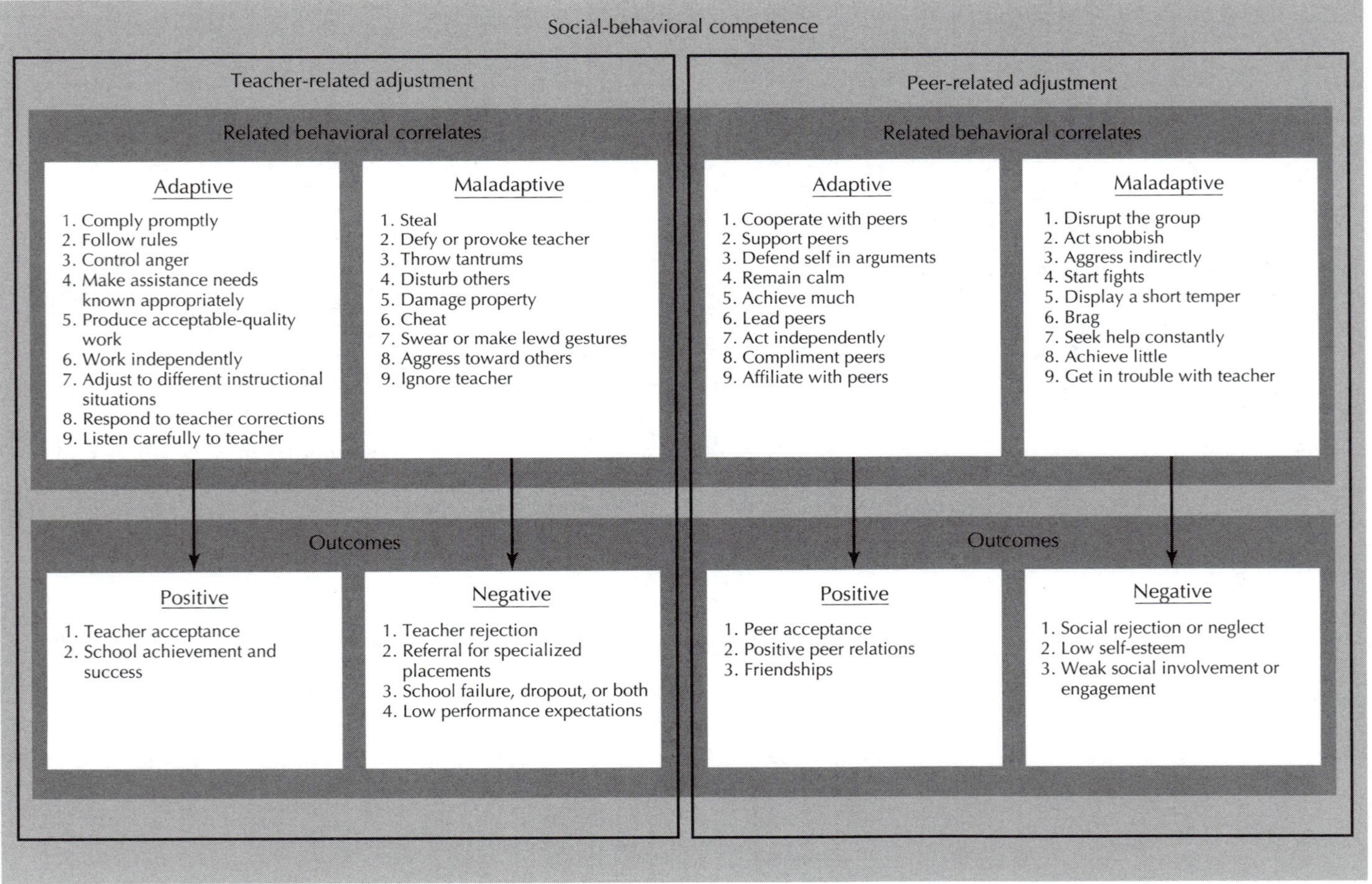

FIGURE 1.1 Model of Interpersonal Social-Behavioral Competence within School Settings.
Source: From "A Construct Score Approach to the Assessment of Social Competence: Rationale, Technological Considerations, and Anticipated Outcomes," by H. M. Walker, L. K. Irvin, J. Noell, and G. H. S. Singer, in *Behavior Modification, 16* (1992), 448–474. Reprinted by permission.

BEHAVIORAL CHARACTERISTICS AND CORRELATES OF ANTISOCIAL BEHAVIOR PATTERNS

Few individuals go through their lives without engaging in some form or type of antisocial behavior on occasion (Bullis & Walker, 1993). This is particularly true of young children who, through the socialization efforts of parents and guardians, gradually reduce their levels of antisocial behavior as they approach school age. However, those children who go on to become conduct disordered usually maintain and actually accelerate their antisocial behavior—especially within the context of school where the opportunities to do so are expanded (Patterson, DeBaryshe, & Ramsey, 1989; Reid, 1993).

In a very real sense, antisocial behavior is about aggression. Aggressive behavior can be expressed in physical, gestural, and verbal forms—all three can be extremely destructive. The aggression that is characteristic of antisocial children and youth is directed at multiple targets, including social agents (peers, siblings, parents, teachers, and other adults), property (vandalism, theft, property destruction, fire-setting), and self (drug and alcohol abuse and impulsive, high-risk behavior). Hunt (1993) recently identified and described five neurobiological patterns of aggression. These patterns and their behavioral manifestations are described in Box 1.2.

There is some degree of overlap among the types of aggression Hunt described; that is, a single aggressive individual rarely manifests the characteristics of only a single pattern. However, these distinctions are a very useful way to characterize the types of aggressive behavior that are seen increasingly in school and community settings. Although the material described in this book has implications for all five patterns of aggression, it is most closely geared to the affective and instrumental types of aggression. Antisocial behavior patterns typically involve a strong investment in the use of instrumental aggression.

Aggressive behavior is highly aversive to others and often leads to rejection and social avoidance. Aggression also produces powerful short-term rewards, including getting one's way, achieving social control over natural situations, and dominating and humiliating others (Walker, Hops, & Greenwood, 1993). The social impact of aggressive children and youth is very powerful and registers strongly within the peer group.

Coie and Kupersmidt (1983) conducted an intriguing study in which they demonstrated just how quickly antisocial, aggressive youth train their peer groups to socially reject them. They identified a group of boys who were highly aggressive and were also socially rejected by their peer groups. They formed play groups of same-aged children, all of whom were unfamiliar with each other, and placed one of these boys in each group. Within a matter of minutes, each of the play groups showed clear signs of rejecting the aggressive boy assigned to them! Reid (1993) argues convincingly that many of these aggressive boys are probably unaware that their own behavior is responsible for such rejection.

Dodge and his colleagues have conducted some important work on how aggressive, rejected children process social information, interpret interpersonal cues, and make decisions based on this information (Dodge, 1985; Dodge, Pettit, McClaskey, & Brown, 1986). These children and youth have serious deficits in this very important area of social

Box 1.2 Patterns of Neurobiological Aggression

- **Over-Aroused Aggression**—This form of aggressive behavior is due primarily to a state of over-arousal, such as that seen in children and youth with attention deficit-hyperactive disorder. Aggressive behavior of this type is largely a side effect of heightened arousal and activity levels and is not characterized by intent to inflict pain or by attempts to use aggression for instrumental purposes. Victims or targets of these aggressive acts are generally randomly involved in the aggressive episode.

- **Impulsive Aggression**—Aggression of this type occurs in a sudden burst, without any identifiable precursors or signs that it is coming. It is thought to be neurologically based and is often associated with irritability or long periods of passivity. Aggressive episodes are very brief in duration and subside as quickly as they emerge. Children and youth displaying this pattern of aggression are subject to frequent and intense mood swings.

- **Affective Aggression**—Aggression arising out of states of intense anger and rage, such as that seen among abused children, is characteristic of this pattern. It is emotionally charged and includes a range of affective states involving intense passion; it is sometimes motivated by vindictiveness or self-protectiveness. Violent episodes are typical of this pattern of aggression. It is highly destructive to both the perpetrators and victims of the aggression. It may be dangerous to be closely associated with such children and youth.

- **Predatory Aggression**—This form of aggression is most prevalent among those at adolescent and adult levels of development. It is often associated with a thought disorder involving paranoia. Such youth have a conspiratorial view of social relations and tend to misinterpret neutral social behavior directed toward them as intentionally harmful. Much of their aggressive behavior is revenge-based and thoughtfully planned. Often it is designed to "settle scores," real or imagined, and contains elements of the predator-prey relationship.

- **Instrumental Aggression**—This very common form of aggression is adopted by many children and youth as a standard way of operating on the social environment (that is, a modus operandi) and involves using aggressive tactics to maximize one's advantage and to get one's way. Instrumental aggression is used to intimidate, humiliate, and coerce others. There is a strong drive to achieve dominance and social control underlying this aggressive pattern. Instrumental aggression has sociopathic tendencies and is commonly viewed as representing a character disorder. Such children and youth often come from unstable, chaotic family environments.

Source: Hunt (1993).

Box 1.3 The Case of Ritchie

The senior author first encountered Ritchie in the process of developing the RECESS program for aggressive children in the K–3 grade range (Walker et al., 1993). Ritchie was in the second grade and was referred for involvement in the program by his school counselor and regular homeroom teacher. Teacher ratings of his classroom and general social behavior were quite negative and were well below normative standards. Direct observations of Ritchie's playground behavior on three separate occasions showed a frequent pattern of coercing peers, dominating playground activities, making up his own rules for games, breaking playground rules, verbally abusing and ridiculing others, and physically provoking smaller and less powerful children.

During one of these observation sessions on the playground, Ritchie began choking a smaller boy (a kindergartner) for no apparent reason. He appeared to have a clear goal of hurting the younger child. The recess supervisor broke up the encounter and called the principal and counselor to deal with the situation. As this entourage was escorting Ritchie into the principal's office to call his parents, I asked him why he was choking the other boy like that. He looked at me in amazement and said, "Well, it was recess!"

relations. For example, they frequently make errors in evaluating the motives and intent of the social behavior directed toward them by peers and adults. They often misinterpret important social cues that guide appropriate responses in everyday situations with peers. They are likely to attribute hostile intentions to accidental or ambiguous behavior from others and respond quite inappropriately as a result. Antisocial children and youth are often frequent teasers of others but respond incompetently to similar provocations from others. Finally, antisocial, aggressive children appear to have quite abnormal standards and expectations regarding their own behavior. These beliefs may, in turn, legitimize much of their deviant, aversive behavior and may also insulate them from accurately decoding negative and disapproving feedback about their behavior. The case of Ritchie in Box 1.3 is a true story that illustrates this point.

By second grade, Ritchie showed all the behavioral signs of being well along the path to antisocial behavior. Students like Ritchie who persist in this behavior pattern into the intermediate grades and who affiliate with a deviant peer group of students like themselves have a severely elevated risk of delinquency (Patterson et al., 1992). We find in our research that we can correctly identify predelinquent children, like Ritchie, in the fifth grade using three easy-to-record measures: (1) a 5-minute rating of classroom-related social skills, (2) the number of discipline contacts in the student's school records, and (3) the total amount of negative social behavior occurring between the student and peers at recess recorded during two, 20-minute observation sessions. The arrest status of antisocial and at-risk students (*N* = 80) who meet cutoff points on these three measures

TABLE 1.1 Standardized Achievement Test Percentile Scores for Antisocial and At-Risk Students Across Grades 5, 6, and 7

	GRADE 5		GRADE 6		GRADE 7	
	Antisocial	*At-Risk*	*Antisocial*	*At-Risk*	*Antisocial*	*At-Risk*
Reading	42.38	56.63	43.36	56.62	37.00	56.46
Math	32.00	58.68	38.36	55.74	23.80	52.18
Total	35.75	58.88	41.59	53.51	28.29	54.15

Source: Walker et al. (1987).

can be accurately predicted in 80% of cases five years later when they are in the tenth grade (Walker & Reid, in press). It is not exaggerating to say that the path to prison begins very early in a child's school career, usually in the elementary grades (Walker & Sylwester, 1991).

This is powerful testimony to the stability of antisocial behavior patterns, and it supports the opinion of many experts that young bullies often get worse, rather than better, as they progress through school. For example, about 50% of children below the age of 10 who get into trouble in school because of their aggressive behavior continue to have very serious behavior problems in adolescence (Kutner, 1993). The stability of very aggressive behavior rivals that of IQs. The test-retest correlation for repeated assessments of intelligence over a ten-year period is about .70; for aggressive behavior over the same period, it ranges from .60 to .80 (Quay, 1986; Reid, 1993).

Most children and youth who are antisocial have well-developed repertoires of bullying others. Increasingly, schools are becoming concerned with the effects of bullying behavior on both its victims and perpetrators. They are investing in social skills training programs to directly teach effective means of reducing aggression and strategies for coping with its occurrence (Hoover & Juul, 1993).

Antisocial children and youth often have moderate to severe academic skill deficits as well as low achievement (see Coie & Jacobs, 1993; Hinshaw, 1992; Offord, Boyle, & Racine, 1991; Reid, 1993). It is not clear whether these academic problems are primarily the causes or consequences of antisocial behavior; however, there is little doubt that they greatly exacerbate it. Table 1.1 contains academic achievement percentile scores in reading, math, and total achievement for a longitudinal sample of 39 antisocial boys and 41 at-risk boys that the senior author and his colleagues have been following since 1984 (see Walker, Shinn, O'Neill, & Ramsey, 1987). Scores are reported for these two groups in grades 5, 6, and 7.

In each year and on each achievement test, the at-risk students were above the 50th percentile; in contrast, the antisocial group, who had much higher levels of antisocial behavior, had average scores that fell well below the 50th percentile, ranging from a low of 23.80 in math during grade 7 to a high of 43.36 in reading during grade 6. These results indicate very serious academic underachievement for the sample of antisocial boys.

Furthermore, as the antisocial boys progressed through their school careers, their academic deficits and achievement problems became even more severe (Walker & Reid, in press).

Classroom Behavior

As a rule, antisocial students make relatively poor adjustments to the demands of schooling and instructional environments that are controlled by teachers. They can put extreme pressures on the management and instructional skills of classroom teachers and often disrupt the instructional process for other students. Antisocial students are quickly referred for specialized services and possible placement outside the regular classroom (that is, self-contained classes, day-treatment centers, residential settings). About two-thirds of the students assigned to self-contained classrooms for severely emotionally disturbed children and youth have acting-out behavior patterns that are labeled conduct disorder (Wagner, 1989).

Generally, antisocial students' classroom behavior deviates too far from expected normative levels to be considered acceptable or appropriate by either teachers or peers. Teacher ratings of antisocial students' social skills are highly predictive of a host of future adjustment problems (Patterson et al., 1992; Walker & McConnell, 1993). We find in our longitudinal research that year after year, regular teachers rate our antisocial students as *very* deficient in their social skills, particularly those skills that support a successful classroom adjustment (for example, cooperates with others, is personally organized, listens carefully to instructions, and so forth).

The amount of time students spend academically engaged in the classroom is an important academic skill that is strongly related to achievement as measured by standardized tests (Rosenshine, 1979). Academic engagement (academic learning time) means that the student is working on assigned tasks, attending to and involved with the assignment, and making appropriate motor responses (for example, writing, computing) (see Brophy & Evertson, 1981; Brophy & Good, 1986). Observational studies indicate that academic engagement levels in the elementary grades vary between about 70 and 90% of allocated instructional time. Rich and Ross (1989) reviewed the research literature on this topic and concluded that about 50 to 60% of the school day is allocated to learning tasks.

In an observational study of 230 elementary school–aged students with disabilities, Rich and Ross (1989) assessed the amount of academically engaged time for portions of this sample that were assigned to regular classrooms (N = 39), resource rooms (N = 55), special classrooms (N = 84), and special schools (N = 52). The academic engagement levels for students in the resource room were highest (93%), followed by the regular classroom (81%). These two placements had higher levels of both allocated and actual engaged time than the other placements; in contrast, the special class placements had the lowest levels on these variables. It should be noted, however, that the students with milder disabling conditions were assigned to resource and regular classrooms and the students with more severe disabilities were in the special class and special school placements.

Academic engagement levels of the antisocial subjects studied by Walker and his colleagues (1987) are consistently lower than standard (that is, the level of behavior, or the average that a group of students produces), averaging between 60 and 70% of observed

TABLE 1.2 Profiles of the Classroom Behavior of Antisocial and At-Risk Students, Grade 5

Code Category	*Antisocial (%)*	*At-Risk (%)*	*Difference (%)*	p
Attending	76.3	86.0	9.7	.0001
Positive initiation to teacher	1.32	.74	.58	.0108
Group compliance	1.25	1.90	.65	.0531
Negative initiation to teacher	.34	.05	.29	.0105
Physical aggression	.21	.07	.14	.0162
Noise	2.80	.46	2.34	.0005
Out of seat	3.40	1.03	2.37	.0005

Source: Adapted from Walker et al. (1987).

time in regular classroom settings. However, the at-risk students in the sample, who have much lower levels of antisocial behavior, average significantly higher levels of academic engagement (between 80 and 90%).

Table 1.2 contains profiles of the behavior of the antisocial and at-risk subjects in the longitudinal study (Walker et al., 1987). These profiles are based on a series of direct observations recorded by professionally trained observers when the target students were in the fifth grade. These observation sessions were conducted during structured academic periods in a regular classroom.

The table contains the average percentage of time spent in three categories of appropriate behavior and four categories of inappropriate behavior. The antisocial students had significantly less favorable profiles than the at-risk students on each of the appropriate categories, except for positive initiation to the teacher. Similarly, the antisocial students had substantially less favorable profiles on all of the inappropriate categories.

Interestingly, the antisocial students had higher rates of positive *and* negative initiations to the teacher. This may be a consequence of the antisocials having relatively low levels of engagement with academic tasks, poor attending rates, and weak academic skills. These factors would cause them to be substantially more dependent on the teacher's assistance in order to perform academically. This profile indicates a very poor classroom adjustment for the antisocial students and a surprisingly good one for the at-risk students.

Playground Behavior

Antisocial students have equally serious adjustment problems with peers on the playground as they do with teachers in the classroom. The aggressive tendencies of antisocial students are more easily expressed in the less structured setting of the playground. Furthermore, the ratio of adults to students on the playground is much less favorable than in the classroom. Studies by the senior author and his colleagues indicate that antisocial children produce anywhere from two to nine times more negative-aggressive behavior than their non-antisocial peers in free-play settings (Walker et al., 1993). Table 1.3 con-

TABLE 1.3 Profiles of the Playground Social Behavior of Antisocial and At-Risk Students

*Code Category**	*Antisocial (%)*	*At-Risk (%)*	*Difference (%)*	p
Negative target verbal	6.2	2.4	3.8	.0407
Negative target physical	.85	.45	.40	.0011
Negative peer verbal	5.5	2.57	2.93	.0041
Negative peer physical	3.9	1.5	2.4	.0007
Ignore	.82	.43	.39	.0252
Positive target verbal	5.6	6.9	1.3	.0124
Structured activity	38.8	50.2	11.4	.0407

*Code categories are defined as follows:

Negative target verbal: Hostile, verbally aggressive language by the target student.

Negative target physical: Hostile behavior involving physical contact by the target student (for example, hitting).

Negative peer verbal: Hostile, verbally aggressive language by a peer of the target student directed toward the target student.

Negative peer physical: Hostile behavior involving physical contact by a peer of the target student directed toward the target student (for example, hitting).

Ignore: A student does not respond to the social initiation of a peer.

Positive target verbal: Positive comments (such as compliments or praise) by the target student directed toward a peer.

Structured activity: An organized game or activity with an identifiable set of rules.

Source: Walker et al. (1993).

tains a profile of the playground social behavior of the antisocial and at-risk students in the ongoing longitudinal study.

The table shows the average percentage of time spent in seven observation code categories (five negative, one positive, and one activity structure code) for the antisocial and at-risk students during a series of behavioral observations recorded on the playground. (Activity structure codes include recess activities—that is, games, free play, and so on.) As in the classroom, the antisocial students had significantly less favorable profiles on each of these categories than the at-risk students. The two groups were much more nearly equivalent in their positive social behavior than in their negative behavior. Furthermore, the antisocial students had substantially more negative social behavior directed toward them than did the at-risk students. Finally, the antisocial students spent substantially less time in structured activities at recess than did at-risk students.

Overall, these studies of the playground social behavior of antisocial students indicate that their positive social behavior nearly matches the levels of normal peers. However, their rate of negative social behavior is much higher than is normal for the playground. Peers tend to reciprocate these students' negative-aggressive behavior at identical levels (Walker et al., 1987). They are strongly biased toward antisocial children because of their

Excluded from recess activities. *Myrleen Ferguson Cate/PhotoEdit*

unpleasant history of having aversive, negative interactions with them. Peers tend to attribute malevolent intent to the neutral social behavior of antisocial children (Hollinger, 1987). This bias may also be reflected in the fact that antisocial students tend to spend substantially less time than either at-risk or non-antisocial students participating in playground activities and games that have formal rules.

Affective Status

Several studies have documented that antisocial children and youth suffer from depression and self-esteem problems. Patterson et al. (1992) report that low self-esteem is a significant correlate of conduct disorder and antisocial behavior patterns. Approximately one-third of adolescent youth who are depressed are also conduct disordered and have well-established antisocial behavior patterns (Chiles, Miller, & Cox, 1980; Kovacs, Paulauskas, Gatsonis, & Richards, 1988). Furthermore, the mixture of affective problems, such as depression, with conduct disorder escalates the degree of risk. The available evidence indicates that youth who are both depressed and antisocial have more substantial adjustment problems than those who are either only depressed or only antisocial (Marriage, Fine, Moretti, & Haley, 1986). Walker, Stieber, Ramsey, O'Neill, and Eisert (1994) found that depression and low self-esteem were strongly associated with status as an antisocial adolescent.

LONG-TERM OUTCOMES FOR ANTISOCIAL AND AT-RISK BOYS

The senior author and his colleagues recently conducted an eight-year follow-up of their ongoing longitudinal sample of antisocial ($N = 39$) and at-risk ($N = 41$) boys (Walker & Reid, in press). These boys were identified in the fourth grade using (1) parent and teacher ratings on the Aggression Subscale of the Achenbach Child Behavior Checklist (Achenbach, 1991) and (2) an antisocial risk index developed by Patterson and his associates (see Capaldi & Patterson, 1989). The relative risk status of the two subject groups was considered extreme for the antisocial boys and minimal for the at-risk boys.

During their high school years, the dropout rate was 62% for the antisocial group and 12% for the at-risk boys. The antisocial boys had a far higher rate of alcohol, tobacco, and drug use than the at-risk boys. Furthermore, half the antisocial boys reported using drugs and 80% of those said they came to school stoned. Between grade 4 and grade 12, the at-risk boys had a total of 45 arrests; the antisocial boys had 350 arrests over this same time span.

Figure 1.2 plots the yearly frequency of arrests for the two groups. The transition from middle school to high school was associated with a dramatic increase in arrest rate for the antisocial boys, perhaps partly due to association with deviant peers (Patterson et al., 1992). The boys in the at-risk group showed only a gradual increase over the high school years. However, by the end of grade 11, the arrest rate for the two groups was nearly equivalent.

Approximately half of all antisocial children go on to become adolescent delinquent offenders, and one-half to three-quarters of adolescent offenders become adult criminals (see Patterson et al., 1989). These authors note that at some point in late adolescence, the incidence of delinquent acts as a function of age begins to drop, and this trend continues into the late 20s. The data in Figure 1.2 show a clear drop-off effect for the sample of antisocial boys. The reasons underlying this phenomenon are not well understood at present. Burnout, among other factors, has been suggested as primarily accounting for this effect. It is likely that those offenders who continue their criminal activity do so at a very high rate.

GENDER, CONDUCT DISORDER, AND ANTISOCIAL BEHAVIOR

Conduct disorder and antisocial behavior have been studied much more intensively among boys than girls, primarily because of the frequency with which boys engage in these forms of behavior and consequently come in contact with police and the juvenile justice system (Zoccolillo, 1993). Furthermore, boys tend to express their antisocial

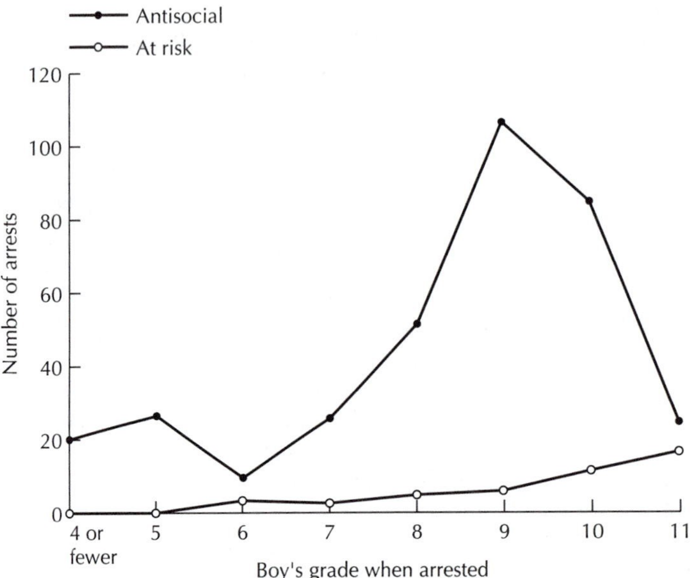

FIGURE 1.2 Frequency of Arrests for Antisocial and At-Risk Boys. *Source:* Patterson et al. (1992).

behavior in confrontational, externalizing (outer-directed) forms, whereas girls are more covert and internalizing (inner-directed) in their behavioral expression of this disorder. In a major review of gender and conduct disorder, Zoccolillo (1993) reports overwhelming evidence of a greater prevalence of antisocial behavior patterns among preadolescent boys than girls. However, some studies show no difference in the prevalence of conduct disorder among adolescent boys and girls. The specific reasons for these discrepant findings between prevalence studies are not currently known.

THE CAUSES AND ORIGINS OF ANTISOCIAL BEHAVIOR PATTERNS

Conduct disorder and antisocial behavior are considered to be multiply determined; a host of constitutional (genetic, neurobiological) and environmental (family, community) factors may influence the development of these behavior patterns (Kazdin, 1985). In terms of causal factors, it is helpful to consider the family situation within a community context. As a rule, the child with conduct disorder is exposed to severe levels of risk at both family and community levels; the development of antisocial behavior patterns is often the unfortunate result of such exposure.

Dodge (1993) has identified three primary types of causal factors that contribute to the development of conduct disorder and antisocial behavior: (1) an adverse early rearing environment, (2) an aggressive pattern of behavior displayed on initial school entry, and (3) social rejection from peers. Dodge describes these major types of causal factors as operating in a temporal sequence. There is compelling empirical evidence that this is actually the case as revealed by the research of Kazdin (1985, 1987), Patterson (1982), Patterson et al., (1992), and Wahler and Dumas (1986).

Patterson and his colleagues (Patterson et al., 1992) have contributed the most complete and detailed explanations of the causal events and processes that account for the development of antisocial behavior patterns. They present a causal model in which a host of family stressors (poverty, divorce, drug and alcohol problems, abuse of family members, and other negative factors) pressure family members severely. Under the influence of these stressors, normal parenting practices are disrupted and family routines become chaotic and unpredictable. Disrupted parenting practices, in turn, lead to social interactions among family members that are reflected in negative-aggressive escalations, the use of coercive techniques to force the submission of others, and the aversive control of behavior by others. Family pathology can become extremely destructive under the influence of these factors. Over time, such conditions provide a fertile breeding ground for the development of antisocial behavior patterns. Children from these homes come to school with negative attitudes about schooling, a limited repertoire of cooperative behavior, and a predilection to use coercive tactics to control and manipulate others.

If a young child brings an antisocial behavior pattern to school and if that pattern is characterized by (1) a high frequency of occurrence, (2) occurrence across multiple settings and contexts, and (3) expression in multiple forms, he or she has a severely elevated risk status for rejection by both peers and teachers. Peer and teacher rejection, in turn, is associated with academic failure, and the child is increasingly isolated. Because of this rejection and social isolation, the antisocial child seeks out others who share the same status, attitudes, and behavioral characteristics. Sociometric studies indicate that antisocial students' best friends are all the other antisocial students in their school (Patterson et al., 1992).

Around grade 4 or 5, antisocial children become eligible for membership in a deviant peer group comprised of other children like themselves. Seventy percent of these children have their first felony arrest within two years of becoming a fully enfranchised member of this deviant peer group. It is important to note that approximately 1 arrest occurs for every 10 to 11 arrestable offenses committed. If the pattern of delinquency continues, it becomes an excellent predictor of adult criminality.

Thus, the path to delinquency, criminality, and ultimately prison begins for many individuals very early in their lives. It starts with the early acquisition of an antisocial behavior pattern within the home and family that is often well developed prior to entering school. If this behavior pattern is elaborated during the primary grades, it leads to social rejection, acceptance by a deviant peer group, and, frequently, to a pattern of criminal behavior. This is a highly predictable path and one that is sadly repeated by thousands and thousands of young people as our societal conditions deteriorate socially, economically, and culturally.

PATHWAYS TO ACQUIRING ANTISOCIAL BEHAVIOR PATTERNS AND CONDUCT DISORDER

Longitudinal and descriptive studies have contributed enormously to our knowledge of the developmental course of conduct disorder and antisocial behavior among at-risk children and youth (see Cicchetti & Nurcombe, 1993). Recent research reported by Patterson et al. (1992) and Loeber et al. (1993) has verified the following observations:

- Many at-risk children demonstrate a progression in their antisocial behavior from *trivial* to *severe* antisocial acts.
- Antisocial children and youth tend to follow one or more of the following paths to conduct disorder: *covert, overt,* and/or *disobedience.*
- Antisocial youth who also follow a path to delinquency can be divided into *early* versus *later* starters.

Patterson and his associates have studied the ecology and dynamics of family interactions of antisocial children and youth more thoroughly than perhaps any group to date (see Patterson, 1982; Patterson et al., 1992; Reid, 1993). They find that many antisocial children progress from trivial to severe antisocial acts over time. Often, this process develops from a situation in which an unskilled parent must care for an infant with a difficult temperament. Tense infant-caregiver interactions and relationships emerge and are damaged by the parents' limited ability to influence the child. This may lead to the child not complying with parental requests, commands, and even demands. Noncompliance eventually turns into oppositional-defiant behavior that can include severe tantrums. The parent may weakly monitor and supervise the child's activities, whereabouts, schedules, and affiliations. This, in turn, can lead to maladaptive behavior involving dishonest acts such as stealing, lying, and cheating. Finally, these forms of behavior are often precursors to delinquent acts, especially if they are accompanied by membership in a deviant peer group.

In an ingenious longitudinal investigation of antisocial behavior patterns, Loeber et al. (1993) empirically identified three pathways to the development of conduct disorder. These pathways are described in Box 1.4.

Some children and youth follow exclusively a covert path, some an overt path, and some a disobedience path. Still others manifest two or all three paths in their progression to conduct disorder. Those who follow a single pathway are much less at risk than are those who follow multiple pathways.

A *covert* path is characterized by stealth and concealment and is directed toward property (vandalism, stealing, fire setting), toward self (substance abuse), or both. In contrast, an *overt* path is directed toward other persons and is characterized by victimization of others, aggressive behavior, the use of coercive tactics to obtain one's way or to force the submission of others. Cruelty, bullying, and fighting are commonly associated with this path. The *disobedience* path involves oppositional behavior (noncompliance, defiance) to adult-imposed rules and behavioral expectations. The dishonesty involved in a covert path (lying, cheating, and stealing) is strongly objectionable to teachers and other school personnel. Aggressive behavior, which characterizes the overt path, leads to rejection by both peers and teachers. Disobedience is an extremely dysfunctional form of student behavior in the context of teaching and managing the classroom environment. Thus, all three of these pathways are very disruptive to school adjustment. They also require slightly different intervention approaches.

Box 1.4 Developmental Pathways to Conduct Disorder

Covert Behavior

Stealing

Lying

Burglary

Drug and alcohol involvement

Overt Behavior

Aggression

Coercion

Bullying

Manipulation of others

Escalated interactions with teachers, parents, and peers

Disobedience

Noncompliance

Oppositional-defiant behavior

Resistant to adult influence

Source: Loeber et al. (1993).

Finally, considerable research interest has developed in the past decade regarding the age of onset of delinquent acts. Juvenile delinquents can be divided into early versus later starters based on the age at which they first begin committing delinquent acts. Early starters are socialized to antisocial behavior from infancy by the family environment and family stressors that disrupt parenting practices. In contrast, later starters are thought to be socialized to delinquency by peer group influences and not by pathological family conditions.

Patterson (in press) and Capaldi and Patterson (in press) analyzed their longitudinal sample of 200 boys and their families according to those who had committed one or more delinquent acts. They found that early starters are substantially more at risk on a host of adjustment measures than are later starters. These authors hypothesize that later starters have not been exposed to negative family conditions and disrupted parenting practices; they also have not experienced academic failure and peer rejection. Thus, their risk profiles are quite different from those of early starters.

The distinction between early and later starters enables us to assess the risk status of antisocial delinquents in a more precise manner. It also has clear implications for intervention.

ANTISOCIAL BEHAVIOR AND VIOLENCE

Our society is consumed, quite justifiably, by fear and concern over the escalating patterns of *violence* that are developing in our society. Violent acts are like earthquakes that are difficult to predict and often seem to strike without warning. Recent studies of delinquency have helped clarify the relationship between violence and antisocial behavior.

Patterson (in press) has shown that youth who are chronic offenders (that is, three or more arrests) are much more likely to be early starters. He found that 100% of boys arrested before the age of 10 had at least three arrests before reaching the age of 17. Capaldi and Patterson (in press) identified 17 boys in their longitudinal sample who had committed violent acts. Each of these 17 boys was found to be a chronic offender. Thus, a severe pattern of antisocial behavior that the child brings to the beginning of the schooling process, coupled with an early start to delinquent acts, identifies a chronic offender. The majority of chronic offenders are perpetrators of violent acts.

The more severe the antisocial behavior pattern and the earlier it begins, the more at risk the child is for delinquency, violence, and a host of long-term, negative developmental outcomes. Gang affiliation is also associated with a huge increase in criminal and violent forms of behavior (Long, 1993).

Violent behavior remains one of the most difficult problems with which our society must cope. In spite of our increasing knowledge of the conditions from which it springs, we are still very limited in our ability to predict and prevent its occurrence.

A recently released study by the National School Boards Association (1993) may prove influential in galvanizing the necessary political action to address this national problem of violence in school. The study involved over 700 school districts nationwide and concluded that (1) violence is more acute now than five years ago and (2) the increase results primarily from the breakdown of the family and the portrayal of violent acts in the media. Other major causes of violence cited in the survey include alcohol and drug abuse, easy access to guns, and poverty.

In the survey and its report, 39% of responding urban districts reported a shooting or knife attack in school during the previous year, and 23% reported drive-by shootings. Suburban and rural school districts also reported an increase in the number and seriousness of violent incidents, including rapes and shootings. More than 80% of the 700 participating districts also reported increases in school violence during the past five years, with 35% noting that the increase was significant. Seventy-seven percent of the districts surveyed cited changing family situations, and 60% cited the media as being primarily responsible for this increase.

The report notes that the most common methods schools use to reduce violence are suspension, increasing police presence on campuses, teaching students alternative ways of handling conflict, and setting up separate schools for disruptive students. Thirty-nine percent of urban schools reported using metal detectors, and 11% have installed closed-circuit television systems. One school district hired a gang member to discourage children and youth from joining gangs.

This report suggests that the issues of violence and school safety must rise to the level of a national emergency. A national plan is needed, along with a significant infusion of resources, to develop effective strategies for coping with this problem that can be broadly disseminated and adopted. It also calls for research on development of new methods for preventing and coping with violent acts in schools.

A PERSPECTIVE ON VIOLENCE

Violent acts committed within the family, school, and community threaten the very fabric of our society. Like tornadoes and earthquakes, violent acts usually occur without warning, do incredible damage, and require long periods for recovery. Just as we know that tornadoes, for example, arise out of volatile thermoconvectional conditions, we understand something of the conditions that are associated with violent acts: (1) family stressors such as poverty, alcohol, and drug abuse; (2) a history of physical, sexual, and/or psychological abuse, neglect, and so forth; (3) depression, frustration, and a sense of hopelessness; and (4) exposure to the modeling or display of violence. As with tornadoes, we can sometimes identify the mix of volatile conditions and triggering events that make violent acts more likely to occur. However, once triggered and unleashed, they run their course and often leave a wake of destruction in their path.

Because violent acts are so difficult to predict and nearly impossible to control once they occur, we believe far greater efforts must be made to prevent or ameliorate the conditions out of which they arise (Schorr, 1988). We have the scientific knowledge and overall capability to address this social problem in an effective manner. Furthermore, it is a *societal* problem that we must solve collectively. Schools have an important role to play in this regard; however, they are by no means responsible for solving this complex problem on their own, nor should they be held primarily accountable for doing so.

Our society's social and economic problems are spilling over into the schooling process in an unfortunate, but highly predictable, manner. They are greatly complicating the basic tasks involved in educating our students. The school's primary task is to facilitate the academic achievement and social development of all students to the maximum extent possible. Students who bring maladaptive behavior patterns to school or who are prone to violence must be *directly taught* a replacement adaptive behavior pattern that will enhance their chances of (1) staying in school for as long as possible (80% of all crimes are committed by high school dropouts), (2) achieving school success, and (3) gaining acceptance from teachers and peers. Even though many children and youth of today come from and return to chaotic home environments on a daily basis, they can still succeed in school if given the proper supports and access to good instruction. Dealing proactively and effectively with this problem is one of the greatest challenges currently facing our schools.

THE COSTS OF ANTISOCIAL BEHAVIOR

Kazdin (1993) argues that the costs of antisocial behavior are nearly impossible to calculate accurately because of their pervasiveness and subtle nature. Antisocial behavior is extremely costly to the individual and to all those (family members, friends, coworkers, educators) who interact with him or her. The lost productivity, the social and economic costs to the individual, and the pain associated with this condition over a lifetime are devastating.

Patterson et al. (1989) note that the United States spends more than $1 billion annually simply to maintain our juvenile justice system. They cite evidence that the annual cost of vandalism approximates half a billion dollars. They note that follow-up studies of antisocial youth show that, as adults, they are severely at risk for accidents, alcoholism, drug abuse and addiction, chronic unemployment, divorce, physical and psychiatric illnesses, and higher hospitalization and mortality rates than normal (Patterson et al., 1989; see also Kazdin, 1985).

Antisocial children and youth are chronic victimizers of others. They tend to use coercive tactics to achieve short-term gains, but they are severe losers over the long-term. In a very real sense, they are also victimized by their own behavior and circumstances. They need substantial assistance to break out of this behavior pattern. Schools can play a pivotal role in this process.

A LOOK TO THE FUTURE

Fisher and Smith-Davis (1990) have described the social and economic trends that are contributing to the collapse of children's services nationally and to the resulting crisis in child development that is broadly recognized. They point to such factors as pervasive poverty, substance exposure and abuse, changing morality patterns among children and youth, child abuse and neglect, the effects of divorce and single-parent homes, teenage pregnancy, school dropout, increasing delinquency rates, expanding needs for mental health services, the sharp increase in homelessness, and the shortage of trained personnel to respond to these critical needs. The effects of these conditions are spilling over into the schooling process and are making the teaching-learning process far more difficult for students and school personnel. Furthermore, in the past two decades, these conditions are largely responsible for the following recently reported statistics on outcomes:

1. Twenty percent of all children under age 18 currently live in poverty.
2. Twelve percent of all children have a diagnosed mental disorder.
3. Twenty-eight percent of all students fail to graduate from high school.
4. Three million children have a serious drinking problem.
5. Fifty-nine percent of all children will live in a single-parent household before reaching the age of 18.
6. Sixteen percent of all children under age 3 suffer abuse and/or neglect.
7. At least 10% of all births in the United States are to drug addicted mothers, thus exposing their babies to serious lifelong health problems.
8. Approximately 6 to 8 million children in our nation who are in need of mental health interventions receive no care whatever; other children, perhaps 50% of those in need of treatment, receive care that is inappropriate for their needs.

The deteriorating conditions of our society, as well as the negative outcomes resulting from them, are a matter of public record. In our view, this is a national emergency that warrants systematic attention at the highest levels of government, advocacy, and policymaking. During 1993, 3 million acts of child abuse were recorded in the United States. A total of 1,299 children died as a result of such abuse (*USA Today*, April 1994). Box 1.5 provides a fact sheet on child abuse and illustrates the pervasive scope of this problem.

Such abuse sets the stage for intense anger, rage, and the development of antisocial behavior. It destroys lives and puts children at risk for a host of negative outcomes. As a society, we seem to be increasingly unable to provide safe family environments and neighborhoods in which to raise our children. Child abuse and antisocial behavior are strongly linked conditions and both flow through generations (from grandparents to parents to children).

Last year, 3 million acts of violence and theft took place in our public schools. Each day, over 100,000 weapons are brought to school, and more than 40 children and youth are either killed or wounded by these weapons. In our country, 1 murder occurs every 20 minutes, resulting in an annual carnage of 24,000 persons who are tragically robbed of the remainder of their lives. FBI statistics show that more than 11,000 persons died between 1980 and 1989 due to homicides committed by high school–aged youth. An elementary school in North Carolina recently reported that 35% of their fifth graders bring weapons to school; half of these children indicated they need the weapons for their own protection! Here are some salient occurrences that typify an average day in the United States (Children's Defense Fund, 1990):

- 135,000 children bring a gun to school.
- 10 children die from gunshots and 30 are wounded.
- 211 children and youth are arrested for drug abuse.
- 1,295 teenagers give birth and 2,795 get pregnant.
- 1,512 teenagers drop out of school.
- 1,849 children are abused or neglected.
- 3,288 children run away from home.
- 2,989 children see their parents divorce.

The specter of random, unprovoked violence has put our society on edge and made our neighborhoods and schools unsafe places to be. The proliferation of gang affiliations is rampant and associated with a dramatic rise in criminal activity among our youth. Juvenile delinquency remains the single best predictor of adult criminal behavior, and the number of youth adopting delinquent life-styles is escalating dramatically (Long & Brendtro, 1992; Patterson et al., 1992).

A 1991 article in the *Los Angeles Times* (cited by Cantrell, 1992) reported that in 1985, there were approximately 500 known gangs in this country with 45,000 members; by 1991, this figure was estimated to have increased to 900 gangs with 90,000 members

Box 1.5 Child Abuse and Neglect Fact Sheet

- Child abuse was formally recognized by the medical profession in 1961 as the "battered child syndrome."
- In 1991, state child protective service agencies received and referred for investigation an estimated 1.8 million reports of alleged child abuse and neglect, involving approximately 2.7 million children. Since 1980, reports of child abuse and neglect have more than doubled.
- Approximately 863,000 children were found to be substantiated or indicated victims of child abuse and neglect in 1991. More than three children die each day in the United States as a result of abuse or neglect.
- Among substantiated cases of child maltreatment in 1991, approximately 44% were for neglect, 24% for physical abuse, 15% for sexual abuse, and 17% for other forms of maltreatment.
- The link between substance abuse and child abuse has strengthened over the years. Parental abuse of alcohol and use of other drugs has been identified as a major factor contributing to child maltreatment and death. It is estimated that nearly 10 million children under age 18 are affected in some way by the substance abuse of their parents.
- Child maltreatment often has negative short- and long-term effects on children's mental health and development. For example, abused and neglected children frequently suffer drops in IQ and an increase in learning disabilities, depression, and drug use.
- The effects of child abuse are sometimes obvious even decades later. The effects are often pervasive: mental, physical, and social in nature. Suicide, violence, delinquency, drug and alcohol abuse, and other forms of criminality are frequently child-abuse-related.
- Studies of adults show that 15 to 38% of women report experiences of various types of sexual victimization during childhood and adolescence, and about 10% of men report sexual abuse during childhood and adolescence.
- Although child abuse occurs in all racial, ethnic, cultural, and socioeconomic groups, physical abuse and neglect are more likely among people in poverty. Reflecting the high rates of poverty among ethnic minorities, minority children enter the child protection system in disproportionately large numbers.

Source: National Clearinghouse on Child Abuse and Neglect Information (P.O. Box 1182, Washington, DC 20013-1182; phone (800) FYI-3366).

(see *Los Angeles Times*, January 1991; Cantrell, 1992). Klein (1994) reports that currently there are *9,000 gangs with 400,000 members nationwide.* This is an astronomical gain over the past nine years. Furthermore, 90% of these gangs are indigenous to the 47 states and 766 cities that currently report having one or more street gangs who define themselves in terms of the ecology of a criminal culture.

Gangs are a symbol, albeit a destructive one, of deterioration in the social structure of our society. Gang membership alluringly offers the promise of identity, belonging, protection, excitement, money, and sex. Membership springs from dysfunctional families, exposure to pervasive poverty, and crumbling social institutions. Gangs provide an organized vehicle for antisocial groups of youth to come together where drug trafficking and violence are normative forms of behavior. (See Cantrell, 1992; for a comprehensive treatment of this topic, see the Spring 1992 special issue of the *Journal of Emotional and Behavioral Problems*).

Gang affiliations of all types are an expression of the need to bond with others for support, safety, friendship, and status. Such affiliations are associated with the destruction of the nuclear or extended family that traditionally has provided for these basic human needs. Given that these needs are invariant and that adequately addressing them is no longer possible by traditional means, alternative procedures must be developed for meeting them in a constructive, positive fashion. This difficult goal will be achieved only by the forging of effective partnerships between schools, families, churches, social agencies, community resources, and the private sector. Most important, children and youth need to access safe places and appropriate peers with whom to "hang out" and do things. Schools can have a substantial impact in solving this problem, but they should not be expected to shoulder the full burden of this responsibility.

Schools are not responsible for the negative societal developments we are experiencing nor for their unfortunate effects. Our schools cannot begin to solve these complex problems alone, yet they are charged with educating *all* children and youth who come through the schoolhouse door. School systems must cope with these challenges as best they can while trying to enlist the support and cooperation of families and other agencies concerned with this problem. At a minimum, the teachers, parents, and peers of these difficult and unfortunate children *must* be affected if acceptable changes for antisocial students are to have any chance of being achieved.

Schools and other institutions in our society tend to blame children and youth having conduct disorders and see them as deliberately choosing to be antisocial and aversive in their daily behavior. In most cases, these children and youth are themselves victims of circumstances beyond their control. Due to prolonged exposure to negative and chaotic environmental conditions, they are inadvertently taught and acquire a destructive, maladaptive pattern of behavior that sets them up for a lifetime of pain, frustration, and disappointment to themselves and others. They are truly among the most challenging students with whom schools must cope.

A great deal is known about how to divert children, youth, and families from the paths leading to these destructive outcomes, and successful model programs in this regard have been noted and described by Schorr (1988), Reid (1993), and Patterson et al. (1992). Systematic intervention and support from *outside the family*, provided early in the life-

The beginnings of a gang. *Tom McKitterick/Impact Visuals*

cycle, can substantially reduce known risk factors and improve the chances of antisocial children and youth being diverted from a path leading to negative, long-term outcomes that may include prison. In her seminal investigative work, Schorr (1988) found that the most effective programs were those that (1) offer comprehensive and intensive services, (2) are able to respond flexibly and promptly to a wide variety of family needs, (3) are open to the diverse needs of a family at risk, and (4) have staff who are able to invest the time and possess the skills necessary to establish relationships based on mutual respect and trust. We believe these program attributes apply equally well to successful school responses to the needs of antisocial students and that they are deserving of access to effective interventions and support within the school setting.

The remainder of this book is devoted to providing perspectives, guidelines, and strategies for use by school personnel in achieving these goals. There are no magic bullets in this material. Dealing with this antisocial student population is difficult, frustrating, and often without identifiable reward. However, of all those who suffer from conditions and disorders that impair school performance, these students are among the most capable, with the greatest capacity for change. We believe antisocial students deserve access to the best practices and model programs—those that have proven to be effective in the past. Our basic purpose here is to describe and illustrate these practices.

RECOMMENDED SOURCES ON VIOLENCE

Violence and Youth: Psychology's Response. Volumes I and II. American Psychological Association Public Interest Directorate, 750 First Street NE, Washington, DC 20002-4242.

Understanding and Preventing Violence. Volumes I, II, and III. National Academic Press, 2101 Constitution Avenue NW, Washington, DC 20418.

STUDY QUESTIONS

1. Define antisocial behavior among children and youth.
2. How extensive is the actual prevalence of antisocial behavior among school-age children and youth?
3. Discuss the responsiveness of antisocial behavior to intervention at preschool, elementary, middle school, and high school levels.
4. How stable is antisocial behavior over a decade as compared to human intelligence?
5. Discuss the connection between antisocial behavior patterns and various types of aggression.
6. Describe the characteristic behavior of antisocial students on the playground. How do peers react to their positive and negative behavior?
7. What are the long-term outcomes and correlates of an early investment in antisocial behavior?
8. Discuss the multiple, potential causes of antisocial behavior.
9. Describe the three major types of antisocial behavior patterns.
10. What is the relationship between antisocial behavior and violence?
11. Discuss the attractions of gang membership to children and youth.

KEY TERMS

abuse
academic achievement
aggression
antisocial
at risk
aversive
conduct disorder
covert–overt
delinquency
neglect
peer acceptance
violence

2 Issues and Procedural Recommendations Regarding Effective Interventions for Antisocial Behavior in School

The School's Role in the Prevention and Remediation of Antisocial Behavior Patterns

The Broader Societal Context and Influence Factors Affecting the Development of Antisocial Behavior

Factors Affecting the Magnitude of Outcomes Achievable by School-Based Interventions

Developmental Continuum of Service Delivery and Expected Outcomes for Antisocial Behavior Patterns

Design and Application of Comprehensive, Coordinated Interventions Applied Early in a Child's School Career

Early Screening and Identification of Antisocial Behavior Patterns

Achenbach Case
Drummond Case
Walker, Severson, and Feil Case

Key Target Areas That Antisocial Interventions Should Address

Universal and Selected Interventions for Addressing Antisocial Behavior Patterns in School

Recommended Intervention Techniques for Use in Designing Interventions for Antisocial Behavior

Guidelines for Implementing Best-Practice Intervention Procedures

Generic Strategies
Implementation Recommendations

Program-Environment Fit or Match Considerations

The NCTV Ten-Point Plan to Sweep Violence off TV and off Our Streets

Conclusion

This chapter sets the stage for using and understanding the rest of the book. It is designed to give the reader an understanding of the culture and social ecology of schools as they relate to implementing interventions for antisocial students. This chapter also offers procedural guidelines and recommendations for the reader to consider in implementing *universal* and *selected* interventions designed to prevent or remediate antisocial behavior patterns. With such knowledge, we believe it is more likely that best-practice interventions for at-risk children and youth can be delivered that will actually have a chance of positively impacting their myriad adjustment problems. The term *school-based interventions* is used to refer to behavior-change procedures that either originate in the school and are extended to other settings or are restricted to implementation within schools. Very often, antisocial students require interventions that address issues and needs extending beyond school boundaries.

Schools provide both an important setting and a powerful context for intervening with antisocial students, but schools are, at once, complex and delicate organizations. Infusing effective interventions for antisocial behavior into the school's ongoing operations requires sensitivity, tact, and careful attention to a host of details. The overall goals of this chapter are threefold: first, we attempt to document the external school factors that impact antisocial behavior patterns and also constrain schools as they respond to them; second, we attempt to create a foundation and context for the school-based delivery of best-practice interventions for antisocial behavior; and third, we describe generic guidelines, recommendations, and resources that will facilitate the identification and implementation of these best-practice interventions for use in reducing and replacing antisocial behavior patterns. Mastery of this information is essential to the effective understanding and use of the material presented in subsequent chapters, which provide detailed information on the critical components of a comprehensive strategy for addressing antisocial behavior patterns (that is, working with parents, developing schoolwide discipline plans, implementing social skills training procedures, investing in violence prevention, and school safety interventions).

This chapter deals with a broad range of topics. Some of the information presented is empirically derived and has stood the tests of replication and time. Other information is experiential in nature and less formal; it reflects the authors' collective experiences as well as those of other professionals who deal with school-based interventions. We believe both types of information are valuable and hold useful wisdom for those who venture bravely into classroom, playground, and other settings intent on improving the adjustment capability of antisocial students.

This chapter begins by describing the roles that schools and educators can play in mounting effective intervention approaches for the prevention and remediation of antisocial behavior patterns among school-age children and youth. The societal context in which schools must function and the social conditions influencing the development of antisocial behavior patterns are also reviewed. Factors affecting the magnitude of outcomes that can be reasonably expected for school-based interventions are discussed, both generically and in relation to antisocial students. A developmental continuum of service delivery and expected outcomes for antisocial behavior patterns is presented. A case is made for the design and application of comprehensive, coordinated interventions that are implemented early in a child's school career. The importance of the earliest possible identification of children at risk for antisocial behavior is discussed, along with recommended practices for doing so. The key target areas that interventions should address are presented and briefly discussed. Both universal intervention approaches (designed for everyone) and selected intervention approaches (designed for individual students) are illustrated along with their appropriate uses. Recommended intervention techniques, and effective combinations of them, are described—as are the sequences in which they should be applied. Guidelines are presented for the reader's consideration in the application of these approaches and techniques. Finally, the extremely important issue of program-environment fit or the "degree of match" between the specific features of an intervention program and the setting in which it is applied is discussed.

THE SCHOOL'S ROLE IN THE PREVENTION AND REMEDIATION OF ANTISOCIAL BEHAVIOR PATTERNS

Policymakers and legislators, at both federal and state levels, view schools as the penultimate vehicle for accessing children who are in need of services, supports, and interventions that can dramatically affect their physical and mental health (for example, medical and sensory screenings, vaccinations, and treatments of various kinds). Schools are also important settings for detecting children who suffer the palpable effects of neglect and various forms of abuse. As families and their members continue to abandon their parenting responsibilities on a broad scale, schools are being asked more and more to assume the role of protector, socializing agent, and caregiver. Instruction in sex education, drug awareness, wellness and health promotion, and rudimentary parenting skills are increasingly in evidence in the curricula of public schools. Soon, schools will be expected and required to instruct children and youth in how to protect themselves from violence.

Schools, especially at the elementary level, are desperate for counseling services to deal with the devastating effects that the deteriorating social and economic conditions of our society have on our young children. Larry Cuban's (1989) prophecy that the school of the 21st century will likely be "a site for the delivery of integrated social and educational services" seems to be unfolding ahead of schedule in many parts of our country. Although most educators would prefer to simply be held accountable for educating our children and youth, we now expect schools to educate them effectively, prepare them for life and careers, *and* compensate for our neglect in preparing them for schooling and providing a safe home in which to develop. In the past, school has been one of the only safe havens available for at-risk children and youth; now, even that safety is being seriously eroded in many urban, suburban, and some rural areas of our country.

Schools have few answers for effectively teaching young children and youth who are hungry; who are unable to sleep well at night because of the myriad anxieties they hold about their personal safety; and who must suffer the indignities of sexual, physical and psychological abuse on a daily basis. If present trends continue, we will have produced generations of children and youth who will be in long-term states of rage and anger at the treatment they have received at the hands of family members, acquaintances, and the larger society. Complex obstacles stand between such children and youth and their

A way station on the path to prison? *Jim West/Meese Photo Research*

achievement of desirable outcomes like school success; selection of and preparation for a career path; and being productive, contributing members of society.

In the face of all these developments, we are (1) reducing our investment in public schools, (2) asking schools to restructure and reform themselves, and (3) becoming more and more vocal in criticizing school systems for their failure to compensate for our failures as a society. Survey after survey shows that we invest far less in our educational system and infrastructure than do other modern, industrialized nations. We also lead the world in the rate of incarcerating our citizens—particularly our youth. In a speech given in the early 1900s near the end of his life, Mark Twain delivered a true anecdote that has compelling relevance for us as we approach the 21st century. He told the story of a farmer in Missouri who had heard that a local township wanted to close some of its schools because they were too expensive. After listening to the debate on this issue at a town meeting, the farmer said, "Well, I don't see how we are going to save any money. For every school we close, we'll just have to build a new jail." At this moment, we are

TABLE 2.1 Literacy-Related Reading Opportunities of Preschool Children

Level	*Time Spent Daily*	*Time Spent Annually*	*Six-Year Cumulative*
High	30–45 minutes	180–270 hours	Over 1,000 hours
Middle	10 minutes	60 hours	360 hours
Low	1 minute	6 hours	36 hours

Source: From *Beginning to Read: Thinking and Learning about Print,* by M. J. Adams. Copyright © 1990 MIT Press, Cambridge, MA. Reprinted by permission.

systematically reducing our fiscal investment in schools and building new jails at a rate perhaps unparalleled in our history!

Schools are, we believe, willing participants in developing solutions to the complex problems that are threatening to overwhelm our society and change our lives in ways we never thought imaginable. However, they cannot do the job alone. They need our investment—our time, money, support, and expertise—as never before. They also need our tolerance and should receive the clear benefit of the doubt as they struggle to educate all children effectively and, at the same time, deal compassionately with the battered victims of many of our incompetent and unspeakably cruel socialization efforts. Our society charges public schools with educating all children who enter the schoolhouse door and to do so in a fair and equitable manner. In the mass processing of children within our school system, educators are faced with increasing numbers of children who are severely disadvantaged in their ability to meet minimal expectations and to compete effectively with their peers. Many at-risk and antisocial children simply do not have the school-readiness skills and preschool experiences that would allow them to be successful as they begin their school careers. Long-term outcomes for these children and youth are often dismal.

Differences among first grade children in beginning reading literacy provide a good example of how many antisocial children from impoverished backgrounds are severely disadvantaged as they begin their school careers. Juel (1988) investigated this problem extensively and concludes that, if you were a good reader in grade 1, the probability of staying a good reader in grade 4 is .87; however, if you were a poor reader in grade 1, the probability of remaining a poor reader at the end of grade 4 is .88. The good news is that if you start school ready to learn and are a good reader, you will remain so; the bad news is that if you start school not ready to learn and you are a poor reader, you will also remain so.

Table 2.1 shows the typical literacy-related reading opportunities (that is, time in which parents either read to or read with their preschool children) that are available for disadvantaged (low) versus advantaged (high) children. These findings reveal huge differences favoring non-at-risk students as they begin their school careers.

Adams (1990) points to the thousands of hours of school-like reading experiences that the disadvantaged children lack upon school entry, as compared with the advantaged children. She questions whether a first grade teacher can make up this difference with a teacher-student ratio of 1:20 or 1:25. Given the demands on teacher resources in grade 1 (that is, from children who are newly adjusting to the schooling experience), this seems extremely unlikely. The key factor is how much time parents and other caregivers spend reading to children in the preschool and school years, as well as whether they discuss the material read. Given the chaotic family environments from which many antisocial children emerge, it is not likely they will have the benefit of this kind of preparation. This is a major factor in explaining the poor record of school performance of antisocial students and calls for the use of peer-tutoring strategies and volunteers in closing this gap.

We believe a two-pronged strategy is required to address the social- and academic-adjustment problems previously cited that are producing droves of young children who are seriously at risk for developing antisocial behavior patterns, conduct disorder, school failure and dropout, delinquency, violent behavior, and adult criminality. It is estimated that 20 to 40% of the school-age population can be considered at risk of school failure and dropout because of long-term exposure to these conditions (OERI, 1994). A significant number of these same children will also follow a trajectory leading to antisocial behavior, conduct disorder, delinquency, and adult criminality.

Congress must galvanize public attention on the true dimensions of the problems we are facing in this regard and declare a national emergency to address them. In our view, these problems are so massive that they will require a coordinated national effort in order to solve them. Public Law 99-457 mandates early screening, intervention services, and supports for children and families who suffer from disabilities and handicapping conditions. We need a parallel law that addresses the needs of young children and families who are at risk for developing antisocial behavior patterns, school failure, violent behavior, and delinquency. Our current legal mandates for providing essential services are not adequate for coping with the rising tide of antisocial behavior problems we are seeing in our schools and society.

Equally important, schools must be broadly supported and perhaps mandated to engage in partnerships with social service agencies that have the capacity to address those critical, unmet needs of children that affect their education and quality of life. School districts and consortia of social service agencies across the country are beginning to develop *school-linked models* of services and supports targeted to families and their children who are at risk. The New Beginnings program of the San Diego, California, school district is an outstanding example of these efforts. The Robert Wood Johnson Foundation has been a highly effective supporter and funder of such models in a number of states including Kentucky and California. The Center for the Future of Children, supported by the David and Lucile Packard Foundation, has produced a major study of school-linked models for at-risk students in which critical issues such as funding, coordination and integration of services, infrastructure, evaluation, and feasible models are examined and reviewed (see *The Future of Children: School-Linked Services*, Spring 1992; available from The David and Lucile Packard Foundation, 300 Second Street, Suite 102, Los Altos, CA 94022). To date, private foundations and local school districts, in collaboration with consortia of social agencies, have taken the lead in developing our capacity in this important domain, and they are to be lauded for their efforts. However, it is essential that federal, state, and local governments invest aggressively in a *school-linked services* approach if we are to have any chance of dealing effectively with the problems confronting us. Schools can play an extremely powerful and critical role in this process if they are allowed to do so and are supported in the process.

THE BROADER SOCIETAL CONTEXT AND INFLUENCE FACTORS AFFECTING THE DEVELOPMENT OF ANTISOCIAL BEHAVIOR

We know a great deal about the societal factors and conditions that accelerate the development of antisocial behavior patterns—which often manifest themselves in violent acts committed against persons or property. For example, the American Psychological Association's recently published analysis of violence among children and youth cites four individual social experiences that seem to accelerate the pace with which our children and youth travel down the path toward antisocial behavior, violence, and ultimately, prison: (1) early involvement with drugs and alcohol, (2) easy access to guns and firearms, (3) association with antisocial groups, and (4) depictions of violent acts in the media (film and television). The authors of this superb document argue that extensive and powerful empirical evidence supports the influential role of each of these factors (see *Violence and Youth: Psychology's Response*; available from the American Psychological Association, Public Interest Directorate, 750 First Street NE, Washington, DC 20002-4242). Similarly, in her seminal work on the societal, at-risk factors that victimize children, youth, and families, Lisbeth Schorr (1988) notes that we *must*, as a society, address three outcomes that are systematically destroying the fabric of our society: (1) school failure, (2) too-early parenthood (that is, teenage pregnancy), and (3) delinquency. She describes these outcomes as time bombs that will have dire consequences now and in the future if we do not get control of them. Also, strong links among these outcomes exacerbate their effects—witness the very strong relationships among school failure, delinquency, and adult criminality. To make matters worse, access to instruction and educational opportunity in many of our prison systems is considered a privilege (to be taken away as a punishment) rather than a mandated right.

The documented role of violent, aggressive acts to which our children are being constantly exposed is receiving increasing attention by legislators and policymakers. Dr. Carole Lieberman, a psychiatrist and noted expert on violence in the media, makes a persuasive case that the media has played a key role in desensitizing our society to violence in such a way that it is now considered by many to be endemic and culturally normative (Lieberman, 1994). However, leaders of this industry continue to deny the overwhelming empirical evidence that such exposure increases violent, aggressive tendencies among children and youth in much the same way that the tobacco industry has denied the health risks of smoking. Box 2.1 presents some facts and Dr. Lieberman's conclusions.

Dr. Lieberman is chair of the National Coalition on Television Violence (NCTV), founded in 1980, which is dedicated to reducing glamorized violence in the media. In 1992, on behalf of NCTV, Dr. Lieberman presented a ten-point plan to the House Judiciary's Subcommittee on Crime and Criminal Justice that is designed to sweep vio-

Box 2.1 Expert Observations Regarding Violence and the Media

- Hundreds of empirical studies have documented that exposure to media violence (video games, TV news, cartoons, children's programs, films, and daily television programs) desensitizes children to violent acts, makes them more likely to behave in an aggressive fashion, and increases the likelihood they will commit violent acts themselves.
- Media violence should be thought of as a highly *addictive* lethal drug that requires ever-higher doses (that is, exposure to more and increasingly graphic violent acts) in order to produce the same rush and to satisfy the addiction.
- The new drug of media violence is flooding our lives and is being sold by the entertainment and news industries 24 hours per day.
- TV news ratings are perceived as being tied to the portrayal of higher levels of violent content. There is evidence that the coverage of violent events by TV news is considerably out of proportion to any increases in the actual rates of violent crimes over the past decade.
- It is very unlikely that the problems of violence in our society can be solved until glamorized media violence is effectively dealt with.

Source: Lieberman (1994).

lence off television. A copy of this plan is presented at the end of this chapter. It contains some excellent and feasible suggestions but does not recommend censorship.

What can schools do about this issue? Perhaps their most valuable contribution would be in teaching students about the risks of consistent exposure to media violence and informing them of its subtle, psychological effects. Students could also be taught about how to become selective in their viewing habits and how to interpret violent events to which they are exposed in the media. Curricula and instructional models for informing students about the health risks of smoking provide an excellent prototype for doing the same thing with media violence.

Media violence is but one of the social toxins that is poisoning the wellspring of our society. Racial discrimination, class conflict, drug and alcohol abuse, political extremism, cultural differences, poverty, domestic abuse, parental neglect, and marital conflict are also powerful contributors to this effect. The "Case of Judge Hargreaves" provides a firsthand look at these problems and how they affect the lives of our children and youth.

Judge Hargreaves is a member of the circuit court of Oregon; however, for the past five years, he has served with distinction as a juvenile court judge in Lane County,

Oregon. The average tenure for juvenile court judges is approximately two years; because of his dedication and commitment, however, Judge Hargreaves served in this role for five years. His experiences therein and his insightful interpretations of them were reported recently in an article he wrote for publication in a Eugene newspaper (*Register-Guard*, April 10, 1994). In his article, which is reproduced in Appendix B, he presents an eloquent analysis of our society's problems through the special vision he has been afforded from his position as a juvenile court judge. Judge Hargreaves makes a persuasive case that we must all assume ownership of these problems and pledge to do something about them. The reader is urged to read and reflect on the content of this article.

The nature–nurture controversy is never more evident than in the debate over the true roots of antisocial behavior. It is difficult to identify and clearly separate the roles of inherited versus social-environmental factors in the development of antisocial behavior patterns; it is even more difficult to reliably isolate an early predilection toward committing violent acts. However, it is possible that such attributes as *activity levels, hormone levels, temperament*, and *impulsivity* are at least partially inherited and could thus serve as precursors (that is, predisposing factors) for the development of agitated, antisocial behavior.

On the nurture side of the issue, there is considerable evidence that the family context and parenting practices play strong, contributing roles in the development of antisocial behavior patterns (see Kazdin, 1987; Patterson, 1982; Patterson, Reid, & Dishion, 1992). The specific parenting practices and family stressors that account for this outcome are reviewed in Chapters 1 and 11 of this book. It is also possible that traumatic head injury and the resulting neurological insults may be a contributing factor in the development of agitation and aggression and could, in some instances, trigger violent episodes.

Schools have to function in the contexts of neighborhoods, community, and the larger society, and they must educate and manage students who are often products of unfortunate family conditions and parenting practices. All of these contexts can, to some extent, influence the development of antisocial behavior patterns. There is very little that schools can do, directly, to reduce the negative impact these contexts have on children's development. Figure 2.1 provides an overview of the factors within and across such contexts that serve as influencing conditions affecting the development of antisocial behavior patterns among children and youth.

As shown in Figure 2.1, social-environmental factors operate at four levels: family, school and neighborhood, community, and society. Family has the most direct influence and is most proximal to the development process, particularly to the origins of the antisocial behavior pattern. Societal factors operate at the most distal level and exert the least direct influence on the development of antisocial behavior. Within each level, we have identified important variables from the literature that seem to suggest a causal role or influence.

Schools can do relatively little on their own to mediate or attenuate the effects of social-environmental factors operating at a societal, community, or neighborhood level. However, with the cooperation and active support of social service agencies, churches, neighborhood associations, volunteer community groups, and families, they can do a great deal. Perhaps, the best chance for a school-based impact in preventing and remedi-

Level One: Family Factors

1. Disrupted and unskilled parenting practices
2. Family stressors: poverty, alcohol and drug abuse, parent criminality, single caregiver, and so on

Level Two: School and Neighborhood Factors

1. Early labeling of antisocial student as deviant
2. Rejection by teachers and peers
3. Social disorganization of neighborhood and loss of ability to monitor, supervise, and control youth

Level Three: Community Factors

1. Crime rate
2. Socioeconomic level
3. Availability of recreation and leisure activities for children and youth
4. Gang activity

Level Four: Societal Factors

1. Problems with job and career-path availability
2. Depictions of violent acts in the media (film, TV programs, and news)
3. Social discrimination and ethnic conflict
4. Lack of cultural cohesion and social harmony

FIGURE 2.1 Social-Environmental Influence Factors in the Development of Antisocial Behavior Patterns among Children and Youth

ating antisocial behavior patterns involves (1) starting as early as possible—in preschool and kindergarten, if possible; (2) working with *all* families to build strong school-home communication bonds that foster cooperation, mutual respect, and positive regard; (3) serving as a site for the delivery and integration of interagency services and resources for dealing with the problems of at-risk students as early as possible in their school careers; and (4) working collaboratively with other agencies to provide distressed families with the supports, technical assistance, and training they need to cope with the stressors and problems that spill over into their children's lives and negatively affect their school performance.

In certain situations, schools may be able to indirectly influence the cohesiveness and social ecology of the neighborhoods they serve by playing a leadership role in (1) developing a sense of community, (2) connecting families and neighborhood members to each other, and (3) making the school a center for neighborhood and community activities. Sociological research indicates that a community or neighborhood's level of *social disorganization* is a strong predictor of gang activity, delinquency, and crime victimization (Sampson, 1992). Social disorganization refers to the absence of a sense of neighborhood cohesion, a lack of neighborhood support networks, conflicting values, and social isolation. This disorganization is directly related to a neighborhood's ability to control delinquency and delinquent activities.

Sampson and Groves (1989) identified three dimensions of social disorganization that are relevant to delinquency. First is the ability of a community or neighborhood to

Social isolation in a neighborhood. *Amy Etra/PhotoEdit*

supervise and control teenage peer groups. Where low levels of cohesion and high levels of social disorganization exist, gangs very often develop from spontaneous play groups. A second dimension consists of local friendship and acquaintance networks that empower neighborhood members to recognize strangers and to engage in guardianship behavior that protects against victimization. Finally, a third dimension relates to participation in formal and voluntary organizations that allows a neighborhood to advocate and defend its local interests. A weak base in this area impairs the neighborhood's ability to exercise effective social control.

The full integration of schools into neighborhood and community life can do much to rebuild the social infrastructure that has been so devastated by the social and economic problems of the past quarter century. The African proverb, "It takes a whole village to raise a child," has special relevance in this context. We must rebuild the village of our society so that we can again provide healthy, nurturing, and safe neighborhoods in which families can raise their children. The field of community psychology offers proven methods for influencing communities to adopt more effective practices (for example, smoking cessation and reduction in drug and alcohol consumption). This field has recently mounted efforts to influence communities to adopt more effective parenting and schooling practices (see Biglan, 1992, 1993; Biglan, Lewin, & Hops, 1990). The methodology of community psychology should be an integral part of any larger attempts to address our societal problems in this area.

FACTORS AFFECTING THE MAGNITUDE OF OUTCOMES ACHIEVABLE BY SCHOOL-BASED INTERVENTIONS

The effectiveness of school-based interventions is an area of continuous debate. It has been described as a search for the "magic bullet"; that is, the magical 5-minute intervention that works every time and lasts forever! Such an intervention is not on the foreseeable horizon for any school-based applications; this is especially true for antisocial students who, as a rule, require implementation of powerful and multiple interventions applied consistently over a long period of time (that is, across school years).

We are too often *not* bound by empirical outcomes vis-à-vis school-based interventions. The most effective interventions are often not those applied most frequently, even though the evidence supports their superior effects. Instead, intervention approaches are selected that allow one to address the problem (by doing something about it) and that appeal, for whatever reason, to the implementer. When dealing with antisocial behavior patterns, we cannot afford the luxury of selecting interventions on this basis. Although no current intervention approach can claim to have effected a "cure" for antisocial behavior, there are some practices that are far more effective than others (Kazdin, 1985, 1987; Reid, 1990, 1993).

Approaches to teaching beginning reading provide a good example of this perplexing educational practice. It would seem practicable to select the approach that produces the lowest rate of reading failure, which happens to be phonics-based approaches. In spite of the accumulated empirical evidence on this question, we continue to invest in a variety of less effective approaches to teach children beginning reading. This is analogous to a surgeon choosing to perform a procedure that has a 19% mortality rate over one that has a 10% rate because (1) it is easier to do, (2) the surgeon is trained in it, and (3) the surgeon just likes it better. Given the stakes involved, it is not possible for the medical field to operate in this manner, yet such a practice continues unabated in many of our schools. It is likely that this practice is driven by educators (1) not being trained in more effective intervention or instructional methods or (2) being invested in philosophical approaches that are counter to more effective approaches and that lead to their rejection.

Given the destructiveness and socioeconomic costs of antisocial behavior patterns, we cannot afford to invest in any but the *best* intervention practices currently available. Figure 2.2 depicts four variables that play instrumental roles in determining the magnitude or effectiveness of intervention outcomes. They are particularly salient when working with students who are invested in antisocial behavior patterns.

It is difficult to differentially weight the importance of these four factors in determining intervention outcomes. In our view, the empirical literature and experiential knowledge have established each of them as extremely important. These factors are applicable to all school-based interventions, regardless of their philosophical underpinnings or bent. However, careful attention to them is of crucial importance in designing and

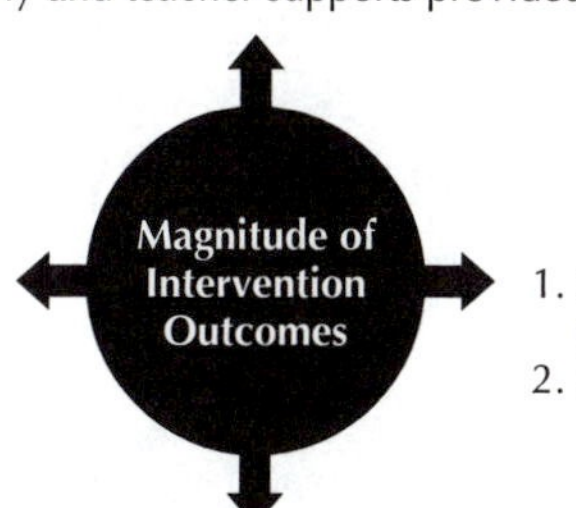

FIGURE 2.2 Factors Affecting the Magnitude of Intervention Outcomes

implementing successful interventions for antisocial students. In a word, such interventions must be *comprehensive, applied according to best-practice standards and guidelines, of maximal power, and of sufficient duration to produce enduring effects.*

Fidelity of intervention is critically important in maximizing outcomes for antisocial students. This dimension simply refers to a careful adherence to best practices in the delivery of instruction and implementing interventions designed to change the behavior of antisocial students. Throughout the remainder of this book, we have attempted to present guidelines and recommendations that will assist educators in achieving this goal.

The entries under each of the four major factors in Figure 2.2 are guidelines for maximizing the influence or power of that factor. If closely followed during the implementation process, they will produce better and more powerful effects across intervention applications. When combined with each other, these four dimensions, or factors, will aggregate to produce the best possible effects for a particular school-based intervention or approach. When working with antisocial students, it is particularly important to carefully monitor their responses to the intervention and to monitor, track, and support their changed behavior over the long-term. This means implementing a low-cost variation of the intervention or an ongoing maintenance procedure for the antisocial student across school years. One-shot interventions, implemented only within the span of a single school year, will not be sufficient to adequately impact antisocial behavior patterns in the vast majority of cases. After mounting an intervention for an antisocial student in a given school year, that student's reaction at the beginning of the next school year (upon seeing the intervention agent) should be something like, "Oh, no! Not you again!" However, it is also conceivable that follow-up in this manner would engender a measure of respect because it would likely be a rare example of consistency and careful monitoring in the student's life.

DEVELOPMENTAL CONTINUUM OF SERVICE DELIVERY AND EXPECTED OUTCOMES FOR ANTISOCIAL BEHAVIOR PATTERNS

Society, generally, and school professionals, in particular, appear to have difficulty in adopting a therapeutic, proactive perspective toward antisocial behavior patterns that many feel are more appropriately punished. Bullis and Walker (1994) note the importance of establishing benchmarks governing intervention expectations for antisocial behavior patterns and deciding how to invest limited resources in their prevention, remediation, and long-term management or accommodation. These authors have proposed a four-stage developmental continuum that addresses: prevention, remediation, amelioration, and accommodation goals. This continuum is illustrated in Figure 2.3, and each of its sequential phases is described briefly.

Before discussing this continuum, it is important to clarify the relationship between *prevention* and *remediation*. In our view, these distinctions share considerable overlap and can, at times, be difficult to distinguish from each other. We see intervention as a valuable tool that can serve either preventive or remedial purposes, depending on the timing of its application. If intervention occurs early in the developmental cycle for a behavior disorder and diverts marginally invested children from a negative path, it may serve a preventive purpose. On the other hand, if intervention occurs later in the developmental cycle, its application would be characterized as remedial. Although we believe it is important to address both prevention and remediation goals, intervention applied early in the developmental cycle of antisocial behavior patterns is of the utmost importance and provides the greatest return on investment.

Figure 2.3 contains four developmental phases relating to services and interventions for addressing antisocial behavior patterns. The actual prevention of antisocial behavior appears to be possible in the preschool to grade 3 age range if a comprehensive, multi-setting (that is, classroom, playground, home) intervention is applied consistently and with high levels of treatment fidelity and integrity. Prevention, in this sense, would be defined as diversion of the at-risk child from the path leading to antisocial behavior and conduct disorder.

Bullis and Walker (1994) recommend an approach involving active remediation of antisocial behavior patterns in the intermediate grades and early middle school years. While a cure is highly unlikely at this developmental level, considerable impact can be achieved upon the deficits associated with this disorder (for example, remediation of social-skills deficits, teaching self-control, improving study and academic skills, and improving peer relations).

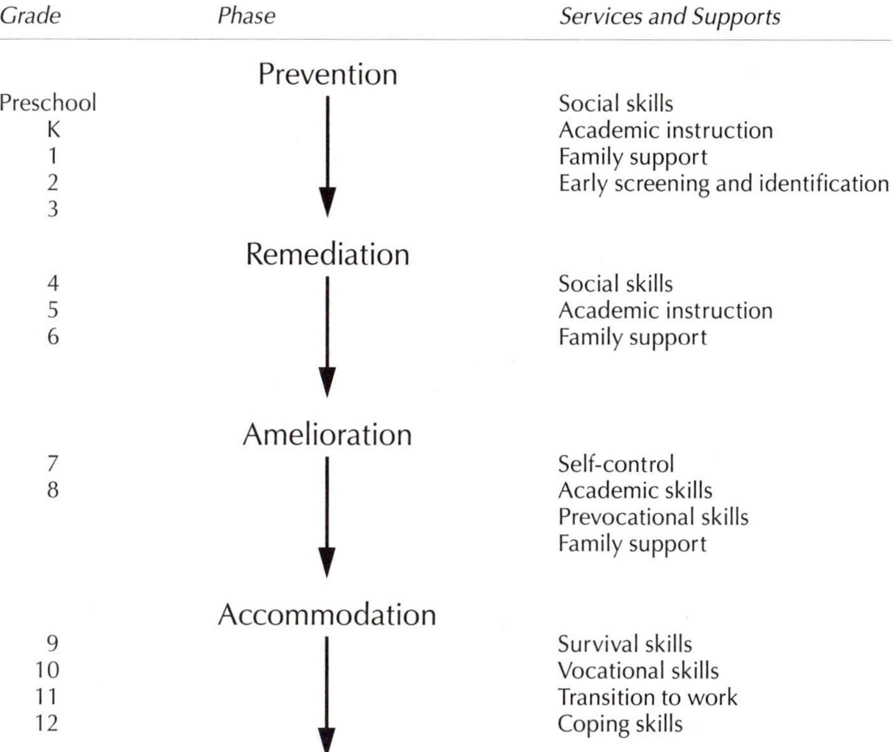

FIGURE 2.3 Developmental Continuum of Services and Expectations for Antisocial Behavior. *Source:* Bullis & Walker (1994).

By grades 7 and 8, goals and expectations should shift from prevention or remediation to attenuation of the negative effects of the behavior pattern on the antisocial student, peers, family members, and the society at large. This developmental phase is referred to as amelioration and focuses on buffering the damaging effects of this disorder through teaching coping and survival skills that will provide some protection against its ravages. Strategies for anger management and control are particularly important in this regard.

Finally, in the developmental period spanning grades 9 through 12, the focus shifts from amelioration to simple accommodation. Bullis and Walker (1994) argue that antisocial students at this stage have a high risk of remaining invested in an antisocial behavior pattern for the remainder of their lives. Realistically, there is relatively little that either schools or social agencies can do at this point to affect the antisocial behavior pattern. Accommodation implies a degree of acceptance that this disorder will likely not change for the better. Efforts should be made to keep these students in school as long as possible and to prepare them, to the maximum extent possible, for the transition from school to work and adult life.

This continuum suggests that far more resources should be invested in the early developmental stages of antisocial behavior patterns than in trying to manage or control their manifestations later on. Making this transition will not be easy, given (1) the numbers of children and youth who are currently antisocial, (2) the intensity and aversiveness of their behavioral acts, (3) the increasingly limited resources that can be dedicated for them, and (4) our seeming reluctance to "catch problems early."

Authorizing legislation and statutes actually prevent a number of federal agencies from engaging in prevention efforts. This is a particularly unfortunate constraint in relation to the task of dealing with antisocial behavior patterns early in their development. Judge Hargreaves notes that children and youth do not begin their delinquent acts by committing serious offenses; they initially become invested in far less serious acts and progress to more serious ones that are ultimately defined as illegal. Similarly, small children begin showing the "soft" signs of antisocial behavior that are relatively trivial (noncompliance, arguing, lying) and gradually progress to much more severe "hard" signs (cruelty, aggression, violence, stealing, fire setting) as they mature (Patterson, 1982; Patterson et al., 1992). Thus, it is extremely important to address the soft, early signs and the less serious acts while we still have a chance to affect them. Danielson (1993) perceptively notes that we wait until it is too late to turn them around before we define behavior disorders as a problem that merits systematic attention and intervention.

DESIGN AND APPLICATION OF COMPREHENSIVE, COORDINATED INTERVENTIONS APPLIED EARLY IN A CHILD'S SCHOOL CAREER

In a seminal review of the empirical knowledge on the prevention of delinquency, Zigler, Taussig, and Black (1992) argue that programs developed specifically for delinquency prevention have produced consistently disappointing outcomes. They evaluated the outcomes associated with juvenile foster homes, diversion programs, and retribution-restitution programs and concluded that none have worked. However, interventions aimed at reducing or preventing the precursors of delinquency (that is, antisocial, aggressive, acting-out, and moody behavior) have shown some promising results (see Michelson, Kazdin, & Marchione, 1986; Patterson, Chamberlain, & Reid, 1982). Similarly, some encouraging work has been conducted in reducing selected aspects of predelinquent behavior by targeting the socializing agents of family, peers, school, and community (see Hawkins, VonCleve, & Catalano, 1991).

Ironically, the most powerful evidence in support of the prevention of delinquency and adult criminality comes from long-term, follow-up studies of early childhood programs targeted for at-risk children early in their school careers. These intervention programs were never designed for delinquency prevention, but rather to prevent the school failure of at-risk populations. Some of the most effective early-intervention programs were multidimensional and included noneducational supports such as providing health care, parent involvement, and offering needed services to families and family members. Zigler et al. (1992) highlight the features of three such programs that have proved effective in preventing the later adoption of a delinquent life-style: The Perry Preschool Project, The Syracuse University Family Development Research Project, and The Yale Child Welfare Research Program. This is an extremely important finding and provides compelling evidence of the importance of prevention efforts achieved through well-designed and implemented early-intervention programs. The widespread replication of the critical features of these successful programs is essential to any effective prevention strategy.

EARLY SCREENING AND IDENTIFICATION OF ANTISOCIAL BEHAVIOR PATTERNS

In order to do early intervention for prevention or remediation purposes, one has to systematically screen and identify at-risk children *early*—some of these children will show only the soft, early signs of antisocial behavior. Preschool children, particularly boys, engage in oppositional, overly active, pestering, random, and unfocused forms of behavior that do not seem serious at this developmental level. However, the manifestations of this behavior pattern in adolescence are *very* different and have great salience and impact—often of a highly aversive nature.

Phil Strain, a distinguished early childhood educator and researcher, is a strong advocate of the earliest possible identification of at-risk children. He has developed a videotape to illustrate its importance for use in in-service training sessions for preschool staff. The videotape opens with some small boys who are arguing, pushing, and shoving each other and being unresponsive to the teacher's attempts to correct their behavior. The next scene shows a female teacher approaching a surly, sulking adolescent. When she attempts to engage him, he suddenly assaults her and breaks her jaw. Strain makes the point that these acts are of the same general type, only separated by about ten years.

It is very important to note that preschoolers who show the early signs of antisocial behavior patterns do not outgrow them. Rather, as they move through their school careers, they grow *into* these unfortunate behavior patterns with disastrous results to themselves and others. This myth that preschoolers will outgrow antisocial behavior is pervasive among many teachers and early educators and is very dangerous because it leads professionals to do nothing early on when the problem can be effectively addressed. These at-risk children need extra attention and assistance just to progress at minimally acceptable rates in meeting teacher expectations and performing academically. Because of their unfortunate beginnings, they have a great deal of ground to make up.

The social behavior of preschool children is sufficiently well differentiated that antisocial behavior patterns are easily identifiable at this developmental stage (Hinshaw, Han, Erhardt, & Huber, 1992). Once children enter elementary school, it is even easier to identify such students because of the more intense performance demands and greater structure operating at this level (Hersh & Walker, 1983). Box 2.2 presents some guidelines for use in the early screening and identification of children and youth who are at risk for developing antisocial behavior patterns. Three options are described for the reader's

Box 2.2 Guidelines for Screening and Identification of Antisocial Behavior Patterns

- A *proactive* rather than a *reactive* process should be used to screen and identify students at risk for antisocial behavior.
- Whenever possible, a multi-agent (teacher, parent, observer) and multisetting (classroom, playground, home setting) screening-identification approach should be used in order to gain the broadest possible perspective on the dimensions of the target student's at-risk status.
- At-risk students should be screened and identified as early as possible in their school careers—ideally at the preschool and kindergarten levels.
- Teacher nominations and rankings or ratings should be used in the early stages of screening and supplemented later in the process, if possible, by direct observations, school records, peer or parent ratings, and other sources as appropriate.

consideration: Options One and Two are designed for use in the elementary grades, and Option Three is designed for use in the preschool years (ages 3–5).

It is extremely important for at-risk students to be screened regularly, using a proactive screening process, to detect those who manifest either the hard or soft signs of antisocial behavior. The earlier such students are identified, the better chance there is for early intervention to help divert them from an antisocial path.

Studies of the referral process in public schools show that (1) general education teachers are involved in the vast majority of school referrals, (2) the referral frequency peaks around grade 2 or 3, and (3) students are far more likely to be referred for academic than social-behavioral problems. In an important study, Lloyd, Kauffman, Landrum, and Roe (1991) systematically analyzed school records to determine how and why a sample of regular teachers referred students in their classes for special education. Their results indicated that 69% of referrals were for boys, two-thirds of all school referrals occurred in grades K–3, and the problems most likely to prompt teacher referrals were academic difficulties (35%), reading problems (31%), and attention problems (23%).

By rank ordering the frequency of each referral reason, these authors found that the seven most frequent reasons involved academic problems; aggressive, disruptive, and delinquent behavior was the tenth most frequent reason given for referral. Thus, it does not seem likely that teachers, on their own, are inclined to refer children, early in their school careers, who may be at risk for antisocial behavior patterns. Yet teachers, more than anyone, have an important reservoir of information concerning the behavioral characteristics of such children. Teachers have the advantage of being able to make literally thousands of normative comparisons among students as they teach and manage the classroom. This information is extremely valuable in making sensitive judgments about the at-risk status of individual students. Left on their own, regular teachers are far more likely to reactively refer students than to proactively screen on a regular basis and refer suspected at-risk students (Gerber & Semmel, 1984). It is essential that such proactive screening be regularly implemented in the preschool and elementary grades and that teachers be intimately involved as suppliers of key information in this process.

Three recommended approaches to this task are described briefly in the form of cases. All three approaches will proactively screen and identify young children at risk for antisocial behavior patterns. They are discussed here, starting with the least labor-intensive approach and progressing to the most labor-intensive one.

Achenbach Case

This approach uses a combination of teacher nominations and teacher or parent ratings on the aggression subscale of the *Achenbach Behavior Checklist* to screen and identify at-risk students (Achenbach, 1991). Teachers can be asked to simply nominate students in

Classroom rulebreakers. *Elizabeth Crews*

their class who match the following profile of the antisocial student: Antisocial students consistently violate classroom and playground rules, display aggressive behavior toward others, sometimes damage or destroy property, take things without permission, and are often in a sullen, agitated emotional state. Teachers should be free to nominate up to five students unless unusual circumstances exist that would indicate a larger number of nominations. They should then be asked to rate each nominated student on the aggression subscale of the Achenbach Behavior Checklist. The teacher form of the Achenbach aggression subscale has 25 items and is essentially identical to the parent form.

The Achenbach Behavior Checklist has set the standard for psychometric excellence in the study of child psychopathology and adjustment problems. It has become a required tool in any scientific study of child psychopathology conducted in either the home or school. Our experience with the aggression subscale indicates that it is highly sensitive in discriminating antisocial from nonantisocial students. Sample items from this subscale include "Defiant, talks back to staff," "Gets in many fights," "Cruelty, bullying, or meanness to others," and "Explosive and unpredictable behavior." Use of this subscale is highly recommended for assessing the behavioral status of potentially antisocial students.

Those students who score two or more standard deviations above the mean of this subscale should be considered seriously at risk for antisocial behavior patterns. If parent ratings also show an elevated profile on the aggression subscale, then the child's at-risk status may be even greater. The students who are identified by this screening process should be exposed to early interventions designed to address their specific adjustment problems and to enhance their ability to cope with the demands of school.

Drummond Case

Systematic research has identified a number of behavioral precursors of antisocial behavior patterns that are highly predictive of the development of conduct disorder and the later adoption of a delinquent life-style (Loeber, 1991; Loeber & LeBlanc, 1990). Adults (parents and teachers) are able to accurately rate these behavioral indicators very early in a child's life (that is, at the preschool level). Drummond (1993) has ingeniously adapted these indicators into a universal, mass-screening procedure for use by elementary teachers in identifying at-risk students. He has extensively developed and researched a seven-item scale for this purpose, called the *Student Risk Screening Scale* (SRSS).

Drummond used the following five criteria to guide development of the SRSS:

1. *Brief.* A screening instrument of this type should have no more than ten items.
2. *Research based.* The items should be those that most powerfully discriminate and predict antisocial behavior patterns.
3. *Easily understood.* The format, scoring, and administration instructions should be clear and as self-explanatory as possible.
4. *Valid.* The instrument should be accurate and valid for the screening–identification of at-risk students.
5. *Powerful.* The instrument should be efficient in identifying those students who are truly at risk and who could benefit from early-intervention programs.

These criteria are carefully reflected in the final form of the SRSS. This instrument has proved to be easy to use, highly effective, and technically sound. It has excellent validity and reliability and powerfully distinguishes non–at-risk students from those who show the early signs of antisocial behavior.

The seven items of the SRSS are listed here:

1. Stealing
2. Lying, cheating, sneaking
3. Behavior problems
4. Peer rejection
5. Low academic achievement
6. Negative attitude
7. Aggressive behavior

Each of the seven items is scored on a 0-to-3 scale in which 0 = never, 1 = occasionally, 2 = sometimes, and 3 = frequently. Total scores on the SRSS can thus range from 0 to 21.

Based on his use of the scale, Drummond has established the following risk-score categories for determining at-risk status: high risk = 9 to 21, moderate risk = 4 to 8, and low risk = 0 to 3. Thus, a student who receives a score of between 9 and 21 should be evaluated carefully for possible early school or family intervention to address the indicated problems.

Form 2.1 illustrates how the SRSS is used to screen an entire classroom. The actual SRSS screening form used by the teacher can accommodate up to 30 students.

All student names for the class are listed down the left side of the form. The SRSS items are listed across the top of the form. The teacher simply evaluates each student on the individual items across the rows and enters a rating (0–3) that characterizes the student's behavior for each item.

The profiles of the three students in Form 2.1 have an elevated risk (that is, high) for antisocial behavior, as indicated by their total scores on the SRSS (12, 11, and 16, respectively). Jamie seems to have more of the indicators of a covert pattern of antisocial behavior, while Fred's profile suggests investment in an overt pattern. Susan seems to have problems that fall in between these two poles; her problems may be more in the realm of disobedience and academic problems.

Table 2.2 illustrates behavioral and academic profiles for three groups of students identified by the SRSS. The profiles of the three student groups in this table indicate that the SRSS has great sensitivity in identifying students whose at-risk status is confirmed by their existing school records.

The SRSS is a highly cost-effective screening instrument that allows teachers to identify at-risk students very early in their school careers so appropriate interventions and support services can be provided for them. Its use is highly recommended as a best-practice.

	ITEMS							
Names	Steal	Lie, Cheat, Sneak	Behavior Problem	Peer Reject	Low Achieve-ment	Negative Attitude	Aggressive Behavior	Totals
Jamie	3	3	2	2	0	1	1	12
Susan	0	0	3	3	2	3	0	11
Fred	1	1	3	3	2	3	3	16

FORM 2.1 SRSS Screening Form for an Entire Class

TABLE 2.2 Academic and Discipline Follow-Up of SRSS Risk Screening

	Low Risk	*Moderate Risk*	*High Risk*
Number of students	117	40	27
Grade point average	3.10	2.43	2.24
Number of classes failed	0.52	1.42	1.88
Standardized test scores: Metropolitan Achievement Test (MAT) < 15th percentile	9%	27%	45%
Academic remediation (percentage of students)	19%	35%	52%
Minor discipline infractions per student	0.76	1.90	2.37
Major discipline infractions per student	0.09	0.30	0.89
Serious academic problems (percentage of students)	22%	48%	67%
Serious discipline problems (percentage of students)	3%	18%	33%
Academic and discipline problems (percentage of students)	0%	10%	30%

Walker, Severson, and Feil Case

Walker, Severson, and Feil (1994) have developed a multiple-gating screening–identification procedure that detects children in the 3–5 age range who are at risk for either externalizing or internalizing behavior problems. *Externalizing* adjustment problems are maladaptive forms of social behavior that are directed outwardly to the external environment. Behavior problems of this type involve a surplus or "too much behavior"; the excess usually violates social norms and is also highly aversive to others. In contrast, *internalizing* behavior problems usually involve skill deficits, are directed inwardly and away from the external environment, and are associated with insufficient amounts of behavior. Examples of externalizing behavior include disruption, oppositional-defiant behavior, and aggression; internalizing behavior involves social avoidance, depression, anxiety problems, phobias, and affective disorders (see Ross, 1980). This bipolar conceptualization captures most of the social-behavioral adjustment difficulties that children and youth experience during their school years.

Figure 2.4 contains a schematic of the three sequential stages or "gates" of the screening procedure referred to as the Early Screening Project (ESP) (Walker, Severson, & Feil, 1994).

In Stage One, the regular teacher nominates and rank orders children whose characteristic behavior patterns most closely match the externalizing and internalizing behavioral profiles. The three highest-ranked externalizers and internalizers then move to Stage Two where their behavior patterns are rated on checklists and Likert rating scales that define their status on specific behavior problems they may be experiencing. Those students who exceed normative criteria on the Stage Two screening measures then move to Stage Three where they are directly observed in both structured and unstructured situations. Structured observations focus on target children's responsiveness to teacher demands and the unstructured observations focus on their peer relations. Parents are also asked to rate their child's behavioral adjustment at this screening stage. As a rule, those children who pass through these three screening "gates" have serious behavior problems and are candidates for early-intervention programs, services, and supports.

Preschool children who are at risk for antisocial behavior patterns will usually be detected by the externalizing path of the ESP screening procedure. Those preschool students whose ESP profiles suggest they are at risk for antisocial behavior should be rated by their teacher, parents, or both on the aggression subscale of the Achenbach Behavior Checklist to confirm their status. Additional, relevant information would be their percentage of negative, aggressive social behavior during social interactions with peers recorded in unstructured situations. If 12–15% or more of their social behavior directed toward peers is negative or aggressive, then another strong indicator of an antisocial behavior pattern is present.

A convenient, and highly recommended, method of recording negative, aggressive social behavior in unstructured situations is to allow a stopwatch to run whenever the child's observed behavior is negative or aggressive and to stop it when it is not. The

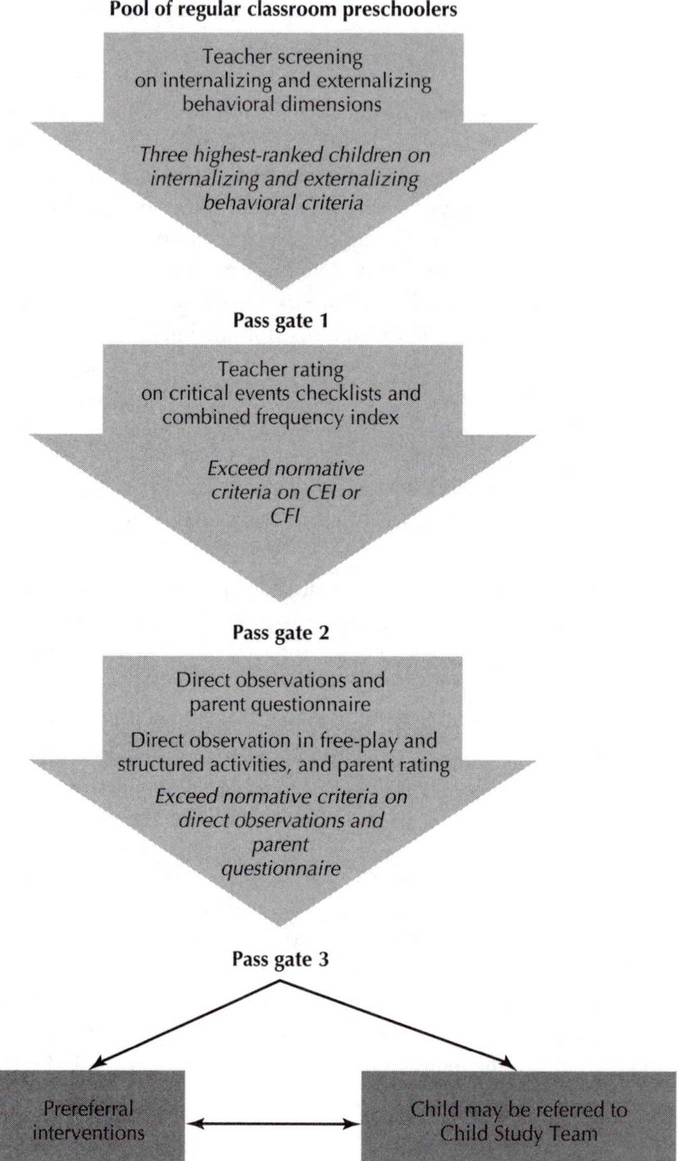

FIGURE 2.4 Schematic of ESP Procedure

percentage of negative, aggressive behavior can be derived by dividing the time on the stopwatch by the length of the observation session and multiplying the result by 100. If 5 minutes of negative, aggressive behavior was observed in a 20-minute period, the percentage would be $5 \div 20 \times 100 = .25 \times 100 = 25\%$ negative, aggressive behavior.

This would be a substantial level of negative, aggressive behavior in comparison to normative standards for preschool children.

The ESP screening procedure, and systems like it, are highly recommended for use at preschool and elementary levels for detecting children who are at risk for antisocial behavior patterns. The ESP is a downward extension of the Systematic Screening for Behavior Disorders (SSBD) procedure developed by Walker and Severson (1990). The SSBD is a proactive, multiple-gating screening system for use in detecting students at risk for externalizing and internalizing problems in grades 1–6. It is highly reliable, and extensive research with preschool populations indicates that it powerfully distinguishes at-risk and non–at-risk children based on their behavioral characteristics.

The three approaches described for screening and identifying preschool and elementary school students who are at risk for antisocial behavior patterns are all reliable, cost efficient, and valid for the uses for which they were designed. Although the key features of these approaches differ from one another, they share a very important characteristic in being proactive rather than reactive screening systems. Each will enable early identification, and each makes excellent use of teacher judgment. In our view, properly structured and elicited teacher appraisal of student adjustment problems is a greatly undervalued and underutilized resource in serving at-risk students in schools.

KEY TARGET AREAS THAT ANTISOCIAL INTERVENTIONS SHOULD ADDRESS

Bullis and Walker (1994) note that a single intervention is insufficient to deal with the complexity and multidimensional nature of antisocial behavior patterns. Children and youth who are at risk for antisocial behavior patterns are also at risk for a host of other negative conditions including (1) academic failure, (2) child abuse and neglect, (3) drug and alcohol involvement, (4) sexually transmitted diseases, (5) accidents, (6) tobacco use, (7) gang membership, and (8) delinquency. Schools alone cannot address all these risk factors, but, in cooperation with families, social service agencies, and communities, they can be effective partners in collaborative interventions designed to impact them.

The first responsibility of schools, in relation to coping with antisocial behavior patterns, should be to teach alternative, replacement behavior patterns that are adaptive and functional. This is a complex process and involves not only direct teaching but also the use of systematic behavior-management methods, positive consequences as well as negative sanctions, and access to counseling. In addition, schools should assume a leadership role in developing intervention strategies for addressing the following intervention target areas in order to help reduce or eliminate associated risk factors:

- Study skills to improve academic performance and competence (see Archer & Gleason. (1989). *Skills for School Success.* Curriculum Associates, 5 Esquire Road N., Billerica, MA 01862-2589; 508-667-8000).

- Social-skills training to improve teacher-, peer- and self-related forms of adjustment (see Alberg, Petry, & Eller. (1994). *A Resource Guide for Social Skills*

Instruction. Sopris West, Inc., 1140 Boston Avenue, Longmont, CO 80501; 303-651-2829).

- Health awareness to identify the consequences of a high-risk life-style (see Severson & Zoref. (1991). Prevention and Early Interventions for Addictive Behaviors: Health Promotion in the Schools. In G. Stoner, M. Shinn, & H. Walker (Eds.), *Interventions for Achievement and Behavior Problems.* National Association of School Psychologists, 8455 Colesville Road, Suite 1000, Silver Spring, MD 20910).

- Strategies for resisting involvement with drugs and alcohol (see Morgan, Likins, Friedman, & Genaux. (1994). *RESIST: Resistance Education Strategies and Interventions Systematically Taught—A Substance Use Prevention Program for Students in Special Education Programs,* available from Family Development Resources, Park City, Utah. *DARE: Drug Abuse Resistance Education* is a superb curricular program developed by the Los Angeles Police Department. It is used by specially trained police officers in collaboration with educators. Information about DARE can be obtained by contacting DARE America at 800-223-DARE).

These four areas or domains have everything to do with the quality of life that antisocial children and youth will experience. They are powerful determinants of the life course and life chances that will affect antisocial students. Whenever possible, social systems and agencies that can provide support, technical assistance, training, and respite to distressed families should be marshaled and coordinated through a school-linked services approach (see Behrmann, 1992). Lisbeth Schorr (1988) argues persuasively that flexible, individually tailored services applied from outside the family can have a positive influence in reducing family stressors and the negative conditions associated with them. School-linked services of this type are likely to be the only effective approach available to us in comprehensively addressing the complex problems of antisocial children, youth, and their families.

Finally, it is crucial to focus on the dimension of resiliency when dealing with antisocial children and youth. As defined by Garmezy (1985), *resiliency* has to do with the interaction between risk and protective factors. A small percentage of children, for example, who have all the risk factors for developing antisocial behavior patterns do not do so. In fact, resilient children and youth often turn out to have productive lives.

Garmezy (1985) has identified three broad categories of nonintellectual, protective factors that are thought to contribute to resiliency: (1) personality dispositions of the child, (2) a supportive family milieu, and (3) an external support system that encourages and reinforces a child's coping efforts. As identified by Rutter (1979), positive temperament of the child is a strong protective factor. Because of their high agitation and irritability levels, antisocial students are severely disadvantaged in relation to this factor. Rutter and his colleagues also found that a family support system characterized by warmth and support operates as a protective factor. However, in terms of the role of schools in developing resiliency, it is most important that careful attention be paid to ensuring that antisocial students (1) recruit and maintain a positive support network of nonantisocial peers and (2) are mentored and socially valued by as many adults and older peers in the school as possible. Assisting antisocial students to become involved in school activities is another method of broadening their social engagement with the school culture. Investment of effort in attempting to increase students' capacity for resiliency will be time well spent and should not be ignored as a viable strategy for use with antisocial students.

UNIVERSAL AND SELECTED INTERVENTIONS FOR ADDRESSING ANTISOCIAL BEHAVIOR PATTERNS IN SCHOOL

Universal interventions are those that are designed to impact all students in the same manner under the same conditions. Examples of universal interventions are school vaccinations; social-skills training of all students in a regular classroom; implementing a schoolwide discipline plan; and developing, posting and monitoring rules governing classroom behavior and performance. In contrast, *selected* interventions are those that are designed for an identified (or selected) target student and the procedures are individually tailored and fine-tuned to fit the specific needs of the target student. Examples of selected interventions are individual counseling, development of a program to remediate an antisocial student's aggressive behavior with peers, and use of time-out. Selected interventions are commonly used as back-ups for universal interventions that prove to be ineffective or insufficient for certain students.

During the Civil War, both Union and Confederate generals planned defensive battle strategy and tactics in a manner that was analogous to the notion of a universal–selected dichotomy. Based on the assumption that a certain number of attacking soldiers would break through the first and second lines of defense, the defending army was deployed so there was a first, second, and even third line of defense. Antisocial students are very likely to "break through" most universal interventions; these strategies will be insufficiently powerful to control or to adequately change the aversive, destructive features of their behavior. Chapter 12 presents a series of case studies that illustrate the application of both universal and selected interventions for antisocial behavior patterns.

Universal interventions are particularly useful for prevention, while selected interventions are more applicable to the remediation of well-established disorders that have proven to be resistant to prior behavior-change efforts. Because universal interventions are generally less demanding to implement and because all students are exposed to them in the same manner, they are more likely to be acceptable to teachers. They do not compromise fairness and equity in the management of individual students, and these are strong values for most teachers. Selected interventions have the disadvantage of appearing to treat individual students in a special manner that is different from that accorded other students. Although a selected intervention can be highly effective and is recommended for use with antisocial behavior patterns, it does have the ability to stigmatize and label the students who are exposed to it.

Universal interventions are less powerful than selected interventions for a given, individual student, and different expectations are associated with their effectiveness. Universal interventions have their greatest impact among students who "are on the margins"—for example, those students who are mildly at risk or who are just becoming invested in an antisocial behavior pattern. Sometimes, systematic exposure to an intervention of this type will be sufficient to tip them in the right direction and divert them from a negative path. Thus, the most appropriate way to judge the effectiveness of a universal intervention is to assess the extent to which it reduces the expected base rate of disorders or problems among groups of students (that is, at classroom, school, or district levels). Selected interventions, on the other hand, are appropriately evaluated in terms of how effective they are in changing the behavior of an individual student. Thus, judgments about the efficacy of selected interventions are usually, though not always, made on a case-by-case basis.

We believe that universal interventions have an important role to play in achieving the two major goals of schooling: academic and social development. These two dimensions are inextricably linked and are facilitative of each other. These twin goals can be achieved by (1) implementing, according to best-practice standards, strategies, and tactics of effective instruction that have been derived through studies of effective schooling and (2) teaching positive mental health principles and interpersonal skills as instructional content and using peer-tutoring strategies to assist in this process.

Algozzine and Ysseldyke (1992) have developed a teaching manual for use in implementing effective instructional practices called *Strategies and Tactics for Effective Instruction* (available from Sopris West, Inc., 1140 Boston Avenue, Longmont, CO 80501). They provide strategies, tactics, and activities to support the application of the following ten principles governing effective instruction and classroom management:

Principles of Effective Instruction

1. Goals and expectations for performance and success are stated clearly and understood by the student.
2. Classroom management is effective and efficient.
3. There is a sense of positiveness in the school environment.
4. There is an appropriate match between student skills and the demands of classroom tasks.
5. Lessons are presented clearly and follow specific instructional procedures.
6. Instructional support is provided for the individual student.
7. Sufficient time is allocated to academics, and instructional time is used efficiently.
8. Student opportunity to respond is high.
9. The teacher actively monitors student progress and understanding.
10. Student performance is evaluated appropriately and frequently.

Adherence to these critical features of effective instruction will benefit all students, and especially those at risk for antisocial behavior patterns. All other things being equal, they will also produce superior academic outcomes across all students. Their systematic use is highly recommended.

The second broad goal of schooling is to facilitate students' positive mental health and to develop a competent repertoire of interpersonal and basic interaction skills. Competent performance in this area can be important to both school and postschool success.

Antisocial students are severely deficient in this critically important performance domain (see Chapter 10). Strayhorn, Strain, and Walker (1993) advocate using peer tutoring to enhance interaction skills and, as a result, facilitate positive mental health. The model they propose is based on the following assumptions:

1. Positive, friendly, kind, and cooperative interactions are highly relevant to the prevention of psychiatric disorders and antisocial behavior.
2. Academic competence (for example, in reading, mathematics, and writing) is also an extremely important psychological health skill for children.
3. Prevention attempts encounter a major obstacle when they depend on programs into which only a fraction of the target population will ever enter, while the prevailing culture of the target population provides massive exposure to hostility.
4. One of the most promising ways of overcoming these obstacles is a transformation and restructuring of schools so that the nurturing and academic training of younger students by older students is part of the daily experience of each student and a training ground upon which important psychological skills can be modeled, instructed, practiced, monitored, and reinforced.

These authors propose a school reorganization plan, based on principles of effective peer tutoring, that would allow this universal intervention to be implemented in a cost-effective manner without unduly burdening teachers and other school personnel. As more and more children enter school with deficits in their basic socialization training, it is essential that schools invest themselves in directly teaching and supporting this type of content.

RECOMMENDED INTERVENTION TECHNIQUES FOR USE IN DESIGNING INTERVENTIONS FOR ANTISOCIAL BEHAVIOR

Literally hundreds of intervention techniques have been reported in the professional literature in the last three decades that are designed to effect changes in the behavioral repertoires of individuals. Our purpose in this section is to focus on a small subset of these techniques that we have found to be highly effective in producing rapid, economical changes in the behavior of antisocial students. The reader is referred to Appendix A of this book for information on the specific details of how these techniques are implemented and the effects they produce among aggressive, antisocial children and youth.

When dealing with well-established antisocial behavior patterns, our experience has been that a combination of (1) systematic social-skills training, (2) behavior-specific praise, (3) positive reinforcement contingencies (individual and group), (4) time-out, and (5) response cost or cost contingency is usually necessary to produce socially valid outcomes (Kazdin, 1977; Wolf, 1978). By socially valid, we mean intervention outcomes or results that justify the time and effort investment of the implementers and that move the antisocial student into the normative range on the target behaviors to which the intervention is applied.

These techniques reduce to classes of positive and mild punishing techniques. It is unfortunate that the behavior patterns of antisocial children and youth are so well developed, aversive, and resistant to tactics of social influence that they require the application of both types of techniques, but in the vast majority of cases they do. The authors do not wish to be perceived as advocates of punishment—indeed, we are not. (See Repp & Singh, 1990, for a seminal treatment of the punishment issue involving vulnerable, at-risk populations; see Horner et al., 1990, for discussion of the details of a technology of nonaversive behavioral support.) However, substantial empirical literature on intervening with this population provides evidence that the combined application of limit setting, aversive consequences, careful monitoring, and reinforcement contingencies is required to have a substantive impact on their behavior (see Kazdin, 1985, 1987; Patterson, 1983; Patterson et al., 1992).

Just as no single intervention is sufficient to solve all the adjustment and life-related problems of antisocial individuals, no single technique (positive or negative) is sufficient to change their behavior satisfactorily. If one's goal is to simply change how antisocial children and youth *perceive* and *talk* about their behavior, then counseling and child psychotherapy will be quite adequate for this purpose. If the goal, instead, is to produce changes in how they *act* and *behave*, then the application of scientifically derived behavior-change procedures is necessary.

In addition to details of procedures contained in subsequent chapters of this book, some excellent resources are available that provide the "nuts and bolts" of the behavior-management mechanics necessary to apply the preceding techniques according to best-practice standards. The reader is referred to the following sources:

- *The Tough Kid Book* (1992), by Rhode, Jenson, and Reavis, available from Sopris West, 1140 Boston Avenue, Longmont, CO 80501. This is a superb treatment of the "tough kid" written for the classroom teacher. It provides extensive coverage of behavioral characteristics, positive intervention procedures, reductive techniques, and advanced intervention procedures and systems for difficult students, including cooperative learning strategies, contracts, social-skills training, home notes, and beeper tapes.

- *Utah's BEST Project: Behavioral and Educational Strategies for Teachers* (1993), edited by Reavis, Jenson, Kukic, and Morgan, available from Ken Reavis, USOE, 250 East 500 South, Salt Lake City, UT 84111, 801-538-7709. This volume is produced by the Utah Department of Education and consists of a series of brief technical manuals, written for teachers, that cover ten strategies for improving behavior and performance in schools. Some of the topics covered include motivation, in-school suspension, time-out, reprimands and precision requests, self-recording, teacher praise, and how to set up and use group contingencies effectively. This volume follows a standard format for each technique and contains a number of very practical strategies and suggestions.

- *The Acting Out Child* (revised, 1994), by Walker, available from Sopris West, 1140 Boston Avenue, Longmont, CO 80501. This book is written for the classroom teacher and other school professionals, including counselors, school psychologists, social workers, diagnosticians, and behavioral specialists. It contains extended treatment of techniques for increasing, decreasing, and maintaining behavior. Case studies of applications of these techniques to typical school situations are also provided. Applications are presented and illustrated for a range of school settings, beginning with the regular classroom and extending to self-contained and resource rooms as well as the playground.

GUIDELINES FOR IMPLEMENTING BEST-PRACTICE INTERVENTION PROCEDURES

The following guidelines are derived from our collective experiences and are presented for the reader's consideration in designing and implementing interventions for antisocial students in school. They are divided into two major types: generic strategies and implementation recommendations. *Generic strategies* have to do with the approach we believe one should take with this population and the kinds of decisions one should make within this context. Implementation recommendations are suggestions for maximizing the cost-effective application of specific intervention techniques and applying them according to best-practice standards.

Generic Strategies

We recommend the following generic strategies for the reader's consideration:

- Begin by conducting a *functional analysis* of the student's behavior to determine the specific purposes or goals that the behavior in question may serve (for example, to avoid a task; to escape from a situation; to establish one's control, power, or dominance over others; or to seek a positive outcome that is valued). Before designing an intervention to change specific behavior, it is essential to know, or at least have some idea about, the purpose the problematic behavior serves. Even problematic behavior that is aversive to others is maintained because it serves the antisocial student's behavioral goals. As a rule, training is required to conduct a functional analysis in a reliable and valid fashion. (See O'Neill, Horner, Albin, Storey, & Sprague, 1990, for an excellent and comprehensive treatment of the issues and procedures involved in conducting a functional analysis of problem behavior.)

- Attempt to build a positive, trusting relationship with antisocial students as a first step in a strategy for positively influencing their behavior and development. Young (1993) refers to this process as an essential step in "setting the stage" for intervening with students in school. Because antisocial students come from such chaotic and unpredictable environments, they need exposure to caring adults who value them and who establish school settings that are consistent, predictable, and supportive (see Young, 1993). This is a highly recommended strategy and should be implemented as a precursor to full intervention. It will not only help to establish a bond, and perhaps friendship, between the student and the interventionist, it will also create the possibility of actually influencing the student's behavior in more positive directions.

- Establish the best universal intervention procedures you can for improving academic performance and social adjustment before resorting to selected interventions.

Teacher screening a student for antisocial behavior patterns. *Kathleen Olson*

- Although there is a high probability that antisocial students will spend some part of the school day, or their school career, in a more restrictive setting, they should have as much exposure as possible to normal peers and general education settings.
- Be sensitive to the *behavioral efficiency* of the student responses you are trying to reduce and replace in comparison to those you are replacing them with. Very often, we

teach adaptive responses and strategies that are far less efficient in producing outcomes desired by the antisocial student than the problematic, aversive ones we are seeking to eliminate. Thus, the adaptive strategies we teach compete poorly with the original, antisocial behavior; thus, newly taught strategies usually fail unless they are strongly supported by the social environment (see Horner & Day, 1991). This situation calls for careful selection of the target responses or strategies, monitoring of their usage, and provision of long-term support to ensure their integration into the student's ongoing behavioral repertoire.

- Begin your intervention approach or strategy with positive procedures only (for example, social-skills training, limits setting, statement of rules, daily debriefings about difficult situations and how they were handled, and school- or home-based incentive systems) and add time-out, brief suspension, or cost contingency procedures if the antisocial student's behavior remains unaffected or marginally so. In most cases, it will be necessary for you to resort to this far more powerful strategy in which adaptive, appropriate behavior is reinforced and supported while maladaptive, inappropriate behavior is *simultaneously* mildly punished and reduced or eliminated (see Appendix A for details of these procedures and their effects).

- Do all that you can to involve the primary caregivers in the intervention process while recognizing that, in some cases, you will receive no cooperation or interest in this regard. Chapter 11 contains suggestions and procedures for approaching this task with parents.

- Systematically screen and begin intervening as early as possible in the school careers of students at risk for antisocial behavior patterns. Preschool and kindergarten are good times to begin. Plan on monitoring, tracking, and reintervening with "booster shots" during the school years following your initial intervention.

- Be sure to teach *empathy* and *socially responsible decision-making* as part of your intervention. Antisocial students tend to be especially weak in these critical social skills. Chapter 10 contains instructions and guidelines for teaching social skills and also references a curriculum, Second Steps, that relates to teaching these two specific skills.

- Be aware that the academic demands and the normal behavioral-control procedures that most teachers and students take for granted as a part of schooling may be highly aversive events for many antisocial students (see Gunter, Denny, Jack, Shores, & Nelson, 1993; Shores, Gunter, & Jack, 1993). Very often, antisocial students display highly agitated forms of behavior that can quickly become out of control due to frustration with their inability to meet minimal academic demands or accept the constraining effects of classroom rules. Very strong links exist between antisocial behavior patterns and school academic failure. Chapters 6 and 7 describe procedures for understanding and responding to these processes.

- It is important to remember that considerable overlap exists between antisocial, aggressive behavior patterns and attention deficit-hyperactive disorder (ADHD). Estimates vary, but experts seem to generally agree that there is a 50 to 60% degree of overlap between these two commonly occurring disorders (see Barkley, 1990; DuPaul & Stoner, 1994; McKinney, Montague, & Hocutt, 1993). Thus, students who are routinely screened or referred for antisocial behavior should also be assessed for ADHD, and vice versa. Barkley, DuPaul, and McKinney, and their respective associates (as previously cited) provide excellent resource material and tools for accomplishing this task. In addition, Pfiffner and her colleagues (Pfiffner & Barkley, 1990; Pfiffner & O'Leary, in press) have contributed some useful recommendations for teachers in managing the behavior of ADHD students within classrooms. The *CH.A.D.D. Educator's Manual*, produced by the national organization, Children with Attention Deficit Disorder (CH.A.D.D.), is essential reading for teachers and other school personnel who are concerned with the problem of ADHD in school and its overlap with antisocial behavior patterns. It contains a superb compilation of research-based, proven strategies for intervening with these students in school. This manual is available from CASET Associates, Ltd., 10201 Lee Highway, #180, Fairfax, Virginia 22030. Finally, the Office of Special Education Programs in the U.S. Department of Education has sponsored a number of forums, research, and materials development projects for addressing ADHD in school. The Chesapeake Institute (2030 M Street NW, Suite 810, Washington, DC 20036) distributes these materials for the cost of publication and mailing. They are excellent materials that are easy to use, practical, and incorporate best practices.

- It is important to remember that a strong connection exists between antisocial behavior patterns and depression (see Kovacs, Paulauskas, Gatsonis, & Richards, 1988). Many antisocial children and youth are at elevated risk for this affective disorder. The material in this book does not address the problem of depression; however, it is important for teachers, counselors, and school psychologists to be on the alert for this disorder among antisocial students and to refer those who are suspected of having it for appropriate evaluation and treatment.

- Antisocial students have a severely elevated risk of school failure and dropout. They have behavioral characteristics that are highly aversive to others and that directly conflict with teacher expectations associated with teaching and managing the classroom environment (see Hersh & Walker, 1983; Walker, 1986). It is strongly recommended that attempts be made to teach antisocial students to understand, accept, and adhere to established classroom rules and teacher expectations. We recognize that this is no easy task; however, it is a most important one that could directly influence the school careers of antisocial students. In this context, we recommend giving careful attention to the issue of antisocial students responding to teacher requests and commands. This is one of *the* most important skills antisocial students can learn and one in which they are very often deficient (see Walker & Walker, 1991).

Implementation Recommendations

Recommendations are presented here for a series of intervention techniques that we and others have found to be highly effective in remediating the behavior problems presented by antisocial students in grades K through 5 or 6. In Appendix A, we illustrate these techniques and present results to demonstrate their efficacy. As a rule, it is unrealistic to expect that a single technique (such as adult praise or time-out) will be effective in having much impact on the behavioral adjustment and teacher or peer acceptance of antisocial students. While guidelines are presented or referenced in other parts of this text for individual techniques, it is very important to remember that one will almost always be simultaneously implementing multiple techniques when dealing with this population.

Adult Praise

Adult praise (from teachers, parents, others) is an extremely powerful form of focused attention that communicates approval and positive regard. It is an abundantly available, natural resource that is greatly underutilized. This is indeed unfortunate because praise that is behavior specific and delivered in a positive and genuine fashion is one of our most powerful tools for motivating students and teaching them important skills. A technical manual on praising, which was developed for Utah's BEST Project, provides detailed guidelines on how to use this technique effectively. Reavis, Jenson, Kukic, and Morgan (1993) argue that praise should be immediate, frequent, enthusiastic, descriptive, varied, and involve eye contact. These are very important keys to making teacher and parent praise effective. We would also suggest that the ratio of praises to criticism and reprimands be at least 4:1, and higher if possible. Finally, it is important to note that antisocial students may not be initially responsive to adult praise incorporated into a school intervention because of their history of negative interactions with the adults in their lives. However, through pairing with other incentives (for example, points exchangeable for privileges at school or home), the positive valence of praise will eventually increase.

Individual and Group Reinforcement Contingencies

A contingency refers to and defines the relationship between a positive consequence and the target behavior of an individual or a group of individuals. It has to do with the arrangement of details between earnable consequences and the performance criteria that must be met to access them. Contingencies can be individual or group oriented. Individual contingencies are a private, one-to-one arrangement between a teacher or parent and a student in which certain consequences (for example, privileges) are made available dependent upon the student's performance. Earning 1 minute of free time for every 10 or 15 math problems correctly solved, or attempted, is an example of an individual contingency. Group contingencies are arrangements in which an entire group of individuals (for example, a class) is treated as a single unit and the group's performance, as a whole, is evaluated to determine whether a positive consequence is earned. For example, if the level of academic engagement for the entire class meets or exceeds 70% for a 30-minute instructional period, then the class earns 5 minutes of extra recess. A combined individual–group contingency arrangement is also possible in which the target student, through acceptable performance, earns a group-activity reward or consequence that is shared equally with the entire class. Applications of these three types of contingency arrangements are illustrated in (1) Appendix A of this book, (2) *Utah's BEST Project Technical Manual*, (3) *The Acting Out Child*, and (4) *The Tough Kid Book*.

Social-Skills Training

Chapter 10 provides extensive treatment of the topic of social-skills training and presents detailed guidelines for effective training. Recommended curricular resources are also provided for use in such training.

Time-Out

Time-out is often a necessary tool for use with disruptive, aggressive students. It refers to removal of students from a particular situation in which (1) they have problems controlling their behavior and (2) the attention of peers is drawn to their inappropriate behavior. They are removed for a brief period of time (usually 5 to 15 minutes). Time-out is a volatile technique, like response cost or cost contingency, that has to be used according to prescribed guidelines to control potential side effects and achieve the desired outcomes (that is, reduction or elimination of undesirable, destructive, or maladaptive forms of behavior). Guidelines are presented in Chapter 11 for the effective use of time-out in home and schools. In addition, *Utah's BEST Project Technical Manual, The Acting Out Child*, and *The Tough Kid Book* also provide guidelines for using time-out effectively. We recommend that (1) procedures be set up to provide for both in-classroom time-out for minor infractions and out-of-classroom time-out (the principal's office) for more serious infractions, (2) students be given the option of electing for brief periods of time-out when they temporarily cannot control their own behavior, and (3) teachers *never* physically engage with any students in order to forcibly put them in time-out.

Response Cost (RC) or Cost Contingency

Unlike time-out, cost contingency (or response cost) removes a privilege or earned points for an infraction. Instead of removing the student from a situation, it removes a point or privilege from the student; thus, it is easier to manage than time-out. Cost contingency is the basis for fines, traffic tickets, yardage penalties in football, and other sanctions in public life that are applied for the purpose of controlling illegal or maladaptive forms of behavior. In combination with praise, a point system, and time-out as a back-up procedure, cost contingency can be extremely effective in reducing maladaptive behavior. The technique is versatile and can be used with equal effectiveness in classroom and playground settings. Appendix A contains a number of studies illustrating the effective use of this technique in the classroom and on the playground. We suggest the following general guidelines be strictly followed in using cost contingency: (1) the RC system should be carefully explained before applying it; (2) RC should always be tied to a reinforcement system, preferably involving points; (3) an appropriate delivery system should be developed; (4) RC should be implemented immediately after the target behavior or response occurs; (5) RC should be applied each time an instance of a target behavior occurs; (6) the student should never be allowed to accumulate negative points (that is, to go in the hole with point totals); (7) the ratio of points earned to those lost should be controlled; (8) the social agent using response cost should never be intimidated from using RC by the target student; (9) subtraction of points should never be punitive or personalized; and (10) the student's positive, appropriate behavior should be praised as frequently as opportunities permit.

PROGRAM-ENVIRONMENT FIT OR MATCH CONSIDERATIONS

A central principle of social ecology is "person-environment fit or match" (Romer & Heller, 1983). This principle relates to the degree to which the person's characteristics (attitudes, skills, performance) fit or match up with the demands and expectations of the environment (a particular setting, such as the classroom or playground). As a rule, the better the fit or match, the more likely that a satisfactory adjustment will be achieved.

Horner, Sugai, and Todd (1994) have recently extended this concept to *programs* that match up or fit with the *contexts* in which they are implemented. *Program-environment fit* is an extremely important dimension that is often ignored in our delivery of interventions in schools. These authors argue persuasively that (1) there is a growing need for the provision of behavioral supports within school settings and (2) too often, our interventions are designed and delivered in a manner that is technically sound but contextually inappropriate.

Unless an intervention is a good contextual fit—in the sense of being acceptable to teachers and students, being consistent with their values and beliefs, not requiring too much effort, being relatively unobtrusive, and holding the promise of effectiveness—it is likely to fail no matter how well it is designed. Knowledge of schools and how they operate is essential if maximally effective interventions are to be designed and implemented effectively for students in general, and especially for antisocial students.

We recommend careful attention to the literature on the acceptability of interventions in schools. Witt and his colleagues have conducted the seminal work in this area (see Witt & Martens, 1983; Witt & Robbins, 1985). This literature indicates that teachers are concerned about the following factors in relation to school-based interventions: (1) risk to the target child, (2) amount of teacher time required, (3) effects of the intervention on other children, and (4) amount of teacher skill required. In regard to reductive intervention techniques, teachers universally find corporal forms of punishment to be unacceptable while differential reinforcement of alternative forms of appropriate behavior are highly acceptable. Teachers reported varying degrees of acceptability for reprimands, staying after school, and time-out. As a general rule, teachers prefer positive, accelerative intervention approaches to negative, reductive approaches.

A careful and sensitive analysis of the influence of the setting on an intervention's potential effectiveness is highly recommended in the design of any intervention. It is absolutely essential that this dimension be attended to carefully in working with antisocial students.

THE NCTV TEN-POINT PLAN TO SWEEP VIOLENCE OFF TV AND OFF OUR STREETS[1]

1. *No censorship.* There should be no government censorship of the media. It must be recognized that upholding the separation of government and media (as well as religion and media) is even more vital to the citizens of the United States than curbing violence.

2. *Ratings system for violence.* A ratings system which describes the violent content of TV shows should be agreed upon by the networks and cable channels. Ratings would delineate the quantity of violence (in terms of violent acts per show) and the quality of violence (in terms of how graphic and lethal the violence is, whether the overall message is pro- or anti-violence, and how gratuitous the violence is). Ratings would be determined by an independent review board comprised of experts in the field of media violence.

3. *Ingredient labels.* Using the precedent of requiring labels on food products which detail the ingredients contained inside, TV shows should be required to broadcast ingredient labels and use them in TV publicity/listings. Such labels would reflect the results of the ratings system: the quantity and quality of the violence contained in the show.

4. *Warning labels on TV shows.* Using the precedent established for products such as cigarettes, TV shows should be required to flash a warning label before those shows rated high in violence. The warning label should read: "The TV show you are about to watch may be hazardous to your psychological and/or physical health due to its highly violent content."

5. *Warning labels on TV ads.* Commercials for war toys (including, but not limited to, action figures, video games, guns, and other weapons) and other violent-themed products would need to carry appropriate warning labels. These would read: "The toy you have just seen advertised may be hazardous to the psychological and/or physical health of a child due to its theme which inspires violent play."

6. *Violence advisors on staff.* At least one psychiatrist and/or researcher on TV violence should be on staff at each network and cable channel to review its shows and determine the psychological impact of any violence portrayed. This person would then advise the producers and TV executives of the findings and make recommendations as to how the violence can be toned down without compromising artistic integrity.

7. *Public service announcements.* Networks and cable channels should be strongly advised to carry PSAs [public service announcements] which educate viewers about the harmful effects of media violence. Each channel would be advised to carry a number of PSAs per day which would be in proportion to how much violent programming it broadcasts.

---

[1]Presented by Dr. Carole Lieberman before the House Judiciary Committee's Subcommittee on Crime and Criminal Justice on December 15, 1992.

8. *"Just say no" in government institutions.* No violent TV programming should be offered to residents of government institutions—such as jails and psychiatric hospitals. These residents are often exposed to countless hours of TV viewing, while in a condition which they are particularly vulnerable to its effect, instead of receiving more appropriate psychotherapy and rehabilitation. No children residing in government institutions should be exposed to TV violence.

9. *Tax breaks.* Tax breaks should be given to networks and cable channels, production companies, foundations, private donors, etc. who provide money to support:

- research and education on the effects of TV violence
- development of nonviolent TV programming for children

10. *Media literacy public health campaign.* A public health campaign should be launched, in the same spirit as campaigns against drunk driving and against the consumption of alcohol by pregnant women, to promote awareness of the effects of media violence. Schools and TV itself would participate in this campaign to create better-educated media consumers. Obviously, safeguards must be built in to disallow government and media resources from promoting self-serving agendas.

CONCLUSION

This chapter has presented information designed to empower the reader to understand the complexity of antisocial behavior patterns and the role of schooling as a powerful context for intervening with antisocial students. Schools can be highly effective partners with families and community agencies in responding to the needs of antisocial children and youth. We have much to learn, but we have also discovered a great deal that is not being applied consistently or effectively in this regard. If we make a good-faith effort to simply implement what we currently know regarding antisocial children and youth, we can collectively make a huge difference in their lives and the lives of those who relate to them. The material in the remainder of this book attempts to make that information accessible to educators and other professionals.

Chapters 3 and 4 deal with an important topic: coping with the acting-out cycle of antisocial students in schools. Antisocial students typically carry high levels of agitation and are usually unskilled at managing their anger. In many cases, they are like powder kegs waiting to explode. Teachers are often drawn, unwittingly, into escalated interactions with these students that end in rage and that can, in rare cases, pose a danger to teacher safety. Chapter 3 provides a seven-phase conceptual model of how these escalated teacher–student interactions are triggered, escalate, and then fade—all within a matter of seconds or minutes. Chapter 4 provides recommended strategies for dealing with each phase of this acting-out cycle. We strongly recommend proactively intervening in the early phases of this behavioral chain so the later, more destructive phases are prevented from occurring.

Antisocial students learn this method of interacting with their parents and siblings through the child-rearing processes to which they are exposed at home. These processes are based on coercion and teach the child that the behavior of others can be controlled by escalating (that is, having tantrums, arguing, being oppositional or defiant) in situations where demands are made upon them or whenever they are faced with a situation from which they wish to escape or avoid. This style of interaction is then generalized to the school setting and applied to interactions with teachers and peers. The antisocial student is usually rewarded for behaving in this way because it provides situational control, social dominance, and escape or avoidance from demands and unpleasant situations. Chapter 11 provides information on the child-rearing practices of the parents of antisocial students and includes suggestions for assisting parents in developing more positive ways of interacting with their children and with school personnel.

STUDY QUESTIONS

1. Distinguish universal from selected interventions. Which is likely to be more effective with the individual student?
2. Discuss the school's role in the prevention and remediation of antisocial behavior patterns.
3. Explain the concept: "School as a site for the delivery of integrated social services."
4. Name four individual, social experiences that serve as "accelerators" in the development of youth violence.
5. Describe how violent acts depicted in the media contribute to increased violence in our society.
6. Name the four levels at which social–environmental influence factors for antisocial behavior operate.
7. Discuss the relationship between the social cohesion of neighborhoods and the development of gangs among youth.
8. After the age of 8, what is the likelihood of a "cure" for an antisocial behavior pattern?
9. Describe elements of a developmental continuum for the progress of antisocial behavior.
10. Briefly describe three different approaches to the early screening and identification of children at risk for antisocial behavior.
11. Discuss some of the key target areas antisocial interventions should address.
12. Provide several examples of universal and selected interventions for antisocial behavior in school.
13. Describe the difference between best practices and implementation recommendations for antisocial behavior.

KEY TERMS

early screening
fidelity of intervention
prevention
program–environment fit or match
remediation
resiliency
school-based interventions
school-linked services
social disorganization

3 The Acting-Out Behavior Cycle of Antisocial Students in the Classroom: A Conceptual Model

Example of an Acting-Out Behavior Pattern Sequence

Indicators of Agitation
Presence of an Escalating Behavior Chain
Presence of Successive Interactions

Seven Phases in an Acting-Out Behavior Cycle

Phase One: Calm
Phase Two: Triggers
Phase Three: Agitation

Phase Four: Acceleration
Phase Five: Peak
Phase Six: De-Escalation
Phase Seven: Recovery

Summary of Phases in the Acting-Out Cycle

Illustration and Application

Conclusion

General education teachers are having to deal with ever-increasing numbers of students who are difficult to manage and teach. In addition, teachers are discovering that the management practices that have worked so well over the years with typical students do not seem to be very effective with these more difficult students. In fact, teachers often report that such practices make situations worse, especially with students who exhibit acting-out or explosive forms of behavior. Antisocial children and youth are very likely to fit this profile.

Table 3.1 presents common assumptions and practices for managing the problem behavior of antisocial students. Four scenarios are described; each scenario contains (1) the commonly held assumption on which the practice is based, (2) the practice that follows logically from the assumption, (3) a classroom example in which the practice is applied, (4) an analysis of the example and the situation, and (5) an alternative approach for dealing with the situation.

In each scenario, problems may arise when commonly used practices are implemented. Some of these problems are predictable while others may be unexpected. First, the students' behavior may escalate unexpectedly. In effect, the teacher addresses one problem and quickly has to deal with a worse problem as a function of the strategies used. Or alternatively, the teacher's strategy may be successful in calming the students down but, in the process, may actually be *reinforcement* of the problem behavior that prompted the situation. Consequently, the next time the students encounter a similar situation, they will be more likely to exhibit the same initial problem behavior in order to engage the teacher. In such situations, it seems patently clear that the students, rather than the teacher, are in control.

The purpose of Chapters 3 and 4 is to illustrate strategies that will enable teachers to understand and effectively address problematic student behavior without causing the behavior to escalate and in a way that solves the situation effectively (that is, both the teacher and the students will be better set up to appropriately manage the situation the next time these circumstances arise). This knowledge is extremely important to teachers as the diversity of classroom environments increases and as more and more students become invested in patterns of antisocial behavior. In this chapter, we present a seven-phase conceptual model to describe the escalation process or *acting-out cycle*. We describe the conceptual model by providing (1) an example of the critical features of an acting-out behavior pattern, (2) a detailed description of the seven sequential phases involved in an acting-out behavior cycle, (3) a summary table describing each phase, and (4) an illustration. In Chapter 4, we describe specific strategies for managing student behavior in each of these phases.

EXAMPLE OF AN ACTING-OUT BEHAVIOR PATTERN SEQUENCE

In the following example, a student in a typical classroom exhibits a range of diverse behaviors in an acting-out behavior cycle. The setting and the interactions between Michael and his teacher are described in Box 3.1.

TABLE 3.1 An Analysis of Common Assumptions and Practices for Managing Antisocial Students

Assumption	*Practice*	*Example*	*Analysis*	*Alternative*
Teachers need to be in *control.*	When problems occur, address them immediately and directly.	The class is working on an independent assignment. Students are working well except for two who are talking. The teacher says very firmly, "You are supposed to be working by yourself; there is to be no talk." One student mumbles under his breath, and the teacher writes his name on the board. The student then curses at the teacher.	The two students are talking, which can be presumed to be positive. The teacher essentially interrupts with a "putdown" or possibly sarcastic comment, "You are supposed to be . . ." There is also a dimension of *confrontation.* The student reacts by mumbling. The teacher interprets the mumbling as insubordination and provides a penalty. The student reacts further with cursing.	The teacher approaches the two students and gently interrupts them, secures their attention, and says, "Look, it is time for math. Please get on with it. You can visit later." Essentially, the teacher redirects the students to the math in a nonconfrontational way and provides them with an alternative (visit later, but it is math now).
Teachers need to establish *authority.*	Students need to be shown "who is the boss."	A student is out of his seat, walking around the room. The teacher tells him to sit down and do his work. The student says he needs to do something. The teacher says to sit down or he will be in trouble. The student keeps walking around the room. The teacher grasps his arm and tells him to sit down. The student swings his arm free vigorously.	Essentially, the teacher is setting the stage for confrontation by not addressing the student's needs and giving no options. The teacher escalates the confrontation by providing a threat and further by grabbing the student's arm.	The teacher could address the student's needs and then provide an option. For example, the teacher could say, "Michael, you should be in your seat working; what's up?" Michael might say, "I need (such and such a book)." The teacher could say, "Well, please go back to your seat and raise your hand for the book." In this way, the teacher addresses the student's need and provides the student with an acceptable strategy for obtaining the need, given the need is reasonable or appropriate.

TABLE 3.1 *(Continued)*

Assumption	*Practice*	*Example*	*Analysis*	*Alternative*
Children must not get away with behavior; otherwise, "what will the other children think?"	Misbehavior needs to be addressed quickly and publicly.	Sarah says she is not going to do her work because it is boring. The teacher says, so all can hear, "Sarah, you need to do the work now or you will stay in at recess to do it." Sarah pushes her materials to the floor.	Sarah makes an engaging statement regarding the work. The *public response* of the teacher provides immediate attention and probably draws the attention of the whole class. Sarah will not back down now that the class is watching the confrontation, so she escalates it by pushing her materials to the floor.	The teacher could ignore Sarah and respond to the students on task, or the teacher could—as privately as possible—redirect Sarah to her work and offer to discuss it with her later if she wishes. (This is a good example of a *private response.*)
Students need to be settled down when they become agitated.	Teachers should approach students with empathy, calm them down, and get them back to work.	Billy is muttering and fidgeting and is on the verge of tears. The teacher goes to him, puts his hand on Billy's shoulder, and says calmly, "I see you are upset. Can I help you?" Billy begins to sob, and the teacher stands beside him and helps him start his work.	The teacher succeeds in calming Billy down and getting him back to work. However, next time Billy is upset, he is likely to exhibit the same tearful, fidgety behavior, and the teacher will use the same calming behavior. The teacher may be setting up "learned helplessness" or be falling into the "rescue" pattern. As a result, Billy might never learn how to solve problems himself. Also, with some students, "rescuing" behavior is highly likely to escalate situations or encourage whining.	The teacher may help to settle Billy down as indicated and redirect him to his work. However, the teacher can visit with Billy later and try to help him solve the problem and come up with strategies for managing the problem next time. If, in the future, Billy resorts to sobbing and fidgety behavior because it worked last time, the teacher could gently remind him of the agreed-upon strategy.

Box 3.1 Example of the Cycle of Acting-Out Behavior

During independent work in math, the class is expected to complete problems that were assigned in the morning period. Michael is sitting slouched in his seat staring at the floor. Look for this chain in the following interaction: agitation, questioning, arguing, noncompliance, defiance, verbal abuse, physical abuse, and assault.

Teacher	Michael	Pattern
"Michael, it is time to get started with your math."	"What math?"	Questions
"The math you didn't finish this morning."	"I did finish it."	Argues
"Well, let me see it then."	Michael has four problems completed.	
"Good. You have done four but you need to do ten."	"I didn't know that."	Continues arguing
"Well, I announced it at the start of the morning that you had to do ten."	"I don't remember that."	Continues arguing
"Look at the board. See math one through ten. It's there every day."	"Oh. I didn't know that."	Continues arguing
"Stop. No more questions. Math one through ten. Do it now."	"I am not going to do that. It's not fair." or	Noncompliance
	"Make me."	Defiance
"If you don't do it now, you will have to do it at recess."	"F—— you."	Verbal abuse
"That language is unacceptable."	"You want math. Here it is." (*throws math book across room*)	Physical abuse

In most schools, the behavior exhibited by Michael would result in an office referral, and the teacher's report would read something like this:

> Michael was sitting at his desk and not working. I approached him to see if he needed help. He asked questions and began to argue. I gave him a clear direction to start work and he refused, saying, "Make me." I followed the usual procedures of giving him a choice of doing the work now or doing it at recess on his time. He

> began to cuss me out and threatened me. I started to fill out an office referral form, and he threw his math book across the room and flipped his desk over. I was worried about the safety of the other students and went to escort him to the office. At this point, he punched me in the face. I have quite a bruise on my face.

The person who has to follow up on this incident, usually the principal or vice-principal, really can only address one item in this disciplinary report—the student hit the teacher. Because of its salience and unacceptability, the principal would be forced to address the last behavior. The hitting could be categorized as assault, and a complaint could be made to the police. If no complaint is made, it is essential that strong negative consequences be delivered, such as suspension and a parent conference. These consequences, if effective, may prevent the student from hitting the teacher again (or they may not). The student may not hit again but may exhibit all of the other behaviors in the behavioral chain leading up to hitting.

Thus, we need to ask the critical question, "What needs to be done to prevent this *whole scene* from happening again?" In this case, we would have to address the beginning of the chain. We can work with Michael in three main areas to effectively address the chain of behavior:

1. Indicators of agitation
2. Presence of an escalating behavior chain
3. Presence of successive interactions

Indicators of Agitation

Michael was sitting in a slouched position, feet outstretched, arms folded, staring at the floor, and basically motionless. These behaviors are general indicators that Michael is having problems coping; it is only a matter of time before his behavior will escalate. There are numerous strategies for addressing his agitation and for assisting him with the problem-solving process. These strategies will be illustrated in Chapter 4 in the section on managing agitation.

Presence of an Escalating Behavior Chain

Michael starts out questioning or challenging the teacher, and each subsequent response from the teacher sets the stage for Michael to argue and ask more questions. Eventually, the teacher tries to terminate the arguing by giving him a clear directive to start work. Michael then refuses, which is called active noncompliance; the "make me" routine is usually referred to as defiance. Michael then moves on or escalates into verbal abuse, intimidation, physical abuse, and finally assault. Each ensuing behavior in this *behavior chain* is more serious than the one preceding it, and the sequence culminates in assaultive behavior. In effect, Michael's behavior began with questioning and finished with assault.

What if the questioning and arguing were terminated early or managed differently? The likely outcome would be that there would be nothing to set the stage for noncompliance. If noncompliance were not present, there would be nothing to set the stage for

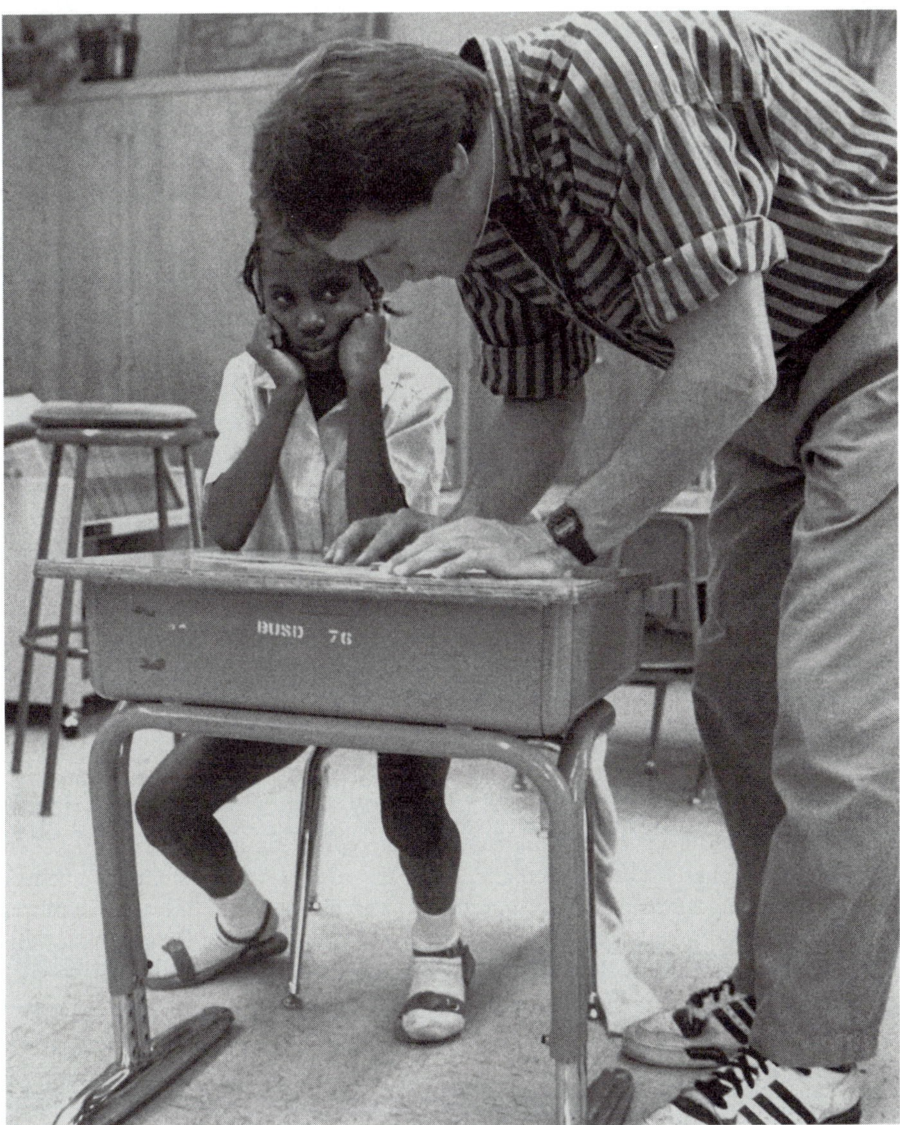

An agitated student resisting her teacher's assistance. *Elizabeth Crews*

teacher defiance and verbal abuse. In other words, if the chain were interrupted at an early stage, there would be nothing to prompt the more serious forms of behavior occurring at the end of the chain. Thus, teacher assault and the other forms of adult confrontation would be prevented. In this chapter, we describe the successive phases in an escalating chain of acting-out behavior involving the teacher and antisocial students. In Chapter 4, we present strategies for intervening early in the chain so as to facilitate prevention of such unfortunate and costly cycles of behavior.

Presence of Successive Interactions

The office report in our example is clear regarding Michael's behavior; however, the specific dynamics of the teacher's behavior are only implied. Unfortunately, in this kind of situation we are looking at a series of *escalating interactions* that involve *both* teacher and student behavior. For each student behavior, there is a corresponding or reciprocal teacher behavior. Each successive student behavior is preceded by a discrete teacher behavior. It could be argued that each teacher behavior sets the stage for the next student behavior. These teacher-student interactions could be described as a series of "my turn, your turn" events. For example, Michael questions the assigned work (math) (Michael's turn). The teacher answers him (teacher's turn). Michael argues (Michael's turn). The teacher directs him to work (teacher's turn). Michael refuses (Michael's turn). The teacher provides choices (teacher's turn), and so on, ending with Michael hitting the teacher.

What if the teacher refused to take a turn? There would be nothing to set the stage for Michael's turn. In other words, Michael's behavior would be eliminated. A critical component in managing this kind of *reactive behavior* pattern is to recognize that we are dealing with *successive interactions*; if these interactions were managed differently (specifically teacher behavior in this case), then the behavioral chain could be dismantled or prevented from occurring.

In effect, this chain of behavior involving Michael and his teacher could have been prevented by using effective strategies to (1) manage Michael's initial agitation, (2) intervene early in the chain, and (3) manage the successive interactions. The dynamics of these critical procedures will be presented more fully in the strategies section of Chapter 4.

SEVEN PHASES IN AN ACTING-OUT BEHAVIOR CYCLE

The escalating behavior pattern exhibited in the preceding example can be illustrated in seven successive phases. The phases that describe the severity or intensity of this behavioral cycle over time are depicted in Figure 3.1. The graph rises as the interaction escalates and falls when it de-escalates. This conceptual model was developed initially by Colvin (1992) to represent the interdependent behavioral dynamics of teacher-student responses occurring during escalating interactions.

Teachers, as well as parents and peers, are often inadvertently trapped in escalating *social interactions* with antisocial students that prove to be extremely disruptive and damaging to relationships. Antisocial students carry high levels of agitation due to the stresses they are under and the neglect and abuse to which they are exposed in nonschool settings. This agitation serves as fuel that drives a coercive behavioral process that is often triggered by innocuous events such as asking questions, making requests, or giving directives. The situation is analogous to a powder keg that is triggered by a spark. The resulting explosion is difficult to control or avoid and does extensive damage. This is exactly the process involved in escalating teacher-student social interactions.

Figure 3.1 illustrates the *escalation* and de-escalation processes involved in this highly coercive process. Understanding this phenomenon is essential to dealing with the intense behavioral challenges presented by antisocial students.

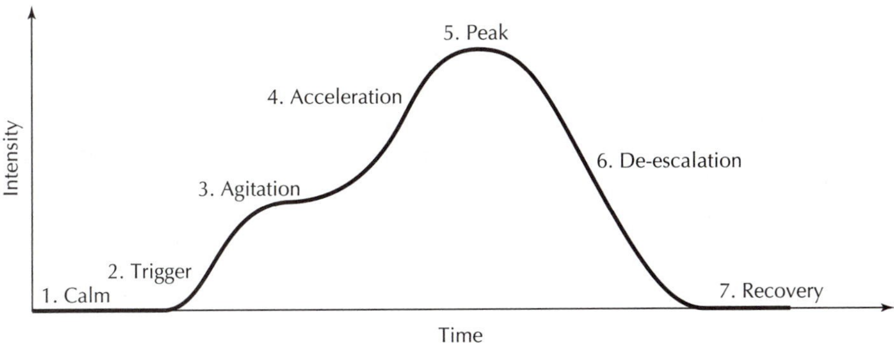

FIGURE 3.1 Phases of Acting-Out Behavior. *Source:* Colvin (1992).

The *behavioral phases* in the chain are described in detail in the following sections. The behavioral content of each phase has been derived from numerous observations made by the authors in working with antisocial students. Typical behavioral characteristics of antisocial students are noted that are associated with their responses to each of the seven phases identified in this acting-out cycle. In most cases, these cycles involve an escalated interaction between the teacher and the antisocial student that is intense, explosive, and highly aversive. In many cases, antisocial students learn this coercive behavior pattern at home in dealing with family members and bring it to school. It represents one of the surest and quickest paths to rejection by school staff and peers.

Phase One: Calm

On-Task Behavior. Antisocial students are relatively calm in the initial phase of the acting-out behavior cycle. To all outward appearances, their behavior is appropriate, generally cooperative, and responsive to teacher-imposed rules and expectations. Teachers often report that "Most of the time, 'So and So' is a delight to have in the classroom but at other times . . ." (which is usually the primary reason for a discipline-referral meeting). Bear in mind that antisocial students may never actually be models of appropriate behavior when compared with other students. However, on occasion, such students may engage in appropriate classroom activities for extended periods and participate, to some degree, in the normal events of the classroom.

Following of Rules and Expectations. In the calm phase, students regard obeying the rules as an accomplishment. They are likely to say, "It made my day." However, later on, these same rules may become the source of severe challenges, limit testing, and teacher confrontations.

Responsiveness to Praise. As with other students, antisocial children and youth need positive attention and adult approval. Teacher praise can be important to them. Unfortunately, the appropriate behavior of antisocial students is often ignored during this phase (probably because the teacher needs a break from dealing with these demanding students).

Initiation of Behavior. When students are relatively calm, they will often initiate appropriate behavior to others (for example, sharing or being of assistance to peers). Thus, it is important to remember that antisocial students can be helpful to others and that they will exhibit these kinds of desirable behaviors on occasion.

Goal-Orientedness. Like everyone, antisocial students need to succeed and have a sense of competence. They will be responsive if appropriate goals can be established that they are likely to meet. In general, this student population does not experience academic or social success in school, so it is critical to provide structures during this phase that will assist them in achieving these extremely important outcomes.

Summary of Phase One: Calm

Overall behavior is cooperative, compliant, and desirable

Phase Two: Triggers

Two sets of triggers operate in this phase: school-based and nonschool-based. These triggers represent pressure points that increase the general level of agitation that antisocial students experience.

School-Based Triggers

Conflicts. The sources of *student conflicts* fall into two broad categories: (1) denial of something the students want or need and (2) something negative is inflicted on the students. In the first case, antisocial students typically do not have good communication skills, so when they need something, their limited verbal skills often do not allow them to communicate effectively (or communicate in a way that is acceptable). If antisocial students perceive their need as being denied, they often react angrily and may be assigned penalties for this reactive behavior. In effect, the original needs or goals are denied and the students end up in trouble for reacting in an inappropriate manner.

In the second case, antisocial students are provoked by a perception that something negative is being inflicted on them—such as a student accidentally bumping into them, refusing to allow them to play in a game, or calling them names. The students then react to such negative events and may experience social or other penalties for the behavior. Antisocial students often become frustrated in this process because they perceive the situation as not being their fault, yet they are victimized via penalties or other sanctions.

Changes in Routine. These students react negatively to sudden changes in routines, especially if the activity is something that has fully engaged them. In general, transitions are difficult for them.

Provocations. Other students see antisocial students as "fair game." These "normal" students can predictably cause their antisocial peers to escalate through provocations, such as name calling, teasing, and interfering with their property. They are viewed as a good tease by peers.

Pressure. School is a high-demand situation in which students are expected to follow a wide variety of directions and complete a number of often complex tasks during the course of a school day. Antisocial students do not manage their time well and have poor planning and adaptive-behavior skills. They are generally poorly organized in a personal sense. The ordinary demands of the school day can set the stage for panic, depression, anxiety, and other emotional behaviors.

Ineffective Problem Solving. Antisocial students have limited strategies for identifying sources of problems, generating adaptive options, evaluating them, negotiating with others, and implementing plans accordingly. Such strategies need to be systematically and directly taught to antisocial students.

Errors. In many cases, antisocial students will stop working when they make errors or will avoid new work because they are likely to make mistakes. Thus, error-correction processes and the assignment of academic tasks are often emotion-laden occasions.

Corrections. Similarly, antisocial students often have problems in accepting assistance after errors have been made or with being required to try a task again. Teacher corrections and debriefings may actually prompt substantial increases in their agitation levels.

Nonschool-Based Triggers

Dysfunctional Homes. Many students who have severe behavior disorders come from needy homes where there may be poverty, unemployment, abuse, neglect, and poor parental modeling of appropriate behavior and positive attitudes toward school.

Health Problems. Parents, in many cases, do not have health insurance and have very limited incomes. An appointment with the doctor could use up several days' income. Consequently, these children may not go to the doctor for the common illnesses, such as viruses and infections, and often come to school sick because their parents cannot afford to stay home with them.

Nutrition. Perhaps as a result of poverty and ineffective parenting, these children do not have regular, well-balanced meals and are often hungry. Severe hunger usually produces an agitated emotional state.

Sleep. Sleeping patterns are often irregular and, in some cases, such children have to sleep in crowded and squalid conditions.

Substance Abuse. Alcohol abuse and use of controlled substances are common problems among these families. A growing population of children are born to substance-addicted mothers. The problem of agitation and attention disorders presented by these children makes them extremely difficult to teach and manage in school. Many are now in public schools, and they often display serious forms of agitated, and sometimes antisocial, behavior.

Gangs. Membership in gangs sets the stage for serious problem behavior at school, especially with school authority and peer relationships. Membership in juvenile gangs is also associated with a dramatic increase in criminal behavior. The safety of adults and students in school becomes a salient issue with gang membership.

Summary of Phase Two: Triggers

Overall behavior involves a series of unresolved problems

Phase Three: Agitation

The agitation phase can last for a considerable amount of time, depending on the events that take place or on which stimuli are present. The graph in Figure 3.1 flattens out during the agitation phase to illustrate the longer duration of this phase.

Students often display high levels of agitation as a function of an inability to effectively manage the triggers identified in Phase Two. *Agitation* is a behavioral term that includes emotional dispositions such as being angry, upset, depressed, worried, anxious, and frustrated. Agitation is manifested both by increases and decreases in student behavior.

Increases in Behavior

Darting eyes. Students look here and there with a certain level of intensity but with little focus or purpose to their eye movements.

Nonconversational Language. Students' responses are such that it is difficult to build a conversation. For example, you greet Tony and ask, "How was your weekend?" He might respond, "Fine." Then you ask, "What did you do?" He answers, "Nothing much." And so on.

Busy Hands. Students are prone to drum their fingers, rub their thighs, tap their pencils, open and close their books, tug at their clothes, and display a general increase in hand movements.

Moving In and Out of Groups. Students will want to join groups and then pull out or will ask to play and then do something else.

Off-Task, Then On-Task Behavior. Students will start a task, stop, do something else, and then start up again. There appears to be little, if any, fixed or sustained attention to academic tasks or related activities.

Decreases in Behavior

Staring into Space. Students appear to be daydreaming and just staring into space.

Subdued Language. Language is largely nonconversational with an extra dimension of weak delivery; that is, one often has to get close to hear what the students are saying (which may upset them more because they usually want to be left alone at this point and maintain their space).

Contained Hands. When agitated, antisocial students often put their hands in their pockets, sit on them, or fold their arms and just sulk.

Withdrawal from Groups. There is a tendency to pull away from a group, to lag behind, and to engage in isolated activities.

Summary of Phase Three: Agitation

Overall behavior is unfocused and off-task

Phase Four: Acceleration

The previous phase, agitation, characterizes students who are unfocused and off-task. By contrast, in Phase Four, student behavior is quite focused. During this phase, antisocial students typically exhibit escalating behavior that assures a predictable and rapid response from the teacher. In other words, students exhibit *engaging behaviors*—that is, behaviors that are very likely to engage some other person (for example, the teacher).

Questioning and Arguing. Students set themselves up to need help or ask questions and then proceed to argue about the responses or details of the task at hand. Typically, the student is not seeking essential information but rather engaging the teacher in a confrontational interaction.

Noncompliance and Defiance. Students refuse to cooperate, usually in response to a teacher directive, demand, or behavioral expectation. For example, the teacher may hear responses such as, "I'm not going to do that," "That's not fair," or "Make me."

Off-Task Behavior. Teachers have a general expectation that students should be academically engaged in assigned tasks or activities. Thus, when students stop working or do not get started promptly with assigned work, the teacher will approach, offer help, or provide a directive to begin work.

Provocation of Others. Students exhibit behaviors that irritate others and perhaps cause them to react strongly (for example, name calling, insults, racial slurs, put-downs, and interfering with other people's property).

Compliance with Accompanying Inappropriate Behaviors. This behavioral event, often called limit testing, has two components: (1) students actually complete the assigned task but (2) exhibit additional social behavior that is unacceptable. For example, Arlene may be asked to sit down. She sits down (compliance) but mutters an obscenity under her breath (additional behavior that is unacceptable).

Criterion Problems. Another form of limit testing, called partial compliance, occurs when students perform at a standard clearly below the expected level. For example, the

An escalating teacher-student interaction. *Kathleen Olson*

teacher may ask for a page of writing, and Carl completes only half a page. Or Marie will write semilegibly (even though prior samples show she can write legibly).

Whining and Crying. This behavior often prompts immediate teacher attention or assistance and may cause adults to show a high level of irritation.

Avoidance and Escape. With these forms of behavior, students are seeking to avoid a current activity or some activity scheduled to occur in the near future. This often puts pressure on teachers or places them in a situation of having to negotiate with students.

Threats and Intimidation. When antisocial students deliver threats, there is the expectation that the threatened person will respond in an intimidated fashion. For example, when the teacher tells Joseph he must complete an assignment either now or after school, he replies, "I know where you live." Such threats are a serious form of implied aggression and pose a potential danger that should not be dismissed.

Verbal Abuse. Similarly, when students use offensive language toward staff, staff will usually respond immediately. They rarely ignore the situation.

Destruction of Property. When students deliberately destroy property, staff always take immediate action.

Serious Behavior in General. Any serious behavior will typically lead to an immediate response from staff, which sets the stage for an escalated confrontation with students.

> **Summary of Phase Four: Acceleration**
>
> **Overall behavior is teacher-engaging**

Phase Five: Peak

All behaviors in this phase are characterized by *serious* disruption and often represent a threat to the safety of others.

Serious Destruction of Property. These behaviors involve substantial and costly damage to property.

Assault. Someone is a target or victim of assault, such as punching, kicking, throwing objects, hair pulling, and even more serious behaviors including assault with objects or weapons.

Self-Abuse. These self-directed behaviors involve hitting, pinching, hair pulling, head banging, and scratching.

Severe Tantrums. Tantrums may not pose a threat to the safety of others, but behaviors such as screaming, yelling, and flailing on the floor will prove to be seriously disruptive.

Hyperventilation. This behavior, though relatively harmless, is an indicator of how stressed or agitated the students may be.

> **Summary of Phase Five: Peak**
>
> **Overall behavior is out of control**

Phase Six: De-Escalation

This phase marks the beginning of the student's disengagement and corresponding reduction in agitation. However, students in this phase are not especially cooperative or responsive to adult social influence.

Confusion. Immediately following a serious incident of being out of control, students sometimes display confused, random behavior, such as wandering around in a circle, staring at the floor, fidgeting, sitting, and standing.

Reconciliation. Some students will want to make up, to see if they are still liked. They will offer to help or come close and stand near the teacher. Some may verbalize that they are sorry for what occurred.

Withdrawal. Students often will put their heads down and try to sleep. In some cases, they may be fatigued from the incident, and in other cases, they may simply need to quiet down. Students will sometimes sleep following a serious incident, which could result from a combination of fatigue, depression, and withdrawal.

Denial. Many students will engage in denial about their behavior, especially regarding the most serious behavioral episodes in the chain. The denial is often paired with blaming someone else.

Blaming Others. Students will frequently become animated as they blame others for the incident in question. For example, a student might say, "Well if she had let me see the nurse, none of this would have happened. It's all her fault." In addition, students will probably talk about the initiating behaviors occurring early in the behavioral chain, when blame can be directed toward some other person.

Responsiveness to Directions. Many supervisors have found that students at this point are sometimes responsive to very concrete directions, such as "Michael, would you sit over there on the bench, please?"

Responsiveness to Manipulative or Mechanical Tasks. In these situations, students often like to become engaged in tasks that are quite mechanical, such as leafing through magazines and playing with Legos.

Avoidance of Discussion. At this point, most students will avoid discussion and opportunities for debriefing unless there is an opportunity to blame others.

Summary of Phase Six: De-Escalation

Overall behavior displays confusion

Phase Seven: Recovery

In this final phase, behavior returns to a nonagitated, relatively normal state and reflects behavioral indicators of recovery.

Eagerness for Independent Work or Activity. Typically, the students will seek some kind of relatively independent "busy work," such as writing, coloring, or looking up words in a dictionary and writing down their meanings. These activities need to be relatively easy; students will tend to avoid difficult tasks or tasks that require teacher assistance.

Subdued Behavior in Group Work. Activities involving interactions with other students are difficult. Strategies such as cooperative learning should not be initiated in this phase.

Subdued Behavior in Class Discussions. Discussions are also difficult and student responses are typically muted and cryptic.

Defensive Behavior. Some antisocial students will display behavior that is very cautious and almost studied. They may be confused or simply may have learned not to say too much at this point.

Avoidance of Debriefing. Students are generally reluctant to talk about an incident (that is, what they did, the events leading up to it, and the alternatives they could have taken).

Summary of Phase Seven: Recovery

Overall behavior shows eagerness for busy work and reluctance to interact or discuss

SUMMARY OF PHASES IN THE ACTING-OUT CYCLE

The summary in Box 3.2 provides an overview of each phase in the acting-out cycle. The lists of behaviors are not meant to be exhaustive; rather, they are examples of a class of behavior for that particular phase.

ILLUSTRATION AND APPLICATION

At this point, we present an illustration of a student who exhibits serious acting-out behavior. Form 3.1 allows us to design procedures for remediating problematic behavior in each phase of the acting-out cycle. The form is divided into two sections: *assessment*, in which the student's specific behaviors are identified for each phase of the cycle, and *strategies* for managing each of the phases. In the next chapter, corresponding strategies will be described for implementation at the onset of each of these identified behaviors. Form 3.2 is a blank version of Form 3.1. Readers can use this form to practice identifying specific behaviors of an antisocial student in each phase.

CONCLUSION

In this chapter, we have presented a seven-phase model for describing serious acting-out social behavior. Behavioral descriptions were culled from a large sample of students who exhibit this behavioral pattern. The primary purpose of classifying behavior in this way

Box 3.2 Summary of the Acting-Out Cycle

Phase One: Calm

1. On-task behavior
2. Following of rules and expectations
3. Responsiveness to praise
4. Initiation of behavior
5. Goal-orientedness

Phase Two: Triggers

School-Based

1. Conflicts
   a. Denial of something they need
   b. Something negative is inflicted
2. Changes in routine
3. Provocations
4. Pressure
5. Ineffective problem solving
6. Errors
7. Corrections

Nonschool-Based

1. Dysfunctional homes
2. Health problems
3. Nutrition
4. Sleep
5. Substance abuse
6. Gangs

Phase Three: Agitation

Increases in Behavior

1. Darting eyes
2. Nonconversational language
3. Busy hands
4. Moving in and out of groups
5. Off-task, then on-task behavior

Decreases in Behavior

1. Staring into space
2. Subdued language
3. Contained hands
4. Withdrawal from groups

Box 3.2 *(Continued)*

Phase Four: Acceleration

1. Questioning and arguing
2. Noncompliance and defiance
3. Off-task behavior
4. Provocation of others
5. Compliance with accompanying inappropriate behaviors
6. Criterion problems
7. Whining and crying
8. Avoidance and escape
9. Threats and intimidation
10. Verbal abuse
11. Destruction of property
12. Serious behavior in general

Phase Five: Peak

1. Serious destruction of property
2. Assault
3. Self-abuse
4. Severe tantrums
5. Hyperventilation

Phase Six: De-Escalation

1. Confusion
2. Reconciliation
3. Withdrawal
4. Denial

Box 3.2 *(Continued)*

5. Blaming others
6. Responsiveness to directions
7. Responsiveness to manipulative or mechanical tasks
8. Avoidance of discussion (unless there is occasion to blame others)

Phase Seven: Recovery

1. Eagerness for independent work or activity
2. Subdued behavior in group work
3. Subdued behavior in class discussions
4. Defensive behavior
5. Avoidance of debriefing

is to enable practitioners to understand the behavioral processes involved in escalating interactions between teachers and students. The descriptions tell the teacher what problematic student behavior to expect at each stage of explosive teacher-student interactions that are increasingly a fact of daily school life. The strategies corresponding to each phase in the acting-out cycle are presented in the next chapter.

STUDY QUESTIONS

1. Why do common or traditional approaches to problem behavior often escalate students with severe antisocial problems?
2. Why is it difficult to change the cycle of acting-out behavior by focusing on the serious behavior component of the chain?
3. What are the main advantages to identifying the behavioral phases in the acting-out cycle?
4. What are the seven phases in the acting-out cycle and common behavioral indicators for each of these phases?
5. What function do successive interactions play in the acting-out cycle?
6. Using a student you have observed or worked with who displays serious acting-out behavior, describe the specific behaviors for each phase of the acting-out cycle.

ACTING-OUT BEHAVIOR

Student Name: *Dominic Smith*
Date: *3/4/93*
Teacher(s): *Walt Jones, Andrea DeForest, Aletia McHenry, Joe Carpenter*
Class: *7th Grade*

ASSESSMENT	STRATEGIES
Calm	**Calm**
Likes to help	
Displays successful work	
Enjoys games	
Likes the computer	
Triggers	**Triggers**
Repeating tasks	
Teasing remarks and putdowns from other students	
Correcting behavior	
Consequences for problem behavior	
Agitation	**Agitation**
Walks around the room	
Scowls at other students	
Pouts and mumbles to himself	
Does not concentrate on his work	
Acceleration	**Acceleration**
Argues and will not quit	
Defiance, "Make me"	
Name calls and threatens students	
Raises his voice and shouts	

FORM 3.1 Description of the Cycle of Acting-Out Antisocial Behavior

ASSESSMENT	STRATEGIES
Peak	**Peak**
Throws objects around the room	
Hits other students	
Yells and screams	
De-Escalation	**De-Escalation**
Goes very quiet, puts his head down	
Complains that no one likes him and that it is not fair	
Talks to himself a lot	
Likes to fiddle with things	
Recovery	**Recovery**
Somewhat subdued	
Likes to work alone	

FORM 3.1 *(Continued)*

KEY TERMS

acceleration phase
acting-out cycle
agitation phase
authority
behavioral phases
behavior chain
calm phase
confrontation
control
de-escalation phase
engaging behaviors
escalating interactions
escalation
peak phase
private response
public response
reactive behavior
recovery phase
reinforcement
social interactions
student conflicts
successive interactions
trigger phase

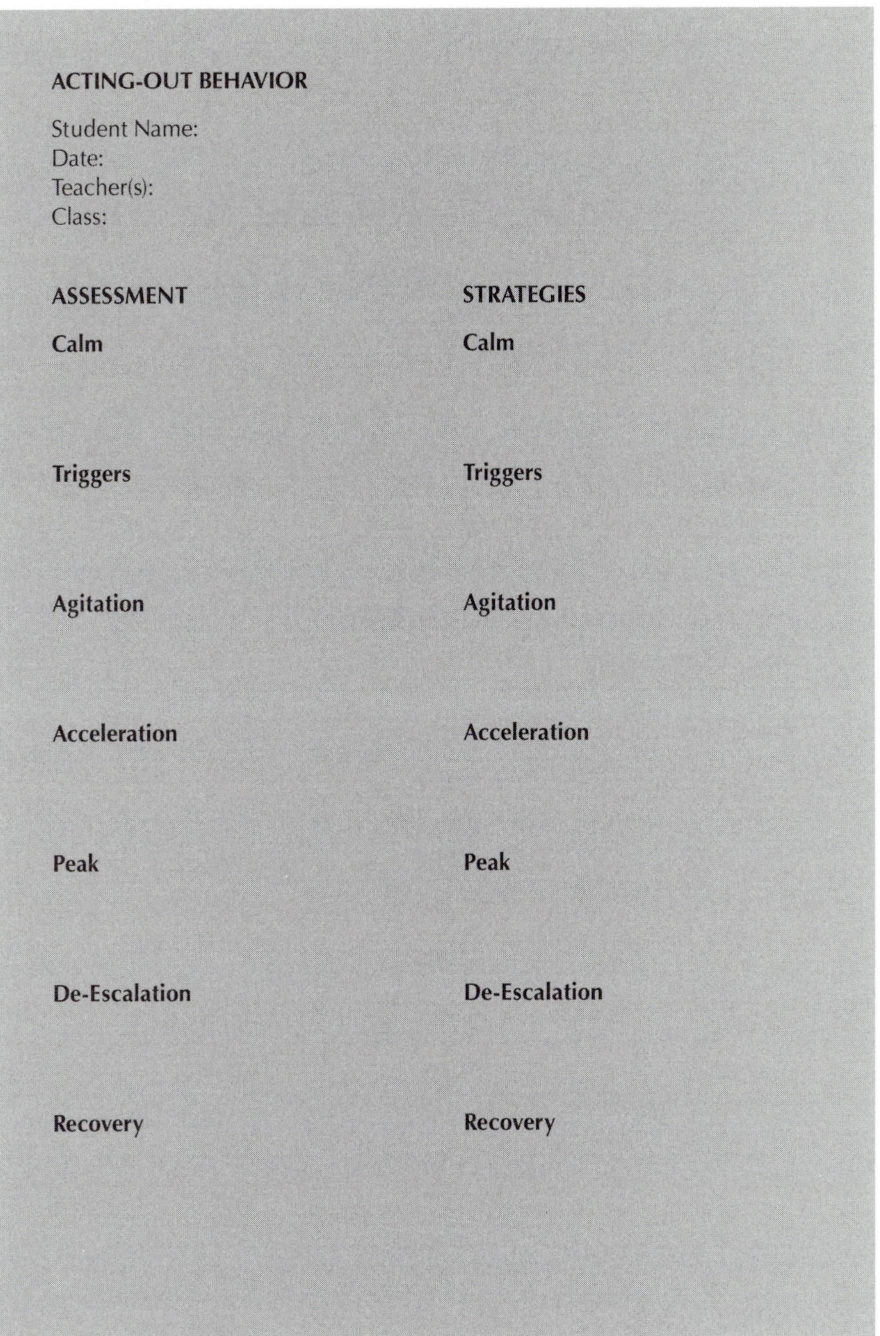

ACTING-OUT BEHAVIOR

Student Name:
Date:
Teacher(s):
Class:

ASSESSMENT	**STRATEGIES**
Calm	**Calm**
Triggers	**Triggers**
Agitation	**Agitation**
Acceleration	**Acceleration**
Peak	**Peak**
De-Escalation	**De-Escalation**
Recovery	**Recovery**

FORM 3.2 Assessment and Intervention Plan for Acting-Out Behavior

4 Strategies for Managing the Phases of Acting-Out Behavior

Strategies for Each Phase of the Acting-Out Cycle

Phase One: Calm
Phase Two: Triggers
Phase Three: Agitation
Phase Four: Acceleration
Phase Five: Peak

Phase Six: De-Escalation
Phase Seven: Recovery

Summary Form and Case Study

Conclusion

In the previous chapter, we presented a seven-phase conceptual model for describing serious acting-out behavior. Each phase represents a link in the behavioral chain. In this chapter, we describe strategies specifically designed for managing problematic student behavior in each of these phases. The basic approach is for the teacher, or other school professional, to effectively manage the behaviors in the early phases of the acting-out cycle so as to prevent the more destructive, subsequent phases. In doing this, the teacher is *interrupting the behavior chain*, thus preempting the later phases, in which more serious behaviors occur.In Phases One through Four (calm, triggers, agitation, and acceleration), the emphasis is on effective teaching and management practices. In the remaining phases, the emphasis is on safety, crisis management, reentry, and follow-up. An illustration (continuing from the previous chapter) is described to demonstrate specific strategies for handling antisocial students in each phase. The seven phases in the cycle of serious acting-out behavior are restated here:

Phase One: Calm

Phase Two: Triggers

Phase Three: Agitation

Phase Four: Acceleration

Phase Five: Peak

Phase Six: De-Escalation

Phase Seven: Recovery

STRATEGIES FOR EACH PHASE OF THE ACTING-OUT CYCLE

Phase One: Calm

It is important for educators to treat the first phase, calm, as a high priority. If effective strategies are applied here, the students' appropriate behavior will likely be maintained, and serious behavior problems may not occur. In addition, the more antisocial students can be maintained in this phase the more they will experience the positive consequences that naturally flow from peers, teachers, and school staff. Four basic strategies for achieving this goal are: (1) classroom structure, (2) quality instruction, (3) providing attention, and (4) teaching social behavior.

Classroom Structure. A number of strategies for establishing *classroom structure* are described in Chapter 6. Students who may exhibit explosive behavior benefit from a predictable environment. The structure provides a sense of security for such students, which helps them to remain calm and reduces the likelihood of unforeseen circumstances arising that may trigger inappropriate behavior. Teachers who have antisocial students should assess the degree to which structural variables are operative in their classroom and the degree to which specific structural variables could assist those students who may potentially exhibit acting-out or antisocial behavior.

CODE: IMPORTANCE	IMPLEMENTATION	
A. Very important B. Somewhat important C. Not important	1. Firmly in place 2. Somewhat in place 3. Not in place	
Structure Variable	**Importance**	**Implementation**
1. Behavior expectations		
2. Reinforcement procedures		
3. Problem-solving correction procedures		
4. Lesson focus specified		
5. Target skills identified		
6. Lesson feedback given		
7. Entry activity utilized		
8. Independent routines targeted		
9. Everyone's attention secured		
10. Students engaged in task immediately		
11. Problems addressed early		
12. Initial explanations brief		
13. Planned variations of instructions used		
14. Dead time avoided		
15. Plan for difficult transitions		
16. Students settled before end of period		
TOTALS		

FORM 4.1 Classroom Structure Implementation

Teachers can assess the extent to which structural variables are in place in their classroom by conducting a self-evaluation or by having someone else (a counselor, another teacher) observe, evaluate, and report back to them. An instrument for assessing classroom structure is presented in Form 4.1. Teachers can use this form to: (1) rate several structural variables according to their *importance* and their *level of implementation* and (2) tally scores for each structural variable.

Once implementation levels of structural variables have been assessed, the next steps are to: (1) analyze why important structural variables are not in place, if they are found to be missing, and (2) develop an action plan to implement the missing variables.

In order to assess which structural variables are more conducive to maintaining calm, on-task behavior with antisocial students, teachers can observe the students under naturally occurring variations in classroom structure and look for differential performance. Alternatively, they can directly manipulate some of the structural variables and observe how they affect students' performance. While many structural variables contribute to the predictability of the classroom environment, the following five are regarded as particularly crucial (these variables are described and illustrated in Chapter 6):

1. Preparation
2. Planned variation in the delivery of instruction
3. Classroom organization
4. Teacher expectations
5. Behavior management system

Quality Instruction. Gettinger (1988) identified *quality instruction* as one of the earliest proactive strategies that should be considered in classroom management. As a rule, if students are successfully engaged academically, there will be fewer associated behavior problems. Similarly, if antisocial students are productively engaged in an assignment or instructional task, there is far less likelihood of other competing classroom stimuli triggering inappropriate behavior.

In a survey of instructional practices in classrooms for students with serious emotional disturbances, Knitzer, Steinberg, and Fleisch (1990) found little evidence of focused academic instruction. Moreover, in an extensive review of the published literature on this topic, Ruhl and Berlinghoff (1992) report a paucity of research on the topic of academic interventions with students having antisocial or acting-out behavior patterns. It appears that the role of effective instructional variables is noticeably absent in much of the published research on students having serious behavior problems.

Colvin, Greenberg, and Sherman (1993) describe the overall *academic profile* of students with problem behavior as having the following key features:

- High rates of off-task behavior
- Poor academic and work-related skills
- Splinter skills in basic academic areas
- Low achievement

These skill deficits can actively interfere with learning and make the delivery of instruction difficult. Thus, managing student behavior often becomes a primary teacher focus at the expense of instruction. One possible remedy for this situation might be to use curricula that directly address the skill deficits exhibited by students with problem behavior. An appropriate curriculum should have the following features:

- Buffer the impact and attenuate the influence of behavioral problems exhibited by students during instruction.
- Enable teachers to instruct antisocial students so that academic achievement occurs at a level commensurate with their ability.
- Strengthen weak academic skills.
- Enable students functioning below grade level to catch up.

Direct instruction has a number of features that are particularly suitable for meeting these challenging needs. Engelmann and Carnine (1982) have presented the critical design components of the direct-instruction model in considerable detail. Some of the features that have particular relevance for instructing students with serious behavior problems are listed here:

- Concepts are presented systematically to control for misinterpretations.
- Skill components are carefully sequenced to ensure that students learn the basic building blocks.
- Procedures are specified in detail to assist teachers in presenting the content.
- Correction procedures are carefully specified.
- Sufficient practice is prescribed.
- Cumulative review and practice are built into the curricula.

In summary, quality instruction is an important tool for maintaining students in the calm phase. However, academic interventions and curricula specifically designed for antisocial students have not been widely addressed to date. It appears that highly structured curricula have considerable potential for improving the academic and behavioral skills of students with problem behavior. Regardless of the curricular approach, it is important to implement the best available practices with antisocial students which we know guide effective teaching and instruction. The support systems inherent in these practices are essential if such students are to progress academically.

Providing Attention. Unfortunately, students who display antisocial behavior patterns are often left alone and ignored when they are calm and on-task. This critical mistake has serious implications for the school adjustment of antisocial students. Teachers may believe that (1) they themselves need a break in such instances because these students take an inordinate amount of teacher time and attention when their behavior is escalating or (2) it is best to leave antisocial students alone when they are calm because teacher attention may prompt their disruptive behavior to occur. This assumption is exactly backward in terms of sound behavior-management theory and practice (Wolery, Bailey, & Sugai, 1988). Essentially, if students receive more attention when they are acting out and out of control than when they are calm, they are *much* more likely to continue the problematic behavior as opportunities allow. Teachers should develop structures to ensure that all students, and especially antisocial students, receive adequate attention during this calm phase. Two basic strategies for *providing attention* are contingent and noncontingent.

Maintaining positive student behavior. *Elizabeth Crews*

Contingent attention refers to attention that is delivered in response to appropriate behavior. For example, if students finish their work on time, they may be allowed a break; or if they stay on-task during a period, they may earn some sort of brief privilege or free-time activity. Contracts may be designed to provide additional structure in order to teach students that positive consequences follow the occurrence of appropriate behavior (Sugai & Tindal, 1993). This arrangement will run counter to most of the prior experience of antisocial students and will need to be consistently applied in order to have the desired effect.

Noncontingent attention refers to strategies designed to provide teacher contacts with students who do not get adequate attention. These strategies provide generalized, noncontingent attention of a positive nature to antisocial students *before* they have had an opportunity to misbehave. Attention of this type serves as a pre-correction geared toward making it unnecessary for antisocial students to act out in order to meet their attention needs. It also serves as a means of communicating positive regard and social interest in antisocial students—a rare event in their lives. For example, the teacher may initiate frequent incidental contact with the antisocial students or give them a regular job of setting up class activities or distributing materials. The regularity of the task ensures that the teacher will have a fixed schedule for making social contact with the students. Teachers should create a list of jobs or activities so that such students can be given specific responsibilities, and opportunities may be provided for the teacher to interact positively with them.

Teaching Social Behavior. In Chapter 10, we present systematic procedures for teaching appropriate social behavior and specific social skills that derive from instructional principles developed for teaching academic skills. Although these procedures are already familiar to many teachers, a problem sometimes occurs in convincing teachers that social behavior needs to be taught in the same way as academic content.

Unfortunately, antisocial children are often inadvertently taught a maladaptive behavior pattern (by parents and others) that is highly aversive and often destructive to themselves, their peers, and teachers. Antisocial students have to be directly instructed and supported in their attempts to replace their maladaptive behavior pattern with an adaptive pattern. As a rule, they cannot do this without assistance from the teacher as well as others (psychologists, parents, peers, consultants). Teachers are well equipped and ideally positioned to assist antisocial students in acquiring and maintaining an appropriate pattern of behavior.

Phase Two: Triggers

Triggers cause or initiate conflicts between teachers and students. The strategies for managing student behavior in this phase use problem-solving and conflict-resolution procedures. We describe three types of strategies: (1) formal problem solving, (2) precorrection, and (3) individual problem solving.

Formal Strategies for Problem Solving

The three most commonly used formal strategies for assisting students to manage triggers are: (1) curricular interventions, (2) individual assistance plans developed from school and district resources, and (3) services purchased from specialists.

Curricular Interventions. Many published and unpublished curricula have been developed for social skills, anger management, problem solving, and responsible decision making (Alberg, Petry, & Eller, 1994; Goldstein, Sprafkin, Gershaw, & Klein, 1980; McGinnis & Goldstein, 1984; Walker, McConnell, Holmes, Todis, Walker, & Golden, 1983; Walker, Todis, Holmes, & Horton, 1988). Antisocial students have serious skill deficits in these areas (Patterson, Reid, & Dishion, 1992). Curricula and effective instructional procedures exist to *directly* teach these skills. Teachers should develop their own library of curricula and adapt their teaching to meet the diverse needs of antisocial students. In a review of studies that examined the effectiveness of social skills programs, Zaragoza, Vaughn, and McIntosh (1991) indicate that a number of programs have been successful with children and youth who have behavior problems. Chapter 10 focuses on social-skills training resources and teaching guidelines for use with antisocial students.

Gleason, Colvin, and Archer (1991) report that students who exhibit problem behavior in the classroom often have serious deficits in study skills as well. Colvin (1988) introduced study skills curricula developed by Archer and Gleason (1989) to students with severe behavior disorders and reported significant gains in their academic performance and appropriate classroom behavior.

Individual Assistance from Schools and District Resources. Schools and school districts typically have specialists, such as behavioral consultants, counselors, social workers, and school psychologists, who work in support roles to teachers. It is often particularly helpful for students with antisocial behavior patterns to work with such specialized staff members to help them unravel escalation triggers and develop strategies to solve them. In addition, these meetings provide students with an opportunity to have some undivided adult attention, which can have beneficial effects.

Services Purchased from Community Specialists. Students with more severe antisocial behavior may need professional expertise beyond that available from school and district resources. These students may exhibit extreme emotional and behavioral problems. In such cases, school districts often contract with specialists from community agencies, such as mental health services, psychiatric hospitals, crisis intervention centers, universities, and private consulting firms. If additional services are obtained from outside the school system, it is important to coordinate them carefully with in-district services (Jones, 1992).

Pre-Correction Plan

The foundation of a *pre-correction* plan is to identify the context in which the predictable problem behavior occurs. In other words, school staff need to identify the specific triggers that set the stage for the occurrence of the problem behavior. The rest of the plan is designed to assist the student in exhibiting expected or adaptive replacement behaviors in these contexts.

Individual Problem-Solving Plan

This strategy is basically a derivation of a pre-correction plan that has a particular focus on implementation procedures applied to the antisocial student and others with moderate to severe behavior problems. The overall steps are: (1) clearly identify the source of the problem, (2) identify possible solutions or options, (3) assist students in evaluating options and selecting an option, (4) discuss results and implications of the choice, (5) develop an implementation plan (that is, specify tasks and who is responsible for each task), and (6) develop criteria for success and specify review dates.

Clearly Identify the Source of the Problem. The purpose of this step is to assist the student in identifying the triggers or sources of the problem. Questions such as "What got you mad in the first place?" "What went wrong for you?" and "What started all of this?" can be very helpful.

Identify Possible Solutions or Options. Once the triggers are identified, the next step is to list possible options. Sample interview questions would include "What can we do about this?" "Instead of doing that, what else could we do?" and "What changes can we make to avoid this next time?" It is important to stress that you are not looking for definite answers at this step; you are just making a list (brainstorming). The two of you will see which option might work best.

Assist Students in Evaluating Options and Selecting an Option. Here the teacher assists the student in examining the pros and cons of each option. Many antisocial students are reluctant to accept responsibility for their own behavior in the discussion of such options. Instead, they are quick to frame options that involve blaming others (parents, teachers, and peers). It is best to hear them out and then gently persist with the options that the student (with your help) can most directly control.

Discuss Results and Implications of the Choice. Even if students verbally agree to a specific plan, they will need assistance to examine implications of the plan. Usually, a plan involves some cost to the student. For example, the source of the problem may be that Alex was behind in assignments, so he agreed to catch up on the work before school. However, the teacher might have to point out that this will mean he will have to get up earlier in order to arrive at school sooner and will not be able to associate with friends before or possibly after school. Teacher support may be needed in accepting such a harsh reality.

Develop an Implementation Plan. In many cases, students with antisocial behavior have limited skills for implementing developed plans. The teacher should spell out key details of the plan, such as specifying tasks and who is responsible for each task. Teachers should identify some tasks for which they will provide assistance, such as visiting with other teachers, talking with the principal, or talking with the parents. In this way, students are visibly supported—it really is a team plan.

Develop Criteria for Success and Specify Review Date. Students need some kind of monitoring plan that includes a regular contact time with the teacher. In setting criteria for success, the teacher should temper the students' goals, as they usually aim too high. A phase-out plan should also be established so that the student can see an end to the program.

Phase Three: Agitation

When students deal ineffectively with triggers or the conflicts associated with them, it is only a matter of time before they begin to exhibit agitated behavior. The primary goal of managing behavior in this phase is to utilize strategies that calm the student down. In general, these strategies are essentially accommodations in which the student's agitation is recognized and dealt with.

Because these strategies are supportive in nature and exceptions to established routines, they must be implemented *before* the onset of serious behavioral episodes; otherwise, the chain of resulting inappropriate behavior may be reinforced. For example, if Patty is already throwing a chair around and cursing the teacher, it is too late to use supportive techniques. However, if she is grimacing, tapping a pencil, or having difficulty getting started, supportive techniques to manage agitation could be applied. The issue is *timing*—such techniques should be implemented at the earliest indications of agitation. These techniques are as follows.

Teacher Recognition. Perhaps the most powerful and supportive strategy available in this stage is for teachers to communicate that they understand the student is having problems. Simple comments such as "Are you doing OK?" "Do you think you can get through the period?" and "You are looking a bit upset today" can help students feel supported and may reduce agitation.

Space. Provide the student with an opportunity to have some isolation from the rest of the class (such as a quiet area, a separate desk, or one near the teacher's desk). Expectations need to be established with the class so that students using the quiet area are left alone by others.

Time. Some students benefit from structured options—for example, to provide alternatives with deadlines, task requirements, and schedules.

Preferred Activities. Allowing students to engage in a preferred activity for a short time may help them focus. It is important to establish clear expectations for how long the students may engage in these activities and to enter the normal routines promptly when asked.

Teacher Proximity. Teacher proximity can help many students relax, especially if they know the teacher is attempting to assist them in addressing their problems. The teacher may stand near the students from time to time and make incidental contact as appropriate. Teachers often underestimate the importance and effectiveness of this strategy; it can be a powerful technique. Unfortunately, many students who act out in the classroom do not have good adult role models. The teacher often becomes their first appropriate role model. Some students, however, prefer isolation or distance from the teacher when they become agitated.

Independent Activities. When students engage in independent activities, they are more likely to become focused on the task and less likely to engage in negative interactions. These tasks should be constructive in nature, and the students should have sufficient skill mastery to engage in the assigned activities without assistance.

Movement Activities. Many students show an increase in their behavioral levels when they are agitated. Activities that require movement are more likely to help them focus than tasks requiring them to sit still at their desks. Examples of movement-oriented activities include errands to the office or other classrooms, helping to distribute materials, and cleaning the chalkboard.

Involve the Student in the Plan if Possible. Because self-management is the ultimate, long-term goal of any intervention program for problem behavior, it is important to actively involve students, when appropriate, in a plan to control agitation. Students often have strategies to help themselves reduce agitation and can contribute to the plan or program. There is a greater likelihood of problem ownership and successful implementation if students can participate in development of the plan.

Relaxation Activities. Teachers have reported that various kinds of relaxation activities are helpful to reduce agitation. These activities include the use of audiotapes, breathing exercises, and relaxation exercises.

Two Possible Problems and Remedies

Because the strategies to reduce agitation are essentially accommodations in an attempt to calm the student, two possible problems may arise: the question of fairness to others and the likelihood of the procedures being used for avoidance purposes.

The Question of Fairness. Peers may question why antisocial students should be getting breaks or privileges. The other students resent having to work hard without access to the same privileges. One possible remedy is to introduce these procedures as exceptions to the general expectations presented to the class. The usual class expectations are explained, and then these procedures are described as exceptions to be used in special circumstances. Exceptions are decided by the teacher on the basis of the individual needs of each student.

Avoidance. Individual students may use these procedures to avoid work; for example, "I don't want to do math today, I'm too mad!" To remedy this problem, procedures can be established that allow the student to make up the time later when agitation levels have subsided.

Phase Four: Acceleration

Applications

The available strategies for managing acceleration behavior can be applied (1) at the onset of peak behavior or (2) during sustained acceleration behavior.

Onset of Peak Behavior. In this application, students are exhibiting signs that out-of-control or peak behavior is highly likely. The strategies to be used at this time are designed to prevent further escalation and to de-escalate the behavior.

Sustained Acceleration Behavior. In this situation, students have been exhibiting the behaviors characteristic of the acceleration phase for quite some time (usually half an hour or more). Although they are unlikely to escalate to the next phase, there is no indication that the students are going to settle down or be cooperative. These strategies are designed to arrest and de-escalate the behavior.

Strategies

The basic strategies are the same for both applications: (1) avoid escalating prompts; (2) maintain calmness, respect, and detachment; (3) use crisis-prevention strategies;

(4) complete exit paperwork; (5) restore the environment as appropriate; (6) return to the original activity or the next activity; and (7) debrief.

Avoid Escalating Prompts. School staff may inadvertently exhibit behaviors that are likely to escalate students. These *escalating prompts* include agitated behavior (for example, shouting), cornering the student, power struggles (for example, "getting in the student's face" and stating, "In this school you will . . ."), touching or grabbing the student, nagging, making statements that may discredit the student in front of peers, and arguing.

Maintain Calmness, Respect, and Detachment. When students are approached in order to address the problem behavior in this phase, there is a high probability that the behavior will escalate. The teacher's behavior at this point needs to be extremely controlled and nonjudgmental. Some guidelines for approaching the student in this situation are as follows:

- *Move slowly and deliberately toward the problem situation.* Walk slowly, and avoid rushing or displaying behavior that indicates panic or anxiety.
- *Speak privately.* Take students aside, and talk quietly. Avoid public statements and loud talk.
- *Speak calmly.* Use a flat, controlled voice. Be as matter-of-fact as possible. Do not threaten.
- *Minimize body language.* Be as still as possible. Avoid pointing, staring at, or crowding the students.
- *Keep a reasonable distance.* Do not get too close and *do not* get "in the student's face."
- *Speak respectfully.* Avoid harsh, angry tones. Use the students' names, and speak in a soft, detached, and respectful manner.
- *Establish eye-level position.* If students are sitting, then sit beside them or squat. If students are standing, then stand. Some students react negatively to anyone towering over them in such situations.
- *Be brief.* Use language that is simple and brief. Long-winded statements or nagging will make some students react negatively.
- *Stay with the agenda.* Stay focused on the problem at hand. Do not get sidetracked. Deal with lesser problems later.
- *Withdraw if problem behavior escalates.* Terminate the discussion if the problem behavior escalates, withdraw from the students, and follow school emergency procedures.
- *Avoid power struggles.* Stay with the problem at hand. Do not be drawn into "I won't, you will" types of engagements.
- *Acknowledge cooperation.* If students cooperate, compliment them and be sure to mention their cooperation in a later report or follow-up to the situation.

The bottom line: Use common sense and approach the problem in a calm, detached, unhurried, respectful, and step-by-step manner.

Use Crisis-Prevention Strategies. *Crisis-prevention strategies* are designed to interrupt the chain of escalating behavior and provide some direction or expectations to students. The three steps in this strategy are (1) establish a negative consequence beforehand, (2) deliver the information to the students, and (3) follow through.

1. *Establishing a negative consequence beforehand.* Negative consequences include office referral, detention, suspension, police call, and parent call. A consequence should be approved by the proper authorities and explained to students before it is implemented. Explaining the consequence in advance helps communicate behavioral limits to students.
2. *Delivering the information.* Information is delivered in the following three steps:
   a. Present the expected behavior and the negative consequence as a choice or decision for the student to make.
   b. Withdraw from the student, attend to other students, or engage in some other task.
   c. Allow some time for the student to decide.

The following are examples of these strategies:

"Michael, you are asked to return to your desk or I will send for the principal." (decision) "You have a few seconds to decide." (time) The teacher then moves to other students. (withdrawal)

"Girls, you are expected to go to class now or we will be looking at detention." (decision) "You have a few seconds to decide." (time) The teacher steps back and looks toward or engages other students. (withdrawal)

Students are likely to exhibit reactive behavior at this point, such as mumbling, facial expressions showing discontent, or sulking. Ignore these behavioral expressions (or address them later if you think they warrant it).

If students escalate (for example, throw a chair or start screaming and yelling), then assume they are entering the next phase (peak), and implement the corresponding procedures (see Phase Five).

3. *Following through.* The next steps taken by the teacher depend on whether students exhibit the expected appropriate behavior or maintain the problem behavior.
   a. If students choose the expected behavior, acknowledge the choice briefly, and continue with the lesson or activity. Conduct a debriefing session later.
   b. If students do not choose the expected behavior (that is, they maintain the problem behavior), deliver the negative consequence. The teacher may clarify the students' choice by saying, "You are telling me to call the principal." Again, conduct a debriefing session later.
   c. If students choose the expected behavior after the allotted time has elapsed, follow through with the consequence.

Complete Exit Paperwork. Paperwork is necessary to document the behavior and to provide information for the debriefing session. Such information is usually collected in

Name: ______________________

Date: ______________________

1. What was your behavior?

____

____

2. What was your concern or need?

____

____

3. What could you do next time that would be acceptable?

____

____

4. What are you expected to do next?

____

5. Can you do it appropriately? ___ Yes ___ No

__________________ Student signature

__________________ Teacher

FORM 4.2 Behavior Form

an incident report or office referral describing the behavior and its relevant circumstances. It is also helpful to have the student complete some kind of *behavior form* that can be used in the debriefing session and for problem-solving purposes. Form 4.2 is a sample behavior form.

Restore the Environment as Appropriate. If students engage in behaviors such as throwing books and pushing desks over, they should be required to restore these objects to their original position or clean up what they have done. If students complete the behavior form, they are more likely to cooperate with this restoration step.

Return to the Original Activity or the Next Class Activity. Once students have completed the form and restored the environment as necessary, the next step is to return to the normal schedule (unless it is more appropriate to maintain the student in isolation).

Debrief. The purpose of the *debriefing* session is to problem solve and prepare students so they will be better equipped to exhibit appropriate behavior the next time a problematic situation arises. Information from the behavior form should help the teacher work through the incident by identifying the context of the problem, the problem behavior, alternative behaviors, and a commitment from students to try an alternative behavior the next time the situation arises.

The debriefing session should be held once the student is back in the original setting. The problem behavior began there, so the remedies should be addressed there, especially if the teacher conducts the debriefing session. If another staff member conducts the debriefing session, the session must be conducted after students have returned to class. It is better to debrief on the day of the incident and at least 20 minutes after the student has returned to class.

Have set questions to discuss with the students, such as:

- What was your behavior?
- What was your concern or need?
- What else could you have done that would have been acceptable and that would have met your need?
- What will you do next time if this situation arises?

Do not be too concerned if you inadvertently assist the student to escalate during this phase—you will get another chance to do it right in the near future!

Phase Five: Peak

When teachers refer to antisocial or acting-out behavior, they typically mean behaviors that occur in the peak phase. These behaviors are serious, disruptive, and can threaten the safety of others. If students get out of control, the classroom is disrupted and the safety of others can be affected. In such cases, the teacher usually tries to remove the students from the classroom. However, students who are out of control can pose a serious threat to the safety of others if attempts are made to remove them (especially if force is used). The basic procedures to consider using are: (1) preparation and precautions, (2) *short-term interventions*, and (3) *long-term interventions* (designed to address safety and disruption as well as follow-up, problem-solving needs). These procedures need to be carefully laid out and rehearsed with staff, students, and parents.

Preparation and Precautions. The procedures used to address peak or out-of-control behavior are typically intrusive (especially if force has to be used). It is critical that a school district or school develop clear procedures for managing student behavior at this point. In most cases, districts and states have guidelines that need to be followed. The following guidelines are recommended:

- Strict criteria should be established for when these procedures are to be used.
- All staff who are likely to use the procedures should be trained to protect all parties. Staff should receive regular review and practice opportunities.
- Two staff members should be involved at the same time.
- Staff need to be designated to monitor the student carefully and to introduce an independent activity as early as possible.
- Careful records need to be kept.
- Parent permission should be obtained. The procedures should be part of school policy and should be in the individual educational plan (IEP) for special-education students who exhibit out-of-control behavior.

Short-Term Interventions. The first step should be to address safety (safety for other students, the involved student, and staff). The *safety procedures* need to be approved, and staff should be familiar with the details of their implementation. The most commonly used safety strategies follow:

- Isolation and removal of other students
- Parent contact
- Police call
- Short-term suspension
- Restraint

Long-Term Interventions. Repeated instances of peak or out-of-control behavior should serve as a red flag that things need to be done differently; that is, that the current plan is failing. Some additional strategies may include the following:

- Plan interventions to address target problem behaviors occurring earlier in the chain.
- Analyze the environment to assess whether escalating prompts are present.
- Assess schoolwork.
- Refer for counseling.
- Refer for evaluation.
- Refer for additional evaluation and services.
- Examine school policy and procedures (if several students are seriously acting out).

Remember: We cannot assume that schools are safe places anymore. School administrators must have clear policies and procedures for managing out-of-control behavior and ensure that all staff (including substitute teachers) receive regular, ongoing training in these procedures.

Phase Six: De-Escalation

The students' behavior will eventually subside either as a result of the strategies used to manage peak behavior or simply through exhaustion. The following steps are designed to manage the students' behavior after a serious incident or peak behavior: (1) isolate the students; (2) allow some time to cool down; (3) engage in independent work for a set amount of time that produces a final product; (4) complete exit paperwork; (5) restore the environment; and (6) resume a regular schedule.

Isolate the Students. The students should be placed in a setting that allows for isolation and supervision. Typically, a room or area near the school office or a specially designated area attached to the classroom will suffice.

Allow Time to Cool Down. Students need some quiet, uninterrupted time for several reasons: (1) to calm down, (2) to avoid the possibility of further escalation, (3) to provide them with a chance to collect themselves, and (4) to save face.

Engage in Independent Work That Produces a Product for a Set Time. The purpose of this task is to establish a basis for cooperation and provide a focus for the students. The task should be relatively easy and mechanical in nature. Assistance should not be provided if at all possible; otherwise, the teacher-student interactions may prompt more problem behavior. A set time, such as 20 minutes, should be established and a product required (such as a page of definitions or a page of math problems completed).

Complete Exit Paperwork. The students complete any necessary paperwork, such as the behavior form described earlier. This task is also useful in assessing the students' level of potential cooperation. For example, if the students complete the form (as well as the product mentioned in the previous step), the teacher has some basis for concluding that they will cooperate with the next step. However, if the students refuse to complete the form or complete it in a shoddy manner, the teacher can likely conclude that they will not cooperate when they return to class. In this event, the students should remain in isolation for a longer period. If students do not have the skills to complete the form, the teacher can use the questions as prompts to query the student for oral answers.

Restore Environment as Appropriate. If the students disrupted the environment, part of the follow-up should be to restore the setting to its original state (for example, picking up chairs, rearranging books, and cleaning up). Again, if the students cooperated with the earlier steps, there is a strong likelihood of cooperation with this step.

Resume Regular Schedule. At this point, the students have been given the opportunity to settle down and have cooperated with three tasks (completing the product, filling out the behavior form and restoring the environment). As a result, they are likely to cooperate when they return to class. Teachers should keep in mind, though, that they may have difficulty with activities that require interaction with other students, such as discussions, and cooperative learning activities. A solitary, independent task is the easiest activity for students at this point.

Phase Seven: Recovery

In this final phase of the acting-out cycle, the students are back in the normal schedule. The procedures to be used in this phase are: (1) assist the student to focus on the activities at hand; (2) reconstruct the acting-out cycle; and (3) develop problem-solving options.

Provide Strong Focus on Normal Routines. The teacher's immediate goal is to assist the students to reenter ongoing classroom activities and maintain on-task behavior. Prompts and brief verbal reinforcements (such as, praise) should be provided. If the students want to talk about the incident, such as what may have happened or who was at fault, the teacher should simply say, "We will talk about that later. Let's get on with our math now."

Do Not Negotiate About the Consequences for the Serious Behavior. Some antisocial students may have learned that if they cooperate in class, they can negotiate about the consequences for their serious acting-out behavior. Teachers should not reconsider the consequences. The consequences are designed to teach limits, that is, to communicate to the students that their behavior is unacceptable. If the consequences are subsequently renegotiated, then students may get a mixed message that it is acceptable to exhibit peak behavior provided they cooperate after the incident has occurred. Teachers should reinforce cooperation after an incident by using other reinforcers, not by modifying the consequences for the previous serious behavior.

Debrief. Unfortunately, this step is frequently omitted by teachers, perhaps because they are pleased the students are back on track, and they do not want to risk escalating them. However, this step is crucial and should not be omitted because the same circumstances or triggers that prompted the chain of escalating behavior are likely to reappear. Some form of debriefing must be conducted with the students to review the chain of behavior, identify the triggers, and establish some alternative responses (for example, to problem solve with the student). The debriefing session should be conducted sometime after the students have been on-task for at least half an hour.

Strongly Acknowledge Problem-Solving Behaviors. When students make chronic errors in academic subjects, teachers praise them for correct responses. The same should apply to problem behavior. When students appropriately handle a certain situation that previously triggered problem behavior, the teacher should provide strong positive reinforcement.

Communicate Expectation That the Students Can Succeed with Help. Students who exhibit antisocial behavior on a regular basis usually have little confidence that they can be successful in their attempts to change the behavior. Many of them have already been exposed to several behavior plans that did not change their behavior. In this step, the teacher tries to: (1) encourage the student to keep trying and (2) identify how the teacher can help the student succeed; that is, how they can work together on the plan.

Establish a Plan with Specific Steps. The debriefing session should have resulted in an agreement that the students will undertake certain problem-solving activities (essentially to identify the triggers and select an alternative response for each). The teacher should ensure that the plan is sufficiently concrete and that a monitoring and review schedule is established.

SUMMARY FORM AND CASE STUDY

Strategies have been presented for managing behavior during each of the seven phases of the acting-out cycle. We return now to the summary form presented in Chapter 3 (Form 3.2) in which a particular student's behavior and corresponding strategies can be listed for each phase (see Form 4.3). The form can be used as a behavior plan for a student who exhibits serious antisocial behavior. It can be used in three ways: (1) at a staff meeting where teachers develop a plan of action for a particular student, (2) in a parent-training session where the parent, with a teacher or consultant, develops a plan for implementation in the student's home, and (3) as a self-management plan for students who are capable of identifying their behaviors at each phase and corresponding strategies for changing them.

The following case study is presented to illustrate these procedures.

Background. Dominic is a 14-year-old seventh grader who has had a long history of problem behavior in public schools. His behavior file has numerous incidents of antisocial behavior, including threatening and abusing staff, throwing materials around the room, and hitting other students during recess. Teachers say he has a very short fuse and is easily upset. He is below average in all subjects and is of average intelligence. He comes from a single-parent home and presently lives with his mother. For some periods of his life, he was in the care of his grandmother and in foster care. After attending several different schools, he was referred to a self-contained school for behavior-disordered students. His mother has steadfastly refused placement outside his local school. She maintains he is a good child but has his bad moments, "Just like his father." He took medication (Ritalin) when he lived with his grandmother, but his mother maintains he does not need medication now. He has been placed in a resource room for reading and math and in a regular classroom for other subjects.

A staff meeting was conducted; the summary form was completed and became Dominic's behavior plan (see Form 4.4; the assessment portion of this form was presented as Form 3.1).

CONCLUSION

Acting-out behavior occurring during teacher-student interactions can be described by a seven-phase conceptual model. Specific behaviors can be identified for each phase of the behavioral chain. Thus, students' place in the acting-out behavior cycle can be determined by their observed behavior. Strategies and procedures can then be implemented for managing student behavior at each phase in the cycle. The basic intent of the strategies is to arrest the behavior at that point in the chain, thereby preventing escalation and, at the same time, setting the stage for students to engage in appropriate alternative behaviors. The overall emphasis is on identifying the early behaviors in the chain, redirecting the antisocial students toward appropriate behavior, and subsequently preempting the acting-out cycle of serious behavior.

Chapter 5 contains guidelines and procedures for developing a schoolwide discipline plan. A well-designed and carefully implemented discipline plan allows teachers and other school staff to proactively deal with situations that have the potential to trigger

ACTING-OUT BEHAVIOR

Student Name:
Date:
Teacher(s):
Class:

ASSESSMENT	STRATEGIES
Calm	**Calm**
Triggers	**Triggers**
Agitation	**Agitation**
Acceleration	**Acceleration**
Peak	**Peak**
De-Escalation	**De-Escalation**
Recovery	**Recovery**

FORM 4.3 Assessment and Intervention Plan for Acting-Out Behavior

ACTING-OUT BEHAVIOR

Student Name: *Dominic Smith*
Date: *3/4/93*
Teacher(s): *Walt Jones, Andrea DeForest, Aletia McHenry, Joe Carpenter*
Class: *7th Grade*

ASSESSMENT	STRATEGIES
Calm	**Calm**
Likes to help	*Contract for successful work*
Displays successful work	*Include computer time in contract*
Enjoys games	*Assist with distributing materials*
Likes the computer	
Triggers	**Triggers**
Repeating tasks	*Pre-correction plan for corrections*
Teasing remarks and putdowns from other students	*Coaching on ignoring and not responding to teasing*
Correcting behavior	
Consequences for problem behavior	
Agitation	**Agitation**
Walks around the room	*Option of quiet area*
Scowls at other students	*Use jobs or errands*
Pouts and mumbles to himself	
Does not concentrate on his work	
Acceleration	**Acceleration**
Argues and will not quit	*Teacher to avoid discussion, etc., when he argues*
Defiance, "Make me"	*Not to respond to name calling, shouting, and disruptive behavior immediately, delay response*
Name calls and threatens students	
Raises his voice and shouts	

FORM 4.4 Case Study: Antisocial Behavior

ASSESSMENT	STRATEGIES
Acceleration *(Continued)*	**Acceleration *(Continued)***
	Use three-step crisis prevention procedure if he persists with disruptive behavior for 20 minutes
Peak	**Peak**
Throws objects around the room *Hits other students* *Yells and screams*	*Use code 1 (emergency) to obtain help from office* *Prompt other students to stay on-task and to stay out of it (if assistant present have assistant take other students to the library or to the designated area)*
De-Escalation	**De-Escalation**
Goes very quiet, puts his head down *Complains that no one likes him and that it is not fair* *Talks to himself a lot* *Likes to fiddle with things*	*Leave alone in isolated area with supervision* *Present a math sheet after 10 minutes of cool-down* *Present behavior form* *Exit to classroom and pick up thrown objects* *Begin classroom activity with independent task if possible*
Recovery	**Recovery**
Somewhat subdued *Likes to work alone*	*Provide independent work for a short time* *Debrief* *Provide strong encouragement*

FORM 4.4 *(Continued)*

escalated forms of behavior. Thus, teachers are able to avoid these unfortunate episodes in many instances.

STUDY QUESTIONS

1. Why is it important to develop effective strategies for intervening early in the chain of acting-out behavior?
2. Why do students with severe antisocial behavior need classroom and school structure?
3. What is the typical academic profile for a student with serious antisocial behavior?
4. What features of an academic curriculum would be beneficial for students with academic deficits?
5. How can attention be used to strengthen target behaviors and weaken problem behaviors?
6. What is meant by noncontingent attention and how can this strategy be used to assist students with frequent problem behavior?
7. What are the critical steps in a problem-solving plan?
8. What is the basic approach in managing student agitation?
9. What are two common problems encountered in using agitation management strategies and what are possible solutions?
10. What are the basic steps in a nonconfrontational crisis-prevention procedure?
11. Why is it important to debrief with a student following a serious incident and what are the main steps in the debriefing process?
12. What are the major steps following a serious behavioral incident?
13. What are the most important steps when a student is back in the regular schedule following a serious incident?

KEY TERMS

academic profile
behavior form
classroom structure
crisis-prevention strategies
debriefing
escalating prompts
interrupting the behavior chain
long-term interventions
pre-correction
providing attention
quality instruction
safety procedures
short-term interventions

5 Establishing a Schoolwide Discipline Plan

Research Findings and Best Practices for Schoolwide Discipline

Discipline Is an Instrument
Proactive Approaches
Visible, Supportive Leadership from the Principal
Collegial Commitment
Staff Development and Effective Teacher-Training Practices
Setting High Expectations
Clear Communication Between Administration and Staff
Strong, Positive School Climate
Interdisciplinary Cooperation and Collaboration
Clear, Functional Rules and Expectations
Data Management and Evaluation

Foundational Phases in the Design of an Effective Schoolwide Discipline Plan

Phase 1: Formulate a Basic Direction for Establishing Expected Behavior and Managing Problem Behavior
Phase 2: Specify Schoolwide Expected Behaviors

Phase 3: Develop Procedures for Teaching Schoolwide Behavioral Expectations
Phase 4: Develop Procedures for Correcting Problem Behavior
Phase 5: Develop Procedures for Record Keeping, Evaluation, and Dissemination

Implementation Steps for a Schoolwide Discipline Plan

Step 1: Establish a Commitment from All Staff to Work Together to Improve the Schoolwide Discipline Plan
Step 2: Establish a Building Team and Operating Procedures
Step 3: Develop or Revise a Schoolwide Discipline Manual
Step 4: Design and Implement a Staff Development Plan
Step 5: Develop a Data Management, Feedback, and Review System

Conclusion

Additional Resources on Schoolwide Discipline

A number of disturbing trends face public schools today that relate to school discipline, violence, gangs, and the management of problematic student behavior. The annual Gallup Poll of the *Public Attitude(s) Toward the Public Schools* consistently identifies school discipline as one of *the* most serious, ongoing problems confronting public school systems. Moreover, communities are becoming increasingly concerned about the physical safety of their students and teachers and about vandalism of school buildings. Incidents of street crime (for example, drive-by shootings, theft, assault, rape) are dramatically increasing and are spilling over into schools with devastating consequences. With the escalating numbers of students who are bringing weapons to school on a daily basis, it can no longer be said that schools are safe havens for anyone. One of our most important goals is to try and make schools secure and parent-friendly places.

Classroom teachers are finding that time spent on instructional activities is being eroded by the need to attend to discipline problems, deal with the effects of parental neglect and abuse, address safety issues, and manage the classroom environment. Cotton (1990) notes that approximately half of all available classroom time is taken up with activities other than instruction and that discipline problems consume most of this precious resource. Due to the unfortunate impact of the deteriorating social conditions of our society on our schools, teachers now have two jobs. Job One is instructing students and facilitating their academic and social development. Job Two involves managing the classroom and coping with often intractable discipline problems that have the potential to escalate into violence. Teachers are having to invest more and more time in Job Two, at the expense of Job One.

Problems with school discipline have reached alarming proportions and are seriously disrupting the education of all our students. As a society and profession, our collective imperative is to accept this challenge and develop effective methods for restoring discipline and reestablishing appropriate school behavior so that (1) our schools can again become safe environments and (2) the essential school functions of teaching and learning can be realized effectively.

In this chapter we present details of schoolwide discipline procedures, based on research and successful practices, that are designed to address antisocial and disruptive behavior problems in public schools. Two major topics are addressed: (1) the foundational steps involved in developing a *schoolwide discipline plan* and (2) implementation procedures for putting the plan into effect and making it work. Every school should establish a schoolwide discipline plan. Some schools are now having to develop violence-prevention plans as well. We believe that a sound discipline plan may reduce the need for developing a companion violence-prevention plan in many instances. This task can be a highly cost-effective investment of staff time and school resources.

Although the discipline problems facing public schools are legion, a number of schools have demonstrated considerable progress in making their buildings safer and more predictable environments, with a strong, positive climate to support instruction and learning. In addition, research over the past two decades has identified promising management strategies and classroom structures that are effective in establishing desirable behavior across *all* children and youth. We suggest three major components that should be addressed in the design of any proactive, schoolwide discipline plan: (1) research findings and best practices on effective schoolwide discipline, (2) the foundational steps involved in the design of an effective schoolwide discipline plan, and (3) the implementation procedures necessary to support the plan. These components are described in this chapter. In addition, we present a case study in Chapter 12 that illustrates the design, implementation, and evaluation of a schoolwide discipline plan in a middle school.

RESEARCH FINDINGS AND BEST PRACTICES FOR SCHOOLWIDE DISCIPLINE

Numerous effective practices are available for managing problematic, antisocial behavior in public schools. They are universal interventions and serve preventive purposes. In this section, we describe those practices that have been validated by research and empirical results with the strong recommendation that they should comprise the cornerstone of schoolwide discipline plans. We also discuss the implied values on which these practices are based.

Discipline Is an Instrument

School discipline is an instrument in that its primary purpose is to allow effective instruction and learning to take place (Colvin, Sugai, & Kameenui, 1992; Jones, 1979). If discipline is viewed as an end in itself, then behavioral control and not student development becomes the primary goal of teaching and management efforts. This can occur at the expense of important instructional goals, such as the academic achievement and social development of all students (Knitzer, Steinberg, & Fleisch, 1990). Discipline should *always* be subordinate to the school's overall mission of realizing these important goals.

Proactive Approaches

An important trend in managing student behavior in schools is the shift toward *proactive approaches*—that is, positive and constructive problem-solving approaches that can serve prevention goals, as distinct from punitive or reactive approaches that focus mainly on simply controlling or suppressing student behavior (Duke, 1989; Gettinger, 1988; Kounin, 1970; Sprick, 1985). Educators are finding that students are generally responsive to these more positive approaches and that even difficult students (for example, antisocial ones) are likely to cooperate with them at some level. In addition, many school personnel argue that these proactive procedures are more consistent with the teaching practices required for effective instruction.

Visible, Supportive Leadership from the Principal

In many respects, the school principal is the key agent in making discipline work. Schoolwide discipline plans need to be carefully planned, adopted, and implemented by all school staff. This will not occur unless the principal takes a highly visible and supportive leadership role.

Collegial Commitment

All school staff need to be actively involved and committed in order to develop, implement, and maintain an effective schoolwide discipline plan. Staff also need to implement the plan with a high degree of adherence to best practices in order to establish a consistent, predictable school environment (Guskey, 1986; Smylie 1988).

Staff Development and Effective Teacher-Training Practices

Research by Smylie (1988) provides convincing evidence that traditional, staff-development activities in the form of in-services, workshops, and consultant-based supports do not bring about significant or durable changes in staff behavior. In a recent review of the literature, Gersten and Woodward (1990) identified three critical factors regarding teacher-training procedures: (1) collegiality, in terms of staff working together; (2) a comprehensive framework or shared philosophy, and (3) the concreteness of the proposed plan. Each of these guidelines should be considered in developing a school discipline plan.

Setting High Expectations

There are many instances in which school staff become acclimated to problematic student behavior and attribute behavior problems to outside factors, over which they have little control. Such factors include the home environment, socioeconomic factors, incompetent parenting practices, and school budgets. In these situations, school discipline can become a *serious* problem. In contrast, when staff expectations for social behavior and learning are high, teachers are more likely to assume greater responsibility for effecting behavior change. Students will usually perform substantially better as a result. In this situation, discipline problems are generally fewer in number and less severe (Duke, 1989; Wong, Kauffman, & Lloyd, 1991).

Clear Communication Between Administration and Staff

School discipline often breaks down when there is no clear understanding among staff in terms of which student behaviors should be referred to the front office and which behaviors teaching staffs should address in the classroom. The school administration justifiably becomes frustrated if too many minor problems are referred to the front office. On the other hand, teaching staff become frustrated when they believe there is insufficient backup or support from the school administration. If not adequately addressed, this perception can escalate into a severe morale issue. Effective school discipline plans must have clear lines of communication between administration and staff in terms of which student behaviors warrant management by staff in the immediate context and which behaviors warrant office referrals (Cotton, 1990; Sprick, 1994).

Strong, Positive School Climate

School must not only be a safe and well-managed environment but should also be a warm, supportive, and friendly place for students and staff. Schools with effective discipline plans have highly visible and creative structures to encourage appropriate social behavior, personal accomplishments, academic achievement, and general quality performance (Hyman & Lally, 1982; Lasley & Wayson, 1982).

Interdisciplinary Cooperation and Collaboration

Effective schools, as a rule, establish organizational structures in which all concerned parties (internal and external) have the opportunity to become involved with the planning, development, implementation, and revision of schoolwide discipline plans. These parties include staff, students, parents, and community agency personnel as appropriate.

Perhaps one of the most significant current trends for effective management practices in public schools is the increase in cooperation and collaboration between school staff and the staffs of various social service agencies (for example, mental health services, disability advocacy organizations, courts, parent support agencies, juvenile or youth service systems, and children's protective services). This trend is evident and clearly more necessary in dealing with the needs and challenges of chronically troubled students who are increasingly populating our schools (that is, those manifesting antisocial behavior patterns and related disorders) (Epstein, Foley, & Cullinan, 1992).

Clear, Functional Rules and Expectations

As noted, rules and expectations for student behavior in a school discipline plan need to be carefully developed with input from all concerned parties. A comprehensive dissemination plan should be in place to communicate these rules and expectations to everyone involved. Structures also should be in place to ensure that the rules are functional, fair, and subject to revision and evaluation as circumstances warrant. There should be a clearly established relationship between students' adhering to these rules and actual accomplishment of the school's goals.

Data Management and Evaluation

Lack of accountability for desired outcomes is one of the major criticisms facing public schools today. Schoolwide discipline plans need to include a systematic data-management system to provide such accountability, to conduct evaluation of the plan, and to identify at-risk students in order to facilitate more timely, proactive interventions. Evaluation and monitoring components of discipline plans should address accountability; goal setting; and teacher, student, and parent satisfaction. Schoolwide discipline should have the same features of accountability as any other school-based system that serves students or staff.

Box 5.1 The Foundational Phases for Designing a Schoolwide Discipline Plan

Phase 1: Formulate a basic direction for establishing expected behavior and managing problem behavior.

Phase 2: Specify schoolwide expected behaviors.

Phase 3: Develop procedures for teaching schoolwide behavioral expectations.

Phase 4: Develop procedures for correcting problem behavior.

Phase 5: Develop procedures for record keeping, evaluation, and dissemination.

FOUNDATIONAL PHASES IN THE DESIGN OF AN EFFECTIVE SCHOOLWIDE DISCIPLINE PLAN

Public schools vary considerably in many domains, such as size, funding levels, age groups served, demographics, socioeconomic factors, and percentage of minority students. The school discipline plan needs to be sensitive to these factors. The following components of a schoolwide discipline plan are *foundational steps* or phases that empirical research has found to be effective. We encourage each school or district to adapt the suggested procedures within these steps to meet their unique needs. Guidelines for appropriate adaptations are presented for each step. Box 5.1 lists the foundational phases of a schoolwide discipline plan in chronological order; detailed descriptions of each phase follow.

Phase 1: Formulate a Basic Direction for Establishing Expected Behavior and Managing Problem Behavior

Schoolwide discipline plans will not be maximally effective if school staff approach behavioral tasks in substantially divergent ways. For example, some staff may want to exclude students who are viewed as not belonging in public schools; in contrast, other staff members may wish to give such students extra assistance in order to keep them in school. Sometimes, certain staff may use rewards to reinforce expected behaviors, while others may avoid or criticize these practices as "bribing the students." Then again, some staff may want to increase punishments for a particular student, while others may be opposed to the use of punishment as a matter of principle. In each of these situations, it would be difficult to develop a consistent schoolwide discipline plan because of unresolved staff differences in approaches and values. These differences need to be resolved beforehand or at least negotiated to some level of agreement.

We recommend two steps or activities for staff to consider in establishing a workable direction for schoolwide behavior management: (1) identify a school mission statement, and (2) specify a purpose statement for the school discipline plan.

School Mission Statement

A school's *mission statement* is designed to capture the broad-based direction and values of the school, staff, and students (Sprick, Sprick, & Garrison, 1992). Staff, students, and parents should have the opportunity to provide input and respond to the school mission statement as it is developed. School discipline is simply one factor, albeit an important one, for assisting the school in accomplishing its overall mission. In other words, the mission statement should give meaning and direction to the schoolwide discipline plan.

The mission statement should be positive, but challenging as well as uplifting; for example:

> We at Lincoln School are committed to providing our students with the behavioral and academic skills required to reason, communicate, and live with dignity in a literate society. This means providing all our students with instruction that will allow them to reach their fullest potential. (Sprick, 1994).

A school motto is sometimes used as an adjunct to the mission statement. The motto is usually a simple statement that can be communicated readily to students and parents. Examples include: "When one succeeds we all succeed," "Cascade is a place to learn," or "Our school is a positive place."

Statement of Purpose

The purpose of a schoolwide discipline plan is to establish and maintain student behavior that allows the accomplishment of school goals. In this sense, discipline provides a structure that enables teachers and students to engage in the learning process necessary to bring about desired academic and social outcomes. For example, many schoolwide discipline plans are designed to establish student behaviors and supportive organizational structures that ensure an environment conducive to teaching and learning. This purpose emphasizes keeping major student disruptions to a minimum and establishing predictable schedules so that effective teaching and learning activities can be conducted in a planned manner.

Discipline also provides a set of procedures that enable teachers and students to work collaboratively and constructively toward solving schoolwide academic and behavior challenges. For example, many schoolwide discipline plans provide specific procedural steps for establishing expected student behaviors and for responding systematically to the full range of maladaptive behaviors displayed by some students.

A sample statement of purpose for a discipline plan follows:

> The **purpose** of the schoolwide discipline plan at Melbourne Elementary School is to:
>
> 1. Establish schoolwide structures and procedures for teachers and students that facilitate teaching and learning
> 2. Encourage student behaviors that enhance the learning environment
> 3. Minimize student behaviors that inhibit teaching and learning interactions

Phase 2: Specify Schoolwide Expected Behaviors

Schoolwide behavioral expectations define desirable behaviors or actions of students that facilitate the teaching and learning process and the efficient operation of a schoolwide discipline plan. In effect, these behavioral targets help the school accomplish its mission. Schoolwide behavioral expectations should be designed for every setting in the school (for example, classrooms, hallways, buses, cafeteria, gymnasium, recess, restrooms, and locker rooms). Some specific school settings have unique features requiring additional behavioral expectations. For example, students are expected to behave in a safe and appropriate manner across all school settings, but noise-level expectations are significantly different in the library and on the playground.

Guidelines

The following guidelines should be followed when identifying and stating schoolwide behavioral expectations:

1. Limit the number of behavioral expectations to four or five.
2. State behavioral expectations in positive terms using simple, understandable language and as few words as possible.
3. Identify specific behaviors to illustrate the range of acceptable variations.
4. Identify clear positive and negative examples to illustrate each behavioral expectation.
5. Define a process and time lines for identifying behavioral expectations:
   a. Identify participants for deciding upon the behavioral expectations (for example, certified and noncertified staff, students, parents, community leaders).
   b. Specify a process (for example, large group, small group, grade level, department).
   c. Specify a plan for training students and staff in the agreed upon expectations and disseminating information about them.

The following list is a good example of general behavioral expectations for Melbourne Elementary School:

1. To provide a safe and supportive environment for learning.
2. To cooperate with others.
3. To manage oneself.
4. To respect the rights and property of others.

Behavioral Expectations for Specific Settings

Specific expectations for school settings with unique requirements for acceptable behavior should be carefully delineated. Settings that require more specific behavioral expectations should be listed. Typically, these settings include hallways, the cafeteria, assemblies, restrooms, gymnasiums, buses, the library, shop, and recess areas. Behavioral expectations for these settings should be identified and stated in the same way as for general schoolwide expectations.

The following list is a good example of specific behavioral expectations for the cafeteria at Melbourne Elementary School:

1. Maintain a clean dining area by busing your table and disposing of your trash appropriately.
2. Maintain a conversational-level voice.
3. Leave the eating area in an orderly manner.
4. Recycle designated materials in appropriate containers.

Students must understand that behavioral expectations may vary depending on the setting. For example, to control conversation volume, students could be required to use an "inside voice" (low volume) in the hallways. However, at recess, students are allowed to use an "outside voice" (high volume). For general guidelines it is best to (1) describe all target settings in observable and unambiguous terms; (2) provide clear descriptions that relate expected behaviors to target settings (for example, "At recess, an outside voice may be used," or "In the cafeteria, you are responsible for properly disposing of your own food"); (3) identify settings where problem behaviors occur more frequently (for example, in the cafeteria or waiting in line for school buses); (4) identify settings where supervision may be a potential problem (for example, isolated corners of the building, in the restrooms, less visible areas of the playground); and (5) identify settings where safety may be a potential problem (for example, using equipment on the playground).

Phase 3: Develop Procedures for Teaching Schoolwide Behavioral Expectations

We recommend addressing three critical steps in developing a continuum for establishing schoolwide behavioral expectations: (1) implement *schoolwide positive structures* to acknowledge students who demonstrate expected behaviors; (2) use a modified behavior-teaching plan; and (3) implement a formal behavior-instruction plan.

Schoolwide Positive Structures to Acknowledge Students Who Demonstrate Expected Behaviors

One of the most common concerns about school discipline plans is that too much emphasis is focused on problematic student behavior. As a result, more attention ends up being given to those students who exhibit problem behavior, while students who demonstrate acceptable behavior tend to be ignored. A school discipline plan should have structures designed to provide a balance between strategies to enhance acceptable behavior and procedures to address problem behavior. One recommended strategy is to develop and implement schoolwide practices for acknowledging acceptable behavior. These practices are called "schoolwide positives" and may include trophies for exemplary leadership, citizenship awards presented at school assemblies, and "caught-in-the-act" coupons distributed in the hallways to students who are following school rules governing hallway behavior. The essential factors to be considered in developing schoolwide positives of this type include (1) award title, (2) award, (3) criteria, (4) presentation, and (5) dissemination.

Title. The awards are given for demonstrations of specific behaviors that staff wish to support and maintain. The title captures the purpose of the award. For example, "Student of the Month" is awarded to the student for excellence in academic performance. "Most Improved" is awarded to the student who displayed the most significant improvements in academic performance or in social behaviors. "Caught-in-the-Act" is an all-purpose award for students who display expected behaviors at any given time.

Award. The award itself refers to the item the student receives, such as a trophy, certificate, coupon, privilege, stickers, or raffle tickets. The awards should be of value to students and should be developed with student input.

Criteria. The criteria define who is eligible for an award, how often an award is delivered, and how many students will receive the award. These criteria should be developed by school staff (with student input as appropriate) and should be implemented consistently. Strict criteria are needed for the more prestigious, public awards (such as "Student of the Month"). Looser criteria may be appropriate for awards that are to be distributed at a higher rate (such as "Caught-in-the-Act" awards) for demonstrations of acceptable behavior at recess.

Presentation. One of the critical features of an award is the recognition it brings to students. The amount of recognition can be controlled by the particular location and form in which the award is delivered. For example, the most public and highly valued recognition might occur at a school assembly. Other awards can be presented in the homeroom. Finally, some awards may be presented privately.

Dissemination. Students who display appropriate behavior can be given recognition in different ways. For example, a student's name may be placed on special sections of school bulletin boards or appear in honor rolls, newsletters, community papers, and parent letters.

Box 5.2 illustrates two types of awards that can have great value for students. In addition to their positive effects on student and teacher morale, they can contribute substantially to improved student behavior.

Modified Behavior-Teaching Plan

The modified *behavior-teaching plan* is designed to provide specific instruction to students in behavioral expectations. The major difference between the modified plan and the next step (formal behavior-instruction plan) is the level of detail. The modified plan has three components (1) remind, (2) supervise, and (3) provide feedback.

Remind. This procedure involves activities that staff engage in with students *before* they have an opportunity to exhibit maladaptive behavior. The purpose is to provide a clear focus on behavioral expectations and to prompt the student about existing rules.

Box 5.2 Example of Schoolwide Positives for Alice Springs Elementary School

Title

"Self-Manager"

Criteria

Satisfactory grades

Follow school rules

No discipline referrals

Class work completed

Five staff signatures (for example, teacher, teaching assistant)

Students listed in office for all staff to review

Presentation

Monthly award assembly

Award

Button

Privileges

- In hallways without pass
- Early release (1–2 minutes maximum) from class where appropriate
- Free seating for assemblies
- Early lunch
- Self-manager lunch table
- Extra computer time

Dissemination

Honor roll list in classroom

Parent notes

"Dolphin Tales"

Title

"Gotcha"

Criteria

Demonstrations of schoolwide expected behavior

Presentation

Individual staff member

Award

Sign in the honor roll log at office

Sticker

Monthly raffle at awards assembly

Dissemination

Signed awards log kept at office (name and room number)

These activities include verbal statements of the rules, announcements, role-plays, discussions, practice, written responses to behavioral expectations, and use of video vignettes.

Supervise. In this step, staff are expected to put themselves in positions where they can observe and monitor student behavior. For example, if hallway behavior is targeted, then staff may position themselves at the doorway or move out into the hallways. As a rule, effective supervision requires direct observation, but this is not always possible.

Provide Feedback. Staff should provide feedback at the earliest opportunity. On the basis of their own observations or reports of others, staff should positively acknowledge those students who demonstrate the expected behaviors but also provide some form of encouragement to those students who do not. Sometimes, specific problems need to be addressed at a schoolwide level. For example, if coming late for class is a schoolwide problem, a behavior-instruction plan could be developed and implemented by all staff to address it. Feedback to all students should be provided regularly on a schoolwide basis as part of the plan's implementation.

Formal Behavior-Instruction Plan

The basic assumption in this approach is that the most efficient method for establishing appropriate behavior on a schoolwide basis is to systematically and directly teach target behaviors that support each behavioral expectation. Effective *behavior-instruction plans* contain the procedural steps typically used in a formal lesson plan (Colvin, Sugai, & Kameenui, 1994).

Step 1: Specify Behavioral Expectations. Behavioral expectations are statements that describe desired, appropriate forms of student behavior. They often are characterized as replacement responses ("fair-pairs") for undesirable or problem behaviors. Behavioral expectations should be described in observable terms; that is, so another person would have no difficulty in identifying their occurrence or absence. Behavioral expectations are often characterized in terms of one or more of the following dimensions: (1) frequency or rate, (2) locus (location, setting), (3) duration, (4) latency, (5) force or intensity, and (6) topography (appearance).

Step 2: Explain the Behavioral Expectations. A specific time, place, and schedule should be established for explaining the identified behavioral expectations. In some schools, a team of teachers may produce a lesson plan for explaining them to students and guiding discussion of their implications. This lesson plan should be distributed to all teaching staff for consistent implementation and follow-up.

As a general rule, all homeroom teachers should explain goals and expected behaviors to their students; however, the school principal, support staff, or groups of students can also provide such explanations to the entire student body during school assemblies or scheduled classroom visits. Explanations should be coordinated so that students receive the same information and within a designated and relatively short time period (for example, within a week). After explanations and examples are provided, adequate time should be allowed for students to ask questions, discuss, and provide input. The amount of time allocated and the level of participation will depend on the students' age and ability to engage in this discussion.

Positive and negative examples for each behavioral expectation or rule should be presented to help students discriminate the differences between expected behaviors and rule violations. For example, in one demonstration the teacher could illustrate how to walk across the room without disturbing others (positive example). In a subsequent example, the teacher could walk across the room while interfering with students by pestering, interrupting, touching them, or taking their possessions without permission (negative example). The essential features of each example should be further illustrated by writing them on a chalkboard, using an overhead projector, or displaying them on wall posters.

After each teacher presentation, students should be asked to model *positive* examples for each behavioral rule. Students do not need to practice modeling or role-playing the negative examples. However, all students should discuss both the positive and negative examples. Special emphasis should be placed on the positive examples and the specific rules that apply to each.

Finally, a summary list or outline of all settings and their corresponding expected behaviors should be developed and discussed. Expected behaviors may be organized according to their commonality across and applicability to a range of school settings. Practice of positive examples of expected behaviors should always accompany this discussion.

Step 3: Provide Structured Opportunities to Practice Behavioral Expectations. A schoolwide schedule should be established to teach and review target behaviors regularly with all students. Some schools have produced schoolwide strategies and lesson plans for conducting these practice sessions. This practice is highly recommended whenever practicable.

Role-playing, simulations, verbal recitals, written statements, and responses to video illustrations should be used as vehicles to practice expected behaviors. For instance, if the school expectation is to "respect the rights and properties of others," a role-play could be structured for a negative example that would involve a teacher who grabs at a certificate earned by a student. A positive example would follow in which the teacher would calmly ask questions about the certificate in an appropriate manner and ask permission to see it.

Provide specific reinforcing or corrective feedback for all accurate displays of expected behaviors in both practice and natural contexts. For example, a teacher not only gives specific praise to students who cooperate and attend during role-play activities, but also provides behavior-specific praise when students display similar expected behaviors while waiting in line in the cafeteria. The teacher should provide specific feedback that highlights information about both positive and negative examples as well as the essential features of the behavioral expectation. For instance, a teacher says, "Grabbing at his certificate is not showing respect for Michael and his property. See the difference when I ask his permission politely? Michael is eager to show what he has earned."

Step 4: Provide Pre-Correction for Problem Settings and Individual Students. Pre-correction strategies should be used when problem behaviors are anticipated. Essentially, staff should correct a potential problem behavior *before* it has a chance to occur. Just prior to students entering the target context, teachers should plan opportunities for them to demonstrate a specific behavioral expectation or make some adjustment in the setting that increases the chances that the expected behavior will occur (for example, increasing supervision, providing more prompts, adjusting the schedule, changing seating arrangements, increasing praise for cooperative behavior). For example, while waiting for the bus, students are likely to engage in unacceptable physical behaviors, such as pushing, pulling, and kicking. To provide a pre-correction, teachers could schedule more practice sessions on the expected behavior of "not provoking others," provide structured activities prior to dismissal, reduce the time required to wait in the bus line, walk with students and wait for the bus with them, and provide strong praise for students who wait appropriately in line on their own.

Reminders are another form of pre-correction. As noted, teachers can remind students of the expected behaviors just before they enter the potentially problematic setting. For example, prior to students finishing their lunch, they are reminded by staff to put leftovers in the garbage containers; or just before recess, students are reminded to use the swings properly and let one person swing at a time. With pre-corrections, the emphasis should be placed only on the expected behaviors, *not* on the undesirable behaviors or their associated negative consequences.

Step 5: Provide Strong Reinforcement for Demonstrations of Expected Behavior. As with the acquisition of academic skill it is important to look for spontaneous displays of expected behavior and to provide behavior-descriptive praise for them. Although the use of positive reinforcement is critical during the acquisition and fluency training of expected behaviors, it is particularly important that staff provide social praise and approval over the long-term for those students who independently exhibit the expected behaviors. Nothing will contribute to maintenance outcomes more directly than this. As a final step, students should be asked to describe expected behaviors and the conditions under which they are displayed to ensure they fully understand them.

Early in the program's implementation, staff should be primed to acknowledge positive behavior in all school settings and as often as possible. Later, after high and stable levels of expected behavior are achieved, the frequency of such acknowledgement can become more intermittent and be gradually scaled back.

Illustration. The fifth grade teachers at a suburban middle school were concerned that many of their students were unable to make orderly transitions. The procedures that teachers followed in individual classrooms were generally not effective in changing this problem behavior. The successful behavior-instruction plan outlined in Box 5.3 was developed and implemented by the entire fifth grade staff to deal with this problem.

Phase 4: Develop Procedures for Correcting Problem Behavior

The most commonly used procedure for managing serious problem behavior in public schools involves an office referral and some sort of correlated consequence. From an analysis of office referrals, Sugai, Kameenui, and Colvin (1993) found that more than 90%

Box 5.3 Behavior-Instruction Plan

Orderly Transitions

Step 1. Specify behavioral expectations
Walk quietly, keeping your body and objects to yourself in transitional settings (reading to math, activity to lining up, circle to center).

Step 2. Explain behavioral expectations
Times: At roll call; in a circle; in a large group; at the start of the day
Procedures: Discussion: Walk, no running or jumping. Talk quietly unless no talking is indicated. Body to yourself; no pushing; hands, feet, and objects to yourself.

Step 3. Provide structured opportunities to practice behavioral expectations
Times: Before each identified transition
Procedures: Explain, discuss, model, role-play.

Step 4. Provide pre-correction for problem settings and individual students
Times: Just before identified transition
Procedures: Remind at least once during period: "Remember to walk quietly and keep your body and objects to yourself."

Step 5. Provide strong reinforcement for demonstrations of expected behavior
Times: As observed
Procedures: Teacher praise, acknowledgement: "Nice job of walking quietly and keeping your body and objects to yourself." Trips, points, group awards, Dolphin awards, and so on.

of school disciplinary actions were in the form of purely negative consequences. A critically important part of an instructional model of classroom management involves the application of nonpunitive correction procedures to the management of inappropriate student behavior. These correction procedures can be translated into the components of a teaching plan for managing problem behavior in a proactive and positive manner (Colvin, Sugai, & Kameenui, 1993).

In most public schools, problem behavior is identified as either a *minor infraction* (that is, student behavior that is managed immediately by staff in the context that it occurs) or a *serious* (sometimes illegal) *school violation* (that is, behavior that involves an office referral and is managed by an administrator). We propose four steps for developing and implementing a plan for addressing and correcting problem behavior: (1) carefully define the minor problem behaviors and serious school infractions; (2) implement procedures for an individual staff member to manage minor problem behaviors; (3) implement procedures for managing minor problem behavior through staff meetings, and (4) implement procedures for managing serious school violations.

Define and Categorize Problem Behavior

The types of correction procedures used to manage inappropriate student behavior will depend on its severity and frequency. School staff must meet and reach agreement on the categories of inappropriate behavior selected to represent minor and serious school violations. The following categories and definitions are recommended:

- *Minor school infractions* are regarded as relatively mild behaviors, but they are disruptive to the teaching and learning process and can easily escalate into more serious behavior problems. Common examples include being tardy for class, talking too loudly in the hallways, not having materials ready for class, and skipping school (truancy). These infractions are typically managed immediately by staff in the context in which they occur.

- *Serious school violations* are usually not illegal but represent substantial breaches of school rules and social norms that seriously disrupt school functioning. Sustained noncompliance and defiance, verbal abuse toward staff, low levels of physical aggression, vandalism, and chronic (that is, repeated) minor infractions are all examples of serious school violations. As noted, target behaviors typically warrant an office referral and are usually managed by the school administration.

- *Illegal behavior* is a violation of the law. Examples include possession of weapons or controlled substances, theft, assault, vandalism, and threats of physical harm or intimidation in school. Each school's definition of illegal behavior should be confirmed with local law enforcement agencies and school district policies. These behaviors almost always warrant office referrals and are managed by the administration (or its designee) in conjunction with local law enforcement agents.

Box 5.4 provides the working definitions of these types of student behavior as developed by a high school faculty.

Procedures for an Individual Staff Member to Manage Minor Problem Behaviors

A range of available procedures is always recommended for an individual teacher to manage relatively minor infractions in the classroom (Wolery, Bailey, & Sugai, 1988). Staff should be expected to seize every opportunity to establish appropriate student behavior (numerous suggestions of such strategies are presented in Chapters 6 and 7). Behavior-management procedures should provide increased positive reinforcement for promoting expected behavior *and* deliver negative consequences, as appropriate, based on severity of the inappropriate behavior. For example, simple reminders may be appropriate for some minor infractions, while loss of privileges, brief time-out, or other penalties

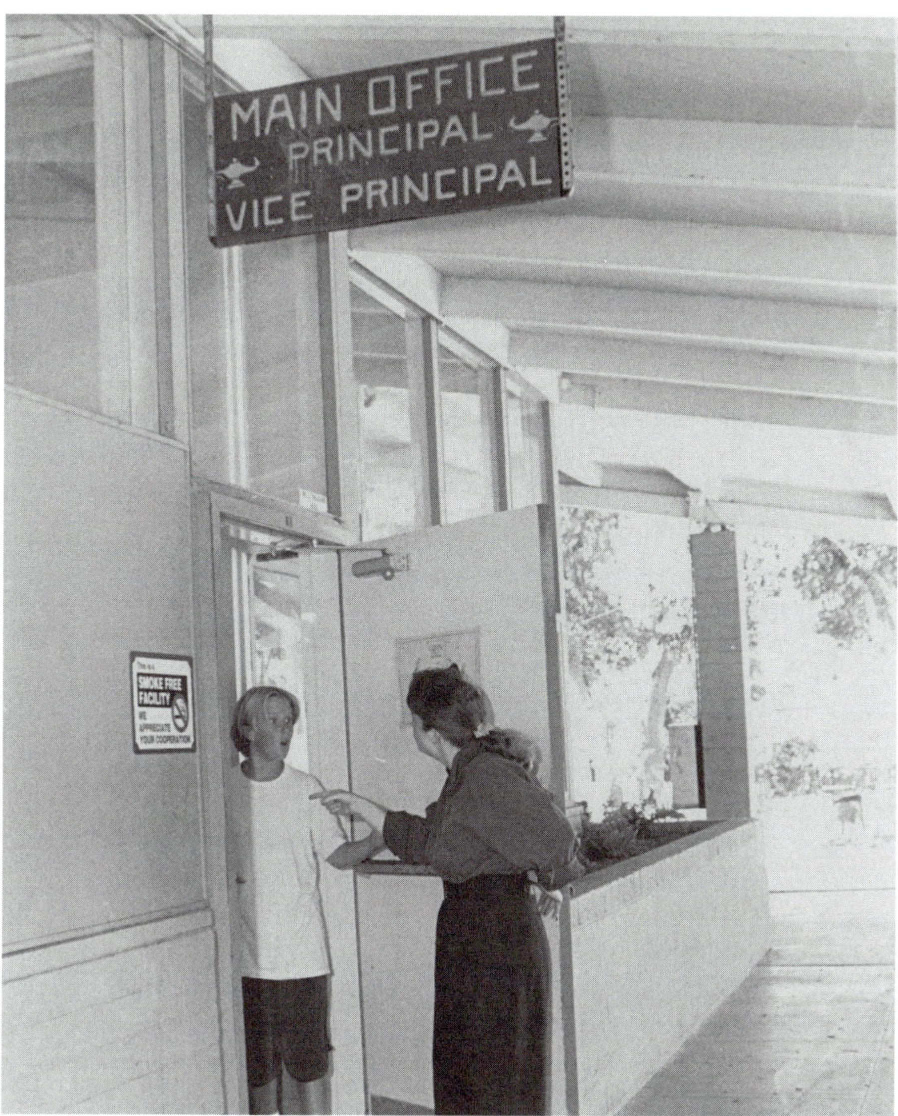

A suspension in the making. *Kathleen Olson*

may be necessary for more serious infractions. Recommended strategies for managing minor behavior problems follow.

1. *Remove adult and peer attention* from the student who is displaying inappropriate behavior and acknowledge other nearby students who are exhibiting the expected behavior. For example, Sarah is talking loudly in class during an individual, seatwork

Box 5.4 Freemantle High School

Working Definitions for Office Referral Infractions

Infraction	Definition
Repeated minor infractions	Recurring problems that have been addressed by teachers with "for the record" documentation or at staff meetings without changing the behavior. Examples: tardies, skipping classes, minor disruptive behavior, profanity, incomplete assignments, minor harassment, and not coming to class prepared.
Fighting	Action involving serious physical contact where injury may occur. Examples: hitting, punching, hitting with an object, kicking, hair pulling, and scratching.
Vandalism	Substantial destruction or disfigurement of property.
Controlled substances	In possession of or using drugs, alcohol, or tobacco.
Serious disruptions	Behavior that causes the class or activity to stop or continue with difficulty. Student does not cooperate and does not make reasonable attempts to disengage or follow directions. Examples: sustained loud talk, noise with materials, horseplay or roughhousing, sustained out-of-seat behavior.
Verbal abuse	Sustained use of profanity or sexual comments directed toward staff or students.
Weapons	In possession of knives, guns, or other items used as weapons.
Defiance	Refusal to follow staff directions, given that reasonable steps (that is, repeating directions one or more times) have been taken.
Off campus	Outside the boundaries of the school grounds without permission.
Theft	In possession of, having passed on, or being responsible for removing someone else's property.
Other	Serious behavior problems that do not fit into the above categories.

assignment. Her teacher turns her back slightly to Sarah and looks at a student nearby who is working quietly. The teacher says, "Students in this row are doing a great job paying attention and working on their assignments."

2. *Redirect student to the expected behavior* with a gesture or verbal prompt and intentionally acknowledge subsequent compliance and displays of expected behavior. For ex-

ample, the teacher gives Sarah a prompt by placing her finger next to her lips and saying, "Remember, Sarah, please use a conversational voice."

3. *Secure the student's attention and inform him or her of the expected behavior,* provide immediate opportunities for practice, and acknowledge compliance and appropriate displays of expected behavior. For example, the teacher says, "Sarah, please listen carefully. If you wish to talk, use a conversational voice. Now, how can I help you?" When Sarah uses a quiet voice, the teacher says, "There you go, Sarah. That was great!"

4. *Deliver a warning by providing an opportunity for the student to choose* between the expected behavior and a penalty or loss of privilege. For example, the teacher says, "Sarah, you need to go to class now or you will miss some recess."

5. *Deliver the penalty or loss of privilege* (for example, loss of some recess time) immediately and in a businesslike manner. Do not linger or nag students.

6. *Use additional resources to address the problem* if there is no improvement in the student's overall behavior after three or four occasions in which a planned intervention has been implemented. At this point we recommend a staff meeting.

7. *Records or documentation of the problem and the interventions* used to address the problem should be developed. Staff should be in agreement on the purpose of these records, dissemination procedures, specification of problem behavior, and the strategies used.

Procedures for Managing Minor Problem Behavior through Staff Meetings

A staff meeting involves a group of teachers, administrators, and other school staff who engage in a problem-solving process and share their suggestions for managing minor problem behaviors. There are several important advantages in staff coming together to address such problem behavior in this manner:

- The meetings provide an opportunity to utilize the ideas of "an untapped resource," namely, other staff.
- When teachers meet in this fashion, there is a greater likelihood of agreed-upon procedures being implemented consistently.
- More intervention options can be generated in this process that may result in fewer office referrals.
- Individual staff members receive support and assistance.
- Ongoing staff development can be facilitated.

These meetings can be called on an informal basis or can be part of a regular meeting that teachers hold (for example, a weekly grade-level meeting). A variety of labels have been used to name this staffing structure (for example, "teacher assistance team," "child study team," "schoolwide behavior committee," and "discipline team").

The following guidelines are suggested for conducting staff meetings:

- A staff meeting should be called by the teacher after three to four documented incidents of the minor problem behavior have occurred.
- The staff meeting should be scheduled on a regular basis during ongoing staff or grade-level meetings.
- A special staff meeting may be called if a teacher needs more immediate support (with as many teachers in attendance as possible).
- A form should be developed and used to document each case and to guide staff meeting activities. Form 5.1 is an example of a staff meeting form for minor problem behaviors. The teacher should complete as much of the form as possible before the meeting, so participants will have some prior information about the case. This information can also serve as the starting point for discussions during the meeting.
- A notetaker and timekeeper should be identified. It is critical to follow the agenda and stay within the allocated time lines.
- Problem behaviors (list no more than two) should be prioritized from most to least important. Descriptions of these problem behaviors should be written in observable forms.
- A specific expected behavior should be paired with each problem behavior and also described in observable form.
- If possible, one to three of the least intrusive and least time-consuming strategies for teaching expected behaviors should be selected. If the expected behaviors do not occur at acceptable levels as a result, more intrusive and time-consuming strategies should be considered.
- Although strategies for teaching expected behaviors should be given the greatest attention, strategies for responding to problem behaviors should also be described. Again, least intrusive and least aversive criteria should always be applied in selecting individual strategies.
- A specific date should be established to review the progress of the strategy in achieving anticipated outcomes. If possible, a plan for collecting and recording data on the effectiveness of the strategies should be developed in this context.

Procedures for Managing Serious School Violations

Serious school violations require actions and follow-up that involve greater teacher effort and more intrusive interventions. The consequences for serious violations should be written into school policy and delivered automatically and consistently. All parents should be informed of the procedures at the start of the school year and should receive a written copy of them. Staff should be clear about what their responsibilities are and who delivers the consequences. Typically, an office referral is made, and an administrative staff person delivers the consequence. Clear guidelines need to be established for student behaviors that warrant office referrals, and all staff must have a clear understanding of which behaviors result in an office referral and the procedures that will be

MOUNT EPSON ELEMENTARY SCHOOL

Student Name: ____________________ Grade: ______ Date: __________

Teacher(s): ____________________ # Previous Behavior Reports/Staff Meeting: ____

Staff Present: ____

____

Problem Behavior(s) (2 minutes) *Expected Behavior(s)* (2 minutes)

Strategies to Teach Expected Behaviors (select 1–3) (3 minutes)

- ☐ Reminders
- ☐ Reinforcers
- ☐ Feedback
- ☐ Contract
- ☐ Practice
- ☐ Individual contacts
- ☐ Monitoring sheet
- ☐ Self-management
- ☐ Parent contact
- ☐ Counseling
- ☐ Tutoring
- ☐ Modified assignments
- ☐ Other ____

Strategies to Correct Problem Behavior(s) (1 minute)

- ☐ Time-out
- ☐ Loss of privilege
- ☐ Parent contact
- ☐ Detention
- ☐ Other ____

Action Plan (5 minutes)

Who	What	When

Student Conference Date: ________ *Start Date:* ________ *Review Date:* ________

Copies to: Office File
Teacher
Other: ______________

FORM 5.1 Staff Meeting Form for Minor Problem Behavior

followed by the office in responding to them. Without clear guidelines for serious school violations, friction may occur between the referring teachers and office staff. Referrals may be made for minor behaviors, or a referring staff person may expect certain consequences to be delivered and they are not. A perception among teachers of a lack of administrative support in managing difficult students is one of the most serious morale issues facing schools today.

Typically, consequences applied for serious school violations include parent conferences, after-school detention, in-school suspension, out-of-school suspension, and expulsion. It is important to keep track of (1) the number of office referrals; (2) the date, period, time, and location of each infraction and consequence; (3) who referred the student to the office; (4) the outcome of debriefing sessions; and (5) follow-up events. Repeated office referrals should be a signal that a student needs more assistance in learning and displaying expected behaviors. Students who have repeated displays of serious school violations should be referred to a schoolwide behavior support team (that is, a teacher-assistance team) to develop a specific, individual plan designed to reduce or eliminate the problem behavior pattern and to establish opportunities for the display of expected behaviors.

Procedures for managing illegal behaviors usually involve an office referral and a police referral. An agreed-upon procedure should be established in advance for handling illegal behavior (for example, documentation and witnesses). Local law enforcement agencies should be contacted for guidelines or criteria about handling illegal behaviors in school and for working with the agencies. Procedures for contacting parents must also be established. We recommend the following procedures for addressing serious school violations:

1. *Identify clearly and define serious school violations.* These definitions should be shared with and reviewed by all school staff. An office referral form should be developed for use in this regard. At a minimum, each form should have (1) identifying information about the student and referring teacher, (2) dates and times of the infraction, (3) identification and descriptions of the infraction, (4) action taken, and (5) procedures for information dissemination. Form 5.2 is an example of an office referral form for a middle school.

2. *Develop a reasonable balance between proactive and reactive consequences for the problem behavior.* Unfortunately, the most common actions taken following office referrals are reactive in nature and often punitive as well (for example, detentions, suspensions, loss of privileges). Students need to know the tolerance levels that define unacceptable behavior and when negative consequences are appropriate and necessary. However, having only negative consequences available for managing serious school infractions creates an ineffective system for remediating behavior problems and developing positive alternatives. The preferred alternative lies in creating a careful balance of proactive and reactive approaches. When we use proactive strategies or actions, we assume that the student needs more help, support, and direction to reduce problem behavior and to learn a more adaptive behavior pattern. These constructive strategies include conferences, pre-correction, instruction (for example, modeling appropriate forms of behavior), counseling, teacher–student contracts, and behavior-instruction plans applied *before* problematic behavior occurs. The

BUNBURY MIDDLE SCHOOL
Phone 555-1234
123 Olga Road
Eugene, Oregon 97403

OFFICE REFERRAL

Student ______________________ Grade 6 7 8 Date __________

Referred By ____________________

Homeroom Teacher ________________

REASON FOR REFERRAL

☐ **Repeated Minor Infraction(s)**

Description: ____

____

____

☐ **For-the-Record and Staffing Plans attached**

☐ **Serious School Violation**

☐ Fighting
☐ Serious Disruption
☐ Off-Campus Violation
☐ Verbal Abuse
☐ Vandalism
☐ Weapons
☐ Controlled Substances(s)
☐ Defiance

☐ Other ______________________

Description: (Specify times, places, those involved, relevant conditions, and initial steps to address problem)

____

____

____

FORM 5.2 Office Referral Form

____

____

____

____

____

____

ACTION TAKEN: (By teacher/person making referral as appropriate)

- ☐ Conference with student
- ☐ Parent contact (phone/note)
- ☐ Contract made with student
- ☐ Parent conference requested/recommended
- ☐ In-house suspension

☐ Other ______________________________

ACTION TAKEN: (By administrator/counselor)

- ☐ Conference with student
- ☐ Parent contacted (phone/note)
- ☐ Referral to School Discipline Team
- ☐ Conference requested with teacher and student
- ☐ Parent conference requested
- ☐ Principal's hearing for possible expulsion
- ☐ Student suspended: __ In-School __ Out-of-School __ Number of days

☐ Other ______________________________

COMMENTS: ______________________________

____

____

____

FORM 5.2 *(Continued)*

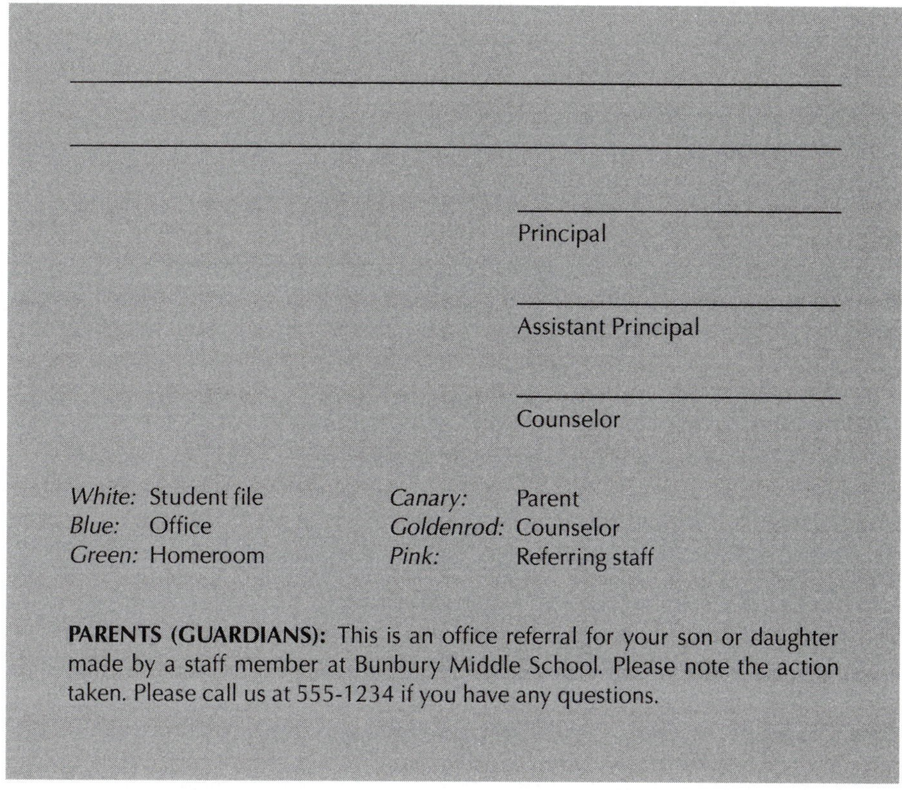

Principal

Assistant Principal

Counselor

White:	Student file	*Canary:*	Parent
Blue:	Office	*Goldenrod:*	Counselor
Green:	Homeroom	*Pink:*	Referring staff

PARENTS (GUARDIANS): This is an office referral for your son or daughter made by a staff member at Bunbury Middle School. Please note the action taken. Please call us at 555-1234 if you have any questions.

FORM 5.2 *(Continued)*

office referral form and the data or tracking system also should reflect the balance between proactive and reactive consequences.

3. *Assemble a schoolwide team* (for example, behavior support team, school discipline team, teacher-assistance team) that has the responsibility of developing a more detailed plan of assistance for students who have recurring, serious school violations. Referrals should be made to this team after the student has had two or three office referrals and has not responded to a combination of proactive and reactive strategies implemented by the administrator or other school staff. It is important that the number of referrals made to this team be controlled or limited to five or six per term; otherwise, the team will not have time to develop and supervise assistance plans for these students. If the number of referrals begins to exceed what the team can handle, it is time to review the relative effectiveness of current, schoolwide practices.

The following guidelines should be considered in forming a schoolwide team: (1) develop a clear statement of purpose and list of team responsibilities; (2) determine who should be on the team and how the selections are to be made; and (3) establish guidelines for meeting days, times, lengths, and agenda items.

Phase 5: Develop Procedures for Record Keeping, Evaluation, and Dissemination

An effective tracking system can be of great assistance in identifying students who exhibit inappropriate behavior on a regular basis. Avoid "punishment loops" in which progressively more intrusive and reactive interventions are required for repeated or escalating episodes of inappropriate behaviors. A strategy for providing direct assistance to students whose behavior does not respond to general schoolwide or classroom procedures is essential. Individual staff members, teacher teams (for example, prereferral or mainstream assistance teams), parents, or cooperating agencies can collaborate in providing this assistance. In addition, referrals for more specialized assistance also may be appropriate (for example, special education, day treatment in alternative schools).

It is important to have a method of tracking student performance in order to monitor the effectiveness of any schoolwide discipline system. Information might be collected schoolwide, in the classroom, or by an individual student or teacher. The information can include a variety of factors, such as (1) attendance patterns, (2) problem behaviors, (3) negative and positive referrals, (4) detentions, and (5) suspensions. Information about which staff persons are involved in discipline-related activities should also be tracked.

Tracking systems are important because they help to (1) ensure that the schoolwide plan is being implemented in a planned, consistent manner, (2) frequently remind staff of the importance of the schoolwide discipline plan, and (3) provide information on whether the plan is accomplishing its goals. The critical components of a tracking system or monitoring plan should include the following items:

- A checklist to measure whether the various steps in the plan have been identified, defined, and implemented.
- Strategies and forms for keeping continuing records of both expected and inappropriate student behavior.
- Decision rules for reviewing and revising the plan.
- A screening system for identifying students who are at risk.
- Procedures and routines for collecting and processing data. (For efficiency, student workers and classified (nonteaching) staff should be trained to enter data into a simple spreadsheet or database program so that data management, analysis, and reporting are simplified.)

Developing Review and Follow-Up Procedures

The success of any plan to teach and manage student behavior in school must include specific procedures for ensuring the accurate and continued implementation of its procedures.

An individual or group should be selected to oversee activities involving maintenance of the schoolwide discipline plan and evaluation of its effectiveness. Procedures should be developed for collecting ongoing and cumulative data on student behavior and staff performance. Questionnaires and interviews can be used to collect information from students, staff, parents, and community representatives for this purpose.

Dissemination Plan

Once components of the schoolwide discipline plan have been developed, the next phase involves developing strategies to disseminate details and procedures of the plan to all concerned parties. A dissemination plan should include a list of the people or groups of people who need to be familiar with or approve the schoolwide discipline plan (for example, administrators, certified and uncertified staff, substitute teachers, district personnel, school-board members, students, parents, community personnel, and staff from cooperating agencies).

IMPLEMENTATION STEPS FOR A SCHOOLWIDE DISCIPLINE PLAN

Even though a schoolwide discipline plan is carefully developed, it may still fail because of ineffective implementation. In this section, we present details of *implementation steps* that should increase the likelihood that a well-designed discipline plan will prove effective.

Step 1: Establish a Commitment from All Staff to Work Together to Improve the Schoolwide Discipline Plan

Substantial changes usually need to occur in staff behavior to effect schoolwide change. It is critical for someone in the building, typically the school principal, to win the support and commitment of the staff to bring about these changes. Cotton (1990) described commitment on the part of all staff to manage student behavior effectively as an "essential precondition of learning." Although such commitment does not guarantee positive changes in student behavior, we believe the principal, or staff leader, needs to work very diligently to secure schoolwide staff commitment as a first and necessary step to ensure the success of any discipline plan.

Step 2: Establish a Building Team and Operating Procedures

As a first step in selecting a building team, the principal or designated school leader should explain the role and responsibilities of the team to all staff. Some of these responsibilities would include meeting once a week for approximately an hour, developing and piloting behavior-instruction plans, and taking a leading role in involving staff at meetings or at other designated times. Composition of the building team should be based on the following criteria:

- Representatives of all staff (general and special educators, support staff, and administration)
- Weighted toward general educators
- Representatives of each grade level
- Credible with all staff
- A combination of voluntary, appointed, and elected members

Step 3: Develop or Revise a School Discipline Manual

A school manual should provide a complete description of the school discipline plan. Details for the five foundational steps of a discipline plan should be delineated. Input should be solicited from all parties involved with the school, such as staff, students, parents, and the community. A procedure needs to be developed by the building team and ratified by staff for reviewing and revising the manual. The procedures should be written in a nontechnical manner so that parents and students can understand their content, and a dissemination plan needs to be developed to communicate details of the plan. Development of the school discipline manual is a *critical* element in implementing and maintaining an effective discipline plan.

Step 4: Design and Implement a Staff Development Plan

It is likely that a school discipline plan will fail unless a staff development plan is carefully designed and implemented as well. The following steps are recommended for designing and implementing such a plan:

1. Specify the roles of all staff members (administrators, teachers, school psychologists, counselors, social workers, paraprofessionals, custodian, nurse, substitute teachers, and other specialists) in making the plan work.
2. Select staff members to serve on the building team.
3. Develop a communication system between the building team and all staff.
4. Prepare and develop all necessary materials and products.
5. Develop a needs assessment for training and skill development.
6. Develop a staff-training schedule.
7. Develop procedures for staff training utilizing existing staff, district consultants, other specialists, or outside consultants.
8. Develop a data-based evaluation system to monitor, evaluate, and review all staff training and implementation procedures.

Step 5: Develop a Data Management, Feedback, and Review System

One of the most important steps in implementing a schoolwide discipline plan is to establish a functional, data-management system. As noted earlier, such a data system helps to ensure that (1) the schoolwide discipline plan is being implemented as designed, (2) staff are frequently reminded of the plan, and (3) feedback is provided to staff on the plan's effectiveness. The following key features should be addressed in setting up and using a data-management system:

- Develop a recording system to chart student behavior (office referrals, attendance, behaviors of concern). Staff need to be identified who will collect and enter such data. The data need to be stored on a computer program that allows easy access and analyses.
- Develop a system to present summary data to staff on a regular basis. These reports can be disseminated at staff meetings, posted, entered in staff bulletins, and distributed to key personnel as appropriate.
- Establish procedures and a schedule to systematically review the data (via the building team, staff meetings, and other structures).
- Use the data to identify at-risk students and chronic problem-behavior students and to develop strategies to provide ongoing assistance to them.

CONCLUSION

Public school personnel are having to manage problem student behavior at ever-increasing levels of intensity and severity. Behavioral episodes are occurring routinely that would have been unthinkable several decades ago. Available research findings on antisocial behavior patterns suggest numerous practices that can be effective for minimizing these problems.

In this chapter, we have described an instructionally based model for managing student behavior on a schoolwide basis that rests on empirically established research practices and that has a strong focus on positive student behavior. This model assumes that proactive strategies for preventing antisocial forms of student behavior are viable, user-friendly, and can be highly cost efficient. We recognize, however, that a schoolwide discipline plan is a universal intervention that will have minimal to no impact on the adjustment status of some highly antisocial students. In such instances, more powerful, selected interventions are required to deal adequately with these students' myriad behavior problems.

In addition to supporting achievement of a school's overall mission, a schoolwide discipline plan is a key back-up resource for all school staff who must deal directly with antisocial students. Inevitably, teachers encounter situations with these students in which back-up consequences beyond the teacher's control must be called into play (for example, suspensions, police contacts, expulsions). Sound operational plans embedded in schoolwide discipline plans allow schools to cope effectively with crisis behavioral episodes and to prevent the occurrence of less severe behavior problems.

The key foundational steps underlying a schoolwide discipline plan were described. The final section of the chapter focused on procedural steps for implementing elements of such a plan.

The next chapter focuses on a more proximal and specific level of intervention with problematic student behavior. Chapter 6 addresses issues and recommended best practices for instructing and managing the classroom environment. If classrooms are structured and managed effectively, substantial amounts of problematic student behavior can be prevented. As a result, the overall qualitative experiences of teachers and students can be improved with a greater likelihood that desirable student outcomes will be achieved.

ADDITIONAL RESOURCES ON SCHOOLWIDE DISCIPLINE

Charles, C. M. (1989). *Building Classroom Discipline: From Models to Practice* (3rd ed.). New York: Longman.

Curwin, R. L., & Mendler, A. N. (1988). *Discipline with Dignity*. Alexandria, VA: Association for Supervision and Curriculum Development.

Nelson, J. (1987). *Positive Discipline*. New York: Ballantine Books.

Sprick, R. (1981). *The Solution Book: A Guide to Classroom Discipline*. Chicago: Science Research Associates.

STUDY QUESTIONS

1. What are the major research findings on best practices for establishing a proactive, schoolwide discipline plan?
2. How are proactive approaches different from reactive approaches to managing student behavior?
3. Why is it critical for staff to establish a basic or common direction in their school discipline plan?
4. What are the major guidelines in establishing schoolwide behavioral expectations?
5. What are the major purposes of schoolwide positives?
6. What is the rationale for using instructional procedures to establish appropriate social behavior?
7. What are the major advantages in utilizing staff meetings to address minor problem behavior?
8. What are the critical pieces of information that should be included on an office referral form?

9. Why is it important to have a record-keeping system and what are the major components of such a system?
10. What are the critical steps in a schoolwide discipline plan?

KEY TERMS

behavior-instruction plans
behavior-teaching plan
foundational steps
illegal behavior
implementation steps
minor school infraction
mission statement
proactive approaches
schoolwide behavioral expectations
schoolwide discipline plan
schoolwide positive structures
serious school violation

6 Instructing and Managing the Classroom Environment

Classroom Structure

Designing the Physical Arrangement of the Classroom
Developing a Checklist of Operating Procedures
Planning Teacher Expectations

Delivering Instruction

Schedule
Instructional Objectives
Teaching to Mastery
Continuous Monitoring of Student Performance
Rates of Success
Pacing
Planned Variation of Instruction
Establishing Independent Routines
Teacher–Student Interactions
Academic Engagement

Managing Student Errors
Shaping Student Responses

Intervening during Instruction

Implement Classroom Expectations or Rules
Frequently Acknowledge Cooperative Students
Establish Consequences for Students Who Do Not Comply with Rules
Establish a Classroom Entry Activity
Keep Initial Explanations Brief
Secure the Attention of All Students before Beginning Explanations
Catch Problems Early
Plan for Difficult Transitions
Use Direct Speech
Avoid Dead Time
Settle Students Down Near the End of Each Period

Conclusion

Teachers increasingly face difficult management tasks and enormous pressures in educating each and every student who comes through the schoolhouse door. More and more children are bringing complex needs to school, and those who are antisocial severely exacerbate the teacher's tasks. Of the many *classroom challenges* that exist today, perhaps no greater challenge currently faces the educational enterprise than developing the academic and social-behavioral potential of these difficult students. To complicate matters further, there are increasing demands from society and local communities to increase the quality of education, raise achievement test scores, and manage an increasingly diverse student population—all with diminishing funds (Hodgkinson, 1991).

There is a strong and continuing movement to require general education teachers to assume more responsibility for the education of students with disabilities, including those with serious behavioral disabilities (Kauffman, 1993; Wang, Reynolds, & Walberg, 1986; Will, 1986). This movement, referred to as the Regular Education Initiative or the Full Inclusion Movement, has been interpreted by many to mean that students with disabilities should be educated to the maximum extent possible in general education settings (Giangreco, Dennis, Cloninger, Edelman, & Schattman, 1993). This policy substantially increases the heterogeneity and diversity of the regular classroom. Providing effective instruction under these conditions becomes considerably difficult and requires a broader array of teacher skills.

Antisocial students, and those with behavior disorders generally, are often deficient in critical academic skills, achieve well below their ability levels, and frequently do not respond well to the instructional process. In order to respond academically, such students usually require investments of more than their share of teacher effort. Because of their aversive behavioral characteristics, many teachers are reluctant to make such investments in antisocial students. However, facilitating the achievement levels of antisocial students is one of the best vehicles we have for diverting them from a path leading to delinquency, school dropout, and adult criminality.

Researchers report that teachers spend from 40 to 75% of available instructional time in activities other than instruction (Goodlad, 1984). Furthermore, Hofmeister and Lubke (1990) report research indicating students spend as little as 17% of their classroom time successfully engaged in academic tasks. In a study of teacher–student interactions, the senior author found that a typical intermediate grade–level teacher averaged only 38 minutes of actual instruction out of a daily 3-hour period (Walker & Buckley, 1973). Cangelosi (1992) appropriately claimed, "As a teacher, you are confronted with more variables to concurrently manipulate than is expected in any other profession" (p. 8).

The purpose of this chapter is to present procedures and strategies for (1) effectively managing problem behavior in the classroom while delivering instruction and (2) increasing the amount of allocated time in which teaching and learning occur. We emphasize strategies for *preventing* problem behavior and for effectively intervening in a safe and timely manner. The topics addressed in this chapter include (1) classroom structure, (2) delivering instruction, and (3) intervening with problem behavior during instruction.

CLASSROOM STRUCTURE

Classroom structure is a term used to describe the manner in which teachers organize the classroom. The overarching goal of establishing structure is to ensure that events in the classroom are as predictable as possible (Paine, Radicchi, Rosellini, Deutchman, & Darch, 1983). Antisocial students, in particular, depend on structure (and its accompanying predictability) in order to cope with the demands and pressures of school. Antisocial students often come from home environments where their daily living needs are not met or attended to on a predictable basis (for example, meals, bedtime, contact with parents). In fact, Wahler and Dumas (1986) conducted a classic review of the family conditions influencing the development and maintenance of aggressive, antisocial behavior patterns among children and youth. They argue persuasively that children in these families are so deprived of predictable circumstances that they often initiate hostile exchanges with family members simply because they know the likely outcomes (punishment, humiliation, negative sanctions). Even though the results are often aversive and painful to the initiating child, this cycle is repeated over and over again because it brings momentary predictability to an otherwise chaotic situation. The ability to predict outcomes and events in one's environment has considerable survival value and appears to be a basic human need.

Classroom structure helps provide antisocial students with the stability they need for controlling their behavior and sets the stage for effective learning. Many strategies are available for enhancing classroom structure; the simple rule to remember is *to provide as much structure as necessary to maintain appropriate student behavior.* Attention to three major strategies is recommended for enhancing classroom structure: (1) designing the physical arrangement of the classroom, (2) developing a checklist of operating procedures, and (3) planning teacher expectations.

Designing the Physical Arrangement of the Classroom

Many different functions and operations take place in the classroom on a regular basis (independent work, group work, transitions, free-time activity, storing materials). Their relative success or failure can depend heavily on the *physical* arrangement of the classroom. It is important to clearly identify all functions necessary for effective instruction to occur and to carefully arrange the classroom so that these functions can be accomplished (Cangelosi, 1993; Colvin, 1993; Paine et al., 1983). Typical functions and corresponding suggested classroom designs are described here:

- *Independent work* requires an area with minimum distractions. It is best to have individual desks to separate students. Areas for independent work should be in a low-traffic section away from materials and from time-out and free-time activity areas.

- *Group-work* areas should ensure that students can easily attend to the teacher and to each other. A semicircle or row configuration of desks can facilitate group-oriented instruction.

If most students are engaged in group work while others are on individual instructional programs, the group instruction should always be conducted in front of the class so the teacher faces the whole room, thus allowing for supervision of the entire classroom. The teacher should take care to keep his or her voice moderately low during group instruction in order to prevent students who are not in the group from being unnecessarily distracted.

- *Free-time activities* are sometimes used for students who finish their work early or as a reward for special achievement. Free time should be restricted to a specific area in the classroom behind or adjacent to the instructional areas. Specific rules of behavior governing free time should also be in effect.
- *Storage materials* should be placed in a low-traffic area to avoid distractions but allow relatively easy access. Ensure that materials are neatly arranged and that they do not block students' view.
- *The teacher's desk* should be out of the path and flow of instruction. It should be located in an area that will safeguard personal property and confidential material.
- *A notice board* should be highly visible in the room and in a high-traffic area, but should also be positioned so it does not divert attention during instruction. The notice board can be divided into sections for specific communications, such as news, projects, rules, and special recognitions.
- *Supervision* is maximized by arranging the room so that all students are in the teacher's view.
- *Quiet-time areas* are used by some teachers to enable students to calm down when they are stressed or agitated. This area needs to be as isolated as possible to prevent interactions with other students and staff.

Attention to these elements can make the classroom a far easier setting to manage. Careful attention to the arrangement of the classroom is usually associated with enhanced outcomes for all students and especially antisocial students.

Developing a Checklist of Operating Procedures

Once the physical layout of the classroom has been determined, the next step is to identify the various details that should be in place before formal instruction and classes begin. A sample checklist of such details follows:

- Post a list of not more than four or five classroom rules.
- Develop a schedule for teaching the different academic subjects and for checking on progress toward long-term objectives.
- Prepare a teacher notebook of essential information. Include sections for anecdotal notes and events; individual education programs (IEPs) for special education stu-

dents; academic and behavioral summaries; and phone numbers, birth dates, important medical information, and parents' names and work phone numbers.

- Review school records from the previous year to determine the students' academic and behavioral levels at the end of the year.
- Develop a menu of rewards (reinforcers), and schedule times for students to use them.
- Establish an effective and easy-to-use discipline plan. (See Chapter 5 on discipline.)
- Post a daily schedule.
- If using point cards (or any other forms), make sure they are printed and ready to be used.
- Decide on a seating plan.

Planning Teacher Expectations

Classroom expectations are designed to provide students with clear information on the kinds of academic and behavioral responses required of them so that instruction and learning can take place in a smooth and efficient manner. A simple rule should be taught that appropriate student behavior results in positive consequences and inappropriate behavior leads to their absence or withdrawal. Some steps that can be used to teach this essential relationship follow:

- *Explicitly state rules* so it is clear to anyone (teacher, student, or observer) when a rule has been followed or broken. For this reason, rules should be precise, practical, and clearly stated.
- *Select functional rules* that focus on student behaviors and responses that facilitate instruction and learning. The following list is a sample of functional rules: (1) Be on time for class. (2) Enter the classroom quietly. (3) Go to your assigned areas promptly. (4) Listen to the teacher's directions or explanations. (5) Raise your hand if you wish to talk or need assistance. (6) Join in the discussion or lesson. (7) Follow the teacher's directions. (8) Organize required materials as directed. (9) Start assigned work on time. (10) Keep working. (11) Ask for help only after you have tried by yourself. (12) Finish assigned work as appropriate. (13) Leave the room punctually and quietly.
- *Establish classroom rules immediately* on the first day of the new school year because any "down time" usually makes it more difficult to establish them later.
- *Rehearse and review the rules* regularly so students are constantly reminded of them. In this way, teachers, as well as students, can identify which rules are not working or need further clarification.
- *Practice frequently broken rules* by simulating situations involving them, providing practice, followed by debriefing.

Teacher reviewing classroom rules. *Elizabeth Crews*

Some teachers prefer to involve students in the development of rules and classroom expectations. In such cases, teachers should have an outline of classroom expectations and procedures for clarifying them.

DELIVERING INSTRUCTION

In an optimally structured classroom, careful attention is given to the use of effective teaching strategies. The strong relationship that exists between effective teaching practices and positive student behavior is well documented (Cangelosi, 1993). If all students are actively engaged in the instructional process, the chances of problem behavior occurring are greatly diminished. Some recommended effective strategies for *instructional delivery* are described in this section.

Schedule

Teachers typically operate their classrooms with a daily schedule in mind. A fixed schedule facilitates the development of routines, punctuality, completion of essential tasks, and personal organization. Once established, this schedule should be broken only when absolutely necessary. Generally, important instructional activities should be scheduled early in the day so that maximum time can be allocated to these essential academic areas.

If a schoolwide schedule exists, teachers need to monitor and control the order of events within particular periods. Activities should provide for immediate review, cumulative review, teacher-directed instruction, student follow-up, debriefing, and practice. Scheduled activities should be established to plan for difficult transitions (such as coming in from recess or going to a less structured program), and the schedule should be posted.

Instructional Objectives

Establishing instructional objectives for students makes intended learning outcomes more likely to occur. Objectives enable measurement of acquisition and allow teaching to mastery. Instructional objectives serve as a road map to show students what they are learning.

Teaching to Mastery

Mastery learning assumes that the vast majority of students can master specific skills if they are given sufficient time to learn them, along with appropriate teacher assistance, feedback, and practice. Antisocial students, as well as those with more generalized behavior problems, typically have an academic profile that reflects "splinter skills"; that is, they have not reached mastery on component skills in subject areas such as math and reading (Gleason, Colvin, & Archer, 1991). Consequently, as new skill areas are introduced, such students have difficulty catching up or staying with the group. The pace of instruction and the rate of content mastery become increasingly difficult for them, thus increasing the risk of academic failure.

Continuous Monitoring of Student Performance

Careful monitoring of student performance ensures that all students can participate in the learning process. It also helps identify errors and allows for their correction. Monitoring of student performance, along with high performance expectations, have been consistently identified as contributors to effective teaching and schooling. Monitoring of student progress can occur informally through the teaching-learning process or formally through curriculum-based measurement (CBM) procedures that provide for continuous and sensitive measurement of student performance (Shapiro, 1989; Shinn, 1989). CBM procedures are highly recommended for use with all students, but especially with antisocial students who tend to be weak academically and need frequent feedback on their performance (Patterson, Reid, & Dishion, 1992). CBM has the following major features:

- Provides for continuous monitoring of individual students' academic progress
- Uses repeated and frequent administration of skill probes taken directly from the curriculum in which the student is being instructed
- Uses short skill probes to facilitate frequent administration
- Identifies academic responses (for example, oral-reading rates) in the basic skill content areas that teachers can measure reliably and validly
- Provides direct, repeated measurement of student performance in the curriculum using production-type responses

Sample CBM measures of student achievement include (1) counting the number of words read correctly in a basal reader for a 1-minute period, (2) counting the number of correctly-solved math problems in a 5-minute period, and (3) counting words spelled correctly in a 2-minute interval (Shinn, 1989).

Rates of Success

Whenever possible, teachers should ensure that antisocial students experience an adequate rate of academic success; otherwise, boredom and frustration are likely to precipitate problem behavior (Smith & Misra, 1992). It goes without saying that planning for student success requires the careful selection of appropriate materials and instructional activities, and the monitoring of student progress.

Pacing

Teachers sometimes wonder whether their instructional presentations are too fast or too slow. This teaching variable, called pacing, deals with the number of per-period opportunities students have to respond academically. Students are generally more attentive, more on-task, and make fewer errors during high-rate teacher presentations than during low-rate presentations.

In general, it's better to be too fast than too slow. A fast pace helps focus student attention, while a slow pace may set the stage for inattentive or inappropriate behavior.

Planned Variation of Instruction

Many strategies exist for delivering instruction, such as teacher-directed instruction, independent work, small-group work, lectures, discussions, and cooperative-learning activities (Cangelosi, 1993). While some of these strategies may be more effective with some classes and types of students than others, the important overall strategy is to use *planned variation*. Students' attention will be lost if any one strategy is used for too long. The teacher should plan and monitor student attention carefully and change the delivery of instruction *before* students' attention wanders or is lost.

Establishing Independent Routines

Independent routines refer to those activities that students complete by themselves. For example, when students finish an assignment, they know to deposit it in the in-basket on the teacher's desk, go to a bookshelf, select a book, return to their desk, and begin reading. Clearly, the more responsibility students can assume in this situation, the less need there is for teachers to provide assistance and supervision, thus freeing them to teach and manage the classroom environment (Smith & Misra, 1992).

Teacher–Student Interactions

Interactions are the exchange of reciprocal social responses between a teacher and a student; they can be initiated by either. If most interactions are student initiated, the question arises, "Who is teaching whom?" On the other hand, if nearly all the interactions are teacher initiated, it could mean that students are too passive or uncreative or that the teacher is too directive or controlling in managing the classroom. Either extreme is unacceptable. So what is an acceptable ratio of teacher-initiated to student-initiated interactions? In a structured classroom, an adequate balance between teacher- and student-initiated interactions is approximately seven (teacher) to three (student) (Engelmann & Colvin, 1983).

Teacher–student interactions can be either positive or negative, depending on whether a teacher is responding to acceptable or inappropriate student behavior. A useful guideline is to expect at least 80 to 85% of all interactions to be positive (Engelmann & Colvin, 1983).

Academic Engagement

Fewer behavior problems occur when students are fully engaged academically. To achieve *academic engagement* among students, a teacher must first secure and maintain students' attention. A teacher needs to stage instruction carefully to capture students' interest and to involve students systematically by actively engaging them in the structured lesson. A realistic expectation for classwide academic engagement (for example, paying attention to the teacher, participating in class discussions, or working independently) is at least 80% of allocated instructional time. Box 6.1 provides a definition of academic-engaged time (AET) and procedures for measuring it in the classroom. A stopwatch is used to record AET for individual students or for an entire classroom, in which case the class is treated as a single unit. In this procedure, the stopwatch is allowed to run whenever the student (or class) is displaying behavior corresponding to the definition. When the target student's behavior is not appropriate, the watch is stopped. When the student's behavior becomes appropriate again, the watch is restarted and allowed to run. At the end of the observation session, the time on the stopwatch (for example, 14 minutes) is divided by the length of the observation session (for example, 20 minutes) to calculate the percentage of AET (for example, $14 \div 20 = 0.7 \times 100 = 70\%$).

Box 6.1 Academic-Engaged Time: Definition and Recording Procedures

DEFINITION OF AET

AET means that the student is appropriately engaged in working on assigned academic material that is geared to his or her ability and skill levels. While academically engaged, the student may exhibit the following activities:

- Attending to the material and the task
- Making appropriate motor responses (for example, writing or computing)
- Asking for assistance (where appropriate) in an acceptable manner
- Interacting with the teacher or classmates about academic matters or listening to the teacher's instructions and directions.

Examples of actions that do not qualify as AET include the following:

- Not attending to or working on the assigned task
- Breaking classroom rules (for example, getting out of one's seat, talking out, disturbing others)
- Daydreaming

AET RECORDING INSTRUCTIONS

Step One. Select a seatwork period in which at least 15–20 minutes of class time has been allocated for independent work on an assigned academic task.

Step Two. Note the hour and minute that you begin observing, and record it.

Step Three. Record the amount of time the student displays behavior consistent with the definition. Let the stopwatch run when the student is academically engaged and turn it off when he or she is not. Restart it when the student is again academically engaged. Repeat this procedure throughout the recording interval.

Step Four. Record the time you stop.

Step Five. Compute the percentage of AET by dividing the time on the stopwatch by the total time observed and multiplying by 100.

Step Six. Record the data from two classroom observations.

Step Seven. Average the two AET observation sessions to obtain an overall AET score. You can do this by averaging the two AET times or by adding the stopwatch times for the two sessions and dividing by the total length of the two sessions.

Managing Student Errors

Correcting student errors is another important part of the instructional process. Error correction procedures need to be systematic, timely, and positive. A simple example is to make the student aware of an error, provide additional information on how to respond correctly, and then test the student on the same academic response or related material later.

Teachers should be highly sensitive to student error rates. A high error rate can mean the material is too difficult and the student may become frustrated. Conversely, a low error rate can mean the work is too easy and boredom may result. In either case, problem behavior may result and divert both teacher and student from a focus on academics.

Teachers also need to track carefully the kinds of errors students make. Analysis of errors and error patterns provides diagnostic information on teacher presentations, choice of examples, error-correction procedures, and rules that may need revision.

Errors provide information to teachers that the student needs more instruction. Unfortunately, teachers in this situation may conclude that the student needs easier work, which soon evolves into watered-down content, and the student loses ground with peers. By contrast, errors should signal that the student is not catching on and may require additional systematic instruction, such as structured practice, additional modeling, more carefully sequenced examples, or more supervision and monitoring before the student is left to practice alone.

Shaping Student Responses

Antisocial students often need to be prompted and encouraged to respond academically. Careful use of teacher attention and approval (for example, "excellent," "good work," "you're improving") can increase student productivity and participation. Use praise or other incentives to shape accuracy in responding. Frequent use of such reinforcement procedures is highly recommended for improving task completion, accuracy, and rate of responding (time to complete a task).

INTERVENING DURING INSTRUCTION

Teachers can prevent a number of problem behaviors by paying careful attention to the strategies just described for managing student behavior while providing academic instruction. In this section, we examine strategies for *intervening during instruction* to prevent problem behavior that may occur during the course of the school day.

Implement Classroom Expectations or Rules

In the first section, we recommended that teachers map out the expected behaviors they would like students to perform. In this section, we look at how to implement these expectations with all students, and especially antisocial ones.

As a first step, teachers should discuss and explain their behavioral expectations to the class. Teachers may wish to develop a set of questions and a script to facilitate class discussion of this topic (Safran & Safran, 1985). There should be opportunities for students to practice the rules via behavioral rehearsal, modeling, simulations, role plays, and other appropriate activities. The rules should be posted and referred to frequently. Students, in general, need reminders, prompts, and consistent feedback; antisocial students are particularly needy in this regard. Teachers should provide high rates of reinforcement to students who exhibit the expected behaviors; this is especially true early in the school year. These expectations should be reviewed on a regular basis thereafter.

Frequently Acknowledge Cooperative Students

Perhaps the most powerful strategy for implementing classroom expectations is to frequently reinforce students who exhibit appropriate behaviors. This procedure calls attention to the appropriate behavior and provides a model for the rest of the class. Whenever possible, acknowledge the positive, cooperative behavior of antisocial students. Sugai, Colvin, and Scott (1993) found very low rates of teacher reinforcement for expected student behavior in a typical middle school. Teachers should develop procedures or structures to remind themselves of the need to frequently look for students who are displaying the expected behaviors. Effective teachers typically use social reinforcers, such as smiles, nods, winks, physical proximity, physical contact (as appropriate), and verbal praise and acknowledgment to encourage and support appropriate student behavior (Alberto & Troutman, 1990).

The following procedures are helpful for reinforcing expected behavior:

- Watch for opportunities to praise students for their special efforts or for cooperative behavior. Teachers need to recognize students who show desirable behavior or approximations thereof. A simple scanning procedure, cued every 5 minutes or so by an audible signal from a watch, can prompt the teacher to search the classroom for a reinforceable example.

- Distinguish between praise for cooperation and praise for acquisition of academic skill. Both forms of achievement need to be equally acknowledged.

- Contact all students. Some students are more visible than others and naturally receive more teacher attention; a special effort is usually necessary to make contact with all students. In this manner, antisocial students may eventually learn that they have the same chance of receiving teacher attention through their positive, cooperative behavior as through their negative, inappropriate behavior.

Establish Consequences for Students Who Do Not Comply with Rules

A careful explanation of the importance of following classroom rules is always recommended; however, it is not sufficient, by itself, to ensure that the rules will be followed.

Teachers should communicate clearly to all class members that there will be positive consequences for following the rules. Negative sanctions for rule infractions should be avoided whenever possible (that is, use selective ignoring if the situation allows it), but sometimes their use is unavoidable. Sanctions such as time-out, response cost (loss of previously earned points), soft reprimands, or loss of privileges should simply be applied as warranted.

We recommend that a correction plan be designed, one that contains a series of steps in which the least intrusive step is used first and more intrusive measures come into play only if the problem behavior persists. For example:

1. Remove attention from the student who is displaying inappropriate behavior, and acknowledge other students nearby who are exhibiting the expected behavior.
2. Redirect the student to the expected behavior with a gesture or verbal prompt, cite the classroom rule being violated, and be sure to acknowledge subsequent cooperation and displays of expected behavior by the student.
3. Secure the student's attention and clearly inform him or her of the expected behavior, provide immediate opportunities for practice, and acknowledge the changed behavior when it occurs.
4. Deliver a brief warning by providing an opportunity for the student to choose between displaying the expected behavior and experiencing a penalty or loss of privilege.
5. Deliver the penalty or loss of privilege in a matter-of-fact manner (for example, time-out or loss of some recess time) and do not argue with the student about details of the penalty.

Establish a Classroom Entry Activity

An independent activity (for example, working on a math puzzle or copying outlines from the overhead) can be effective in settling students down as they come into class. These activities provide a focus for the students, assist them in getting organized, and provide an occasion for the teacher to prompt a task. These entry activities are particularly important when the lesson at hand involves some set-up time, such as in a less structured art class.

Keep Initial Explanations Brief

Teachers should keep in mind that lengthy explanations at the beginning of an academic lesson or task set the stage for inattentive and disruptive student behavior. The more promptly students engage in a structured activity, the less likely they are to problem behavior. If several pieces of information must be presented, they should be distributed over the instructional period. The skillful management of academic start-up activities and transitions between activities or periods will pay huge dividends in improving the quality and productivity of the instructional environment.

Secure the Attention of All Students before Beginning Explanations

In general, it is important to secure everyone's attention before beginning the explanation of a lesson; otherwise, students may learn that they do not need to listen and may come to rely on teacher redirections and repeated explanations in order to get up to speed. Classroom observations show that antisocial students have a higher than normal overall rate of appropriate initiations to the teacher, primarily because of their general inattentiveness and weak academic skills (Walker, Shinn, O'Neill, & Ramsey, 1987). Considerable amounts of teacher time and effort are needlessly invested in this management process. It is far better to obtain everyone's attention initially—prior to beginning the instructional process.

In order to gain students' attention initially, teachers should position themselves so they can see the faces of all their students and ensure that all students are looking at them. Some teachers use signals to gain students' attention; examples include the use of standard directions such as "Everyone listen," changes in voice volume, holding up one's hand, scanning the whole class and looking toward nonlistening students to get their attention, and acknowledging students who are attending. Sometimes, however, it may be necessary to get the class moving into an activity, then reinforce the cooperative students and redirect the students who are not engaged.

Catch Problems Early

Teachers need to act quickly at the onset of inappropriate behavior and immediately begin the appropriate correction procedures specified earlier. In this way (1) students learn that the teacher is serious about implementing the expected behaviors; (2) the behavior may be prevented from escalating; and (3) the procedure may prevent other students from joining in with the inappropriate behavior.

Teachers can maintain attentive student behavior by frequently scanning the whole class and not turning their backs to students for lengthy periods. As one expert has noted, the teacher "must have an automatic scanner going at all times" (Cummings, 1983, p. 65). If possible, other staff should be used to assist slower students or to keep the body of the class working in an independent activity so additional attention may be given to individual students.

Teachers should act quickly if students are engaging in activities that involve (1) misusing equipment, (2) threats to the safety of others, and (3) changing a prescribed activity. Cangelosi (1993) added an interesting dimension to catching problems early. He recommended that teachers should "deal with misbehavior well before 'they get to you'" (p. 203).

Algozzine (1993) refers to the teaching and management of students as war. He notes that "there are more of them than there are of you and they are better armed!" This metaphor, though greatly exaggerated, does have relevance in describing the daunting challenges with which teachers are confronted daily in educating classrooms of high-energy students.

The most effective strategies for quickly addressing problem behavior require directly attending to the students who are cooperative and academically engaged and redirecting those who are not. If further consequences are necessary, they should be delivered in a brief manner. *Remember not to lecture or give lengthy explanations.* In this process, teachers should simply state the rule infraction and the corresponding consequence or sanction that is associated with it.

Plan for Difficult Transitions

Transitions are probably the most common time for problem behavior to occur in most classrooms. Problems will often arise if these transitions are not carefully planned (Cangelosi, 1993; Cummings, 1983). Antisocial students have great difficulty with transitions between academic periods and activities. Transitions can be managed effectively by introducing intermediate steps, providing advance prompts and reminders, and reinforcing students who cooperate.

Teachers should frequently examine their instructional programs to identify difficult transitions and make the appropriate adjustments. Many problems arise from inadequate planning that results in students having to rush at the end of one activity and scramble to the next one. If students begin to get out of control or diverge significantly from a planned activity, consider introducing another independent activity (for example, students could be directed to write some responses in their workbooks). Once students have calmed down, teachers can resume the activity or move on to another one. Teachers should also have a set signal for stopping an activity, such as an arm raised or a verbal cue.

Use Direct Speech

Language should be kept as simple, respectful, and direct as possible. Teachers should avoid using questions that require an answer if they really want to give the student a direction. Also, long and lengthy explanations in the context of correcting a student may cause additional problem behavior.

Avoid Dead Time

Students need to know what they should be doing at all times; otherwise, they may generate their own activities. Except for planned downtime, students should be kept busy as much as possible.

It is helpful to have back-up or "sponge" activities readily available in case a lesson is completed before the end of a period. Alternative activities should also be ready for students who finish an activity early while others need extra assistance. As the name suggests, "sponge" activities can be used to engage students during transition times. These activities should be constructive and somewhat reinforcing; the students involved should require only minimal assistance while doing these activities.

Settle Students Down Near the End of Each Period

Teachers should have a planned routine to settle their students down before the end of a class period. Teachers appreciate colleagues who send students to other classes and activities in a calm rather than a rushed, agitated, or excited manner.

A standard exit routine for students in transition should be established between teachers. For example, after a special activity under the direction of another teacher, it should be clear whether the students' regular teacher will come to retrieve the class or whether the other teacher will supervise the returning students.

CONCLUSION

As the diversity of classrooms increases dramatically, teachers face accelerating pressures to teach and manage their students effectively. In addition, one of the many challenges teachers must address is the increasing complexity of the social-behavioral problems children and youth bring to school. Historically, we have used reactive and, in many cases, punitive measures to manage problem behavior in school. These strategies, although still widely used, are becoming less effective as the intractability of these problems increases and fiscal resources are being reduced. Whenever possible, teachers need to turn to more positive and proactive strategies that emphasize prevention.

In this chapter, we recommended the use of prevention procedures related to the design and proper functioning of the classroom environment. By systematically utilizing these strategies, students are provided with a stable, predictable environment that will generally facilitate desirable behavior and minimize problem behavior. We recognize that some students will be unresponsive to these proactive procedures that are applied to all students. In these instances, an optimally designed and operating classroom will be insufficient to maintain the adaptive behavior of antisocial students. It will be necessary to directly teach adaptive forms of behavior to these students. Chapter 7 describes procedures and guidelines for accomplishing this important task.

STUDY QUESTIONS

1. What are the major factors that, in combination, seriously challenge a teacher's ability to teach effectively?
2. What are the major reasons for providing students, especially antisocial students, with a high degree of classroom structure?
3. What are important guidelines for designing the physical arrangement of a classroom?
4. What are the major steps for establishing classroom expectations?
5. What is the relationship between academic engagement and problem behavior?
6. What are the major strategies teachers can use to manage problem behavior in the context of instruction, with the specific goal of continuing instruction and managing the behavior?

KEY TERMS

academic engagement
classroom challenges
classroom expectations
classroom structure
instructional delivery
intervening during instruction
physical arrangement

7 An Instructional Approach to Teaching Adaptive Behavior Patterns

Teaching Adaptive Behavior

Instructional Steps for Teaching Adaptive Behavior
Application of a Behavior-Instruction Plan

Pre-Correction: Anticipating Problem Behavior

Pre-Correction Procedures
Application of Pre-Correction Procedures

Conclusion

Strategies for managing problem behavior in the classroom are increasingly emphasizing *directly teaching* adaptive behavior patterns (Colvin & Sugai, 1988; Cummings, 1983; Evertson, Emmer, Clements, Sanford, & Worsham, 1984; Kameenui & Darch, in press; Sprick, 1985). A basic assumption underlying this trend is that many students, particularly at-risk students, have not learned the essential competencies required for school success (see Hersh & Walker, 1983; Walker, 1986). These students exhibit critically important competencies at such a low rate that they do not access the usual positive consequences associated with school success.

Cotton (1990) argues persuasively that effective classroom management, especially in the early grades and for students from lower socioeconomic backgrounds, is much more an *instructional* than a *disciplinary* enterprise. The purpose of this chapter is to make the case that the same procedures used for delivering instruction can and should be applied in providing *behavior instruction* that supports school success. We describe two procedures for teaching such adaptive behavior: instructional steps for teaching adaptive behavior and pre-correction strategies for anticipating problem behavior.

TEACHING ADAPTIVE BEHAVIOR

A broad range of *instructional steps* can be considered for teaching adaptive forms of student behavior. In this section, we describe eight steps for teaching adaptive behavior and provide an illustration of a behavior-instruction plan.

Instructional Steps for Teaching Adaptive Behavior

The eight steps for teaching adaptive behavior are listed here and described in this section:

Step 1: Specify expected behaviors

Step 2: Identify explanation times and procedures

Step 3: Identify practice times and procedures

Step 4: Specify reminder times and procedures

Step 5: Identify reinforcement procedures and contingencies

Step 6: Decide on correction procedures

Step 7: Identify feedback times and procedures

Step 8: Design student monitoring and review procedures

Step 1: Specify Expected Behavior

In this initial step, teachers identify the expected behaviors they want students to demonstrate in the classroom. Typically, these are the classroom behaviors that support academic performance and reflect teacher expectations of all students. Common expectations include following directions, coming to class prepared, doing your best work, cooperating with each other, and making assistance needs known appropriately.

Teacher directly teaching adaptive behavior patterns to one of her students.
Gale Zucker

Step 2: Identify Explanation Times and Procedures

Teachers should involve all students in a group discussion and development of classroom rules that reflect teacher expectations and that students regard as fair and reasonable (Algozzine & Ysseldyke, 1992; Smith & Misra, 1992). The teacher should also specify the overall goals that provide the direction or focus for the behavioral expectations (for example, "We are here to improve math skills. What do we have to do as a class to make sure we learn math?"). In this step, the teacher earmarks available discussion times and guides the discussion as appropriate.

Step 3: Identify Practice Times and Procedures

Teachers should provide regular practice opportunities for their students to facilitate skill acquisition, behavioral mastery, and maintenance. Given that most teachers want students to exhibit adaptive forms of behavior as fluently as possible, practice opportunities should be provided frequently. Teachers can use techniques such as role-plays, behavioral rehearsals, and simulations for this purpose. The times and purpose of these practice activities should be clearly identified and described.

Step 4: Specify Reminder Times and Procedures

Effective classroom managers frequently remind students of classroom expectations (Brophy, 1986; Doyle, 1989). Such reminders are more effective if they are presented to students before, rather than after, they have had a chance to exhibit inappropriate behavior.

Step 5: Identify Reinforcement Procedures and Contingencies

A fundamental law of learning is that behavior is more likely to be repeated if it is reinforced. *One of the most critical mistakes made in classroom management is to take appropriate student behavior for granted.* Under these conditions, students will quickly learn that inappropriate behavior gets teacher attention and appropriate behavior is ignored. Instead, students need to learn that appropriate behavior is just as likely to earn prompt teacher attention or approval as behavior that violates classroom rules and teacher expectations.

Antisocial students have usually experienced an unfortunate learning history in this regard. Because of their high levels of aggression and skillful use of coercive tactics to manipulate and force the submission of others, antisocial students can generate a rich schedule of attention (albeit mostly negative attention) from their teachers, peers, and parents. This process gives antisocial students temporary control (and dominance) over many situations involving these social agents. While such control provides short-term rewards, it usually leads to severe long-term costs in the form of teacher, peer, and sometimes parental rejection.

Our experience has been that most antisocial students will respond positively to an instructional approach to behavior change that is applied completely and correctly, monitored carefully, and revised or fine-tuned as needed. However, it is important to note that behavioral gains achieved in the classroom will not automatically transfer to other school settings unless procedures are in place to prompt and support such transfer (Morgan & Jenson, 1988). School and home rewards to support student behavior also need to be arranged and implemented.

Typically, regular teachers make use of three types of *behavioral incentives* to motivate students: *social reinforcers* (praise, teacher acknowledgment or student recognition, displays of student work, positive facial expressions), *tangibles* (stickers, cards, tokens, points, and other preferred items), and *privileges* (extra time at the computer, reading, special projects, free time, and approved break activities). An array of rewards should be selected, and the conditions or contingencies under which they are to be delivered at school or home should be clearly specified. Finally, the reinforcement system should be carefully explained to all students.

Step 6: Decide on Correction Procedures

Just as teachers are quick to provide assistance in order to correct student errors during instruction, they also need to be ready to correct problem behavior promptly. A *correction procedure* is purely functional; that is, the correction is judged to be successful if the student exhibits appropriate behavior instead of inappropriate behavior at the next opportunity to respond. Teachers should have a planned strategy for correcting problem behavior. Unless the inappropriate behavior is serious, the first step in correcting inappropriate behavior should be directly acknowledging nearby students who are exhibiting the expected behaviors.

Step 7: Identify Feedback Times and Procedures

At the close of a lesson or period, teachers generally provide students with feedback about their performance. Similarly, teachers should let their students know how they did on the expected behaviors and provide social reinforcers or privileges as indicated. If the students in question exhibited the expected behaviors at unacceptable levels, the teacher should debrief with them, make suggestions for improvement, and provide encouragement for the next period.

Step 8: Design Student Monitoring and Review Procedures

Skilled teachers usually have some way of assessing skill acquisition in the subject areas they teach. Typically, they use informal methods for determining whether their students are catching on and more formal methods for assessing mastery at the end of an instructional unit. Similarly, teachers need to know how their students are performing on the expected behaviors daily as well as over more extended time periods. These monitoring systems need to be simple and should take as little time as possible. Checklists, simple frequency counts, time samples, stopwatches, and informal judgments can be used for this purpose. In some cases, it is appropriate to assign data collection tasks to the students themselves. Teachers should develop a workable monitoring system, specify implementation procedures to support it, and review times and procedures as necessary. Curriculum-based measurement procedures are highly recommended for this purpose (Shapiro, 1989; Shinn, 1989).

Application of a Behavior-Instruction Plan

The eight steps involved in teaching social behavior are illustrated in the behavior-instruction plan in Form 7.1. A seventh grade teacher wanted to teach her students to bring all necessary materials to class. An eight-step behavior-instruction plan was developed to teach the target behavior of "coming to class organized and prepared" (Colvin, Braun, DeForest, & Wilt, 1993). Behavior-instruction plans of this type are highly recommended for teaching specific forms of adaptive social behavior.

PRE-CORRECTION: ANTICIPATING PROBLEM BEHAVIOR

Students inevitably make errors even though teachers typically use a number of effective instructional practices. Correction procedures are usually applied to help students make correct responses after they have made errors. However, if the teacher anticipates errors, *pre-correction procedures* can be used to make adjustments before the students have a chance to respond inappropriately. For example, if students are required to read a paragraph containing two or three difficult words, the teacher may preteach those words first and then have the students read the passage. This technique is known as *pre-correction* (Kameenui & Simmons, 1990).

This same strategy for anticipating errors can be applied to social behavior. If a teacher anticipates the likely occurrence of problem behavior, strategies can be applied *before* the students in question have a chance to respond inappropriately. For example, the teacher might suspect that students will return from the gymnasium and enter the classroom in a noisy manner. In this situation, the teacher could remind them before they go to the gymnasium, meet them at the door, and have an entry task ready for them upon entering the classroom. In this way, the teacher anticipates problematic behavior and makes some adjustments beforehand. This strategy of making adjustments beforehand, based on anticipated or predictable problem behavior, is highly recommended for reducing the likelihood of having to respond *reactively* to inappropriate student behavior after the fact (Colvin, Sugai, & Patching, 1993). In this section, we describe the necessary procedural steps for developing a pre-correction plan and provide illustrative applications of a pre-correction plan.

Pre-Correction Procedures

The seven steps of a pre-correction plan are listed here and described in this section:

Step 1: Identify the context and the likely problem behavior

Step 2: Specify expected behaviors

Step 3: Systematically modify the context

Step 4: Conduct behavioral rehearsals

Step 5: Provide strong reinforcement for expected behaviors

Step One: Expected Behaviors

Bring necessary supplies (notebook, pencil sharpener, homework, textbook)

Materials to be in reasonable shape

Notebook organized

Step Two: Explanation Times and Procedures

Time: First opportunity at the beginning of the first class

Explain purpose as related to school success. Supply list described, notebook organization described. Letter of explanation sent to parents.

Step Three: Practice Times and Procedures

Time: First class and twice weekly for three weeks (Monday and Thursday), once weekly for the term (Monday)

Positive and negative examples presented. Discussion, training time allocated for notebook organization.

Step Four: Reminder Times and Procedures

Verbal reminders twice weekly at the end of the period for the next period.

Self-check sheet developed for each student. Chart developed by students and posted on notice board.

Step Five: Reinforcement Procedures and Contingencies

Verbal praise to acknowledge students prepared for class.

Distribution of reward stars. If 80% of class prepared, free time allocated for the last 10 minutes of class.

Step Six: Correction Procedures

Provide verbal praise to students prepared. Remind students not prepared. Provide warning for second occurrence and loss of break time for third occurrence.

Step Seven: Feedback Times and Procedures

Use chart to provide feedback at the beginning of the period on how well class was prepared.

Step Eight: Monitoring and Review Procedures

Use of chart (frequency count of number of students prepared for class).

Raised criteria for class reward to 90% after three weeks. Chatted with two students who were consistently unprepared to provide encouragement and help. Sent results to parents and principal.

FORM 7.1 Illustration of a Completed Behavior-Instruction Plan: Coming to Class Prepared

Step 6: Prompt expected behaviors

Step 7: Monitor the plan

Step 1: Identify the Context and the Likely Problem Behavior

The context for a particular problem behavior can be an event, task, condition, setting, or circumstance. Both formal and informal methods can be used to identify situations that seem to reliably elicit inappropriate student behavior.

Informal methods include simple observation and recall. For example, a teacher might notice that students are very noisy when they return from recess and it takes some time for them to settle down as they reenter the classroom. The context would be the transition from recess to class, and the target behavior would be the noisy entry of students and their initial off-task or disruptive behavior.

Formal methods are designed to obtain more precise information. For example, through direct observations, accompanied by procedures for the functional analysis of behavioral and environmental events, a trained observer notes each student's behavior and records the corresponding antecedent (prior) and consequent (following) events surrounding the target behavior (Sugai & Colvin, 1989; Wolery, Bailey, & Sugai, 1988). A typical situation in which these procedures are applied follows: The teacher uses class discussion to have students answer the first three questions from a history book. The teacher then says,"I want you to finish the remainder of the questions by yourself. So everyone do questions 4 through 20 in your workbook, please." After a few seconds, Tommy looks around and makes a face at Mary. Mary grins. Tommy then calls out, "Boy, this is boring! Why can't we do something that's fun?" Some students, including Mary, laugh and the teacher says, "Tommy, you need to finish the assignment. Please begin your work now."

A functional analysis of this situation suggests that Tommy's off-task behavior is tied to an independent-work situation. This analysis might also show that peer attention reinforces and supports his inappropriate behavior (that is, gaining the teacher's attention in an unacceptable manner). Repeated observations conducted over multiple occasions may be necessary to confirm these initial judgments.

Step 2: Specify Expected Behaviors

When students exhibit inappropriate behaviors in a given classroom context, the adaptive *replacement* behaviors for that context also need to be clearly specified (Brophy, 1983; Sprick, 1985; White & Haring, 1980). For example, if Fernando talks out to get teacher assistance during independent work, the replacement behavior could be to raise his hand. If JoAnn interrupts others during class discussions, the replacement behavior might be to wait before speaking or to allow others to finish talking before speaking out. A number of recommended guidelines for selecting such expected replacement behaviors follow:

1. Describe the expected replacement behavior in *observable* terms (for example, raise your hand if you wish to speak).

2. Select behaviors that are *incompatible* with the problem behavior (for example, wait your turn instead of interrupting) (Engelmann & Colvin, 1983; Evans & Meyer, 1985; Horner & Billingsley, 1988).
3. Select behaviors that are *functional replacements* for the problem behavior (for example, staying on-task—replacement behavior—results in positive teacher attention) (Carr & Durand, 1985).

Step 3: Systematically Modify the Context

The purpose of modifying the context in which problem behavior occurs is to increase the likelihood that the expected replacement behaviors will emerge and persist. Numerous dimensions of the behavioral context can be modified (for example, instructions, explanations, tasks, activities, scheduling, seating arrangements, reminders, and curriculum). Modification of these factors should be based on findings from a prior functional analysis and should be carried out in as normal and unobtrusive a manner as possible. For example, given that Sally disrupts Harry, the context could be modified by simply changing the seating arrangements, or by giving Sally (or Harry) a specific task (collecting homework, taking attendance) to do upon entering the classroom.

If substantial contextual changes must be made, a systematic plan should be developed to move students back from the restricted or modified context and toward the original or normal context. For example, if Jaime disrupts large-group instruction, it may be necessary to have him participate in small-group work on a restricted basis (for example, either with one or two other students or for shorter periods of time). The level of restriction should be reduced as Jaime begins to exhibit the expected behaviors in large-group work. The number of students in the group and the length of group instruction should be increased gradually as his performance allows.

Step 4: Conduct Behavioral Rehearsals

Once a student enters a classroom context in which problem behavior is likely to occur, the use of behavioral rehearsals should be conducted to prevent its occurrence. Essentially, behavioral rehearsals involve presenting target students with some type of training in the expected behaviors just before they enter the target context, if at all possible (Engelmann & Colvin, 1983; Sugai & Tindal, 1993). This training may take several forms, such as having the students recall, read, or demonstrate the expected behaviors to the teacher. In some cases, it may be necessary to have the students relearn and practice the expected behaviors beforehand. For example, if Sarah tends to interrupt other students during group instruction, the teacher can catch her just before the session begins and say, "Now remember, Sarah, please wait until someone is finished before you speak. Now tell me what you will do if you wish to speak." The assumption is that she will be more likely to remember and perform the expected target behaviors if prompted just before entering the target context.

Step 5: Provide Strong Reinforcement for Expected Behaviors

Students frequently have a long history of exhibiting inappropriate behavior in the target context. Because of this powerful learning history, it may be difficult to replace an established behavior pattern with a new one. In other words, the new behavior will be in competition with the old inappropriate behavior, which has been reinforced intermittently over time (Horner & Billingsley, 1988). Thus, in order to replace this well-established behavior pattern, strong reinforcement (that is, frequent and of high magnitude) must be provided for the target or replacement behaviors.

Step 6: Prompt Expected Behavior

Although a specific target behavior may have been rehearsed and carefully reinforced, students still may exhibit problematic behaviors in the target context. One reason for this may be that the pretraining or behavioral rehearsal was conducted outside the target context. Teachers need to be *very* sensitive to antisocial students who find it difficult to exhibit the expected target behaviors. This is especially true in new contexts or in situations where competing responses have been successful in the past. The following procedures are designed to provide additional assistance to such students:

1. Acknowledge target students *immediately* when they exhibit the expected behaviors. For example, the teacher may say, "I appreciate the way you are raising your hand," or "Minh, I like the way you're getting ready for the math assignment."
2. Provide reminders of expected behaviors as part of directions given in an instructional lesson. For example, in a geography lesson on capital cities, the teacher might say, "Could someone raise his or her hand and tell me the capital city of Australia?" Students who reply correctly should be given immediate and positive acknowledgment.
3. Should the predictable inappropriate behaviors occur, use the following correction procedures:
   a. *First occurrence*: Ignore the first occurrence of the inappropriate behavior. If the student talks out, the teacher should continue with instruction and attend to other students who are on-task or are exhibiting the expected behaviors.
   b. *Second occurrence*: Provide a two-part signal for the second occurrence of the problem target behavior. For example, if the student talks out again (which is likely), the teacher (1) puts a finger to her or his lips to signal not talking out and (2) raises his or her hand to model the expected behavior. The teacher then provides immediate approval when the student complies and demonstrates the expected behavior.
   c. *Third occurrence*: Present a verbal warning for the third occurrence of the inappropriate behavior. The warning is presented in the form of a decision or choice to be made by the student. For example, the teacher says, "Jimmy, you need to raise your hand to speak or you will have to leave the group [or some other penalty]." It is imperative to provide choices that are familiar to the student and are logical and fair, and to follow through on the choice the student makes.

Step 7: Monitor the Plan

A monitoring procedure needs to be developed and implemented in order to ensure ongoing supervision and evaluation of a behavior-instruction program. A complete monitoring plan consists of at least two parts. The first part is a checklist that contains a description of what the teacher will do at each of the seven steps of the pre-correction procedure. When first learning or implementing this procedure, teachers may find it helpful to use the checklist as a prompt or script. Later, a teacher's aide or second teacher can use the checklist to see that the plan is being implemented accurately, consistently, and completely.

The second part of the monitoring plan provides a record of the student's performance (that is, frequency counts of expected and problem behaviors). Data should be collected on a regular basis to determine whether the procedure is effective in reducing the problem behavior and increasing the expected behavior. The complete seven-step procedure can be converted into a checklist that is useful for structuring staff meetings focused on dealing with the problem behaviors. It can also be used as an outline for development of a behavior intervention plan.

Application of Pre-Correction Procedures

Dominic is a fifth grade student who tends to come into class very noisily. He takes considerable time to settle down and becomes agitated when the teacher attempts to direct him to sit down and begin his schoolwork. A seven-step pre-correction plan for Dominic is illustrated in Form 7.2.

CONCLUSION

Many students in today's public schools exhibit problem behavior at unacceptably high rates. A constructive interpretation of this situation suggests that these students have not learned the appropriate target behaviors or social competencies required for school success. The remedy for this situation is to provide such students with systematic instruction in these adaptive behaviors, to use pre-correction procedures as appropriate, and to assist them with their behavioral mastery. We have presented an instructional model for teaching adaptive behavior. Once students learn these adaptive social behaviors and become fluent in their use, they are in a stronger position to experience both social and academic success in school.

Chapter 8 extends this basic approach to managing the antisocial student's social behavior on the playground. Antisocial students typically have a higher than normal rate of rule infractions on the playground and tend to display high levels of negative-aggressive behavior directed toward peers. Behavior problems of antisocial students are most difficult to manage in the unstructured context of the playground during ongoing recess activities. Accomplishing this task successfully requires careful monitoring, direct teaching, coaching, and prompting, as well as the use of both positive and negative sanctions.

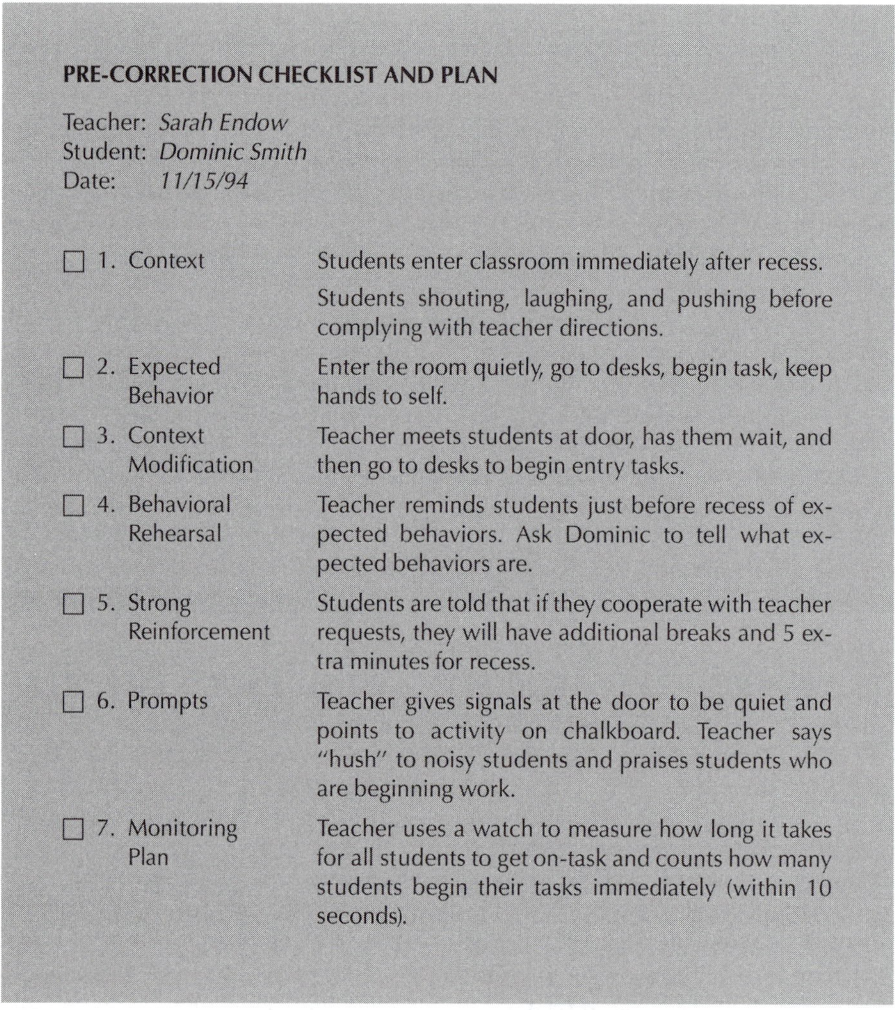

PRE-CORRECTION CHECKLIST AND PLAN

Teacher: *Sarah Endow*
Student: *Dominic Smith*
Date: *11/15/94*

☐ 1. Context	Students enter classroom immediately after recess. Students shouting, laughing, and pushing before complying with teacher directions.
☐ 2. Expected Behavior	Enter the room quietly, go to desks, begin task, keep hands to self.
☐ 3. Context Modification	Teacher meets students at door, has them wait, and then go to desks to begin entry tasks.
☐ 4. Behavioral Rehearsal	Teacher reminds students just before recess of expected behaviors. Ask Dominic to tell what expected behaviors are.
☐ 5. Strong Reinforcement	Students are told that if they cooperate with teacher requests, they will have additional breaks and 5 extra minutes for recess.
☐ 6. Prompts	Teacher gives signals at the door to be quiet and points to activity on chalkboard. Teacher says "hush" to noisy students and praises students who are beginning work.
☐ 7. Monitoring Plan	Teacher uses a watch to measure how long it takes for all students to get on-task and counts how many students begin their tasks immediately (within 10 seconds).

FORM 7.2 A Pre-Correction Checklist and Plan for Dominic

STUDY QUESTIONS

1. What is the rationale for using instructional procedures to teach social behavior and to remediate serious antisocial behavior?
2. What are the critical steps in an instructional plan for teaching social behavior?
3. Why is the "practice" step so important in teaching social or adaptive behavior?

4. Why do teachers often omit the step of providing incentive procedures for demonstrations of acceptable behavior in the classroom? Why is this step so critical?
5. What are the critical outcomes in the design of correction procedures?
6. How is pre-correction different from traditional correction procedures?
7. What are the major steps in a pre-correction plan?

KEY TERMS

behavioral incentives
behavior instruction
correction procedures
instructional steps
pre-correction procedures

8 Instructing and Managing the Antisocial Student on the Playground

Bullying by Antisocial Students and Resulting Peer Reactions

Playground Situations That Are Particularly Difficult for Antisocial Students

Generic Strategies and Procedures for Preventing and Remediating Negative-Aggressive Behavior and Rule Infractions on the Playground

Teaching Normative Standards
Teaching Adaptive Strategies for Specific Social Situations
Teaching Generic Social Skills
Teaching Anger Management and Conflict-Resolution Strategies

RECESS: A Comprehensive Intervention for Aggressive Behavior

Conclusion

Recommended Resources for Use in Addressing Teasing, Bullying, and Negative-Aggressive Forms of Student Behavior

How *not* to join a playground activity in progress. *Elizabeth Crews*

Antisocial students have their most difficult adjustment problems on the playground, where adult supervision and monitoring are weakest. Adults have little to say or do about what happens among peers in this setting. Only the most obvious behavioral examples of abuse, conflict, humiliation, and hostile social exchanges normally come to the attention of adult playground supervisors. Teasing, bullying, intimidation, and even humiliation are common occurrences, and antisocial students are often at the core of these unpleasant and unfortunate circumstances. To make matters worse, many teachers are able to avoid playground duty; thus leaving this important task to untrained personnel who are ill equipped to deal with the severe behavioral challenges that commonly occur in this setting.

Collectively, the authors of this book have spent hundreds of hours observing the playground behavior of antisocial, aggressive students and supervising implementation of intervention programs designed to change or improve it. The relatively unstructured nature of this setting, combined with low levels of adult monitoring and supervision, provide a fertile breeding ground for *peer conflict*. As a rule, antisocial students require structure in order to manage and control the aversive and impulsive features of their

TABLE 8.1 Playground Social Behavior: Means and Standard Deviations for Playground-Code Categories by Student Group

Playground Social Behavior Dependent Variable	EXTERNALIZERS (N = 73)		INTERNALIZERS (N = 76)		NORMAL STUDENTS (N = 152)	
	$\bar{X}$	SD	$\bar{X}$	SD	$\bar{X}$	SD
1. Social engagement (SE)	30.1	16.8	27.4[b]	13.1	35.1	15.3
2. Social involvement (SI)	32.9[a,c]	15.6	43.9	15.3	40.9	16.2
3. Participation (P)	22.6[a,c]	28.7	7.4	16.1	14.2	22.6
4. Parallel play (PLP)	5.8[c]	7.5	10.7[b]	10.6	4.9	7.5
5. Alone (A)	6.1[a]	8.3	8.6[b]	10.0	3.5	5.5
6. No codable response	1.5	1.7	1.7	3.6	1.3	2.0
7. Total negative behavior	6.0[a,c]	7.9	1.8	4.2	1.9	5.6

[a]Externalizers vs. unranked students $p < .05$.
[b]Internalizers vs. unranked students $p < .05$.
[c]Externalizers vs. internalizers $p < .05$.

behavior. Thus, the playground is an especially difficult setting for them in which to display and maintain self-control, cooperative overtures to others, and positive social behavior.

The profile of antisocial students that emerges from studies of their social behavior on the playground is characterized by coercion, conflict, playground rule infractions, and instrumental as well as reactive forms of aggression. Table 8.1 profiles the playground behavior of elementary school students representing the following three types of behavior patterns: (1) *externalizing* behavior, (2) *internalizing* behavior, and (3) "normal" behavior patterns.

These behavioral profiles were generated through the national standardization process for the Systematic Screening for Behavior Disorders (SSBD) screening–identification procedure developed by Walker and Severson (1990). Playground observations were recorded on a large sample of students in the primary and intermediate grades, representing 20 school districts and 10 states. Teacher rankings and ratings were used to assign students in their classrooms to externalizing, internalizing, and "normal" groups based on standardized behavioral definitions and descriptions provided to each participating teacher. Externalizers exhibited acting-out, aggressive, and antisocial behavior patterns; internalizers represented socially isolated, avoidant, depressed, and phobic students; normal (average) students were judged to represent the entire class as indicated by teacher nominations.

These students were observed during regular playground activities in the absence of any interventions. The authors and the professionally trained observers were blind as to the group designation of the target students. During each 10-second interval, the observer coded one of the following six categories that best represented the student's behavior during that interval: social engagement, social involvement, participation, parallel play, alone, and no codable response. The first three categories could be coded as either positive (+) or negative (−), while the remaining three were coded with a slash if they occurred. *Social engagement* is coded to capture free-play exchanges among peers in which the target student engages in verbal behavior; social involvement is coded when the target student exhibits nonverbal, peer-related social behavior; participation refers to involvement in structured games and activities with identifiable rules; parallel play means that two students are engaged in the same activity within close proximity but are not communicating or interacting with each other; alone means the target student is socially isolated and not interacting with anyone; and no code means the student is doing something (for example, talking with an adult) that cannot be recorded with the coding system being used.

Inspection of Table 8.1 indicates that externalizers had a far less favorable social-behavioral profile than either internalizers or normal students. They had much higher than normal rates of negative social behavior directed toward peers, and they spent less time socially engaged than normal students, primarily due to their aversive behavioral characteristics. Internalizers, in contrast, had very low levels of negative social behavior but spent substantially more time alone and in parallel play than did either externalizers or normals. Across these code categories, the normal students appeared to have relatively positive and adaptive behavioral profiles on the playground.

It is remarkable to note just how positive the social behavior of "normal" peers is at recess (see behavioral profile for normal students in Table 8.1). In spite of the lack of structure in most playground settings, most children are, as a rule, quite positive with each other—that is, except those who fit the profile of the antisocial, aggressive student. This is one major reason why the social behavior of antisocial students has such salience in free-play settings—it stands in stark contrast to what is normal for this situation.

These observations do not completely characterize the playground behavior of antisocial students because the sample of externalizers included other, related behavior problems and disorders (that is, acting-out, at-risk, hyperactive, and disruptive students). However, the observations provide a useful context for comparing the social behavior of students in these settings who consistently violate consensual social norms with those who subscribe to them. The importance of positively influencing the playground social behavior of antisocial students cannot be overemphasized.

Peer-related social adjustment is determined primarily by the social exchanges and impressions that occur among peers within unstructured, free-play settings at school. Antisocial students are severely at risk in this regard. Carefully conducted empirical research indicates that antisocial students have high rates of aggressive behavior at recess and in other unstructured school and nonschool settings (see Cicchetti & Nurcombe, 1993; Kazdin, 1985, 1987; Pepler & Rubin, 1991). Furthermore, this evidence indicates that they develop negative reputations among their peers that persist long after their antisocial behavior has improved (Hollinger, 1987).

This chapter focuses, in considerable detail, on the playground social behavior of antisocial, highly aggressive students in elementary grades. Topics covered include (1) the bullying behavior of antisocial students, associated peer reactions to bullying, and discussion of the structure of best-practice interventions for dealing with the resulting conflicts; (2) playground situations that are particularly difficult for antisocial students; (3) generic strategies and procedures for preventing the occurrence of teasing, bullying, negative-aggressive behavior and playground rule infractions; and (4) key features of a comprehensive intervention program for remediating aggressive behavior on playgrounds.

BULLYING BY ANTISOCIAL STUDENTS AND RESULTING PEER REACTIONS

One of the behavioral tendencies that seems to be characteristic of antisocial students is *bullying*. It is a form of highly aggressive behavior that involves coercion, intimidation, and threats to one's safety or well-being. Bullying can involve one-on-one situations but more often involves intimidation of a single individual by a hostile group of peers. An estimated 160,000 students miss school each day due to the fear of being bullied (Lee, 1993).

Mean-spirited *teasing* is often a precursor to bullying, which is more likely to occur if the person being teased overtly reacts to the teasing (that is, counterteases, gets angry, or shows obvious fear). Because of their tendency to affiliate with others who share their deviant behavioral characteristics, antisocial students are more likely to find themselves in school situations that prompt such teasing and bullying (for example, associating with other antisocial students on the playground and ganging up on single peers).

Studies of bullying in European and U.S. schools indicate that bullying is more prevalent in this country, perhaps due to our increasing cultural acceptance of violence as an expected, normative form of behavior (Hoover & Juul, 1993; Shelly, 1985). Studies of bullying in Scandinavian schools indicate that between 5 and 9% of school-age students are regularly bullied before, during, and after school; about the same proportion of the school-age population acts as perpetrators of bullying (Munthe, 1989; Olweus, 1987).

Shelly (1985) found that approximately 80% of high school students and 90% of elementary and middle school students in the United States reported that they had been bullied at some point in school. The advent of gangs both on and off school grounds provides an ominous new dimension to the historic problems of bullies and bullying. A significant number of students who bring weapons to school do so because they feel they need them for protection. Many schools have become trading centers for the exchange and sale of weapons; most of the student body is usually aware of these activities. Students frequently believe that school officials and other adults cannot adequately protect them from bullying and the specter of gang victimization; in many cases, they are right. Thus, the behavioral interactions that occur between antisocial and non-antisocial students under adult supervision (for example, in the classroom) are mediated and strongly affected by what has occurred or may occur between them in unsupervised situations where adults are not present. It is important for school staff and parents to be aware of such constraints in the ongoing peer relations of children and youth.

A student can play one of three roles in a bullying situation: victim, nonparticipant, or perpetrator. Antisocial students are rarely victims of bullying. Although victimization does happen to them occasionally, they are much more likely to be actively involved in the bullying of others. The preferred role for most children and youth is avoidance of bullying (that is, as a nonparticipant). However, being a nonparticipant or a victim is often not a choice that one can voluntarily make. Students who have a disability or who have unusual attributes (for example, having thick glasses, strange names, atypical dress, being shy and timid, or appearing "nerdlike") are especially vulnerable as targets of teasing and bullying. Bullying that occurs in the context of gang activity seems to operate in a more random fashion in which the victims are often selected by chance and circumstance.

The safety of both students and teachers is an issue that has assumed paramount importance in our society within the past decade. One of the strongest fears that parents have about their children in school is the fear for their children's safety. There is a growing and alarming concern among both educators and parents regarding school safety; these concerns are exacerbated by the high rate of injuries suffered by students during recess. Thompson (1991), for example, reported that more than 170,000 children are injured annually on the playgrounds of U.S. schools, a total that includes accidents.

Students are not the only victims of intimidation, threats, and bullying in many of our schools. The U.S. government continues to invest millions of dollars annually in trying to control threats to the safety of teachers and other support staff. Passage of the National School Safety Act of 1994 is an attempt to redress this issue. Unstructured and lightly supervised areas of the school (for example, playgrounds) are especially problematic in protecting the security of school staff. Many schools have had to resort to using electronic communication devices and video cameras in order to monitor low-traffic areas. The dollar costs of these security systems run into the hundreds of millions annually.

High rates of bullying in a school are often a precursor to violence and should be a red-flag indicator that immediate and drastic actions need to be taken to reduce them. A schoolwide approach, involving parents whenever possible, is the best answer to coping with this problem. The student body must also be directly involved in developing workable solutions to this problem. Gagnon (1991) argues persuasively that *the* most important ingredient in effective interventions for bullying is to directly involve all parties in the solution (that is, teachers, students, parents, and neighborhood or community). A positive school climate in which mutual respect exists between students and staff and where there is a strong feeling of cohesion, inclusion, and fairness constitutes a powerful preventive force against bullying. Creating a schoolwide awareness of the problem of bullying and developing and enforcing rules, limits, and sanctions against it are also extremely important measures.

Olweus (1991) conducted the seminal work to date in developing effective interventions against bullying in schools. His universal interventions designed to reduce bullying in schools have produced substantial reductions in rates of both being bullied and bullying others; these results have been replicated for boys and girls and across school sites. His interventions for bullying are based on the following key principles:

- It is important to create a school (and home) environment that is characterized by warmth, positive social interest, and involvement from adults *but that sets firm limits for unacceptable behavior.*
- When violations of these limits occur, then nonhostile, nonphysical sanctions should be consistently applied.
- Careful monitoring and surveillance of student activities should occur within and outside the school.
- Adults should act as responsible authorities during all adult–child interactions, and especially when bullying occurs.

Olweus used these general principles to develop specific intervention techniques for addressing bullying at school, classroom, and individual levels. He argues that two important prerequisites for determining the effectiveness of these intervention components are awareness and involvement; that is, all parties (teachers, parents, and students) must assume ownership for the problem of bullying and for developing workable solutions to it.

Table 8.2 presents the intervention components developed by Olweus for use at school, classroom, and individual levels. This is a universal intervention for bullying that requires the complete involvement of the entire school and the development of ongoing working relationships with parents. However, it is likely that some antisocial, aggressive students will require intensive, selected interventions in order to bring their bullying and mean-spirited teasing under control and into the normal range of expected behavior. Some highly recommended resources for preventing and intervening with bullying are listed at the end of this chapter.

Antisocial students, particularly those in middle school and high school, are often key perpetrators of actions that threaten the safety of peers and adults in school. However, their investment in this behavior pattern begins much earlier, as they enter school, and escalates through negative social behavior, teasing, and bullying to levels of intensity where it is perceived as a threat to the safety and well-being of others. When this occurs, antisocial students are at risk for suspension and permanent expulsion from school; placement on home-tutoring regimens; and assignment to specialized settings such as day treatment, alternative schools, or residential-care facilities.

Antisocial students can generally be expected to receive the same kind of treatment they administer to others and also to be socially avoided whenever possible. Both the short- and long-term costs of such *social reciprocity* are generally severe for the antisocial student. Our observations of antisocial students and their interactions with non-antisocial peers in free-play settings, such as recess, indicate that (1) their levels of positive social behavior are approximately equal to or slightly below those of peers, (2) their levels of negative-aggressive social behavior are substantially higher than those of peers, and (3) the levels of positive and negative social behavior directed toward peers by antisocial students are perfectly matched by the behavioral reactions and social behavior directed toward them by peers. For example, Walker and his colleagues systematically observed the playground social behavior of a sample of antisocial (N = 39) and at-risk control (N = 41) students when

TABLE 8.2 Olweus Program Components for Bullying at School, Class, and Individual Levels

School Level	*Class Level*	*Individual Level*
• School conference day on bully/victim problems • Better supervision of recess • More attractive school playground • Contact telephone • Meeting staff—parents • Teacher groups for the development of the "school climate" • Parent circles (study and discussion groups)	• Class rules against bullying: clarification, praise, and sanctions • Regular class meetings • Cooperative learning • Meeting teacher—parents/children • Common, positive activities • Role playing • Literature	• Serious talks with bullies and victims • Serious talks with parents of involved children • Teacher use of imagination • Help from neutral students • Advice to parents (parent brochure) • Discussion groups with parents of bullies and victims • Change of class or school

Source: From "Bully/Victim Problems among School Children: Basic Facts and Effects of a School-Based Intervention Program," by D. Olweus. In D. J. Pepler & K. H. Rubin (Eds.), *The Development of Childhood Aggression*, pp. 411–446. Copyright © 1991 Lawrence Erlbaum. Reprinted by permission.

they were in the fifth grade. The two groups of students differed in terms of their relative risk status for antisocial behavior and the development of both conduct disorder and delinquency (that is, extreme versus minimal) (see Shinn, Ramsey, Walker, Stieber, & O'Neill, 1987; Walker, Shinn, O'Neill, & Ramsey, 1987).

Table 8.3 contains means and standard deviations for positive and negative playground behavior of the antisocial and at-risk control students as well as of respective, interacting peer partners. In terms of overall percentage or level, Table 8.3 indicates that there was a relatively small difference in positive social behavior directed toward peers by the antisocial and at-risk students. In contrast, the negative behavior of antisocial students was more than double that of the at-risk students. Interestingly, the interacting peers (partners) of antisocial and control students in these observations directed similar levels of positive social behavior toward antisocial and control students. However, the interacting peer partners exhibited almost the same level of negative social behavior to antisocial students as the antisocial students had directed at them (that is, 8.10 versus 9.92). A similar effect was noted for the at-risk control students (that is, 3.42 versus 4.05). Thus, non-antisocial peers appear to reciprocate both the positive and negative social behavior of

TABLE 8.3 A Comparison of Means and Standard Deviations of Students' Percentage of Time Observed for Playground Coded Variables

	GROUP			
	ANTISOCIAL (*N* = 39)		AT-RISK CONTROL (*N* = 41)	
Variable	$\overline{X}$	*SD*	$\overline{X}$	*SD*
Total positive behavior by target toward peers	38.36	13.5	44.06	17.8
Total negative behavior by target toward peers	9.92	10.7	4.05	5.2
Total positive behavior by peers toward target	31.26	12.8	33.83	15.0
Total negative behavior by peers toward target	8.10	8.0	3.42	3.4

Source: Shinn et al. (1987).

antisocial and at-risk students, even though the levels of negative behavior dispensed by the antisocial students were more than double that for the at-risk controls.

These results suggest that non-antisocial peers are strongly oriented toward social reciprocity and the matching of negative-aggressive initiations and social responses occurring during their social exchanges with antisocial and at-risk students. Non-antisocial peers are often drawn into hostile social exchanges with antisocial students and can display substantial negative behavior in extricating themselves from such situations. In our coding systems, we record this behavior in a discrete category we call "adaptive negative." Both peers and antisocial students are often quick to escalate initially negative situations of a mild nature into hostile exchanges involving anger and physical aggression. The residual social costs of such exchanges are reflected in social avoidance, negative reputations, biased responding, and negative interpretations of the behavioral intentions of antisocial students.

Thus, it is strongly recommended that the non-antisocial peers of antisocial students be involved in any attempts to remediate the negative-aggressive features of antisocial behavior in free-play and other settings. We believe that peers must be trained in many of the same social skills as the antisocial student, be provided opportunities to rotate through the roles of special helper or behavioral monitor on the playground, and to share equally in group activity rewards earned for the whole group by the antisocial student for engaging in positive, cooperative behavior. The RECESS program for aggressive behavior, which is profiled later in this chapter, incorporates these critically important features and was expressly designed for this negative-aggressive target population.

PLAYGROUND SITUATIONS THAT ARE PARTICULARLY DIFFICULT FOR ANTISOCIAL STUDENTS

Research by Dodge and his associates (see Dodge, 1980; Dodge, Coie, & Brakke, 1982) indicates that antisocial, aggressive children and youth experience great difficulty with three social situations involving peers and adults: (1) joining ongoing peer groups, (2) responding to teasing and *provocation*, and (3) complying with commands and requests. Failure in any one of these social domains can be costly and opens the door to school failure and ultimate rejection by peers and teachers. Studies of antisocial children and youth indicate that (1) they tend to be extremely unskilled in their attempts at accessing ongoing (already formed) peer groups that have come together around an activity; (2) they respond to teasing and provocation by others with intense anger accompanied by threats and sometimes tantrums; and (3) they often do not comply with requests and commands from teachers and peers. These responses put the social adjustment and acceptance of antisocial students at serious risk.

As part of a federally funded project on assessing children's social perceptions, flash points (tolerance limits), and knowledge of strategies appropriate for use in these three areas, Walker and his colleagues conducted a series of focus groups on responding to teasing and provocations and joining ongoing peer groups (see Irvin et al., 1992; Irvin & Walker, 1993; Walker, Irvin, Noell, & Singer, 1992). As part of the focus-group procedure, groups of primary- and intermediate-level students were interviewed about their knowledge and impressions regarding these social domains. They also coded video scenes illustrating situations in both domains; the researchers involved in these studies also coded the videos independently. The results of these activities were most instructive and interesting. The findings are reported in Tables 8.4–8.7.

TABLE 8.4 General Observations about Peer-Group Entry Resulting from Focus Groups and Scoring of Video Scenes

1. 8–10-year-olds are far more sensitive to subtle social cues and nuances of social situations than expected.
2. The researchers' choices of when it is appropriate to join peer-group activities were uncorrelated with those of 8–10-year-olds.
3. 8–10-year-olds believe it is OK to interrupt a peer-controlled activity and ask to be involved if:
   a. Peers are organizing for or setting up the activity.
   b. The ongoing activity involves parallel play (for example, a puzzle).
   c. The activity involves two persons and turn-taking.
4. 8–10-year-olds display considerable resilience and persistence in the face of rejection of their social bids.
5. Opposite-sex social bids appear to be more likely to be rejected than same-sex bids.

These findings result from extensive contact with multiple focus groups of children that included boys and girls and teasers and teasees. This information sheds light on the beliefs and normative standards that children hold about responding to teasing and provocations and about joining ongoing peer groups. Tables 8.4 and 8.5 report conclusions based on what these children told researchers in the focus groups and on the video scene codings by both the focus-group members and researchers. Overall, the children were impressively sensitive to the nuances and subtle features of the social-situational dynamics

TABLE 8.5 General Observations about Teasing and Provocation Resulting from Focus Groups and Scoring of Video Scenes

1. Some teasing is friendly and some is mean and provocative. Most teasing among 8–10-year-olds seems to be of the mean, provocative type. This appears true for boys and girls.
2. Friendly, acceptable teasing appears more characteristic of adolescents.
3. Teasing among boys involves themes of intimidation, power, domination, control, humiliation, and threats to one's safety. In contrast, teasing among girls involves themes of social cruelty, deception, hurt feelings, subtle rejection, manipulation, and being left out.
4. Some teasing appears to be deliberate; other teasing is primarily prompted by circumstances or the situation and is largely spontaneous or accidental.
5. Everyone is teased at some point, but there are children who are heavy-duty targets of teasing and those who are high-rate teasers of others.
6. Factors that increase one's probability of being teased include:
   a. Extreme reactions (tantrums)
   b. Being atypical or not fitting in with social norms or dress codes
   c. Having atypical physical or behavioral attributes (being short, wearing glasses, needing a hearing aid, or having strange habits)
   d. Being socially and athletically unskilled
7. Most teasing is done by groups to an individual who is selected as a target.
8. Teasing among friends is sometimes OK teasing while teasing among strangers or just acquaintances is often not OK.
9. Size is a major factor in teasing among boys.
10. 8–10-year-olds are not analytical or reflective about teasing; their responses to it and attitudes about it are mostly emotional.
11. Adaptive responses to teasing seem to be ignoring, asking the persons to stop, leaving the situation.
12. Maladaptive responses to teasing seem to include teasing back, name calling, getting mad or crying, hitting or having tantrums, threatening harm.
13. 8–10-year-olds have firm beliefs in the effectiveness of strategies for stopping teasing that have no effect or actually make it worse.

TABLE 8.6 Peer-Group Entry Do's and Don'ts Resulting from Analysis of the Literature and Focus Groups

Do's	*Don'ts*
• Hover and wait.	• Ask informational questions.
• Help others, be of assistance.	• Talk about yourself.
• Make group-oriented, positive statements.	• Disagree with those in group.
• Initiate only during natural breaks.	• Interrupt the group.
• Respond promptly to invitations.	• Seek attention.
• Say, "Can I play?" If not, act disappointed.	• Brag.
• Take any offer—even for partial involvement (for example, referee).	• Instruct those in the game.
• Tell name, say you're new or visiting, and ask to play. If refused, ask others to play.	• Barge in and say, "I'm playing!"
• Select a game that is fun. If refused, go look for someone who has no friends.	• Make threats—"Let me play or I'll tell someone you hit me!"
• Play by yourself as an alternative.	• Be persistent—tag along and persist until you finally get to play.
• Take whatever is offered to you.	
• Know the game you select and know rules; don't play unless you do.	
• Get someone to teach you the rules quickly.	

involved in joining peer groups and dealing with teasing and provocation. The social judgments of the senior author and his colleagues were essentially unrelated to those of focus-group members regarding when to attempt joining ongoing peer groups. The social norms of peers as to the timing of such approach behavior is clearly divergent from that of adults. There was considerably more agreement among the adults and peers on which approach strategies were adaptive and which were maladaptive.

Table 8.6 contains a list of do's and don'ts about peer-group entry gleaned from an analysis of the professional literature and from the focus groups. Table 8.7 contains a similar list about teasing and provocation. Some of the strategies contributed by the focus groups appear to be ingenious and potentially effective; others would appear to have no effect or to actually make the situation worse (for example, walk away and get a friend to scream at them).

Substantial literature is available on joining ongoing peer groups and compliance with requests and commands; however, the empirical and conceptual literature currently

TABLE 8.7 Teasing and Provocation Do's and Don'ts Resulting from Analysis of the Literature and Focus Groups

Do's	*Don'ts*
• Ignore.	• Cry.
• Leave the situation.	• Get visibly angry or lose temper.
• Protect self.	• Escalate (move up a notch).
• Rebuff in a firm manner.	• Counteraggress (match).
• Get help (call teacher or supervisor).	• Say, "Get out of here!"
• Tell the teacher.	• Walk away and get a friend to scream at them.
• Request that the teasers stop; if it doesn't work, then tell the teacher.	• Gang up on them; spread the word, and get them to isolate the teaser or provoker.
• Request that the teasers stop; walk away; if it doesn't work, go tell someone.	• Tease back.
• Just walk toward the teacher, but don't tell unless they follow.	• Call the teasers names.
• Give warnings, but stop after two.	• Act hurt or serious.

available on teasing and provocation appears to be considerably less well developed. Focus groups with primary-level and beginning intermediate-level students indicated that this area is in need of systematic investigation and research. Interviews with focus groups of randomly selected boys and girls indicated that (1) all viewed themselves as having been victims of teasing by others; (2) fear of teasing was a major social constraint in their lives, especially for girls; (3) they would go to great lengths to avoid situations in which they were likely to be teased; and (4) none would admit to teasing others.

In order to gain the perspectives of the *teasers*, the researchers asked teachers to nominate children in the primary and intermediate grades who were high-rate teasers. Focus groups were scheduled with the six children who were nominated (all boys in grades 3 and 4). The comments and body language of these boys were most interesting and strongly suggested that self-disclosure of numerous incidents of mean-spirited teasing may be a marker for children who are invested in overt, antisocial behavior patterns. Box 8.1 provides a first-person account, by the senior author, of the initial exchanges between these boys and the three adults who were conducting the focus group. It is important to note that none of the boys or adults involved had ever seen each other before.

One of the characteristic features of antisocial behavior patterns is noncooperative behavior and a tendency to not comply with commands and requests, especially from adults. Given the importance of joining ongoing peer groups, teasing and provocation, and compliance with commands and requests to both peer- and teacher-related forms of adjustment, it is extremely important that all antisocial students (1) be assessed as to their

Box 8.1 The Case of the Teaser Terrorists

The six boys, displaying aggressive body language, entered the room in which the focus group activity was to be held. It was as though the James Boys, Ike Clanton, and the Cole Younger Gang had all walked into a room at once. Within 5 minutes, I thought we needed more than just three adults to handle the situation. Each of the six boys looked like a behavioral escalation waiting to happen.

The focus group leader said we were here to talk about teasing and provocation. Immediately, two hands shot up—those of two boys who were eager to tell their stories. One commented that he teased a lot and was *really* good at it! The focus group leader said we would get to each boy but asked that we first go around the table, tell our names, and state where we were from; she began by introducing herself. Two boys introduced themselves as Jason and Jeremiah; they were from two local elementary schools. I was next in line and introduced myself as Hill Walker from the University of Oregon. Immediately, they all looked at me and one of the boys said, "Hill Walker? What kind of stupid name is that?"

I was stunned at the boldness of the question because I was an adult and they'd never seen me before. I was also momentarily speechless and had no response to the query. However, it made a lasting impression.

These boys went on to relate a litany of cruel stories about how they had victimized others. They seemed to be competing among themselves to see who had committed the most outrageous acts of teaser-terrorism. Although it was impossible to verify the truth or accuracy of their accounts, it was clear that they had not the slightest remorse about the acts they described.

competence levels in these areas and (2) that prompt and thorough intervention efforts be initiated to remediate identified deficits. Any attempts to address the playground behavior of antisocial students should incorporate systematic attention to these critically important domains.

As a rule, antisocial students do not use approach strategies that are likely to help them join groups of peers involved in an ongoing activity. The resulting rejection confirms the antisocial students' feelings of alienation and rejection, thus further isolating them from the social mainstream. As noted earlier, antisocial students are likely to be high-rate teasers; however, their responses to teasing and provocations by others are usually extremely maladaptive (for example, throwing tantrums, getting visibly angry, yelling, and making threats). Finally, the sulking, "chip on the shoulder," oppositional behavior of antisocial students in classrooms often leads to hostile, escalated interactions with their teachers. The outcomes of these episodes can be seriously damaging to the school careers and academic success of such students, and they effectively poison the teacher–student relationship.

GENERIC STRATEGIES AND PROCEDURES FOR PREVENTING AND REMEDIATING NEGATIVE-AGGRESSIVE BEHAVIOR AND RULE INFRACTIONS ON THE PLAYGROUND

The authors recommend the following four general approaches for preventing negative-aggressive behavior and rule infractions on the playground: (1) teaching antisocial students and their peers normative standards regarding social relations with peers and playground rules; (2) teaching adaptive strategies regarding joining already-formed peer groups, dealing with teasing, and compliance with commands and requests; (3) teaching generic social skills that will improve their chances for social acceptance and social engagement; and (4) teaching anger management and conflict-resolution strategies. Each of these approaches is discussed in this section.

Teaching Normative Standards

Walker, Hops, and Greenwood (1984, 1993) found that the standards extremely aggressive children hold governing peer relations and rules are often quite divergent from those of other children. It is likely that these aggressive children come from home environments where the behavioral standards to which they are exposed are not normative and where they are not taught to respect formal rules. In implementing intervention programs to improve the quality, or positive valence, of aggressive children's social behavior, it is necessary to preteach these *normative standards* and behavioral expectations because their ability to meet the minimal criteria for reinforceable responses during the intervention is too limited.

Walker and his associates developed a social-skills training (SST) procedure in which they used direct-instruction procedures to teach awareness and understanding of playground rules as well as normative standards governing peer relations. Lists of playground rules were solicited from a series of elementary schools and a generic set of rules was developed that would apply to most recess periods. When using this list with a given student in a particular school, the generic rules were reviewed with teachers and playground supervisors and fine-tuned to fit the idiosyncratic requirements of that school. The target student was then instructed in each rule on the list by teaching differences between acceptable and unacceptable examples of the rules, and thorough use of discussion, role-plays, coaching, and debriefing. Sometimes peers were used as instructional assistants in this teaching process; at other times, just the teacher or consultant and the target student were involved.

A similar procedure was used to teach target students clear discriminations between positive and negative forms of verbal, physical, and gestural social behavior. This instructional procedure proved to be highly effective in facilitating the necessary discriminations in the role-playing situation. For both playground rules and peer-related social behavior, this training procedure was followed by an incentive-based, behavior-management system on the playground. This general approach of preteaching rules and social behavior, combined with a behavior-management procedure to support their applications, was an extremely effective approach. It dramatically reduced the amount of time required for aggressive children to acquire a much more adaptive and prosocial behavior pattern.

Teaching Adaptive Strategies for Specific Social Situations

Antisocial students, as well as at-risk students in general, often do not have good information about *adaptive strategies* for joining peer groups, handling teasing, or complying promptly, fully, and appropriately with commands and requests from others. This is probably due to such factors as (1) a failure by the adults in their lives to teach such skills directly, (2) a lack of response opportunities to learn and demonstrate these skills, and (3) limited opportunities for observational learning.

Figures 8.1–8.3 provide schematic representations of the critical features involved in joining in, teasing and provocation, and compliance. These schema are built on the information-processing model developed by Dodge and his associates (see Dodge, 1986) and were created to guide research in the assessment and development of social competence (Irvin et al., 1992). They provide useful conceptual road maps for structuring instruction–intervention efforts that are geared toward improving the social skills and competence of antisocial students.

For example, in Figure 8.1, three different situations are used to teach discriminations between interruptive and noninterruptive ways of approaching and seeking to join

Scenarios

1. Group game ("Drop the Flag")
2. Group or dyadic/cooperative (puzzle)
3. Dyadic/competitive (darts)

Times and ways to join in

	Positive	Neutral	Negative
Interruptive	Polite request	Positive verbalization	Physical aggression
Noninterruptive	Polite request	Wait	Threaten or brag

Response options

1. *Externalizing:* brag, instruct, barge in
2. *Internalizing:* hover, ask questions
3. *Appropriate:* ask to join in

How others might react

1. Ignore
2. Invite
3. Reject
4. Defer

FIGURE 8.1 Joining-In Overview

ongoing peer groups. There are some general prerequisites for successfully joining already-formed groups of peers engaged in an ongoing activity: (1) be sure the student knows the rules of the target game or activity and has the necessary skills to participate in it; (2) the student should not ask questions of the members of the group that require an answer; (3) hovering around the activity and waiting for an invitation can be a successful strategy; (4) asking to join should be timed to coincide with natural breaks in the activity; and (5) bragging and instructing members of the group should be avoided at all costs. In the instructional procedure, positive, neutral, and negative examples of interruptive strategies are contrasted with noninterruptive strategies, and the distinguishing features of each are illustrated. The probable reactions of peers to each of these strategies are also addressed.

Figure 8.2 illustrates the instructional approach as applied to typical situations involving teasing and provocation. Examples of strategies for coping with teasing and provocation are provided for five situations ranging from ambiguous, to accidental, to hostile. The strategies for coping with teasing and provocation involve two critical dimensions: engagement and quality. Responses to teasing and provocation can be positive or negative and can either engage or disengage the teaser.

Scenarios*

1. Ambiguous
2. Ambiguous/accidental
3. Accidental
4. Friendly
5. Hostile

Response options

	Engaged	Disengaged
Positive	• Countertease • Don't take too seriously	• Leave situation • Ignore completely
Negative	• Fight and chase • Get angry and cry	• Threaten to summon adult authority • Ask person to stop teasing

*Girls' and boys' scenarios vary in thematic content.

FIGURE 8.2 Teasing and Provocation Overview

As a rule, disengagement with the teaser terminates the teasing episode and is a desirable strategy. Positive techniques for dealing with teasing and provocation include ignoring the teasing (if possible); counterteasing (but only under certain conditions that do not prompt escalation of the teasing into bullying); walking away from the situation; asking the teaser to stop in a direct manner; and threatening to or actually seeking assistance from an adult if the teasing persists, becomes severe or escalates into bullying, or becomes a threat to one's safety and well-being. Undesirable responses to teasing include getting mad and crying, giving chase to the teaser, and fighting or threatening to fight.

The adaptive and maladaptive features of each strategy are discussed in considerable detail with target students. Aggressive, antisocial students are taught to resist their urges to engage in spontaneous teasing as part of this instructional process as well. However, because of the powerful situational triggers that are associated with teasing, the emotional arousal that the process of teasing can generate, and the social rewards that accrue to the teaser (for example, dominance, attention, submissive behavior by the teasee), it can be very difficult to get many children and youth to voluntarily refrain from this form of abusive playground behavior.

Figure 8.3 presents a template for dealing with compliance. Situational determinants that mediate compliance with teacher and peer directives are represented in this schematic as (1) clear versus unclear; (2) distinctions between requests, commands, and demands; (3) directives applied to individuals versus members of groups; and (4) commands given within the context of orderly versus disorderly environments. Strategies are reviewed and discussed during the instructional procedure that range from immediate, direct compliance to outright defiance. Target students are urged to adopt the strategies of direct compliance, request for clarification, negotiation around the command or request, and simple refusal (but with a reason given for the refusal). Students are urged to carefully avoid the responses of passive noncompliance (that is, partial compliance) and outright defiance.

We believe that systematic instruction in these three domains, combined with coaching, debriefing, and incentive systems applied within natural settings, can have a powerful effect on the teacher- and peer-related adjustments of antisocial students. In some schools, the necessary resources and expertise may not be available to systematically teach adaptive strategies in this manner. In such cases, playground supervisors should, at a minimum, use cuing, prompting, debriefing, and behavior-specific praise to support antisocial students in improving their coping skills.

Teaching Generic Social Skills

Antisocial students are often deficient in the *generic social skills* that support teacher and peer acceptance and that contribute to school success. These core skills are particularly important for peer relations and mediate the student's ability to gain access to peer-controlled social networks and to recruit and maintain friends. Chapter 10 provides general information, identification, and instructional–intervention procedures, as well as recommended guidelines for the development of social competence through social-skills training.

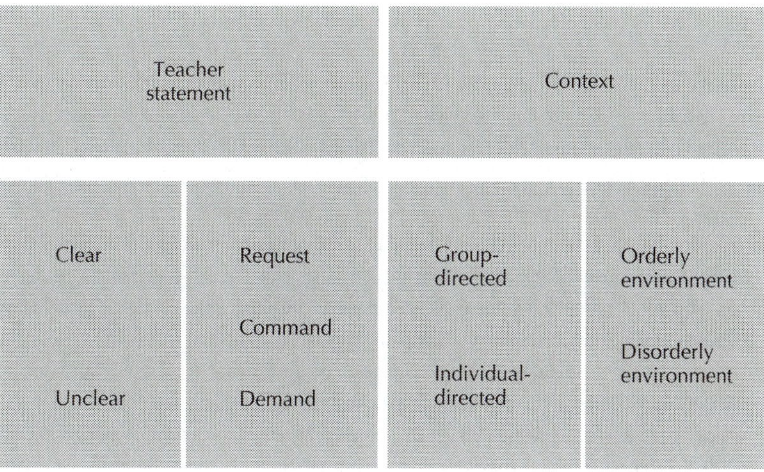

Response options*

Compliance	1. Compliance
	2. Request for clarification
	3. Negotiation
	4. Simple refusal (with reason)
	5. Not meet expected standards
	6. Passive noncompliance
Noncompliance	7. Defiance

*Response options sample 3 alternatives from list: 2 inappropriate and 1 appropriate for each item.

FIGURE 8.3 Compliance Overview

For elementary school students, it is essential directly to teach the social skills that support both teacher- and peer-related adjustment. For middle and high school students, it is also important to teach social skills that support self-related adjustment. The skills that support these three forms of social adjustment are described in Williams, Walker, Holmes, Todis, and Fabre (1989) and are reviewed in Chapter 10. Peer-related and self-related forms of adjustment have the most direct relevance for free-play settings involving peer relations.

Teaching Anger Management and Conflict-Resolution Strategies

One of the characteristic features of an antisocial behavior pattern is a high level of agitation that often leads to conflict with peers and adults. Antisocial children and youth carry intense levels of anger, and sometimes rage, due to the social and environmental conditions of abuse to which they have been exposed. Antisocial children and youth also carry feelings of alienation. Many have great difficulty controlling and managing their anger effectively. Most have not been taught appropriate methods of expressing anger and dissatisfaction.

The intense expression of anger and the initiation of conflict with others can have powerful instrumental effects that are personally rewarding. Tantrums, sulking, and direct confrontations are generally effective means of controlling the behavior of others. Antisocial children are masters at escalating these emotional conditions to a point where the social exchange becomes so aversive that peers, teachers, and parents give in or withdraw from the situation. Thus, these emotional states come to have a powerful value for antisocial students because they allow them to shape the social environment to their liking. For example, if a student chooses to resist a demand, the sudden escalation of anger often causes the demand to be withdrawn, deferred, or renegotiated.

It is important to the long-term development of antisocial students that they learn how to recognize and control their anger and to avoid the initiation of spontaneous and unnecessary conflicts with others. They must also learn to resolve conflicts without resorting to the use of coercion, threats, and physical force. Highly aggressive children and youth tend to view the world as a more dangerous and hostile place than other children do; they are also more easily provoked into responding physically as a means of resolving perceived problems.

Anger management and anger control, as well as conflict resolution, are ideal subject matter for systematic social-skills training. Chapter 10 lists some social-skills curricula that are especially designed for addressing these themes.

In the area of anger management and control, it is important to teach antisocial students (1) how to recognize both when they are angry and the emotional-psychological arousal that accompanies intense anger, (2) to identify the situations and events that seem to trigger their intense anger, (3) to recognize the unpleasant consequences that can result from intense expressions of anger, and (4) to learn appropriate methods of expressing anger and dissatisfaction. Many aggressive children resort to coercive tactics and strategies because they do not have the necessary social skills to cope with important social tasks and demands (Coie, Underwood, & Lochman, 1991). Thus, anger-management training should always be accompanied by systematic, social-skills training.

Coie et al. (1991) report a comprehensive intervention for improving social relations with peers and reducing aggressive behavior in schools. Their intervention consists of four major components: (1) social problem-solving skills, (2) positive-play training, (3) group-entry skill training, and (4) dealing with strong, negative feelings. This is a well-conceptualized approach for improving the social adjustment of antisocial, aggressive children. The social problem-solving component of this intervention is designed to teach and assist aggressive children to generate alternatives to difficult situations that are adaptive, but that still efficiently produce valued outcomes. Positive-play training is designed to strengthen target students' repertoires of positive, prosocial behavior (for example, turn taking, following the rules of games and activities, sharing, and cooperating). Group-entry skill training is extremely important in that it provides a vehicle for accessing peer-controlled activities in an acceptable manner. Finally, strategies for controlling emotions are taught in order to assist the student in managing anger and coping with intensely negative feelings.

Anger-control strategies typically consist of self-talk, cognitive mediation, relaxation training, behavioral rehearsal, and opportunities to control emotions and manage negative feelings in a range of social situations, including difficult ones. Coie et al. (1991) cite evidence that emotional control techniques of this type can be effective in coping with negative feelings and reducing aggression (see Lochman, Burch, Curry, & Lampron, 1984). The investment of time and effort in anger management and control strategies for antisocial students is highly recommended.

Antisocial students are in dire need of strategies for dealing with their frequent conflicts involving peers and adults. Social problem-solving strategies in which students are taught to generate alternatives for solving the conflict are invaluable. Students also need process skills required for effective conflict resolution; these include negotiation skills, cooperation, listening, turn taking, ability to assume the other person's perspective, and a positive attitude.

We strongly recommend the use of *peer-mediation* strategies, whenever possible, to resolve conflicts that antisocial students experience in their social relations with peers. Schrumpf, Crawford, and Usadel (1991) have developed an excellent program that uses peer mediation for this purpose. They define peer mediation as a voluntary method for resolving peer conflicts and disputes without resorting to coercion. The peer mediator must be an unbiased, empathic listener and respectful of all parties to the process. Mediators are expected to remain neutral and objective and to maintain confidentiality of information; those involved in the process are not allowed to interrupt when someone else is talking, and the parties involved must also agree to cooperate. The program developed by Schrumpf and colleagues for peer mediation consists of the following steps:

Peer-Mediation Steps

1. Open the session
2. Gather information
3. Focus on common interests
4. Create options
5. Evaluate options and choose a solution
6. Write the agreement and close

RECESS: A COMPREHENSIVE INTERVENTION FOR AGGRESSIVE BEHAVIOR

The Reprogramming Environmental Contingencies for Effective Social Skills (RECESS) program is a comprehensive intervention designed for aggressive children in grades K–3 (Walker et al., 1993). RECESS is a behavior-management package that teaches prosocial forms of peer-related behavior and applies sanctions (loss of points, time-out) for negative-aggressive behavior, rule infractions, teasing, and bullying.

RECESS consists of four major program components: (1) systematic training in cooperative, positive social behavior via prepared scripts, discussion, and role playing for the aggressive child and all other class members; (2) a response-cost point system in which points are subtracted for inappropriate social behavior and rule infractions; (3) praise by the RECESS consultant, teacher, and playground supervisor for positive, cooperative, interactive behavior; and (4) concurrent group and individual reinforcement contingencies with the group-activity rewards available at school and the individual rewards (privileges) available at home. RECESS focuses on the aggressive child's peer-related social behavior with the goals of decreasing negative-aggressive social initiations and responses to within normal limits and teaching a positive, constructive pattern of relating to others.

RECESS consists of four sequential phases: (1) recess only, (2) classroom extension, (3) fading, and (4) maintenance. During the recess-only phase, the program operates only during recess where the consultant has responsibility for monitoring the target child's behavior and interactions with peers; this phase lasts for 10 days. In the last three days of this phase, the RECESS consultant teaches the playground supervisor to operate the program, and the supervisor is monitored and supervised carefully while doing so. In the classroom-extension phase, the program is extended to the classroom if necessary; if not, the program is continued during recess periods as in phase one. This phase lasts approximately 15 days. During the fading phase, which lasts about 15 days, the major components of the program are eliminated, with the goals of making the program easier to manage and reducing the target child's dependence on external support procedures. The first three phases last approximately 40 days. The final phase, maintenance, continues indefinitely and consists of a low-cost variation of the intervention procedures in which praise and a surprise group-activity reward are made available if covert monitoring of the aggressive child at recess indicates that his or her social behavior falls within the normal range.

RECESS is a powerful intervention program that will have a substantive impact on the social behavior of aggressive children in grades K–3. It is a complex behavior-management package that is based on a reduce-and-replace strategy. That is, the target child's negative-aggressive behavioral repertoire is reduced or eliminated and replaced with an adaptive, prosocial behavior pattern. The RECESS referral graph in Figure 8.4 illustrates why RECESS is framed in this manner. That is, the negative-aggressive rate of most antisocial children is eight to nine times higher than that of their peers.

The information in this figure is based on systematic playground observations of 19 negative-aggressive primary school students and 21 socially "normal" students who were nominated by their teachers. The shaded area at the top of the graph defines the normal range of positive social responses displayed by the normal students; the average of this group is indicated by the white line. The average rate of positive social responses for the 19 aggressive students is indicated by the dotted line at the top, which shows that the positive response rate was nearly identical for the two groups.

Similarly, the shaded area at the bottom of the graph defines the range of negative social responses for normal students, with the white line indicating the average rate for this group (that is, .11 per minute or about one negative-aggressive social response every 9 minutes). In contrast, the average rate for aggressive students was eight to nine times higher than for normal students. The data plotted for John (shown by the solid line) are typical of the profile for aggressive, antisocial students in this range.

These results indicate that the most important task in dealing with such children is to reduce their rate of negative-aggressive social responses to within normal limits, as

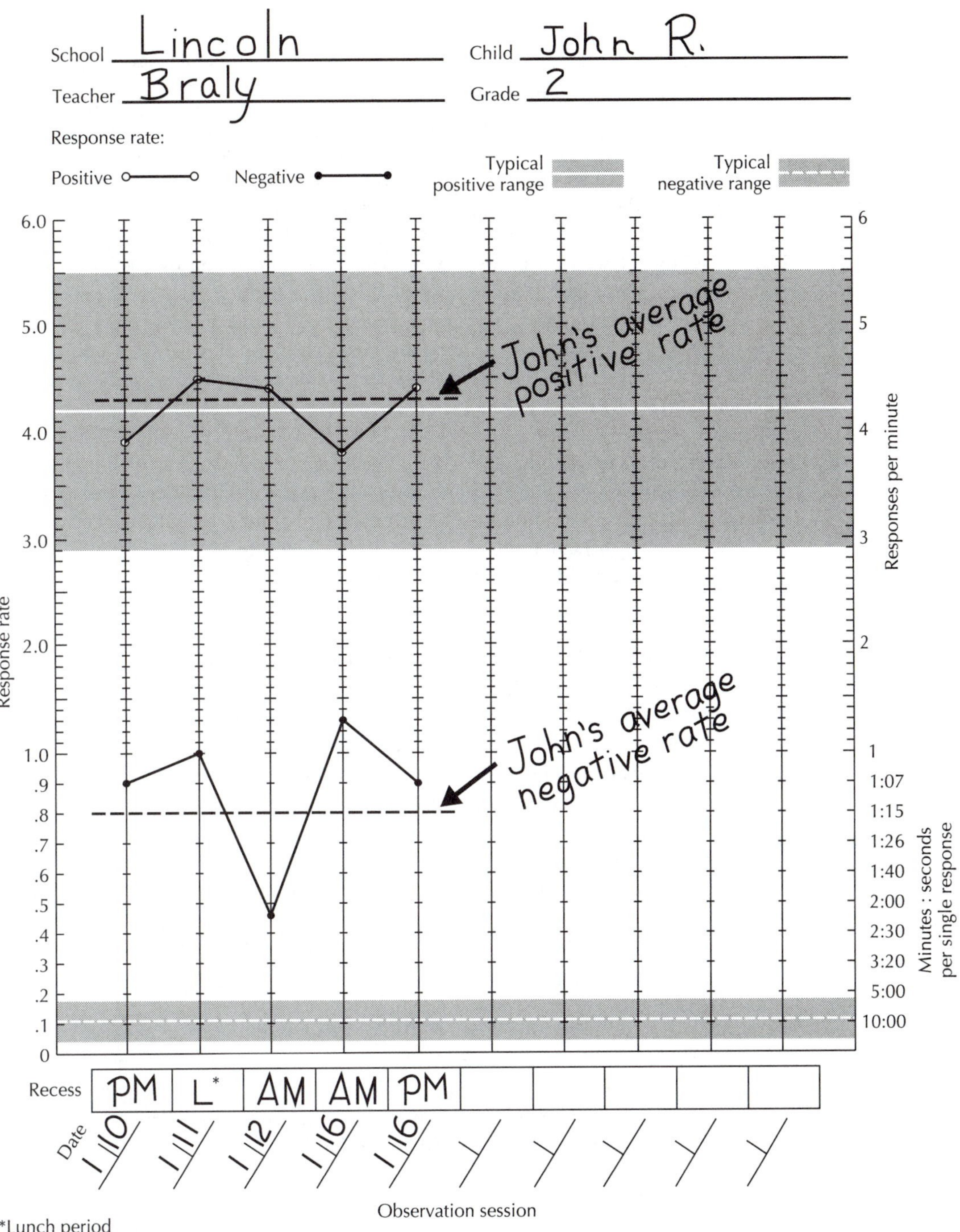

FIGURE 8.4 RECESS Referral Graph

defined by the social behavior of non-antisocial peers. Once the aversive, antisocial features of their behavior is under control, they are in a position to learn and practice an adaptive, prosocial behavior pattern. RECESS accomplishes this goal efficiently for most aggressive students to whom it is applied in grades K–3. This is the ideal developmental window in which to intervene effectively with negative-aggressive students.

Form 8.1 is a sample of a completed RECESS Point Record Form; Form 8.2 is a blank copy for the reader's use. This form is the essence of the program's implementation and provides for the delivery of behavior-specific praise and bonus points, and subtraction of previously awarded points for negative-aggressive behavior and rule infractions. It can be attached to a clipboard and used throughout recess periods on the playground. One point for each 5 minutes of recess is awarded on the point record form prior to the beginning of the recess period. The target student's task is to keep these points by behaving positively and avoiding rule infractions. For each instance in which a point is subtracted, it is important to inform the student of the event and why the point was subtracted.

Tables 8.8–8.10 display results of the RECESS program's application for ten highly aggressive students enrolled in grades K–3. These tables display target students' performance across program phases on three measures: (1) rate per minute of negative-aggressive social responses, (2) rate per minute of positive social responses, and (3) rate of playground and classroom rule infractions.

Table 8.8 indicates that RECESS had a powerful effect in reducing the target students' rates of negative-aggressive social behavior from baseline (preintervention) to the recess-only phase. These rates increased only slightly as the playground supervisor was trained to assume control of the program. Over the long-term, negative rates of these aggressive students stayed in the normal range, as defined by the negative-response rate of nonaggressive peers (that is, .11 per minute). In contrast, RECESS had no discernible or predictable effect on the positive-response rate of these students (see Table 8.9). This is likely a result of their already being within normal limits as defined by the social behavior of peers. Finally, Table 8.10 indicates that the program had a strong positive impact in reducing the frequency of playground and classroom rule violations.

It is rare to find a consultant-based, selected intervention program that is more effective than RECESS with antisocial, aggressive students in grades K–3. This program was developed and systematically tested and revised over a five-year period (see Walker, Hops, & Greenwood, 1984, 1993). It has been applied successfully to the behavior of hundreds of antisocial, aggressive students during and following its publication.

If implemented correctly, RECESS will have a powerful impact on the social behavior of most aggressive students who qualify for it. Only the most aggressive, antisocial students in grades K–3 qualify for RECESS, due to the power of the intervention program and the time and effort required to implement it (that is, 40 to 45 hours of consultant time over a 2- to 3-month intervention period). In spite of the powerful effects produced by the program, experience indicates that long-term maintenance procedures must be built in to preserve behavioral gains achieved during the intervention. It is extremely important that the maintenance phase of RECESS be implemented over the long-term, following completion of the first three program phases. Maintenance should

RECESS

Name *John* Date *5-24-94*

	Regular points	Bonus points and description	Count / Praise / Initial
Morning recess	///	1-Stayed calm when ball hit him in the face	/// G.W
Lunch recess	//// (one crossed out)		/// // G.W
Afternoon recess	////	1-Helped Jimmy when he fell.	/// / G.W

INSTRUCTIONS FOR RECESS SUPERVISORS

A. Praise: Give praise frequently during each recess (at least once every 5 minutes). Keep tally in circle provided. Initial tally at end of each recess. (During days 1–7, the consultant should praise every 2 or 3 minutes.)

B. Bonus points: If child is extra-thoughtful or handles a difficult situation admirably, give a bonus point, tell the child, and, if possible, jot down a brief description.

C. Point losing: Cross out one point for every rule broken. Tell child as soon as possible (see rules on clipboard).

D. Timeout: If all the *regular* points are lost during a given recess, have the child sit out for the duration of that recess (bonus points are not lost). If child doesn't cooperate with this, inform the teacher or consultant.

FORM 8.1 Completed Point Record Form. *Source:* From *RECESS: A Program for Reducing Negative-Aggressive Behavior*, by H. Walker, H. Hops, and C. Greenwood. Copyright © 1993 by Educational Achievement Systems, Seattle, WA. Reprinted by permission.

RECESS

Name ______________ Date ______________

	Regular points	Bonus points and description
Morning recess		COUNT PRAISE INITIAL
Lunch recess		COUNT PRAISE INITIAL
Afternoon recess		COUNT PRAISE INITIAL

INSTRUCTIONS FOR RECESS SUPERVISORS

A. Praise: Give praise frequently during each recess (at least once every 5 minutes). Keep tally in circle provided. Initial tally at end of each recess. (During days 1–7, the consultant should praise every 2 or 3 minutes.)

B. Bonus points: If child is extra-thoughtful or handles a difficult situation admirably, give a bonus point, tell the child, and, if possible, jot down a brief description.

C. Point losing: Cross out one point for every rule broken. Tell child as soon as possible (see rules on clipboard).

D. Timeout: If all the *regular* points are lost during a given recess, have the child sit out for the duration of that recess (bonus points are not lost). If child doesn't cooperate with this, inform the teacher or consultant.

FORM 8.2 Blank Point Record Form. *Source:* From *RECESS: A Program for Reducing Negative-Aggressive Behavior,* by H. Walker, H. Hops, and C. Greenwood. Copyright © 1993 by Educational Achievement Systems, Seattle, WA. Reprinted by permission.

TABLE 8.8 Negative-Response Rate During Preintervention and Intervention Phases of RECESS for Ten Socially Negative-Aggressive Children During Recess and Classroom Periods

	SUBJECTS										TOTAL GROUP	
Phases	*1*	*2*	*3*	*4*	*5*	*6*	*7*	*8*	*9*	*10*	$\bar{X}$	*SD*
Recess												
Baseline	.91	.99	.85	.97	1.05	.34	.55	.22	.47	.11	.69	.35
1a Consultant-operated	.01	.07	.06	.02	.01	.11	.01	.04	.03	.03	.04	.03
1b Recess-supervisor-operated—consultant present	.17	.04	.03	.05	.06	.02	.02	.02	.01	.00	.05	.04
2 Recess-supervisor-operated—extended to classroom	.02	.05	.11	.24	.32	.09	.07	.01	.18	.14	.14	.09
3 Fading	.08	.12	.13	—	.38	.13	.10	.02	—	—	.12	.11
Classroom												
B1 Prerecess program	.00	—	.28	.11	.22	.25	.00	.46	.41	.10	.26	.16
B2 Postrecess program	.02	.19	.15	.25	.07	.28	.00	.15	.26	.07	.15	.10
2 Class extension	.00	.06	.04	.18	.09	.08	.00	.05	.06	.05	.07	.05
3 Fading	.01	.00	.01	—	.04	.13	.00	.12	—	—	.05	.05

Source: From *RECESS: A Program for Reducing Negative-Aggressive Behavior,* by H. Walker, H. Hops, and C. Greenwood. Copyright © 1993 by Educational Achievement Systems, Seattle, WA. Reprinted by permission.

stay in effect for at least the remainder of the school year in which the program is implemented.

Children who are at serious risk for developing antisocial behavior patterns at the K–3 developmental level are often expected to "grow out of it." That is, maturity and the growth process are somehow expected to work a magical transformation in diverting the aggressive child from a path leading to antisocial behavior, conduct disorder, and delinquency. The evidence shows that young bullies often get worse and that instead of growing out of it, they actually grow into it! The best answer we seem to have is to attack this problem as early as possible. This means identifying it early, recognizing it for what it is, and intervening comprehensively and consistently. There is no better place to start than on the playground, where this behavior pattern develops in a most unfortunate manner but which affords numerous opportunities for teaching a prosocial behavior pattern with peers and adults.

TABLE 8.9 Positive-Response Rate Across Program Phases for Ten Socially Negative-Aggressive Children in RECESS

	SUBJECTS										TOTAL GROUP	
Phases	*1*	*2*	*3*	*4*	*5*	*6*	*7*	*8*	*9*	*10*	$\overline{X}$	*SD*
Recess												
Baseline	3.07	3.91	5.30	5.23	3.18	4.08	1.56	1.91	5.00	3.50	3.92	1.30
1a Consultant-operated	2.37	5.70	5.98	5.31	2.53	4.47	1.90	1.60	5.10	2.89	3.88	1.69
1b Recess-supervisor-operated—consultant present	2.91	5.73	6.15	6.12	3.65	3.95	2.32	1.22	4.65	2.43[a]	4.12	1.72
2 Recess-supervisor-operated—extended to classroom	3.03	3.79	5.64	4.63	2.44	4.54	1.80	1.88	5.13	3.88	3.83	1.34
3 Fading	3.17	3.81	5.61	—	2.90	3.77	2.00	2.01	—	—	3.26	1.24
Classroom												
B1 Prerecess program	.29	—	3.04	3.14	1.30	2.98	.18	2.98	3.51	1.82	2.46	1.28
B2 Postrecess program	1.86	1.31	2.85	2.02	1.42	2.40	.43	1.98	3.67	1.80	2.09	.88
2 Class extension	.57	1.27	2.66	2.13	2.18	1.77	.18	1.68	1.96	.74	1.75	.79
3 Fading	.75	1.10	1.10	—	2.36	2.49	.55	2.48	—	—	2.35	.86

[a]One data point only.
Source: From *RECESS: A Program for Reducing Negative-Aggressive Behavior,* by H. Walker, H. Hops, and C. Greenwood. Copyright © 1993 by Educational Achievement Systems, Seattle, WA. Reprinted by permission.

CONCLUSION

The social behavior of antisocial students on the playground can be extremely problematic for peers and a most intractable behavior-management problem for school staff. Mean-spirited teasing, bullying, and negative-aggressive forms of behavior violate social norms

TABLE 8.10 Rule-Breaking Rate in Recess and Classroom Settings for Ten Socially Negative-Aggressive Children in RECESS

	SUBJECTS										TOTAL GROUP	
Phases	*1*	*2*	*3*	*4*	*5*	*6*	*7*	*8*	*9*	*10*	$\overline{X}$	*SD*
Recess												
Baseline	.20	.88	.52	.66	.21	.06	.07	.17	.19	.31	.30	.27
1a Consultant- operated	.02	.04	.02	.01	.01	.05	.02	.09	.02	.02	.03	.02
1b Recess-supervisor-operated—consultant present	.05	.03	.02	.10	.03	.02	.00	.17	.00	.05	.04	.05
2 Recess-supervisor-operated—extended to classroom	.08	.04	.16	.16	.07	.03	.01	.01	.02	.06	.07	.05
3 Fading	.02	.04	.04	—	.19	.01	.01	.04	—	—	.04	.06
Classroom												
B1 Prerecess program	.00	—	.03	.05	.01	.00	.00	.10	.05	.00	.03	.03
B2 Postrecess program	.19	.08	.00	.13	.09	.01	.00	.15	.00	.00	.06	.07
2 Class extension	.00	.02	.04	.03	.12	.03	.00	.02	.00	.01	.03	.03
3 Fading	.00	.00	.01	—	.46	.02	.00	.01	—	—	.04	.17

Source: From *RECESS: A Program for Reducing Negative-Aggressive Behavior,* by H. Walker, H. Hops, and C. Greenwood. Copyright © 1993 by Educational Achievement Systems, Seattle, WA. Reprinted by permission.

and lead to strong rejection by peers and adults alike. These target behaviors are ideal candidates for prevention and remediation by using a combination of universal and selected interventions that also involve parents, neighborhoods, and the community.

The next chapter focuses on defining social skills, documenting their importance, and describing procedures for their assessment. Chapter 10 presents instructional guidelines and procedures for teaching social skills systematically and facilitating their generalization across settings and maintenance within settings. Social-skills training that emphasizes cooperation, empathy, communication, acceptance, socially responsible decision making, self-esteem, and positive regard for others is one of the best vehicles we have for teaching adaptive, prosocial behavior patterns to all students. More than any other group, antisocial students are in need of exposure to such training.

RECOMMENDED RESOURCES FOR USE IN ADDRESSING TEASING, BULLYING, AND NEGATIVE-AGGRESSIVE FORMS OF STUDENT BEHAVIOR

Materials describing the RECESS program include detailed procedural manuals for program consultants, cooperating teachers, and playground supervisors plus a packet of program consumables (forms, charts, and wall posters). The total cost of the program is approximately $125. This material is available through Educational Achievement Systems, Inc., 319 Nickerson, Suite 112, Seattle, WA 98109. Once purchased, RECESS can be used for repeated program applications. Additional packets are also available from Educational Achievement Systems.

Bully Proofing Your School is a comprehensive program for preventing and intervening effectively with bullies and is a valuable best practice in addressing this problem. It involves school staff, students, parents, and the community. This program notes that a "silent majority" of 85% of students are bullied at some point in their school careers; it attempts to marshal the social power of this majority in supporting and protecting the victims of bullies while simultaneously defusing their power. The authors of this program also provide an extensive resource guide of videotapes, books, and other materials for use by parents, students, and schools in addressing this problem. *Bully Proofing Your School* is available from Sopris West, Inc., 1140 Boston Avenue, Longmont, CO 80501, 303-651-2829.

Valerie Besay, a British school psychologist, is an outstanding expert on school bullying. She has written a highly respected book on bullying in schools and has also developed a school-based, staff-development program for use in coping with bullying. Her book *Bullies and Victims in Schools: A Guide to Understanding and Management* provides both a comprehensive treatment of the topic and numerous suggestions for coping with bullying. The book is divided into two parts: Part One focuses on understanding bullying and Part Two focuses on what to do about it. The U.S. distributor for her book is Taylor and Francis, Inc., 1900 Frost Road, Suite 101, Philadelphia, PA 19007, 215-785-5800. Besay's staff-development training program for controlling bullying in school, *We Don't Have Bullies Here*, is structured around a typical school day and explains how daily procedures can be organized and coordinated for reducing bullying. Her staff-development program is a universal intervention and involves a whole-school approach. This program is available from V. E. Besay, 57 Manor House Road, Jesmond, Newcastle upon Tyne, NE2 2LY, England.

The National Center for School Safety publishes an 18-minute film, *Set Straight on Bullies*, designed to assist school administrators in educating teachers, parents, and students about the severity and implications of the schoolyard bullying problem. This Emmy-award-winning film tells the story of a bullying victim and how the problem adversely affects his life as well as the lives of the bully, other students, his parents, and teachers. The film is available for purchase by contacting the National School Safety Center at 4165 Thousand Oaks Boulevard, Suite 290, Westlake Village, CA 91362.

STUDY QUESTIONS

1. Antisocial students have their most difficult adjustment problems on the playground. Why?
2. Under which behavioral classification does antisocial behavior fall: externalizing or internalizing?
3. Distinguish teacher-related from peer-related forms of social adjustment.
4. Define bullying.
5. How do teasing and bullying differ from each other?
6. How likely are antisocial students themselves to be victims of bullying?
7. What is the relationship between bullying and violence?
8. List four key principles of effective bullying interventions.
9. Describe three playground situations that are particularly difficult for antisocial students.
10. Describe four strategies for preventing and remediating negative-aggressive behavior on the playground.
11. Describe the key elements of the RECESS program for aggressive students.

KEY TERMS

adaptive strategies
anger management
bullying
externalizing
generic social skills
internalizing
normative standards
peer conflict
peer mediation
provocation
social engagement
social reciprocity
teasing

9 Social Skills: Importance and Assessment

The Social Status, Social Skills, and Social Adjustment of Antisocial Children and Youth

Methods for Identifying Students in Need of Social-Skills Training

Definition and Conceptualization of Social Skills

Criteria and Procedures for Targeting Specific Skills for Training

Ascertaining Specific Skill Deficits

Social Validity
Assessment

Recommendations and Best Practices for Evaluating Social-Skills Interventions

Documenting Skill Acquisition
Evaluating Outcomes of Social-Skills Interventions

Conclusion

Considerable research over the past two decades has clearly demonstrated what many teachers have known for a long time: Antisocial students consistently fail in their social relations with other children, youth, and adults (see Parker & Asher, 1987). Aggressive behavior is the single most important reason for a child's rejection by peers (Coie, Dodge, & Kupersmidt, 1990). Higher than normal rates of aggression are also a powerful factor in teachers' lack of acceptance of antisocial students. In surveys of teacher expectations and tolerance levels, aggressive behavior consistently ranks as one of the most objectionable forms of student behavior (Hersh & Walker, 1983; Walker, 1986).

Antisocial students often do not display age-appropriate social behavior; they tend to be extremely immature in almost all of their social interactions with peers and adults in school. As young children become socialized to the norms and behavioral standards of our society, they gradually reduce their levels of aggressive behavior when school age approaches. However, older students with antisocial behavior patterns display rates of aggression that are more typical of 3- and 4-year-olds (Patterson, 1982). Rarely are such students helpful or cooperative in their social exchanges. In fact, antisocial students seem to have a singular disinclination to cooperate with others in peer-controlled activities. These students seem to bring a contentious, "chip on their shoulder" set of attitudes to many social situations. Such students often have poor adult models for positive, appropriate social behavior in the home; furthermore, parents of antisocial children do not usually teach prosocial forms of behavior that facilitate positive peer and teacher relations. Unfortunately, parents of many antisocial children often model negative attitudes toward school. As a result of this unfortunate learning history, antisocial students often display behavioral characteristics that cause them to be viewed as hostile and socially unskilled by peers and adults alike.

This chapter focuses on procedures, guidelines, resources, and recommended best practices for screening and assessing the social-adjustment problems that antisocial students experience in school. The material in this chapter is designed to provide a comprehensive treatment of this topic because we believe social skills and social competence are domains in which antisocial students are often severely deficient. These deficits, in turn, place their school and life adjustments at severe risk of failure. Topics covered in this chapter include (1) a review of the social-adjustment and social-behavioral characteristics of antisocial students, (2) methods for the identification of students in need of social-skills training, (3) definitions and conceptualization of social skills, (4) criteria and procedures for targeting specific skills for training, and (5) recommendations and best practices for evaluating social-skills interventions and their outcomes in school.

THE SOCIAL STATUS, SOCIAL SKILLS, AND SOCIAL ADJUSTMENT OF ANTISOCIAL CHILDREN AND YOUTH

In *sociometric* assessments (that is, peer-popularity ratings and nominations), antisocial students are consistently rated negatively by their peers and are also socially rejected. Peers often identify antisocial students as undesirable classmates and playmates (Dodge, Coie, & Brakke, 1982; Parker & Asher, 1987). Similarly, teacher ratings of antisocial, aggressive students reflect a widely held perception among educators that they lack social

Counselor recording social behavior at recess. *David Young-Wolff*

skills and that they violate social norms and behavioral expectations (Gresham & Elliott, 1990). These perceptions, by both peers and teachers, seem to remain true throughout grades K–12 (see Sabornie & Kauffman, 1985; Sabornie, Kauffman, & Cullinan, 1990).

Walker and his colleagues (Walker & McConnell, 1993; Walker, Shinn, O'Neill, & Ramsey, 1987) found that regular teachers rated the social skills of antisocial students, in both elementary and middle schools, approximately one standard deviation below the mean for nonantisocial students. For example, the mean social-skills rating score for a sample of 762 elementary students was 159.78 (SD = 33.16); the mean score for a sample of 39 antisocial elementary students was 134.94 (SD = 33.74) (see Walker et al., 1987). A similar discrepancy was found when these students were in middle school, as indicated by an ongoing longitudinal study of antisocial and at-risk control boys (see Walker, Stieber, & O'Neill, 1990).

A number of well-controlled studies show that antisocial children will characteristically misinterpret neutral situations as being hostile or negative (Dodge & Frame, 1982;

Hollinger, 1987). They are quick to attribute hostile intentions to peers, even when there is no basis for doing so. Take Jason Black, for example.

> Jason is a second grader at Pleasant Mountain Elementary School. He is having a hard time this year, especially with the other children in his classroom. Jason often has temper tantrums during recess and at lunchtime. The playground supervisor reports he spends little time interacting with other second graders. The supervisor described a recent incident involving Jason as follows: "Jason approached a group of children playing 4-square. Jason's turn came and when the ball was bounced his way he missed it. Several children giggled. Suddenly Jason began screaming at the children playing the game, 'You threw it so I wouldn't get it! You're cheats—all of you!' Jason then pushed another child and stomped off."

This example typifies antisocial children's often-cited inability to correctly interpret and react to naturally occurring social situations. To complicate matters further, they are sometimes physically unskilled and often do not take the time to learn the rules of games and activities thoroughly. Not surprisingly, Jason, and other students like him, are quickly shunned by nonproblem children in their classroom. Eventually, antisocial students are reduced to interacting only with other deviant students. As a rule, the best friends of antisocial students are all the other antisocial students in their school (Patterson, Reid, & Dishion, 1992). Although this process satisfies the friendship needs of antisocial students, it also identifies a group of students who associate with one another regularly and who have negative reputations with peers and teachers.

Antisocial students bond together as a group, hang out together during and after school, and create the foundation for future associations as a deviant peer group or gang. Longitudinal work shows that antisocial students spend significantly less time participating in structured games and activities at recess than do at-risk control students of the same age and sex whose behavioral profiles are similar to those of well-adjusted children (Walker et al., 1987; Walker, Stieber, & O'Neill, 1990). Antisocial students tend not to have interests in structured playground activities that have identifiable rules and are controlled by peers; instead, they usually spend their time associating with each other in free play. The degree to which they are monitored and supervised in this situation is minimal. As a rule, they have low levels of social engagement in mainstream playground activities. Research has shown that gangs can develop from unsupervised, spontaneous play groups of this nature (Crowe, 1994).

Antisocial students like Jason report that acting aggressively comes easily, that it is difficult to inhibit aggressive impulses, and that aggressive acts usually get them what they want (Perry, Perry, & Rasmussen, 1986). Some highly aggressive children can consciously verbalize the instrumental benefits of aggression as early as grade 2. In explaining the RECESS program for aggressive behavior (see Walker, Hops, & Greenwood, 1993) to primary-level target students who qualified for this intervention, the senior author has, on several occasions, encountered a situation in which the target boys commented on the attractiveness of the program's extensive home and school rewards but noted that it did not compare favorably with what they currently had going for them. The instrumental benefits of peer-directed aggressive behavior are substantial (for example, dominance, power, control of social situations) and help explain why a well-developed pattern of aggressive behavior is so difficult to change.

By the time Jason Black left Pleasant Mountain Elementary, he had been evaluated by a school-based child-study team and was labeled as "seriously emotionally disturbed." When asked to describe himself, Jason chose words like, "ugly," "stupid," and "nobody likes me." While claiming that no one liked him, he was always quick to add, "Who cares?" His only real friend was a middle school boy who had already been picked up by police for shoplifting. Teachers at Pleasant Mountain actually felt relieved knowing Jason would not be returning for the next academic year.

The words Jason used to describe himself reflect the poor self-image and low self-esteem that is characteristic of many antisocial children (Patterson et al., 1992). Such a self-assessment is to be expected, given the constant barrage of criticism and negative messages they receive from teachers and peers. Furthermore, antisocial students do not see school as a friendly place or as a setting in which they can demonstrate much mastery and experience success. Studies indicate that students like Jason are frequently exposed to control, containment, and punishment strategies by school systems (Neel & Rutherford, 1981). Furthermore, Walker, Block-Pedego, Todis, and Severson (1991) found that students with externalizing, acting-out behavior patterns are often denied access to school-based support services, such as counseling, social-skills training, values clarification, and speech and language training. The aversive nature of their behavioral characteristics and their low likability quotients are probably responsible, at least in part, for this outcome. A disproportionately large percentage of antisocial students are excluded from school and placed on home-tutoring regimens.

Social-skills deficits and a failure to abide by rule-governed teacher expectations are the root causes of the adjustment problems experienced by antisocial students. Antisocial students, through their general behavioral inclinations, set up social environments that severely punish them. They victimize others, especially peers, at extraordinarily high rates; yet they perceive themselves as victims and as not being treated fairly. Ironically, antisocial students, who are the greatest victimizers of others in school, see themselves as the ultimate victims. In one sense, this is true because the long-term consequences of an antisocial behavior pattern are highly victimizing to the perpetrator. As noted in Chapter 1, antisocial students have a high risk for experiencing long-term negative outcomes that include life failure in many areas, as well as higher hospitalization and mortality rates.

Antisocial children and youth seem to have an extremely well-developed capacity for accurately interpreting social contingencies in naturally occurring situations and for taking full advantage of them. They are especially sensitive to the nuances, gray areas, and seams (that is, inconsistencies and weaknesses) of social-control systems that operate in home, school, and community settings. As a rule, they are able to overwhelm the intended socialization or disciplinary features of these systems, and they can be quite ingenious in so doing. The resulting behavioral effects maximize the antisocial child's short-term advantages, but they result in severe long-term social costs that are reflected in the active disapproval and lack of acceptance by parents, teachers, peers, and others.

Antisocial students' heightened sensitivity to how the social environment affects them is matched only by their insensitivity to the effects of their behavior on the social environments in which they travel. This outcome may be due partially to their general tendency to resist tactics of social influence directed toward them by adults and peers (that is, a determination not to be controlled or affected by the formal and informal rules governing social interactions and cooperative, appropriate behavior). It may also be the case that the home environments of many antisocial children are so chaotic and unpredictable that they learn to resist such influence in order to cope and survive. In all probability, this insensitivity is also due to a faulty learning history in which antisocial students have not been exposed to conditions that require and teach the importance of social rules.

Coie, Dodge, Ladd and their colleagues have conducted the seminal work to date on how aggressive, socially rejected students decode, process, and interpret social information (see Coie, Belding & Underwood, 1988; Dodge, 1980, 1986; Dodge & Frame, 1982; Ladd & Oden, 1979). Their research shows that such children and youth make many errors that prove to be highly significant in their decoding and interpretation of the social information and behavioral feedback they receive. These errors cause them to misread the motivations and intentions of peers and adults. When antisocial children base their subsequent behavioral actions on such errors and misinformation, the resulting behavioral effects can be potentially disastrous. Perhaps because of these misinterpretations of social cues, antisocial students often respond inappropriately to well-intentioned social bids from others. This tendency, combined with their generally aversive behavioral characteristics, can lead to social rejection by peers and teachers; such rejection can form rather quickly. Evidence shows that teacher and peer rejection is nearly an inevitable consequence of displaying a characteristic pattern of antisocial behavior in school (Patterson et al., 1992).

Hollinger (1987) has reviewed this evidence in the context of mainstreaming and social integration. He concludes that aggressive, antisocial students are at a severe disadvantage in their peer-related adjustment within mainstreaming settings because of their deficits in social perception and social skills. Similarly, more than a decade of research by Walker and his associates on teacher reactions to the mainstreaming and social integration of students with disabilities indicates that regular teachers are extremely intolerant of the behavioral characteristics of antisocial students (Gersten, Walker, & Darch, 1988; Hersh & Walker, 1983; Walker, 1986).

Sometimes, students like Jason will receive special school services before being labeled "seriously emotionally disturbed." For example, near the end of second grade, Jason participated in a social-skills training program initiated by the district school psychologist. Jason made a number of positive changes during this social-skills training program. He practiced listening, cooperation, and turn-taking skills with two other difficult students. Unfortunately, when he returned to the regular free-play setting during recess, his behavior immediately deteriorated, due to a lack of coordination and follow-up from the training setting to recess. Even when Jason would ask to join an ongoing playground activity in a polite and appropriate manner, his peers would still reject and ignore him. In the classroom, Jason was similarly unable to maintain the social gains he had demonstrated in the training situation.

This behavioral effect is commonly observed following systematic social-skills training with many aggressive, antisocial students. Jason's difficulties are not at all uncommon in this regard. An inability to generalize newly learned social skills from the training setting to the classroom or playground is often reported by educators (see DuPaul & Eckert, in press). Too often, newly acquired cooperative and positive behaviors will last only several days following their initial instruction and demonstration. The failure to generalize or maintain these critical skills over time is a serious obstacle to the effectiveness of systematic, social-skills training and needs to be addressed by researchers and educators alike.

The specific reasons underlying this generalization and maintenance failure of social-skills training are complex and not completely understood. Acquiring and then integrating a new set of social skills into one's behavioral repertoire is difficult, requires extensive practice and support, and must be worthwhile to the individual. Many social-skills programs fail due to one or more of these factors (Schloss, Schloss, Wood, & Kiehl, 1986). However, students like Jason face an added burden in this regard. Hollinger's (1987) review of social-skills and social-perception biases in the context of mainstreaming suggests some plausible explanations as to why the efforts of students like Jason to use prosocial skills often end in failure. Aggressive students develop negative reputations among their peers and suffer from *social-perception biases* that cause peers to continue rejecting them.

Hollinger cites evidence by Dodge (see Dodge & Frame, 1982) showing that peers are more likely to attribute hostile intentions to the behavior of rejected and aggressive boys than to nonaggressive boys. Peers also tend to remember the negative behavior and to forget the positive behavior of aggressive boys. Finally, peers are likely to interpret the neutral behavior of aggressive boys as negative, while they interpret it as positive for nonaggressive boys. Thus, social-perception bias of this type can be a powerful factor in partially explaining why it is so difficult to change the sociometric status of aggressive, antisocial boys by using social-skills interventions. As a rule, antisocial students continue to be socially rejected and isolated, even after receiving extensive training in social skills. It is our view that social-skills training is necessary but not sufficient for changing the social status and social competence of antisocial students. We will deal with social-skills training in substantial detail in Chapter 10.

Compelling research by Patterson and his associates (see Patterson, 1988; Patterson & Bank, 1989; Patterson et al., 1992) indicates that social rejection by peers and teachers provides an important contribution to the negative developmental path that many antisocial children and youth follow. It is a path that usually begins early in a child's life and, tragically, is often the path that also leads to prison and a host of life failures. Displaying prosocial skills, developing friendships and social-support networks, and being responsive to teachers' behavioral expectations can do much to help offset this trajectory. In this regard, we believe that antisocial students are well worth the investments that systematic social-skills training and intervention require. If implemented correctly, they can produce outcomes that have considerable promise (see Barton, 1986; Ladd, 1981; Pepler & Rubin, 1991).

METHODS FOR IDENTIFYING STUDENTS IN NEED OF SOCIAL-SKILLS TRAINING

As a general rule, nearly all aggressive, antisocial students will be able to derive some benefit from social-skills intervention. However, antisocial students are not the only ones in most regular classrooms who are in need of systematic social-skills training. Students in nearly all recognized categories of disability display deficits in their social skills (Merrell, 1993; Walker & McConnell, 1988). Many students who do not have disabilities or at-risk conditions also have deficits in specific areas (for example, getting along with others, coping with not getting one's way, or making assistance needs known appropriately).

Because of their knowledge of individual students, regular teachers are excellent judges of which students are in need of social-skills training (Gresham & Elliott, 1990; Maag, 1989). Teachers are in an ideal position to identify target students for such training due to the normative comparisons they are able to constantly make among students. Four methods, and various combinations of them, have been reported in the professional literature for identifying socially unskilled students: teacher rankings, teacher ratings, sociometric techniques, and direct observations recorded in natural settings. There are clear advantages and disadvantages associated with each method.

Teacher *rankings* and ratings are the least expensive and least intrusive of the four methods; sociometric measures and direct observations are more intrusive and more expensive to record than teacher-supplied measures. Sociometric procedures will identify rejected and neglected students who can benefit from systematic social-skills training; direct observations will identify students who behave negatively with peers or have low rates of social contact with them. Teacher rankings will identify children who are unskilled, unpopular, or socially withdrawn, depending on the dimensions used to rank the students. Teacher ratings will identify students who have social-adjustment problems; they have the added advantage of pinpointing specific skills in need of remediation.

We recommend a combination of either teacher rankings and ratings or teacher nominations and ratings for the purpose of identifying students in need of social-skills training. Whenever possible, we also recommend that direct behavioral observations be recorded in the target student's recess periods. These observations should assess two important variables that often serve as red-flag indicators of social-skills or social-acceptance problems: time spent alone and percent of total behavior that is negative. Greenwood, Walker, Todd, and Hops (1979) have used these combined methods with considerable success in screening and identifying young children who have social-skills deficits and who can benefit from social-skills training.

In the nominations and ratings procedure, the teacher reviews the behavioral characteristics of all students in the class and identifies those who are most at risk. From this group of high-risk students, those most at risk are systematically evaluated on a teacher

Box 9.1 Walker-McConnell Sample Items

Elementary	**Never...Sometimes...Frequently**
1. Shares laughter with peers	1..........2..........3..........4..........5
2. Controls temper	1..........2..........3..........4..........5
Adolescent	
1. Makes friends easily	1..........2..........3..........4..........5
2. Shows sympathy for others	1..........2..........3..........4..........5

Source: Walker & McConnell (1993).

rating instrument for social skills (see Gresham & Elliott, 1990; Walker & McConnell, 1993). In the ranking and rating procedure, the teacher rank orders all students on a social-adjustment dimension (that is, social skills, social competence, social rejection or isolation) and then rates the social skills of those who achieved the highest or lowest ranks (Greenwood et al., 1979).

A number of social-skills rating scales are available for use by teachers. The *Buros Mental Measurements Yearbook*, available in any university library, is an excellent source for evaluative information on the technical features of social-skills rating scales. The *Social Skills Rating System* (SSRS) by Gresham and Elliott (1990) and the *Walker-McConnell Scale of Social Competence and School Adjustment* (SSCSA) by Walker and McConnell (1988, 1993) are two rating systems for social skills that have excellent psychometric properties and national, normative databases. The SSCSA contains an elementary-scale version (grades K–6) and an adolescent version (grades 7–12). The SSRS has preschool-, elementary-, and secondary-scale versions; it has the added features of a parent rating scale and, beginning in grade 5, a self-report version for use by individual students in appraising their social skills.

These instruments elicit teacher judgments of students' social skills by using a Likert rating scale based on frequency of occurrence. Sample items from the elementary and adolescent scales of the SSCSA are presented in Box 9.1.

The authors of the SSCSA and the SSRS have used correlation and factor analysis procedures to identify clusters of social skills that hang together and to measure subdomains of social competence, such as school adjustment, cooperation, assertion, peer relations, empathy, self-control, and responsibility. These subdomains allow for diagnosing and pinpointing the specific areas in which a student is having problems. They can be used effectively to guide the direction and content of social-skills interventions and should be considered carefully in evaluating students' overall social competence.

Box 9.2 Definitions of "Alone" and "Negative Social" Behavior

Alone—The student is alone when he or she is not within 10 feet of another student, is not engaged in any organized activity (that is, with identifiable rules), and is not exchanging social signals (verbal or nonverbal) with any other students.

Negative Social—The student is engaging in negative social behavior when he or she displays hostile behavior or body language toward peers; attempts to tease, bully, or otherwise intimidate others; reacts with anger or rejection to the social bids of peers; or displays aggressive behavior with the intent to inflict harm or force the submission of peers.

For recording *direct observation* of the target student's social behavior in free play (for example, recess periods), we recommend that things be kept as simple as possible. A stopwatch and a definition can be used to code and record playground social behavior with great sensitivity and accuracy. Workable definitions for when to code students as being alone and when to code them as exhibiting negative social behavior are provided in Box 9.2.

These two dimensions should be observed and recorded separately. However, if two stopwatches are available, they can be coded simultaneously. The recording–coding rule to remember is: *Let the stopwatch run when the target student is meeting the requirements of the definition (that is, his or her behavior conforms with the definition) and stop it whenever this is not the case. Restart the stopwatch and let it run when the student's behavior is again meeting the requirements of the definition.* The stopwatch is started and stopped throughout the observation period as the student's social behavior dictates. At the end of the period or session, the time on the stopwatch is divided by the length of the session (that is, the total time observed) and multiplied by 100 to obtain a percentage estimate of either alone or negative social behavior.

We highly recommend this method because it is inexpensive, easy to use, and extremely accurate. Antisocial students tend to spend more time alone and to be more negative than nonantisocial students. As a general rule, it is a red flag if a target student spends more than 12 to 15% of a recess period in solitary activity. Similarly, if the student is negative more than 10% of the time, it is also a red flag. Nonantisocial students in general rarely spend time alone at recess, and they are positive with each other approximately 90 to 95% of the time.

Once a pool of students has been selected to receive social-skills training, the next task is to determine which skills to teach them. There are a number of viable approaches to this task that are discussed later in this chapter in the section on targeting social skills for instruction.

DEFINITION AND CONCEPTUALIZATION OF SOCIAL SKILLS

Interest in social skills can be traced to the 1930s and the work of Moreno (1934). He assessed peer popularity and social preferences via sociometric techniques and identified the social-behavioral correlates of popularity and social rejection. Over the next four decades, a number of developments stimulated and maintained professionals' interest in social skills. These developments included (1) the work of behavior therapists in isolating and teaching discrete forms of social behavior, (2) the assertion-training and affective-education movements in psychology and education, (3) deinstitutionalization and mainstreaming, and (4) the regular education and full-inclusion initiatives. All of these developments tended to highlight the critical importance of social competence as a foundation for school and postschool success.

There are a variety of overlapping definitions of social skills reported in the professional literature (Gresham, 1986; Hollinger, 1987; Maag, 1989). Walker and his colleagues (Walker et al., 1983) have defined *social skills* as a set of competencies that (1) allow an individual to initiate and maintain positive social relationships, (2) contribute to peer acceptance and to a satisfactory school adjustment, and (3) allow an individual to cope effectively and adaptively with the larger social environment. This definition encompasses the following three essential elements of social competence: (1) to recruit social-support networks and friendships, (2) to meet the demands of teachers who control classrooms and peers who control playgrounds, and (3) to adapt to changing and difficult conditions in one's social environment.

McFall (1982) has contributed the most powerful work to date in the conceptualization of social competence and social skills. McFall refers to *social competence* as an overall, summative judgment that key social agents (parents, teachers, peers) make regarding the social effectiveness of one's behavior. Social skills, on the other hand, are the specific strategies and tactics that individuals use to respond to daily social tasks, such as making friends, communicating requests, and responding to social initiations by others. The effectiveness of these skills in producing key social outcomes (teacher and peer acceptance) are used by social agents as a basis for making social competence judgments.

Gresham (1986) has made an important distinction between social-skill deficits and performance deficits. Children with social-skill deficits do not actually have the necessary skill levels to perform in a socially competent fashion. Examples of skill deficits include not knowing how to make friends, being unable to carry on a conversation, or having no idea about how to join an ongoing peer group. Gresham notes that the criteria for determining a *skill deficit* is that either the child does not know how to execute the skill or the child has never previously demonstrated the skill. In contrast, a *performance deficit* means the child has the social skill in his or her repertoire but does not perform it or does not do so at acceptable levels. Likely causes of performance deficits are motivational problems or a lack of opportunities to perform social skills.

Social-skills deficits require a direct teaching approach, while performance deficits require an incentive-based, management approach. Techniques for use with skill deficits include direct instruction, coaching, modeling, and behavioral rehearsal; in contrast, techniques for use with performance deficits involve prompting, cuing, reinforcement, prompted social initiations, home and school rewards, and both individual and group contingencies. In evaluating students' social effectiveness, it is important to determine whether the deficits are skill based or performance based.

CRITERIA AND PROCEDURES FOR TARGETING SPECIFIC SKILLS FOR TRAINING

At least two major criteria are available for selecting the specific social skills to target in social-skills training efforts. These criteria relate to (1) ascertaining specific skill deficits and (2) determining social validity.

Ascertaining Specific Skill Deficits

The students who receive the training must be deficient (skill or performance based) in the target skills selected, and this deficiency must create problems, of some sort, either for the target student or for key social agents (that is, parents, teachers, or peers who interact with them). This requirement may seem unnecessary; however, one of the factors contributing to the less than robust effects achieved from some social-training efforts is that students are instructed on social skills they already perform at acceptable levels. Too often students are instructed in areas in which deficits do not create problems or in which they already perform at criterion levels. In these situations, the incentives for behavior change are quite weak at the outset. *It is essential to determine that a deficit in a particular skill or domain actually exists and that it creates problems and also to determine whether it is a skill-based or performance-based deficit.* Finally, the importance of the skill deficit to the student's daily functioning and to achieving long-term valued outcomes (that is, social acceptance, effective adjustment, satisfactory mental health) must be assessed.

Social Validity

Social validity refers to consumer evaluations and reactions involving the selection of social skills as training targets, as well as the assessment and intervention procedures used. Consumer, as used in this context, refers to the recipients of social-skills interventions or to the social agents (parents, teachers, and peers) who are affected by it and are in a position to judge its impact.

Social validity has been conceptualized by Gresham (1986) as having three components: social significance, social importance, and social acceptability. *Social significance* has to do with consumers' perception of the goals or purposes of social-skills intervention. Increasingly, we must be sensitive to contextual factors in establishing such goals that (1) account for the rights of students and parents, (2) are culturally sensitive and appropriate, and (3) do not conflict with the values and preferences of parents, especially with their moral and religious values. Educators who advocate for social-skills interventions in school need to have a clear rationale for why social skills are being taught, which social skills are being taught, and what the expected outcomes are.

We believe a useful, overarching rationale, in this regard, concerns the dual goals of schooling (that is, the social and academic development of all children and youth). Schools are expected to develop students' potential to the maximum extent possible in these two areas, but we tend to emphasize academic development to the exclusion of social development and competence. Socially effective behavior lays the groundwork for success in and out of school and throughout one's life. We have the ability to teach the social skills that underlie socially effective behavior in the same way that we teach the academic skills that account for academic achievement. In addition, the more socially competent students are in school, the greater will be their degree of school success and academic achievement (Coie & Krehbiel, 1984; Pepler & Rubin, 1991). Social skills are also directly related to one's ability to develop friendships and social-support networks, both of which are important to one's overall quality of life.

Social importance refers to the nature of the behavior change achieved and whether it makes a difference in a student's life. Is its overall impact positive or negative? Does it contribute to achievement of social outcomes that are valued, such as teacher and peer social acceptance, school success, and improved friendships? Maag (1989) notes that social-skills training efforts too often focus on social skills that have no demonstrated relationship to improved social outcomes. Even the best social-skills interventions will have only limited effects if the intervention is applied to skills that bear weak relationships to important social outcomes. Thus, in evaluating social-skills curricula for use in such interventions, it is extremely important to carefully review the rationale and procedures used by the authors to select the target skills. Several examples of how this is done are briefly described.

Sheldon, Sherman, Schumaker, and Hazel (1984) described the procedures they used in developing their adolescent social-skills curriculum called ASSET (Hazel, Schumaker, Sherman, & Sheldon-Wildgen, 1981). They provide an excellent model of how target skills should be selected. These authors consulted the following three primary sources for information to guide their selection of the target skills included in ASSET: published literature on social skills; social-validation ratings by parents, teachers, and students; and judgments of professional experts. Once they had developed a core of social skills for curricular inclusion, they had the skills evaluated by a panel of experts who were also asked to identify situations where the skills could be appropriately applied. As a result of these efforts, the content validity of ASSET is considered to be outstanding.

As an initial step in designing the ACCESS curriculum, Walker and his colleagues (Williams, Walker, Holmes, Todis, & Fabre, 1989) conducted an extensive survey of the professional literature on social skills and also of existing curricula for use at the secondary level. They constructed comparable social validation surveys for use by teachers and their students. These surveys were self-report instruments designed to measure teacher and student opinions regarding the importance of each social skill listed. Skills were grouped into the following three adjustment types: teacher-related, peer-related, and self-related. The surveys were completed by 183 teachers (regular and resource room) and by 437 adolescents, divided into students having mild disabilities and those without disabilities.

Across all three sections of the surveys (that is, teacher-, peer-, and self-related) there was moderate to high agreement between general and special-education teachers, between male and female students, and between general and special-education students.

Among all students and all teachers, there was relatively high agreement in assigned importance ratings for teacher-related adjustment with an agreement index of .83. For peer-related adjustment, the agreement index was .39; and for self-related adjustment, it was .03. These results were replicated within both general and special-education teacher–student groups.

Thus, this study indicated that teachers and students attach similar levels of importance to social skills that support teacher-related forms of adjustment (for example, compliance with teacher requests, making assistance needs known appropriately, self-control). However, they showed relatively low levels of agreement on skills supporting peer-related adjustment (for example, being able to start a conversation, accepting yourself for what you are, feeling free to do what is best for you) and almost no agreement on skills supporting self-related adjustment (for example, trust your decisions, have a great personality, be honest in your behavior). These results indicate that teachers and students attached some degree of importance to all the skills listed in the survey; however, the relative importance attached to them varied between teachers and students across the three adjustment areas.

Social acceptability is the final component of social validity. Are the methods and techniques used to teach social skills acceptable to the target students, parents, and teachers involved? Were the target students embarrassed or otherwise made to feel uncomfortable in the process of receiving the training? Did the students and instructional personnel like the procedures, curricular materials, and formats for instruction that were used? Would they use this approach and materials again? Informal interviews and surveys can be used to get at these important consumer questions, and their use is highly recommended.

Assessment

As noted in an earlier section, teacher ratings of social skills are an excellent resource both for selecting students in need of social-skills intervention and for identifying the domains (areas) and skills in which deficiencies exist. The next task is to prioritize these skill deficits and then decide which ones to teach. One should select a curriculum that teaches the skills in which the student is deficient.

Gresham and Elliott (1990) designed the SSRS social-skills assessment system so that information is generated by teacher ratings on two key dimensions of social skills: (1) frequency of occurrence and (2) perceived importance of the skill. This procedure allows the teacher first to determine whether an individual student has a deficit on a particular skill and then to judge the relative importance of the social skill. The importance rating for each social skill makes it possible to rank-order and prioritize which skills to teach first or to teach at all. An example of this dual-rating procedure is illustrated in Box 9.3. This rating procedure provides a systematic vehicle for combining the dimensions of frequency of occurrence and social importance into effective decision making in the area of social skills. Its use is highly recommended.

A number of author teams have developed assessment systems to accompany their social-skills curricula (Elliott & Gresham, 1991; Stephens, 1992; Walker et al., 1983; Walker et al., 1987). Both the assessment systems and the curricula to which they are tied can be used independently of each other, as stand-alone systems; however, these compo-

Box 9.3 SSRS Ratings of Frequency and Importance

Scale Item	Frequency	Importance
1. Makes friends easily	1.....2.....3	1.....2.....3
2. Makes good decisions	1.....2.....3	1.....2.....3

Frequency: 1 = never, 2 = sometimes, 3 = always

Importance: 1 = not important, 2 = important, 3 = very important

Source: Gresham & Elliott (1990).

nents are most effective when they are used in tandem. Some curricular programs provide Likert rating systems, of a criterion-referenced nature, that convert each social skill in the curriculum into an assessment item. This rating system is usually built into the curriculum. The teacher or social-skills instructor rates the target students' behavioral status on each skill contained in the curriculum and uses this information to decide which skills to teach and in which order. If the curriculum of choice does not provide an assessment option of this type, a Likert scale continuum can be applied to each skill, and selected target students (or all students in the class) can be rated on them. We recommend using either a *frequency of occurrence* dimension or a descriptive or true dimension for this purpose. Examples of each are provided in Box 9.4.

Either of these dimensions will work well for assessing student status on the social skills contained within most available curricula. We strongly recommend that a formal, rather than an informal or subjective, process be used to determine which skills to teach to which students.

In any classroom of students, there is likely to be a small number of *core skills* in which a substantial portion of the students are deficient, and most students could benefit from systematic instruction in them. In addition, there is likely to be a small pool of students who could benefit from instruction in nearly all the core skills listed in a given curriculum program. The remainder of the students would likely fall in between these two points. A useful procedure for identifying which skills should be taught to which students is to rate all students in the class on all skills contained in the curriculum. A matrix with social skills listed down the side and student names listed across the top can be used for this purpose. A numerical rating, ranging from 1 to 5, is then assigned to each student for each listed skill. Form 9.1 contains an example of a completed social-skills matrix; Form 9.2 is a blank copy of this form. In this example, the regular classroom teacher rates each student individually on a skill dimension. A rating of 1 equals unskilled, a rating of 3 equals moderately skilled, and a rating of 5 equals very skilled.

The information contained in Form 9.1 can be very useful for (1) determining which skills should be taught to all students using a universal instructional approach, (2) determining which students should receive instruction in all the listed skills in the

Box 9.4 Likert Scales for Frequency of Occurrence and Descriptive or True Ratings

Frequency of Occurrence. (How often is the skill displayed?)

	Never	**Sometimes**	**Frequently**
1. Concentrates well	1.............2.............3.............4.............5		

Descriptive or True. (How descriptive or true is this skill of the student's characteristic behavior?)

	Not Descriptive or True	**Moderately Descriptive or True**	**Very Descriptive or True**
1. Accepts others	1.............2.............3.............4.............5		

curriculum, and (3) for grouping students by skill deficits for the purpose of forming small groups in which targeted skills can be taught efficiently. We recommend that any skill on which 70% or more of the class members receive a rating of 3 or less should be taught to everyone as a core skill. Any student who receives teacher ratings of 3 or less on 75% or more of the listed social skills should be exposed to all skills contained in the curriculum. This would be considered a selected intervention because the target student is "selected out" by the assessment procedure for an individually tailored intervention that is more intensive than that applied to other class members. It is likely that nearly all antisocial, aggressive students will require exposure to a selected intervention at some point.

Inspection of Form 9.1 indicates considerable variation in the teacher's ratings in terms of (1) individual student performance across skills (that is, within students) and (2) skill levels across students on the listed social skills (that is, within skills). Across all students and skills, the average teacher rating was 3.1, indicating a moderate level of skill mastery for the class as a whole. However, the instructional relevance of the matrix information emerges only when the profiles of individual students and skills are examined.

From Form 9.1, for example, it is apparent that the entire class could benefit from instruction in the skills of joining in, complimenting, expressing anger, following rules, and disagreeing with others. Average scores for the class on these skills were all less than 3, and most of the students were assigned ratings of 3 or less on them. Similarly, it is clear that the following students could likely benefit from intensive social-skills training in either small-group or one-to-one instructional formats: Jeff, Sarah, Jerry, Ed, Tom, and Kate. The average scores of these six students across the listed skills ranged from 1.7 to

Social Skills	Student Names																						Average Social-Skill Score
	Jenny	Jeff†	Julie	Mary	Sarah†	Frank	Dave	Suzy	Jerry†	Eiji	Myles	Ed†	Ann	Maria	Bonnie	Carl	Kelly	Phillip	Vicki	Tom†	Kate†	Will	
1. Listening	4	2	3	3	3	4	2	5	1	3	3	2	4	5	3	2	4	3	5	3	2	4	3.2
2. Greeting others	3	1	3	4	2	3	5	3	1	4	3	3	5	3	2	4	3	4	4	3	2	3	3.1
*3. Joining in	3	2	3	3	1	3	4	3	2	3	2	1	4	3	2	1	3	4	3	2	1	3	2.4
*4. Complimenting	3	3	2	3	2	4	3	4	1	3	3	2	3	4	3	3	2	3	4	3	1	2	2.8
*5. Expressing anger	3	1	3	4	2	3	4	4	1	3	3	1	3	4	3	3	3	4	4	3	2	3	2.9
6. Keeping friends	3	2	4	4	1	4	4	3	2	4	3	2	4	4	4	3	4	4	4	3	2	4	3.3
7. Doing quality work	3	3	3	4	2	4	3	4	1	4	4	3	3	4	3	4	4	4	3	3	3	4	3.3
*8. Following rules	4	2	3	3	1	3	3	3	2	3	3	3	4	4	3	3	3	3	2	2	1	3	2.8
9. Using self-control	3	3	3	4	1	4	4	4	2	4	3	2	5	5	3	4	3	3	3	2	1	4	3.1
10. Offering assistance	4	3	4	4	2	4	5	3	2	5	4	3	4	3	4	4	3	3	5	2	2	4	3.5
*11. Disagreeing with others	3	2	3	3	1	3	4	3	2	3	4	2	3	3	3	3	3	4	3	3	2	3	2.9
12. Being organized	4	3	4	4	2	4	4	3	3	5	4	2	4	4	2	3	4	3	4	3	3	4	3.5
13. Having conversations	4	2	3	3	3	3	4	4	2	4	4	3	4	3	3	4	3	4	4	3	1	3	3.2
Average Student Score	3.4	2.2	3.1	3.5	1.8	3.5	3.8	3.5	1.7	3.7	3.3	2.2	3.8	3.8	2.9	3.2	3.2	3.5	3.7	2.3	1.8	3.4	

*Low average social-skill score.

†Low average student score.

FORM 9.1 Sample Completed Form for Determining Social-Skills Target Deficits for Use in Whole-Class, Small-Group, and One-to-One Instruction

Social Skills	Student Names	Average Social-Skill Score
1. Listening		
2. Greeting others		
3. Joining in		
4. Complimenting		
5. Expressing anger		
6. Keeping friends		
7. Doing quality work		
8. Following rules		
9. Using self-control		
10. Offering assistance		
11. Disagreeing with others		
12. Being organized		
13. Having conversations		
Average Student Score		

FORM 9.2 Sample Blank Form for Determining Social-Skills Target Deficits for Use in Whole-Class, Small-Group, and One-to-One Instruction

2.3, indicating very low overall skill levels when compared to peers. Finally, the information in Form 9.1 can be used to construct small groupings of students based on their shared skill deficits. For example, Jeff, Dave, Jerry, Ed, Carl, and Kate would be candidates for membership in a small group for instruction in listening skills. Similarly, Jeff, Sarah, Jerry, Ed, and Kate would comprise a small group to learn the skill of expressing anger. Finally, on the skill of following rules, the small group would be composed of Jeff, Sarah, Jerry, Vicki, Tom, and Kate.

Although the student membership of these small groups will vary from skill to skill, there will tend to be some recurring overlap within them due to the presence of a small number of students with low average skill levels (for example, Jeff, Sarah, and Ed in our example). It is a good idea for the group membership to change from skill to skill, but more socially skilled students should be included in these groups as appropriate to (1) reduce the possibility of stigma and labeling from peers being associated with such instruction and (2) to take advantage of the expertise and assistance of more skilled peers as both behavioral models and as special helpers and instructional assistants. Again, the matrix information in Form 9.1 provides a solid means of identifying skilled students to play such roles (for example, Ann, Kelly, Maria, Suzy, Will).

The matrix information can also be useful in forming student groups in order to use cooperative-learning strategies for social-skills training. In forming such student groups for academic instruction, teachers usually assign an A, B, C, and D student to each group. Similarly, student groups reflecting unskilled, minimally skilled, moderately skilled, and very skilled levels can be identified from the matrix and assigned accordingly for social-skills instruction. A universal, classwide social-skills intervention is described in Chapter 10 that utilizes this general approach.

Another assessment strategy is to use the universal intervention as a means of identifying those students who need a selected intervention. That is, a core set of skills, judged to be appropriate for all students, could be taught effectively to the entire class as an instructional unit. Those students who do not respond to such instruction could then be selected for either small group or individually tailored social-skills instruction.

As is obvious from the foregoing discussion, numerous options exist for selecting and prioritizing social skills to be taught in both universal and selected interventions. The rule to remember in this regard is: *Avoid subjectivity in decision-making and adopt a formal, structured process for making this important set of judgments.* Time invested in this process will be well spent and will make the social-skills training that does occur far more effective.

RECOMMENDATIONS AND BEST PRACTICES FOR EVALUATING SOCIAL-SKILLS INTERVENTIONS

The two major indications of the success or failure of any systematic social-skills training effort are (1) whether the target student acquires and demonstrates previously unlearned social skills or uses already-acquired skills in a more competent fashion and (2) whether the skill-acquisition process leads to improved social effectiveness and acceptance by key social agents in the student's life. A variety of assessment approaches have been used in attempts to answer these two fundamental questions. Some of these approaches are briefly discussed in this section.

Documenting Skill Acquisition

Methods that are frequently used to document the acquisition of social skills include behavioral role-plays, ratings of the observed frequency of specific social skills or the degree of skill demonstrated in their occurrence, and direct behavioral observations recorded in natural settings (for example, recess, classroom, other school settings). More recently, computer-based videodisc technology has been used for this purpose. Problematic social situations are displayed, and students are asked to indicate their knowledge or judgments of the situations via a touch-screen (see Irvin et al., 1992).

Of these methods, ratings by others is perhaps the least sensitive in detecting changes in specifically taught social skills. Direct observations, behavioral role-plays and demonstrations, and touch-screen video measures are far more sensitive. However, these methods have the disadvantage of producing information that has only weak validity in predicting long-term outcomes associated with social effectiveness.

Evaluating Outcomes of Social-Skills Interventions

Assessments of the *social outcomes* of social-skills training efforts are additive, rather than formative. They are focused on the products or results of the training and assess their social impact as registered with teachers, peers, and parents. In contrast, formative evaluation is focused on the process of social-skills training and whether specific skills or strategies were actually acquired as a result. Outcome-based assessments typically rely on sociometric measures (for example, nominations and ratings by peers), teacher and parent ratings of social skills and overall social competence, and school records analyzed over time (for example, referrals, discipline contacts). Outcome assessments are usually recorded after the training is concluded and are designed to measure the overall impact of the intervention on the target student's social competence and effectiveness. Direct, behavioral observations are also used for this purpose in order to measure the behavior-change process that may or may not be reflected in greater social acceptance and effectiveness.

We recommend that multiple methods, agents, and settings be used to evaluate the results of social-skills training efforts. Whenever possible, a combination of direct observations, parent and teacher ratings, and sociometric procedures should be used for such assessments. This combined approach provides the most comprehensive measurement of potential outcomes, solicits the perspectives of multiple social agents who are important in the student's life, and samples the primary settings (classroom, playground, home) in which the student's social behavior is most important. Maag (1989) has contributed an excellent review of approaches and techniques for conducting social-skills competence assessments.

CONCLUSION

In a book of this type, attention to the systematic assessment and development of socially competent performance is of paramount importance. Antisocial students are regarded by teachers as among the least socially skilled of all at-risk student groups (Walker & McConnell, 1988). Careful screening and identification of the social-skills deficits of this student population enables cost-effective, social-skills instruction. Too often, systematic, social-skills training is misguided because skill and performance deficits are not carefully identified and tied directly to the instructional process.

Chapter 10 focuses on recommended strategies and procedures for systematically training antisocial, as well as non-at-risk, students to be more socially perceptive and effective. Both universal- and selected-intervention approaches are described and illustrated. Recommended resources for conducting such training are also provided.

STUDY QUESTIONS

1. Why do antisocial students have such negative attitudes toward schooling?
2. Why are antisocial students likely to suffer rejection by both teachers and peers?
3. Describe the benefits that the aggressor experiences as a result of an aggressive behavior pattern.
4. Name two of the root causes of the adjustment problems experienced by antisocial students.
5. Why do antisocial students seem to be so insensitive to the effects of their behavior on others?
6. Why do antisocial students develop such negative reputations among their peers?
7. Briefly describe four methods for identifying socially unskilled students.
8. Name two dimensions that effectively identify socially rejected and neglected students at recess.
9. Describe the relationship between social skills and social competence.
10. Define the concept of social validity.
11. Describe two major indications of the success or failure of any systematic social-skills training effort.

KEY TERMS

core skills
direct observations
frequency of occurrence
performance deficit
rankings
social acceptability
social competence
social importance
social outcomes
social-perception bias
social skills
social validity
sociometrics
skill deficit

10 Social Skills: Implementation and Generalization

Approaches to Teaching Social Skills

Contextual Factors Mediating the Teaching of Social Skills

A Universal Approach to Teaching Social Skills: Example and Guidelines

The Playground Behavior Game
Getting a Universal Social-Skills Program Going in Your Classroom

Example of a Selected Approach to Teaching Social Skills

Use of Opportunistic Teaching Methods to Facilitate the Display of Previously Taught Social Skills

Recommendations and Guidelines Governing Best Practices in Social-Skills Interventions in Schools

Resources for Evaluating Curricula and Conducting Social-Skills Training

Conclusion

For years, professionals were unsure that children's social behavior could be assessed, taught, and changed in the same way that academic performance is responsive to these processes. Social-affective behavior was considered to be a product of one's temperament, personality, and upbringing; therefore, the idea of directly teaching improved or more skillful forms of it was slow to catch on. It has now been clearly established that the content of social behavior can be taught effectively using exactly the same principles and techniques as for teaching academic concepts.

The purpose of this chapter is to describe best-practice procedures and recommended guidelines for *implementation* of social-skills training. Both universal and selected approaches to social-skills training are illustrated. Topics covered include (1) approaches to teaching social skills, (2) contextual factors mediating the teaching of social skills, (3) an example and guidelines for a universal approach to teaching social skills, (4) an example of a selected approach to teaching social skills, (5) use of opportunistic teaching methods to facilitate the display of previously taught social skills, (6) recommendations and guidelines governing best practices in social-skills interventions in schools, and (7) resources for evaluating curricula and conducting social-skills training.

APPROACHES TO TEACHING SOCIAL SKILLS

Two major approaches to improving social behavior can be identified in the professional literature: social-skills training and interpersonal cognitive problem solving, or *social problem solving* (Hollinger, 1987). The former strategy is skills based, while the latter is strategy based. Social-skills training assumes that key skills underlie social competence and that these skills can be identified and systematically taught. In contrast, social problem-solving focuses on teaching generic strategies for responding to social situations. These strategies are adaptive, and their use reflects social competence. *Skills-based approaches* tend to rely on direct instruction, while strategy-based approaches focus on developing improved cognitive awareness of social situations and understanding adaptive strategies for responding to them. Target students in this approach are taught to generate a range of alternatives for dealing with social situations.

Zaragoza, Vaughn, and McIntosh (1991) reviewed 27 studies (involving a total of 574 students) that used primarily skills-based approaches to develop the social competence of students in both clinical and nonclinical samples. Ager and Cole (1991) did a similar review of 22 studies that used primarily cognitive problem-solving approaches. Zaragoza et al. (1991) found that the most frequently used intervention techniques were coaching, modeling, behavioral rehearsal, feedback, and reinforcement; other techniques included videotape depictions of social situations, role playing, and discussion. Overall, all but one of these studies reported positive results of the social-skills training on some measure and at some level; however, only four of the studies yielded significant positive gains in peer acceptance. Peer ratings proved to be the most resistant to change of all the measures used across these studies. Only one of the 27 studies attempted to assess the types of social difficulties the participants were experiencing and then design an intervention based on these specific problems. Also, only one study attempted to verify that the behavior-problem students involved actually had social-skills deficits and were in need of systematic social-skills training.

Ager and Cole (1991) critically analyzed studies involving cognitive social problem-solving approaches to improving social competence. However, some of these studies could also be characterized as skills based. Thus, both approaches to teaching social skills appeared to be represented in this review. Strategies used in the studies included social problem-solving, modeling, coaching, and self-instruction; there was an underlying theme in the strategy-based studies of assisting target participants to recognize critical features of problematic social situations, to generate response alternatives to them, and to think through solutions to the situations. No clear advantages for either skills-based or strategy-based approaches emerged from the Ager and Cole review and analysis; results for both approaches were mixed. A number of methodological issues relating to social-skills training were raised by these authors.

Hollinger (1987) conducted a similar review of the empirical evidence underlying the effectiveness of these two approaches. He also found mixed results but concluded that there were sufficiently promising outcomes for both approaches to justify further investments in them. Nearly all reviews of social-skills approaches have noted problems with achieving a durable, long-term impact on social competence and with producing generalization of effects (that is, behavioral gains) from training to nontraining settings. Achieving durable, significant changes in peer acceptance remains one of the most difficult, but important, goals of the social-skills training process. Studies are also highlighting the importance of tailoring social-skills training efforts to the specific deficits of target students and identifying the particular types of social-adjustment problems students have in order to adjust the intervention accordingly. Methods and examples of conducting systematic social-skills training are described in this chapter.

CONTEXTUAL FACTORS MEDIATING THE TEACHING OF SOCIAL SKILLS

The formats used to conduct social-skills training have involved one-to-one, small-group, and whole-classroom instructional arrangements. Research is not clear on which method is best; it is likely that the effectiveness of a particular method depends greatly on the needs and characteristics of the target students. Ideally, all students should be taught in large-group, entire-classroom arrangements; however, given the diversity of today's classrooms, it is not likely that this universal approach will be effective for all students.

Generic social-skills training should be thought of as a three-step process. In Step One, all students in a classroom should be exposed to a core set of skills from which all students can benefit. These skills can be identified by social-skills ratings of the entire class, as described in Chapter 9. Strayhorn, Strain, and Walker (1993) recently made a case for the systematic instruction of all children and youth in the social goals of kindness, cooperation, and positive social behavior. It was suggested that peer tutoring could be used to absorb the costs of exposing all students to such an approach. Those students who are not responsive to such a universal instructional procedure become candidates for Step

Teaching social skills in a small-group format. *Robert Finken*

Two (small-group instruction), Step Three (intensive, one-to-one instruction), or both. As noted earlier, small-group instruction works best when students are grouped together according to shared skill deficits. Several nontarget students of the same age or sex should participate as peer models and instructional assistants in such small-group instruction. Those students who need more intensive instruction and support than can be provided in a small group thus "select themselves out" by their unresponsiveness to small-group instruction. As noted earlier, antisocial students are likely to be members of this final group of target students.

Box 10.1 contains a nine-step instructional procedure, taken from ACCEPTS, a social-skills intervention program developed for elementary-age students by the senior author and his colleagues (see Walker et al., 1983). This procedure is based on principles of instruction designed to directly teach essential social skills and to help target students clearly discriminate instances of the target skill from noninstances and discuss situations in which the new skill can be applied. If combined with *cuing, coaching, debriefing, feedback,* and *reinforcement* in natural generalization settings, this approach can be powerful

Box 10.1 The ACCEPTS Instructional Sequence

The ACCEPTS instructional sequence was modeled after a direct instruction teaching procedure. By following scripted formats, each of the 28 ACCEPTS skills is taught individually, with a maximum of nine instructional steps. The basic instructional sequence is standardized across all 28 teaching scripts; however, the actual number of steps involved in the instructional sequence varies according to the difficulty of the individual skill. The instructional sequence outlined here includes the maximum number of teaching steps contained in any one teaching script.

Step 1: Definition and Guided Discussion

a. Teacher presents skill definition, followed by student oral response.
b. Teacher leads students in a guided discussion of skill application and a range of examples.

Step 2: Positive Example

a. Teacher presents first videoscene example showing appropriate skill application, *or*
b. Teacher models an example of appropriate skill application.
c. Debrief episode.

Step 3: Negative Example

a. Teacher presents second videoscene (nonexample) demonstrating failure to use skill or incorrect skill application, *or*
b. Teacher models a nonexample demonstrating failure to use skill or incorrect skill application.
c. Debrief episode.

Step 4: Review and Restate Skill Definition

a. Teacher reviews skill definition.
b. Student oral response.

Step 5: Positive Example

a. Teacher presents a third videoscene of appropriate skill application, *or*
b. Teacher models a second example of appropriate skill application.
c. Debrief episode.

Step 6: Activities

a. Teacher *models* a range of activities that exemplify or expand upon skill production.
b. Teacher presents students with *practice* activities and role-play situations designed to build skill mastery.

Box 10.1 *(Continued)*

Step 7: Positive Example

a. Teacher presents final video-scene example, if called for in the script, *or*
b. Teacher models final, positive example as needed.
c. Debrief as needed.

Step 8: Criterion Role-Plays

a. Teacher presents students with criterion role-play calling for skill demonstration.
b. Teacher judges students' quality of skill performance. If acceptable, proceed to next step. If unacceptable, recycle students through an abbreviated instructional sequence, present a second role-play, and reassess students' performance.

Step 9: Informal Contracting

a. Teacher presents students with a situation or rule for trying out the skill in a natural situation prior to the next session.
b. Students respond with a verbal commitment.

Source: From *The Walker Social Skills Curriculum: The ACCEPTS Program (A Curriculum for Children's Effective Peer and Teacher Skills),* by H. M. Walker, S. McConnell, D. Holmes, B. Todis, J. Walker, and N. Golden.

for improving social competence. This instructional sequence is appropriate for use with universal, small-group, and one-to-one instructional formats.

There are several reasons why isolated social-skills programs, in which a student is pulled out of the regular classroom, may not be the best approach for improving the social competence of antisocial students. First, even when antisocial students change many of their social behaviors, they continue to be faced with peer groups that are unwilling to allow them to alter their long-standing negative reputations (see Hollinger, 1987). Thus, involving the peer group in the training and implementation of social-skills interventions may be a highly advisable strategy when working with students who are antisocial or aggressive.

In their review, Zaragoza et al. (1991) found that, although social-skills interventions for children with behavior problems resulted in improvements, the children's reputations among peers remained the same. These authors concluded that peers' perceptions of a student with behavior problems are extremely resistant to change. Peers rarely change their attitudes toward and expectations of antisocial students, even when their social behavior is clearly altered in positive directions. Thus, negative reactions by peers may elicit negative behaviors on the part of the target student, thereby providing continuing support for the antisocial student's problem behaviors—and justifying the peers' negative perceptions.

The second reason why "pull-out" social-skills programs may be insufficient for antisocial students is that these programs are often limited to a single *context* in which the negative behaviors are embedded. When social-skill improvement efforts are restricted to one context, generalization will likely not extend to the regular classroom, the playground, or the lunchroom. Whenever possible, it is desirable to train, cue, prompt, and coach antisocial students in a variety of contexts in which their social skills are likely to play instrumental roles in determining their acceptance and social adjustment.

Third, peers have great sensitivity to the differential treatment of students in their midst, and this sensitivity increases with age and maturity. Students who are pulled out of the classroom on a regular, predictable schedule carry some risk of being stigmatized by the attention associated with this procedure. When combined with their already negative reputations and aversive behavioral characteristics, antisocial students may be at risk for further stigmatization as a part of the social-skills intervention. If pulling the antisocial student out of class is the only alternative, then steps should be taken to attenuate the possibility of stigma (for example, vary the schedule or change the reasons for the pull-out).

Another important contextual factor relates to who provides the instruction for the social-skills training. Most often, instruction is conducted by the school or districtwide counselor or psychologist. At other times, a temporary position is filled and the instructor is employed only for the duration of the social-skills program. These instructors are generally unable to observe antisocial students for sufficient periods of time as they interact in the classroom and on the playground. Instead, they see children only for the actual social-skill instruction.

The expertise of classroom teachers is rarely fully utilized for social-skills instruction. This occurs despite the findings of a recent teacher survey indicating the strong need for effective social-skills curricula. Both special- and regular-education teachers in this study believed that social-skills training should be an integral part of the regular school curriculum (see Bain & Farris, 1991).

Finally, most social-skills programs simply do not include adequate techniques, time, and resources for promoting the generalization and maintenance of learned social skills. Specific techniques must be included in these programs to maximize generalization and maintenance; otherwise, the social validity of many social-skills interventions will continue to be unacceptable.

A UNIVERSAL APPROACH TO TEACHING SOCIAL SKILLS: EXAMPLE AND GUIDELINES

This section describes a universal approach to teaching social skills. The focus is on the entire classroom; it is a global, or universal, intervention that targets all students. Regular classroom teachers and playground supervisors play critical roles in the implementation of this universal intervention.

The individual classroom is an ideal place to focus interventions that either prevent or decrease antisocial school behavior. Classroom-level interventions offer access to all students in a uniform manner. All the students are in one place and thus no one (parents, counselors, or the individual child) needs to be counted on to remember an appointment. Classrooms and playgrounds are two of the main arenas for social-interaction training involving peers and adults. There is tremendous potential for students to learn and practice new social skills at school. Finally, teachers and students generally feel comfortable with this approach, especially when it is presented along with other learning experiences and activities and is integrated into the ongoing academic program.

The following description of this *whole-class approach* is derived from an ongoing prevention project for conduct disorders funded by the National Institute of Mental Health (see Reid, 1990). The purpose of this project is to prevent antisocial behavior patterns from leading to conduct disorder in elementary school children (specifically, students in grades 1 and 5). It is a multifaceted approach that includes parent education and social-skills training for all students. The social-skills program and the parent-education component run simultaneously in order for information and procedures to be replicated for target children in school and at home and thus to increase the likelihood of achieving behavioral consistency across settings. However, conducting classroom social skills without parent education is still a viable intervention option.

This whole-class approach is designed around 20 lessons lasting 1 hour each. Many components of the intervention can be easily utilized in the regular academic curriculum, and thus be reinforced throughout the school year. This program was designed for the regular classroom teacher and includes all students in the class. *Generalization* and *maintenance* of social skills is a primary focus of this approach. All children are included in order for nonproblem students to learn ways of including and supporting their peers (that is, those who have behavior problems and those who do not). The classroom teacher is the primary instructor, which means that skills such as cooperation and listening can be practiced and reinforced throughout the instructional day.

Finally, the playground (or other free-play settings) serves as the context for ongoing generalization-training efforts. The classroom teacher and playground supervisors work closely together on an incentive system (the Playground Behavior Game) to ensure continual practice of newly acquired skills within natural settings. Before starting this program, students are assigned to teams of four to six students each. Teams should have roughly equivalent numbers of boys and girls and be composed of popular as well as rejected or neglected children. Friends can occasionally be paired in teams, especially if one of the students only feels comfortable participating with that other student. If possible, desks for each team should be placed together. Group selection does not necessarily have to remain fixed. If it appears that a particular group is having difficulty achieving success, then the groups should be reconfigured to achieve a more even performance among all groups. If a group or cooperative approach of this type is used throughout the entire school year in academic subjects, consider reconfiguring the groups every two or three months.

Teaching social skills in a normative peer group has one main advantage: Students can observe the behavior of each other during skill-practice sessions. In addition, less successful groups can observe the interactions and end products of more successful groups. Cooperative peer groups have been shown to support and motivate change in academic achievement, as well as in social competence (Johnson & Johnson, 1986; Slavin, 1984). The simple act of pairing unpopular children with popular children will significantly improve the social interactions of both and can lead to increased acceptance of unpopular children (Bierman, 1986; Bierman & Furman, 1984). Students have the opportunity to pool their knowledge and skills while completing a project or assignment together. For example, during one "Dealing with Anger" lesson, student teams are instructed to create a 5-minute video depicting positive ways of dealing with an anger-provoking situation. Students take different roles (director, actor, camera person) and work on a script as a group. During the lessons on cooperation, teams must build a structure, as a group, out of nothing but spaghetti and gumdrops. All decisions need to be consensual.

Many of the whole-class social-skill lessons are based on teaching those things in which antisocial students are traditionally weak. Students spend 45 minutes to 1 hour each week engaged in role-plays, dramatizations, and other cooperative activities that address the following topics:

Following rules

Listening

Study skills

Listening and asking questions

Identifying feelings

Compliments (giving and receiving)

Cooperation

Joining a group

Including new people

Dealing with anger (2 lessons)

Almost all social-skills curricula can be adapted to meet the needs of an entire class. Lessons were developed for this whole-class approach by examining several curricula and adapting activities so that all students in any classroom could participate. Each teacher knows what will work best in his or her classroom and should use adaptations accordingly.

In addition to traditional social-skills lessons, this whole-class approach calls for students to gather in a classroom meeting once each week. There are two goals for these class meetings. One is to give each student an opportunity to speak to the rest of the class while all other students listen. This is an especially useful activity for both antisocial students and neglected students. The second goal of the class meeting is to provide an opportunity to teach problem-solving skills. Once the problem-solving procedure is taught and the students and classroom teacher feel comfortable with all the steps involved, the class meeting becomes a forum for solving student problems. Appropriate problems for the focus of this activity generally involve social-interactional or rule-compliance issues.

Students begin each class meeting with a review of the social skills introduced up to that point. For example, during the sixth week of class meetings, the teacher begins with a quick review in the form of a question and answer game about rules, listening, pinpointing feelings, and asking appropriate questions. Following this review, each student "checks in." Students are invited to share examples from their own lives in which they used a particular social skill. They briefly describe the situation and then identify the skill involved (more review and practice).

Over time, students use the check-in procedure to identify problems that can then be worked through using the problem-solving strategy. After check-in, students either engage in learning one of the four problem-solving steps or use the entire process to actually solve problems. The steps in the process have been simplified, but cover the basic strategies usually employed when teaching problem solving.

Students learn the following problem-solving steps:

1. Clearly state the problem
2. Brainstorm solutions
3. Evaluate solutions
4. Try out a solution

Most antisocial students have no idea about how to solve problems effectively; they devote little time to thinking through problems, tend to jump in with both feet, and end up doing something completely inappropriate (for example, yelling, fighting, or giving up). Not only are these students given an opportunity to learn a much more effective problem-solving procedure, they can practice again and again and observe how their peers use problem-solving strategies. Nonproblem students learn effective ways of working through problems with aggressive or antisocial students, as well as techniques for looking at issues in their personal lives.

The classroom teacher is active during the initial class meetings. He or she needs to teach the four problem-solving steps, provide opportunities for practice, and monitor progress. Eventually, however, the classroom teacher gradually withdraws and students take over and facilitate the meetings.

As noted, one of the most important components of this whole-class approach is a focus on generalization and maintenance processes. The playground or other free-play setting serves as the primary context for generalization and maintenance training in the area of peer relations. The Playground Behavior Game, described in the following section, is a simple approach to ensuring carryover of learned skills. It requires the classroom teacher to work closely with the people whose responsibility it is to monitor the behavior of students in free-play or recess situations. In this chapter, we refer to these people as the "playground supervisors."

The Playground Behavior Game

We strongly recommend using an additional incentive system when first implementing a social-skills program on a classwide basis. During each classroom lesson, the teacher's regular disciplinary practices should be used, but on the playground most students have no or only limited experience with adults attending to their behavior. On the playground, the norm is for most social behaviors (positive and negative) to go unnoticed, with the exception of only the most violent or seriously inappropriate incidents warranting the attention of school personnel. To ensure generalization of learned social skills, some form of extra motivation in free play is generally required. The incentive system presented here provides students with team and class rewards for positive play with peers during free play.

As mentioned, each classroom is divided into four or five small groups for in-class social-skills training activities. On the playground, rewards and incentives can be earned for each team, depending on the quality of their behavior with one another. Both positive and negative forms of behavior are addressed in the Playground Behavior Game.

The Playground Behavior Game is substantially more difficult to describe than it is to implement. It is our experience that, once in place, the game has a tremendous impact on the social behavior of most students, including antisocial ones. Adult playground supervisors are also positively affected by this activity. Without the Playground Behavior Game or some other free-play incentive system, generalization and maintenance of newly learned skills is highly unlikely. And without providing for generalization outcomes, the teaching of social skills is not really a good investment of teachers' and students' time.

Component I: Positive Behavior

Although positive behavior on the playground is acknowledged for the individual student, the rewards are earned for all students. When a predetermined criterion is met, the entire class earns a more valuable group reward. The playground supervisors circulate among the students during recess looking for examples of positive, prosocial behaviors, such as:

- Interacting nicely with peers
- Following directions
- Playing properly on playground equipment
- Staying within designated boundaries

The playground supervisors must move around a great deal in order to observe and reinforce positive behavior. When the supervisors observe a student engaged in appropriate behavior, they should call attention to the desired behavior and present the student with an armband.

During any given free-play period, playground supervisors might distribute anywhere from 20 to 50 armbands for instances of positive student behavior. The classroom teacher can assist the playground supervisors by having them focus only on certain target social skills for reinforcement. For example, some classrooms may have problems in quietly and quickly lining up after recess. The supervisors can be instructed to make a special effort to acknowledge positive "line behavior." Or, if the social-skill lesson that week is "accepting new people into games," the playground supervisors can make this the primary target behavior for which students receive armbands.

Another variation for distributing positive incentives involves including student representatives of the class. Select two or three students in the class to distribute armbands to their classmates for positive behaviors and target social skills. Do not attempt this, however, until students are familiar with the Playground Behavior Game. Rotate the selected students so that everyone has a chance to distribute positive incentives to their classmates. This technique works well with all ages of elementary school students. It relieves the playground supervisors of some of the monitoring burdens and makes the students more and more responsible for their own behavior. The armbands are collected at the completion of the recess period.

Component II: Negative Behavior

Negative social behavior is addressed in a group format, although student behavior is tracked individually. Monitoring student behavior on the playground requires a score sheet for each class. Student names are listed by team (see Component IV: Materials). The playground supervisors use this score sheet to track any occurrences of negative behavior.

All teams are to be given the same number of points at the start of the recess period. The class should be told that all groups have been given all of the possible points because you (the classroom teacher) trust that they will not engage in negative behaviors or break the playground rules during recess. Explain that if individual students should engage in negative behavior with other students or break any playground rules during the recess period, they will lose one of the team's points for each occurrence. If, at the end of recess, the total points remaining for a group is greater than a predetermined criterion, each member earns a sticker and the group's success is recorded on a large progress chart displayed in the classroom (see Component IV: Materials). Over the course of the year, the criteria for earning a reward should get more and more difficult as students become more socially skilled.

Students can lose points for behaviors such as teasing, arguing, name calling, leaving the boundary area, entering the building, fighting, not coming at the signal, not using playground equipment properly, not following directions. It is important to mark off points for small infractions. The playground supervisors should not wait for a physical fight to occur but should intervene early in the behavioral chain and mark off points for name calling, arguing, or teasing. This early intervention can prevent the confrontation from escalating into a fight.

Classroom teachers should work closely with playground supervisors in creating a list of social behaviors and skills that will cause students to lose points. Let students know that not all negative behaviors, rule infractions, or even attempts to use the positive behavior taught during social-skills lessons will be seen every time but that, over time, many of these behaviors will be recorded.

Component III: Debrief

As recess is ending, the playground supervisors hand the score sheet to the classroom teacher. The score sheet is the mechanism for communication between the supervisors and the teacher. A few examples of both positive and negative recess behavior can be noted on it.

As students enter the classroom following recess, they drop their armbands into a large jar. A short class discussion should take place in which students are praised for specific positive behaviors on the playground. During this discussion, it may be appropriate to refer to a student by name, especially if an antisocial student displayed positive behavior on the playground. Or, a more general statement can be made to a group, such as, "I heard that someone on the Green Team did an excellent job of including someone else in their game."

It is also important to point to specific examples of negative behavior. Students should not be referred to individually (for example, avoid saying "The Red Team lost two points, one point when Jason left the boundary area and one when Jane teased Alex."). For one or two of the incidents, it is important to ask students how a negative situation might have been handled in a more positive way.

Students can earn small rewards for good performance in a number of ways. First, the entire class can earn a prize of some type when the jar of armbands is full. Second, group members can earn stickers for meeting the daily criteria. Vary the order and choice for prizes, stickers, and progress charts in order to keep student motivation high.

Component IV: Materials

The following materials are needed for the Playground Behavior Game:

1. Large poster displayed in the classroom listing playground rules
2. Nylon armbands (or substitute any tangible reward that can be distributed easily on an individual basis)
3. Jar for collecting armbands
4. Classwide prizes for distribution when the jar is full (examples include plastic animals, lunch coupons, stickers, extra free time, and snacks)
5. Score sheet divided by team and listing all students—for example:

Red Team	*Blue Team*	*Green Team*
Jason	Elena	George
Laura	Seth	Liz
Jane	Kyle	Lee
Jose	Donna	Ashley
Judy		

6. Clipboard and pencil
7. Progress chart for tracking group progress

Getting a Universal Social-Skills Program Going in Your Classroom

The aims or goals of any social-skills program is to modify students' interpersonal behaviors with peers and adults and to improve the effectiveness of their social behavior. Valued social outcomes include acceptance in peer groups, acceptance by significant adults, good school adjustment, better mental health, and lack of contact with the juvenile court system (see Gresham, 1986). We believe the universal (whole-class) approach to teaching social skills and the accompanying incentive system to ensure generalization and maintenance is an ideal way of reaching these goals. As we have noted, this universal approach may not work for the most seriously antisocial student, but it is a logical and natural starting point for intervening with such students.

Almost any social-skills curriculum can be adapted for a whole-class approach. Begin by creating cooperative teams. Next, develop activities that include all students. Ideas can be found in almost any social-skills or team-building curriculum. Finally, do not ignore an incentive system for free-play settings. Students engage in negative social behaviors primarily in unstructured, free-play settings.

The classroom teacher has the following responsibilities in setting up a classwide social-skills program:

One Month Prior

- Review age-appropriate social-skills curricula
- Make a list of students for each team (remember four to six students, equal mix of males and females, and only one or two rejected students per group)
- Prepare materials for the Playground Behavior Game (or other free-play incentive system)
- Meet with playground supervisors to review playground rules and the incentive system
- Make 1–2 hours available during the weeks of social-skill instruction

One Week Prior

- Order relevant lessons
- Prepare a 1- to 2-minute description of the lesson's skill
- Prepare a short demonstration or role-play of the lesson's skill (3–5 minutes)
- Prepare group activity related to the lesson's skill (most curricula provide activities that are easily adaptable)
- Let students and parents know what is coming

Day One

- Move desks
- Introduce the social-skills program
- Begin Lesson One

Ongoing

- Continue to plan new group activities
- Monitor Playground Behavior Game
- Provide rewards earned during Playground Behavior Game
- Reconfigure groups as necessary

EXAMPLE OF A SELECTED APPROACH TO TEACHING SOCIAL SKILLS

We believe that social-skills training should, whenever possible, occur within the context of natural school settings and be embedded within the target students' peer group. The whole-class approach is an excellent means of doing this; however, it is by no means the only way. The peer group can be involved in both one-to-one and small-group instructional formats as instructional assistants, as special helpers on the playground and in the classroom, and as peer mentors and models. The rule to remember is that *isolated, pull-out approaches divorced from the peer group are to be avoided whenever possible.* However, it is also important to remember that social-skills interventions are generally more effective when (1) they are individually tailored, (2) they take into account the specific deficits and adjustment problems of target students, and (3) generalization and maintenance effects are planned for and actively pursued. An example of a one-to-one, small-group format for teaching social skills is presented in this section to provide a contrast with the universal approach described earlier.

The ACCEPTS program is a comprehensive social-skills intervention package designed to teach mastery of the following three skill clusters or areas: (1) classroom skills, (2) relating to others, and (3) coping skills (Walker et al., 1983). The program contains 28 social skills that are sequenced so that they build on one another in order to form more complex skills. Classroom skills involve meeting the teacher's minimal behavioral demands necessary for delivering and managing instruction (for example, complying with requests, and working on assigned tasks); relating to others includes friendship-making and getting-along skills as well as basic social-interaction skills; coping skills consist of strategies for dealing with not getting one's way and coping with teasing. ACCEPTS was designed primarily for use in one-to-one and small-group instructional formats; however, its content and instructional procedures can easily be adapted for whole-group, entire-classroom instruction and has been used in this fashion by numerous consumers.

ACCEPTS is appropriate for use in grades K–6; the companion ACCESS social-skills program covers grades 7–12. ACCEPTS provides an eight-step instructional procedure that provides intensive coverage of each social skill, including defining the skill, providing examples and nonexamples of the skill, showing and discussing video examples of the skill being applied (both correctly and incorrectly) in a range of social situations, and the use of modeling and behavioral rehearsal to further build conceptual and initial behavioral mastery. Cuing, coaching, debriefing, and feedback are implemented extensively within target natural settings to assist the student in applying previously taught skills correctly and appropriately. One to two 45-minute, daily lessons are usually required to initially teach each ACCEPTS skill; however, some of the more complex skills, such as making friends, can require longer periods for mastery. If the program is used with more severely disabled students, skill mastery trials and lesson times will expand considerably. ACCEPTS is geared for primary use with general-education students and those having mild to moderate disabling conditions.

ACCEPTS has two major components: *instruction* and *behavior management*. The instructional component occurs in a classroom of some type and usually consists of the target students and, depending on user preference, nontarget peers who serve as instructional assistants during training and as special helpers at recess. The behavior-management component is designed to facilitate the transfer and generalization of the initially learned social skills to classroom and playground periods. The procedures of this component also support and further instruct the target student in variations of the skill required by differing social situations that occur in classroom and playground settings.

In the classroom, the regular teacher acknowledges, praises, and provides a rating (0–5) for appropriate demonstrations of the previously taught classroom skills (for example, listening to instructions and directions or making assistance needs known). At the end of the instructional period in which the rating is awarded, the teacher debriefs the student about her or his behavior and relates the assigned rating to this debriefing. The rating is exchanged for points that count toward a school or home reward activity for the child.

On the playground, a single focus skill is identified for each day of the program (that is, the skill currently being taught in the ACCEPTS curriculum); during the recess period, the program supervisor (counselor, teacher, school psychologist, other school staff) and the regular recess supervisors look for appropriate displays of the skill in the student's ongoing social interactions. These instances are noted, described, and praised as they occur, with care being taken not to disrupt ongoing social exchanges or organized play activities. The target student is also praised during the recess period for engaging in social exchanges with peers and participating in games and structured playground activities. Special helpers play an important role in this process as mentors, playmates, and guides to the nuances of peer-controlled activities. The focus is on inclusion of the target student in a full range of social activities at recess. At the end of the recess period, the target student's playground behavior and use of the focus skills are reviewed with him or her and points are awarded for both positive social engagement and appropriate displays of the focus skill. The earned points are then exchanged for a group-activity reward that is shared equally with class members.

Form 10.1 is an example of a completed point-recording form used at recess in the ACCEPTS program. Focus skills are listed on the form; in any recess period, there is always one focus skill and two review skills, which are the preceding skills in the instructional sequence. The form contains instructions for the program or recess supervisor to use in debriefing and awarding points to the target student for both social engagement and skills usage. A blank copy of this form is included as Form 10.2.

The ACCEPTS program illustrates many of the practices we have been advocating throughout this chapter. Potential target students are evaluated on the ACCEPTS placement test, which converts each social skill in the curriculum to a Likert rating of 1 to 5. This information is used to (1) determine whether the students can profit from the program and (2) place the students appropriately in the ACCEPTS curricular sequence. This information is also useful in constructing small groups of students who share common skill deficits. An intensive instructional procedure is initiated, which is then followed by a behavior-management support system that builds behavioral mastery of the skill in classroom and playground generalization settings. Only in this way do the target students stand a chance of fully integrating the target skills into their behavioral repertoire so that they become functionally useful.

The ACCEPTS social-skills training and behavioral-mastery processes are carefully embedded in the peer-group context by (1) involving peers as special helpers, behavioral models, mentors, and special helpers during the instruction and behavior-management phases of the program and (2) having the target students earn group-activity rewards that are shared equally with peers. These features provide strong motivation for peers to support the target students' attempts to use the skills appropriately and are powerful in reversing their negative perceptions of antisocial, aggressive students whose behavioral characteristics are so aversive to them. When the program is implemented only during the morning recess, we find positive spillover effects in the noon and afternoon recesses (see Appendix A). Once positive social exchanges occur reliably between aggressive students and peers and the negative perception biases are attenuated, it is likely that peers will respond reciprocally to the positive social initiations of the target students. For this behavioral effect to occur indefinitely, it is critical to build in a long-term maintenance program to provide the necessary levels of monitoring and support.

USE OF OPPORTUNISTIC TEACHING METHODS TO FACILITATE THE DISPLAY OF PREVIOUSLY TAUGHT SOCIAL SKILLS

A number of strategies and techniques have been reported in the literature over the past decade that are designed to facilitate the transfer of behavioral gains across settings and to produce durable, enduring effects over time. Some excellent examples of techniques that facilitate the generalization of social skills can be found in well-controlled studies by the following authors: Stokes and Osnes (1986); Paine et al. (1982); Dougherty, Fowler, and Paine (1985); Sasso, Melloy, and Kavale (1990); Schumaker and Ellis (1982); and DuPaul

COMPLETED ACCEPTS RECESS RATING FORM

Child's Name Jamie Curtis Date 3-7-94

Rater's Name Ms Vamoski

General Instructions. The target child's *social participation* and *social-skill level* are rated in a single, daily recess period. a new form should be used for each daily rating. Specific instructions for making these ratings and for using e form are provided below.

Social Participation

Rater: The child's social participation is evaluated and rated in 5-minute segments throughout the recess period. "YES" is circled if the child has interacted appropriately for *at least half of the 5-minute period.* Appropriate interaction includes (1) active involvement in a game, (2) participation in an organized playground activity, or (3) talking to peers. "NO" is circled if the child does not interact with peers for more than half of the 5-minute period *or* if the child engages in negative, inappropriate interacions for at least half of the period. Negative, inappropriate interaction includes such behaviors as arguing, teasing, hitting, and obstructing games.

To the child: Before recess, review with the child:

A. Things to do to *earn* free time

1. Play with friends (monjey bars, sandbox, foursquare, etc.)
2. Play games (baseball, dodgeball, Red Rover, etc.)
3. Talk to friends

B. Things that *don't earn* free time

1. Being alone
2. Watching games, but not playing
3. Arguing with or teasing other children
4. Hurting people

Rating

Recess Period	*Points Earned*	
1st 5-minute period	YES	(NO)
2nd 5-minute period	(YES)	NO
3rd 5-minute period	(YES)	NO
4th 5-minute period	YES	(NO)
5th 5-minute period	(YES)	NO
6th 5-minute perioid	(YES)	NO

$\frac{1}{2}$ minute of free time is earned for each YES circled.

TOTAL free time earned for playing with friends 2

FORM 10.1 Completed ACCEPTS Recess Rating Form. *Source:* From *The Walker Social Skills Curriculum: The ACCEPTS Program (A Curriculum for Children's Effective Peer and Teacher Skills)*, by H. M. Walker, S. McConnell, D. Holmes, B. Todis, J. Walker, and N. Golden.

SKILL-LEVEL RATING AND REVIEW

Rater: At the end of each of each recess period, the target child is evaluated and rated on the use of specific social skills taught in the ACCEPTS curriculum. This rating focuses on the use of a smaller number (3) of social skills. As these may be difficult for the child or newly learned, it is important that he or she be rewarded for using them. When you see the child engaging in one of the skills listed below, provide brief, verbal praise. At the end of the recess period, indicate skills used by circling "YES" on the appropriate line. If the skill was not exhibited, circle "NO."

Skills to Focus On

1. Talk as much as you listen (YES) NO
2. Join in YES (NO)
3. Help others (YES) NO

Review with the child the "Skills to Focus On" before recess. Tell the child you will be watching especially for skills, but you want to see other skills used appropriately also.

1 minute of free time is earned for each YES circled.

TOTAL free time sarned for focus skills 2

Also at the end of recess, the child's overall social-skill level is evaluated and rated on a scale of 0 to 5 ("0" representing unskilled and "5" highly skilled). This rating should reflect the *degree* to which all social skills are displayed and the child's *skill level* in applying them.

Overall Skill Level

Unskilled *Highly Skilled*

0. . . . . .1 . . . . 2 . . . . (3). 4 5

1 minute of free time is earned for each point on the scale.

TOTAL free time minutes earned for Overall Skill Level 3

After recess spend a moment with the child to:

1. Ask questions abput the activities completed and skills used. Prompt and praise the child for accurately describing his or her behaivior during recess.
2. Debrief and provide feedback to the child, detailing (1) activities or skills you observed, (2) skills the child successfully applied, and (3) skills the child should have applied or instances where skills were not properly used.
3. Explain the ratings you have recorded for the child. Whenever possible, praise the child for positive aspects of his or her performance.

FORM 10.1 *(Continued)*

COMPLETED ACCEPTS RECESS RATING FORM

Child's Name ____________________ Date ____________________

Rater's Name ____________________

General Instructions. The target child's *social participation* and *social-skill level* are rated in a single, daily recess period. a new form should be used for each daily rating. Specific instructions for making these ratings and for using e form are provided below.

Social Participation

Rater: The child's social participation is evaluated and rated in 5-minute segments throughout the recess period. "YES" is circled if the child has interacted appropriately for *at least half of the 5-minute period.* Appropriate interaction includes (1) active involvement in a game, (2) participation in an organized playground activity, or (3) talking to peers. "NO" is circled if the child does not interact with peers for more than half of the 5-minute period *or* if the child engages in negative, inappropriate interacions for at least half of the period. Negative, inappropriate interaction includes such behaviors as arguing, teasing, hitting, and obstructing games.

To the child: Before recess, review with the child:

A. Things to do to *earn* free time

1. Play with friends (monjey bars, sandbox, foursquare, etc.)
2. Play games (baseball, dodgeball, Red Rover, etc.)
3. Talk to friends

B. Things that *don't earn* free time

1. Being alone
2. Watching games, but not playing
3. Arguing with or teasing other children
4. Hurting people

Rating

Recess Period	*Points Earned*	
1st 5-minute period	YES	NO
2nd 5-minute period	YES	NO
3rd 5-minute period	YES	NO
4th 5-minute period	YES	NO
5th 5-minute period	YES	NO
6th 5-minute perioid	YES	NO

$\frac{1}{2}$ minute of free time is earned for each YES circled.

TOTAL free time earned for playing with friends ______

FORM 10.2 Blank ACCEPTS Recess Rating Form. *Source:* From *The Walker Social Skills Curriculum: The ACCEPTS Program (A Curriculum for Children's Effective Peer and Teacher Skills),* by H. M. Walker, S. McConnell, D. Holmes, B. Todis, J. Walker, and N. Golden.

SKILL-LEVEL RATING AND REVIEW

Rater: At the end of each of each recess period, the target child is evaluated and rated on the use of specific social skills taught in the ACCEPTS curriculum. This rating focuses on the use of a smaller number (3) of social skills. As these may be difficult for the child or newly learned, it is important that he or she be rewarded for using them. When you see the child engaging in one of the skills listed below, provide brief, verbal praise. At the end of the recess period, indicate skills used by circling "YES" on the appropriate line. If the skill was not exhibited, circle "NO."

Skills to Focus On

1. ______________________________ YES NO
2. ______________________________ YES NO
3. ______________________________ YES NO

Review with the child the "Skills to Focus On" before recess. Tell the child you will be watching especially for skills, but you want to see other skills used appropriately also.

1 minute of free time is earned for each YES circled.

TOTAL free time sarned for focus skills ______

Also at the end of recess, the child's overall social-skill level is evaluated and rated on a scale of 0 to 5 ("0" representing unskilled and "5" highly skilled). This rating should reflect the *degree* to which all social skills are displayed and the child's *skill level* in applying them.

Overall Skill Level

Unskilled *Highly Skilled*
0. . . . . .1 . . . . 2. . . . . 3 . . . . 4. 5

1 minute of free time is earned for each point on the scale.

TOTAL free time minutes earned for Overall Skill Level ______

After recess spend a moment with the child to:

1. Ask questions abput the activities completed and skills used. Prompt and praise the child for accurately describing his or her behaivior during recess.
2. Debrief and provide feedback to the child, detailing (1) activities or skills you observed, (2) skills the child successfully applied, and (3) skills the child should have applied or instances where skills were not properly used.
3. Explain the ratings you have recorded for the child. Whenever possible, praise the child for positive aspects of his or her performance.

FORM 10.2 *(Continued)*

and Eckert (in press). Superb compilations of both generalization and maintenance strategies applicable to social-skills training have been contributed by Horner, Dunlap, and Koegel (1988) and Albin, Horner, Koegel, and Dunlap (1987).

The literature to date indicates that systematic social-skills training shows promise, but it has not generally produced the robust intervention effects that this approach potentially can yield. We believe social-skills training and intervention, when implemented according to best-practices standards, is one of the most potentially effective tools available to educators for ensuring some degree of success for most students who experience adjustment problems as a part of schooling.

A strategy known as *opportunistic teaching* is highly recommended for developing socially competent performance and is an important adjunct to the direct teaching of essential social skills and problem-solving strategies. This technique is most appropriately used to prompt, cue, coach, shape, and praise demonstrations of previously taught social skills and strategies, or approximations thereof, in natural settings. This incidental-teaching approach was originally developed by Phillips, Phillips, Fixsen, and Wolf (1974) and takes advantage of "teachable moments" when interactive situations occur in natural settings, such as the playground, hallways, lunchroom, and classroom. This technique can also be used to prompt students as to when social skills should be used (that is, opportunity to respond).

Young (1993) has identified three appropriate uses of opportunistic teaching: (1) to prompt students who have missed an opportunity to use a social skill, (2) to provide correction to a student who applies a skill incorrectly or inappropriately, and (3) to debrief with a student who engages in inappropriate behavior in a situation where an alternative social skill would have worked equally well. In such situations, a brief teaching sequence should be initiated in which feedback is given and discussed, alternative responses are discussed and, when possible, actually practiced on the spot. This procedure can greatly enhance the transfer of skills from the original instructional situation to natural contexts and also facilitates incorporation of the skill into the student's ongoing behavioral repertoire (see Black, Downs, Bastien, Brown, & Wells, 1987; Oswald, Lignugaris-Kraft, & West, 1990; Young, 1993). It is strongly recommended that practitioners of social-skills training consider integrating opportunistic teaching into their intervention procedures.

RECOMMENDATIONS AND GUIDELINES GOVERNING BEST PRACTICES IN SOCIAL-SKILLS INTERVENTIONS IN SCHOOLS

Based on extensive reviews of the professional literature and on direct experience in developing and implementing social-skills interventions, the senior author has constructed a list of cardinal rules for conducting generic social-skills training (see Walker, 1988; Walker, Schwarz, Nippold, Irvin, & Noell, 1994). We believe these rules approximate *best practices* currently used in the area of social-skills intervention (see Box 10.2).

These rules assume that users are committed to achieving high-quality outcomes in the realm of social competence and are willing to make the necessary investments to achieve this goal (Walker et al., 1994).

RESOURCES FOR EVALUATING CURRICULA AND CONDUCTING SOCIAL-SKILLS TRAINING

Sugai and Fuller (1991) have contributed an excellent decision model and process for the evaluation of social-skills curricula. This model provides criteria and procedures for comparing and selecting social skills curricula that are appropriate for specific students and settings. As such, it meets a critical need in our field and fills a void that has long existed. These authors also include procedures for conducting a cost-benefit analysis that juxtaposes demands of the curricular approach or program with likely benefits that can be expected from its implementation. This decision model and process is highly recommended to the consumer who is evaluating social-skills curricula for possible selection.

Perhaps the most complete resource developed to date for guiding social-skills training efforts from assessment through intervention is *A Resource Guide for Social Skills Instruction* by Alberg, Petry, and Eller (1994). This guide was developed under the auspices of a three-year grant from the U.S. Office of Special Education Programs of the U.S. Department of Education. The guide is extremely detailed and has been through a number of focus-group reviews by target audiences (for example, general- and special-education teachers and administrators, parents, and related services personnel). It has also been reviewed extensively by a panel of national experts in the area of social-skills training.

A Resource Guide for Social Skills Instruction lists and describes a number of techniques for use in facilitating the generalization and maintenance of social skills, including: (1) teach skills that will be supported in a variety of settings, (2) involve the student, (3) take advantage of "teachable moments," (4) teach a variety of responses, (4) teach in different settings with a multitude of persons, (5) fade consequences, and (6) teach students self-management techniques. These are excellent strategies and their application is illustrated in the resource guide.

This resource guide contains chapters on (1) the need for social-skills instruction, (2) social-skills instructional guidelines, and (3) selecting a social-skills program and preparing for its implementation. One appendix provides program summaries and highlights representative social-skills programs geared for four developmental levels (preschool, elementary, middle or junior high school, and senior high school or postsecondary). The second appendix contains an annotated bibliography of available social-skills programs.

The following publishers who market to the educational community carry substantial inventories of social-skills products: American Guidance, Inc.; Psychological Assessment Resources, Inc.; PRO-ED, Inc.; Research Press, Inc.; and Sopris West, Inc. Each of

Box 10.2 Cardinal Rules for Conducting Social-Skills Training

- Social skills should be taught as *academic* subject matter, using instructional procedures identical to those for teaching basic academic skills (for example, reading, language, mathematics).
- Whenever possible, social skills should be directly taught along with possible variations in their appropriate application.
- The critical test of the efficacy of social-skills training is the functional integration of newly taught skills into one's behavioral repertoire and their demonstration and application in *natural* settings.
- Both the social context and situational factors mediate the use of social skills and must be taken into account systematically in facilitating students' use of them.
- Social-skills training procedures are not an effective intervention for complex behavior disorders or problems. They represent only a partial solution and should not be used by themselves to remediate aggressive or disruptive behavior patterns.
- Social-skills training can be an important complement to the use of behavioral-reduction techniques in that it teaches adaptive alternatives to maladaptive or problematic behavior.
- The instructional acquisition of social skills does not guarantee either their application or topographic proficiency in applied settings.
- There is considerable inertia operating against the behavioral integration of newly taught social skills into one's ongoing behavioral repertoire, as is the case with any newly acquired skill.
- To be effective, social-skills instruction must be accompanied by the provision of response opportunities, feedback, and incentive systems in natural settings to provide for their actual demonstration and mastery.
- Social validation of social skills by target consumer groups is a critical step in both the selection and training of social skills.
- There are two types of deficits in social-behavior adjustment: skill deficits (cannot do) and performance deficits (will not do). These deficits should be assessed and treated differently, as they require different forms of intervention for effective remediation.

Source: From "Social Skills in School-Age Children and Youth: Issues and Best Practices in Assessment and Intervention," by H. M. Walker, I. E. Schwarz, M. Nippold, L. K. Irvin, and J. Noell. In *Topics in Language Disorders: Pragmatics and Social Skills in School Age Children and Adolescents,* 14(3), 70–82. Copyright © 1994 by Aspen Publisher, Inc., Gaithersburg, MD. Reprinted by permission.

Box 10.3 Social-Skills Curricula for Antisocial, Aggressive Students

The social-skills curricula and programs listed here are especially designed for students who fit the profile of the aggressive, antisocial student. They emphasize anger management and control, resolution of social conflicts, and social problem-solving and responsible decision-making—all areas in which this student population is characteristically deficient.

Managing Anger Skills Training (MAST), by Leona Eggert. Available from National Educational Service, 1610 West 3rd Street, P. O. Box 8, Bloomington, IN 47402

Second Step: A Violence Prevention Curriculum Committee for Children. 172 20th Avenue, Seattle, WA 98122

Aggression Replacement Training: A Comprehensive Intervention for Aggressive Youth, by Arnold Goldstein and Barry Glick. Available from Research Press, Inc., 2612 North Mattis Avenue, Champaign, IL 61821

Peer Mediation: Conflict Resolution in Schools, by Fred Schrumpf, Donna Crawford, and H. Chu Usadel. Available from Research Press, Inc., 2612 North Mattis Avenue, Champaign, IL 61821

Helping Kids Handle Anger: Teaching Self-Control, by Pat Huggins. Available from Sopris West, Inc., 1140 Boston Avenue, Longmont, CO 80501

The Tough Kid Book: Practical Classroom Management Strategies, by Ginger Rhode, William Jenson, and H. Kenton Reavis. Available from Sopris West, Inc., 1140 Boston Avenue, Longmont, CO 80501

these publishers carries an excellent line of social-skills curricular programs that would be appropriate for use with antisocial students and those who experience more generic behavioral-adjustment problems in school.

Finally, Box 10.3 lists some curricular programs that are geared especially for use with aggressive, potentially violent students. These programs may be particularly effective with antisocial students; consideration of them is highly recommended when antisocial, aggressive students are the targets of social-skills intervention efforts.

CONCLUSION

In our view, social-skills issues and social-skills interventions are perhaps the most important topics to be covered in a book of this type that focuses on antisocial behavior patterns among children and youth. These students have pervasive social-skills and performance deficits that severely hamper their school adjustment and increase the chances that they will become delinquent, ultimately drop out of school, and experience a life filled with failure and frustration. The resulting social costs to the students, teachers, peers, and parents involved are enormous. The economic and social costs to our society are soaring to an astronomical level that we can no longer afford (Schorr, 1988). Many of these students are likely to become violent offenders (Capaldi & Patterson, in press; Patterson, Reid & Dishion, 1992). Our best hope for diverting young children from this unfortunate life trajectory is to systematically intervene early in their lives and school careers and to teach them, in cooperation with their parents and guardians, the critical skills that will support their academic and social development. The earlier we intervene in this regard, the better chance we have of achieving desirable outcomes—preschool and kindergarten are none too soon!

For antisocial students, intervention in school is but one piece of the puzzle for diverting them from a path leading to a host of negative developmental outcomes. Their parents and primary caregivers are a major potential resource for contributing to this process. Unfortunately, this resource is not often used well in efforts to change the behavior patterns of antisocial students. Chapter 11 details procedures and guidelines for improving parents' ability to influence their children's behavior in a positive way.

STUDY QUESTIONS

1. Describe the key features of the two major approaches to teaching socially effective behavior. How are they similar and different?
2. Describe the three-step process involved in teaching generic social skills.
3. Identify the three social skills that Strayhorn and his colleagues say should be taught to all children and youth.
4. How sensitive are peers to the differential treatment of students by others?
5. Who, in your judgment, is the best and most qualified person in school to carry out social-skills training activities?
6. Describe a whole-class approach to teaching social skills.
7. Describe the problem-solving skills of antisocial students.
8. Is the ACCEPTS program an example of a selected or universal approach to teaching social skills?
9. Define opportunistic teaching methods.
10. To what extent do previously taught social skills show evidence of spontaneous generalization to other settings and situations?

KEY TERMS

best practices
coaching
context
cuing
debriefing
feedback
generalization
implementation
maintenance
opportunistic teaching
reinforcement
skills-based approaches
social problem solving
whole-class approach

11 Parent Involvement in the Schooling of Antisocial Students

The Role of Parents

Improving Ongoing Interactions with Parents

Developing a Positive Attitude toward Parents
Regular Communication
A Problem-Solving Approach
Home–School Interventions

Encouragement at Home
Discipline at Home
Coping with Noncompliance
Preventing Abuse

Conclusion

Recommended Resources on Parent Practices

It is an unfortunate fact that the origins of antisocial behavior patterns in school are often embedded in the family conditions to which antisocial children are exposed. While there is evidence that antisocial behavior patterns are causally related, in varying degrees, to such factors as neurobiology, temperament, and hormonal levels (Kazdin, 1985), there is broad documentation that these behavior patterns are often strongly associated with pathological family conditions (Patterson, 1982). This is particularly true of children and youth for whom the signs of antisocial behavior begin early in their lives (that is, well before they start formal schooling). Such children are referred to as "early starters." Evidence indicates that they are socialized to antisocial behavior patterns by the family conditions and parenting styles to which they are exposed from earliest infancy. Early starters have severely elevated risk status for a host of long-term, negative developmental outcomes, including school failure, delinquency, and adult criminality (Dishion, Patterson, & Griesler, in press; Dishion, Patterson, Stoolmiller, & Skinner, 1991; Patterson, Reid, & Dishion, 1992).

Because of the central role that family and home conditions play in the etiology of many antisocial behavior patterns, families must become partners with schools and other social agencies if satisfactory solutions to this problem are to be found. For reasons described in this chapter, it is extremely important to enlist *parent involvement* in and support of school interventions for antisocial students. Although it is possible to effect positive behavioral changes in school without involving parents in the intervention, any behavioral gains achieved in a school-only intervention will likely be specific to that setting. Whenever possible, parents of antisocial students should participate in the planning and implementation of school interventions because (1) many of the adjustment problems that antisocial students experience at school have their origins in the home; (2) the more settings in which interventions for antisocial behavior can be implemented, the more likely there is to be a substantive, overall impact on the student's total behavior; (3) parental support in coordinating the school and home components of an intervention (for example, monitoring, praising, debriefing, delivery of home rewards) can significantly increase the effectiveness of any school intervention; and (4) parent involvement sometimes opens the door for parent education that can lead to more effective parenting practices, positive parent-child interactions, and improved student self-esteem.

As noted in Chapter 1, normal parenting practices are severely disrupted in families that are stressed by such factors as divorce; poverty; physical, sexual, or psychological abuse; drug and alcohol abuse; conflict; unemployment; and other negative factors. Disrupted parenting practices, in turn, provide a fertile breeding ground for the development of antisocial behavior patterns in young children (Loeber & Dishion, 1983; Patterson, 1983; Patterson et al., 1992). Five parenting practices are critical to the development of adaptive, prosocial patterns of behavior among children and youth: (1) appropriate and fair discipline; (2) monitoring and supervising the child's whereabouts, activities, and peer affiliations; (3) involvement in the child's life and investment of time and energy in his or her development; (4) use of positive family-management techniques of encouragement, support, praise, positive regard and valuing, and appropriate structure and consequences governing the child's daily behavior; and (5) ability to resolve conflicts among family members and to manage crises. Family environments that lack these parenting profiles are often chaotic, unhealthy settings in which to rear children. Children emerging from them are ill prepared for the complex demands associated with schooling and face likely rejection by both peers and teachers. The best window of opportunity to divert these children from an antisocial path is to intervene effectively during grades K–3.

Professionals increasingly believe that successful treatment of antisocial behavior among children and youth requires comprehensive interventions coordinated across home and school settings (Patterson et al., 1992). Furthermore, Reid and Patterson (1991) note that intervention efforts for antisocial behavior must address the three social agents who have the greatest impact on the child's behavior (that is, parents, teachers, and peers). If intervention occurs early in a child's school career and involves a family–school partnership, there is a much greater likelihood of achieving a positive result. The experience of the authors is completely in accord with this view.

This chapter presents information and guidelines on two important topics: (1) how to involve parents in supporting their child's school adjustment to teachers and peers and (2) how to achieve positive teacher–parent interactions on an ongoing basis. These are important outcomes for school personnel to strive for, not only for antisocial students but for all students. The first section describes the role of parents in effective parent–teacher communication; the second section presents specific techniques and guidelines for achieving this goal.

THE ROLE OF PARENTS

What would you say is the number one way to raise students' achievement at school?

1. Lengthen the school day
2. Decrease class size
3. Increase parent involvement
4. None of the above

If you chose 3, "increase parent involvement," you are not alone in your thinking. Results of a 1989 national survey indicated that most educators believe "more parent involvement" is the best way to improve student achievement. At the same time, 90% of all teachers surveyed in a Gallup poll on this topic reported not getting needed support from parents (Clapp, 1989).

We do not know of a single teacher, school administrator, or school psychologist who does not believe that a student's parents can make a huge contribution to a child's positive emotional and academic development. Furthermore, these professionals agree that parent support and involvement in their child's schooling can have a significant impact on their school success. Many teachers depend on parent involvement for their students to complete homework and class extras, such as special projects. One of the key elements of effective schooling is regularly assigned and completed homework. The teacher's ability to call on parents for their support in coping with student behavior problems at school is equally important. In a Phi Delta Kappa poll representing over 20,000 students and their teachers, the number-one intervention strategy teachers

Parent and child talking about school. *Charles Gupton/Uniphoto*

reported using when dealing with students at risk for behavior problems was notifying and conferring with parents (Lombardi, Odell, & Novotny, 1990).

Unfortunately, parents and families can contribute, albeit often unknowingly, to a student's development in a most negative fashion. The nature of young children's behavior at home usually typifies what can be expected as they progress through school. Research has shown that a preschooler's noncompliance to parent directions is the cornerstone or "gatekey" behavior for the further development of antisocial behaviors (Loeber & Schmaling, 1985). That is, noncompliance serves as the first step in a chain of increasingly aversive behavioral events that ultimately place the child at severe developmental risk. While the great majority of young children's interactions with their parents are affectionate and positive, studies show that even nonproblem boys demonstrate an aversive act of some type about once every two minutes (Patterson, 1982). As young children approach school age, however, most will cut their rates of aversive behavior approximately in half through the socialization efforts of parents. Unfortunately, this is not true for antisocial children, whose rates actually accelerate over the course of their

Box 11.1 The Case of Sam, the Cookie Monster

By age 4, Sam Jackson's parents already knew he was "difficult." His almost constant whining and arguing had his parents feeling overwhelmed and depressed. A typical example of an interaction with his parents begins with Sam asking for a snack. His mother says, "No." Next, Sam climbs onto the counter and his mother says in a louder and firmer voice, "No, get down now." Sam continues to badger his mother. His mother then goes on to explain that dinner is coming, that she is saving the cookies, and that he has already had three. Finally, she gets to the point of being unable to stand the nagging and screams at Sam, "You are a terrible whine! I am so sick of this! Go ahead and get a cookie. Your dad will deal with you later." Sam almost always gets his cookie; and in this particular example, it took only about 10 minutes of tantrum throwing. After hundreds of these types of interactions, Sam learns that he needs only to escalate quickly to extreme forms of negative behavior in order to get what he wants. Sam's parents give in to him and do not understand there are other options for dealing with the situation.

school careers. Thus, children with high rates of negative, coercive social behavior when entering school are likely to start their educational careers off on the wrong foot. Unfortunately, they very often go downhill after that (Parker & Asher, 1987).

Many researchers have characterized the family as providing the early training ground for delinquency; there appears to be considerable truth to this observation. Wahler and Dumas (1986) cite extensive evidence that parents who have criminal records produce children who have a greater chance of becoming delinquent. For example, in a follow-up study of 350 children through age 18, West and Farrington (1977) found that 37% of sons whose fathers had criminal records became delinquent; the equivalent figure for sons of fathers who had no criminal record was 8%. An early pattern of well-developed antisocial behavior is often the single best predictor of later delinquency, which in turn is the best predictor of adult criminality (Patterson et al., 1992).

As already noted, parents of antisocial children tend to use harsh and inconsistent disciplinary practices, are usually not involved in a positive manner in their children's lives, and do a poor job at monitoring and supervising their children's daily activities (Loeber & Dishion, 1983; Patterson et al., 1992). In addition to these negative parenting factors, what seems to differentiate nonantisocial from antisocial children is how parents respond to their child's aversive behavior. Parents of antisocial children are more often inconsistent and noncontingent both in their praise and in their punishment of their children's behavior. That is, their use of praise and punishment bears no logical relationship to the child's actual behavior. These parents often give in to their child's coercive, demanding behavior, which usually escalates the negative behavior they were trying to stop in the first place. Box 11.1 is a typical incident in the home of a somewhat troublesome preschooler.

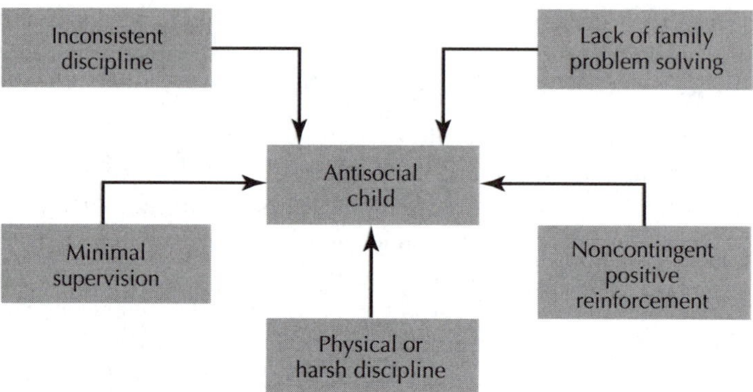

FIGURE 11.1 Typical Parenting Practices Used by Parents of Antisocial Children

Through this process, Sam, and other children like him, learn to control all their family members through similarly aggressive and aversive means. To make matters worse, antisocial children get little, if any, instruction in *prosocial* behavior—that is, in how to be positive and cooperative in their interactions with others. Observations of distressed families show that, when it does occur, the positive behavior of antisocial children often goes unnoticed or is responded to inappropriately (for example, with criticism such as "You picked up your room but you never do it when I ask you.") (see Patterson, 1982; Patterson et al., 1992). So it seems that parents of these children often lack many of the *parent management skills* necessary for dealing with behavior problems. Figure 11.1 sums up what researchers have found so far about the parenting practices used by parents of antisocial children.

Figure 11.1 depicts the problems most parents of antisocial children display in their parenting practices. To make matters worse, antisocial children often live in families where unemployment, poverty, and stress are common events. Of course, it is important to remember that many children who live in poverty or in divorced families do not become chronic delinquents and often do relatively well in school and in their peer relations. Such children and youth are called "resilient" in that they do well in their lives in spite of being exposed to substantial risk factors that seem to negatively influence others. So far, relatively little is known about the protective factors that seem to insulate such children from the debilitating effects of the conditions to which they are exposed. However, the children who live in disadvantaged conditions with parents who are marginal in their ability to discipline, monitor, and provide positive support for their children are at high risk for developing antisocial behavior and eventual delinquency in adolescence (Kazdin, 1985).

Where does this leave you as Sam Jackson's teacher? Should you give up, decide there is nothing you can do, or simply blame his mother and father? If you do these things, Sam will most certainly fail at school. We believe there are a number of positive things you can do for Sam by engaging his parents in his education, even if he comes from a highly stressed home environment. The next section of this chapter outlines specific and practical steps for improving school and teacher interactions with all parents, especially those like Sam's.

IMPROVING ONGOING INTERACTIONS WITH PARENTS

Few would deny that, over the course of their development, children's parents are the most consistent and important caretakers in their lives. Parents generally have a substantial impact on a child's social and academic growth. They are obviously in a position to exert tremendous influence on their children's development. Teachers need to do everything possible to involve parents in the schooling process and to assist them in using this influence to motivate their children's school performance. Canter and Canter (1991) recently reported that only 25% of parents receive specific guidelines from teachers on how to assist their children at school. However, when asked if they would provide additional help to their children at home, more than 85% of the parents surveyed said they spent at least 15 minutes each day working with them. This has proven true in our own experience as well. To the maximum extent possible, teachers and schools should use parental resources in fostering their children's development within school. It appears that most parents are willing to invest time and effort in fostering their children's school success.

Teachers and schools are legally required to involve only those parents of students who have been certified as "handicapped" and are receiving special-education services at school. Schools tend to resist offering special-educational services to most at-risk, antisocial students in the elementary years; yet these students' parents are available and are often willing to be involved in their children's schooling. And for those families where parent involvement might appear hopeless, remember that even the smallest changes in an unhealthy parenting cycle can produce momentous changes down the road. This section will provide guidelines and easy-to-follow techniques for involving all parents in their children's schooling.

Developing a Positive Attitude toward Parents

The importance of approaching parents in a positive manner seems almost too obvious to merit discussion. However, our observations of parent–teacher interactions tell us that far too many teachers are often frustrated in their interactions with parents and with trying to involve them in their child's schooling. Old baggage from previous experiences with difficult parents is often brought to these new interactions.

It is well known that schools are not friendly places for parents of difficult students. Many parents of these children and youth were themselves difficult in school and may carry negative, hostile memories of their school experiences. Thus, they are distrustful of the school setting and often expect the worst when they are required to have contact with school personnel. Such parents are not necessarily all that supportive of school and may actually foster negative attitudes toward school among their children.

Unnecessary conflicts sometimes arise between the school and home. A teacher, for example, can quickly become discouraged with parents who are unavailable for classroom volunteering, who fail to respond to notes or forms that are sent home, or who have difficulty finding time to attend parent–teacher conferences. Often, these parents are labeled as "uncooperative" by school personnel, which leads teachers to become even more frustrated with their misbehaving child. This, in turn, leads the school to complain and the parents to feel as if they are being falsely blamed for their child's difficulties at school. A vicious cycle quickly ensues.

Positive parent involvement must begin early in a child's school life. Those first interactions between parents and the kindergarten teacher, the school principal, and even the school secretary are extremely important. From then on, parent contacts with teachers, the counselor, principal, and other school personnel should be respectful and friendly. As a first step, every effort should be made to create a school atmosphere in which all parents are respected, valued, and made to feel welcome. This task should be a major responsibility of the school principal and supported fully by teachers.

Whenever possible, school contacts with parents should begin with discussion of the child's strengths. Too often, school professionals let personal beliefs about parents (for example, that they are uncooperative, hostile, or too demanding) get in the way of effective interactions and parent–teacher working relationships. Parents deserve to be treated at least as well as you would want to be treated if your child were in the classroom. If your child were a student, which of the following would you want from their teacher?

To hear from them at the beginning of the year

To know specific expectations of the student

To learn problems before things get out of hand

A general idea of what is happening in the classroom

To know when a child is doing well

Positive communication with parents can quickly demonstrate a teacher's competence, professionalism, and concern for students. It can establish the foundation for an effective working relationship between schools and families that can yield enormous benefits for both.

Regular Communication

Positive communications with parents need to begin on the first day of school. Schools should always make the first move; *never* wait until something goes wrong to begin school–home communications with parents. To make regular communication easier, contacts do not always have to be an individual letter or phone call to a parent; simple letters, short memos, or general newsletters that all students take home work well. Consider mailing notes home as well. It costs less than $10.00 to mail a note to 30 different households. A quick, positive note expressing your enthusiasm about the upcoming year

Box 11.2 Sample Letter of Introduction

Dear Parents:

Just a quick note to welcome you and your child to my classroom. I am looking forward to the 1993–1994 school year and to getting to know each one of you.

Always feel free to leave a message for me at 555-6451, and I will get back to you as soon as I can. Over the first few weeks of school, we will be reviewing fractions, starting the book, *The Celery Stalks at Midnight* by James Howe, and pairing up for a science fair project.

Sincerely,

is all that is needed to establish your reputation as a teacher who communicates positively with parents. A sample letter of introduction is provided in Box 11.2.

Calendars

In addition to short letters or memos sent to all parents (throughout the year), another easy technique to use is a monthly, bimonthly, or weekly newsletter or *classroom calendar.* Calendars are easily created from your own planning books. They are especially useful to parents because specific information will enable them to ask their children questions about school and classroom activities. No longer will parents be faced with blank faces because all they can ask children is "What did you do in school today?" If the calendar shows that on Wednesday students reviewed a spelling test, practiced using a compass, and were introduced to their new science component, the Rain Forest, parents are armed with much more specific information about what is happening in school.

The other advantage of an up-to-date calendar is that it gives parents information about school tasks that students need to prepare for. For example, it is most helpful if parents know in advance about homework assignments, upcoming tests or quizzes, field trips, and other special classroom or schoolwide activities. Box 11.3 is a sample calendar.

Newsletters

Newsletters work in much the same way as calendars. Many teachers already use this technique and have included their students in helping to create the news items. Box 11.4 is a sample newsletter.

Box 11.3 Sample Calendar

NOVEMBER

Monday	*Tuesday*	*Wednesday*	*Thursday*	*Friday*
6	*7*	*8*	*9*	*10*
PE Computer lab Homework: Read chapters 8 & 9 Math fact sheet	Homework: Study for spelling test	Begin section on Japan Spelling test Homework: None	Library Homework: Math—do review questions	Homework: Finish reading *Charlotte's Web*

Good News Notes

Good news notes (sometimes called "school–home notes") are another great way to provide positive information to parents. Parents and students like to see positive accomplishments and special contributions acknowledged in this way.

Once you copy a supply of good news notes, it takes virtually only seconds to jot down a few positive words about a student's school behavior or academic performance. Use your attendance record as a way of tracking who has had a good news note sent home recently. Form 11.1 is a sample form for a good news note.

These notes have been used extensively to improve the academic and behavioral functioning of students as well as to improve communication processes between parents and schools (see Kelley, 1990). Aside from their positive communication value, perhaps the greatest advantage of school–home notes is that they allow parents to deliver appropriate consequences at home for successful school performance. Thus, a wide range of home-based incentives can be accessed to support a student's school behavior and performance.

Phone Calls

One of the most effective, yet underutilized parent communication techniques is a quick phone call home. Parent phone calls are not for long conversations, just for quick updates on how that parent's child is doing in your classroom. Getting in the habit of phoning

Box 11.4 Sample Newsletter

4th Grade News: February 1–15, 1994

Editor: Mr. Rodriguez
Assistant Editors: Ashley Clien, Jason Smith, and Steven Johnson

Letter from the Editor

Dear Parents,

Happy Valentine's Day. We will be exchanging valentines on Friday, February 12. If you would like to volunteer to help at our party, please drop me a note.

Students finished "The Celery Stalks at Midnight," and have book reports due next Wednesday.

Everyone is enjoying our new time in the computer lab.

Sincerely,
Don Rodriguez

Upcoming Trip

Seattle Art Museum
March 2, 1993
Permission Slip
Attached—Return by February 25, 1994

New Activity

Computer lab began last Monday. We will have computer lab every Monday.

Book Report

By: Laura Ringsmann
Book: *Little House in the Big Woods*
Author: Laura Ingalls Wilder

This was a book about a little girl named Laura and her sisters, Mary and Carrie. Everything happened a long time ago. Laura's father had to shoot animals for food and her mother had a large vegetable garden. I liked this book because it had lots of interesting stories about the olden days and because the girl's name was Laura.

parents with positive comments about their child leads to tremendous perks down the line, and makes subsequent phone calls about problem behavior a lot easier. If a teacher makes just two calls each afternoon, they will have made ten calls in a week. One teacher can reach an entire classroom in just two or three weeks. At regular intervals, teachers should set a goal for themselves of reaching two to three parents by phone each day.

Early in the year, a good way to start a phone call with a new parent might be to ask how their child is responding to school. By so doing, each parent is able to talk about their child without the teacher leading the parent one way or the other. These calls also let parents know that the teacher will use the phone to touch base with them every once in a while so they can work together to create the most positive school experience for their son or daughter.

GOOD NEWS

Name: ______________________

Date: ______________________

____

____

____

____

____

Sincerely: ___________

____

FORM 11.1 Sample Good News Note

Start parent phone calls by briefly describing some recent positive behavior by the student. An open-ended question about the parent's perception of some recent classroom assignment or activity is another good topic to cover. Occasionally, these phone conversations may lead to effective problem solving, particularly if there is a concern or problem at school for which parent input is important.

One of the authors of this book recently participated in a program that tested the idea of using phone-answering machines in target classrooms. Teachers provided daily information regarding classroom activities and take-home assignments via recorded telephone messages. Parents, in turn, could access the recorded message using their phone and then leave specific questions or concerns as messages for their child's teacher. It was not necessary for the parent and teacher to talk directly in order for this procedure to work. Finally, the teacher had a quick and easy avenue for communicating with parents on an individual, personalized basis.

Once the phone was installed in the classroom, teachers sent letters to all parents letting them know about the new phone-answering machine. An easy solution to misplaced phone numbers was sending home a sticker or refrigerator magnet with the teacher's name and number printed on it. Every teacher we've known who has a phone-answering machine has greatly appreciated the ease and convenience of this communication technique. Most found that it increased their frequency of parent contacts two- or threefold.

How much does it cost? Approximately $40.00 per month per classroom in most areas. If the school lacks funds for this purpose, there are other alternatives. We have seen teachers secure outside funding, apply for funds from the district or local school–parent group, or initiate their own fund-raising program to get the program started. This investment will be well worth the effort and is a significant procedural advance in the quality and effectiveness of parent–teacher communication.

A Problem-Solving Approach

Antisocial children and youth pose many obstacles to teachers' effective management of the classroom. Sometimes, no matter how much you try to prevent problems, you will have a student who constantly challenges you and disrupts the classroom. In such cases, you should not wait too long to call on the student's parents for assistance. Waiting until a student needs to be removed from school before contacting the parents is clearly not an example of effective parent involvement. We recommend a structured *teacher–parent problem-solving* approach when the need arises to involve a parent because of the child's antisocial behavior in the classroom or on the playground.

School personnel may have been exposed to problem-solving techniques through their pre- or posteducational training, and some may use problem-solving strategies in their professional interactions. However, relatively few teachers or school administrators use this simple approach when working with parents.

The problem-solving worksheet in Form 11.2 is useful whenever the need to communicate with a parent arises over a student's problem behavior. The worksheet will help keep you focused on finding solutions instead of on reviewing the student's problem and its possible causes. The latter focus is usually not productive and can lead to scapegoating and blaming the parents—both of which are poisonous to positive parent–teacher relations. Parents tend to feel as if teachers are blaming them or somehow expecting them to magically solve their child's behavior problems at school when called by an overwhelmed or agitated teacher. On the other hand, a parent who receives a solution-focused call from a teacher is much more apt to participate in finding a workable answer to the problem. The key lies in not blaming parents, but focusing instead on solutions and keeping reviews of the problems to a minimum.

Each component of the worksheet comes with its own set of "Do's and Don'ts" (see Box 11.5). Briefly review these, then use the worksheet and make it yours. This problem-solving form provides a useful structure for conducting parent–teacher meetings. Its use will maintain a focus in seeking a solution and will help keep the process positive.

Box 11.5 Do's and Don'ts of Problem Solving

Step 1: State the Problem

Do

- Stay calm
- State the problem using clear and specific words
- Start by taking some responsibility

Don't

- Blame the parent
- Go on and on
- Use jargon

Step 2: Brainstorm Solutions

Do

- Stay calm
- Be specific
- Generate many possible solutions

Don't

- Evaluate too soon
- Be defensive
- Lecture
- Bring up the past
- Stop thinking of new solutions just because one sounds good

Step 3: Evaluate Solutions

Do

- Stay calm
- Talk about the future
- Allow each person an equal say
- Start small

Don't

- Ask parents to do things they cannot
- Skip advantages or disadvantages

Step 4: Pick a Solution

Do

- Stay calm
- Combine solutions

Don't

- Leave without a solution to try
- Give up

Step 5: Write an Agreement

Do

- Stay calm
- Make a time to follow up
- Take responsibility for success of intervention
- Be ready to try problem solving again

Don't

- Blame parents for failures

STEP 1: STATE THE PROBLEM

____

____

STEP 2: BRAINSTORM SOLUTIONS

1. ________________	5. ________________
2. ________________	6. ________________
3. ________________	7. ________________
4. ________________	8. ________________

STEP 3: EVALUATE SOLUTIONS

a. Can we agree to cross any solutions off the list?
b. What are the advantages and disadvantages of each solution?

Solution: ________________

Advantages	**Disadvantages**
________________	________________
________________	________________

Solution: ________________

Advantages	**Disadvantages**
________________	________________
________________	________________

FORM 11.2 Problem Solving Worksheet

Solution: ____________________

Advantages	**Disadvantages**
____________________	____________________
____________________	____________________
____________________	____________________

STEP 4: PICK A SOLUTION

____

____

STEP 5: WRITE AN AGREEMENT

(Include who will do what by when.)

____

____

____

____

FORM 11.2 *(Continued)*

Home–School Interventions

A problem-solving meeting or phone call often will culminate in some type of home–school intervention. Many parents are willing to be actively involved in a partnership and provide more structure at home; however, they may need a teacher's guidance for doing so. The home is a potential resource for influencing behavior change and generalization of gains that is ignored when an intervention focuses only on the school and individual student.

Social-skills training to improve students' social competence and school adjustment is an excellent area in which to conduct joint school–home interventions. Students can be taught specific social skills at school (for example, eye contact, turn taking, cooperative-

Name: ______________________ Date: __________

	Monday	Tuesday	Wednesday	Thursday	Friday
Paid attention					
Turned in assignments					
Worked independently					
Raised hand					
Had materials					

Comments:

Code:
4 = excellent
3 = satisfactory
2 = needs improvement
1 = unacceptable

______________________ ______________________

Teacher's Name Parent's Initials

FORM 11.3 Home–School Card

ness, sharing, and negotiating), and parents can prompt and reinforce the appropriate display of these skills in the home and community. Home rewards can also be delivered if the student's school and home performance meet preestablished standards or criteria. This can be an extremely effective way to conduct systematic social-skills training; however, it requires (1) careful monitoring and supervision, (2) frequent communication between teachers and parents, and (3) joint planning and implementation. Procedures and guidelines for conducting social-skills training are presented in Chapter 10.

Home–School Cards

Home–school cards are an excellent way for parents to stay in close touch with their child's school performance and to be informed of progress. Begin by using the card on a daily basis. The student is responsible for carrying the card between school and home. Form 11.3 is one example of a home–school card, but teachers and parents will need to work together to create a card that works for each particular student.

At first, parents should be encouraged to reinforce (praise) their child simply for bringing the card home. Eventually, they may want to reinforce, with praise or privileges, better and better school performance. Teachers can also provide support, praise, or privileges to the antisocial student for returning the card from home to school as well as for school performance. The parent should initial the card to indicate that it has been reviewed and discussed.

Teachers should use their own judgment when meeting with parents to plan a home–school intervention involving the use of home–school cards. Not all parents are ready or willing to provide tangible rewards to their children for school performance. When a parent is open to doing so, you should be prepared with a list of ideas for home incentives and estimates of how much each is worth in terms of the student's school performance. Remember to individualize the list for each set of parents with whom you work. Based on the parents' knowledge of their child and your observations at school, an appropriate list of home rewards should be relatively easy to create. As part of this process, however, it is important to establish the cost of each reward option on the list in terms of points earned at school or the number of good home–school cards brought home. Low-value items should be relatively easy to earn (15 minutes of extra TV time) and higher-value items (having a friend over, a movie, a family outing) should require much greater amounts of acceptable performance.

A sample list of home rewards and incentives is provided in Box 11.6.

Home–School Contracts

A more formal home–school contractual arrangement may result from a problem-solving meeting with parents, especially when the student is included in developing solutions. A *school contract* is simply a formal, written agreement among the student, parent or parents, and the teacher. The contract can focus on almost any student behavior appropriate to the context of school (for example, paying attention, doing assignments, getting along with peers, and complying with teacher requests and commands). The contract also includes an agreement about specific student, parent, and teacher behavioral responsibilities necessary to make the solution work. A simple contract that meets these specifications is shown in Box 11.7.

Contractual arrangements of this type are an excellent way to precisely define expectations and standards of behavior. They provide a public commitment to a solution that has been cooperatively derived by the parties to the agreement; as such, they can serve as strong motivation for students to change their behavior.

Encouragement at Home

Parents sometimes turn to their child's classroom teacher for assistance with behavior problems at home. Teachers are viewed by many parents as child-development experts and as highly skilled in the management of child behavior. Although a teacher may feel comfortable dealing with students' classroom behavior, giving advice to parents may appear to be a wholly different matter. Probably the most important message a teacher

Box 11.6 Sample List of Home Reinforcers

Food

Dried fruit as snack

Popcorn in the evening

Choosing dinner one night

Getting to take a special lunch to school

Small cookie, gum, cake, pie, etc.

Going out for pizza with family

Choosing dessert for evening meal

Baking (brownies) or cooking with parents

Parent Time

Playing one 5-minute game with parent(s)

Having story read

Taking a walk with parent(s)

Being taken out to a movie

Going out with parent(s) for ice cream

Special night out with one parent

Going to the park with parent(s)

Baking (brownies) or cooking with parent(s)

Shopping with parent(s)

Using special "grown up" toy that requires parental supervision for ________ (specified time limit)

Riding motorcycle with parent or other adult

Resources

Nintendo or other TV game

Choosing a special TV program

Taking bottles and cans back to the store and keeping or splitting the refund

Using special "grown up" toy that requires parental supervision for ________ (specified time limit)

Using Mom's makeup

Using parent's tools

Box 11.6 *(Continued)*

Privileges

Choosing a special TV program

Having shared bedroom to self for 1 hour a day

Having first dibs on bathroom in the morning for ________ (specified time)

Nintendo or other TV game

Telephone time

Permission to go to a special event (party, dance, etc.)

Privacy time

Staying up half an hour later

Choosing from a grab bag of small items all wrapped up

Going swimming

Going out to play

Having a friend over for the evening

Having a friend spend the night

Watching cartoons

Visiting grandparents, uncle, aunt, etc.

Making a craft project (woodwork, weaving, etc.) (work on it for 15 minutes a night with one parent)

Looking at a book in bed before lights out

Help cook or bake

Riding bike

Pushing grocery cart

Going fishing

Going hiking

Going to a friend's house to play

Using parent's tools

Lottery: earning tickets that can be drawn for larger prize

Scavenger hunt

Costs Money

Renting a video

Nintendo or other TV game

Box 11.6 *(Continued)*

Costs Money *(Continued)*

Choosing from a grab bag of small items all wrapped up

Going out to a movie

Getting a comic book

Going out for ice cream with parent(s)

Earning articles of clothing for self

Shopping with parent(s)

Earning money (allowance)

Going ice skating or roller skating

can give to a parent in this context is that the confidence and encouragement they show toward their child can be a powerful tool for developing positive behavior. Parents and teachers need to encourage children's efforts and achievements, *no matter how small.* As adults, we tend to overlook children's positive behavior and focus too often on the things they do wrong. Children need and want their parents' vote of confidence; it helps build self-esteem and makes them feel valued.

Too often parents withhold their encouraging words until their child "achieves" (for example, a better grade in math, a neat room at home, a week with no arguing). When parents hold out for high achievement in this manner, some children conclude they are not good enough, and they feel they have to approximate perfection. The child who has

Box 11.7 Sample Student Contract

I, Lisa, agree to sit quietly and do my assignment during math and to show my math note to my parents each day.

I, Ms. Wilson, agree to provide math assignments that Lisa is capable of doing and to send a math note home each day.

We, Mom and Dad, agree to let Lisa stay up an extra 15 minutes each day she brings her math note home.

Box 11.8 Handout of Guidelines for Setting Up Contracts at Home

Helping Contracts Go Smoothly

1. Have I chosen a behavior that my child is capable of doing?
2. Have I broken it down into small steps?
3. Have I specified a time to check the behavior each day?
4. Have I come up with an incentive or list of incentives?
5. Have I talked with my child and explained what each of us will do each day?

difficulty in math may never learn to multiply if the parent fails to notice his or her efforts to improve. Encouragement implies reasonable expectations; recognition of small goals or steps is important in this regard.

Teachers can help parents focus their encouragement on one behavior at a time by teaching them how to set up behavioral contracts with their children, be it for getting along with others, following directions, or cleaning up the bedroom. Some parents may resist the idea of contracting with their children. In these cases, it helps to point out how they use informal contracts on an everyday basis with their children. For example, a parent might say, "Help me with the groceries and then you can play," or "When you finish your homework, you can watch TV." These are informal, daily contracts that are commonly used by almost all parents.

Formal contracts or charts are a means of providing children with recognition for their positive behavior. Many parents find these techniques helpful for teaching new skills or for learning a new routine. Other parents use contracts to help children get back on track when they are having a hard time with something they already know how to do, like school work or doing chores without being asked. Give parents a handout like the one shown in Box 11.8 to help guide them in the use of contracts and point charts at home. In addition, setting up a formal contract or chart involves at least six steps (Clark, 1985):

1. Select a target behavior.
2. Make a point-reward chart.
3. Write a reward menu.
4. Keep track of the points earned.
5. Adjust the contract or chart.
6. Discontinue the program.

Select a Target Behavior

Parents should start by choosing one behavior for the child to work on. The behavior needs to be observable and countable. For example, "show respect" might actually be "follow directions within 10 seconds without arguing." Describe the target behavior in positive rather than negative terms. Break the behavior or task down into easy-to-accomplish steps. For example, cleaning the child's room might include five steps: putting trash in the wastebasket, pulling up the comforter, putting the pillow on the bed, putting dirty clothes in the hamper, and folding or hanging up clean clothes.

Make a Point-Reward Chart

Write down the target behavior on a chart. Make sure everyone understands all the components of the chart. Also, write down the time when the parent will check to see whether or not the behavior has occurred. Next to each behavior, list the number of points (for example, checks or stars) the child can earn for that behavior. The number of points for a particular behavior will depend on its difficulty. Forms 11.4 and 11.5 provide examples of easy-to-understand charts and contracts.

Write a Reward Menu

Parents should sit down with their child and discuss the reward menu. Box 11.6 contains many ideas for home rewards that are inexpensive or that only involve parents' time. Some parents will be uncomfortable rewarding their child's behavior. Encourage these parents to just give the system a try and to only pick rewards with which they feel comfortable. Consistently recognizing and noting the child's behavior is the most important component of this system. The rewards will only get a child going; eventually, these new behaviors will become a part of the child's own repertoire of behaviors. Point out to resistant parents that many adults also work for extra incentives or rewards (for example, bonuses, commissions, recognition, or extra privileges).

Keep Track of the Points Earned

When a child earns a point, record it on the chart with lots of enthusiasm. When he or she has enough points for a reward, be sure the parent can make it available. For example, don't offer 30 minutes of time with a parent who usually has to work late.

Adjust the Contract or Chart

Have parents keep the old charts and look at them from time to time to see how much progress their child has made. To improve the program, make the behavioral definitions clearer, add new rewards to the menu, or make the reward slightly more difficult to attain.

_______________ **Point Chart**
(Name)

Week of _______________

Tasks	Mon	Tues	Wed	Thur	Fri	Sat	Sun

I, _______________, will earn a point for each of the tasks noted above. At the end of the day, if I have earned 4 of the 6 points, I will receive a star for the day. If I have earned 5 stars by Sunday, I can choose one of the rewards from the list.

I, _______________, will check each day at 7 P.M. to record ___________'s points on each task. I will give rewards as specified above, offering the weekly reward by Sunday at 10 A.M. if 5 stars have been earned for the week.

Reward list: _______________ _______________

_______________ _______________

_______________ _______________

_______________ _______________

_______________ _______________

_______________ _______________

FORM 11.4 Sample Point-Reward Chart

MY CONTRACT

I, ______________, agree to do the following chore: ____________________

Step 1: ______________________________

Step 2: ______________________________

Step 3: ______________________________

Step 4: ______________________________

Step 5: ______________________________

For each step completed, I can earn ____________________________

This chore needs to be completed by ____________ (time)

If I can do it without being reminded, I can earn ____________________

____
Child's signature

I, ________________ (parent), agree to check the chore by ____________

(time), and will reward each step completed with ______________________.
This can be exchanged for items in the grab bag.

____
Parent's signature

FORM 11.5 Sample Point-Reward Chart

Parents and children spending time together.

Myrleen Ferguson Cate/PhotoEdit
Michael Newman/PhotoEdit
Tony Freeman/PhotoEdit
Myrleen Ferguson Cate/PhotoEdit

Discontinue the Program

Do not have parents keep a point chart or contract indefinitely, just until the child's behavior improves or until he or she has learned the new routine. Let the child know that the chart helped her or him to make improvements and that he or she has grown and added a good skill or behavior to all the things he or she already knows. Parents should continue to praise improved behavior and newly acquired skills, but phase out the chart. Consider having a family party, special dinner, or extra treat to celebrate the child's "graduation" from the chart or contract.

Discipline at Home

Parents will also look to their child's classroom teacher for assistance with discipline at home. Three noncorporal discipline strategies that have proven easy to learn and use by parents are time-out, privilege removal, and work chores. The following material was designed so that you can distribute it to parents as you deem appropriate.

Time-Out

Time-out is a commonly used discipline technique that works well for children ages 2 through about 12 or 13. Often, teachers use time-out in the classroom, so teaching parents of difficult-to-manage students to use this technique at home makes a great deal of sense. Go over the simple instructions that follow with parents *and their child* prior to implementing the time-out procedure at home. The following key features should be remembered in using the time-out procedure:

1. Stay calm when asking a child to go to time-out.
2. Start with a 5-minute time-out.
3. Add 1 minute each time a child does not comply with time-out—up to a limit of 10 minutes.
4. After 10 minutes, if a child still will not go to time-out, take away a privilege (see privilege-removal section).
5. Do not lecture a child once time-out is over.

It is a good idea to observe and monitor the children's behavior closely following time-out so as to identify an instance of behavior that is reinforceable with praise. In this way, the children learn that their behavior determines the use of positive and negative consequences and that holdover anger will not occur. Because of residual anger, children are sometimes ignored for long periods by parents and teachers following time-out. If this occurs too often, children learn that inappropriate behavior is more likely than appropriate behavior to produce adult attention (even though negative in tone). This is an unfortunate lesson indeed and one that should be avoided at all costs.

Box 11.9 reviews the time-out procedure and Box 11.10 provides recommended general guidelines in administering time-out. You should share this material with parents as you deem appropriate; however, you should be sure to discuss it and answer any questions parents have prior to, during, or following its use.

Box 11.9 The Time-Out Procedure

One of the most important things to remember about using time-out is to *use it*, do not just threaten to use it. Once you have decided to use time-out, follow these simple steps:

1. *Label the problem* with a simple statement such as, "You didn't stop arguing. That's a time-out."
2. *Wait 10 seconds* for your child to go.
3. *Set a timer* or check your watch for 5 minutes.
4. *Remove yourself* and do not talk to or check on your child during the time-out period.
5. *Stay neutral* when time-out is up and avoid discussion of the event causing the time-out.
6. *Carry on* with regular activities with the child when time-out is over.

Box 11.10 Guidelines for Time-Out

1. Select a place.
2. Prepare the room (take out any dangerous or valuable items).
3. Explain the procedure to child or children.
4. Practice time-out beforehand.
5. Label the behavior that earns time-out.
6. Be consistent.
7. Don't talk to children when they are in time-out.
8. Be calm or neutral when giving time-out.
9. Use a timer, if possible.
10. When time-out is over, don't make children apologize.

What to Do When Children Refuse to Enter Time-Out

1. Stay calm.
2. Add 1 minute for each instance of noncompliance.
3. Add up to 5 extra minutes.
4. Remove a privilege.

Box 11.11 Privilege Removal

Before you begin using time-out, decide which privileges to use as back-ups. Privilege removal is a back-up consequence to use when your children refuse to go to time-out. Eventually, they learn that it is easier to go to timeout for 5 minutes than to lose a privilege for an hour or two.

The privileges must be under a parent's control. Make sure that you monitor the privilege you remove. For example, if you take away the bike for an hour, know where the bike is. Lock it up if necessary. If you cannot control the privilege, do not put it on your list!

Common privileges to remove. Many parents remove the following privileges: TV time, playing with a favorite toy or piece of sports equipment (bike, skateboard, soccer ball), playing with a friend, using the stereo or radio, goodies in the refrigerator, going to a planned activity, using the phone, going out to play.

Remove the privilege for no more than 1 to 2 hours. Lengthy privilege removal builds up resentment.

Follow through. When you say that a privilege will be lost, do it that day.

Remove the privilege as soon as possible. The sooner the discipline issue is over, the easier it is to have a pleasant family atmosphere.

Privilege Removal

If children fail to comply with time-out, then the parents need to be prepared to use *privilege removal* as a back-up consequence to the time-out. The following scenario serves as an example:

> Sarah Tenor just asked Justin to clean up his Legos and set the table for dinner. Justin is sitting playing, but not following his mother's direction. Sarah says, "That's not minding, Justin. Take a time-out." Justin continues to ignore her, so Sarah says, "Justin, you have 6 minutes in time-out." Justin now starts to pound the floor and accuses his mother of picking on him. Sarah adds another minute to time-out. This continues until Sarah gets to 10 minutes. Sarah gives Justin one last chance: "Justin, that's 10 minutes; either you pick up your Legos now and set the table or go to time-out." Justin continues his tantrum, so Sarah says, "OK, Justin, you just lost TV time after dinner."

The handout shown in Box 11.11 will help you work with parents as they determine which privileges to remove should their children refuse to go to time-out. Have parents create a list of possible privileges to remove before they begin using time-out. The critical thing to remember about time-out is *staying calm*! In addition, be sure parents take away or limit something they can actually control. For example, taking away Justin's TV time would not have been a good idea if Sarah had had to go to work that evening and would not have been around to supervise her son.

Work Chores

The *work chore* is usually one of the more effective discipline strategies for use with older children. Work chores function in much the same way as time-out; instead of going to time-out, however, children do some kind of "job" around the house. Work chores should be short, requiring 5 to 10 minutes to complete the job. Work chores should also involve some household (or outside) chore that the child is not usually required to do. The list of possible work chores must be individualized by child and household. In one family, cleaning the tub might never be a job the child needs to do, so using it as a work chore would be a good idea. In another home, cleaning the tub might be a regular child-assigned chore, so another activity would be needed as a work chore. A sample list of chores is provided in Box 11.12 to help parents start thinking about ideas for chores; but the best way to generate a list is for parents to walk around the house with a pad of paper and write down the little jobs that take about 5 or 10 minutes to complete. Parents should have the list ready and refer to it if their children misbehave; for example, do not follow directions, talk back, or fight with brothers or sisters. If children do not complete work chores, then parents need to remove a privilege (see previous section).

Parents of difficult children are often deficient in the parenting practices listed earlier in Figure 11.1 (discipline monitoring, positive family-management techniques, parent involvement, and problem-solving and conflict resolution). If anything, they tend to overuse punishment. It is always important to encourage parents to use positive strategies when there is a problem, although this does not come naturally for even the most skilled parent. However, many behavior problems can be addressed effectively using such a positive approach. The case in Box 11.13 illustrates this point.

Box 11.14 is a handout for parents on how to perform key parenting skills correctly and effectively. If possible, all parents should receive a copy of the handout, but it is critical that parents and primary caregivers of antisocial students be exposed to this information.

Ideally, the teacher should schedule an appointment to discuss these practices and the handout. If parents are receptive to learning more about effective parenting, the resources listed at the end of this chapter can be recommended to them.

Coping with Noncompliance

As discussed briefly earlier in this chapter, noncompliance with adult requests, commands, and demands is one of the more frustrating child behaviors with which parents and teachers have to cope. Furthermore, noncompliance often serves as a gatekey behavior for the development of far more serious behavioral tendencies. Patterson and his associates

Box 11.12 Examples of Long and Short Work Chores

Short Chores

1. Clean kitchen or bathroom sink
2. Sweep floor
3. Clean bathroom mirror
4. Empty dishwasher
5. Fold one load of laundry
6. Vacuum carpet in one room
7. Dust one room
8. Wipe down one wall
9. Sweep front or back sidewalk
10. Clean tub or shower
11. Clean out a kitchen cabinet
12. Clean out the refrigerator
13. Scrub floor
14. Polish furniture
15. Water plants
16. Clean out garbage can
17. Pick up litter in yard
18. Take out garbage
19. Wipe down kitchen cabinets
20. Wash dishes
21. Bring firewood in
22. Wash car
23. Clean up dog "dirt" in the yard
24. Clean toilet
25. ______________________
26. ______________________
27. ______________________

Long Chores

1. Wash windows
2. Clean mold off tiles in shower
3. Clean mold off windows
4. Scrub the outside of pots and pans
5. Rake leaves
6. Vacuum house
7. Pull weeds
8. Chop wood and/or stack it
9. Mow the lawn
10. Clean the oven
11. ______________________
12. ______________________
13. ______________________

Box 11.13 Case: How Michael Got the Hang of It

Michael is 7. His mother wants him to hang up his coat when he gets home from school each day. She has tried talking, yelling, and even not letting him watch TV at night when he forgets. Now she is ready to try a more positive approach. She first puts in a new hook right at his level. Michael really likes charts with stars, so she decides to give him a star each time he remembers to hang up his coat. The next time Michael comes in, his mom is on the phone. She excuses herself and gets a star out of the box. Michael kind of throws his coat at the hook. His mother says, "I'm glad you tried to hang your coat up. Here is a star for your chart. Let's pick up your coat together this time." Later that evening when Michael comes in, he drops his coat in the hallway. His mother ignores this. The next afternoon he does hang his coat on the new hook and his mother gives him the star. Several days later, when Michael is remembering well, his mother lets him hang up his coat without the star. She is careful, though, to praise him for hanging up his coat without being told; she says, "Michael, I'm glad you hung up your coat. I don't have to give you a star each time. I think you're really becoming more responsible."

(Morgan & Jenson, 1988; Patterson, 1983) have clearly shown that one path to an antisocial behavior pattern involves progression from trivial, maladaptive forms of behavior to more disruptive and deviant forms. Thus, persistent noncompliance, as an example, can lead to tantrums, followed by oppositional-defiant behavior, then verbal and physical aggression, then stealing, and finally delinquency. This is a most destructive and costly progression. In some instances, it is possible to prevent these outcomes by dealing effectively with the noncompliance so that the more serious forms of maladaptive behavior do not come into play.

Antisocial children are particularly vulnerable to having problems in complying with adult directives (Patterson, 1982). They are inadvertently taught a pattern of noncompliance through the manner in which their parents frame and deliver such directives to them and the manner in which they respond if the child refuses to comply. Essentially, they learn that they often do not have to comply because parental follow-through rarely occurs; however, such children intermittently comply just often enough so that the parents' rate of giving such directives is maintained. Children who have been taught such a behavior pattern bring it to school and try it out on teachers and other school personnel. Unfortunately, teachers, who are busy instructing large groups of students, have the same problems of framing, delivering, and following through on their directives as do parents.

Box 11.14 Tips for Parents on Effective Family-Management Techniques

Research on parenting has identified five key parenting practices that are important in the upbringing of well-adjusted children. Each of these practices is briefly discussed here.

1. *Discipline.* Parental discipline needs to be fair, consistent, and predictable. It should *never* be harsh or punitive. There should be a logical relationship between child behavior and the consequences that are supplied to it.

2. *Monitoring.* Careful parental *monitoring* of children's activities, whereabouts, and friendships and peer associations is one of the single most important things that parents can do to ensure that their children grow up healthy, well adjusted, and safe.

3. *Parent Involvement.* This practice involves simply spending time with your children in either structured or unstructured activities. The parent-child contact is the important thing and the activity chosen is usually incidental to the time spent together and the positive interactions that occur.

4. *Positive Parenting Techniques.* Positive parenting means being supportive and encouraging of your children. It is important to establish a warm, caring relationship that involves mutual respect and affection. In this way, you will be better able to influence your children in the right directions using techniques such as social interest, praise and approval, persuasion, and logical thinking—without resorting to punishment and other negative methods of behavioral control.

5. *Problem Solving, Conflict Resolution, Crisis Intervention.* During their upbringing, children experience many minor crises that, nevertheless, loom very large in their lives. When they bring problems to their parents for assistance, it is extremely important that they be responded to immediately and completely. Alternatives should be developed for them to consider in solving the problem and they should be encouraged to choose one that is acceptable and that works for them. Children should always have the confidence that such problems will receive a fair hearing and that they will have access to your assistance as needed.

Adherence to these simple, yet critically important, practices in your parenting efforts will have a positive impact on your children and your relationship with them. Furthermore, they will contribute to a much more positive set of family dynamics. The following rules are offered for your consideration in parenting your children. They can be helpful in the prevention of adjustment problems later.

- Set up a daily debriefing time in which you review your children's day and what it was like. Questions like, "Tell me what you did today?" "What did you do that was fun or interesting?" "Who did you play or talk with?" "Did anything happen that was a

Box 11.14 *(Continued)*

problem or that you didn't like?" are excellent ways to conduct such a debriefing. Why should you debrief? First, it tells children you care for them and are concerned about what happens in their lives. It is also an excellent method for screening to detect problems that you might not discover otherwise. Once children start school, it is extremely important to conduct a daily debriefing of this type on an ongoing basis.

- Monitor your children's activities, behavior, schedules, whereabouts, friendships and associations carefully. It is important to provide such monitoring in a positive, caring manner but to do so in a way that is not smothering or unpleasant. Careful monitoring of this type can be a powerful protective factor. As children grow and mature, such monitoring may have to change form and become more subtle and less direct; however, it is extremely important that it occur, especially as they enter adolescence, when the risks of problems are so much greater.
- Children should be taught positive attitudes toward school, and school should be perceived as a highly valued activity. A pattern of cooperative, prosocial behavior will do a great deal to foster a good start in school that will ensure both academic achievement and social development over the long-term.
- The most important skill you can teach your children prior to entering school is listening as you read to them. Your children should see the material you are reading and associate the sound of the words with their symbols on the page. This activity is an important precondition for developing children who are good readers and who are interested in reading. It is one of the best things that can be done to prevent later school failure and to help ensure academic success.

Noncompliance is one example of a maladaptive behavior that is too often strengthened and maintained both at home and in school.

Whether or not a child complies with an adult directive has as much to do with how the command is framed and delivered as it does with the consequences, or lack of them, that follow the delivery. The most commonly cited definition of noncompliance is by Schoen (1986): noncompliance refers to a situation in which an adult makes a request or gives a command that directs another individual's behavior toward some end or goal and

(1) the individual refuses to comply with the request, (2) no response to the command occurs within a specified time period (usually 5 or 10 seconds), or (3) some unrequested behavior occurs instead. If the command or request is given in response to an aversive behavior or act, it is usually in the form of a terminating directive designed to stop it. If the command or request is directed toward an appropriate task or goal, it is usually delivered in the form of an initiating directive designed to start or continue the behavior. Both parents and teachers frequently fall into the trap of issuing far more terminating than initiating commands; in the process, they focus too much on negative, inappropriate behavior and deliver too many critical statements. This is a cycle that is all too common in the interactions of parents and teachers with antisocial children and youth and ultimately reduces the social influence these agents can have in shaping behavior toward positive ends.

It is also important to distinguish *alpha commands* from *beta commands.* Alpha commands involve a clear, direct, and specific command with minimal verbalization and allow a reasonable time for compliance to occur. Examples of alpha commands would include, "Roberto, will you close the door, please?" or "Jenny, if you open your book to page 49, you'll find the answer to your question." In contrast, beta commands are vague, overly wordy directives that often contain multiple instructions to do something. As a rule, they do not allow ample time or opportunity for compliance (see Forehand & McMahon, 1981; Walker & Walker, 1991). Examples of beta commands include, "Jamie, you are always talking when you're supposed to be working. How many times have I told you to do your work instead of talking all the time. I'm warning you; you'd better shape up!" or "Michiko, I don't care how many times you ask, I'm not going to let you go on the bus trip until you change your ways. You're sassy and arrogant. When I see an attitude adjustment, we'll talk about it." Additionally, beta commands are usually accompanied by more anger and emotional venting than are alpha commands, which also further reduces their effectiveness. As with the commonly observed ratio of terminating to initiating commands, adults often fall into a trap of giving more beta than alpha commands. As a result, the children may feel they are constantly being lectured to and reject the feedback as a matter of course.

Doing all you can as a teacher to facilitate students' compliance with your directives and assisting parents in doing the same is one of the most important contributions you can make to your students' social and academic development. Of course, children and youth should also be taught to discriminate the appropriateness of commands they receive from their peers or strangers. Clearly, nonresponsiveness to inappropriate commands is an important skill and requires the exercise of good judgment.

Box 11.15 is a handout of guidelines for giving commands that should be studied carefully and shared with parents as you deem appropriate. Follow-up discussion of this material with parents is highly recommended. As a teacher, you can request the parents' assistance in facilitating their child's compliance with teacher directives. The best way for parents to accomplish this is to implement these guidelines in their interactions with their children at home. This investment will be well worth the effort.

Box 11.15 Guidelines for Giving Commands

1. Beta commands are to be avoided at all costs—give clear, crisp alpha commands whenever possible.
2. Whenever possible, the ratio of initiating to terminating commands should not be less than 4 or 5:1.
3. Children and students should be praised promptly following acceptable compliance with a command.
4. Give only one request or command at a time.
5. Be precise in your description and delivery of the command.
6. Use language the child can understand.
7. Ensure that the child understands exactly what is expected.
8. Ensure that the child is capable of doing what is being asked.
9. Do not reissue the command more than once.
10. Never allow yourself to be drawn into arguments or confrontations about the command.

Sources: Forehand & McMahon (1981); Morgan & Jenson (1988); Walker & Walker (1991).

Preventing Abuse

Antisocial children and youth are masters at provoking parents and teachers into fits of anger and sometimes rage. They often find these outcomes rewarding and see adult anger as an indication of their social control over authority figures. Sometimes, the resulting escalated interactions between the adult and these children and youth can become abusive or approach abusive levels. The information on child-abuse prevention in Box 11.16 is designed to assist parents who may find themselves in this situation. Dissemination of such information to parents of antisocial children and youth is optional and depends on the teacher's judgment as to how it would be received.

Box 11.16 Guidelines for Prevention of Child Abuse

PARENTS ON THE VERGE OF ABUSE

STOP and:

- Call a friend
- Go to your room and take ten deep breaths (and then ten more)
- Play some music
- Exercise
- Take a shower
- Sit down, close your eyes, and think of a pleasant place

NATIONAL CHILD ABUSE HOTLINE

(A FREE CALL)

1-800-422-4453

CONCLUSION

This chapter has focused on the importance of (1) communicating effectively with parents regarding their children's school behavior and performance and (2) utilizing parents as a resource for managing antisocial students in school. Though often a challenge, engaging such parents in school–home interventions designed to improve students' school achievement and behavioral adjustment can yield major dividends. Our experience indicates that the resulting outcomes are well worth the investment of time and energy.

Chapter 12 presents a number of case studies that illustrate some of the best practices described in this book. Several illustrate the roles that parents can assume as effective partners with schools in responding to the behavioral challenges presented by antisocial students. The reader is urged to review these case studies carefully.

RECOMMENDED RESOURCES ON PARENT PRACTICES

Some excellent resources on effective parenting practices have been developed over the past two decades. Many of the best materials have been produced by Gerald Patterson and his associates of the Oregon Social Learning Center. Sources for accessing such materials are listed here.

Northwest Media, Inc. Northwest Media develops videotapes, manuals, and newsletters emphasizing practical skill-building tools for natural, foster, and adoptive parents and for children of all ages. They are also quite useful for related-services personnel and educators. Available materials address the following topics: creating safe environments, study skills for success, young children in court, drug use during pregnancy, teaching new behavior, parents and friends, confidence building, limit setting, problem solving, and getting ready for school. Ordering information and a catalogue can be obtained by contacting Northwest Media directly at P.O. Box 56, Eugene, OR 97440.

Castalia Publishing Company. Castalia carries some of the best materials for teaching parents effective parenting skills. Available materials range in scope from scientific research volumes to books, manuals, and videos designed specifically for parents. Castalia Publishing Company can be contacted at P.O. Box 1587, Eugene, OR 97440; phone: 503-343-4433.

Research Press Publishing Company. Research Press Publishing Company has a long tradition of publishing excellent materials for clinicians, parents, and educators. They publish a broad array of materials for use in training parents in effective practices. Their address is 2612 N. Mattis Avenue, Champaign, IL 61821; phone: 217-352-3273.

STUDY QUESTIONS

1. Why is parent involvement so crucial?
2. Name five common characteristics of families with severely antisocial children.
3. Describe how parents can inadvertently increase a child's antisocial behavior.
4. What are several techniques for improving teacher–parent interactions?
5. Describe the problem-solving process.
6. With regard to parenting, what role can encouragement play with antisocial students?
7. Describe the process for helping parents set up a formal contract or chart.

KEY TERMS

alpha commands
beta commands
classroom calendar
good news notes
home–school cards
monitoring
parent involvement
parent management skills
privilege removal
school contract
teacher–parent problem solving
time-out
work chore

12 Case Studies of Best Practices with Antisocial Students

Jamie: Reducing High-Risk Life-Style Factors

Background
Intervention
Results
Discussion

Bobby and Greg: Increasing Positive Peer Interactions

Background
Intervention
Results
Discussion

Charlotte: Encouraging Positive Behavior at Home and School

Background
Intervention
Discussion

Second Steps: Implementing Classwide Social Skills

Background
Intervention
Results
Discussion

Project PREPARE: Establishing a Schoolwide and Classroom-Level Management System—A Building-Team Approach

Project PREPARE
Background
Intervention
Results
Discussion

Jimmy: Early Intervention for the Prevention of Antisocial Behavior among Kindergartners—The First Steps Program

The First Steps Program
Background
Intervention
Results
Discussion

Billy: Victim of Circumstances and Victimizer of Others

Background
Discussion

Conclusion

This chapter presents case studies of effective practices with antisocial students in school. These case studies are based on real events that reflect the diverse experiences of the authors in designing and implementing school-based interventions. Those case studies that contain graphic presentations of data reflect direct observations of students' behavior recorded in classrooms and on playgrounds, analysis of existing school records, or informant ratings of the effects of interventions. Our intention is to illustrate a range of school interventions (both selected and universal) for addressing antisocial behavior patterns and to highlight the key features that account for their effectiveness.

JAMIE: REDUCING HIGH-RISK LIFE-STYLE FACTORS

Background

Jamie was a fifth grade boy at Elmwood Elementary in Creswell, Oregon. Creswell is a small rural town of approximately 7,000 people. Three elementary schools serve the schooling needs of the Creswell population. The town economy is dominated by a lumber mill that has fallen on hard times as a result of the severe restrictions placed on the available timber supply in the Northwest. Each year, the labor force in Creswell shrinks due to mill layoffs, and the unemployment rolls increase accordingly.

Jamie came from a difficult family situation. His father and mother were divorced when he was 3 years old—following years of abuse, conflict, intermittent poverty, and involvement with drugs and alcohol. Jamie's mother struggled to raise three children, Jamie and two younger sisters, on an income that was just above the poverty level. The family had been listed with the Oregon Children's Services Division because of the severe economic and social stresses and pressures the family had been suffering. Because of reports of severe parental neglect, Jamie's mother had her parenting rights reviewed by the court on several occasions. Jamie had poor monitoring and supervision at home and in his neighborhood, and his behavior pattern reflects it.

Jamie was a troubled boy whose school history reads like a patchwork quilt of erratic attendance, repeating a grade, high rates of discipline contacts with the principal, negative comments by his teachers in his cumulative folders, and frequent school suspensions. He had a negative reputation with most of his current and former teachers because of his sullen attitude, weak academic performance, tendency to engage in confrontations with adults that verge on being "out of control," and failure to respond to either teacher directives or teacher attempts to correct his academic mistakes. Things were not much better with his peers, who tended to avoid him whenever possible and disengage rapidly when they got involved in social exchanges with him. Although Jamie pretended not to care about his negative reputation and social isolation, it was clear that he was extremely hurt by it. However, he had very little idea about how to change the situation.

School officials at Elmwood reported that Jamie had major behavior problems since the first grade, when he missed nearly a third of the school year because he disliked school so much. The slightest demands on Jamie would often result in defiance that if responded to, would quickly escalate into violent tantrums. Through this process, Jamie learned that he could acquire a substantial degree of control over his school environment, and he engaged in the process at the slightest provocation. By the third grade, Jamie was largely alienated from his teachers, peers, and most of what happened at school. School officials indicated that if an alternative school or day-treatment placement were available, Jamie would probably have been assigned to it several years earlier.

Jamie, as it turns out, was a major factor in the reassignment of the Elmwood vice-principal. His behavioral episodes in his regular classroom, on the playground, in the hallway, and in the lunchroom resulted in so many visits to the vice-principal's office that a computer program was developed to record his disciplinary infractions. Mr. McDaniels, the vice-principal, was frustrated with his inability to get Jamie to "listen to reason" and change his ways. At the beginning of the fifth grade, Jamie was testing his new teacher through subtle provocations and passive noncompliance. Mr. Rexius lost his patience and sent Jamie to the vice-principal's office after a shouting episode that followed one of Jamie's more memorable tantrums. As Jamie walked into the office, Mr. McDaniels asked him, "Well, what've you done this time?" whereupon, Jamie replied with, "None of your —— business, you ——!" Mr. McDaniels lost his temper and struck Jamie on the side of the face, breaking his jaw in two places. The vice-principal was subject to school board disciplinary actions; he was eventually reassigned to a fourth grade classroom as a regular teacher.

In the past year and a half, Jamie had been associating with several other boys who share his background and many of his behavioral characteristics, though none approach his levels of defiance and alienation. On several occasions, they have been suspected of being behind some incidents of vandalism at the high school, but sufficient evidence to corroborate their involvement was not available. A neighbor recently told Jamie's mother that she has heard that Jamie and these boys are experimenting with alcohol and drugs.

Intervention

The principal and staff of Elmwood School were exasperated with Jamie. Everything they had tried seemed to either have no effect or actually make Jamie's resistance to positive influence by adults greater. Home tutoring, suspensions, counseling, and values clarification had all been tried with Jamie to no avail.

Jamie was referred by his fifth grade homeroom teacher, Mr. Rexius, for evaluation as emotionally disturbed according to the procedures and criteria of the Individuals with Disabilities Education Act (IDEA). The child study team reviewed the test results prepared by the school district psychologist (Ms. Moraga) and also examined Jamie's school history as part of the IDEA eligibility process. Although many of Jamie's behavioral characteristics suggested he was socially maladjusted and, therefore, ineligible for certification as handicapped, there was sufficient evidence for a diagnosis of emotional disturbance because he (1) showed clear signs of depression, (2) was very impulsive, and (3) had great difficulty controlling his anger and related emotions. Thus, Jamie was certified as handicapped and, thereby, became eligible for the protections of IDEA and the additional resources provided under this legal mandate.

It was decided that Jamie's counselor, in consultation with the school psychologist and child study team, should design an individually tailored program for Jamie that would attempt to reduce his risk of (1) school failure and dropout, (2) drug and alcohol involvement, (3) sexually transmitted diseases, and (4) delinquency. Jamie's counselor, Mr. West, spent the past summer in a special institute learning how to work with high-risk youth such as Jamie. During his training, he discovered the following facts about risks faced by students like Jamie:

1. Antisocial students tend to be at risk for multiple rather than single negative developmental outcomes. Thus, students who show signs of being at risk for conduct disorder are also very likely to be at approximately equal risk for drugs, alcohol, and tobacco use; accidents; delinquency; and sexually transmitted diseases.
2. Students who are antisocial or have deficits in their ability to self-regulate their own behavior have a greatly elevated risk for later involvement with drugs (Dishion & Andrews, 1994). Miller and Brown (in press) report that self-regulation deficits are associated with a cognitive-behavioral profile of addiction.
3. Because of their alienation from adults and the formal behavioral-control systems that operate in schools and because they have learned successfully to resist social influence tactics from adults, it is very difficult to change the behavior of children like Jamie.

Mr. West decided to make a long-term investment in Jamie by acting as a monitor, mentor, teacher, and resource for helping Jamie learn the skills that would reduce his risk status. He made a commitment to work closely with Jamie for the five months remaining in the fifth grade and to follow up with the middle school counselor in the next academic year. Mr. West divided his approach into four phases: (1) relationship building and general counseling; (2) self-esteem building; (3) skill building in the areas of relating to others, academic achievement, and refusing drugs, tobacco, and alcohol; and (4) self-control and self-regulation. The intervention program began with relationship building and followed in sequence through the remaining phases; however, elements of each previous phase were continued into the next so as to build on and maintain the gains realized in the earlier phases.

Mr. West was realistic enough to know that his efforts were unlikely to guarantee a reversal in Jamie's trajectory toward a life of trouble, failure, and frustration. However, he wanted to reduce Jamie's risk as much as possible in order to give him a chance to access a more positive life course. Thus, he felt that, while the investment was perhaps risky, it was worth doing.

Mr. West began by scheduling a regular meeting time each week with Jamie that lasted an hour to an hour and a half. Sometimes they met in his office and at other times they spent time doing a variety of activities (for example, playing basketball or video games, taking walks, or just talking). The counselor's goal was simply to establish a positive, trusting relationship with Jamie that would allow him to have some social

Student sharing concerns with the school counselor. *David Grossman*

influence with him. He would counsel Jamie during these sessions in an indirect rather than direct way. Slowly, over time, Jamie opened up and relaxed somewhat in his sessions with Mr. West. Initially, Jamie had been reluctant to attend the sessions with Mr. West, but he eventually began to look forward to them.

Jamie felt rejected, criticized, and devalued because of his negative family and school histories. Given the treatment he had received, his feelings in this regard were realistic. During the sessions in Phase One, it was clear that Jamie had an extremely low opinion of himself and had experienced little success in his young life. He showed clear signs of adolescent depression in self-report assessments administered by Mr. West. Mr. West talked in general terms with Jamie regarding his good points and his potential. His most difficult task was to get Jamie to see that he had *any* value and that his problems stemmed from the behavioral choices he made rather than from rejection of him as a person. This was a difficult discrimination for Jamie to make, but he eventually seemed to realize and accept it, at least intellectually.

Mr. West had Jamie develop a list of his good points and strengths and then rank order them according to which he felt were his strongest and most valued attributes. Although this process took a great deal of time and effort, and was difficult for Jamie, it proved to be a therapeutic exercise. Mr. West used Jamie's list as a means of pointing out examples of his competence and skills during some of their outings.

Skill building was the most difficult and time-consuming phase of Mr. West's intervention program. Mr. West believed that Jamie had to dramatically improve his competence in three crucial areas: (1) developing social relationships with peers and adults; (2) learning to resist peer pressures to use drugs, alcohol, and tobacco and to engage in illegal activities; and (3) improving his academic performance. Mr. West selected a well-known social-skills curriculum to use in directly teaching Jamie social skills that would support his peer- and teacher-related social adjustments. He used a combination of role-plays, videotaped simulations, and homework assignments to teach Jamie social skills in the areas of problem solving, anger management and conflict resolution, making friends, coping with frustration, meeting teacher expectations, and having a positive outlook.

In the area of dealing with peer pressures, Mr. West decided to enroll Jamie in an excellent, schoolwide prevention program developed by the Oregon Research Institute (Severson & Zoref, 1991). This program teaches students (1) essential health facts associated with drug usage and high-risk behavior, (2) awareness of sources of influence that subtly shape people to engage in these activities and (3) knowledge and use of refusal skills for resisting social bids to become so engaged. As part of this program, students are taught a set of refusal skills that involve different ways to say no. Examples of these refusal skills include (1) refusing but giving a reason (for example, "I'm on the track team so I can't do it"), (2) changing the topic of the conversation, (3) thinking of another activity and suggesting it, and (4) saying you can't do it but giving the persons permission to do so if they wish. Mr. West supplemented this instruction, as well as the material from Jamie's regular, schoolwide sex-education classes, in his counseling sessions with Jamie.

Finally, Mr. West set up a monitoring and academic support system for Jamie with all his teachers. His daily academic performance was rated by each teacher and the ratings turned in to Mr. West. If Jamie achieved a certain average rating for the week, he earned a special-activity reward. Mr. West also monitored Jamie's homework assignments and his completion of them.

Mr. West taught Jamie some strategies for monitoring his own behavior and making good decisions in difficult situations. A key strategy was called the Triple A Routine. Whenever Jamie was confronted with a potentially difficult situation, he was taught to run through this problem-solving procedure in his mind: (1) *assess* the situation and collect information in order to make a sound behavioral choice, (2) consider alternatives, select one, and then *act* on it, and (3) evaluate how it worked and then *amend* his actions, if necessary, in order to better adapt to the situation. Thus, assess, act, and amend became a reliable strategy that Jamie learned to apply to just about any situation that he perceived held potential problems for him.

Results

Jamie responded reasonably well to Mr. West's efforts. Most of all, he was flattered by the consistent, positive attention he received from Mr. West, who was the one individual Jamie felt had really tried to understand him. A genuine feeling of respect and affection had developed between them.

Jamie lost his sense of helplessness and victimization through the efforts of his counselor. He was learning skills that were functional and that he could rely on to deal with difficult situations. He had even begun to anticipate these difficult situations and to take preventive actions to deal proactively with them. In this sense, he felt empowered to cope with the daily challenges of living as never before.

Jamie still had occasional lapses with his temper and the surly attitude that resulted from his long sense of alienation and rejection by most of the people in his life. Though greatly improved in this respect, Jamie's lapses were just enough to provide justification for his teachers and peers to maintain their negative biases toward him. Jamie's most difficult problem seemed to be coping with the consistently negative expectations of him that his long pattern of aversive behavior had established. Mr. West spent a great deal of their counseling sessions on this issue and tried to get him to see that eventually people would change their images of him, if he continued along the positive, adaptive path he was following. Jamie wasn't so sure, but he did not argue the point.

Jamie had superior academic potential and responded well to the academic monitoring and support arranged by Mr. West. He began completing all his homework and generally received excellent marks on his schoolwork. His teachers were delighted with these signs but remained wary of his volatile behavioral repertoire. Jamie was pleased with their positive reactions to his academic success, but he tried hard not to show it.

Over the summer, Mr. West continued to call Jamie weekly, unless he was out of town; they also got together occasionally. Jamie had some real worries about moving to middle school in the upcoming school year and encountering new teachers and new peers. However, Mr. West pointed out that this was a great opportunity to start fresh and to build a new, more positive reputation with peers and teachers. Jamie promised that he would try his hardest. He said he wanted to stay in contact with Mr. West, who agreed to do so. Mr. West said he would alert his new counselor to the arrangement they had had over the past year.

Discussion

Jamie fits the profile of the typical upper-elementary student who is on a path leading to antisocial behavior, conduct disorder, delinquency, and adult criminality. Mr. West made a good start at diverting Jamie from this path and invested an exceptional amount of effort in doing so; however, it is very unlikely that Mr. West's efforts, as excellent as they are, will be sufficient to turn Jamie around and to ensure his positive adjustment and school success. For this to occur, systematic efforts would have to be made to involve Jamie's mother and his peers directly in a comprehensive intervention program that spans multiple school years.

Jamie would have had a far greater chance of overcoming this unfortunate behavior pattern if Mr. West had implemented his program when Jamie was just beginning his school career (in kindergarten or grade 1). Jamie's unfortunate experiences with his teachers and peers actually strengthened the antisocial behavior pattern he brought to the schooling experience. Over the next five years, he learned that his coercive tactics and oppositional behavior allowed him to control, through aversive means, his social environment at school—and it became his primary means of coping. Jamie had little idea of the enormous social costs that this interactive style would hold for him in his future life.

BOBBY AND GREG: INCREASING POSITIVE PEER INTERACTIONS

Background

Bobby and Greg were referred to an ongoing project, directed by the senior author, on remediating aggressive behavior problems of students in grades K–3. These boys were enrolled in different second-grade classrooms at Twin Oaks Elementary School. This Eugene, Oregon, elementary school served a rural population. As a small school, it had a relatively low incidence of disciplinary problems; school safety was not an issue, and there were few recurring, serious behavior problems among its students.

Bobby and Greg stood out among their peers because of their tendency to bully and tease other children. Both boys were larger than most students of the same age. They were often abusive as well as quite negative in their interactions with classmates in the classroom, on the playground, in hallways, and in the lunchroom. Although they were enrolled in different classrooms with separate teachers and different peer groups, Bobby and Greg were best friends. They spent almost all their available time together at recess and tended to associate with a small number of children who seemed to share their aversive behavioral characteristics. Because of their negative and coercive behavioral tendencies, Bobby and Greg were often excluded from peer-controlled activities and rarely participated in structured games and activities at recess. Both boys were socially rejected by the vast majority of their peers, who tended to avoid them whenever possible.

Bobby and Greg's teachers were thoroughly familiar with the behavior problems presented by these two boys and were distressed by their consistently aggressive behavior. Like most teachers, they were extremely intolerant of aggressive behavior, even when it was not directed at them. Teacher ratings of Bobby's and Greg's social behavior indicated a consistent pattern of engaging in provocative social behavior and the use of coercive tactics designed to force the submission of others. Their levels of aggressive, negative, and hostile behavior were rated by teachers as well above normal when compared to that of their nonaggressive peers.

Because Bobby and Greg had spent all of their school careers at Twin Oaks, the entire school staff and most of the student body were well aware of their behavior patterns. Unfortunately, both boys had already developed well-established reputations as bullies and troublemakers by the second grade; they were well on their way toward school failure, even at this early point in their schooling experience.

The home backgrounds of Bobby and Greg showed some similarities. Bobby came from a chaotic family that placed him at serious risk. Greg's family situation was much less serious but involved severe problems in supervision and monitoring. Bobby's parents were under tremendous stress from a host of problems (drug and alcohol abuse, long-term poverty, and a father-absent family situation). Bobby's father had spent considerable time in jail. Bobby had two younger siblings who also showed the damaging effects of these family conditions. Bobby came to school with a strong pattern of oppositional and coercive behavior, while Greg's problems were of a more covert nature (taking things without permission while others weren't looking, lying, and escaping responsibilities for his actions through avoidance and denial).

A series of observations was recorded for Bobby and Greg in their homeroom and on the playground. These observations revealed that the two boys would qualify for and probably benefit from a systematic, structured program to teach them a prosocial, adaptive pattern of peer-related behavior. Preintervention observations conducted over a two- to three-week period indicated that, on average, 72% of Bobby's social interactions with peers were positive and 28% were negative; the comparable figures for Greg were 91% and 9%. As a rule, primary-grade students are approximately 95% positive in their interactions with peers across school settings (that is, classroom and playground). Bobby had a more serious problem with negative-aggressive behavior than Greg in terms of its overall frequency; however, when he was having a bad day, Greg would tend to engage in violent episodes that seemed to come out of nowhere and were of a relatively short duration. Thus, both boys needed access to an effective intervention that would teach them a more adaptive approach to peer relations and also increase their overall rates of positive social interaction. A relatively intensive, selected intervention was designed and implemented to focus on their peer-related social behavior in the classroom; it could later be extended to other school settings.

Intervention

Although their patterns of negative-aggressive behavior were somewhat different, Bobby and Greg were exposed to an intervention that was comprised of identical components. This intervention appeared to be sufficiently versatile to accommodate the aggressive behavior problems of both boys. The intervention was implemented over four consecutive phases that ranged in length from six to fourteen days and was individually tailored for each boy.

In the first intervention phase, behavior-specific praise and accompanying points were awarded for positive social exchanges with peers; earned points were also simultaneously subtracted for each instance of negative-aggressive behavior directed toward peers. Earned points could be exchanged for individual rewards, delivered at home, and for a group activity reward shared equally with peers at school (for example, a game of 7-Up or Simon Says). Thus, Bobby and Greg were earning points for positive social behavior and were also losing them for negative-aggressive behavior during this phase.

In Phase Two, the intervention procedure was simplified in order to make it easier to manage. A total of 15 points was given noncontingently (that is, awarded freely) at the beginning of the treatment period (one point for each minute); the boys did not have to earn points as in the previous phase—they just had to avoid losing them. The boys' task was to keep the points and to avoid losing them by not engaging in negative-aggressive behavior or playground rule infractions during the 15-minute intervention period.

In Phase Three, only a praise and bonus-points procedure was in effect in which Bobby and Greg were awarded bonus points for outstanding examples of either positive social behavior or a refusal to respond to provocative situations that normally precipitated hostile or aggressive social behavior. Individual rewards were eliminated during this phase and only an occasional group reward, shared equally with peers, was made available.

In the fourth phase, the point system was faded out and daily feedback from the teacher, regarding peer-related social behavior, was the only intervention in effect.

This intervention was coordinated and delivered by a behavioral consultant (district behavioral specialist) who visited Twin Oaks on a daily basis. The intervention was in effect for only a brief, 15- or 30-minute period daily and spanned approximately a two-month period. It was introduced for Bobby following the fourteenth day of baseline observations and for Greg following the twenty-third day of baseline observations. Figure 12.1 shows that the intervention had a positive effect on Bobby's and Greg's social behavior.

As a first step in implementing the intervention, the teacher consultant carefully reviewed with Bobby and Greg the instances of negative-aggressive behavior that were of concern to their teachers and peers. These instances were role-played, as were positive examples of social exchanges with peers. The intervention was explained in detail to Bobby and Greg and reviewed until they understood it. After all their questions had been answered, they helped the consultant and teacher present the plan to the entire class. Peers were encouraged to contribute ideas as to how they might help Bobby and Greg become more positive in their daily behavior. Following these sessions, the intervention was implemented in a daily activity period in the homeroom, where peer interactions were allowed to occur within the context of a variety of quasi-free-play activities involving low levels of classroom structure. Permission for Bobby's and Greg's participation in the intervention was obtained from their parents following a meeting in which the program was explained. As per the consultant's request, Greg's parents agreed to grant home rewards (for example, extra TV time, and special privileges) contingent upon his school performance. Bobby's parents were opposed to home rewards of any kind and refused to participate in this part of the program; however, they did not object to Bobby earning individual rewards at school (for example, playing computer games).

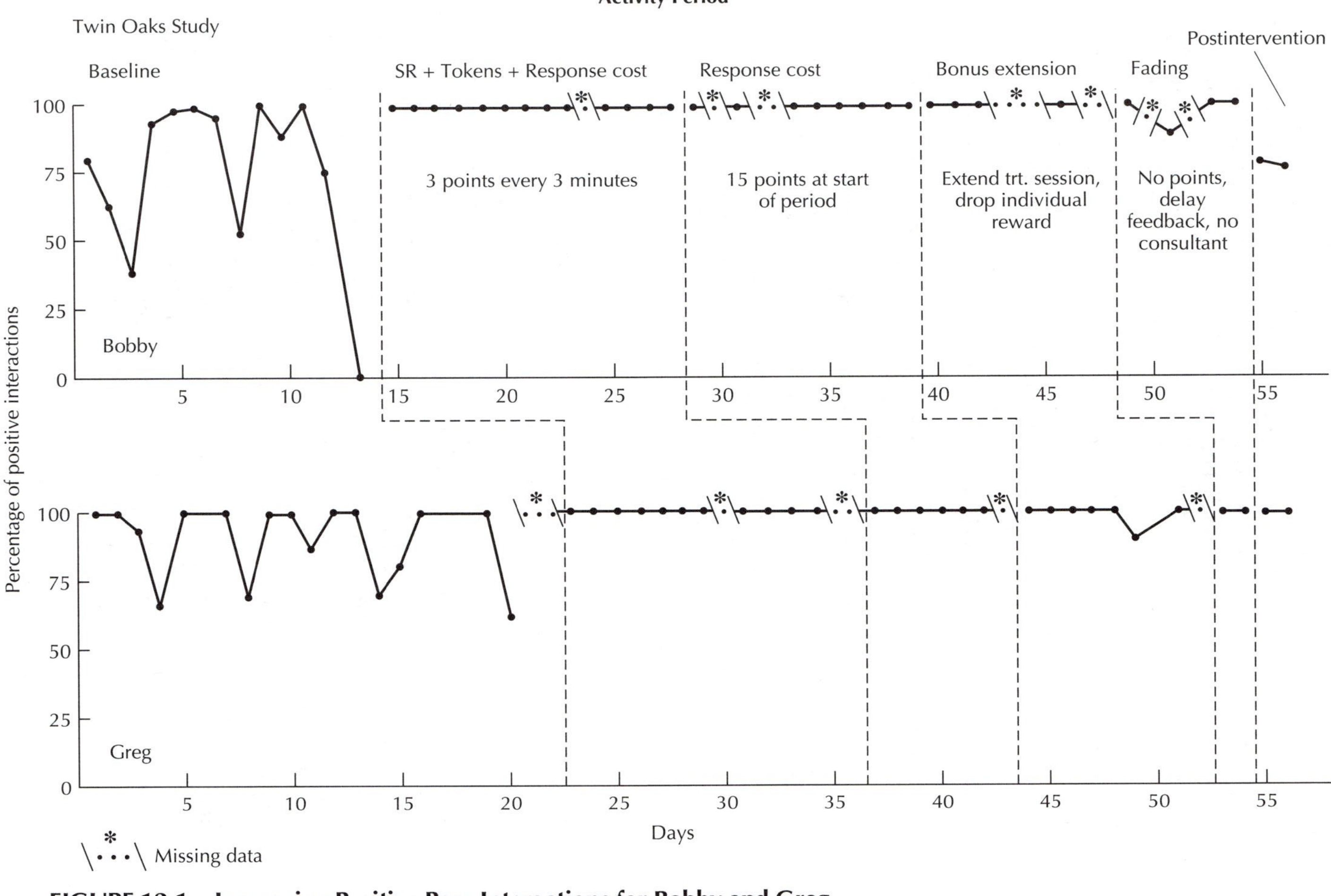

FIGURE 12.1 Increasing Positive Peer Interactions for Bobby and Greg

Results

Figure 12.1 indicates that the intervention program had a powerful effect for both Bobby and Greg in dramatically increasing their rates of positive interactions with peers. The intervention essentially eliminated negative-aggressive behavior for the two boys in the first three intervention phases. Bobby began to show some slight deterioration in his positive social interactions during the fading period as well as during postintervention observations. Greg seemed to maintain a consistent pattern of positive social interactions with his peers throughout the study.

The daily observations reported in Figure 12.1 were recorded by professionally trained observers throughout the duration of the study. Observers achieved and consistently maintained an interobserver agreement standard of better than 80% across all phases of this study. Observers were not informed about any details of the study. Teacher ratings of Bobby's and Greg's behavior also showed improvements that were consistent with the observational results.

Following termination of the study, the teacher was coached in techniques for maintaining the behavioral gains achieved over the long-term. These techniques included (1) the consistent use of praise and approval for examples of positive social behavior involving peers, (2) covert monitoring of Bobby's and Greg's social behavior, (3) regular debriefing sessions on their peer relations, and (4) occasional, surprise group-activity rewards made available for exceptional weeks of positive social interactions. Our experience indicates that the application of such techniques is necessary to maintain behavioral gains over the long-term following even the most successful of interventions.

Discussion

The intervention in this case study proved to be highly effective for Bobby and Greg. It was an expensive intervention, and would require minor adaptations in order to cover all settings throughout the school day. To address this issue, we have successfully used a procedure where the full intervention is first applied in a homeroom period or in the first morning recess. It is then extended to other school settings and periods using a low-cost variation of the intervention procedures where the teachers or supervisors in these settings simply rate the child's overall performance on a card as either + or −, or sometimes using a 1–5 rating scale (a rating of 1 is poor performance and a rating of 5 is excellent performance). The card is then returned to the homeroom teacher at the end of the school day and the results are used to determine home and school rewards. This extension procedure is highly efficient, easy to use, and seems to work well.

A series of studies on reducing negative-aggressive behavior among K–3 students found that awarding points at the start of a period and then subtracting them as required for each rule infraction or for each instance of maladaptive behavior is as effective as simultaneously awarding and taking away points throughout the period (see Appendix A). This is an important finding because the former procedure is far easier for teachers and other school personnel to manage than is the latter. Chapter 2 contains an extensive discussion of response cost (subtracting points), including recommended guidelines and issues to consider when using this highly effective technique.

The key ingredient that accounts for the power of this intervention was the *combination* of simultaneously applying praise and points (exchangeable for home and school rewards) and response cost (loss of points) for instances of negative-aggressive behavior. Either one of these procedures, in isolation, would not have produced a treatment effect of this magnitude. However, it is a relatively complex and labor-intensive procedure, so it should be simplified, as in this example, as soon as possible. Reducing negative-aggressive social behavior initially requires an intensive intervention, but its intensity can be faded out relatively quickly if some variation of the procedures remain in effect over the long-term (for example, praise, careful monitoring, debriefing, and occasional school or home rewards). Positive-only procedures are highly effective for maintaining behavioral gains following the initial use of a combination of positive and mild punishment procedures (response cost).

CHARLOTTE: ENCOURAGING POSITIVE BEHAVIOR AT HOME AND SCHOOL

Background

Charlotte is a third grader at Mildred Elementary School who has experienced academic and social difficulties since first beginning kindergarten. Her attention span is limited, and, according to her first and second grade teachers, she often acts inappropriately during class and on the playground. Charlotte has a high frequency of classroom rule infractions and has difficulties handling free play.

When she is working on an independent writing assignment, Charlotte can stay on-task for only 3 to 5 minutes. Then, she might abruptly get out of her seat, walk to the back of the room, and start eating part of her lunch. When told to go back to her desk, Charlotte usually sneers and tells her teacher something like, "I don't have to listen to you; I can do what I want." As a rule, further warnings are futile. Linda Evans, Charlotte's teacher, now handles the inevitable conflict by sending Charlotte to the principal's office. This provokes Charlotte more; she throws down her pencil and yells, "I hate you!" as she stomps off to the office with the classroom aide.

In the second grade, Charlotte was evaluated for learning disabilities; however, the examining school psychologist decided her difficulties were primarily social-behavioral in nature, thus she did not qualify for any handicapping condition. The school psychologist recommended several small-scale, prereferral interventions, such as after-school friendship groups, so that Charlotte might learn to be more cooperative in the classroom and develop a better sense of self-esteem. Ms. Evans thought that she would do better in a resource or self-contained classroom and was disappointed when Charlotte was declared ineligible for special education. Although she stayed in her second grade classroom for the remainder of that year, neither Charlotte's teacher nor the school psychologist noticed much improvement.

The teachers at Mildred and the school psychologist know little about Charlotte's home life. Her mother did not attend the child study team meeting when the school psychologist presented his test results. Nonetheless, all of Charlotte's teachers have expressed concerns at one time or another about her home life. Her daily appearance indicates little in the way of consistent care or a daily routine. Her hair is usually uncombed, and most days she is tired when she arrives at school. Charlotte has great difficulty focusing and sustaining her attention, possibly because she suffers from poor nutrition. Teachers believe there is little discipline or effective supervision and monitoring in Charlotte's home. Ms. Evans has not tried to call Charlotte's mother this year, mostly because past efforts by teachers and administrators have been unsuccessful. Ms. Evans does send home weekly schoolwide bulletins for parents and monthly classroom newsletters, but she doubts that Charlotte's mother reviews the information.

Citing Charlotte's lack of progress and poor response to the classroom interventions proposed by the school psychologist, Ms. Evans expressed concern that Charlotte is falling so far behind academically that she is in danger of having to repeat third grade. Furthermore, Charlotte's negative attitude and difficult behavior are taking too much of Ms. Evans's time away from her ability to teach the other students in class. It seems that Charlotte has been in the principal's office at least once a week since October. Ms. Evans recommends to Allan Otis, Mildred's new school counselor, that she either be assigned to a resource room or that arrangements be made to give her supplementary academic instruction.

Intervention

While Mr. Otis can see that Charlotte is falling further and further behind, he thinks they should try again to establish better home–school communication before referring Charlotte to the school psychologist. Mr. Otis offers to take charge of the communication process and development of subsequent intervention plans. He has some specific ideas in mind, and Ms. Evans is more than glad to have him take charge.

Mr. Otis's initial conversation with Charlotte's mother is tense, but civil. The mother sees Charlotte's difficulties as a school problem and insists she has no behavior problems with Charlotte at home. Mr. Otis is genuinely interested in hearing more about how things work in Charlotte's home and asks if he might visit with the mother in her home for about 30 minutes.

The home visit enables Mr. Otis to not only see Charlotte's home environment firsthand but allows him to be more persuasive as well. This face-to-face contact gives him a chance to talk with Charlotte's mother in her home where she is naturally more relaxed and comfortable. In this atmosphere, Mr. Otis has a chance to explain Charlotte's academic and behavior problems in greater detail. Charlotte's mother is more forthcoming, and he is finally able to persuade her to monitor Charlotte's daily school efforts through a weekly home–school report.

The plan is simple. The school will send home a weekly summary of Charlotte's school behavior that describes how she performed across the following four areas for each of the five school days:

1. Followed directions
2. Completed homework
3. Kept hands and feet to herself
4. Raised hand when there was a problem

Without using any incentives to encourage or increase her performance, Ms. Evans will simply track Charlotte's behavior in each area and give her a score of 1 (Poor), 2 (Fair), or 3 (Excellent). Charlotte's mother must sign the report and see that Charlotte returns it to school. A chronology of some key developments in the intervention is described here:

Week 1: Mr. Otis calls to remind Charlotte's mother that the school-behavior report is coming home.

Week 3: Mr. Otis asks Ms. Evans to call the mother and thank her for signing the school-behavior notes. Mr. Otis is hoping to build up a more positive relationship between Ms. Evans and Charlotte's mother.

Week 5: Ms. Evans invites Charlotte's mother in for a meeting with her and Mr. Otis. The purpose of the meeting is to discuss the home–school behavior-note system, as well as ways it might be improved.

Mr. Otis begins the meeting by thanking Charlotte's mother for her participation and describing the purpose (or problem) of today's discussion: "We greatly appreciate your support with Charlotte's school-behavior notes. Charlotte is doing a fine job taking the notes between home and school. We wanted to meet today to talk about ways to improve the system."

Fifteen minutes of brainstorming lead to some creative solutions. Charlotte's mother, it turns out, would like to see the notes from school more often and wonders if she could provide a small reward if the notes are positive. Mr. Otis, Ms. Evans, and Charlotte's mother brainstorm some small home rewards that might be appropriate for good behavior. Ms. Evans agrees to send the notes home daily; she also asks if she can call home in about a week to see how the new system is working.

Another meeting was scheduled for next month to follow up and make necessary changes in the home–school note system. Once Charlotte's mother is using the home-note system consistently, Mr. Otis plans to talk with her again about discipline issues and strategies at home. The goal is not to change her parenting style or her value system but to make essential information on parenting practices available to her if she is interested.

Discussion

Charlotte's pattern of problem behavior would be classified as mildly antisocial at best; it is unlikely that her problems are severe enough to warrant a diagnosis of conduct disordered or antisocial. Her major problems seem to be (1) noncompliant and occasionally oppositional behavior directed toward her teacher, (2) difficulty in focusing and sustaining her attention, (3) poor social skills, and (4) lack of motivation for academics and homework. Although not considered of an antisocial nature per se, these behavior problems are difficult for teachers who must manage a class of 20 to 30 youngsters.

The intervention proposed by Mr. Otis was on the lower end of the intensity scale and was only slightly intrusive into the teacher's management of the classroom. It was a largely private arrangement among Charlotte, her mother, her teacher, and Mr. Otis. As interventions go, it was not especially powerful; however, it was just the ticket in Charlotte's case, as she responded very favorably. The intervention involved all parties in a positive school–home monitoring procedure in which a great deal of positive attention was focused on Charlotte's school behavior and academic performance. It was also accomplished with only a minimal reliance on privileges and rewards; Charlotte responded well to adult praise, approval, and attention—which does not often occur with antisocial students. The cross-setting monitoring and accountability component of this intervention and the positive attention from adults were probably the factors that were most responsible for the positive outcomes. It is *extremely* important to continue this sort of monitoring and supervision, albeit at a reduced level, over the long-term in order to solidify and preserve Charlotte's gains.

SECOND STEP: IMPLEMENTING CLASSWIDE SOCIAL SKILLS

Background

Cliff Heights Elementary School is located in a working-class neighborhood in Chicago, Illinois, and serves approximately 800 students from low- to middle-income families. Violent behavior, including random acts of assault and vandalism and occasional drive-by shootings, characterizes the daily life of this neighborhood. These volatile social conditions are spilling over into Cliff Heights and affecting what goes on there.

Cliff Heights teachers and staff are frustrated with the number of students in their classrooms who have low academic skills and poor school-adjustment records. The teachers also complain about having to spend most of their available time dealing with behavioral issues. There are playground fights almost every day, despite the new requirement that two classroom teachers supervise these periods. There are increasing concerns about children bringing weapons to school. Each day, pairs of teachers monitor the playground during recess periods, in addition to the three regular playground supervisors. The problems are so bad that children as young as 6 and 7 are getting suspended for engaging in unacceptable playground behavior.

At the same time, a small, vocal group of parents is asking Cliff Heights to do something about the situation. They are very concerned about drugs, gangs, and the disrespectful behavior toward adults and property that they see in the school. Cliff Heights is lucky to have Joyce Gilfrey, a full-time counselor, who runs anger-management, social-skills, and self-esteem student groups. They seem to be effective and are popular with teachers, parents, and students; however, only a small number of students in the school are reached by each group. It is clear that another strategy is needed if the problems at Cliff Heights are to be adequately addressed.

Intervention

Ms. Gilfrey, together with the principal, Ms. Abbott, decide to devote an entire staff meeting to a problem-solving session focused on what the school can do to decrease and prevent the high levels of negative, undesirable, and sometimes dangerous student behavior. Teachers expressed concern that the pattern of letting kids out of class to attend groups is becoming more and more difficult to accommodate. These are the very students who need academic instruction and support the most.

Ms. Gilfrey describes a new violence-prevention curriculum, called Second Step, she learned about at a recent conference. This curriculum is designed for an entire class, rather than for a small group of students. Second Step focuses on three main areas: empathy development, problem-solving skills, and anger-management techniques—all of which are important dimensions in the prevention of violent and antisocial of behavior. The Cliff Heights teachers are interested but also hesitant to take on anything more, as they are extremely stressed by increasing class sizes, the complex needs of their students, reduced resources, and the diversity of backgrounds and behavioral characteristics in their classes.

Ms. Gilfrey recommends that Second Step be used on a schoolwide basis. In this way, it is more likely that most students will learn the skills and concepts and that classroom expectations will carry over across grade levels.

Ms. Gilfrey is determined to make a violence-prevention program work at Cliff Heights. She recognizes how much more effective a classwide approach of this type can be as compared to her small pull-out groups with five or six students each. Too often, she has helped students make positive behavioral changes, yet they continue to face peer groups that resist these changes. Another recurring problem has been that even when students are able to improve socially, the improvement tends to be restricted largely to her office (that is, the training setting). Generalization of these behavioral effects to other school settings tends to be difficult and the improvements usually prove ephemeral.

Following the staff meeting, however, Ms. Gilfrey realizes that schoolwide implementation will need to be put on hold. Instead, after conferring with Ms. Abbott, she decides to approach just the third-grade teachers.

Third grade marks a major change in how children are socialized. They depend much less on their parents for guidance and tend to look more to their peers for feedback and acceptance. As a corollary, they are increasingly influenced by what peers think, value, and do in their daily behavior. Ms. Gilfrey believes, as do the developers of Second Step, that all children of this age could benefit from practice and training in using empathy, problem-solving, and anger-management skills, given the sometimes difficult changes and choices they now face. Empathy, in particular, seems to be a skill or attribute in which antisocial students are seriously lacking (Walker, Stieber, Ramsey, & O'Neill,

1990). Such skills can assist all children in building up their coping ability as they begin this new stage of socialization. Curricula like Second Step have the potential to assist students in feeling better about themselves and getting along with others, including their families.

Ms. Gilfrey meets with the third grade teachers and introduces Second Step. She agrees to take primary responsibility for preparing the lessons if classroom teachers will make 30 minutes of class time available twice each week for two months. Teachers are also asked to participate in all role-play activities included in the lessons. After two lessons, one classroom teacher, Mr. Michaelson, decides he would like to teach the curriculum himself. There are modifications he would like to make, and he would also like to teach the lessons at different times during the day. Ms. Gilfrey agrees and makes herself available for support, discussion, and questions.

Results

After one month of leading students through the curriculum and demonstrating how to teach it, Joyce asks the other teachers to teach the lessons themselves. She agrees to stay in the classroom and help when necessary as the teachers assume teaching responsibility for Second Step. Apparently, the third grade teachers have spoken with Mr. Michaelson, who has been pleased with the program, and he has encouraged the three to take charge of teaching it. It quickly becomes clear that Ms. Gilfrey's presence is not needed to teach and manage Second Step successfully. These teachers, who are highly skilled, are able to integrate Second Step materials into their ongoing instructional programs. In addition, they are able to review, practice, and reinforce the skills taught as students display them throughout the school day.

During this time, Ms. Gilfrey provides a training session for all playground supervisors, as well as the school principal. Her goal is for everyone (herself included) to be in a position to help the third grade students use and practice the key social skills they are learning—especially when conflict arises.

Mr. Michaelson, the three third grade teachers, and the playground supervisors all report that they can see some positive effects in the peer relations and classroom adjustment of many of the students who are participating in Second Step. The fact that everyone gets involved in Second Step (students, teachers, the principal, and Ms. Gilfrey) is a positive feature of the program. Within two months of Second Step's implementation, Ms. Abbott observes a substantial decline in office referrals and the number of playground incidents reported to the front office.

Next year, the third grade teachers will teach Second Step and even provide some guidance to teachers at two other grade levels. A new committee, a teacher-assistance team, has been formed at Cliff Heights to support teachers' efforts to implement the curriculum. This committee is made up of a parent, two third-grade teachers, Ms. Gilfrey, Ms. Abbott, and one playground supervisor. The committee has the goal of effecting schoolwide implementation of Second Step, but for now they are taking it one class at a time.

Discussion

Some key features of the Second Step program are: (1) the core skills areas it teaches (empathy, problem solving, anger management), (2) the fact that is a universal intervention to which all students are exposed, and (3) its involvement at a schoolwide level. There are no skills more important in the prevention of antisocial and violent, aggressive forms of behavior among children and youth than those in these three areas. However, it is extremely important that each student be recognized and praised by teachers, counselors, playground supervisors, the principal, and school support staff for displaying these skills in natural school settings.

Second Step represents an important advance in the direct teaching of social skills that facilitate positive peer relations and that also contribute to meeting teacher expectations for classroom behavior and academic performance. It is designed for integration into the ongoing curricula of most elementary programs. It is most important, whenever possible, that curricular content of this type be taught to all students on a schoolwide basis. Universal interventions like Second Step are most important for those students, such as Charlotte, who seem to be on the margin of school failure. That is, they show signs of adjustment problems and often accompanying academic failure but at a level that is still within the range of recovery. Those students with fully developed antisocial behavior patterns will usually require follow-up, selected interventions in order to divert them from a path that too often leads to unfortunate long-term outcomes, including prison.

PROJECT PREPARE: ESTABLISHING A SCHOOLWIDE AND CLASSROOM-LEVEL MANAGEMENT SYSTEM—A BUILDING-TEAM APPROACH

Project PREPARE

Increasingly, educators are having to deal with the criticism that our schools do not enforce adequate discipline. Lack of adequate discipline in public schools consistently ranks as one of the most often cited concerns of Gallup poll respondents in surveys of attitudes toward education. As a matter of course, we are seeing spiraling occurrences of student behavior that significantly impact the safety of both staff and students. They include assault, possession of weapons, gang behavior, threats to adults and students, substance abuse, physical abuse, and occasionally sexual abuse.

Sugai, Kameenui, and Colvin (1990) have developed a schoolwide intervention model, called Project PREPARE, to enable special and general educators to meet classroom and schoolwide disciplinary needs. This project was developed and tested through a Special Projects grant from the U.S. Department of Education (Office of Special Education and Rehabilitative Services).

Project PREPARE (**P**romoting **R**esponsible, **E**mpirical, and **P**roactive **A**lternatives in **R**egular **E**ducation) for students with behavior disorders is designed to develop, evaluate, and disseminate an instructional model that will enable special and general educators to meet the classroom and schoolwide behavior-management needs of all students. It is a universal intervention to which all staff and students are exposed in the same fashion. The three central elements in the Project PREPARE intervention model are: (1) a behavioral-instruction approach, (2) a schoolwide focus on the prevention and remediation of problem behavior, and (3) staff development provided through a building-team approach.

The behavior-instruction approach for establishing classroom and schoolwide discipline is based on the same procedures that serve as the foundation for teaching academic skills (Colvin & Sugai, 1988, 1992). In academic instruction, teachers generally complete a number of preparatory steps before students are required to demonstrate a skill independently. The preparatory steps usually involve clarifying the goals and objectives of instruction, specifying the content, selecting examples, explaining the skills to be learned, modeling the skills, providing supervised practice, providing corrective feedback, and furnishing opportunities for independent practice. These same steps can be operationalized for teaching and establishing appropriate behavior at classroom and schoolwide levels in exactly the same manner as for academic development. The instructional sequence governing the application of these procedures in teaching adaptive student behavior was described and illustrated in Chapter 7, "An Instructional Approach to Teaching Adaptive Behavior Patterns."

This behavior-instruction teaching model was designed to achieve two major goals: (1) to teach and establish appropriate behavior, usually referred to as *prevention* and (2) to correct inappropriate behavior after it occurs, usually called *remediation.* In the PREPARE model, all school settings are targeted for intervention (that is, classrooms, hallways, the cafeteria, restrooms, library, bus stop areas, the playground, and the gymnasium). In addition, each student in the school is targeted for exposure to the intervention regardless of their school placement (general education, resource room, special education). Furthermore, regardless of the degree to which students display appropriate or inappropriate behavioral levels, they receive identical exposure to the intervention because of its schoolwide and universal nature. Thus, when Project PREPARE is implemented prior to or at the beginning of the school year, it serves primarily a prevention function. When it is implemented during the school year, in response to a school crisis, it serves a remedial function.

Cotton (1990) reported a crucial research finding that influences effective schoolwide discipline practices. She describes such practices as *commitment,* on the part of all staff, to establishing and maintaining appropriate student behavior. Given this, two questions arise: "How do you get all staff to agree to certain practices?" and "How do you get staff to reliably implement what they agree to?"

Answers to these kinds of questions fall under the framework of staff development. However, to date, the results of research on effective staff-development procedures or models has not been very encouraging. According to Guskey (1986), "Nearly every major work on the topic of staff development has emphasized the failings of these efforts" (p. 5). Smylie (1988) empirically tested a staff-development model and identified the following three factors that appear to be very important in bringing about teacher change at a schoolwide level:

1. Personal teaching efficacy, which refers to teachers' perceptions of their ability to directly affect student performance
2. Characteristics of teachers' classroom environments, which include class size, class academic heterogeneity, and concentrations of low-achieving students
3. Interactive contexts of schools, which refer to leadership from the principal and collegial support

Project PREPARE incorporates several of the key features recommended by Smylie (1988) for staff-development models. Essentially, Project PREPARE is to be implemented by a building team, referred to as a "teacher-assistance team." The building team is designed to carry out the following tasks and functions:

- Afford representation of all staff
- Provide a structure for administrative support
- Pilot or field test certain strategies, such as the behavior-instruction plans, to teach appropriate behavior
- Provide collegial support for staff
- Serve as a catalyst for ongoing review of procedures
- Secure open channels for staff communication
- Facilitate participatory decision-making by staff as appropriate
- Provide a structure to enable the process of staff development to advance at an appropriate pace
- Assume responsibility for direct training of staff in the procedures, especially the behavior-instruction plans. The overall responsibility of the team is to bring the staff along, as opposed to doing the job for them.

Project PREPARE is a staff-development model designed to enable educators in a school to manage problem behavior more effectively. It is also designed to handle as many problems as possible at the school level, rather than referring them to a central district. Such latter solutions are often problematic in that (1) they are an admission of the school's inability to cope effectively with disciplinary problems, (2) district solutions are frequently divorced from the nuances of the conditions at the local school that frame the problem, (3) such solutions can be very expensive, and (4) school staff often do not own the proposed solutions because they were not involved in their development.

The basic assumptions underlying Project PREPARE are twofold: (1) effective schoolwide discipline can be achieved by applying the principles of instruction to teaching appropriate behavior and managing inappropriate behavior and (2) the proper target for designing and implementing a schoolwide discipline program is the school staff—not the students. The critical mechanism for implementing this project is utilization of a building-level team. The remaining sections of this case study provide details of Project PREPARE's implementation at Hamilton Middle School.

Background

Hamilton Middle School is located in a peripheral section of Eugene, Oregon—a city of 125,000 people located in a metropolitan area of 200,000. The school district has approximately 20,000 students in grades K–12; Hamilton enrolls approximately 450 sixth, seventh, and eighth graders. Hamilton's socioeconomic status is relatively low, ranking 50th out of 368 schools in Oregon (that is, 172 students qualify for free lunches, representing 39% of the student body). Many of the students come from shelter homes and low-rent motels or low-income apartments and housing (approximately 20%). One-third of the families have been classified as transient, based on school turnover rates. The student body at Hamilton is predominantly Caucasian, with slightly less than 2% representing minority groups.

The high rate of recidivism for front office referrals prompted the administrators and staff of Hamilton to seek involvement with Project PREPARE. In addition, approximately 80% of these referrals were coming from 10% of the school population. Thus, a relatively small number of students was consuming a significant amount of Hamilton's administrative resources and causing continuous and severe disruptions in overall school atmosphere, as well as in individual classrooms. After several schoolwide problem-solving sessions, in which Project PREPARE was one of the options discussed, the school principal approached Project PREPARE staff to request information on procedures for participating in the project.

Intervention

The project manager presented an overview of Project PREPARE to the school administration and representative staff. The role and responsibilities of the building team were defined. Some of these responsibilities included meeting together once a week for approximately an hour, developing and piloting behavior-instruction plans, taking a lead role in involving teachers and other school staff at regular staff meetings or at other designated times. The principal then presented this information to the Hamilton staff. After some discussion, they decided to give Project PREPARE a try and contacted the project manager who had initially presented the program.

The initial step in implementing Project PREPARE is to identify a building-level teacher-assistance team (TAT). Criteria for forming the team are developed; membership is usually based on the following guidelines:

1. Includes representatives of all school staff (general and special educators, support staff, and administration)
2. Is weighted toward general educators
3. Includes representatives of each grade level
4. Has credibility with staff
5. Selection process combines voluntary, appointed, and elected options

The Hamilton building team was ultimately comprised of nine staff members: the vice-principal, the school counselor, five general-education teachers with representatives from each grade, and two special-education teachers. In the development of Project PREPARE, careful attention was devoted to the need for working with and within existing structures, wherever possible. To this end, procedures were developed to assess disciplinary structures and practices already in place and the extent to which they were achieving intended goals. Thus, our first step was to develop a survey to assess the effectiveness of Hamilton's existing schoolwide discipline plan in relation to prevention and remediation achievable at a schoolwide level.

The survey was distributed to all Hamilton staff, and approximately 50% were returned. The results of the four content areas of the survey are presented here:

1. *School Manual about Discipline.* Staff agreed that a manual existed. There was considerable variability in staff responses as to how this product was developed and the extent to which it is disseminated to all students, staff, and parents. Most Hamilton staff indicated that the manual is in need of revision and that the revision process itself needs clarification.

2. *Content of the Schoolwide Discipline Plan.* Staff were in agreement on the philosophical basis underlying the plan and with the delineation of behavioral expectations. (These are extremely important areas on which to reach staff agreement as they are fundamental to the success of any schoolwide discipline plan.) There were several staff responses addressing perceived needs, such as: (1) more structures for acknowledging students who demonstrate expected behaviors, (2) a greater continuum of back-up consequences and more involvement of staff in follow-up related to the delivery and effectiveness of such consequences, and (3) clarification of the referral and record-keeping processes.

3. *Implementation.* Staff responses were mostly in the area of "somewhat in place." The need was expressed to establish more consistency and to develop structures that provide regular updates to staff and students.

4. *Monitoring System.* Staff members indicated they were not typically informed of the school's monitoring system or kept up to date on any regular basis. An overall concern of all staff was the need to address Hamilton procedures for managing students who exhibit high rates of problem behavior.

The building team used results of the survey to begin the process of planning procedures for enhancing the effectiveness of its schoolwide discipline. The basic process used was to identify key priorities with staff; develop draft proposals; and then take the drafts to all staff for discussion, revision, and adoption. Three major priorities were identified: (1) the need to develop and implement behavior-instruction plans on a schoolwide basis, (2) clarification of behaviors that warrant office referrals and administrative intervention as distinguished from behaviors that should be managed directly by staff, and (3) procedures and strategies for staff to work together to manage persistent but minor behavior problems.

An important early task in PREPARE's implementation is to develop and apply behavior-instruction plans in all classrooms. Hamilton building-team members facilitated this process at each grade level. Team members selected "Coming to Class Prepared" as the initial target behavior they wished to teach all students. Details of the behavior instruction plan designed for this purpose are presented in Box 12.1.

Each Hamilton teacher reported considerable student gains for "Coming to Class Prepared," which is so important to school success and meeting behavioral expectations. The average improvement across all classrooms for the percentage of students coming to class prepared was 21%; the baseline average of 74% increased to a postintervention average of 95%.

The second key task was to clearly define and categorize problem behaviors so they could be dealt with effectively by Hamilton staff. One of the most crucial steps in any school discipline plan is to establish agreement among staff on which student behaviors warrant office referrals and which should be managed directly by staff at a classroom level. Failure to manage this step often leads to (1) staff dissension, (2) a breakdown in trust between staff and administration, and (3) inconsistent practices throughout the school. To this end, staff must meet and reach agreement on categories of inappropriate behavior. It is important to develop a list that represents a sampling of the full range of indicator behaviors for each category. The following categories are recommended for this purpose:

- *Minor school infractions* are regarded as relatively mild behaviors, but they are disruptive to the teaching and learning process. Furthermore, they can easily escalate into more serious behavior if not handled correctly; this is especially true for antisocial students who carry high levels of agitation. Common examples of minor school infractions include being tardy for class, talking too loudly in the hallways, not having materials ready for class, and skipping school (truancy). These behaviors are typically managed by staff within the immediate context in which the problem behavior occurs.

- *Serious school violations* are not necessarily legal infractions (most often they are not), but they represent serious breaches of school rules and involve forms of behavior that seriously disrupt school functioning. Examples include sustained noncompliance and defiance, verbal abuse toward staff, low levels of physical aggression, vandalism, and chronic (repeated) minor infractions. These behaviors typically warrant an office referral and are managed by the administration or its appropriate designee.

- *Illegal behavior* violates the law. Examples include possession of weapons or controlled substances, theft, assault, vandalism, and threats or intimidation. This list should be confirmed with local law-enforcement agencies and district policies. These behaviors typically warrant office referrals and are managed by the administration (or designee) in conjunction with local law-enforcement agents.

Using these categories, the staff at Hamilton identified and defined behaviors that should be referred to the office. Subsequently, the office-referral form was revised to reflect these changes, and the definitions were printed on the back of the form. The revised office-referral form and definitions of office-referral behaviors are presented in Forms 12.1 and 12.2, respectively.

Box 12.1 Behavior-Instruction Plan—"Coming to Class Prepared"

Phase One: Goals

Be prepared for class with necessary materials (second period)

Phase Two: Expected Behaviors

1. Bring necessary supplies (notebook, pencil sharpener, paper, homework, textbook)
2. Materials to be in reasonable shape
3. Notebook organized

Phase Three: School Settings

Classroom

Phase Four: Instruction Plan

1. Explaining goals and expected behaviors
   a. Preparation related to success in class
   b. Supply list described
   c. Notebook organization described
   d. Letter of explanation sent to parents
2. Identifying positive and negative examples
   a. Positive example: Materials organized, complete, and good quality
   b. Negative example: Incomplete and poor-quality supplies
3. Providing practice opportunities
   a. Class discussion on what is needed
   b. Training time allocated to check notebook
   c. Chart preparedness
   d. Review weekly
4. Providing reminders and pre-correction
   a. Positive verbal reminders
   b. Self-check sheet
   c. Charting
5. Providing acknowledgment of demonstrations of expected behaviors
   a. Verbal praise
   b. Reward stars (80% prepared) for access to free time, computer time, treats

Phase Five: Correction Procedures

1. Reinforce students who are prepared
2. Remind students who are not prepared

Box 12.1 *(Continued)*

Phase Five *(Continued)*

3. Provide warning
4. Implement negative consequence if needed

Phase Six: Record-Keeping System

Use of chart (frequency count of students prepared for class)

Phase Seven: Procedures for Review, Follow-up, and Evaluation

1. Raise criteria from 80 to 90% class prepared
2. Assigned homework
3. Letter to parents

Form 12.3 is a sample recording form and Box 12.2 provides definitions of the consequences and outcomes listed on the form. It is very important to record not only the frequency of specific infractions on a schoolwide basis but also to record how each office referral was dealt with.

If minor problem behaviors still persist after a staff member has made several documented attempts to correct them, the next step involves setting up a staff meeting. The following guidelines are suggested for conducting such meetings:

1. A staff meeting should be called by the teacher after three to four documented incidents of the minor problem behavior have occurred and attempts at remediation have failed.

2. The staff meeting should be scheduled on a regular basis during staff or grade-level meetings.

3. A special staff meeting may be called if a teacher needs more immediate action (with as many teachers in attendance as possible).

4. A form should be developed and used to document each case of the problem behavior and to guide staff-meeting activities. Form 12.4 is an example of a staff-meeting form for use in planning actions for minor problem behaviors. The teacher should complete as much of the form as possible before the meeting, so participants will have some information about the case. This information also can serve as the starting point for discussions about a plan of action to be developed during the meeting.

5. A notetaker and timekeeper should be identified. It is critical to follow the agenda and keep on the time lines in order to prevent meetings from lasting too long and

HAMILTON MIDDLE SCHOOL
Phone 555-8245
1525 Echo Hollow Road
Eugene, Oregon 97402

OFFICE REFERRAL

STUDENT ____________ GRADE 6 7 8 DATE ______

REFERRED BY __________ HOMEROOM TEACHER __________

REASON FOR REFERRAL
Repeated minor infraction(s) ☐
For-the-Record and Staffing Plans attached ☐
Parent contacted ☐

Description: ____

____

____

SERIOUS SCHOOL VIOLATION

- ☐ Fighting
- ☐ Serious disruption
- ☐ Controlled substance(s)
- ☐ Verbal abuse
- ☐ Vandalism
- ☐ Off-campus violation
- ☐ Harassment/hazing
- ☐ Defiance
- ☐ Weapons
- ☐ Other ________________

Description: (Specify times, places, those involved, relevant conditions, and initial steps to address problem)

____

____

____

____

FORM 12.1 Office-Referral Form

____

____

ACTION TAKEN: (By teacher/person making referral as appropriate)

- ☐ Conference with student
- ☐ Parent contact (phone/note)
- ☐ Parent conference request
- ☐ Made contact with student
- ☐ Other ______________

ACTION TAKEN: (By administrator/counselor)

- ☐ Conference with student
- ☐ Parent contacted (phone/note)
- ☐ Student suspended ___ number of days
- ☐ Referred to School Behavior-Support Team
- ☐ Principal's hearing for possible expulsion
- ☐ Conference requested with teacher and student
- ☐ Parent conference requested
- ☐ Detention ___ number of days
- ☐ Police contact
- ☐ Lane County Youth Services contact
- ☐ Other ______________

COMMENTS: ______________________________________

____

____

____

White—Student file
Blue—Office
Green—Homeroom
Canary—Parent
Goldenrod—Counselor
Pink—Referring staff

____
(Principal, Assistant Principal, Counselor)

PARENTS (GUARDIANS): This is a copy of an office referral for your son or daughter made by a staff member at Hamilton Middle School. The action is noted. Please call us at 555-8245 if you have any questions.

FORM 12.1 *(Continued)*

HAMILTON MIDDLE SCHOOL
OFFICE REFERRAL
WORKING DEFINITIONS FOR INFRACTIONS

REPEATED MINOR INFRACTIONS

Recurring problems that have been addressed by teachers with for-the-record documentation, such as tardies, skipping classes, minor disruptive behavior, profanity, incomplete assignments, minor harassment, and not coming to class prepared.

FIGHTING

Action involving serious physical contact that may cause injury (such as hitting, punching, hitting with an object, kicking, hair pulling, and scratching).

VANDALISM

Substantial destruction or disfigurement of property.

CONTROLLED SUBSTANCES

In possession of, or using drugs, alcohol, or tobacco.

SERIOUS DISRUPTION

Behavior causing class or activity to stop, or continue with difficulty. Student does not cooperate with reasonable attempts to disengage or follow directions. These behaviors include sustained loud talk, noise with materials, horseplay or roughhousing, sustained out-of-seat behavior.

VERBAL ABUSE

Sustained profanity or sexual comments directed toward staff or students.

HARASSMENT OR HAZING

Sustained or intense verbal attacks based on ethnicity, gender, disabilities, or other personal matters.

FORM 12.2 Definitions of Office-Referral Behaviors

WEAPONS

In possession of knives, guns, or other items used as weapons.

DEFIANCE

Refusal to follow staff directions given reasonable steps have been taken.

OFF CAMPUS

Off campus without permission.

THEFT

In possession of, having passed on, or being responsible for removing someone else's property.

OTHER

Serious behavior that does not fit into the above categories (such as setting off fire alarms, indecent exposure).

FORM 12.2 *(Continued)*

discussions from straying. Schools that adhere to the time lines continue, as a rule, to have the staffings.

6. Problem behaviors (list no more than two or three) should be prioritized from most to least important. Descriptions of these problem behaviors should be written in specific, observable form.

7. An expected (that is, adaptive) behavior should be paired with each problem behavior.

8. If possible, one to three of the least intrusive and time-consuming strategies for teaching expected behaviors should be selected. If the expected behaviors are not observed at acceptable levels and the problem behavior does not respond, more intrusive and time-consuming strategies can be considered.

9. Although strategies for teaching expected behaviors should be given the greatest attention, specific strategies for responding to problem behaviors should also be described. Again, the least intrusive and least aversive strategies possible should be selected.

CONSEQUENCES

	Sep	Oct	Nov	Dec	Jan	Feb	Mar	Apr	May	Jun	Total
Office conference											
In-school suspension/ detention											
Out-of-school suspension											
Loss of privileges											
Parent telephone call											
Expulsion											
Police contact											
OFFICE OUTCOMES											
Staffing											
Tutoring											
Contract											
Counseling											
Parent meeting											
Other											

Consequences: These refer to the action or outcomes for the infractions noted on the Office–Referral Form.

FORM 12.3 Recording Form

10. A specific date should be established to review the progress of the strategy selected. If possible, a plan for collecting and recording data should be developed to measure progress.

11. All paperwork should be completed and distributed immediately after the staff meeting.

Box 12.2 Definition of Consequences and Office Outcomes

OFFICE CONFERENCE

A conference occurs between the student and office staff (principal, assistant principal, or designee). The conference may involve the following or any combination of the following: verbal reprimand, censure, warning, pep talk, plan for doing better.

IN-SCHOOL SUSPENSION/DETENTION

Any placement outside the normal placement for a set period of time, such as detention, after-school detention, placed near the office, sent to another room, Saturday morning school, lunch detention.

OUT-OF-SCHOOL SUSPENSION

Student is denied access to school and school property for a set period of time.

LOSS OF PRIVILEGES

Student is denied access to school privileges or activities such as sport teams, games, social events, off-campus privileges, recreation room.

EXPULSION

Student is expelled from the school following district guidelines.

POLICE CONTACT

Police are called and report filed.

STAFFING

A staff meeting is called to generate a plan to address the problem behavior and remediate the problem.

TUTORING

Student is given additional assistance with school work.

Box 12.2 *(Continued)*

CONTRACT

An individual contract is made for the student by staff.

COUNSELING

Counseling is scheduled for the student and a problem-solving plan is developed.

PARENT TELEPHONE CALL

A telephone call is placed to parents or guardian (contact is made, a message is left, or records indicate attempt to call).

PARENT MEETING

A meeting is called involving staff and parents.

OTHER

Information is too vague to classify, or consequence is not listed.

12. It is important to note that a parent contact needs to be made before an office referral can occur, provided the staffing plan is not successful in changing the student behavior in question.

Staff at Hamilton Middle School scheduled staffings to occur during their regular grade-level meetings (every other week), as a first option, and then informally, on an as-needed basis.

Results

Office-referral data were used to assess the effectiveness of the Project PREPARE school-wide discipline plan at Hamilton Middle School. An archival data-recording instrument was designed for this purpose, with categories that recorded the reasons for referral and the actions taken.

HAMILTON MIDDLE SCHOOL
STAFFING PLAN
☐ BEHAVIOR PROBLEM
☐ ACADEMIC PROBLEM

Student Name: ____________________ Grade: ________ Date: ________

Homeroom Teacher: ______________ # For-the-Record Reports: ________

Staffing Plans: ________________

Staff Present: ____

____

Problem Behaviors (2 minutes)

Expected Behaviors (2 minutes)

Strategies to Teach Expected Behaviors (select 1–3) (3 minutes)

☐ Reminders
☐ Reinforcers
☐ Feedback
☐ Contract
☐ Practice
☐ Individual contacts
☐ Monitoring sheet
☐ Self-management
☐ Parent contact
☐ Counseling
☐ Tutoring
☐ Modified assignments

☐ Other ____

Strategies to Correct Problem Behaviors (1 minute)

☐ Time out
☐ Loss of privilege
☐ Parent contact
☐ Detention

☐ Other ____

FORM 12.4 Staff-Meeting Form

Action Plan (5 minutes)

Who	**What**	**When**
________	____________________	________
________	____________________	________
________	____________________	________
________	____________________	________

Student Conference Date: ________ *Start Date:* ________

Review Date: ________

Copies to: Office file
Teacher(s)

Other: ____________________

FORM 12.4 *(Continued)*

Office-referral data were collected at Hamilton Middle School (the target school) and at another middle school (the control school) of similar size, location, and student demographics (low socioeconomic status, transient population, and a small number of students responsible for the most serious problem behavior occurring in the school). Pre–post measures were recorded over a one-year period (1992–1993) for the two schools. Adjustments were made to the data for slight differences in school populations and number of school days. Three major outcomes of the effects of PREPARE were observed; they are described here and shown graphically in Figures 12.2, 12.3, and 12.4.

1. There was an overall reduction in office referrals at the target school of 51% compared to an increase of 12% at the control school (see Figure 12.2).

2. Figure 12.3 shows percentage change in the categories and frequencies of office referrals for the two schools. Hamilton showed substantial reductions in disruption, harassment, fighting, defiance, and other categories; the control school showed increases in each of these categories.

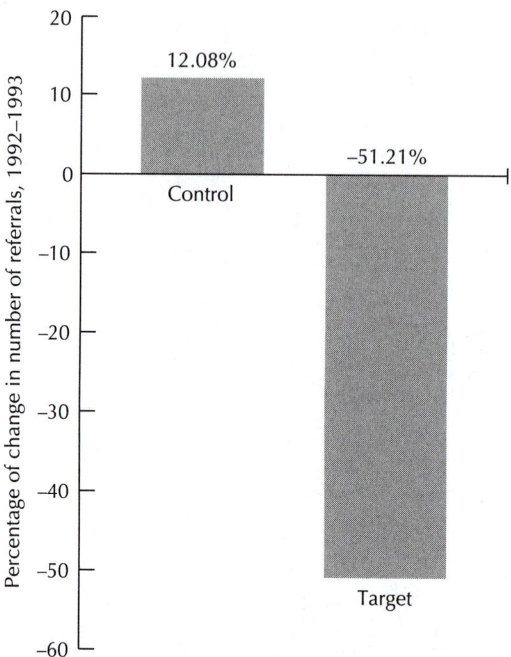

FIGURE 12.2 Change in Number of Office Referrals: Hamilton versus Control School

3. Figure 12.4 shows the types and frequencies of school consequences implemented for office referrals in Hamilton and the control school over the one-year period. At Hamilton, there was a decrease in the use of all categories of consequences. At the control school, there were decreases for all categories of consequences except detention and other.

Staff at Hamilton Middle School implemented a proactive, schoolwide discipline plan comprised of three major components: (1) schoolwide strategies to teach expected behaviors, (2) clear delineation of student behaviors that warrant office referrals with the expectation that other behaviors are managed directly by staff, and (3) structured opportunities for teaching staff to address persistent minor problem behavior as a team. The essential ingredient for implementing the plan was the formation and operation of a schoolwide building team. Results showed substantial reductions in Hamilton office referrals, in general classroom disruptions and teacher and staff defiance, and a substantial reduction in school suspensions. One year later, the Hamilton staff was committed to

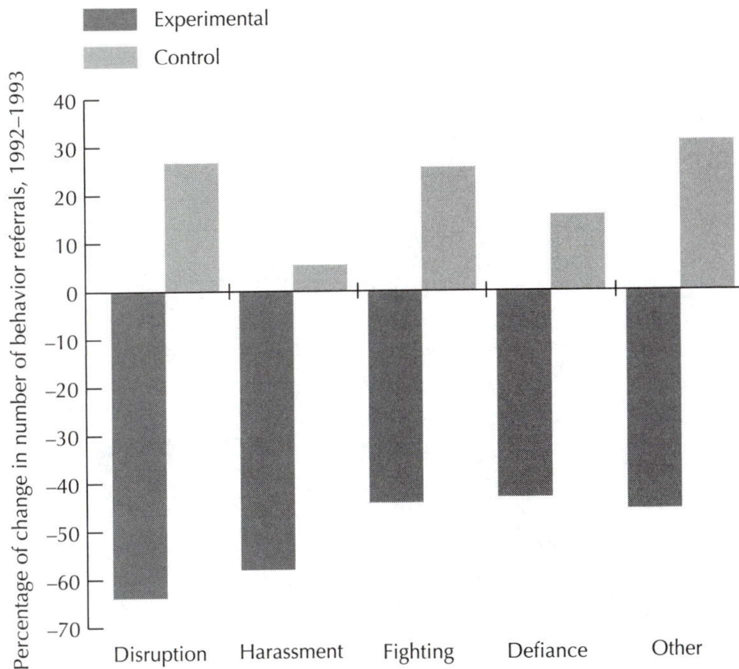

FIGURE 12.3 Change in Frequency of Referrals by Type: Hamilton versus Control School

maintaining the building team and the three components of teaching behavior, managing minor problem behavior at a staff level, and dealing with serious forms of student behavior at the office level.

Discussion

Project PREPARE proved to be robust in terms of empowering the staff of Hamilton to deal more effectively with disruptive and out-of-control student behavior. The results in Figures 12.2–12.4 are persuasive in this regard. They also reflect a considerable savings in staff time in dealing with disruptions occurring in the classroom and other school settings. Probably the most important factor in accounting for this positive outcome was the full commitment of all staff to making the system work. There was an unusual degree of cooperation and shared decision making among teachers, the principal, office staff, and members of the teacher-assistance team. Also, the structure and uniform recording

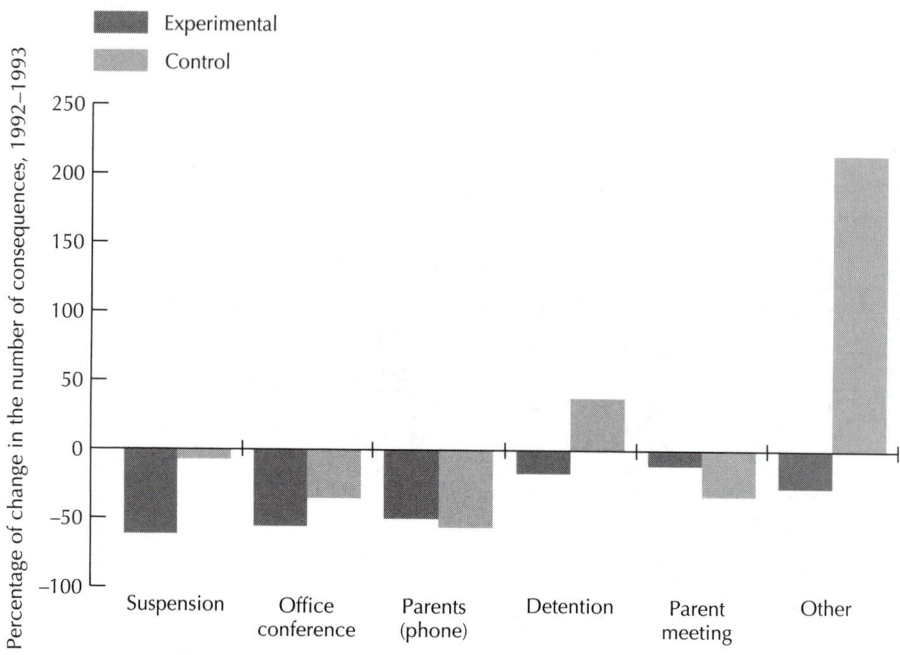

FIGURE 12.4 Change in Frequency of Consequences by Type: Hamilton versus Control School

and decision-making provided by PREPARE greatly facilitated the communication processes. Essentially, a schoolwide monitoring, recording, and consequation system was established for dealing with student behavior problems. The staff of Hamilton was pleased with the results of PREPARE and plan to continue its implementation into the foreseeable future.

JIMMY: EARLY INTERVENTION FOR THE PREVENTION OF ANTISOCIAL BEHAVIOR AMONG KINDERGARTNERS—THE FIRST STEPS PROGRAM

The First Steps Program

First Steps is a coordinated school and home intervention designed to prevent the development of antisocial behavior patterns among kindergartners who have an elevated risk for this disorder. First Steps was developed and tested over a four-year period and was supported by a four-year grant to the Eugene School District from the U.S. Office of Special Education Programs. Thomas Henry, Director of Elementary Education for Eugene School District 4J, and the senior author jointly directed this program.

First Steps consists of three modules that can be implemented separately or as a combined unit. These modules deal with: (1) school intervention, (2) family support and parent training, and (3) support and assistance from community social service agencies. Collectively, the components of the First Steps program provide a comprehensive intervention for the prevention of antisocial behavior patterns among kindergartens. The program was designed to pick up at-risk children at the moment they begin their formal school careers and work with them, their parents, teachers, and peers intensively over a period of more than one year to ensure that they get off to the best start possible in meeting the demands of school. Details of each of the First Steps components follow.

School Intervention

The CLASS (Contingencies for Learning Academic and Social Skills) Program for Acting-Out Children comprises the school intervention component of First Steps (Hops & Walker, 1988). CLASS requires 30 school days for implementation. It is designed as a behavior-management template that overlays onto the curricula and instructional routines of regular educational settings; however, it can be easily adapted for effective use in more restrictive placement settings (for example, resource or self-contained settings, day-treatment centers, and residential programs).

CLASS is divided into two major phases: consultant and teacher. The consultant phase lasts five program days and is characterized by proximal and intense monitoring of the target student's classroom behavior. Red and green signaling cards are used for this purpose during two, 20- to 30-minute periods daily; points and praise for following classroom rules and remaining academically engaged are awarded frequently during these periods (every 1 to 2 minutes). The red side of the card is used to signal inappropriate behavior or that the target student is not academically engaged. If the red side is showing when it is time to award a point, then the point goes on the red rather than green side and serves as a form of cost contingency (that is, loss of points). Eighty percent of the available points have to be awarded on the green side of the card (that is, for appropriate behavior) in order to earn a group-activity reward that immediately follows the period. If the target student meets the reward criterion for both daily sessions, then a special privilege or reward, prearranged with the parents, is delivered at home. The student takes the card home, signed by the teacher, as a record of the day's events and performance at school; the parents, in turn, review and sign the card, and it is returned to school the next day.

The teacher phase of the CLASS program lasts from day 6 to day 30 and is divided into reward and maintenance conditions. The reward condition lasts from program days 6 through 20 and involves continued use of home and school rewards and the awarding of points; the maintenance phase (program days 21–30) relies only on teacher and parent praise to maintain the behavioral gains achieved in the previous phase. Brief time-out procedures (spent either in room or at the front office of the school) are implemented to deal with such things as teacher defiance, fighting, property destruction, and having severe tantrums.

On program day 6, the regular teacher assumes primary control of the CLASS program's daily procedures with the support and assistance of the teacher consultant (usually a school counselor, school psychologist, behavioral specialist, resource teacher, diagnostician, or other school professional). By this point in the program, the monitoring, point awarding, and praising requirements of CLASS have been reduced to levels where the teacher can manage the program as part of her or his regular teaching duties. The teacher phase begins with intermittent use of the red and green point card for monitoring and awarding points but is completely faded out by program day 15. The magnitude of available rewards at home and school both increase as the program progresses, as does the length of the intervals required to earn them. For example, during days 16–20, the student must work for five full school days in order to earn the reward criterion.

The CLASS program was developed and tested over a five-year period under the auspices of a large grant from the U.S. Office of Special Education Programs (see Walker, Hops & Greenwood, 1984). It has been used extensively throughout the United States, Canada, and Australia; in addition, CLASS has been translated into Spanish and successfully replicated in Costa Rica. CLASS is a powerful intervention for changing the behavior of acting-out children in grades K–3 who are oppositional or defiant. It is geared primarily for those students who have problems with rule-governed behavioral demands imposed by teachers and other adults early in their school careers.

Family Support and Parent Training

The second component of First Steps is the parent training module called *Homebase.* Homebase is a parent skill-building program that is based on over 25 years of research and clinical trials at the Oregon Social Learning Center—a group of researchers and specialists who conduct research on deviant families (that is, those who produce antisocial, delinquent offspring). Homebase is a child-focused program for improving adjustment to kindergarten. The program includes six sessions in the home and a midweek call to discuss parent and child practice of the lesson content previously taught. Homebase is implemented over consecutive weeks to maximize parents' mastery of the material and corresponding parenting skills. The Homebase lessons are designed to complement the CLASS program and are organized around the following basic components of school adjustment: following rules, cooperation, listening, and getting along with other children.

Each in-home meeting follows a standard format. The skill is presented by the consultant, and a rationale is provided for its importance. Then the parent and consultant complete a current skill-level assessment for the child. Some lessons are enhanced through videotape examples that are shown during the home visit. Activity cards and other instructional materials for the week's lesson are presented and reviewed with the parents. A daily time is chosen for practice of the skill. Barriers to practicing the exercises are then discussed and strategies for implementation are developed that are fine-tuned to the parents' preferences and skill levels.

Following the six weeks of skill development, groups of parents may meet monthly to share their successes and discuss strategies for responding to difficulties they encounter during the daily practice sessions geared toward managing the child's behavior problems at home. Groups also discuss their successes and difficulties experienced in collaborating with the school intervention component of First Steps. This is an extremely important part of First Steps and is appreciated by the parents of kindergarten children in the program.

Box 12.3 contains a brief description of the content of each Homebase lesson, in the order in which they are taught.

Support and Assistance from Community Social Service Agencies

The third component of First Steps is optional and is the least well developed of the three modules. This component attempts to match up family needs with available community support services for which the family may qualify. Many of the First Steps parents represent families and households that are extremely stressed by such factors as poverty, abuse, alcohol and drug problems, and single caregiver situations. During the Homebase part of the program, parents are asked if they want to hear about community service programs for which they might qualify. If they do, then a standard interview is conducted by the Homebase consultant to (1) provide information for determining eligibility for services and (2) identify agencies that offer services and supports that match the family's needs. The case study that follows provides a profile of Jimmy—an antisocial kindergartner who participated in First Steps program.

Background

Jimmy was commonly referred to as a "terror" soon after entering kindergarten; it did not take him long to establish a reputation as one of the most difficult children in the school's morning and afternoon kindergarten classes. He entered school with a well-developed pattern of oppositional and extremely noncompliant behavior. Jimmy had a short attention span and was agitated much of the time—popping off at the drop of a hat. Academic tasks and appropriate group behavior (for example, participating in circle time and listening to the teacher in small groups) were extremely difficult for Jimmy. He could not seem to keep his hands off others and was constantly pestering his classmates and their materials.

Box 12.3 Instructional Content of Homebase Lessons

Homebase is a brief program designed as a bridge between home and school that helps parents guide children's behavior and support and supplement school programs and expectations.

Homebase consists of a basic program for parents and a follow-up enhancement program. The basic program is delivered in the home over a six-week period.

The Six Skills Lessons

1. *Talking about school—"How's school?"* Skills for gathering information, listening, and problem solving.
2. *Building self-confidence—"You're great and you can do it."* What you can do each day to improve your child's self-confidence in school (encouraging school) by identifying and encouraging your child's strengths and helping him or her try out new activities and skills.
3. *Teaching cooperation—"I appreciate your cooperation."* Teaching school-related skills of cooperation with directions, sequencing activities, spending time doing school-related activities.
4. *Teaching self-control—"Remember the rules."* In combination with cooperation, being able to control and manage behavior and emotions in the class and on the playground can be practiced at home by the rules you set up for good behavior.
5. *Problem solving—"Let's figure it out."* Help your child learn to look at a problem as something to solve rather than as an obstacle. We provide some simple skills that parents can practice at home with their children. We also teach strategies to help children work out problems away from home.
6. *Playing well with other children—"If you're nice to them, they'll be nice to you."* This is always an important concern for parents and one that they may not feel able to help with. We provide activities parents can do with their children to help in friendship initiation and maintenance.

Jimmy's peer relationships were a disaster. He was informally labeled as "undesirable" by peers because his highly aversive social behavior was so intolerable; they avoided him whenever possible, often going to extraordinary lengths to do so. Jimmy was aggressive, controlling, and bullying in his peer-directed social behavior—and his peers responded in kind. Based on peer popularity ratings he was the most disliked student in the kindergarten class.

Ratings of Jimmy's aggressive behavior on the Achenbach Child Behavior Checklist showed that he scored at the 99th percentile for boys of his age on the aggression subscale. Observations of his playground and classroom behavior revealed a high rate of rule infractions and negative-aggressive social behavior, as well as low levels of academic engagement during instructional periods. Jimmy easily qualified for the First Steps program, based on his screening-evaluation profile and the program's selection criteria.

Jimmy's parents were divorced when he was 2. They were both from Montana and came from ranching backgrounds. After the divorce, Jimmy's mother moved to Oregon with Jimmy and his older sister. They settled in a trailer house on the outskirts of Eugene, where Jimmy's mother raised wolves as a combined occupation and hobby. The family's income fluctuated between just above and just below the poverty level. Jimmy and his sister were left alone and unsupervised for long periods while their mother attempted to make ends meet.

When the First Steps consultant conducted a home visit to explain the program and the parent's role in it, she was confronted by a pack of nine timber wolves who were wandering in and out of the house and yard. Jimmy's mother reassured her they were harmless. She noted that Jimmy had difficulty understanding why he could not take his favorite wolf, Tundra, to school for show-and-tell. From this point on, in staff meetings, the First Steps consultant affectionately referred to Jimmy as the "wolf kid."

Jimmy's mother said she did not care if he participated in the school intervention part of the program, but after hearing about the parent component of First Steps, she said she wanted no part of Homebase. She felt that her relationship with Jimmy was fine and that she did not need to develop her parenting skills further. The program consultant agreed to implement the school intervention part of First Steps but asked Jimmy's mother to agree to provide home privileges and rewards, as the CLASS program requires, and to monitor his school performance. She agreed to do so.

Intervention

The CLASS program was explained to Jimmy, his teacher, and his peers according to guidelines contained in the program. Jimmy's classmates were somewhat skeptical about the program's ability to improve his behavior—as was his kindergarten teacher, Mr. Spira. However, three months into the school year, he was willing to try almost anything to improve Jimmy's daily school behavior.

Jimmy made the reward criterion for the morning session of program day 1 but failed to make the second session's reward criterion. Thus, he earned an activity reward for himself and his classmates after the morning session but missed the afternoon reward opportunity and the home privilege for that day. He came to school in a sullen, agitated state on day 2 and failed to achieve the criterion for both sessions. At the beginning of day 3, the procedures for CLASS program day 2 were repeated. Jimmy said that he did not think the program's available reward options were attractive enough and was not sure he wanted to continue.

The program consultant talked with him and said that the available rewards in the CLASS program were the same for him as for other children who participate in the program. She agreed to review the list of school and home rewards that had been developed to add options that were of greater interest to Jimmy, but she refused to increase their magnitude, as Jimmy originally wanted. Jimmy seemed pleased with this effort and agreed to continue the program. He made the daily reward criterion for all sessions for program days 3–5 after successfully completing program day 2. On program day 6, Mr. Spira assumed control of the program under the consultant's supervision. Jimmy had some difficulty with this transition, failing to make the criterion for that day. However, he did well from program days 7 through 10 when the program was extended to the playground, lunchroom, and gym.

From day 10 to day 15, Jimmy had to repeat, several times, program blocks that are required in this part of the CLASS program in order to meet the reward criterion. However, he negotiated the more difficult, five-day program block (program days 15–20) on the first try and did quite well in the process. He earned nearly all the available points for this five-day period and seemed to enjoy the recognition and praise that he received from his peers, teachers, and his mother. During the maintenance phase of the CLASS program (days 21–30), Jimmy was working for teacher and parent praise only. His performance was somewhat irregular over this ten-day period, but his overall behavioral level was still substantially above his pre-intervention level.

The CLASS program was terminated following this phase; however, the First Steps consultant strongly encouraged Mr. Spira to continue praising Jimmy as much as possible for good academic work, appropriate classroom behavior, and positive social behavior directed toward peers. He agreed to provide a weekly review and debriefing for Jimmy regarding his social behavior and academic performance. The consultant arranged with Jimmy's mother to make a surprise home privilege available from time to time when the reports of Jimmy's school performance were positive.

The program consultant explained to Jimmy's mother that support from community agencies was available through the First Steps program. Jimmy's mother expressed considerable interest in this option and asked for further information on available supports and services and how to qualify for them. The consultant promised to look into the matter and get back to her regarding specifics.

Results

Mr. Spira was asked to rate Jimmy's behavior on the Achenbach Aggression Subscale after the CLASS program had been concluded. His ratings indicated that Jimmy's overall level of aggression was reduced from the 99th to the 70th percentile. An analysis of archival school records for Jimmy showed that the number of discipline contacts with the princi-

TABLE 12.1 Profile of Jimmy's Classroom and Playground Behavior

Code Category	*Preclass*	*During Class*	*Postclass*
Academic engaged time	47%	82%	74%
Negative social behavior	17%	2%	7%
Playground rule infractions	.27 per minute	.06 per minute	.09 per minute

pal's office averaged 3.5 per week in the month immediately preceding the CLASS program; discipline contacts averaged 0.3 per week the month following termination of the program. Table 12.1 provides a profile of Jimmy's classroom and playground behavior prior to, during, and following CLASS.

Jimmy's levels of maladaptive behavior showed substantial decreases across the various phases of the CLASS program; however, there was some recovery of preintervention baseline levels in the month following termination of CLASS. This is typical for antisocial children who are exposed to programs like CLASS. As a rule, there is substantial residual gain during follow-up if low-cost maintenance procedures are put into effect and remain in place over the long-term.

Discussion

While Jimmy had a reasonably positive response to the CLASS program, it is unlikely that the First Steps intervention alone, as implemented herein, would turn his school adjustment around. His risk of school failure and teacher–peer rejection was attenuated somewhat in kindergarten by exposure to this program. However, in order for him to be diverted from a path leading to a host of negative school and nonschool outcomes, it is essential that a coordinated home, school, and peer-group intervention be implemented over the long-term (that is, across school years). It is rare for schools to make an investment of this magnitude in students such as Jimmy; however, results of our best efforts are increasingly leading us to the conclusion that such an investment is necessary in order to divert children from a path leading to antisocial behavior, conduct disorder, delinquency, school dropout, adult criminality, and related problems.

BILLY: VICTIM OF CIRCUMSTANCES AND VICTIMIZER OF OTHERS

Background

Billy Smoot was born into a family that had lived on the margins of poverty for generations. Daily life in the Smoot family was chaotic, unpredictable, harsh, and often cruel. Psychological and other forms of abuse (sexual and physical) were routine occurrences in the family. Billy was severely beaten as a child for offenses that most children commit at one time or another (for example, arguing, taking things without permission, refusing to comply promptly with requests, fighting with siblings and peers and being late). He came to expect harsh punishments as a natural part of his life and developed a high tolerance for abuse and physical pain. His later responses to psychological therapy, however, would reveal that he did not tolerate well the severe psychological abuses that he experienced growing up.

Billy's parents, uncles, older siblings, and cousins had frequent contact with police about a variety of offenses ranging from minor to extremely serious. Several of Billy's uncles were known drug dealers as well as users; they were frequently involved in disputes with their clients over drug money and the associated exchanges. Billy's family seemed to define itself in terms of criminal behavior and exhibited attitudes of alienation, hostility, exploitation, and manipulation for personal gain without regard for the consequences to others.

When Billy was 9 years old, one of his uncles shot and killed Billy's father in a dispute that escalated into a murderous rage. The uncle concealed the body and attempted to hide the incident from the attention of police. He managed to do so for approximately two weeks before word of the murder got out; he was arrested and charged and was eventually convicted and sent to prison. Billy was acutely aware of all these events as they unfolded; although their impact on him was severe, his overt behavior did not seem to change noticeably as a result of his exposure to them.

From about the age of 3, Billy was regarded by all who knew him outside the family as an extremely disturbed little boy. He suffered the classic profile that is associated with the development of antisocial behavior patterns (harsh punishments, infrequent monitoring and supervision, weak parent involvement, lack of positive parenting, and an inability to rely on family members for assistance in problem solving and crisis resolution). Billy had an aura of great sadness about him, but mixed in with dangerous passive-aggressive tendencies. To some, he behaved much like an abused animal in his interactions with strangers and acquaintances (wary, afraid, and equally quick to avoid contact or to strike first in anticipation of punishment from others). Billy suffered the classic symptoms of severe psychological distress, including bedwetting, nightmares, delusional speech that was not connected to real events, fire-setting, stealing, and extreme cruelty to animals.

Billy was referred for a psychological evaluation during the first month of kindergarten. Kindergarten was mandatory in the school district in which he lived, and this was his first experience with schooling. The school was in shock over exposure to much of Billy's characteristic behavior. Billy's mix of bizarre, aggressive, and oppositional behavior was unacceptable to his teachers and peers. The school's attempts to further understand and work with Billy's mother regarding his school behavior were futile. Billy was quickly rejected by nearly everyone in his school; he, in turn, viewed school as a hostile place that constantly picked on him for no good reasons. He had mastered elaborate verbal schemes for justifying his own actions and blaming others for his problems.

Billy's school records file was nearly 3 inches thick by the time he was in middle school. It was filled with archival accounts and documentation of his unfortunate and destructive path through the school system. In his elementary experience, each teacher who was to receive Billy the following year lived in dread of having to deal with him. They rarely underestimated the severity of the challenges that Billy presented. Although bright, Billy's performance always hovered around barely passing in his academic subjects; however, not a single teacher recommended that he repeat a grade.

Billy joined a gang in the fifth grade and had his first felony arrest within a year. He told his school counselor that he could have been arrested 15 times during this period but that he outsmarted the cops. Billy was exposed to about every available school-based service there was during his first five years in school (that is, counseling, Chapter One, values clarification, social-skills training, resource-room and self-contained placements, and referral to psychological and psychiatric services external to the school)—all to no avail. In the sixth grade, he was the target of a court-ordered interagency hearing to determine the next step for him. A decision was made to send him, at public expense, to the secure-treatment unit of a residential facility for extremely disturbed and criminal children and youth. Billy was assigned to this program for three and a half years and was neither the worst nor the best student among those in the program.

Billy was considered a reasonable risk by the staff of the residential facility and was returned to his family and home district during the middle of his sophomore year. He seemed to adjust well for a while, until he reconnected with his former peers—most of whom were now habitual, chronic juvenile offenders. During the summer between his sophomore and junior year, Billy was arrested for shooting at a local church with another student from his school. Eight shots from semiautomatic weapons were fired into the church. Fortunately, the shooting occurred during the week when the church was only occupied by staff, none of whom were injured. Billy and his accomplice were tried and sentenced to four years in prison.

Discussion

Billy was on a path to personal destruction and a chaotic, unfortunate life almost from birth. He had no chance for a normal upbringing, and he reacted to the conditions of his daily life as most children would—he adapted to them as best he could and learned from what he experienced. Unfortunately, the values he was taught and the survival skills he acquired are extremely dysfunctional in the normative, mainstream of our culture.

An episode that occurred in one of his sessions with a psychologist illustrates the nature of the ecology in which Billy was immersed. Billy and the psychologist were discussing his family, and Billy asked if the therapist would like to see a picture of his family. The picture was taken when Billy was about 8 years old and showed his father, older sister, and Billy with their arms around each other. Billy's 15-year-old sister was holding her year-old, illegitimate daughter, and both Billy and his father were each holding an Uzi.

Billy told the psychologist that he did know that his sister, at least, loved him. The psychologist asked how he knew that, and he told the following true story: "One day, my sister and I were running from the cops after we robbed a store. As we came around this corner, the door on my side flew open. She reached over, grabbed me, and kept me from falling out of the car." Nothing about the situation appeared out of the ordinary for Billy.

It is unlikely anything could have been done to save Billy from the path he followed, the excruciating experiences he had, and the pain he inflicted upon others. The financial and social costs resulting from Billy's situation will be enormous and, in many respects, essentially incalculable. Our society seems to be producing children and youth like Billy at a far higher rate than is generally known or believed. Each Billy we produce and fail to divert from the path to prison is a potential time bomb that will wreak enormous damage on our society and collective quality of life. Responding to the problems posed by the Billys of our society involves far more than just working with at-risk families; a coordinated federal, state, and local response is necessary to address the myriad stresses, dysfunctional attitudes, and unfortunate traditions of such child-rearing situations. Failure to do so puts our nation and our way of life at serious risk. We think this is a national emergency that warrants development of a national plan to guide state and local efforts in addressing this critical problem.

CONCLUSION

With the exception of the case of Billy, the preceding case studies are intended to provide helpful illustrations and details relating to the application of many of the principles described in this book. The procedures described represent best practices with antisocial students, as illustrated in the professional literature and as judged by the authors. As noted, the studies are based on real events and applications in which the authors have been involved. We hope they are of value to the reader in bridging the often difficult gap that exists between knowledge and effective practice.

Chapter 13 addresses an issue that is assuming paramount importance in our schools and the larger society—preventing school violence and ensuring school safety. We are experiencing an epidemic of violence among school-age children and youth, and societal concern about its potential impact is at an all-time high. The seeds that spawn this violence are sewn at national, state, and local levels, and each level of government must play a role in its solution. Until a coordinated national plan is developed to systematically address this problem, schools must take the necessary steps to protect themselves and to work collaboratively with parents and community agencies in realizing this goal and preventing future school violence.

13 School Violence, Gangs, and Safety: Toward Proactive Strategies

Violence: Characteristics, Causes, Trends, Societal Factors, and Recommendations

- Dimensions of Violence
- Causal Factors
- Trends
- Societal Changes Associated with Increases in Violent Behavior
- Recommended Methods for Reducing Violence

Gangs and Gang Activity

School Safety

Conclusion

Resources on Violence, Gangs, and School Safety

Additional Resources

> Violence is a public health and safety condition which results from individual, socio-economic, political and institutional disregard for basic human needs. Violence includes physical and nonphysical harm which causes damage, pain, injury and fear. Violence disrupts the school environment and results in the debilitation of personal development which may lead to hopelessness and helplessness. (School Violence Advisory Panel of the California Commission on Teacher Credentialing, 1994, p. 4)

> We are in no danger of becoming a nation of wimps; we are in imminent danger of becoming a nation of thugs. We know the details of violence among children and youth in our society. We recite the litany of this violence with shame, sorrow, disgust, and terror. However, for decades we have failed to act on what we know about the causes of violence and aggression. We cannot afford to delay effective action any longer. (Kauffman, 1994, pp. 25–27)

This chapter addresses the volatile issue of *violence*, particularly as it affects our school systems and the quality of life of students and school staff. School violence, gangs, and school safety are strongly linked dimensions of a larger societal problem for which we seem to have no effective solutions. Schools are no longer the safe havens they once were. In many urban and suburban centers, they are primary sites for the exchange of weapons and drugs as well as centers of gang activity and recruitment. A number of observers have noted that violence seems endemic to our society and is increasingly a normative form of behavior for many.

The two opening quotes define what is meant by violent behavior and provide an urgent call for a plan to address it. As we have noted on several occasions in this book, violent, aggressive, and antisocial forms of behavior constitute a national emergency in this country, and we need a national plan of action to address it. The National Centers for Disease Control has concluded that violence is one of our society's chief public health concerns. Billions of dollars are spent annually in dealing with the medical and health-related effects of interpersonal violence.

This chapter is divided into three major sections dealing with school violence, gangs, and school safety. The first section characterizes violence, profiles its recent trends, and describes the conditions that seem to account for its occurrence. This section also profiles recommended approaches and strategies for coping with violence both in schools and outside of schools. Finally, a model program, called Fast Track, is featured that involves teachers and parents working together to prevent violence among antisocial children who are early in their school careers. The second section focuses on *gangs* and gang activity. The characteristics, types, and activities of gangs are described along with strategies for dealing with them. The third section describes school *safety* issues and practices designed to ensure that safety risks to students and school staff are reduced to a minimum.

VIOLENCE: CHARACTERISTICS, CAUSES, TRENDS, SOCIETAL FACTORS, AND RECOMMENDATIONS

Dimensions of Violence

Violence is usually thought of as an extreme form of physical aggression, sometimes involving weapons, that is directed toward others. Vandalism is also considered a serious form of violent behavior, and, increasingly, verbal harassment and intimidation are defined as violent forms of behavior. Focus groups of students reveal that psychological intimidation and harassment (for example, ridicule, name calling, and cursing) are frequent and salient forms of violence to which they are exposed (Stephens, 1994). Physical and psychological violence are destructive to one's self-esteem and emotional well-being and place severe constraints on normal, day-to-day activities. This is particularly true of intimidation and harassment directed toward females. Box 13.1 profiles some key assumptions and facts regarding violence, as developed by the School Violence Advisory Panel of the California Commission on Teacher Credentialing (Dear, Scott, & Marshall, 1994).

The *New York Times* ("Profile of Youth," 1993) recently profiled youth violence and provided an in-depth study of children who grow up in a culture of urban violence. This investigative piece provided a case study of a teenage murderer who noted that a gun was as easy to get in his neighborhood as a quart of milk! Children and youth who grow up surrounded by violence struggle just to survive and have a probability of encountering death or serious injury that is roughly equivalent to that of a combat zone.

Handguns and easy access to alcohol and drugs provide an explosive and often lethal mixture that accounts for a large proportion of the violent acts that occur between people. Farrar (1994) notes that 1,000 guns are purchased daily in California. There are currently more firearm dealers in California than teachers. The rate of youth homicide is escalating dramatically, due primarily to the involvement of *weapons* in disputes, particularly handguns. Only 19% of handguns are purchased through black market contacts; the majority of juveniles access guns through their parents and primary caregivers.

Approximately 14% of incarcerated juveniles are considered to be violent offenders (DeComo, 1994). Fifty percent of these violent offenders report that they were under the influence of alcohol when they committed violent acts. A Los Angeles study of homicides showed that 79% of violent offenders had drugs or alcohol in their systems at the time of arrest.

Juveniles under the influence of *drugs* are often violent offenders. As a rule, alcohol and crack cocaine are the drugs involved in such episodes (Bostic, 1994). There is a tendency for alcohol to be associated with violent crimes, and illegal drugs with property crimes.

Truancy is also a factor that indirectly exacerbates the occurrence of both violent and nonviolent acts (Bostic, 1994). Over 90% of daytime burglaries are committed by truant youth. If they are also involved in drugs and alcohol and are carrying weapons, the possibilities for the commission of violent crime are greatly increased.

Box 13.1 Assumptions and Facts about Violence

- The historical development of this society has been based on violence, and violence continues to be a cultural norm.
- Society is diminished when an individual is damaged by violence.
- Violence is reciprocal and communicable. Violence is contagious. It is transmitted by overt, indiscriminant aggression and in subtle, unintentional ways.
- Violence is not the human condition. It is learned behavior that is preventable.
- Violence cuts across all lines of culture and ethnicity and is not exclusive to any single group or class.
- Prevention of violence requires education of and by all segments of society. It requires a reassessment of how conflict is viewed and resolved.
- Individuals should be educated to understand that they have choices in the way they behave and express their feelings and that they are responsible for the consequences of their actions.
- Effective resolution of violence requires early intervention that respects the integrity and dignity of all concerned.
- In order to establish safe schools, school personnel need to be increasingly aware of the nature and implications of violence upon schools and should be trained in ways to deal effectively with that violence.

Source: Dear, Scott, & Marshall (1994).

The conditions and outcomes just described provide an overview of the dimensions of violence in our society, particularly as they relate to violent juvenile crime. Violence is an unfortunate behavioral response that is learned by some individuals as an option for dealing with certain highly charged, interpersonal situations. It is not an inevitable, endemic attribute of our society that we are obligated to accept as the status quo. The presence of drugs, alcohol, weapons, and triggering events greatly increases the chances that violent acts will be committed.

Stephens, Butterfield, and Arnette (1994) recently conducted a review and analysis of school crime and violence. They included 29 studies and surveys that had been conducted over the last four years. The results provide overwhelming evidence of a dramatic rise in school crime and violence. Ironically, surveys of school staff and students report that a clear majority (75% and above) do not feel their safety is threatened by these developments and that violence in their schools is not a significant problem (Dear, Scott, & Marshall, 1994; Leitman & Binns, 1993). These results may be partially explained by the sectors of our society that were and were not included in the study samples.

Other sources indicate that students and school staff *are* concerned about their personal safety. Safety is a concern both on school grounds and on the way to and from school where victimizations are more likely to occur. Most such victimizations of students are not self-reported. Individuals with disabilities are especially vulnerable in this regard (Crowe, 1994).

As many experts have noted, we must teach our children and youth to eschew violence in all its forms and develop alternative strategies for problem solving and resolving disputes and conflicts with others. This instruction needs to occur in all settings and at all ages, but it is essential that we begin immediately to build it into our core curricula in school and to encourage parents to teach it as a normal part of socializing their children to the norms and values of our society.

Causal Factors

Complex causes associated with violence involve social, environmental, and individual factors. To complicate matters further, this society seems, at least passively, to accept violence. Specific causal factors of violent behavior include: poverty; prejudice and discrimination; unemployment; despair and hopelessness; access to drugs, alcohol, and violence; gang membership and activities; the presence of mob violence; cultural values; and *media violence*—that is, exposure to violent episodes by the mass media (see American Psychological Association, 1994). Violent acts can also be precipitated by the following three events or factors and combinations thereof: (1) temporal proximity, (2) situational risk factors, and (3) activating events. Temporal proximity refers to predisposing factors that precede the violent event. Situational risk factors are circumstances that surround an encounter between persons and that increase the chances that violence will occur. Finally, activating events are those that immediately precede the violent act and trigger its actual occurrence (see Roth, 1994).

The following example illustrates these three factors: Jamie is a fifth-grade boy with a history of severe antisocial behavior problems in school and who has suffered teacher and peer rejection (temporal event). Of late, Jamie has been teased by some of his classmates about his appearance, especially his style of dress (situational risk factor). At recess, several boys are looking at him, pointing, and laughing (activating event). Jamie walks over in a rage and attacks one of the boys.

High levels of agitation and feelings of alienation are strong precursors of violent behavior, particularly among youth. If these factors lead to membership in a gang, there is a dramatic escalation of criminal behavior—much of it violent in nature (Klein, 1994). Drug and alcohol use, combined with limited skills for resolving disputes and conflicts, provides a potent mixture that can easily trigger violence.

Trends

Bureau of Justice statistics indicate that the rates of violent *crime* have remained relatively stable for the past 15 years; however, public awareness and concern about violence has increased dramatically in the past several years (Furlong, 1994). Much of this concern may have been stimulated by the extensive media coverage that the problems of crime and violence have received in the last decade (Lieberman, 1994).

Violence is an extremely serious social problem in this country. In 1990, 23,438 Americans were murdered—a rate of 9.4 for every 100,000 persons. An estimated 2.9 million nonfatal violent acts (rape, robbery, aggravated assault) also occurred in 1990. These rates of violent crimes are among the highest in the industrialized world (Roth, 1994).

Statistics regarding the stability of violent crimes can be somewhat misleading. Nearly all studies of trends in violent criminal behavior show that it has remained fairly stable during the past 15 years, in spite of harsher sentences that have been meted out during this same period (see Furlong, 1994; Roth, 1994). However, Wilson and Howell (1993) reviewed evidence that shows violent juvenile crime (that is, aggravated assault, robbery) is increasing substantially. For example, juvenile arrests for violent crimes increased 41% from 1982 to 1991, reaching its highest level in history during 1991. During this same period, the number of arrests for murder and aggravated assault increased by 93% and 72%, respectively (Wilson & Howell, 1993). Changes in our society associated with increased violence are discussed in the next section.

Societal Changes Associated with Increases in Violent Behavior

Antisocial behavior and the conditions associated with it (that is, stressed families, weak parenting practices, poverty, social fragmentation, and ethnic conflicts) provide a fertile breeding ground for juvenile crime and violence, gang membership, and the use of drugs and alcohol (Crowe, 1994; Stephens, 1994). The huge increase in the juvenile crime rate in the past 50 years is primarily the result of the deteriorating social and economic conditions of our society. Since 1987, the crime rate for 14–17-year-olds has doubled, while their percentage of the population has declined. By 2005, however, the cohort of 14–17-year-olds will increase by approximately 23% (Coie, 1994). Furthermore, it is estimated that in 1997, we will have the largest group of unemployed and underemployed youth in our history (Crowe, 1994). These demographic trends are associated with ominous social consequences for our quality of life and call for a major societal response to prevent their occurrence.

John Coie, a noted researcher on antisocial behavior and violence, recently gave an address on the prevention of violence at a national research conference (Coie, 1994). He described some key facts and changes that account for the dramatic increases we have seen in juvenile crime and violence; they are listed and described in Box 13.2.

Recommended Methods for Reducing Violence

As a society, we have become strongly invested in the use of suppression strategies (for example, incarceration) to cope with the increasing tide of violence, especially juvenile violence, that is a dominant focus of our justice system. As noted, much harsher sentences for violent acts were the standard practice of the justice system between 1975 and 1989

Box 13.2 Key Facts and Changes Associated with Increases in Juvenile Violence

1. Adolescents are killing their friends. Fifty-five percent of juvenile homicides involve friends and acquaintances. Only 30% involve assaults on strangers.

2. There has been a huge surge in reactive aggression among children and youth that is qualitatively different from anything we have seen before. This surge is associated with the following developments: (1) youth today are much more likely to respond with a rage reaction to situations in which they feel violated or victimized, (2) the anger flashpoint has lowered dramatically—youth today take offense much earlier and to things that were previously ignored, and (3) youth feel an obligation to retaliate when they perceive provocations from others.

3. In the past 20 years, youth have moved from fists, to knives, to handguns, to automatic weapons in settling their conflicts.

4. There are two pathways to the development of a violent behavior pattern among children and youth. Both pathways show a rise in violence with a subsequent dropoff after age 17. The more serious path involves the early-starter group (ages 6–8) who are most violent and are likely to continue their violent behavior into young adulthood. The other path involves later starters (early adolescence) who are less violent and whose violence does not persist.

5. Two key risk factors associated with the development of violent behavior are (1) a child with high irritability and temperament problems and (2) stressed families with primary caregivers who feel pressured and overwhelmed. This mix often leads to a highly negative and coercive pattern of family interaction resulting in violent episodes.

6. Parents of such children have a firm belief that the harsher the punishment they mete out, the more likely it is the child will remember it and that it will be effective. Such parents were often exposed to harsh punishment themselves and tend to replicate it with their own children.

7. Antisocial, violent children and youth often go to overcrowded schools where there is a high density of students like themselves. They tend to use aggression to solve problems with their peers and suffer rejection by peers as a result. These students then bond with others like themselves—a bonding that provides the foundation for deviant peer-group affiliation with associated violence and gang activity.

8. Schools with high concentrations of antisocial, violent students tend to have poor resources and employ teachers who are inexperienced and who become overly stressed and burned out. These teachers' frustrations in dealing with such students parallels the students' home experiences involving child irritability and parents who are overly stressed with weak child-management skills. Such teachers become highly frustrated, are often unsuccessful, and get angry at these difficult students.

Box 13.2 *(Continued)*

9. These students view teacher and peer rejection as unfair and undeserved, and they react accordingly. If they perceive bad things happening to them, they (1) get angry, (2) think the other person meant it, and (3) retaliate, often with violent behavior. This behavior, in turn, confirms teacher and peer expectations of them.

10. Children who are antisocial in home and at school by age 6 or 7 are 50% more likely to become violent. Parent–teacher conferences to resolve these emerging problems often escalate, degenerate into blame fixing, and further polarize the school and family relationship.

11. During the elementary school years, parents gradually lose the ability to influence and control such children effectively. Parents start giving up hope by early adolescence and begin to reduce their involvement with the child. This translates into reduced monitoring and supervision of the child's activities, whereabouts, and affiliations. Consequently, the risks for juvenile violence, involvement with drugs and alcohol, criminal behavior, gang membership, and use of weapons can escalate dramatically.

Source: Adapted from Coie (1994).

(see Roth, 1994). However, the rate of violent crimes did not decrease during this period. This suggests that harsher sentences do not deter violent crimes and that other strategies for preventing the spread of violence must be investigated. Many experts now argue that we need a science of prevention for addressing violent behavior and its many ramifications.

Intervention Approaches

Coie (1994) strongly emphasizes that solutions to the complex problems of juvenile violence will not yield to either simple or unidimensional approaches. From our experiences in dealing with this problem, most knowledgeable experts in the areas of law enforcement, corrections, juvenile justice, criminology, and psychology agree on the following points:

1. Incarceration alone does not work, and we cannot build a sufficient number of incarceration facilities to solve the problem.
2. By the time the legal system actually punishes juvenile offenders, they have much too long a criminal history to turn around.

3. Most of our suppression programs are retaliative in nature and turn out to be training grounds for crime.
4. Boot camps do not affect recidivism rates more favorably than other programs for antisocial and delinquent youth.
5. Day-treatment programs, with educational and rehabilitative components, appear to be far more effective than incarceration but are only rarely available for juvenile offenders.
6. The best time to intervene with this population is at school entry or in preschool.

An effective, overall strategy for dealing with the problem of juvenile crime and violence will require different approaches in the way many of our key agencies and institutions respond. For example, the juvenile justice system has a characteristic practice of warning rather than consequating first-time juvenile offenders—especially if they are young. This practice is based on the quite reasonable assumptions that (1) first-time offenders should be given second chances and (2) admonishments may be effective in this regard. However, this pervasive practice may be the exact opposite of what is needed.

In a recent eight-year follow-up of 80 boys at elevated risk for antisocial behavior, Walker and Reid (in press) found that the best predictors of these boys' arrest rate between grades 6 and 12 were (1) the severity of the first arrest and (2) the boy's age at the time of the first arrest. The more severe the first offense and the younger the boy when it occurred, the greater the number of arrests occurring between grades 6 and 12. These boys had a total of 395 felony arrests between grades 6 and 12. Using first-arrest severity (among other factors) and age of onset as predictors, we obtained a better-than-chance prediction of their subsequent arrest frequency.

This result suggests that the first arrest should be taken extremely seriously by prosecutors and the juvenile court system—particularly if it is severe and occurs early. It is likely that such children and youth will require direct consequation of their emerging criminality that could involve appropriate sanctions, parent obligations, careful monitoring and supervision, and probation. Assignment to day-treatment or other rehabilitative programs may be indicated as well. Such a reversal of traditional practices has significant implications for resource allocation decisions, juvenile accommodations, and current professional practices with this population.

School practices will also have to change as part of any overall effective strategy for addressing this problem. In our traditional practices, (1) schools do not assume any ownership of this problem; (2) students showing such signs are typically exposed to control, containment, punishment, and push-out strategies; and (3) in many cases, students are denied access to therapeutic support services during their school careers, which puts them even further at risk. With 4 to 6 million of these students currently populating our schools, we can no longer afford the luxury of such problem avoidance and neglect. Schools, like other agencies concerned with this population, will need to alter their typical practices if we are to be successful. Specifically, schools should (1) be the focal point of coordinated, comprehensive interventions involving the family and other agencies;

Box 13.3 Steps for Reducing Violence in Our Society

Step 1. Provide effective consequences of aggression.

Step 2. Teach nonaggressive responses to problems.

Step 3. Stop aggression early, before it takes root.

Step 4. Restrict access to the instruments of aggression.

Step 5. Restrain and reform public displays of aggression.

Step 6. Correct the conditions of everyday life that foster aggression.

Step 7. Offer more effective instruction and more attractive educational options in public schools.

Source: Kauffman (1994).

(2) begin identifying, tracking, and intervening with at-risk students at the beginning of school entry; (3) assume a proactive, supportive posture with these students and their families rather than a rejecting, punishing one; and (4) stop assuming that such students can solve their problems without assistance from school professionals. Changes along these lines will go a long way toward giving at-risk children and youth a reasonable chance of achieving school success—a critical ingredient in realizing a productive life in today's world.

We discuss recommended strategies for two levels of prevention–intervention efforts that need to occur in order to reduce violence: (1) societal-community level and (2) individual-school level.

Societal-Community Level. In a recent discussion of the problem of violence in our society, Kauffman (1994) argues persuasively that violence and aggression have no single cause or single solution. He notes further that, as a society, we must make a commitment to become a less violent society and to implement, on a broad scale, the actions that we know will contribute to its reduction. Box 13.3 lists the seven steps Kauffman suggests be taken to address this problem.

These recommendations have broad policy implications that, if adopted, could have a powerful effect on this societal problem. Their adoption requires development of a national consensus as well as a national commitment and strategy to ensure they will have an impact. Our educational system and the resources of the media will be key instruments for realizing this goal. The success of media and educational campaigns to reduce tobacco, alcohol, and drug use are examples of the possibilities that can be achieved in this regard.

A strong consensus appears to be emerging among experts in juvenile crime and violence that we cannot build a sufficient number of prison beds and incarceration facilities to cope with our society's problems with juvenile crime and violence. The sheer numbers continue to be overwhelming and the costs beyond our collective means (Bostic, 1994). Steinhart (1994) suggests there will be a renaissance of interest in prevention as public agencies and our society become aware of the astronomical costs of punishing violence. The dominant focus of our efforts to deal with juvenile crime and violence to date has been on the application of negative adult sanctions to juveniles. One state has developed a proposal to put 12-year-olds into adult courts for suspected gang activity. Increasing incarceration time for juveniles and overinvesting in incarceration for this population have had no effect in stopping juvenile crime and violence. Locking young people up seems to have no to minimal deterrent value in preventing violence and juvenile crime.

Steinhart (1994) suggests four foundational elements that must be included in a comprehensive strategy to prevent violence: (1) a recognition that violence arises from multiple risk factors, including child abuse, school failure, family criminality, media violence, and drug abuse and its ramifications; (2) multiple strategies must be applied to address multiple risk factors; (3) an early start is necessary to intersect the trajectory of children and youth headed toward a violent life-style; and (4) whole communities need to be involved.

The American Psychological Association's Commission on Violence and Youth offers a number of universal recommendations that should be considered in controlling the individual and social factors that contribute to youth violence (American Psychological Association, 1993) (see Box 13.4).

Bostic (1994), who is the Los Angeles Police Department's Commander of Juvenile Operations, recently gave an address on gangs, narcotics prevention, and their relationship to violence at a conference on school violence. He is an expert with the Justice Department's DARE (Drug Abuse Resistance Education) program to teach resistance to drugs and gang involvement, which now includes a curricula component on violence prevention. He argues that (1) we must keep youth out of the juvenile corrections system; (2) we must funnel offending youth to diversion and community-based programs that have rehabilitation and educational emphases in order to keep them out of this system; (3) we need to use blended-funding strategies from different agencies so that money follows at-risk youth and families and not agencies; (4) we must identify at-risk children and families early and get them involved in after-school programs, sports, and school activities; (5) we must create a safe haven for youth and families for after-school activities; and (6) we must push as many resources as possible onto school campuses where they can be used effectively and in a coordinated fashion. As part of this effort, at-risk youth must be taught mediation skills, problem-solving competencies, and how to make personally responsible, adult decisions. A comprehensive strategy of this type is being implemented in a number of urban centers and appears to be successful in keeping many at-risk children and youth out of gangs.

Bostic (1994) also provides a compelling argument that certain youth are beyond hope and should be written off, in terms of exposure to this comprehensive approach.

Box 13.4 American Psychological Association's Recommendations for Reducing Violence

- Early childhood interventions in the form of extensive support services and training to teach all families and child-care and health-care providers how to deal with early childhood aggression.
- Developmentally appropriate school-based interventions in classroom management, problem solving, and violence prevention.
- Sensitivity to cultural diversity through community involvement in the development of violence-prevention efforts.
- Mass media cooperation in social responsibility to both limit the depiction of violence during child viewing hours and educate children about violence-prevention efforts.
- Limitation of firearm accessibility to youth, and teaching firearm-violence prevention.
- Reduction of alcohol and other drug use among youth.
- Mental health services for perpetrators, victims, and witnesses of violence.
- Prejudice-reduction programs that defuse hate crimes.
- Cooperative mob-violence prevention efforts through police and community leaders.
- Individual and professional commitment from the psychological community to reduce youth violence.

Source: American Psychological Association (1993).

They are the third generation of gang members, many of whom are born to drug-affected mothers. They are dangerous to the public safety, have no conscience, are drug-affected themselves, and are not afraid of anything or anyone. He cites an incident in which some gang members pursued other gang members into a police station and conducted a shoot-out on the premises!

School systems are having to invest in extremely restrictive educational programs to accommodate children and youth of this type. These programs are at another level of intensity and restrictiveness beyond alternative schools for disruptive youth and, in some instances, approximate boot camps. Increasingly, these placement programs are having to be mounted at the elementary-school level.

Wilson and Howell (1993), of the Office of Juvenile Justice and Delinquency Prevention in the U.S. Department of Justice, have proposed a comprehensive strategy for serious, violent, and chronic juvenile offenders. This strategy has two principal components: (1) preventing youth from becoming delinquent by focusing prevention programs on at-risk youth and (2) improving the juvenile justice system's response to delinquent

Box 13.5 Key Principles for Preventing and Reducing Delinquency

- Strengthen families.
- Support core social institutions.
- Promote prevention strategies and programs.
- Intervene immediately and effectively when delinquent behavior occurs.
- Identify and control the small percentage of serious, violent, and chronic juvenile offenders.

Source: Wilson & Howell (1993).

offenders. This strategy targets five groups of influence factors that include individual characteristics, family influences, school experiences, peer-group influences, and neighborhood and community. Wilson and Howell argue that interventions must be developed to counter the risk factors associated with each of these influence factors. Their strategy contains five key principles for preventing and reducing *delinquency*, which are listed in Box 13.5.

The "macro-strategies" described thus far are essential for addressing violence and its prevention at a global, societal level. At best, schools are collaborative partners with a host of other agencies in implementing such complex strategies. Obviously, they cannot do it by themselves. However, there are things that schools can do on an individual basis to address their share of the problem and to make schools safer and more productive environments for learning and child development. Some recommended strategies are discussed in the next section.

Individual-School Level. Proactive, school-based strategies for preventing violence generally focus on curricula, staff development, and administrative procedures. It is essential that units on violence prevention be incorporated into curricula that address (1) peer *mediation*; (2) conflict resolution; and (3) social and emotional skills for managing anger, negotiating, adopting another child's perspective, and developing alternative solutions to disagreements (Van Steenbergen, 1994). The National Association for Mediation (NAME), an advocacy organization for mediation approaches, indicates that schools have set up conflict-resolution programs in the last decade. The advantages of mediation approaches are listed in Box 13.6.

Increasingly, curricula are available that include units specifically geared toward violence prevention and that provide direct instruction to students in how to cope with

Box 13.6 Advantages of Peer Mediation

- Mediation is more effective than suspensions or detentions in promoting responsible behavior.
- Mediation reduces violence, vandalism, and absenteeism.
- Mediation reduces the time teachers and administrators must spend dealing with discipline problems.
- Mediation promotes peace and justice in our multicultural world through mutual understanding of individual differences.

Source: Van Steenbergen (1994).

its occurrence. Ways need to be found to incorporate this instruction into academic curricula so that all students are exposed to it. Curricula components should be developed to teach students how to avoid fights and to train peers to intervene, when possible, so that no fight occurs—instead of focusing on reconciliation efforts afterwards. Some universal strategies for reducing the conditions that often prompt student altercations include avoiding long periods of unstructured time, use of staggered lunches, peer counseling, and mentoring-confidant programs.

Staff-development training is essential to instruct staff in how to prevent and cope with violence at an individual, teacher–student level. It is extremely important that staff know how to recognize when students are agitated, when they are likely to escalate, when not to press them over an issue, and how to develop and maintain positive interactions with all students. Chapters 3 and 4 are devoted to these topics.

Teachers are also key participants in the development of a positive school climate where all students, and their families, are made to feel welcome and valued. Development of a schoolwide discipline plan and, where necessary, a violence-prevention plan are essential elements of developing and maintaining such a school climate.

It is essential that a responsive and prompt crime-reporting system be developed by each school. Schools have been criticized for underreporting crimes occurring on their campuses and for failing to carefully distinguish school misconduct from criminal behavior (Maddox, 1994; Weaver, 1994).

Box 13.7 contains a school-crime assessment tool that can be used to assist schools in measuring their crime-vulnerability status. This instrument was developed by the National School Safety Center; ideally, it should be administered twice each year (for example, October–November and March–April). An elevated score indicates the need to develop a prevention–intervention program in cooperation with law enforcement personnel.

Box 13.7 School-Crime Assessment Tool

The National School Safety Center has developed the following school-crime assessment tool to assist school administrators in evaluating their vulnerability to school-crime issues and potential school-climate problems.

1. Has your community crime rate increased over the past 12 months?
2. Are more than 15% of your work-order repairs vandalism-related?
3. Do you have an open campus?
4. Has there been an emergence of an underground student newspaper?
5. Is your community transiency rate increasing?
6. Do you have an increasing presence of graffiti in your community?
7. Do you have an increased presence of gangs in your community?
8. Is your truancy rate increasing?
9. Are your suspension and expulsion rates increasing?
10. Have you had increased conflicts relative to dress styles, food services, and types of music played at special events?
11. Do you have an increasing number of students on probation in your school?
12. Have you had isolated racial fights?
13. Have you reduced the number of extracurricular programs and sports at your school?
14. Has there been an increasing incidence of parents withdrawing students from your school because of fear?
15. Has your budget for professional development opportunities and in-service training for your staff been reduced or eliminated?
16. Are you discovering more weapons on your campus?
17. Do you have written screening and selection guidelines for new teachers and other youth-serving professionals who work in your school?
18. Are drugs easily available in or around your school?
19. Are more than 40% of your students bused to school?
20. Have you had a student demonstration or other signs of unrest within the past 12 months?

Box 13.7 *(Continued)*

Scoring and Interpretation

Multiply each affirmative answer by 5 and add the total.

0–20 Indicates no significant school safety problems

25–45 An emerging school safety problem (safe school plan should be developed)

50–70 Significant potential for school safety problem (safe school plan should be developed)

Over 70 School is a sitting time bomb (safe school plan should be developed immediately)

Finally, experts note that racially based violence among children and youth is an emerging problem that has the potential to transcend our current preoccupation with gangs and drugs (Bell, 1994). Increasing tensions, conflict, and violence are being observed in our urban centers among White, Latino, African American, and Asian American children and youth. This is, in part, a result of the rapidly increasing diversity of our student population; currently, one in three residents of San Francisco is foreign born (Winokur & Marimucci, 1994). Our schools and our society are well behind the curve of effectively accommodating this great challenge.

A recent survey of high school students (cited in Winokur & Marimucci, 1994) reveals the basic dimensions associated with this issue (see Table 13.1). These are scary statistics and suggest reasons why students band together in ethnically based gangs and other affiliations to achieve acceptance, status, and protection. Winokur and Marimucci (1994) argue persuasively that severely overcrowded schools and busing are two factors that greatly exacerbate these problem schools. However, the design and effective use of school space to enhance school safety is an issue that has received scant attention to date from school professionals (Crowe, 1994). Students who are bused to schools outside their neighborhoods tend not to feel a sense of pride in or commitment to the schools to which they are transported.

There are some positive steps that schools can take to deal with this emerging and potentially explosive problem. The curricular and administrative-teaching practices of the school should accommodate cultural and ethnic differences in the most sensitive, respectful manner possible. No member of an ethnic group should feel unwelcome or undervalued by the school atmosphere. Teaching time and activities must be devoted to educating students about other cultures as well as their own. Finally, student leaders of different ethnic groups should be brought together in nonconfrontational, problem-solving forums to get to know each other and to develop respect for each others' background, cultural heritage, and values.

TABLE 13.1 How High School Students View Their World

Nearly 5,000 students from the 1993 edition of *Who's Who Among American High School Students* were demographically selected to participate in the 24th annual Survey of High Achievers. Nationally, 1,957 students completed and returned the questionnaire. Here are some of their responses:

	Students Who Think Race Relations in the United States Are Getting Worse	*Students Who Have Felt Racial or Ethnic Discrimination*	*Students Who Admit to Using a Derogatory Word to Refer to a Member of a Different Racial or Ethnic Group*
All students	53%	40%	48%
African American	58%	71%	51%
Asian American	58%	79%	38%
White	52%	33%	49%
Latino	50%	60%	57%

STUDENTS WHO REPORT GANGS AT THEIR SCHOOL (I)				STUDENTS WHO REPORT GANGS AT THEIR SCHOOL (II)		
All Students	*Suburban*	*Urban*	*Rural*	*Public*	*Parochial*	*Private*
17%	24%	23%	9%	20%	13%	6%

Of students who report gangs at their school, those who report a violent incident:

Frequent Fights between Students	*Student Attacking a Teacher*	*Knife Fights between Students*	*Rape or Sexual Assault*	*Shooting on School Grounds*	*Teacher Hitting a Student*	*Mugging*
79%	31%	19%	18%	16%	13%	11%

Source: From *Who's Who among American High School Students.* Copyright © 1993 Educational Communications, Inc., Los Angeles. Adapted by permission.

Fast Track: Families and Schools Together

The Fast Track program was designed to prevent antisocial behavior and violence. This model program represents the best effort to date to prevent this unfortunate disorder.

The Fast Track program is a multi-site, collaborative study funded by the National Institute of Mental Health. Fast Track is designed to prevent antisocial behavior patterns, violence, and juvenile crime by (1) identifying at-risk children and families as early as possible and (2) intervening intensively with parents and schools at the point of school entry.

At-risk children are selected from neighborhoods with high crime rates. At-risk children in the schools serving these neighborhoods are screened and identified at the end of the kindergarten school year. Children who are antisocial at both home and school are selected for participation. These children are 50% more likely to become violent than those who are antisocial in only one setting.

Both universal and selected target interventions are used in this prevention effort. Schoolwide interventions are implemented in target schools designed to make the classroom and school environment more accepting, more instructionally effective, more disciplined, and more socially responsive to the needs of children. Selected target interventions for the at-risk children include academic tutoring, social-skills training, and problem-solving sessions. Parent groups are held regularly; in these groups, parents are assisted in helping their children make a good transition from kindergarten and to get off to a good start in first grade. The focus is on what parents can do. Teachers also participate in these parent focus groups so effective partnerships can develop in the absence of a crisis atmosphere. Teachers are given staff training, support, and technical assistance from Fast Track staff to assist them in more effectively teaching and managing the participating at-risk students. Finally, the target children are followed up intensively and given support at key transition points (for example, at entry into middle school).

The authors of Fast Track expect to follow up these students through 2005. This study is an extremely well-designed prevention effort and should greatly enhance our knowledge regarding whether and how we can prevent this unfortunate disorder. If it succeeds, ways will have to be found to adapt it so its key features can be used by interested communities.

GANGS AND GANG ACTIVITY

The control of gang activity, as well as the symbols of such activity on school campuses, is of critical importance. Often gangs are infused into the social structure of a school before staff are fully aware of the problem. The National School Safety Center has developed the Gang Assessment Tool to assist communities in determining the extent of gang activity in the vicinity of a school. (For more information, contact the National School Safety Center, Pepperdine University, 4165 Thousand Oaks Boulevard, Suite 290, Westlake Village, CA 91362.) This assessment tool is presented in Box 13.8. As with the School-Crime Assessment Tool, its use is highly recommended.

Each "yes" response earns the indicated number of points. The total score is an assessment of the severity of the problem and can suggest the possible need for school security measures: 0–15 points indicate no significant gang problem; 20–40 points indicate an emerging gang problem; 45–60 points indicate a significant gang problem for which an intervention–prevention strategy should be developed; and 65 points or higher indicate an acute gang problem that requires urgent attention and intervention.

Box 13.8 Gang Assessment Tool

1. Do you have graffiti on or near your campus? (5)
2. Do you have crossed-out graffiti on or near your campus? (10)
3. Do your students wear colors, jewelry, clothing, flash hand signals or display other behavior that may be gang-related? (10)
4. Are drugs available near your school? (5)
5. Has there been a significant increase in the number of physical confrontations or stare downs within the past twelve months in or around your school? (5)
6. Is there an increasing presence of weapons in your community? (10)
7. Are beepers, pagers, or cellular phones used by your students? (10)
8. Have you had a drive-by shooting at or around your school? (15)
9. Have you had a "show-by" display of weapons at or around your school? (10)
10. Is the truancy rate of your school increasing? (5)
11. Are there increasing numbers of racial incidents occurring in your community or school? (5)
12. Is there a history of gangs in your community? (10)
13. Is there an increasing presence of "informal social groups" with unusual names—for example, "Woodland Heights Posse," "Rip Off and Rule," "Females Simply Chillin'," or "Kappa Phi Nasty" ? (15)

Source: National School Safety Center (1992).

In the past 25 years, our society has become increasingly fragmented and divided into factions. We divide ourselves by ethnicity, religion, gender, sexual orientation, class, politics, and so on. As a result, our society has experienced unprecedented social conflict during this period. These developments have provided a fertile breeding ground for gang affiliations wherein youth seek social support, shared values, and a sense of acceptance.

In many ways, gangs are an expression of modern tribalism. Anthropology has much to offer us in understanding the tribal structure and dynamics of modern gangs. Some shared features between ancient tribes and organized street gangs include (1) dialects, (2) visual signs, (3) dress, (4) marking of territory, (5) codes of behavior, (6) intertribal conflicts, (7) peace treaties, and (8) tribal cohesion and loyalty of tribal members. Developing attractive alternatives to such powerful affiliations is a daunting challenge. Box 13.9 contains a list of gang characteristics, types, and activities. This list represents a

Box 13.9 Fact Sheet on Gang Characteristics, Types, and Activities

- Gangs have been with us since the beginning of organized society. The Book of Proverbs contains descriptions of elders being victimized by youth groups.
- Gang proliferation and growth are associated with a breakdown of the family; increased urbanization; the advent of crack cocaine; tax limitation measures that eliminate youth programs; reduction of meaningful jobs for youth and young adults; and racial discrimination, alienation, and conflict.
- Gang members are three times more likely to be violent than nongang members.
- Gang violence is a community problem that requires a multi-agency, community-based solution. It is not exclusively a police or school problem.
- Incarceration and suppression strategies alone will never solve the U.S. gang problem; community organization, outreach programs, and vocational training programs are also required to effectively treat and prevent gang problems.
- Much of gang activity is driven by control issues (of members, neighborhoods, and turf) and by manipulation of others' fear. Gangs capitalize on the natural fears community members have of them.
- In the past decade, 11,000 individuals have been murdered by gang members and 15,000 have been seriously injured.
- Gangs are highly cohesive and communicate through marking, graffiti, dress, language (verbal and nonverbal), tattoos, hand signs, and behavioral codes or rules.
- Eighty-three percent of the largest U.S. cities ($N = 79$) report having a gang crisis.
- Males outnumber female gang members by 20 to 1; however, female gangs are a fast-growing problem.
- There are two major types of gangs: traditional (neighborhood based) and nontraditional (profit oriented and organized around drug dealing, car theft, and burglary).
- Ethnic orientation, among other factors, can be an organizer for gang development and identification and often leads to gang-related, racial violence.
- Schools are heavy recruiting sites for new gang members. Gangs are often the leading competitors with communities for the hearts and minds of young people. Peer pressures to join gangs can be extremely powerful and difficult to resist.
- Incentives for gang membership include: recognition, peer status, social support, shared values, family tradition or history, protection, and perceived opportunity.
- In the past two decades, the U.S. gang problem has worsened significantly: (1) instruments of war (Uzis, AK-47s) are now being used by gangs, (2) victims are often shot multiple times with powerful, automatic weapons, (3) many gang members are totally desensitized to violence and care nothing for their victims.

Box 13.9 *(Continued)*

- Gang members generally range in age from 12 to 40. The average age of gang members is increasing, with many maintaining their gang membership well into their 30s.
- Hate crimes committed by loosely affiliated youth groups and gangs are increasing rapidly in our society.
- Gang members have a low rate of participation in school activities. Rarely do gang members bond or identify with a significant adult at school.
- Neither programs nor people change gang membership. Individual gang members must see a window of opportunity to change and be supported in that decision. Youth need alternatives to gang membership that are attractive and accessible.
- Currently, Latino gangs are the largest in the United States.

synthesis of the core knowledge currently available regarding gangs. It has considerable relevance for educators in understanding and coping with the challenges of gang activity.

A prevention–intervention strategy for gangs should be developed in close collaboration with law-enforcement authorities, parents, and other agencies as appropriate. The DARE program, in which specially trained police officers play key instructional and security roles on school campuses regarding drug resistance and violence, is highly recommended as a part of any comprehensive school strategy. Gang insignias, clothing, graffiti of any kind, jewelry, or other gang symbols should not be allowed on school campuses; in addition, formal programs should be in place to divert students from gang membership.

Box 13.10 contains guidelines and recommended strategies for preventing and intervening with gang activity on school campuses. Both universal (gang-prevention curricula) and selected (for example, graffiti removal) strategies should be incorporated into a comprehensive gang strategy. In addition, a strategy needs to be in place for responding immediately to gang incidents at school that involve violence or drugs. Law enforcement must be a key player in this strategy.

The reader is referred to two superb sources on strategies for coping and intervening with gangs on school campuses. Natalie Salazar, coordinator of community partnership programs for the Los Angeles County Sheriff's Office, is a nationally recognized expert on gang prevention–intervention. She has developed a model program entitled "Rising Above Gangs and Drugs," developed through a grant from the U.S. Department of

Box 13.10 Recommendations for Schools in Preventing and Intervening in Gang Problems

1. Gang prevention efforts must begin as early as possible in a child's school career—some kindergartners and first graders show clear signs of emerging gang involvement. Early intervention is more likely to divert children from later gang involvement.
2. The social cohesion of neighborhoods and communities must be improved if gangs are to be controlled. Schools are important partners with families, police, churches, courts, corrections, and social service agencies in working toward this goal.
3. A comprehensive, interagency system for sharing records and information must be developed to effectively address gang problems that will allow early intervention and guide prevention efforts.
4. Any successful gang prevention–intervention strategy must have three components:
   a. A strong law enforcement component that allows detection and detention of chronic gang members
   b. An intervention component that controls gang activity on school campuses and allows gang members to escape gang involvement
   c. A prevention program to positively influence vulnerable children and youth who are on the cusp of gang activity
5. Students vulnerable to recruitment by and involvement in gangs should be exposed to (1) adult and peer mentoring, (2) academic tutoring and added support as needed, (3) strategies for fully engaging them in the schooling process including participation in school activities, (4) social-skills training geared toward recruiting and maintaining friendships, and (5) effective home–school communication and collaboration.
6. Multicultural sensitivity, awareness, tolerance, acceptance, and respect must be taught. Ensure that the behavior of school staff and students reflect these values on a daily basis.
7. The teaching of morals, values, and socially responsible decision making should be reinstituted in the school curriculum.
8. After-school recreation and leisure programs should be available to students and their families.
9. Sports programs should be maintained whenever possible.
10. At-risk students should have access to computers, labs, and instructors.
11. School service clubs should be strengthened and made broadly accessible.
12. A reasonable and enforceable dress code should be developed.
13. A false sense of security that leads to the denial of the subtle signs of emerging gang activity should be avoided.

Box 13.10 *(Continued)*

14. Strong positive role models must be available at school.
15. Transferring gang members between schools should be carefully considered, as such transfers may help spread gang activity.
16. Consider developing a gang-prevention policy on the school campus in collaboration with law-enforcement officials and other agencies as appropriate. Implement a gang-prevention curriculum as part of this effort.
17. *All* graffiti should be confronted and immediately removed on school buildings. Gang-related graffiti found on students' persons should be confiscated. Building graffiti should be removed within 12 hours.
18. A comprehensive set of gang prevention–intervention school strategies should include (1) clear behavioral expectations, (2) visible staff, (3) parent involvement, (4) in-service training, (5) graffiti removal, (6) cooperation with law enforcement, (7) existence of a gang-prevention plan, and (8) community involvement and coordination.

Justice. This model program is packaged in a highly readable, user-friendly operational manual. (Information about this program can be obtained by writing to Natalie Salazar, Community/Law Enforcement Partnership Programs, 4700 Ramona Boulevard, Monterey Park, CA 91754-2169, (213) 526-2169.) The National School Safety Center's *Gangs in Schools* publication is an excellent resource for schools in developing gang prevention–intervention strategies. (It can be purchased from the NSSC, 4165 Thousand Oaks Boulevard, Suite 290, Westlake Village, CA 91362.) Additional resources on gangs are provided at the end of this chapter.

SCHOOL SAFETY

A number of steps can be taken to increase the safety and security of school campuses. Violence from neighborhoods and communities spills over onto school campuses in the same way that episodes of weapons possession are relatively frequent occurrences on school grounds. It is essential that schools take steps to deal with these issues in terms of prevention, intervention, and suppression.

Control of weapons on school campuses is an issue of excruciating national concern; it is estimated that approximately 22% of students bring weapons to school. A strategy that combines multiple components is essential to address this problem. Metal detectors are required in some schools; in others, locker searches are routine and required. Some schools do not allow book bags because they can be used to conceal weapons. Perhaps the key element in any strategy of this type is to set up a reporting system for students in which individual students are urged to report a weapon at the first sighting. Some schools award a cash bounty to students for reporting weapons (Cubbage, 1994).

An information-sharing system that tracks individual students is urgently needed that connects the school, the juvenile *courts*, and law-enforcement agencies. Ideally, a tracking and information-sharing system of this type reports the student's educational status to other agencies, and the student's criminal or mental health records are reported to the host school. Juvenile court judges have historically been reluctant to share this information because of fears about abuse of the information and stigmatization. The juvenile justice system protects the privacy of offenders in a way that often puts school staff and society at risk. There is a serious issue of teacher and student safety when students who are guilty of crimes such as murder, assault, and rape are placed in schools without reporting their backgrounds to school authorities. Unknowing teachers or other staff could walk into escalated interactions with agitated students of this type and would be immediately at serious risk for their safety. At a minimum, they have a right to know the backgrounds and status of such students. State and federal laws allow for more latitude in this regard than is generally known (Finley, 1994). In addition, a number of state laws are being reviewed and new ones proposed that will allow for the disclosure and interagency sharing of juvenile criminal records and case histories.

The *School Safety Checkbook*, produced by the National School Safety Center, provides a host of recommended strategies for developing and maintaining safe schools for students and staff. Topics include school climate and discipline, school attendance, personal safety, and school security. This document is available for purchase from the NSSC.

Box 13.11 contains a list of recommended strategies for developing safe school environments and ensuring the security of staff and students. Their successful implementation requires the cooperation of school staff, students, parents and law-enforcement authorities.

Crowe (1994), a national expert on school safety and the analysis and prevention of criminal behavior, argues that too often we search for complex external strategies to the problems of school safety, violence, and gang-related activity. He notes that effective solutions are sometimes very simple, sitting under our noses, and are present within the school. The Case of the Savvy Custodian (Box 13.12) makes this point very well.

As the case illustrates, the school can be viewed as a large extended family. It is important that everyone therein be valued and that the potential contributions of all staff be recognized in solving problems confronting the school.

Crowe (1994) has developed a model program called Crime Prevention Through Environmental Design (CPTED) in which innovations in the design and utilization of school space are applied to increase school safety (see Crowe, 1990). The CPTED process begins with an assessment of how school space is currently used. Answers are sought to the following questions during the assessment:

Box 13.11 Safe School Recommendations

- Regularly review board of education policies with school staff regarding pupil safety and protection, pupil discipline, and staff responsibilities
- Discuss school crisis-intervention plans with all staff and volunteers.
- Assign staff to supervise the school campus, focusing on entrances, exits, and problem areas. Chart assignments on a map of the school.
- Enlist formal and informal student leaders, staff, and parents to communicate student behavior and dress-code expectations (that is, intercom announcements, student and parent letters, newsletters, and posted signs).
- Maintain a zero tolerance for weapons, threats, intimidation, fighting, and other acts of violence.
- Post signs requiring all visitors to sign in and out at the office and to obtain a visitor or volunteer button or ID card.
- Train and encourage all staff to personally contact visitors and refer them to the office.
- Minimize the number of unlocked entrances; post signs referring people to unlocked entrances.
- Involve volunteer or volunteer and staff teams to monitor entrances, exits, and halls for students and visitors.
- Require students to have a hall pass when moving about the school during class sessions.
- Limit hall passes to an absolute minimum.

1. What is the designated purpose of the space?
2. How was it originally intended to be used?
3. How well does the space support its current and intended uses?
4. Is there conflict?

Additional information is obtained on ownership of space, its definition, and needed changes in the design, redesign, and utilization of the space.

The design and use of school space is directly related to student discipline and criminal behavior. Problem areas commonly identified by CPTED assessments include: school grounds, parking lots, locker rooms, corridors, classrooms, and restrooms. Crowe (1994) recently reported survey data indicating that 21% of U.S. students are afraid to use school restrooms.

Box 13.12 The Case of the Savvy Custodian

A problem developed in a middle school involving lipstick marking of school surfaces as well as of individuals and their clothes. Girls, and some boys, would apply heavy amounts of lipstick and brand their peers and school surfaces (windows, lockers, doors) with kisses. Students, teachers, and a few parents began to voice complaints. Teachers were asked to warn their students to discontinue the practice—to no avail. Next, the school administration sent a letter to the parents of all students describing the problem and imploring them to have their children stop "kissing"—or not start if they were not already doing it. This produced another increase in the rate of kiss-marking. After a 2-hour faculty meeting on this issue, the principal gave the student body a 20-minute lecture at an assembly on why this practice must stop. The lecture was followed by daily reminders over the intercom for the next week. The latter was associated with a wildfire of kiss-marking!

The school custodian went to the principal (now in desperation) and asked if she might try something. She was most deferential of the expertise of the principal and school staff and apologized for her lack of education. After hearing her proposal, the principal endorsed it.

The custodian stationed herself in the girls' bathroom during the morning recess. She was holding a bucket and a sponge. A group of girls came in, smeared on gobs of lipstick, and proceeded to kiss-mark the mirror and walls—even the paper towel dispenser. The custodian calmly observed this activity and did not try to stop it. As the girls finished, she went over to a toilet, scooped up a bucket of toilet water, and proceeded to swab down the walls and mirror of the bathroom. Very quickly, rumors were flying throughout the school that the custodian was seen carrying buckets of toilet water and cleaning up lockers and wall surfaces throughout the school. The rate of kiss-marking dropped to zero within less than a day!

Strategies exist to effect improvements relating to school safety in each of these problem areas. Effective use of lighting, designation of gathering areas, location of restrooms, management of school supervision resources to maximize surveillance, and use of barricades to close off unnecessary entrances are just a few examples of successful CPTED strategies. The work of Crowe (1990) and other experts in the areas of school design and space utilization has much to offer in the improvement of school safety.

CONCLUSION

The school of the future will likely look very different from the school of today. If present trends continue, it will be a coordinated site for the delivery of integrated social and educational services that may include health, wellness, welfare, family support, and mental health services. Many schools will also have to add significant involvement with law-enforcement agencies and juvenile court systems to this list.

A number of promising strategies for coping with violence, gangs, and criminal behavior among our children and youth are being developed. Inventories of these strategies and practices are currently being assembled by the U.S. Congress, the U.S. Justice Department, and the U.S. Centers for Disease Control. The reader is referred to these organizations for compilations of this information.

RESOURCES ON VIOLENCE, GANGS, AND SCHOOL SAFETY

Some highly-recommended sources on violence prevention were listed at the end of Chapter 1. Additional resources are described here.

1. *Alienated America: Racial Division and Youth Violence.* This special issue of *Spectrum* (Vol. 66, No. 3, Summer 1993) is devoted to the causes of violence and strategies for preventing it. This issue of *Spectrum* is available by writing to The Council of State Governments, 3560 Iron Works Pike, P.O. Box 11910, Lexington, KY 40578-1910.
2. *The National School Safety Center:* This center assimilates, develops, and disseminates high-quality information on school violence and safety. It is located at Pepperdine University and is jointly funded by the U.S. Departments of Justice and Education. The NSSC has a large inventory of useful staff-development materials and publishes the *National School Safety Center News Journal.* The NSSC's address is 4165 Thousand Oaks Boulevard, Suite 290, Westlake Village, CA 91362.
3. *Office of Technology Assessment*: This research arm of the U.S. Congress is currently compiling a national bibliography of research and effective practices with juvenile offenders. Its report will be comprehensive, extremely valuable, and is highly recommended.
4. *Office of Juvenile Justice and Delinquency Prevention*: This branch of the U.S. Department of Justice is a repository of knowledge on this topic. This office produces publications that compile new information on promising practices in this area.

ADDITIONAL RESOURCES

American Association of School Administrators. (1991). *Beyond the Schools: How Schools and Communities Must Collaborate to Solve the Problems Facing America's Youth.* AASA Stock Number: 021-00313.

Arthur, R., & Erickson, E. (1992). *Gangs and Schools.* Holmes Beach, FL: Learning Publications.

Brendtro, Brokenleg, & Van Bockern. (1990). *Reclaiming Youth at Risk: Our Hope for the Future.* Bloomington, IN: National Educational Service.

Canadian Education Association, Toronto, Canada.

Carly, C., Kelly, P., Mahanna, P., & Warner, L. *Street Gangs: Current Knowledge and Strategies.* Washington, DC: National Institute of Justice.

Curcio, J. L., & First, P. F. (1993). *Violence in the Schools: How to Proactively Prevent and Defuse it. Roadmaps to Success: The Practicing Administrator's Leadership Series.* Newbury Park, CA: Corwin Press.

Furlong, M. J., & Morrison, G. M. (1994). School Violence and Safety in Perspective (9-article miniseries). *School Psychology Review, 23*(2), 139–261.

Gaustad, J. (1991). Schools Respond to Gangs and Violence. *OSSC Bulletin, 34*(9).

Lal, S. R., et al. (1993). *Handbook on Gangs in Schools: Strategies to Reduce Gang-Related Activities.* Newbury Park, CA: Corwin Press.

Landon, W. (1992). Violence and Our Schools: What Can We Do? *Updating School Board Policies, 23*(1), 1–5.

MacDougal, J. (1993). *Violence in the Schools: Programs and Policies for Prevention.*

Menacker, J., Hurwitz, E., Ward, W., Pascarella, E., & Herzog, L. (1990). *Using the Law to Improve School Order and Safety: Final Report on Grant 87-MU-0004.* Chicago: University of Illinois, College of Education.

National Center on Educational Outcomes. (1992, June). *Promoting Safe, Disciplined, and Drug-Free Schools: National Education Goal 6 and Students with Disabilities* (Brief Report 7). Minneapolis, MN: National Center on Educational Outcomes.

Nicholson, G. (1985). Safe Schools: You Can't Do It Alone. *Phi Delta Kappan, 66*(7), 491–496.

Prophet, M. (1990). Safe Schools in Portland. *American School Board Journal, 177*(10), 28–30.

Prothrow-Stith, D. (1987). *Violence Prevention Curriculum for Adolescents.* Newton, MA: Education Development Center.

Riley, K. W. (1991). *Street Gangs and the Schools: A Blueprint for Intervention.* Bloomington, IN: Phi Delta Kappa Educational Foundations.

Stephens, S. (1990). Making Schools Safe: The Role of the Modern Business Officer. *School Business Affairs, 56*(9), 24–27.

Van Acker, R. (1993). Dealing with Conflict and Aggression in the Classroom: What Skills Do Teachers Need? *Teacher Education and Special Education, 16*(1).

STUDY QUESTIONS

1. Define violence and give examples of different forms of it.
2. Name three factors that greatly enhance the likelihood of violent behavior occurring.
3. Describe some key facts and assumptions that have been learned about the nature of violence.
4. What percentage of incarcerated juveniles are violent offenders?

5. How is truancy related to criminal behavior?
6. Name three types of causal factors associated with violence.
7. Has the rate of violent acts increased or decreased in the United States over the past two decades?
8. Name the two levels at which interventions must occur if we are to reduce violence in our society.
9. Do you think some youth are so invested in criminal behavior and violence that they are beyond hope? If so, why?
10. List five key principles for preventing delinquency.
11. What role can peer mediation play in reducing violence?
12. In your view, what is the most effective strategy for increasing the safety of schools?

KEY TERMS

courts
crime
delinquency
drugs
gangs
mediation
media violence
safety
truancy
violence
weapons

EPILOGUE

Appendix C contains a reprint of a recent article that appeared in the *San Francisco Examiner* entitled "Generals in the War on School Violence" (Marinucci & Winokur, 1994). This investigative piece profiles the strategies and attributes of educational leaders (principals, counselors, and teachers) who are struggling to cope with violence on school campuses in the urban centers of our society. This article clearly shows that many urban schools are, in fact, war zones, and they reveal the tragedy of school violence and its interpersonal effects.

The educational leaders who are profiled in the "War on School Violence" have great courage and are to be commended for their dedication and skill. However, they are engaged in a holding action, at best. Many middle and high schools are held hostage by a relatively small group of antisocial, potentially violent students. They poison the schooling atmosphere for everyone. Such students need caring adults in their lives, but they must be held accountable for their actions and evicted from schooling if they pose threats to the safety of other students and school staff. In our view, students who choose to bring weapons to school, who physically intimidate and assault others, and who attempt to hold the school hostage through use of terror tactics forfeit their rights of access to that setting. Such students should also experience the full force of available legal sanctions for these forms of behavior.

Truly effective answers to the problems of intimidation, threats to physical safety, drugs and weapons on campus, and disruptions of the educational process, as described in this article, rest in the early school histories of such youth. As we have said over and over in this book, early interventions that are comprehensive, multidimensional, and carefully coordinated are essential to address this severe and growing problem in our society. A way must be found to provide access to such programs for at-risk children and their families on a broad scale. Unless we do, many of our schools will continue to be way stations along the path to prison for a significant subgroup of the school-age population.

APPENDIX A

Empirical Foundations in Discriminating, Predicting, and Changing Aggressive, Antisocial Behavior in School and at Home

This appendix describes empirical investigations conducted primarily by the senior author and his colleagues as part of their ongoing research. The methods used in these studies, and the outcomes reported for them, provide scientific support for many of the intervention procedures described in this book. They also provide important information about the nature and developmental characteristics of aggressive, antisocial behavior in children and youth. Key studies are summarized in a series of exhibits. These exhibits are analogous to the descriptions of the research notes, sources, and annotations that many writers include in the appendices of major historical works.

Each exhibit follows a standard format (preface, results, and comment). The preface briefly introduces the study and explains how it was set up, the results section reports the outcomes, and the comment section interprets the results and describes their relevance to aggressive, antisocial behavior patterns.

It is not essential that you completely understand or even review this material in order to effectively use the procedures described in this book. These exhibits are presented for the reader who is interested in empirical outcomes derived from the longitudinal and scientific study of antisocial, aggressive behavior, particularly in schools.

Some of the exhibits are brief presentations of previously published research.

EXHIBIT 1: THE INFLUENCE OF ARREST STATUS AND SPECIAL EDUCATION CERTIFICATION ON ADJUSTMENT STATUS FOR AT-RISK STUDENTS: MARKERS FOR NEGATIVE DEVELOPMENTAL OUTCOMES

Preface

As part of a long-term study of antisocial behavior patterns among children and youth, the senior author has collaborated with the Oregon Social Learning Center in the longitudinal investigation of the adjustment status of a sample of 200 boys and their families. The boys in this sample, who were selected in 1983 and 1984 when they were in the fourth grade, were chosen according to the number of police contacts registered in the neighborhoods serving their respective elementary schools. Schools serving neighborhoods with higher than normal rates of police contacts were selected as sites for recruiting this sample.

When the boys were in the ninth grade, school and court records were inspected to determine those who (1) had been arrested one or more times and/or (2) had been referred, evaluated, and certified as eligible for special education. Using these criteria, the sample of 200 boys was divided into four groups: (1) arrested and special education ($N =$ 38), (2) not arrested and special education ($N = 35$), (3) arrested and no special education ($N = 42$), and (4) not arrested and no special education ($N = 74$). (Complete data are not available for 11 subjects.) These groups were then compared on six child adjustment measures (academic skills, antisocial behavior, child depression, association with deviant peers, peer relations, and self-esteem) and three parental variables (parental discipline; parental monitoring of child activities, affiliations, and location; and parental depression).

Table A.1 profiles the four subject groups across these measures using standard scores. A negative coefficient means the measure is not characteristic of the group of subjects; a plus coefficient means the measure is characteristic of the group of subjects. The larger the coefficient, the more characteristic (plus coefficient) or uncharacteristic (negative coefficient) the measure is of a given subject group.

Results

The distribution of scores and their valences (+ or −) are presented in Table A.1 for the four groups. The *no arrest/no special education* group has the ideal profile on these nine measures. That is, boys in this group are academically skilled, not antisocial, not depressed, do not associate with deviant peers, are exposed to positive, effective parental discipline and monitoring practices, their parents do not suffer from depression, and they have positive peer relations and positive self-esteem. In stark contrast, boys in the *arrested/special education* group show an extremely negative and problematic profile across these measures. In fact, their valences or signs on these measures are the exact opposite of those for the *no arrest/no special education* group in every case. The remaining two groups show more problematic profiles on these adjustment measures than do the *no arrest/no special*

TABLE A.1 Adjustment Measures of At-Risk Students Grouped by Arrest Status and Special Education Certification

Adjustment Measure	*Arrested/ Special Ed. (N = 38)*	*No Arrest/ Special Ed. (N = 35)*	*Arrested/ No Special Ed. (N = 42)*	*No Arrest/ No Special Ed. (N = 74)*
Academic skills	−.85	−.33	−.21	+.69
Antisocial	+.61	−.22	+.28	−.36
Child depressed	+.37	+.03	+.22	−.34
Deviant peers	+.70	−.29	+.41	−.46
Parental discipline	−.35	−.03	+.08	+.17
Parental monitor	−.47	+.25	−.17	+.20
Parental depression	+.29	−.06	+.03	−.10
Peer relations	−.50	−.03	−.06	+.29
Self-esteem	−.39	−.05	−.13	+.30

education group; however, the "arrested/no special education" group appears to have a much more serious adjustment profile than the "no arrest/special education" group.

Comment

The results of this study indicate that at-risk youth who experience one or more arrests by grade 9 have serious academic and social-behavioral adjustment problems. One of the powerful risk factors to which they are exposed is especially ineffective parenting practices, which places them at even further risk for a host of negative developmental outcomes, including school failure. Furthermore, when arrest status is accompanied by special education certification, this combination of events seems to identify youth who have an extremely high-risk status for serious, negative developmental outcomes. Given these findings, *all* potentially at-risk youth in the upper elementary and middle school grade ranges should be screened systematically on these two factors (arrest status and eligibility for special education certification) and appropriate remedial actions should be initiated for those students who are positively identified by this process.

Long-term studies of outcomes for students in special education are often negative and fall well below minimal expectations (Wagner, 1989). At-risk students are particularly vulnerable to problems occurring during the transition from school to work and adult living. Outcomes for students certified as severely emotionally disturbed (SED) are discouraging in this regard, with approximately 20% being arrested during school and 43% arrested within two years of leaving school. Collectively, these results argue for the early identification and intervention of children and youth who are at risk for delinquency and school failure. This deadly combination is a harbinger of costly and unfortunate outcomes later in life.

EXHIBIT 2: REGULAR CLASSROOM BEHAVIORAL PROFILES OF NEGATIVE-AGGRESSIVE VERSUS ACTING-OUT/DISRUPTIVE STUDENTS IN THE PRIMARY GRADES

Preface

Since 1966, the senior author and his colleagues have been studying and developing intervention programs for children and youth having conduct problems. The adjustment problems of some children are characterized primarily by aggressive behavior directed toward their peers. In contrast, other children have serious adjustment problems primarily involving their interactions with adults, particularly teachers. Such children act out against adult-imposed rules, oppose or defy teacher authority, and disrupt classroom routines. A small subset of these two target groups display both aggressive and acting-out behavior patterns. They tend to be rejected by both teachers and peers and are serious behavior-management challenges for teachers and often parents. The study described here was designed to examine behavioral similarities and differences between groups of students representing these two behavior patterns.

Table A.2 profiles the appropriate and inappropriate behavior of a group of six negative-aggressive elementary students and a group of six acting-out/disruptive elementary students in regular classrooms. A combination of teacher nominations, ratings, and direct behavioral observations was used to select the two groups. Direct observations of classroom behavior were recorded by professionally trained observers.

The numbers in Table A.2 are frequencies for each code category, expressed as rate per minute.

Results

The rate per minute of the subjects' behavior for each of the 12 observation code categories (six appropriate and six inappropriate) is listed in Table A.2. On average, negative-aggressive students had substantially higher overall rates of appropriate behavior in the classroom than did acting-out/disruptive students. Acting-out/disruptive students had substantially higher rates of inappropriate behavior than the negative/aggressive students.

Comment

These results are not surprising, given that the behavior problems of acting-out students primarily involve teachers and the classroom. It would have been interesting to assess

TABLE A.2 Appropriate and Inappropriate Behavior by Negative-Aggressive and Acting-Out/Disruptive Students

Appropriate Behavior	*Negative-Aggressive (N = 6)*	*Acting Out/Disruptive (N = 6)*
Individual work	.95	1.25
Group work	1.45	1.04
Vocalization to teacher	.26	.14
Vocalization to peer	.18	.03
Positive physical	.01	.01
Appropriate movement	2.40	.30
Average	.88	.46
Inappropriate Behavior		
Nonattending	1.80	2.50
Noisy	.24	.80
Vocalization to teacher	.17	.27
Vocalization to peer	.80	1.00
Physical	.20	.15
Movement	1.85	2.75
Average	.84	1.25

the two groups in a playground setting. We suspect the aggressive students would have had much higher rates of antisocial and coercive behavior in free-play settings and the acting-out students would likely have had higher rates of playground rule infractions. However, we do not have direct observation results to either confirm or disconfirm these predictions.

Results of the current study suggest that acting-out students are impaired primarily in their teacher-related adjustment and aggressive students are impaired primarily in their peer-related adjustment. Interventions for acting-out students should focus on teacher–student interactions; they should begin in the classroom and be extended to other school settings as needed. In contrast, interventions for aggressive children should focus on peer-to-peer interactions and should begin on the playground where peer social exchanges can occur in an unconstrained manner. Variations of these intervention procedures should be extended to other school settings as required.

EXHIBIT 3: COMPARISONS OF THE SCHOOL ADJUSTMENT STATUS OF MIDDLE SCHOOL AT-RISK BOYS WHO ARE DEVIANT IN TWO OR MORE SETTINGS, DEVIANT IN ONLY ONE SETTING, OR DEVIANT IN NO SETTINGS

Preface

As part of our longitudinal research with antisocial and at-risk boys, the senior author and his colleagues compared the behavioral adjustment status of students in their sample and divided them into three groups: (1) those who were deviant in both the classroom and playground setting when compared with peers ($N = 14$), (2) those who were deviant in one setting (classroom or playground) when compared with peers ($N = 29$), and (3) those who were not deviant in either setting based on normative peer comparisons ($N = 31$) (Walker, Shinn, O'Neill, & Ramsey, 1987; Walker, Stieber, Ramsey, & O'Neill, 1991). The adjustment status (academic and social) of these three groups of boys was examined on measures other than those used to define their levels of deviance in these settings. These were (1) a global measure of academic performance (academic skills) and (2) four observation code categories derived from direct observations in the classroom (academic-engaged time), on the playground (total target positive and total peer positive), and at home (total positive home behavior).

Results

Table A.3 profiles performance of the three groups on these five adjustment measures. Means and standard deviations are presented on each variable for each subject group (see Columns 4 and 5 of the table). Differences between the groups on each of the five variables were tested for statistical significance; the results are reported in Column 6.

Table A.3 indicates clear differences in adjustment status among these three groups, with students who are deviant in two settings having the most serious problems. There were statistically significant differences on three of the five adjustment variables used; in each case, the students who were deviant in two settings had the most negative or maladaptive scores.

Comment

This finding is consistent with other results reported in the literature indicating that individuals who experience adjustment problems in multiple settings (for example, home and school) are likely to be more deviant than those who experience problems in only one setting. For example, Loeber and Dishion (1984) found that boys who fight at home and school are more deviant than those who fought either at home or at school. Thus, it is important to assess behavioral status in all important target settings and to intervene in those settings where the student's behavior falls below normative or expected standards. It is extremely unlikely that intervention in one setting will affect performance in other settings, even if the settings show some degree of similarity with each other.

TABLE A.3 Adjustment Measures of At-Risk Boys Showing Deviance in Two or More Settings, One Setting, or No Settings

Variable	*Group*	*Number of Subjects*	*Mean*	*Standard Deviation*	*Probability*
Academic-engaged time	Two settings	14	58.50%	16.70%	<.001
	One setting	29	73.98%	17.03%	
	Not deviant	31	88.48%	8.45%	
Academic skills	Two settings	14	−.34	.61	<.02
	One setting	29	−.05	.79	
	Not deviant	31	+.35	.87	
Total target positive	Two settings	14	38.35%	13.08%	N.S.
	One setting	29	38.44%	16.67%	
	Not deviant	31	45.97%	16.61%	
Total peer negative	Two settings	14	12.47%	8.18%	<.001
	One setting	29	5.91%	6.00%	
	Not deviant	31	2.21%	2.28%	
Total positive home behavior	Two settings	14	.39	.16	N.S.
	One setting	29	.40	.15	
	Not deviant	31	.38	.14	

EXHIBIT 4: ADJUSTMENT PROFILES OF ANTISOCIAL AND AT-RISK MIDDLE SCHOOL BOYS

Preface

Since 1984, the senior author and his colleagues have been engaged in a longitudinal study of the school adjustment of 39 antisocial and 41 at-risk boys (Shinn, Ramsey, Walker, Stieber, & O'Neill, 1987; Walker, Shinn, O'Neill, & Ramsey, 1987; Walker, Stieber, & Eisert, 1991). The antisocial boys have a highly elevated risk status for developing an antisocial behavior pattern and subsequent delinquency; the at-risk boys have much lower risk status but are more vulnerable to these outcomes than normal students. Tracking of these boys began when they were in the fourth grade. The Oregon Social Learning Center studies these same boys and their families in home and community settings.

Each fall and spring, a series of measures (direct observations, school records, and teacher ratings) is recorded on these boys; at the end of the school year, an exhaustive search of their school records for the past nine months is done. Court records and police contacts are also reviewed for the past year. Students' performance can be compared (1) between home and school, (2) within school (that is, fall to spring), and also (3) across school years.

Table A.4 presents information for these two groups on a series of behavioral adjustment measures recorded at the end of grade 5. The second part of the table profiles the performance of these two groups across an additional set of adjustment measures that have a classroom/academic performance focus.

Results

All measures indicate that the antisocial students have many more as well as much more serious adjustment problems than at-risk students. This discrepancy appears to intensify as the two groups of students progress through their school careers. Furthermore, the at-risk students are either close to or within the normal range on most adjustment measures. By the end of the eighth grade, only 3 of the at-risk students had been arrested, with 1 arrest each. In stark contrast, 21 of the 39 antisocial students had been arrested at this point, with a total of 68 arrests. It is estimated that there is only 1 arrest for every 10 to 11 arrestable offenses actually committed.

Comment

The antisocial students were selected for inclusion in this study because teachers and parents gave them extremely high scores on the aggression subscale of the Achenbach Child Behavior Checklist (CBC). The at-risk students had CBC aggression subscale scores that were much closer to the normal range. The aggressive behavior patterns of the antisocial students and the unfortunate parenting practices and home conditions to which they were exposed appear to set them up for a host of school-related problems including (1) rejection by peers and teachers, (2) low academic achievement, and (3) assignment to restrictive placements. School archival records indicate a host of school adjustment problems. The huge difference in the number of discipline contacts between the antisocial and at-risk students is a measure of how serious the school adjustment problems of antisocial students are. Furthermore, inspection of Table A.4 indicates that the negative behavior of antisocial and at-risk students is almost perfectly reciprocated or matched by the peers with whom they interact in free play. This may be a key factor in the social rejection of antisocial children and in the severe difficulties involved in changing the negative bias and impressions of them held by peers.

TABLE A.4 Behavioral Adjustment and Classroom/Academic Performance of Antisocial and At-Risk Students

Behavioral Adjustment Measure	*Antisocial Students*	*At-Risk Students*
School discipline contacts	476	14
Attendance (total days missed)	526	281
Number receiving special education services	14	6
Number retained at least one grade	6	2
Negative social behavior on the playground:		
Target students	9.93%	4.05%
Peers of target students	8.09%	3.41%
Classroom/Academic Measure		
Reading achievement	42.38 (Percentile)	56.63 (Percentile)
Math achievement	32.00 (Percentile)	58.68 (Percentile)
Total achievement	35.75 (Percentile)	58.88 (Percentile)
Resource/Chapter One	14 (Number Receiving)	6 (Number Receiving)
Retained more than one grade	2	0
Time engaged in assigned academic tasks	68%	85%
Total social skills teacher rating score	121.09	164.59

It is important that school interventions focus on reducing and replacing the aggressive forms and levels of behavior displayed by these students. The aggressive and coercive behavioral tendencies of these students are highly aversive to peers and often lead to peer avoidance, neglect, and even victimization. As a first step, this behavior pattern needs to be either eliminated or greatly reduced in scope. Next, their consistent tendency to use coercive, provocative strategies with key social agents (teachers, parents, and peers) needs to be replaced with proactive strategies that emphasize cooperation and do not precipitate the negative outcomes of the type previously described. Powerful interventions, applied consistently over time and settings, are necessary to achieve this goal.

EXHIBIT 5: POSITIVE VERSUS NEGATIVE SOCIAL BEHAVIOR IN DISCRIMINATING ANTISOCIAL AND AT-RISK STUDENTS IN PLAYGROUND AND CLASSROOM SETTINGS

Preface

Research with aggressive, antisocial children has found consistently that negative social behavior has far more discriminant and predictive power than does positive social behavior. Research indicates that the negative social behavior of aggressive students is considerably more stable over time than their positive social behavior. Furthermore, actual rates per minute of positive social responses for aggressive students, occurring in ongoing peer exchanges on the playground, are relatively unaffected by implementation of powerful interventions that reduce their negative behavior. For example, Walker, Hops, and Greenwood (1981) describe an experimental evaluation of the RECESS intervention program for reducing negative-aggressive behavior among aggressive, antisocial children in grades K–3. The RECESS intervention program had the following effects on the average negative, aggressive response rates of ten antisocial children across baseline, intervention, and fading phases, respectively: .69, .05, and .14. The positive response rates of the same ten students across these identical phases were 3.92, 3.88, and 3.83, respectively. Thus, while the intervention had a very powerful effect in reducing the students' negative, aggressive behavior, it had no effect on their positive social behavior.

As a rule, the positive social behavior of aggressive, antisocial children is often within the normal range when directly observed and recorded in natural settings (for example, the playground) and compared with that of non-antisocial peers. However, their rates of negative-aggressive behavior can be up to nine times higher than that of non-antisocial peers under the same conditions on the playground (Walker & Hops, 1993).

To investigate this question further, the positive and negative social behavior of aggressive and at-risk students was assessed in both playground and classroom settings. Each of the 39 antisocial subjects and 41 at-risk subjects in the ongoing longitudinal study was observed on multiple occasions on the playground and in regular classrooms.

Results

Tables A.5 and A.6 present the results of these assessments using *t*-tests and discriminant function analysis procedures for direct observation data. The observation code used to record playground observation data provided for coding social behavior as either positive or negative. Similarly, the classroom code used provided for recording appropriate and inappropriate behavior, so there was an equal probability of occurrence for coding either.

However, in both the classroom and playground, inappropriate and negative social behavior, respectively, were the most powerful in discriminating the antisocial from the at-risk students. Furthermore, in every case except one (positive initiation to teacher), antisocial students had more negative, maladaptive levels or rates on these code categories than at-risk students. Antisocial students may initiate to teachers at higher rates (both positive and negative) because they are more dependent on teacher assistance due to their deficient academic skills.

On the playground, seven of the code categories that significantly discriminated the two groups were negative in their valence, as opposed to positive (see Table A.5). When these discriminating code categories were ranked according to their correlational magnitude with the discriminant function, the five most powerful code categories were all

TABLE A.5 Playground Behavior of Antisocial and At-Risk Students

Playground Code Category	*Antisocial Students*	*At-Risk Students*	*Probability*
Negative target verbal	6.2%	2.4%	<.0002
Positive initiated target verbal	5.6%	6.9%	<.01
Negative initiated target verbal	.85%	.45%	<.01
Negative target physical	5.42%	1.99%	<.001
Negative peer verbal	5.50%	2.57%	<.004
Negative initiated peer verbal	.68%	.39%	<.006
Negative peer physical	3.90%	1.50%	<.0007
Ignore	.82%	.43%	<.02
Activity 3	38.8%	50.2%	<.04

Code Category Variable	r *with Discriminant Function*
Negative target verbal	−.50
Negative peer physical	−.46
Negative target physical	−.44
Negative peer verbal	−.39
Negative initiated peer verbal	−.36
Positive initiated target verbal	.33
Negative initiated target verbal	−.33
Ignore	−.30
Activity 3	.27
Positive target physical	.21
Activity 1	−.20

TABLE A.6 Classroom Behavior of Antisocial and At-Risk Students

Classroom Code Category	*Antisocial Students*	*At-Risk Students*	*Probability*
Activity 1	44.6%	58.7%	<.003
Activity 2	54.9%	40.2%	<.002
Attending	76.3%	86.0%	<.0001
Positive initiated to teacher	1.32%	.74%	<.01
Negative initiated to teacher	.34%	.05%	<.01
Individual noncompliance	.12%	.02%	<.01
Group compliance	1.25%	1.90%	<.05
Negative physical	.21%	.07%	<.01
Noise	2.8%	.46%	<.0005
Inappropriate locale	3.4%	1.03%	<.0005

Code Category Variable	r *with Discriminant Function*
Nonattending	.50
Inappropriate locale	.43
Noise	.43
Activity 2	.38
Activity 1	−.37
Negative initiated to teacher	.32
Positive initiated to teacher	.32
Individual noncompliance	.31
Physical negative	.30
Group compliance	.24

negative (see the "Code Category Variable" section of Table A.5). Similarly, in the classroom, five of the eight discriminating code categories (excluding the two activity structure codes) measure inappropriate behavior. When ordered by their correlation with the discriminant function, the first four categories were inappropriate, as opposed to appropriate.

Comment

These results replicate previous findings on this question and those of Patterson, Reid, and Dishion (1992). They strongly suggest that, unlike many other disorders of adjustment, antisocial students require direct interventions designed to reduce or eliminate their negative-aggressive social behavior. Attempting to reduce or eliminate negative, aggressive or inappropriate behavior using only positive interventions with this student population is an extremely weak strategy. Our experience suggests that antisocial, aggressive children need to be exposed *simultaneously* to an intervention that (1) *directly* reduces maladaptive behavior, (2) implements a social-skills intervention to teach proactive alternative methods of coping with social situations and responding to social tasks and demands, and (3) provides support and incentives for the target child and peers to change their characteristic ways of interacting with each other over the long term. Subsequent exhibits in this appendix illustrate research studies that provide empirical support for this approach.

EXHIBIT 6: DIFFERENTIAL PARENTING PROFILES THAT DISCRIMINATE ANTISOCIAL AND AT-RISK STUDENTS

Preface

Patterson and his colleagues (1982, 1992) and other investigators (Kazdin, 1985; Wahler & Dumas, 1986) have developed overwhelming empirical evidence that harsh and incompetent parenting practices play an instrumental role in the development of aggressive, antisocial behavior patterns in children. Patterson et al. argue persuasively that normal parenting practices are severely disrupted, and often qualitatively changed, by a host of negative stressors including alcohol and drug abuse; physical, psychological and sexual abuse of children and mothers; poverty; unemployment; and depression. Under these conditions, essential parenting practices, such as discipline and monitoring, are often harsh, unfair, random, or nonexistent; furthermore, they are often highly ineffective.

Patterson et al. have identified five key parenting practices that are extremely important in children's development. Competent performance of these parenting practices tends to produce well-socialized children who achieve adequately in school and relate well to teachers, peers, and parents. Incompetent performance of these practices places children at risk for a host of negative developmental outcomes, including the development of antisocial behavior patterns. These practices include (1) *discipline* that is fair, timely, and consistent; (2) *monitoring* of children's activities, whereabouts, and affiliations; (3) *positive behavior-management techniques* that involve support, encouragement, and valuing of the child; (4) *parent involvement* in the child's life and daily activities; (5) *problem-solving* and *crisis-management skills* that can assist the child in resolving conflicts. It has also been demonstrated that when parents are taught to effectively implement these practices, the overall behavioral adjustment of their children improves substantially (Patterson, 1982).

As part of our longitudinal study of antisocial and at-risk students, Ramsey and Walker (1988) examined the family-management practices to which the two groups were exposed. We expected that the parents of antisocial students would display less favorable profiles on the Patterson et al. parenting practices than would parents of the at-risk students. Each of these practices is assessed by a multimethod–multimeasure construct score that has been validated and standardized on normal families.

The families of each of the students in our 80-case sample (39 antisocial and 41 at risk) are formally assessed by Patterson and his associates every two years as part of their ongoing, longitudinal study. Using results from these assessments, we were able to profile the parents of our two groups.

Results

Figure A.1 profiles the family-management styles of parents of the two subject groups using average z scores for each group. Parents of the at-risk students had more favorable profiles than the parents of the antisocial students on each of the five parenting practices. Differences were statistically significant, favoring the at-risk group, on the construct scores representing each parenting practice, with the exception of parent involvement. These results indicate clearly that the antisocial students in our study were exposed to much less competent parenting practices than were the at-risk students.

Comment

The adjustment status of our antisocial students, already problematic when they were selected for our study, continues to deteriorate over their school careers. In contrast, the at-risk students have maintained a more favorable position, relative to children who are not at risk, in terms of their adjustment status. These divergent trends may be related to the different parenting practices and family conditions the two groups have been exposed to during their preschool and school careers. These results suggest that any comprehensive intervention approach designed to alter these students' antisocial behavior patterns would have to include a strong parent training and intervention component.

EXHIBIT 7: THE PATH FROM FAILED PARENTING TO ANTISOCIAL BEHAVIOR IN SCHOOL TO DELINQUENCY IN ADOLESCENCE

Preface

For many students, schooling serves as an unfortunate transition between negative family conditions, deficient parenting practices, and the adoption of a delinquent life-style in adolescence. Patterson (1982) found that negative disciplining and monitoring practices by parents are especially powerful in fostering the development of antisocial behavior in the home. If children bring an antisocial behavior pattern to school, it is likely to be

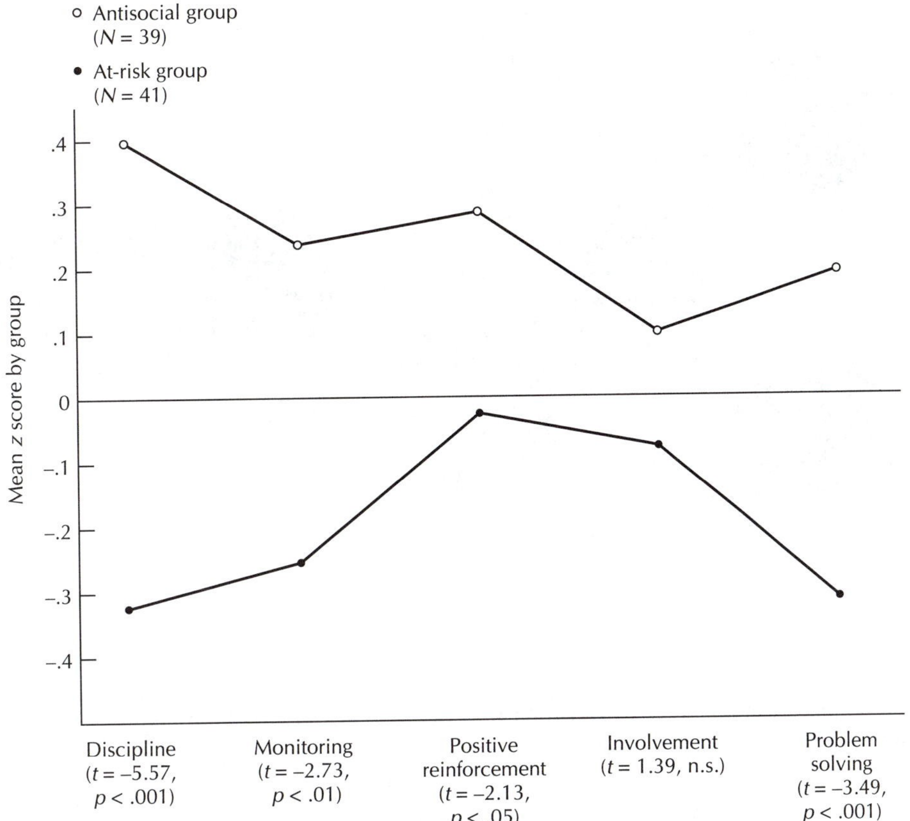

FIGURE A.1 Profiles of Family-Management Style for Parents of Antisocial and At-Risk Students. *Source:* From "Family Management Correlates of Antisocial Behavior among Middle School Boys," by E. Ramsey and H. M. Walker. In *Behavioral Disorders, 13*(3), 1988, 187–201. Reprinted by permission.

maintained and strengthened there. This well-established antisocial behavior pattern in school is strongly associated with membership in a deviant peer group and subsequent delinquency in adolescence.

Ramsey, Patterson, Bank, and Walker (in press) investigated the path that exists from incompetent parenting practices to antisocial behavior in school to delinquency in adolescence. The collaborative longitudinal studies of Patterson and Walker and their respective colleagues (Patterson & Bank, 1986; Walker et al., 1987) made this study possible. Eighty subjects were shared between the two studies in which data were obtained from homes, schools, and juvenile court records. This study was conducted over a three-year period.

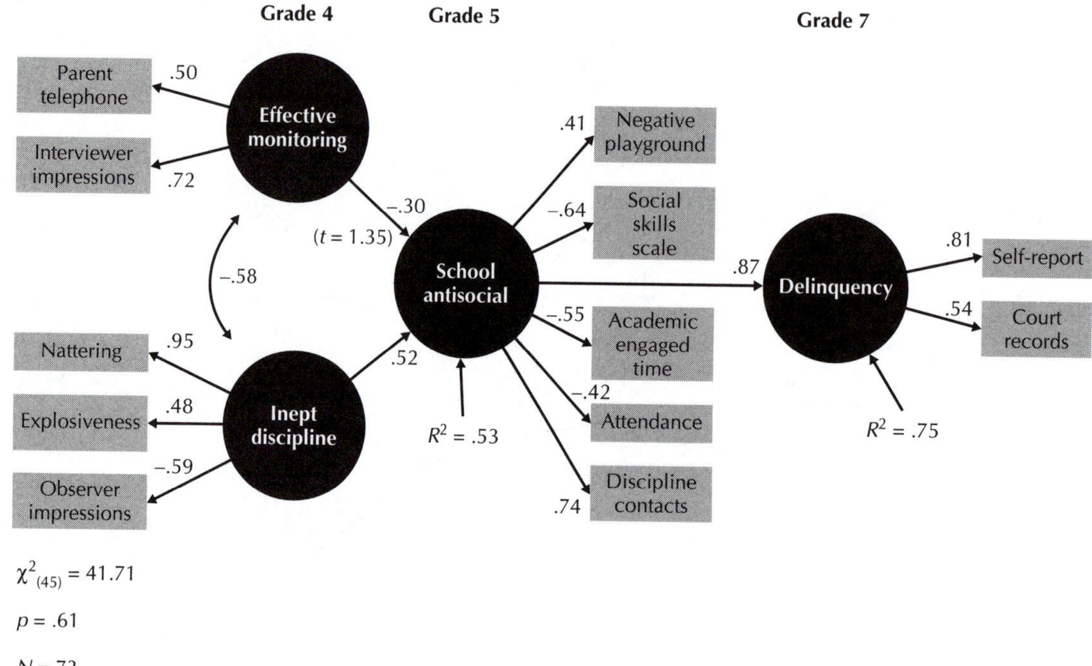

$\chi^2_{(45)} = 41.71$

$p = .61$

$N = 73$

FIGURE A.2 Path from Parenting Practices to School Antisocial Behavior and Later Delinquency

When the subjects (39 antisocial and 41 at risk) were in grade 4, their parents' skills in discipline and monitoring were assessed. In grade 5, a global, antisocial score was developed that measured each student's investment in antisocial behavior patterns at school. Finally, in grade 7, the students' delinquency was assessed using court records and self-reports of delinquent acts.

Results

Figure A.2 reveals a direct path from parenting practices to antisocial behavior in school and subsequently to delinquency. Low to moderately strong relationships existed between parental monitoring and discipline in grade 4 and school antisocial behavior in grade 5. A well-established pattern of antisocial behavior in school by grade 5, however, is highly predictive of delinquency by grade 7. The path coefficient of .87 in Figure A.2 between school antisocial behavior and delinquency over a two-year period is an exceptionally strong relationship. This result suggests that a well-developed pattern of antisocial behavior in school may serve as an important precursor for subsequent delinquent life-styles.

Comment

The results of this study indicate that antisocial behavior patterns show substantial evidence of cross-setting consistency as a function of incompetent parenting practices. Parenting practices seem to set the child up for antisocial behavior in school, which is often associated with both teacher and peer rejection. Teacher rejection can contribute to school failure and peer rejection and is often a precursor of association with deviant peers, which in turn is strongly associated with delinquent acts. This study suggests that early intervention for school antisocial behavior may be an extremely important factor in preventing later delinquency.

EXHIBIT 8: GENERALIZATION OF ANTISOCIAL BEHAVIOR PATTERNS FROM HOME TO SCHOOL

Preface

Considerable debate has occurred over the past two decades regarding the origins of antisocial behavior patterns. A concurrent debate has focused on the extent to which such behavior patterns are influenced by the demands and attributes of different situations (Mischel, 1968). In other words, to what extent is a child's behavior in a given situation a function of the nature of that setting and to what extent is it a function of the behavioral history and inclinations the child brings to that situation? In the area of antisocial behavior, this debate has turned on the question of whether aggression is situationally specific or more accurately characterized as having traitlike status (that is, a generalized attribute that can be expected to occur in any setting).

Ramsey, Patterson, and Walker (1990) investigated the extent to which the antisocial behavior of the 80 students showed evidence of generalization from home to school. Multimethod and multi-agent construct scores for home and school antisocial behavior were developed in order to investigate this question. At-home behavior was assessed when students were in grade 4; school behavior was measured in grade 5.

Results

Figure A.3 presents (1) factor loadings that define the contribution of each indicator measure to its respective construct score in the home or school and (2) the path coefficient between home antisocial behavior in grade 4 and school antisocial behavior in grade 5. The path coefficient between home and school antisocial behavior was .72, which indicates that 52% of the variance in school antisocial behavior in grade 5 could be accounted for by home antisocial behavior one year earlier.

Comment

The results of this study provide considerable evidence for the cross-setting generality of antisocial behavior for the sample. This level of stability for antisocial behavior across home and school settings, over a one-year period, provides support for the accumulating

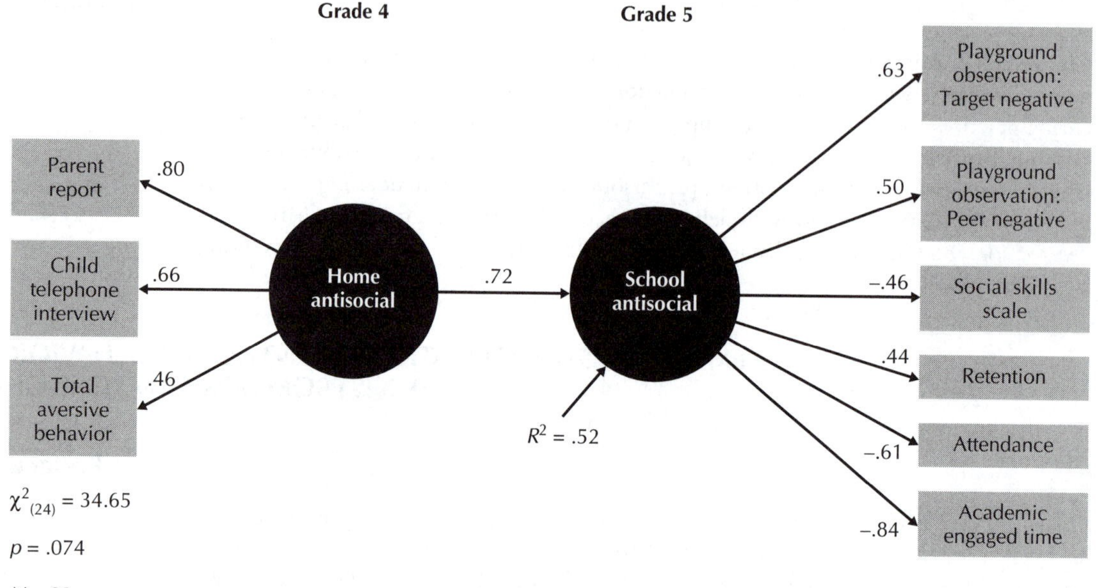

FIGURE A.3 The Relationship Between Antisocial Behavior in the Home and School

evidence that antisocial behavior patterns perform in a traitlike fashion. The authors believe there is empirical evidence both for the situational specificity and the traitlike performance of antisocial behavior. However, the more severe the antisocial behavior pattern becomes, the more likely it is to behave like a trait, independent of setting characteristics. Over a decade, severely aggressive and antisocial forms of behavior show stability levels that match or exceed those for IQ (Quay, 1986). This level of stability and cross-setting consistency presents severe challenges to interventionists charged with making permanent changes in this behavior pattern.

EXHIBIT 9: THE EFFICACY OF PRAISE, TOKEN REINFORCEMENT, AND COST CONTINGENCY IN REDUCING NEGATIVE-AGGRESSIVE SOCIAL INTERACTIONS AMONG ANTISOCIAL BOYS

Preface

The senior author and his associates conducted a series of experiments on reducing negative-aggressive behavior among elementary school–age boys. This research was the initial step in the research and development of the RECESS program for remediating aggressive behavior patterns in school (Walker & Hops, 1983). The purpose of the studies was to assess the efficacy of adult praise, token reinforcement procedures, and cost contingency (loss of previously earned or awarded points), singly and in combination, in reducing negative-aggressive social interactions among antisocial boys. The overall goal of this research was to identify a powerful, yet economical, combination of intervention procedures that could be adapted for effective use in regular classrooms and on playgrounds.

Two groups of six boys each were recruited from local school districts and placed in an experimental classroom full-time for approximately three months. Group I students were assigned to the experimental setting from October to January and Group II students from February to May. Students were selected because they displayed much higher than normal rates of aggressive behavior in class and on the playground. Children were referred for consideration by elementary school counselors who were aware of the intervention program and who responded to a specific, written description of the behavior problems and types of students being recruited. Teacher ratings and direct behavioral observations of social-interactive behavior in free-play settings were used to select students for inclusion in each group. Baseline rates of positive and negative interactions were recorded for each student in his regular class prior to assignment to the experimental class (see baseline 1 in Figures A.4 and A.5). Following assignment to the experimental classroom, a second baseline phase (baseline 2) was instituted for each subject group in order to establish a behavioral standard or level for evaluating subsequent intervention phases in that setting.

An intensive academic program focusing on basic skills in reading, math, and language was developed and implemented for each subject group. In addition, three, 30-minute activity periods were established daily in which students were allowed to engage in free-play social interactions or in a variety of games and activities that facilitated peer-to-peer social exchanges.

Group I was exposed to a series of daily intervention procedures during these activity periods in which social praise (hereafter called "social"), token reinforcement, and cost contingency were applied in various combinations in response to their interactive behavior. Brief baseline phases were alternated with the intervention procedures in the following sequence: baseline 2, social 1, baseline 3, social 2, social plus tokens, social 3, social plus tokens 2, social plus tokens plus cost contingency, social plus tokens 3, and social plus tokens plus cost contingency 2. This design allowed the specific and combined effects of these intervention procedures to be isolated in a highly controlled, experimental setting. Following the last phase, Group I returned to their referral school and was monitored and followed up continuously (via behavioral observations) for a one-month period. No post-integration interventions or follow-up transition procedures were implemented for either Group I or Group II. Both groups were also followed up briefly at three- and six-month periods following the end of experimental classroom intervention.

Group II provided an intersubject replication for Group I results. In contrast to Group I, Group II was exposed to the intervention procedures of praise, token reinforcement, and cost contingency only in a combined fashion (see Figure A.5). After the second baseline was recorded, the full combination of intervention procedures (social, tokens, cost contingency) was implemented for approximately one week. This initial exposure to the intervention was followed by a brief baseline phase and a return to the full intervention for a three-week period. A four-week fading phase was then implemented in which the number of available daily points (points awarded daily for good academic and social behavior) was reduced by 20% each week. Finally, the Group II students were returned to their school settings and followed up continuously for a one-month period.

With the exception of the fading phase for Group II, the procedures and contingencies operating within each phase were explained to both subject groups as they occurred. Praise was applied to their positive interactive behavior during and following ongoing, peer-to-peer social exchanges. The teacher and teacher's aide in the experimental class were instructed to find and positively reinforce 30 instances of praiseable, interactive behavior for each student during the three activity periods during the day. They were monitored and supported in this task by the experimental classroom supervisor. Tallies of delivered praise were kept for each student to ensure that this daily goal was met.

In the phases in which token reinforcement was used, it was always paired with and delivered in conjunction with teacher praise; that is, students knew during these phases that they had earned two points each time they were praised for their positive interactive behavior directed toward a peer. During the phases in which cost contingency was also used, four previously earned points were subtracted for each instance of negative, aggressive, verbal, physical, or gestural social behavior. Thus, the ratio of point loss to point earning was set at 2:1 to ensure that the display of negative-aggressive forms of social behavior would be perceived as costly and thus discouraged. If a student's total points would drop below zero with a given application of cost contingency, a brief time-out was used to discourage further instances of negative-aggressive behavior until additional points were earned.

Results

Results for these experiments are presented in Figure A.4 and Table A.7 for Group I and in Figure A.5 and Table A.8 for Group II. Daily observation data, averaged across students within each subject group, are presented in Figures A.4 and A.5; phase means and standard deviations are presented in Tables A.7 and A.8 for each subject group. Table A.9 summarizes the follow-up results for each subject group and provides normative data for comparative purposes.

Figure A.4 provides a daily average for all six subjects across all baseline, intervention, and follow-up phases. As a general rule, the performance of individual subjects approximated closely the group effects depicted in Figure A.4 and Table A.7. Baseline and follow-up data were recorded in the referral setting for the target subjects and same-sex peers who were nominated by teachers as representing the peer-group average in terms of normative social behavior. During baseline 1, approximately 60% of the subjects' interactions with peers were positive as recorded in free-play settings (see Figure A.4); for same-sex peers under identical conditions, approximately 95% of their social interactions with peers were positive. During a second baseline (baseline 2), recorded in the experimental class, the target students averaged approximately 80% positive social interactions with each other. As a rule, their social behavior was not consequated during this

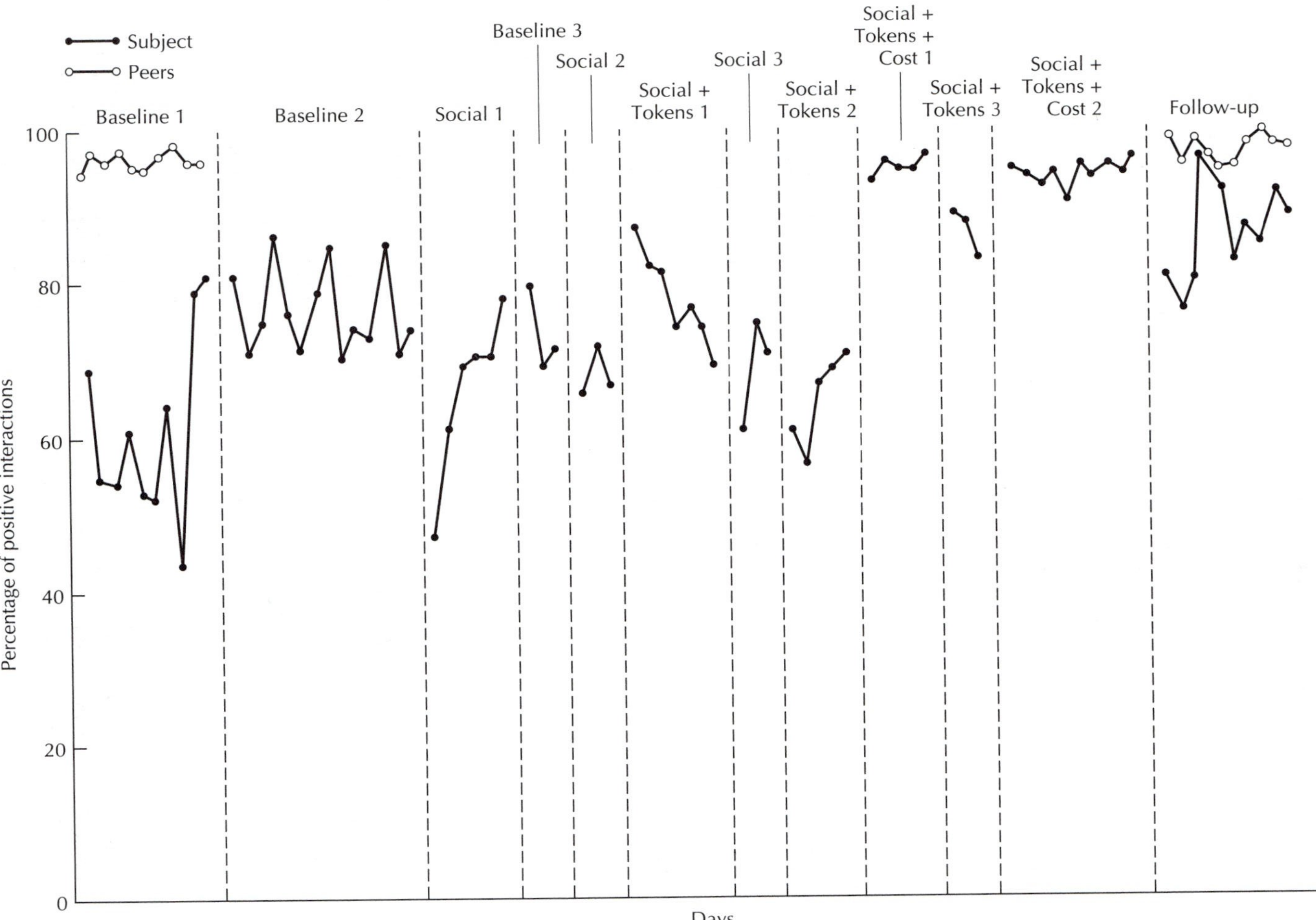

FIGURE A.4 Group I: Positive Interactions during Baseline, Intervention, and Follow-Up Phases

TABLE A.7 Phase Means and Standard Deviations for Group I

	REGULAR CLASSROOM—BASELINE 1					
	RATE OF POSITIVE INTERACTIONS		RATE OF NEGATIVE INTERACTIONS		PERCENTAGE POSITIVE INTERACTIONS	
	Mean	*SD*	*Mean*	*SD*	*Mean*	*SD*
Subjects combined	.34	.27	.24	.06	59.00	12.36
Peers combined	.58	.14	.02	.01	96.00	1.19

	EXPERIMENTAL CLASSROOM					
	RATE OF POSITIVE INTERACTIONS		RATE OF NEGATIVE INTERACTIONS		PERCENTAGE POSITIVE INTERACTIONS	
Phase	*Mean*	*SD*	*Mean*	*SD*	*Mean*	*SD*
Baseline 2	1.37	.22	.29	.09	82.69	4.32
Social 1	1.43	.23	.54	.21	72.77	9.36
Baseline 3	1.95	.29	.45	.13	81.28	3.53
Social 2	1.41	.21	.47	.10	75.00	2.52
Social + Tokens 1	1.73	.23	.35	.09	83.19	5.15
Social 3	1.51	.01	.54	.16	73.73	5.65
Social + Tokens 2	1.64	.32	.64	.19	71.84	4.61
Social + Tokens + Cost 1	2.81	.22	.09	.03	96.79	.90
Social + Tokens 3	2.44	.37	.27	.08	90.11	2.27
Social + Tokens + Cost 2	2.28	.45	.07	.02	96.87	1.07

phase unless it threatened to escalate into physical aggression. Agitated affective states, name calling, provocations, and aggressive posturing with each other occurred at high rates during this phase; the target students' interactions required close supervision in the absence of behavioral contingencies for consequating and controlling their negative-aggressive features.

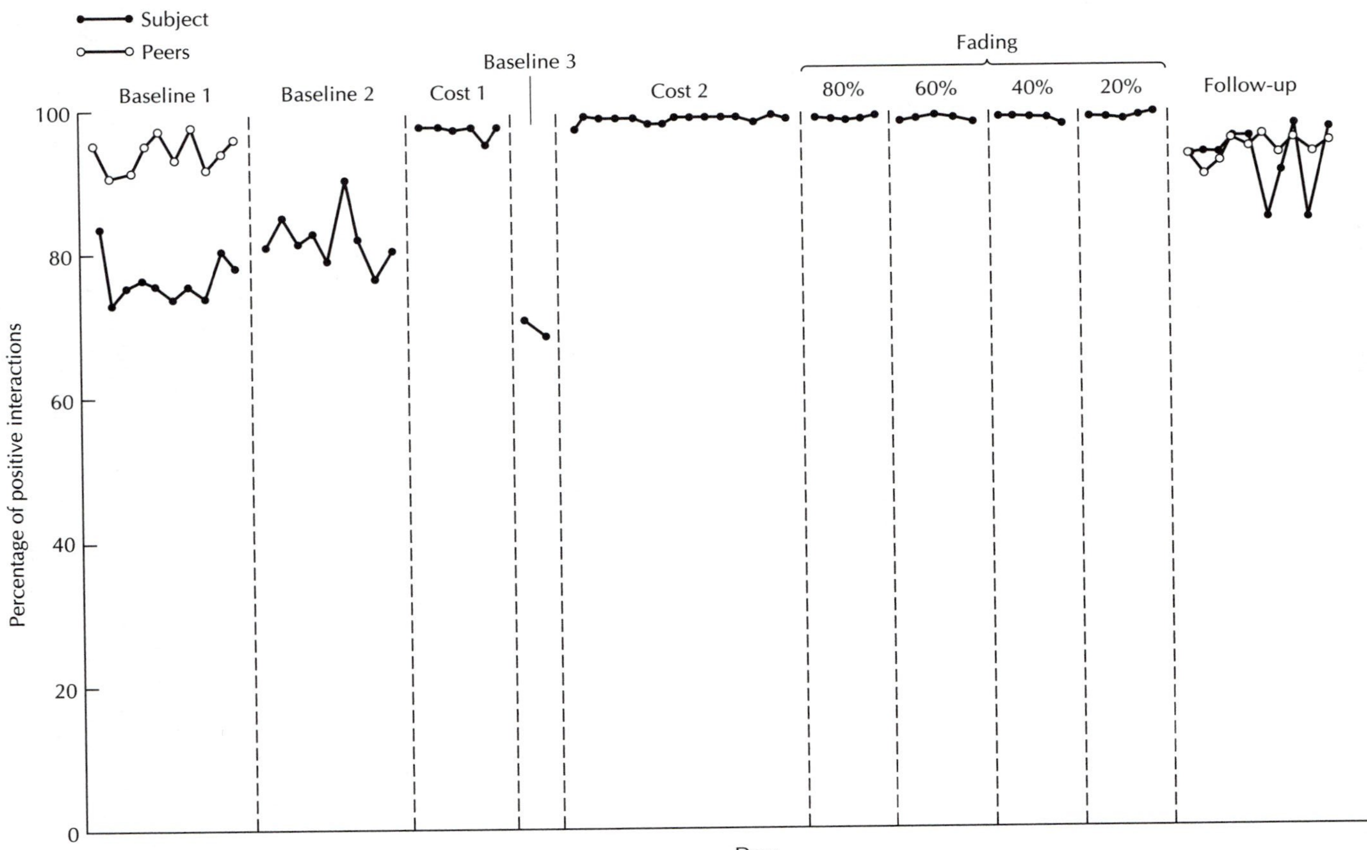

FIGURE A.5 Combined Effects of Social Praise, Tokens, and Cost Contingency for a Second Group of Target Subjects

TABLE A.8 Phase Means and Standard Deviations for Group II

	REGULAR CLASSROOM—BASELINE 1					
	RATE OF POSITIVE INTERACTIONS		RATE OF NEGATIVE INTERACTIONS		PERCENTAGE POSITIVE INTERACTIONS	
	Mean	*SD*	*Mean*	*SD*	*Mean*	*SD*
Subjects combined	.81	.31	.24	.12	75.36	11.22
Peers combined	.60	.14	.02	.01	96.44	1.19

	EXPERIMENTAL CLASSROOM					
	RATE OF POSITIVE INTERACTIONS		RATE OF NEGATIVE INTERACTIONS		PERCENTAGE POSITIVE INTERACTIONS	
Phase	*Mean*	*SD*	*Mean*	*SD*	*Mean*	*SD*
Baseline 2	2.54	.73	.55	.25	82.19	4.40
Social + Tokens + Cost 1	2.32	.54	.06	.03	97.62	.89
Baseline 3	3.74	.16	1.62	.10	69.75	2.15
Social + Tokens + Cost 2	2.58	.69	.03	.02	98.72	.48
Fade-out Week 1 (80%)	2.25	.32	.03	.01	98.70	.48
Fade-out Week 2 (60%)	3.12	1.03	.05	.01	98.46	.57
Fade-out Week 3 (40%)	3.24	.69	.04	.01	98.81	.68
Fade-out Week 4 (20%)	2.93	.23	.04	.01	98.77	.44

In the remaining phases, we systematically evaluated the effects of praise alone and praise in combination with token reinforcement and cost contingency. Inspection of Figure A.4 indicates that neither praise alone nor praise in combination with token reinforcement proved effective in controlling negative-aggressive behavior and in substantively increasing positive social interactions. In fact, praise alone seemed to increase rates of negative-aggressive behavior initially. Social combined with tokens increased positive interactions initially but the effect proved ephemeral. Only when negative-aggressive behavior was consequated *directly* with cost contingency was there a powerful, durable effect on the students' overall social, interactive behavior. Furthermore, in the phases in which cost contingency was in effect, negative-aggressive behavior was virtually eliminated and was well within the normal range, as defined by normative peer data.

During the one-month follow-up, there appeared to be a slight accelerating trend for positive social interactions for the target students, but this trend was no longer evident at three- and six-month follow-up periods. Data recorded at these, more distal, post-intervention time points indicated that the behavioral levels of the target students approximated those during the preintervention, baseline phase recorded in the referral setting.

Table A.7 contains phase means and standard deviations for the Group I students for (1) positive interaction rate, (2) negative-aggressive interaction rate, and (3) percentage of positive interactions. These statistics are presented for target students and peers in the referral school and for target students in all experimental class, baseline, and intervention phases. These data indicate that (1) the combination of social, tokens, and cost contingency had a very powerful effect in reducing negative-aggressive interaction rates, (2) there appeared to be a strong spillover effect on positive interaction rate associated with this reduction, and (3) the overall percentage of positive interactions showed a substantial increase during the phases in which cost contingency was combined with social and tokens.

Figure A.5 presents observational data and results for Group II. As noted, this experiment was designed to replicate results of those phases for Group I in which the combination of social, tokens, and cost contingency was in effect. The study also examined the extent to which the daily number of points could be gradually reduced without affecting behavioral levels (students were not informed of these changes).

Figure A.5 indicates that a very powerful treatment effect was achieved when the combination of social, tokens, and cost contingency was introduced. We removed this combination for a two-day period and then reinstated it to establish a causal relationship between the intervention and the subjects' interactive behavior. During the next three weeks, in which the full intervention was in effect, negative-aggressive behavior was virtually removed from the subjects' behavioral repertoires. The fading phase indicated that daily point totals could be gradually reduced to 20% of their prior levels over a four-week period without changing the students' behavior.

Upon initial return to their referral schools, maintenance levels for the target students were substantial; however, they began to show signs of deterioration about halfway through the month-long, initial follow-up period. Follow-up into the next school year indicated that these effects did not last over the long-term.

Table A.8 contains means and standard deviations for Group II in the referral school and experimental class. As with Group I, exposure to the combination of social, tokens, and cost contingency produced a powerful treatment effect whenever it was implemented. Overall, Group II students had a higher rate of positive social interactions across all study phases, while their negative-aggressive rate was much more similar to that of Group I students. Their responses to the presence and absence of the intervention procedures were nearly identical.

TABLE A.9 One-Month Follow-Up Measures of Experimental Subjects and Their Peers in Referral Classrooms

	GROUP I					
	RATE OF POSITIVE INTERACTIONS		RATE OF NEGATIVE INTERACTIONS		PERCENTAGE POSITIVE INTERACTIONS	
	Mean	*SD*	*Mean*	*SD*	*Mean*	*SD*
Subjects combined	.50	.15	.08	.04	86.00	6.61
Peers combined	.38	.14	.01	.01	97.00	1.50

	GROUP II					
	RATE OF POSITIVE INTERACTIONS		RATE OF NEGATIVE INTERACTIONS		PERCENTAGE POSITIVE INTERACTIONS	
	Mean	*SD*	*Mean*	*SD*	*Mean*	*SD*
Subjects combined	.82	.33	.09	.08	90.11	5.59
Peers combined	.51	.07	.04	.04	92.73	6.72

Table A.9 provides means and standard deviations for target students and their peers in the one-month follow-up period. Follow-up behavioral observations were conducted on both target students and their peers immediately following reintegration into the referral classroom. As the follow-up summary data in Table A.9 indicate, both subject groups were moved substantially closer to their peer-group levels in terms of their overall percentage of positive interactions—presumably as a result of their exposure to the intervention procedures in the experimental classroom. However, these effects did not maintain over the long-term (that is, at three- and six-month follow-up intervals), thus replicating the empirical literature that indicates that it is extremely difficult to produce behavioral changes in an intervention setting and expect spontaneous or subsequent generalization of them to nonintervention settings.

Comment

A number of investigators have examined the role of positive-only, negative-only, and combined positive and negative approaches to behavioral interventions. As a general rule, results of these investigations indicate that combined positive and negative approaches produce superior and more powerful effects than positive-alone or negative-alone approaches (Shores, Gunter, & Jack, 1993). For example, Rosen, O'Leary, Joyce, Conway, and Pfiffner (1984) found that a positive-only approach was not effective when applied to the behavioral repertoires of hyperactive students. Similarly, Pfiffner, Rosen, and O'Leary (1985) investigated the efficacy of positive-alone versus positive and negative procedures in combination and found clearly superior effects for the latter procedure. Finally, Pfiffner and O'Leary (1987) found that the addition of negative consequences (mild reprimands) to enhanced positive reinforcement procedures (praise and stars exchanged for back-up rewards) produced an immediate increase in on-task behavior and accuracy of academic performance. These authors demonstrated that, following gradual fading of the negative consequences, the behavioral levels of their subjects could be maintained successfully through the use of positive-only procedures.

Pfiffner et al. (1984) make the case that children and youth with oppositional behavior disorders probably need positive *and* negative procedures together in order to assist them in acquiring adaptive behavior patterns or learning new classroom or playground rules. However, once the acquisition process is complete, previously acquired academic and behavioral gains can be maintained without applying negative consequences. All research conducted by the senior author and his associates confirm these findings for severely aggressive and acting-out students (Walker, Hops, & Fiegenbaum, 1976; Walker & Hops, 1993).

The results of the current investigation provide strong replications of the findings by Pfiffner and others (see Shores, Gunter, & Jack, 1993 for a recent review). Social praise alone was found to be extremely ineffective in promoting positive interactions among subjects. In fact, the rate of *negative* social interactions nearly doubled over baseline levels during the social 1 phase (see Table A.7). When paired with social praise, token reinforcement procedures proved to be initially effective, but these results did not persist. It was hypothesized that during this phase, students could earn and accumulate sufficient tokens over successive days to exchange points for the least expensive back-up reinforcers from the reward menu. Thus, it was not necessary to maintain a higher level of responding in this phase in order to secure access to the available reinforcers; it only required patience. However, with the addition of cost contingency, whose application involved a considerable response cost (that is, a 2:1 ratio) to the students for engaging in negative or aggressive social behavior, there was an immediate and persistent increase in positive interaction rate and a corresponding decline in negative interaction rate. The withdrawal and subsequent reintroduction of cost contingency established its causal role in this regard.

Experimental results with Group II proved that the combination of social praise, tokens, and cost contingency was an extremely powerful intervention in reducing negative-aggressive behavior among antisocial students. Furthermore, it was possible to fade substantially the number of tokens (points) available daily and still maintain high levels of positive interactive behavior. These results suggest that, once established, high levels of appropriate behavior can be maintained with a much reduced and less costly variation of the original, full intervention procedures. It is likely that by this point in the intervention process, the students' positive social behavior was not being substantially maintained or supported by the point system.

For both Groups I and II, generalization and maintenance effects were short-lived upon return to the referral setting. As the empirical literature has demonstrated, producing such effects requires considerable behavioral engineering and transition planning (Morgan & Jenson, 1988).

The intervention model developed and evaluated in this investigation produced powerful effects that were specific to an experimental class setting. However, these results set the stage for a series of investigations in regular classrooms and playgrounds in which these procedures were successfully adapted for use with highly aggressive children. These studies and their results are described in Exhibits 10 and 11. They provided an important conceptual and empirical foundation for development of the final prototype version of the RECESS program for remediating aggressive behavior in schools (Walker & Hops, 1993).

EXHIBIT 10: APPLICATION OF REINFORCEMENT AND RESPONSE COST IN REDUCING NEGATIVE-AGGRESSIVE SOCIAL INTERACTIONS IN REGULAR CLASSROOMS

Preface

As part of the research and development process for the RECESS program for K–3 aggressive children, Walker and his associates (Walker, Hops, & Greenwood, 1981) conducted a series of experiments in regular classroom and playground settings. Intervention components of social praise, token reinforcement, and response cost were adapted for use in regular school settings. A combination of group and individual contingencies was used to deliver the reinforcement procedures. Fading procedures were also evaluated as part of these experiments. Multiple-baseline designs across subjects and periods were used to establish causal relationships between the intervention procedures and observed changes on the dependent measures used.

Three experiments are reported involving five highly aggressive students enrolled in the primary grades. In Experiment I, two aggressive boys (Paegan and Chuck), who had been referred by their regular teachers, were exposed to a multicomponent, full program during a daily 30-minute activity period in the regular classroom. A 30-minute, no-treatment generalization period immediately followed the intervention period. This study involved eight sequential phases: baseline; full program; generalization bonus; fading phases 1, 2, and 3; praise only; and follow-up (see Figure A.6). Experiment II provided an intersubject replication study of the effects of Experiment I involving two aggressive students (Robert and Gregory). As with Experiment I, a multiple-baseline design across subjects was used to establish causal relations. Experiment II consisted of six sequential phases: baseline, full program, free points plus response cost, generalization, bonus, fading and postintervention (no treatment). Experiment III involved one student (David) and used a multiple-baseline design across periods (homeroom, math, and playground during recess). This study had seven phases: baseline; full program; free points plus response cost; fading 1, 2, and 3; and postintervention (no treatment).

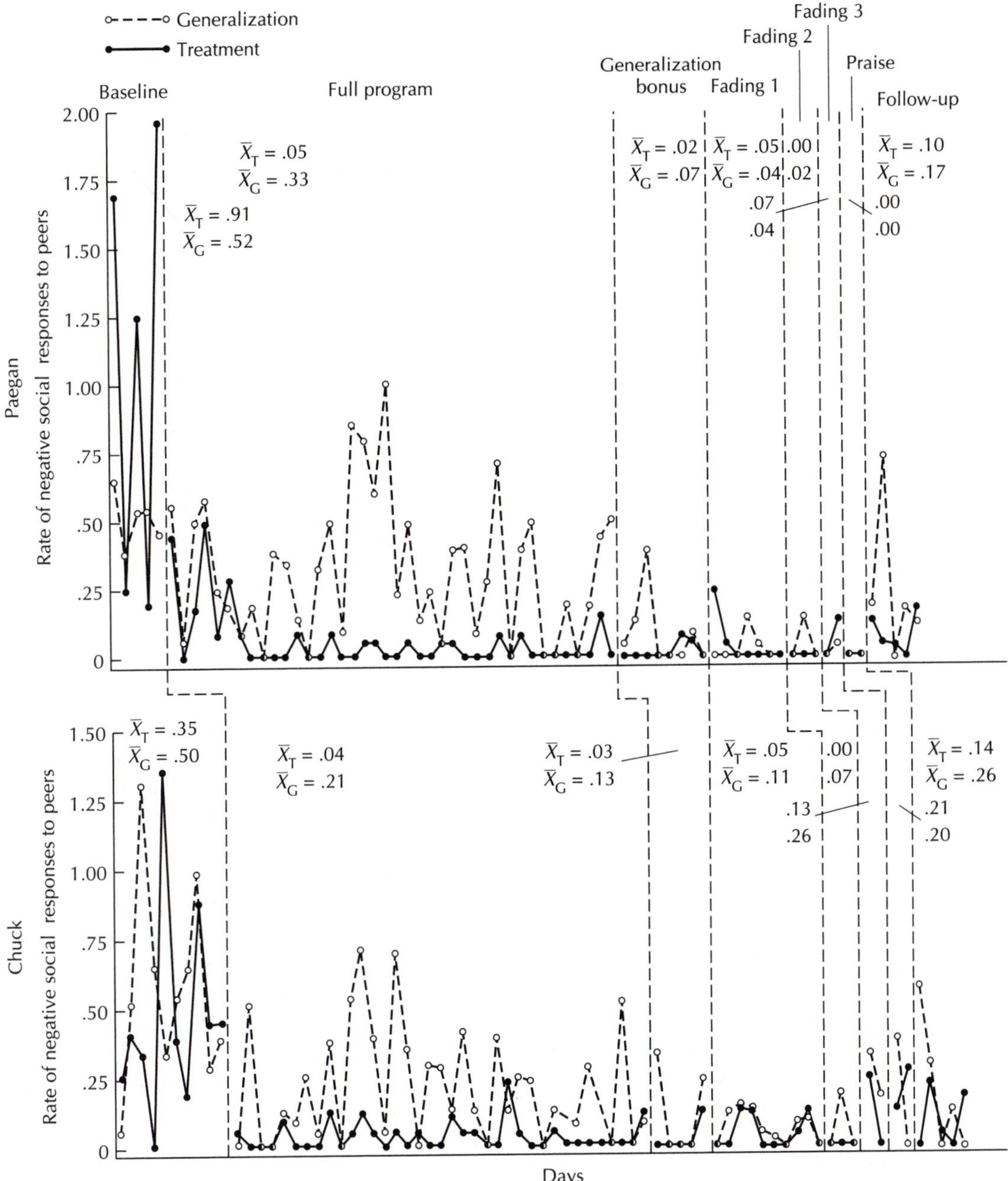

FIGURE A.6 Experiment I: Paegan and Chuck—Rate of Negative Social Responses to Peers ($\bar{X}$ = average rate of negative social responses, T = treatment period, and G = generalization period)

The generalization bonus phase provided an incentive for students to match their intervention levels in the activity (treatment) phase with equivalent behavioral levels during the generalization period that immediately followed. The free points plus response cost phase involved a shift from students earning points for positive interactive behavior and losing them for negative-aggressive behavior to having points awarded noncontingently at the start of the period (one point for each 5 minutes) and losing them whenever instances of negative-aggressive behavior occurred. Fading involved a gradual reduction in the number of points that could be earned daily.

Students in these experiments could earn social praise and points, on an intermittent basis, for engaging in positive, socially appropriate, interactive behavior. Behavior-specific praise always preceded awarding of the points for reinforceable instances of the target behavior. If the target student met the reward criterion, a group activity was earned and shared with the entire class later in the day; if not, the student could keep the points that were earned and accumulate them toward an individual home reward.

The rate of negative and positive responses was recorded by professionally trained observers across experimental phases.

Results

Figure A.6 presents results of the intervention for Paegan and Chuck (Experiment I). The data are plotted and graphed across phases by treatment and generalization periods, which were recorded daily. The average negative rate per phase is also presented by treatment and generalization periods.

Introduction of the full intervention procedure was associated with a substantial reduction in the negative response rate for both subjects. Over the six-week, full intervention period, the negative response rate was consistently lower in both treatment and generalization periods than during the no treatment, baseline phase. The generalization bonus phase was designed to reduce the remaining discrepancy between the generalization and treatment periods. The addition of this contingency, which remained in effect throughout the fading periods, appeared to be generally successful; however, it proved to be relatively more effective for Chuck than for Paegan. The fading of points and major program components were tolerated better by Paegan than Chuck, whose performance began showing some deterioration in the second fading phase. During the immediate, postintervention follow-up period, the students' behavioral levels were higher than during the generalization bonus and fading phases, but approximated those that occurred during the full implementation phase.

The results of this study were generally encouraging. The intervention produced a relatively powerful reduction of negative-aggressive behavior and showed evidence of generalization to an immediately following, no treatment, activity period. The fading procedure used was only partially successful in maintaining full intervention behavioral levels. A decision was made to replicate this study with another pair of aggressive subjects using a similar, multiple-baseline design across subjects.

Figure A.7 contains results of the replication experiment for Robert and Gregory (Experiment II). The intervention was extremely effective in reducing negative-

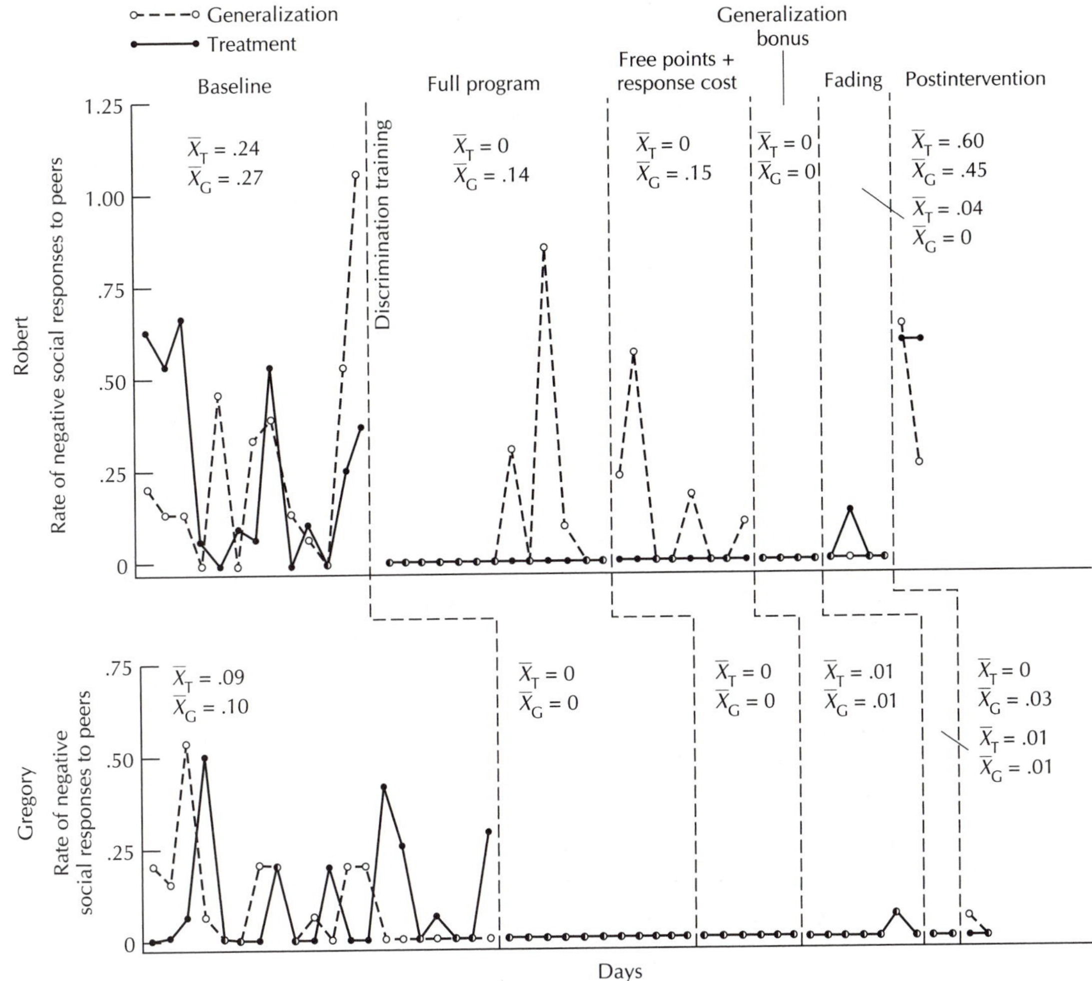

FIGURE A.7 Experiment II: Robert and Gregory—Rate of Negative Social Responses to Peers ($\overline{X}$ = average rate of negative social responses, T = treatment period, and G = generalization period)

aggressive behavior for both students, virtually eliminating it during the treatment period. Robert's performance showed evidence of discriminated responding between treatment and generalization periods while Gregory's did not. Gregory's performance was consistent across all study phases following introduction of full intervention. Although Robert responded well during the treatment period across all study phases, he showed no maintenance effects and his performance during the generalization period was erratic and unpredictable from session to session.

To provide yet another replication of the intervention procedures, we conducted a third study involving a multiple-baseline design across periods (homeroom, recess, and math seatwork) for one student, David. Results of this study are presented in Figure A.8.

The results of this experiment indicate that the full intervention produced a powerful and immediate treatment effect whenever it was introduced. The coincidence of behavior change with exposure to the intervention established its causal role in all three intervention settings. Following its introduction, the rate of negative-aggressive responses was reduced to and maintained at near-zero levels during treatment periods. However, generalization effects were sporadic and more difficult to predict. The fading procedures were generally effective in maintaining low levels of negative-aggressive responses while reducing or eliminating program components.

Comment

These experiments were valuable in illustrating the efficacy of the intervention procedures, providing information on key implementation issues and successfully adapting the procedures for effective use in regular classroom and playground settings. Clear evidence of strong intervention effects was generated, but evidence in support of spontaneous, unprogrammed generalization effects was weak. These results led to the design of a playground intervention in which a low-cost variation of the response cost procedure was evaluated in a multiple-baseline design across recess periods. The purpose of this study was to devise methods for maximizing the intervention power of response cost while making its delivery as efficient as possible within regular school settings. This experiment is reported in Exhibit 11.

EXHIBIT 11: THE EFFICACY OF A RESPONSE COST INTERVENTION IN INCREASING POSITIVE SOCIAL INTERACTIONS IN FREE-PLAY SETTINGS

Preface

Playground interventions must have certain attributes in order to be successful. They must: (1) be relatively easy to implement, (2) have sufficient power to effect behavior change in a complex, uncontrolled setting, and (3) provide for the careful monitoring and consequation of the target behavior. Previous experiences suggested that a response cost intervention would meet these intervention requirements.

The senior author and his associates designed an intervention in which the target student was awarded (noncontingently) one point for each 5 minutes of recess at the beginning of the recess period. Points were then subtracted for rule infractions and for each instance of negative-aggressive social behavior (verbal, physical, or gestural) that occurred during the period. If all points were lost during a given recess period and the student's behavior required the application of response cost, the student sat out the re-

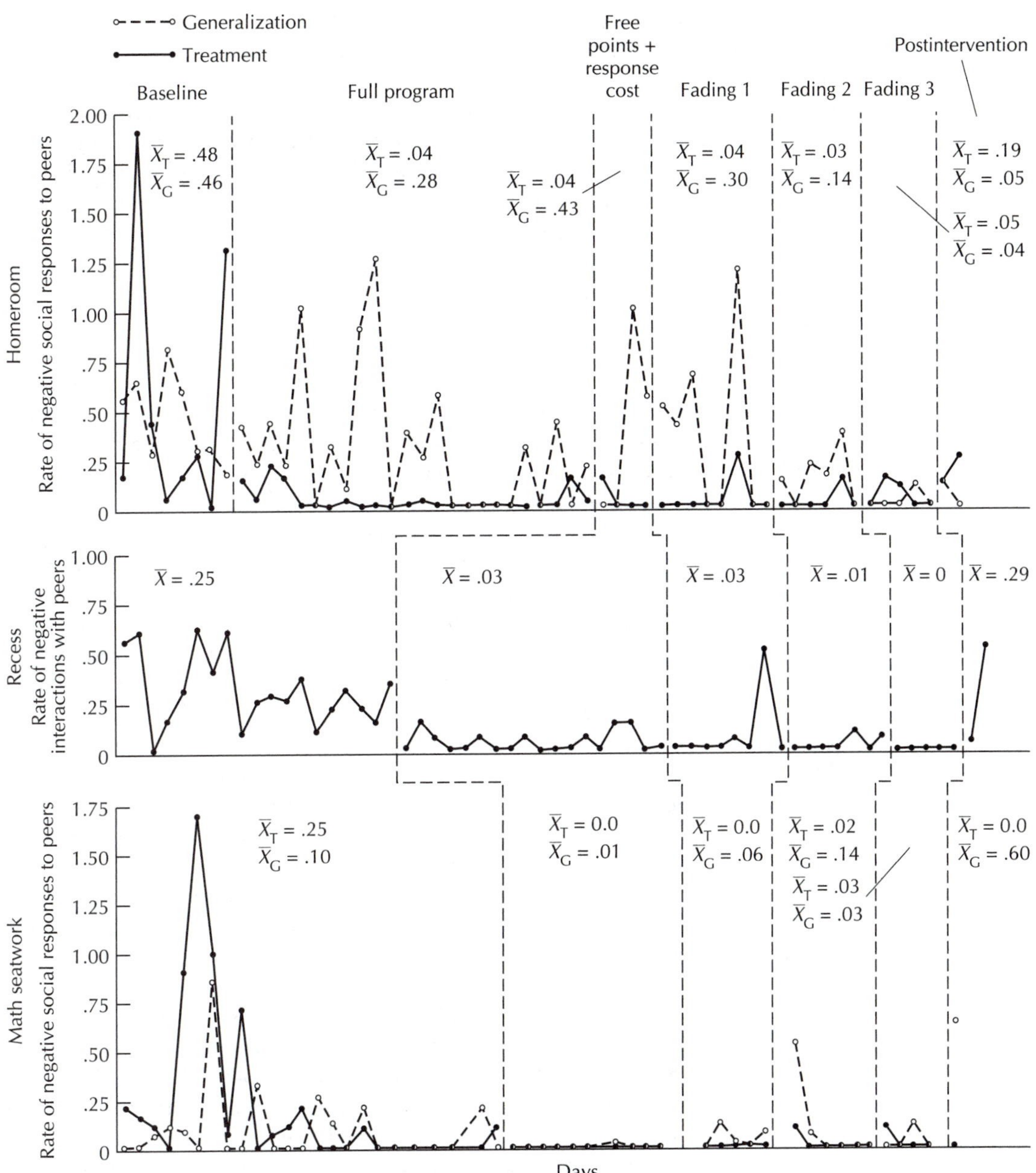

FIGURE A.8 Experiment III: David—Rate per Minute of Negative Social Responses to Peers (*upper and lower panels*) and Negative Social Interactions with Peers (*middle panel*) ($\bar{X}$ = average rate of negative social response, *T* = treatment period, and *G* = generalization period)

mainder of that recess. If no more than two points were lost in two of the three daily recesses, a group-activity reward was made available at the end of the school day that was shared by the target student and all classmates. If the target student failed to earn the group reward, he or she could exchange whatever points were retained across the three daily recess periods for movie tickets that could accumulate toward earning prearranged home rewards. Praise for instances of positive social behavior were given intermittently throughout each recess period and bonus points could be earned for outstanding examples of positive, cooperative behavior.

Results

Figure A.9 reports results of this experiment. This intervention proved to be relatively easy to implement and was highly effective in reducing negative-aggressive behavior and increasing positive, social interactions with peers. Once implemented, the intervention virtually eliminated negative-aggressive behavior for the target subject. In addition, there appeared to be some spillover from recess periods 1 and 2 to period 3. This partially compromised replication of the causal influence demonstrated for the intervention procedure in recess periods 1 and 2. Due to the elevated baseline level in the afternoon recess period, it was possible to demonstrate only a modest increase in performance following introduction of the intervention procedure (see Figure A.9). During the three fading phases, the intervention components were successfully reduced and eliminated while maintaining high levels of positive behavior. However, a return to baseline conditions in follow-up showed clear evidence of some behavioral decay.

There was no unequivocal evidence of generalization from the playground intervention to the classroom during the treatment and fading phases. However, inspection of the bottom graph in Figure A.9 suggests that there may have been some carryover effects of the playground intervention to the classroom, in which a daily sample of the target student's behavior was recorded during a teacher-led instructional activity. The more positive level of the target student's classroom behavior, beginning around program day 33, may represent playground spillover effects from the playground intervention; however, we are unable to verify this observation given the experimental design that was used in this study.

Following the baseline 2 phase, we implemented a low-cost variation of the intervention procedure designed to maintain the behavioral levels achieved during intervention. It involved daily, covert recording of the target student's behavioral level in a randomly selected daily recess. A stopwatch was used for this purpose and the recording process was not visible to the target student or peers. If the target student met the daily reward criterion in the target recess for four of five days each week, a group-activity reward was delivered at the end of the week. This variation of the intervention was highly effective in reestablishing behavioral levels obtained during the full program. Data for this second baseline phase are not shown in Figure A.9; however, this covert procedure reestablished approximately 80% of the target student's original behavioral level, as averaged over the full intervention period.

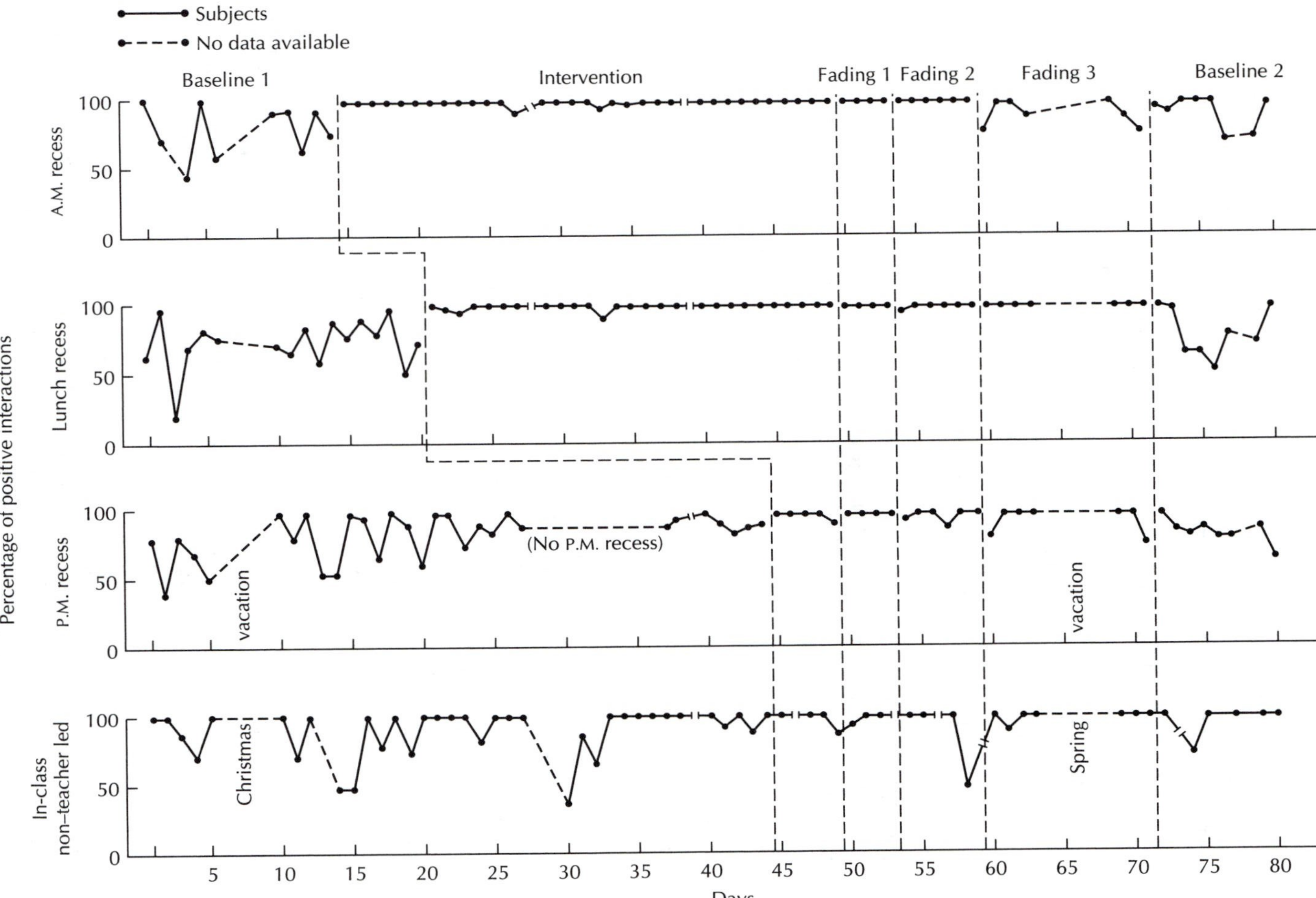

FIGURE A.9 Response Cost in Intervention in Playground Settings: Percentage of Positive Interactions

Comment

This intervention was highly successful and served as a prototype for the design of the RECESS program for negative-aggressive child behavior (Walker & Hops, 1993). The intervention was highly effective, yet of low cost to implementing agents (that is, behavioral consultants and playground supervisors). A more elaborate version of this intervention was successfully applied to ten aggressive students in a subsequent study using a multiple-baseline design across subjects. Across these ten students, their negative-aggressive rate was reduced from .69 during baseline to .04 during full program implementation. When the RECESS program consultant turned complete control of the program over to the recess supervisor, the negative-aggressive rate increased slightly and stabilized at .14. The average rate of negative-aggressive social responses for nonaggressive K–3 students in playground settings is approximately .11.

EXHIBIT 12: RESPONSE COST AND ITS REQUIRED FREQUENCY OF USE IN MAINTAINING BEHAVIORAL LEVELS OF STUDENTS

Preface

One of the advantages of adding mild reprimands or response cost to an intervention program containing positive contingencies is that their necessary frequency of use tends to decline over time. Pfiffner and her colleagues (Pfiffner & O'Leary, 1987; Pfiffner, Rosen, & O'Leary, 1985) found this to be the case with mild reprimands; they also found that it was possible to maintain behavioral gains effectively following a combined positive–negative intervention with primarily positive procedures.

As part of a larger study involving reduction of acting-out behavior in the classroom, Walker, Hops, and Fiegenbaum (1976) investigated the frequency with which it was necessary to use response cost within and across a group of severely acting-out, primary school students. Intervention occurred in a highly controlled experimental class to which the subjects were referred by their local schools for a period of approximately three months. Response cost was applied systematically to the following classes of maladaptive student behavior: talking back (−1), talking out (−1), not attending (−1), fighting or throwing objects (−4), swearing (−3), out of seat (−1), teacher defiance (−2), disturbing others (−1), and playing with objects (−1). Students were able to earn a maximum of approximately 35 points daily for appropriate academic and social behavior.

Daily records were kept of the number of points earned and lost by individual students ($N = 5$) for each target behavior to which response cost was applied.

Results

Results of the daily recordings are presented in Tables A.10 and A.11. The data in Table A.10 indicate that (1) the five students showed considerable variation in terms of the number of times response cost had to be applied to their maladaptive behavior, (2) the

TABLE A.10 Frequency of Response Cost per Student during Successive Days of Intervention

	DAY							
Student	*1*	*2*	*3*	*4*	*5*	*6*	*7*	*Total*
1	11	9	8	11	6	6	0	51
2	6	6	4	4	3	7	2	32
3	2	2	8	3	4	0	*	19
4	2	1	1	1	0	2	2	9
5	17	1	12	9	7	4	6	56
Total	38	19	33	28	20	19	10	167

*Absent

TABLE A.11 Frequency of Response Cost per Student for Each Target Behavior

	STUDENT					
Behavior	*1*	*2*	*3*	*4*	*5*	*Total*
Talk-outs	23	4	11	4	26	68
Not attending	9	10	2	2	9	32
Fighting	1	0	1	0	0	2
Swearing	0	0	0	0	0	0
Out of seat	1	0	0	1	3	5
Teacher defiance	4	1	3	0	0	8
Disturbing others	5	6	0	0	12	23
Playing with objects	8	11	2	2	6	29
Total	51	32	19	9	56	167
Daily average	7.28	4.57	3.16	1.28	8.00	

behavior of all five acting-out students came in contact with the contingency from day one of intervention, and (3) the frequency with which it was necessary to use response cost across the first seven days of intervention showed a steady decline. These data suggest that the combined positive and negative features of the intervention were powerful in teaching a more adaptive pattern of classroom behavior to these students. As a group, these five students averaged approximately 85% appropriate behavior during the first seven days of the intervention.

Table A.11 contains the total number of times response cost was applied for each student for each target behavior and the daily average that it was used per student during the first seven days of intervention in the experimental classroom. Response cost was never applied to swearing, but it was applied to talk-outs a total of 68 times over a seven-day period. The five students varied from 1.28 to 8.00 in the daily average with which response cost was applied to their behavior in the classroom.

Comment

These data reveal some important features about the use of response cost in reducing maladaptive student behavior. If response cost is applied correctly and consistently, it is likely that the necessity for its use will decline significantly over time, following acquisition of a more adaptive pattern of behavior. Furthermore, its presence has the effect of preventing the occurrence of maladaptive behavior that may have occurred previously at relatively high rates. In addition, these data indicate that students having the same levels of maladaptive behavior will vary considerably in the number of times their actual behavior has to be directly consequated by response cost before it is reduced and stabilizes at reduced levels. Finally, the number of times that response cost has to be applied to specific target behaviors is a function both of the behavior's relative frequency of occurrence and its resistance to punishing consequences. These are, in turn, established by the reinforcement and punishment histories associated with each target behavior.

The results of this study again highlight some of the benefits of response cost as a mild form of punishment when used in combination with positive reinforcement to reduce maladaptive classroom behavior. It is particularly noteworthy that many acting-out and aggressive students will maintain levels of appropriate behavior with relatively low frequencies of response cost application.

EXHIBIT 13: EXTERNAL REPLICATIONS OF THE RECESS PROGRAM FOR AGGRESSIVE STUDENTS

Preface

Fowler and her associates (Dougherty, Fowler, & Paine, 1985; Fowler, Dougherty, Kirby, & Kohler, 1986) used the RECESS program as a vehicle for investigating peer-monitoring and self-control procedures among elementary school–age students. These studies, by independent investigators, provided powerful, external replications of the effectiveness and versatility of RECESS for reducing negative-aggressive peer interactions. Two of these studies and their respective results are described here.

Dougherty et al. (1985) investigated the efficacy of the RECESS program with a mildly retarded child (Dennis) during daily recess periods. Substantial reductions in this student's negative interactions were maintained during the initial implementation of RECESS. These reductions were maintained when peer-monitoring and self-monitoring were implemented in subsequent morning recesses. In the afternoon recess, peer monitors were used to reduce the student's negative interactions. Finally, in the noon recess, the target student was appointed as a peer monitor for a moderately developmentally disabled classmate (Ed). The target student's negative interaction rate was quickly reduced following his appointment as a peer monitor.

In this study, peer monitors essentially served as behavioral consultants in monitoring and implementing the RECESS program in the same way as adult, behavioral consultants do. Their implementation behavior, however, was carefully monitored and supervised by the authors of this study.

Results

Results for the target subject (Dennis) and his moderately retarded peer (Ed) are presented in Figures A.10 and A.11. The data in these figures not only powerfully replicate intervention effects attributable to the RECESS program but also demonstrate the efficacy and cost effectiveness of self- and peer-monitoring procedures in maintaining behavioral gains following intensive intervention. These findings are especially important for implementing procedures in free-play, recess settings where the ratio of adult supervisors to children is extremely low.

In a subsequent study, Fowler et al. (1986) extended these findings further with three disruptive 7-year-old boys who had no other handicapping conditions. Fowler et al. investigated the efficacy of the following conditions: *adult monitor* (an adult implements the RECESS program), *peer monitor* (target student serves as the implementor of the RECESS program), and *monitored by peers* (target students' peers operate the program).

Results for this study are presented in Figure A.12. They indicate that all three conditions were highly effective in changing or maintaining the target students' positive, social interactions with peers.

Comment

These studies significantly extend the utility, efficacy, and external validity of the RECESS program. They are especially valuable in demonstrating how an abundant resource, peers, can be trained to serve as effective agents for behavioral change in natural settings. Furthermore, these investigators demonstrated that serving as a monitor–manager of the social behavior of others has a positive effect on the behavior of the monitor–manager. Finally, a child with cognitive impairments was able both to respond to the RECESS program and to successfully apply some of its monitoring components to the behavior of a peer.

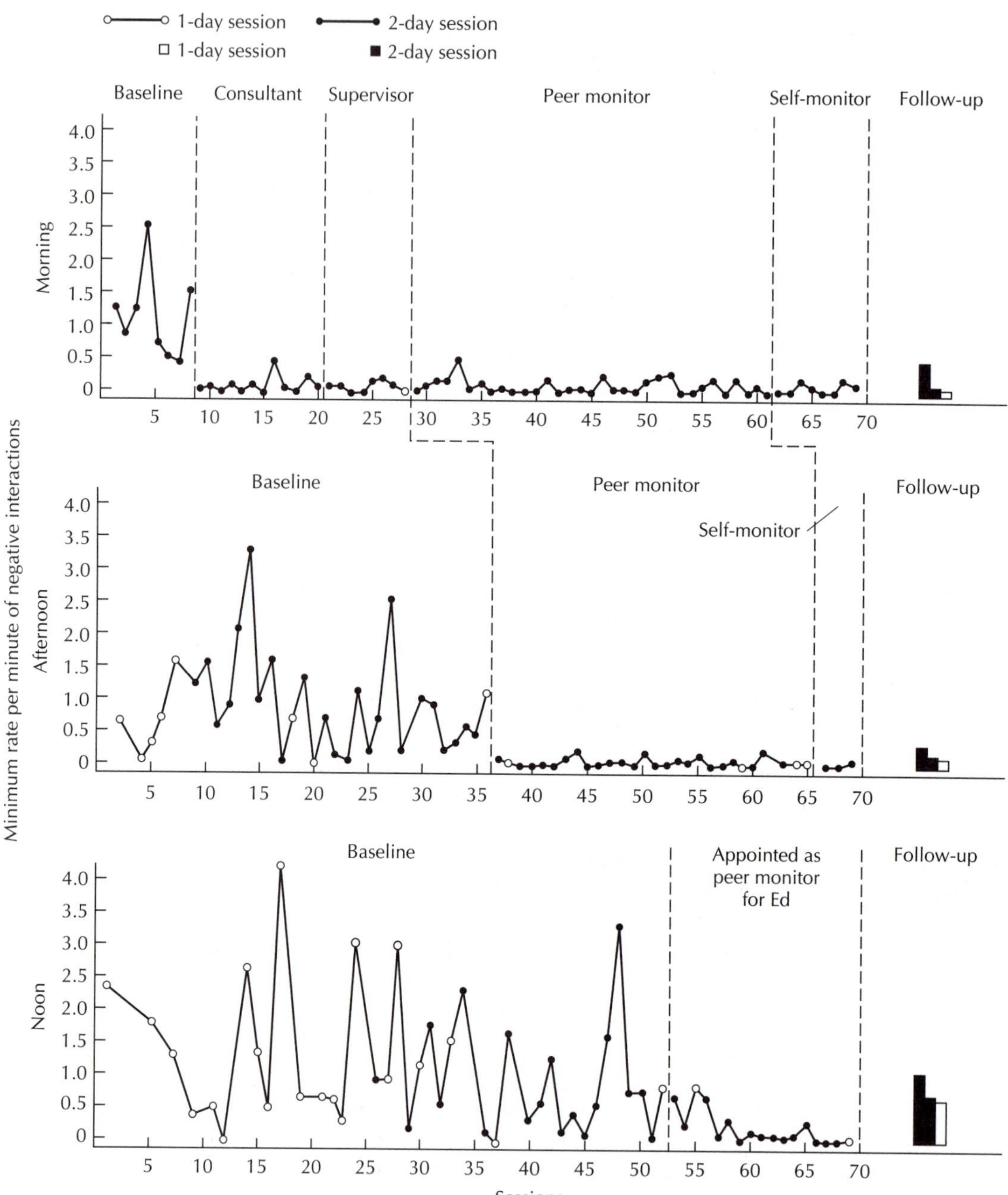

FIGURE A.10 Minimum Rate per Minute of Negative Interactions Exhibited by Dennis. Closed dots represent an average of two sessions; open dots represent one session. Follow-up sessions are represented by histograms: Shaded histograms represent 2-day sessions; open histogram represents one-day session. *Source:* From "The Use of Peer Monitors to Reduce Negative Interactions during Recess," by B. S. Dougherty, S. A. Fowler, and S. C. Paine. In *Journal of Applied Behavior Analysis, 18,* 1985, 141–153. Reprinted by permission.

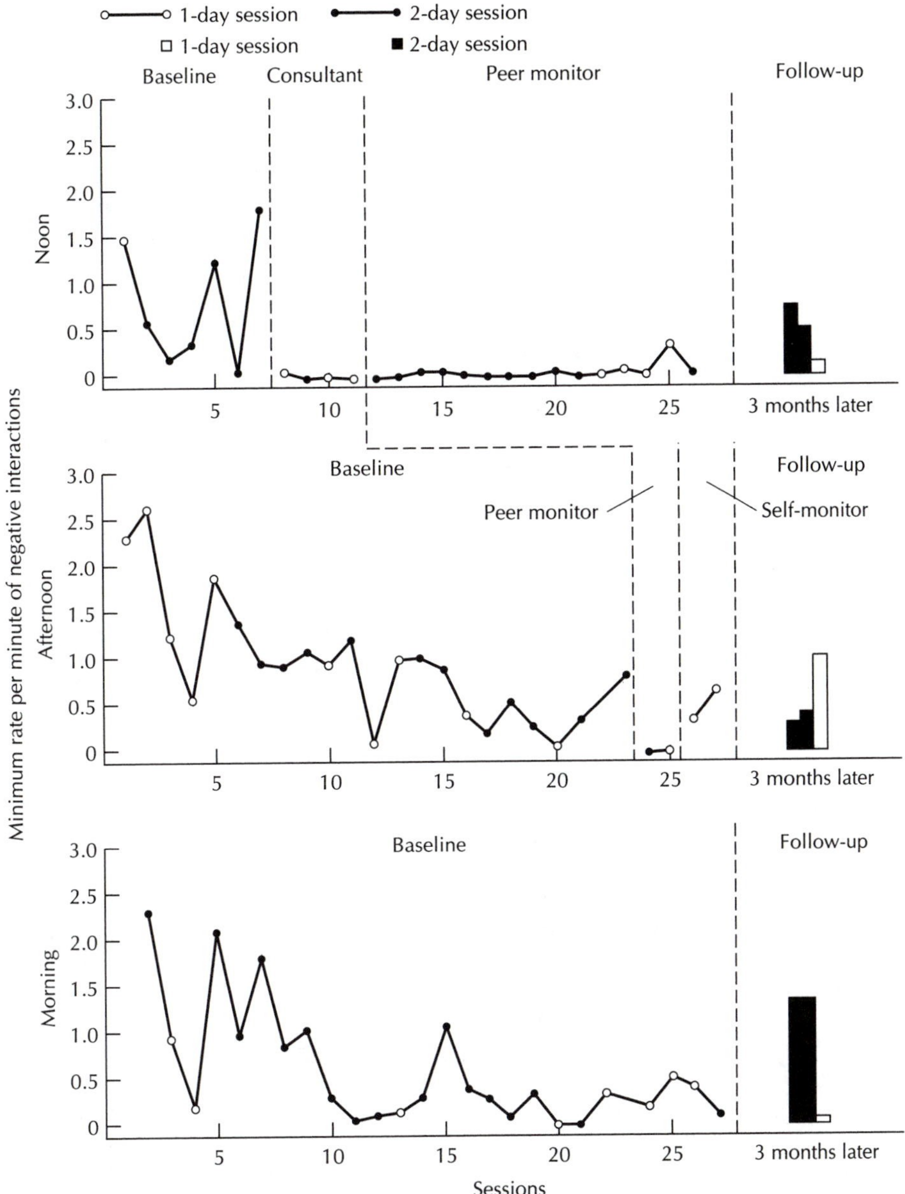

FIGURE A.11 Minimum Rate per Minute of Negative Interactions Exhibited by Ed. Closed dots represent an average of two sessions; open dots represent one session. Follow-up sessions are represented by histograms: Shaded histograms represent 2-day sessions; open histogram represents one-day session.
Source: From "The Use of Peer Monitors to Reduce Negative Interactions during Recess," by B. S. Dougherty, S. A. Fowler, and S. C. Paine. In *Journal of Applied Behavior Analysis, 18,* 1985, 141–153. Reprinted by permission.

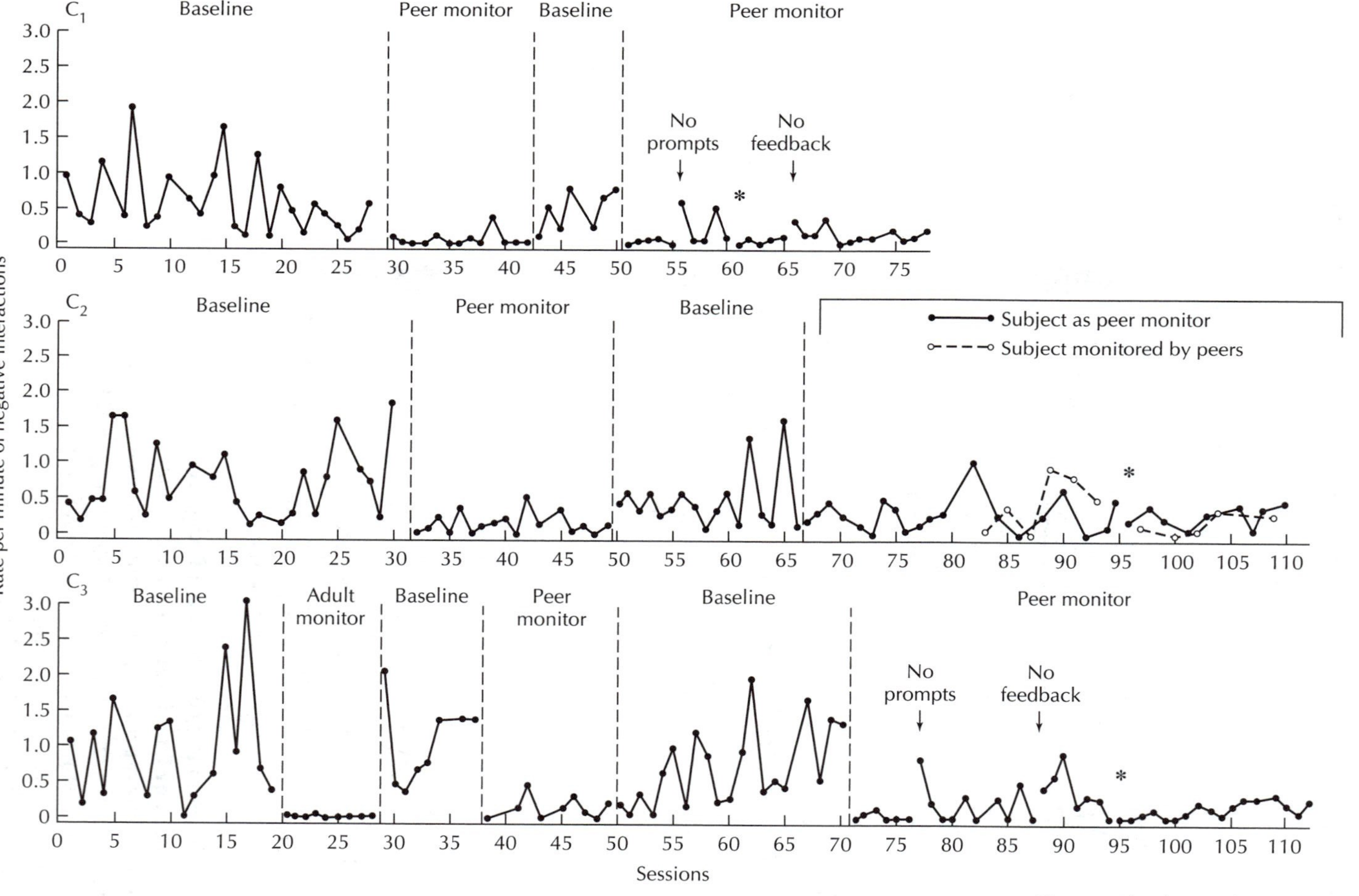

*Peer monitor in morning recess

FIGURE A.12 Minimum Rate per Minute of Negative Interactions Using Adult Monitoring, Peer Monitoring, and Monitoring by Peers. *Source:* From "The Use of Peer Monitors to Reduce Negative Interactions during Recess," by B. S. Dougherty, S. A. Fowler, and S. C. Paine. In *Journal of Applied Behavior Analysis, 18,* 1985, 141–153. Reprinted by permission.

APPENDIX B

The Case of Judge Hargreaves: Society Is Failing Its Children, Forsaking Its Future

Juveniles: Our culture is going to have to change the way it thinks about and reacts to its problems, a judge says.

In 1993 in juvenile court in Lane County, there were 395 petitions filed to protect abused and neglected children. If it had not been for severe budget constraints imposed on the state Children's Services Division, which files most of these petitions, the number would have been much larger. The petitions filed represent a response to only the very worst cases.

In 1993 in Juvenile Court, there were 465 petitions filed charging juveniles with crimes. Almost all were for felony-level crimes. In ad petitions the number of petitions filed represented only a small percentage of the felony charges referred to the Juvenile Department by police agencies. There simply are not enough intake workers, counselors, staff, beds in the detention facility or programs to deal with any more.

WHERE ARE WE GOING?

An absolutely staggering number of children, beginning as early as age 3, 4 or 5, are being physically or sexually abused by a parent or the partner of a parent. When this abuse comes to light within the family unit, commonly no professional help is sought and no effective action is taken to help the child deal with the experience. In addition, in most cases, no effective action is taken to deal with the abuser, who simply moves on to another relationship and abuses other children.

Boys, and a growing number of girls—12, 13, 14, 15 years old—are being charged with raping, sodomizing or otherwise sexually abusing their brothers, sisters, cousins or

---

From "Society Is Failing Its Children, Forsaking Its Future," by James Hargreaves. In Eugene *Register-Guard,* Sunday, April 10, 1994, page 1B. Reprinted by permission.

neighbors. Many of these kids sit for months in detention waiting for a bed to become available in the few residential facilities available around the state. Many more continue in the community in their own homes or the homes of friends or relatives while receiving long-term treatment. These young people represent a significant risk to the community and most would not be in the community if treatment alternatives were available.

WHERE ARE WE GOING?

During the last five years, on the average, at least one petition every two weeks was filed with the court because a baby was born drug-addicted or drug-affected. The first of the wave of drug-affected babies has now reached school age. Their lack of impulse control and other deficits often require special classes and teachers, as well as intensive personal attention, to attempt to control their behavior and meet their educational needs.

On almost a daily basis, the Juvenile Court must deal with families where children have to be placed in some sort of foster or shelter care because the drug or alcohol use of one or both of the parents is at such a level that they cannot provide a safe home. At the same time, the waiting period for an opening in a treatment program that may be able to help these people control their addiction and resume the role of parent is frequently many months long. Often, just to stay on the waiting list the person is expected to call in on a weekly basis. Expecting someone addicted to follow up in this fashion is unrealistic.

WHERE ARE WE GOING?

Over the last five years, the number of armed robberies, assaults and other serious crimes committed by teenagers in Lane County has grown rapidly, in some crime categories as much as 100 percent. At the same time, we have had to reduce by about one-half the number of juveniles held in secure detention in the county and at the State Training School. At the State Training School, for every new child admitted, one must be released. The same situation is common at the county level.

At any given time, we have about 400 children in foster homes in Lane County. They are there because their parents cannot or will not create a safe environment in their own homes. Within the last few months, the Children's Services Division had to hold a special "media event" to draw attention to the fact that additional foster parents were desperately needed.

We have a number of programs in the area that have demonstrated their effectiveness in teaching people to become better parents and, through that process, have created safer environments for hundreds of children. Unfortunately, the number of families who need and want the help that these programs can provide far exceeds the capacity of the programs. The number of families on waiting lists is often in the hundreds.

WHERE ARE WE GOING?

I can keep giving examples of the problems that we in Lane County face in relation to children and families almost indefinitely. I can keep asking, "Where are we going?" The thing that I can't do is answer the question. I don't know the answer to the question because I don't know how long we as a society are going to be willing to keep going along this path. The one thing that I do know is that the path we are following is not taking us anywhere that I want to be!

So, how did we get into this mess and how do we get out of it?

It is my belief that the main reason we got into this mess is that, as a society, we put our emphasis on reacting to problems that could no longer be ignored rather than trying to prevent the problems or deal with them when they were small. Let me give a couple of examples.

I stated earlier that in delinquency matters, we are dealing almost exclusively with kids committing serious felonies and don't have the resources left over to deal with those committing less serious offenses. The problem is, very few of these kids start getting into trouble by committing serious felonies. Most who commit serious felonies start small and work their way up.

There was a time, 15 or 20 years ago, when we had the ability to deal with kids who were committing relatively minor offenses. The number being referred to the Juvenile Department for criminal behavior was much lower. The level of seriousness of crimes being committed by juveniles was also much lower. Funding at both the state and local level was more adequate to allow for a response to both major and minor criminal activity. Then several things happened.

In 1985, the Legislature decided that it would be a good idea for the counties to deal with more delinquents in the community, rather than having them committed to the State Training School. As a part of putting this idea into practice, the Legislature set a limit of 513 on the population of the Training School. This was a reduction of 237 beds. To help work with these more difficult kids in the community, the Legislature was going to provide the counties with additional funds. The kids stayed in the community. Very little money ever arrived.

In the first half of the decade of the '80s, Lane County's economy fell on hard times, led by the decline of the timber industry. The general fund budget for Lane County dropped sharply because of the loss of . . . revenue from the decreased timber harvest. During that time, major budget cuts resulted in substantial reductions in both staff and programs within the Juvenile Department. Those reductions have never been restored. In fact, further cuts have been made, including a $200,000 reduction in the latest budget. The staff of the Juvenile Department is now about 60 percent of what it was in 1980.

Following rapidly on the heels of these budget cuts of the 1980s and the reduction of bed space at the Training School came an ever-accelerating increase in both the amount and seriousness of juvenile crime. Much has been written about the reasons for this dramatic change. For the moment, it is enough to say that this increase in juvenile crime is real, it is continuing and it has forced a difficult choice to be made.

The choice was between trying to provide immediate community protection from the largest number of the most serious offenders, or taking a longer range approach by putting more of the limited resources into early intervention to help reduce the number who reach the level of serious crime. Given the magnitude of danger to the community and the resources available, it is hard to fault the decision that evolved: that immediate community protection was more important than long-term prevention.

If we put a lot of effort into dealing with kids at the early stages of their involvement with the law, I do not know anyone who works with the problem who is not convinced that we could substantially reduce the number who go on to commit felonies. Unfortunately, we are so heavily invested in dealing with the kids who are committing serious felonies, we can't deal with those at a level in which we have a better chance of success.

We are trapped. We can't take the services away from the kids committing serious felonies and lower the level of community protection, and there is no more money to provide services to prevent them from eventually committing serious felonies. Dealing only with the kids who are committing serious felonies is not reducing juvenile crime. It is not even slowing the rate of increase. It will only be when we add prevention through early intervention that we will begin to stem the rising tide of juvenile crime.

With kids who are abused or neglected, the system has developed along much the same lines. We have reacted to the biggest or worst problems and have not put sufficient effort into identifying and resolving problems before they reach major proportions. Again, we are trapped. By making the decision to use limited resources to react only to the worst problems, we have left little to deal with prevention. Until we have both effective prevention and reaction systems in place, the tide will continue to rise.

As the tide of abused and neglected children continues to rise, it feeds the growing pool of young people who resort to crime to display their anger, frustration and lack of caring for themselves and others. This pool of delinquent youth in turn becomes a breeding ground for the plague of adult crime afflicting our country.

How do we get from our current position of dealing with the problem from what I see as the back end to dealing with it from the front end?

I know that there are those who would say that the answer is simple. Lock up more kids for longer periods when they commit crimes. If parents abuse or neglect their children, take the children away. If we did this enough, people would get the message and change the way they behave.

Here are just a few of the things wrong with that approach:

- The expense to house and care for all of the children that would be affected would be staggering.
- We already incarcerate adults and children at a rate higher than any other country in the Western world, and our crime rates have not declined.
- Taking children away instead of trying to teach people how to be better parents will create a huge segment of society that has not grown up in a family setting and whose members are even less prepared to be parents themselves than were their parents.
- There is simply no evidence to suggest that such an approach has any setting affect on others, beyond the child or family directly involved.

Doing more of the same things that have gotten us to where we are seems unlikely to produce positive change. Indeed, some say that one definition of insanity is doing the same thing the same way 20 times, and getting the same results each time, and then doing it the 21st time and expecting a different result.

I submit that long-range plans must be developed at both the state and county levels for making this transition. These plans must carry with them substantial increases in funds committed to prevention. That funding must continue until the combination of prevention and reaction reduces the number of serious problems that occur. As the number of serious problems that call for reaction is reduced, money can be diverted to prevention.

I suggest that to accomplish this transition will require some radical changes in a number of societal norms.

One radical change must be in the way that the Legislature and the governing bodies of the counties relate. They will have to demonstrate unprecedented cooperation and coordination to produce integrated plans. Without consensus and a unified approach at both state and local levels, nothing will be accomplished. With the diversity of Oregon's 36 counties, this will be a particularly difficult challenge.

Once the Legislature and the governing bodies of the counties adopt plans, they will have to leave them alone for a substantial number of years to allow them to work. Annual or biannual tinkering to adapt the plans to the fancies of new legislators or commissioners, or the winds of political change, will only produce failure. Long-range planning, let alone the carrying out of long-range plans, has never been a strong suit of either state or local governments.

Radical change also will need to occur in our educational system. Our system needs to begin at the earliest occasion to teach kids about personal boundaries and touching, about violence, about drug and alcohol abuse, about sex and parenting, about being healthy and responsible. I am not talking about education by way of a class now and then on these topics when kids reach "the right age." I am talking about an education system built around a core of these things—a system that continually delivers these messages, in age-appropriate fashion, from kindergarten through 12th grade.

Another needed change: Society should reject the notion that just because two people have the ability to conceive a child, they also have the innate skills and ability to parent that child in an adequate manner. The fallacy of that assumption is demonstrated on a daily basis in juvenile courts all across the country, and still the notion persists. It is critical that early identification of girls and women who are pregnant take place so that parent education and other support services can be offered before the birth of the child. Once the child is born, ongoing services must be available and encouraged. It doesn't work to wait until something goes noticeably wrong before the community takes note that there is a new parent in its midst.

Placing a high priority on identifying the fathers of children and seeing to it that they take responsibility for their children is yet another change that must occur. Men cannot be allowed to father children and then simply walk away to leave the mother or the rest of the community to meet the needs of the child. We must view the responsibility of the father of a child, regardless of his age, as co-extensive with the responsibility of the mother. Fathers will have to be able to demonstrate the ability to adequately parent their children and be prepared to do so as required.

The most radical change will have to be in the way that we think about children and families. We are going to have to abandon the notion that children are like cars or furniture or houses, to be owned and controlled and that this ownership and control is not to be interfered with by the state except under the most limited of circumstances. There is an old African saying, "It takes a whole village to raise a child." I believe we are going to have to adopt that concept and recognize that children belong to the community and that it is up to the community to see that they are raised in a fashion that is most likely to produce healthy, productive adults.

The most vital component of the concept of children belonging to the community is each member of the community accepting personal responsibility for the well-being of each child in the community. This means no more looking the other way as some young mother with several kids in tow stands in the aisle of the grocery store and repeatedly slaps one of them to try to make the child stop crying. It means no more shaking the head and simply walking away wondering how people can live like that when we see filthy, undernourished children living in squalid apartments or falling down houses. It means doing more than just hoping that at some point someone will do something about the kid down the block who is involved in petty thefts in the neighborhood. It does mean developing a societal attitude that it is not only all right but in fact expected that each individual will take responsibility for identifying children or families who are in need of help and either offering that help or bringing the need to the attention of someone who can do something about it.

What I am suggesting is the creation of a culture in which the very first priority truly is producing healthy, well-adjusted children who, in turn, will be able to grow into healthy, productive adults. Talking about children as the first priority has recently been in vogue in this state. Unfortunately, talk is pretty much all it has been. The application of the financial resources of the state and the county to back up this talk has not happened.

This is not a situation in which we can do more with less. We can't even do more with the same amount or even a little more. It is going to take the spending of a lot more money now, to save a lot more money in the future. Hard choices will have to be made by our legislators and county commissioners. This is not a situation where there is not enough money. It is simply a question of priorities. How is the money that is available going to be spent? Who is going to be first?

The future is a resource to be managed and children are the foundation of the future. Legislators and commissioners will have to decide what things state and county government will not do so that adequate funds can be invested in the future. They will have to give up the time-honored approach to hard financial times of trying to continue to do everything, but just not do it as well.

Can this magnitude of change in our society be accomplished? Maybe, given enough commitment by enough people. Will it be accomplished? Probably not in my lifetime, if at all. If the current situation is so bad and the likelihood of change so far in the future and so problematic, why do all the people who work with kids and families continue to do it? I can't answer that question for anyone but myself. The reason I did it for five years is found in a story told to me by a counselor in the Lane County Department of Youth Services on a day when I was feeling overwhelmed by the whole problem.

He told me of a morning on a beach after a ferocious storm. The beach was miles long and littered from one end to the other with starfish that had been washed up on the sand by the storm. An old man made his way down to the beach and began slowly making his way from one starfish to another picking each up in turn and tossing it back into the water. A young man stood on a sand dune and watched in silence for some time as the old man continued his slow journey from starfish to starfish. Finally, he could stand it no longer. He approached the old man and asked, "Old man, there are miles of beach and thousands of starfish; at your slow pace, what possible difference can you make?" The old man looked at the young man and then at the starfish he held in his hand and said softly, with a smile, "I suppose it will make a difference to this one," and tossed the starfish back into the water.

We have been engaged in picking up starfish one at a time for a long time. All we need to do is to look around us to see what that has produced for our society. My greatest fear is that we will continue to do what we have been doing and continue to go where we are going—and get there!

Be for the future. Put children first.

APPENDIX C

Generals in the War on School Violence

For Garo Mirigian, principal of Fremont's Centerville Junior High School, it was a typical day.

He checked rumors that a 13-year-old boy had brought a gun to school, drafted a letter to a student's probation officer, prepared for a gang-intervention meeting, patrolled the playground and tried to calm a gang member's enraged relative.

"It's 2:30," Mirigian said afterward, "and I still haven't done any academics."

In the war against school violence, Mirigian is one of hundreds of California educators on the front lines. Because of his high-visibility post in an urban school, he is also one of the most important.

Successful violence prevention "centers around really successful leaders," said Ronald Stephens, director of the National School Safety Council in Westlake Village, Los Angeles County. "They convey to the kids that they really care about them."

While questions remain about the effectiveness of the many differing philosophies and programs aimed at quelling violence, experts agree that leaders are critical—perhaps the single most important factors, in the absence of any proven systems approach.

"There are a lot of studies of good schools. They have parental involvement, good communication—and strong principals," said Nancy Guerra, a violence-prevention researcher at the University of Illinois at Chicago.

For some leaders, it's personal charisma that changes young lives and turns schools around; for others, it's a program they've backed.

Some are nationally known figures whose stories have been the stuff of newspaper articles and movies. Others labor out of the limelight, quietly coping with tight budgets, difficult students, angry parents and politicians who have their own agendas.

From "Generals in the War on School Violence," by Carla Marinucci and Scott Winokur. In *The San Francisco Examiner,* Sunday, June 5, 1994, page B-1. Reprinted by permission.

INSPIRATION AND CHOKEHOLDS

Jaime Escalante is the inspirational teacher whose efforts to get Latino gang members in Los Angeles interested in algebra and calculus were the subject of the film *Stand and Deliver.*

Now a math teacher at Sacramento's Hiram Johnson High School, Escalante requires his 120 students and their parents to sign a contract committing themselves to his demanding program for four years, including summers.

In turn, Escalante promises to make them more proficient in mathematics than they ever imagined possible.

But school alone "cannot educate," Escalante said.

"No matter how much money and programs, it won't work—unless they understand respect and discipline in the classroom."

Students don't have to be gifted, he added, just willing to play by the rules.

"I tell them, 'I'm going to give you the *ganas,*'" he said.

Ganas, Spanish for "hunger" or "will," is written on a sign hung in Escalante's classroom as a reminder of the potential for success in even the most troubled youth.

As principal of Overfelt High School in San Jose, a school once plagued by violence, Ruben Trinidad wouldn't hesitate to get physical himself.

Gang members learned that the day they covered the school with graffiti. Trinidad grabbed one, threw him off his bike and pedaled six blocks after another.

"I almost fainted," he recalled, "but I caught him."

During his seven-year stint at Overfelt, Trinidad took no prisoners—and no excuses. Once, while trying to eject a violent nonstudent, he was attacked with brass knuckles.

"I cold-cocked him, like a football lineman would block someone with an elbow," Trinidad said.

"Then I jumped on him and used a policeman's chokehold—and pressed charges."

The principal's toughest job, he said, may be determining who can be saved and who has to go.

"There's always going to be about 25 kids who make an effort to hold any campus hostage," Trinidad said.

"You have to look for the legal ways to make them straighten out, or get them to move on, because any student who wants an education deserves to be in a safe environment," said Trinidad, today principal of Carleton High School in Belmont.

"NEVER EASE UP"

Pacifica retiree Bob Arata was a teacher, counselor, assistant principal and principal in San Francisco middle schools. His last post was principal of James Lick Middle School.

Arata earned a reputation during his 37 years in the district as a tough guy with a good heart and an open mind.

"He was a throwback, like the old, small-town principal who knew all the parents," said police officer Rich Quesada, who worked with Arata at Lick. "Fair, but very strict. He defined the rules and stuck by them."

Arata never attracted the attention that prompts movie treatment, but he's a walking repository of information on how to keep the peace.

Maintain a High Profile

"Get the hell out of your office. That's the last place you want to be. At 8:00 A.M. I was in the yard for the early arrivals. You say hello, then go to the street and see the kids as they get off the Muni bus. As soon as they see you, you make contact."

"Two or three times a day, you walk around the outside of the school, so all of the kids in the gym classes see you, also the outsiders coming around. And the minute they get out of school you want to be on the street or in the yard."

"You walk by like a cop on the beat. Every day, this is your routine. You never ease up."

"It's a constant reminder to the screw-ups, the kids prone to violence, that you're there. They feel uncomfortable—but the great number of kids who aren't screw-ups feel safe."

"The word gets out that you're always outside—and inside. Finally, they come to realize you're all over."

Identify Likely Victims and Victimizers

"You know within two to three weeks who your victims are because they walk around with 'Victim' written on their forehead."

"Normally, it's the quiet kid, the loner who can't make friends. He could be a good student, but a lot of the time he's a slow learner."

"No matter where he goes, someone will push, shove and kick him. The belligerent kids and the cowards will go after him. They're the kids with low self-esteem who use these kids to gain some type of notoriety. Victimizers travel in packs and they help each other by identifying the easy marks. I would always get them real quick and lay out my expectations."

Get Close to the Kids Psychologically

"It starts the minute the kid walks into your office. From then on, you monitor every move he makes. Fear is a great motivating device to get them to behave."

"But on the other side of the coin, if a teacher makes an accusation and your investigation proves the kid right, you walk through the streets of hell to make sure the thing is rectified. You don't nail the kid for something he didn't do."

"Once you do that, you're an extension of the kid's family. In fact, many times you're the *only* family the kid has."

OUT OF THE LIMELIGHT

In the San Jose Unified School District, "We don't have a Jaime Escalante, but there are lots of people helping kids who aren't on the cover of *People* magazine," said Gunderson High School teacher Bill North.

One of them is Kate Lenox, who manages counseling and peer helping programs at Hoover Middle School.

Lenox has all the right academic credentials and state certifications, but what makes her stand out, like the other effective leaders, is personal chemistry.

She is a witty, energetic woman who uses charm, persuasion and the sheer power of authority to get errant kids to do better.

Her high-pressure job requires her to constantly think on her feet in order to avert disputes that have sent Hoover students to the hospital in the past. Yet Lenox manages to retain a sense of humor and an informality students like.

"You guys want to spend time with the most gorgeous counselor on the planet?" she asked one group of teens in the midst of a nearly violent crisis.

The effect is disarming. More often than not, students offer no resistance and disputes are resolved peacefully.

Even so, Lenox is aware that some situations can't be prevented from going from bad to worse.

"All conflicts don't have happy endings," she said. "There's 1,200 kids at this school—and me. Honestly, I think it's almost humanly impossible to do this job well.

"How many kids am I not getting to? I love the kids and I love the work I do, but I wonder sometimes: How effective can I be?"

IRON FIST IN A VELVET GLOVE

Mirigian, the Fremont principal, knows his authority doesn't stem from his style or appearance.

"I'm not cool, I'm overweight and I'm balding," he said.

But he doesn't worry about it. The bottom line, he knows, is winning the war against violence.

When he intervened in one campus skirmish this last school year, it took all of his considerable skills to avert serious violence.

A gang fight had erupted and eight youths were suspended. There were rumors of retaliation and talk of an impending drive-by shooting.

Mirigian moved swiftly, activating a phone tree and calling a parents' meeting to quell fears and come up with a strategy.

The upshot was an offer by parents to patrol the campus and donations for a walkie-talkie system totaling $1,200.

The next day, Mirigian invited three of the suspended youths to breakfast. Over pancakes, he led a discussion about their future.

"I want you guys to stay at this school," he said. "I will be loyal to you, if that's what it takes for you to succeed. If I see you make the effort, I will make it.

"But if you screw up," he warned, "I will lose no sleep over kicking you out."

Grateful for a chance to regain the principal's trust, one boy came up to Mirigian afterward and asked him to keep an eye on him. The principal said he would.

REFERENCES

Achenbach, T. (1985). *Assessment and taxonomy of child and adolescent psychopathology.* Beverly Hills, CA: Sage.

Achenbach, T. M. (1991). *The child behavior checklist: Manual for the teacher's report form.* Burlington: University of Vermont, Department of Psychiatry.

Adams, M. (1990). *Beginning to read: Thinking and learning about print.* Cambridge, MA: MIT Press.

Ager, C., & Cole, C. (1991). A review of cognitive-behavioral interventions for children and adolescents with behavioral disorders. *Behavioral Disorders, 16*(4), 276–287.

Alberg, J., Petry, C., & Eller, A. (1994). *A resource guide for social skills instruction.* Longmont, CO: Sopris West.

Alberto, P. A., & Troutman, A. C. (1990). *Applied behavior analysis for teachers.* Columbus, OH: Charles E. Merrill.

Albin, R., Horner, R., Koegel, R., & Dunlap, G. (1987). *Extending competent performance: Applied research on generalization and maintenance.* Eugene: University of Oregon, Specialized Training Program.

Algozzine, R., & Ysseldyke, J. (1992). *Strategies and tactics for effective instruction.* Longmont, CO: Sopris West.

American Psychological Association. (1993). *Violence and youth: Psychology's response.* Washington, DC: Author.

American Psychological Association. (1994). *Violence and youth: Psychology's response.* Washington, DC: Author.

Archer, A., & Gleason, M. (1989). *Skills for school success (grades 3–6).* North Billerica, MA: Curriculum Associates.

Bain, A., & Farris, H. (1991). Teacher attitudes toward social skills training. *Teacher Education and Special Education, 14,* 49–56.

Barkley, R. (1990). *Attention deficit hyperactivity disorder: A handbook for diagnosis and treatment.* New York: Guilford Press.

Barton, E. (1986). Modification of children's prosocial behavior. In P. Strain, M. Guralnick, & H. Walker (Eds.), *Children's social behavior* (pp. 331–372). New York: Academic Press.

Behrman, R. (1992). *The future of children: School-linked services.* Los Altos, CA: Center for the Future of Children, The David and Lucile Packard Foundation.

Bierman, K. L. (1986). Process of change during social skills training with preadolescents and its relation to treatment outcome. *Child Development, 57,* 230–240.

Bierman, K. L., & Furman, W. (1984). The effects of social skills training and peer involvement on the social adjustment of preadolescents. *Child Development, 55,* 151–162.

Biglan, T. (1992). Family practices and the larger social context. *New Zealand Journal of Psychology, 21*(1), 37–43.

Biglan, T. (1993). A functional contextualist framework for community interventions. In S. C. Hayes, L. J. Hayes, H. Reese, & T. Sarbin (Eds.), *Varieties of scientific contextualism* (pp. 251–276). Reno, NV: Context Press.

Biglan, T., Lewin, L., & Hops, H. (1990). A contextual approach to the problem of aversive practices in families. In G. Patterson (Ed.), *Depression and aggression: Two facets of family interactions* (pp. 103–129). Hillsdale, NJ: Erlbaum.

Black, D. D., Downs, J., Bastien, J., Brown, L. J., & Wells, P. (1987). *Motivation systems workshop manual.* Boys Town, NE: Father Flanagan's Boys' Home.

Bostic, M. (1994, May). *Juvenile crime prevention strategies: A law enforcement perspective.* Paper presented at the Council of State Governments Conference on School Violence, Westlake Village, CA.

Brophy, J. E. (1983). Classroom organization and management. *Elementary School Journal, 83,* 265–285.

Brophy, J. (1986). Classroom management techniques. *Education and Urban Society, 18,* 182–194.

Brophy, J., & Evertson, C. (1981). *Student characteristics and teaching.* White Plains, NY: Longman.

Brophy, J., & Good, T. (1986). Teacher behavior and student achievement. In M. Wittrock (Ed.), *Handbook of research on teaching* (3rd ed., pp. 328–375). New York: Macmillan.

Bullis, M., & Walker, H. M. (under review). *Characteristics, causal factors, and school-based interventions for children and adolescents with antisocial behavioral disorders.* Proceedings of the Shaker Town Annual Conference, Lexington, KY.

Bullis, M., & Walker, H. M. (1994). *Comprehensive school-based systems for troubled youth.* Eugene: University of Oregon, Center on Human Development.

Cangelosi, J. S. (1992). *Systematic teaching strategies.* New York: Longman.

Cangelosi, J. S. (1993). *Classroom management strategies: Gaining and maintaining students' cooperation.* White Plains, NY: Longman.

Canter, L., & Canter, M. (1991). *Parents on your side: A comprehensive parent involvement program for teachers.* Santa Monica, CA: Lee Canter & Associates.

Cantrell, M. (1992). Guns, gangs and kids [Guest editorial]. *Journal of Emotional and Behavioral Problems, 1*(1), pp. 4–5.

Capaldi, D. M., & Patterson, G. R. (1989). *Psychometric properties of fourteen latent constructs from the Oregon Youth Study.* New York: Springer-Verlag.

Capaldi, D., & Patterson, G. R. (in press). Interrelated influences of contextual factors on antisocial behavior in childhood and adolescence for males. In D. Fowles, P. Sutker, & S. Goodman (Eds.), *Psychopathy and antisocial personality: A developmental perspective.* New York: Springer.

Carr, E. G., & Durand, V. M. (1985). Reducing behavior problems through functional communication training. *Journal of Applied Behavior Analysis, 18*, 111–126.

Chiles, J., Miller, M., & Cox, G. (1980). Depression in an adolescent delinquent population. *General Psychiatry, 37*, 1179–1184.

Cicchetti, D., & Nurcombe, B. (Eds.). (1993). Toward a developmental perspective on conduct disorder [Special Issue]. *Development and Psychopathology, 5*(1/2).

Clapp, B. (1989). The discipline challenge. *The Instructor, 99*(2), 32–34.

Clark, L. (1985). *S.O.S.! Help for parents.* Bowling Green, KY: Parents Press.

Coie, J., Belding, M., & Underwood, M. (1988). Aggression and peer rejection in childhood. In B. B. Lahey & A. Kazdin (Eds.), *Advances in clinical child psychology.* New York: Plenum.

Coie, J. D., Dodge, K. A., & Kupersmidt, J. (1990). Peer group behavior and social status. In S. R. Asher & J. D. Coie (Eds.), *Peer rejection in childhood.* New York: Cambridge University Press.

Coie, J., & Jacobs, M. (1993). The role of social context in the prevention of conduct disorder [Special Issue]. *Development and Psychopathology, 5*(1/2), 263–276.

Coie, J., & Krehbiel, G. (1984). Effects of academic tutoring on the social status of low-achieving, socially-rejected children. *Child Development, 55*, 1465–1478.

Coie, J., & Kupersmidt, J. (1983). A behavioral analysis of emerging social status in boys' groups. *Child Development, 54*, 1400–1416.

Coie, J., Underwood, M., & Lochman, J. (1991). Programmatic intervention with aggressive children in the school setting. In D. Pepler & K. Rubin (Eds.), *The development and treatment of childhood aggression* (pp. 389–407). Hillsdale, NJ: Erlbaum.

Colvin, G. (1988). *Lane School annual report* [unpublished document]. Eugene, OR: Lane Educational Service District.

Colvin, G. (1993). *Managing acting-out behavior.* Eugene, OR: Behavior Associates.

Colvin, G., Braun, D., DeForest, D., & Wilt, J. (1993). Establishing a proactive school-wide and classroom management system: A building team approach. In J. Marr, G. Sugai, & G. Tindal (Eds.), *The Oregon conference monograph 1993* (pp. 144–149). Eugene: University of Oregon, College of Education.

Colvin, G., Greenberg, S., & Sherman, R. (1993). Improving academic skills for students with serious emotional disturbances: The forgotten variable. In J. Marr, G. Sugai, & G. Tindal (Eds.), *The Oregon conference monograph 1993* (pp. 9–14). Eugene: University of Oregon, College of Education.

Colvin, G., Kameenui, E., & Sugai, G. (in press). Instructional classroom management: Towards a reconceptualization of integrating and managing students with behavior problems in general education. *Education and Treatment of Children.*

Colvin, G. T., & Sugai, G. M. (1988). Proactive strategies for managing social behavior problems: An instructional approach. *Education and Treatment of Children, 11*(4), 341–348.

Colvin, G., & Sugai, G. (1992). Schoolwide discipline: A behavior instruction approach. In J. Marr & G. Tindal (Eds.), *The Oregon conference monograph 1992* (pp. 41–45). Eugene: University of Oregon, College of Education.

Colvin, G., Sugai, G., & Kameenui, E. (1992). Staff survey on school-wide discipline. Unpublished manuscript. *Project PREPARE: Promoting responsible, empirical and proactive alternatives in regular education for students with behavior disorders.* University of Oregon, College of Education, Eugene, OR.

Colvin, G., Sugai, G., & Kameenui, E. (1993). An instructional approach for developing school-wide discipline plans. Unpublished manuscript. *Project PREPARE: Promoting responsible, empirical and proactive alternatives in regular education for students with behavior disorders.* University of Oregon, College of Education, Eugene, OR.

Colvin, G., Sugai, G., & Kameenui, E. (1994). Curriculum for establishing a proactive school-wide discipline plan. Unpublished manuscript. *Project PREPARE: Promoting responsible, empirical and proactive alternatives in regular education for students with behavior disorders.* University of Oregon, College of Education, Eugene, OR.

Cotton, K. (1990). Schoolwide and classroom discipline. *School improvement research series: Close-up #9.* Portland, OR: Northwest Regional Educational Laboratory.

Crowe, T. (1994, July). *A statistical profile of juvenile crime.* Paper presented at the Institute on Gang and Drug Policy, Office of Justice and Delinquency Prevention, San Jose, CA.

Cuban, L. (1989, April). *School reform in the 21st century.* Portland, OR: Portland State University.

Cummings, C. (1983). *Managing to teach.* Snohomish, WA: Snohomish Publishing.

Dear, J., Scott, K., & Marshall, D. (1994). An attack on school violence. *National School Safety Center News Journal, 3,* 4–8.

DeComo, R. (1994, May). *Reinventing juvenile corrections.* Paper presented at the Council of State Governments Conference on School Violence, Westlake Village, CA.

Dishion, T., & Andrews, D. (1994). *A multicomponent intervention for families of young adolescents at risk: An analysis of short term outcomes.* Eugene: Oregon Social Learning Center.

Dishion, T., Patterson, G., & Griesler, P. (in press). Peer adaptation in the development of antisocial behavior: A confluence model. In L. R. Huesmann (Ed.), *Current perspectives on aggressive behavior.* New York: Plenum.

Dishion, T., Patterson, G., Stoolmiller, M., & Skinner, M. L. (1991). Family, school, and behavioral antecedents to early adolescent involvement with antisocial peers. *Developmental Psychology, 27,* 172–180.

Dodge, K. (1980). Social cognition and children's aggressive behavior. *Child Development, 51,* 1162–1170.

Dodge, K. (1985). A social information processing model of social competence in children. In M. Perlmutter (Ed.), *Minnesota symposium in child psychology* (Vol. 18, pp. 107–135). New York: Academic Press.

Dodge, K. (1986). Social information processing variables in the development of aggression and altruism in children. In C. Zahn-Waxler, E. M. Cummings, & R. Ianotti (Eds.), *Altruism and aggression: Biological and social origins* (pp. 280–302). New York: Cambridge University Press.

Dodge, K. (1993). The future of research on conduct disorder. *Development and Psychopathology, 5*(1/2), 311–320.

Dodge, K., Coie, J., & Brakke, N. (1982). Behavior patterns of socially rejected and neglected adolescents: The roles of social approach and aggression. *Journal of Abnormal Child Psychology, 10,* 389–410.

Dodge, K., & Frame, C. L. (1982). Social cognitive biases and deficits in aggressive boys. *Child Development, 53*(3), 620–635.

Dodge, K., Pettit, G., McClaskey, C., & Brown, M. (1986). Social competence in children. *Monographs of the Society for Research in Child Development, 51*(2, Serial No. 213).

Dougherty, B. S., Fowler, S. A., & Paine, S. C. (1985). The use of peer monitors to reduce negative interactions during recess. *Journal of Applied Behavior Analysis, 18,* 141–153.

Doyle, W. (1989). Classroom management techniques. In O. C. Moles (Ed.), *Strategies to reduce student misbehavior* (pp. 11–31). Washington, DC: Office of Educational Research and Improvement.

Drummond, T. (1993). *The Student Risk Screening Scale (SRSS).* Grants Pass, OR: Josephine County Mental Health Program.

Duke, D. L. (1989). School organization, leadership and student behavior. In O. C. Moles (Ed.), *Strategies to reduce student misbehavior* (pp. 31–62). Washington, DC: Office of Educational Research and Improvement.

DuPaul, G., & Eckert, T. (in press). The effects of social skills curricula: Now you see them, now you don't. *School Psychology Quarterly.*

DuPaul, G. J., & Stoner, G. (1994). *Assessment and management of ADHD in school.* New York: Guilford Press.

Elliott, S., & Gresham, F. (1991). *Social skills intervention guide.* Circle Pines, MN: American Guidance.

Engelmann, S., & Carnine, D. (1982). *Theory of instruction: Principles and applications.* New York: Irvington.

Engelmann, S., & Colvin, G. (1983). *Generalized compliance training.* Austin, TX: PRO-ED.

Epstein, J. (1983). *Effects on parents of teacher practices in parent involvement.* Baltimore, MD: Johns Hopkins University, Center for Social Organization of Schools.

Epstein, M. H., Foley, R. M., & Cullinan, D. (1992). National survey of educational programs for adolescents with severe emotional disturbance. *Behavioral Disorders, 17*(3), 202–210.

Evans, I. M., & Meyer, L. H. (1985). *An educative approach to behavior problems: A practical design model for interventions with severely handicapped learners.* Baltimore, MD: Paul H. Brookes.

Evertson, C. M., Emmer, E., Clements, B. S., Sanford, J. P., & Worsham. (1984). *Classroom management for elementary teachers.* Englewood Cliffs, NJ: Prentice-Hall.

Farrar, D. (1994, May). *Violence, guns and alcohol: Tailoring the solutions to fit the problems.* Paper presented at the Council of State Governments Conference on School Violence, Westlake Village, CA.

Fisher, J., & Smith-Davis, J. (1990). *Children of the inner cities: A NASDSE seminar.* Washington, DC: National Association of State Directors of Special Education.

Forehand, R., & McMahon, R. (1981). *Helping the noncompliant child.* New York: Guilford Press.

Forness, S. (1992). Broadening the cultural-organizational perspective in exclusion of youth with social maladjustment. *Remedial and Special Education, 13*, 55–59.

Fowler, M. (1992). *CH.A.D.D. educator's manual.* Fairfax, VA: CASET Associates.

Fowler, S., Dougherty, B., Kirby, K., & Kohler, F. (1986). Role reversals: An analysis of therapeutic effects achieved with disruptive boys during their appointments as peer monitors. *Journal of Applied Behavior Analysis, 19*(4), 437–444.

Furlong, M. (1994). Evaluating school violence trends. *National School Safety Center News Journal, 3*, 23–27.

Gagnon, C. (1991). School based interventions for aggressive children: Possibilities, limitations and future directions. In D. Pepler & K. Rubin (Eds.), *The development and treatment of childhood aggression* (pp. 449–450). London: Lawrence Erlbaum.

Garmezy, N. (1985). Stress-resistant children: The search for protective factors. In J. E. Stevenson (Ed.), *Recent research in developmental psychopathology* (pp. 213–233). Elmsford, NY: Pergamon Press.

Gerber, M. M., & Semmel, M. I. (1984). Teacher as imperfect test: Reconceptualizing the referral process. *Educational Psychologist, 19*(3), 137–148.

Gersten, R., Walker, H. M., & Darch, C. (1988). Relationships between teachers' effectiveness and their tolerance for handicapped students. *Exceptional Children, 54*(5), 433–438.

Gersten, R. G., & Woodward, J. (1990). Rethinking the Regular Education Initiative: Focus on the classroom teacher. *Remedial and Special Education, 11*(3), 7–16.

Gettinger, M. (1988). Methods of pro-active classroom management. *School Psychology Review, 17*, 227–242.

Giangreco, M. F., Dennis, R., Cloninger, C., Edelman, S., & Schattman, R. (1993). "I've counted Jon": Transformational experiences of teachers educating students with disabilities. *Exceptional Children, 59*(4), 359–372.

Gleason, M. M., Colvin, G. T., & Archer, A. L. (1991). Interventions for improving study skills. In G. Stoner, M. Shinn, & H. Walker (Eds.), *Interventions for achievement and behavior problems* (pp. 137–160). Silver Spring, MD: National Association of School Psychologists.

Goldstein, A., Sprafkin, R. P., Gershaw, N. J., & Klein, P. (1980). *Skillstreaming the adolescent: A structured learning approach to teaching prosocial skills.* Champaign, IL: Research Press.

Goodlad, J. I. (1984). *A place called school: Prospects for the future.* New York: McGraw-Hill.

Greenwood, C. R., Walker, H. M., Todd, N. M., & Hops, H. (1979). Selecting a cost-effective screening device for the assessment of preschool social withdrawal. *Journal of Applied Behavior Analysis, 12*, 639–652.

Gresham, F. (1986). Conceptual issues in the assessment of social competence in children. In P. S. Strain, M. J. Guralnick, & H. M. Walker (Eds.), *Children's social behavior: Development, assessment, and modification* (pp. 143–179). New York: Academic Press.

Gresham, F. M., & Elliott, S. (1990). *The social skills rating system (SSRS).* Circle Pines, MN: American Guidance.

Gunter, P., Denny, R., Jack, S., Shores, R., & Nelson, M. (1993). Aversive stimuli in academic interactions between students with serious emotional disturbance and their teachers. *Behavioral Disorders, 18*(4), 265–274.

Guskey, T. (1986). Staff development and the process of teacher change. *Educational Researcher, 15*(5), 5–12.

Hawkins, J. D., VonCleve, E., & Catalano, R. F., Jr. (1991). Reducing early childhood aggression: Results of a primary prevention program. *Journal of the American Academy of Child and Adolescent Psychiatry, 30*, 208–217.

Hazel, J., Schumaker, J., Sherman, J., & Sheldon-Wildgen, J. (1981). *ASSET: A social skills program for adolescents.* Champaign, IL: Research Press.

Hersh, R. H., & Walker, H. M. (1983). Great expectations: Making schools effective for all students. *Policy Studies Review, 2*(Special No. 1), 147–188.

Hinshaw, S. (1992). Externalizing behavior problems and academic underachievement in childhood and adolescence: Causal relationships and underlying mechanisms. *Psychological Bulletin, 111*, 127–155.

Hinshaw, S., Han, S., Erhardt, D., & Huber, A. (1992). Internalizing and externalizing behavior problems in preschool children: Correspondence among parent and teacher ratings and behavior observations. *Journal of Clinical Child Psychology, 21*(2), 143–150.

Hodgkinson, M. (1991). Reform versus reality. *Phi Delta Kappan, 73*, 9–16.

Hofmeister, A., & Lubke, M. (1990). *Research into practice.* Boston: Allyn & Bacon.

Hollinger, J. (1987). Social skills for behaviorally disordered children as preparation for mainstreaming: Theory, practice and new directions. *Remedial and Special Education, 8*(4), 17–27.

Hoover, J., & Juul, K. (1993). Bullying in Europe and the U.S. *Journal of Emotional and Behavioral Problems, 2*(1), 25–29.

Hops, H., & Walker, H. M. (1988). *CLASS: Contingencies for Learning Academic and Social Skills.* Seattle, WA: Educational Achievement Systems.

Horne, A., & Sayger, T. (1990). *Treating conduct and oppositional disorders in children.* Elmsford, NY: Pergamon Press.

Horner, R. H., & Billingsley, F. F. (1988). The effect of competing behavior on the generalization and maintenance of adaptive behavior in applied settings. In R. H. Horner, G. Dunlap, & R. L. Koegel (Eds.), *Generalization and maintenance: Lifestyle changes in applied settings* (pp. 197–220). Baltimore, MD: Paul H. Brookes.

Horner, R. H., Dunlap, G., & Koegel, R. L. (Eds.). (1988). *Generalization and maintenance: Lifestyle changes in applied settings.* Baltimore, MD: Paul H. Brookes.

Horner, R. H., Dunlap, G., Koegel, R. L., Carr, E. G., Sailor, W., Anderson, J., Albin, R. W., & O'Neill, R. E. (1990). Toward a technology of nonaversive behavioral support. *Journal of the Association of the Severely Handicapped, 15*, 125–132.

Horner, R. H., Sugai, G., & Todd, A. (1994). *Effective behavioral support in schools.* Field Initiated Research proposal submitted to U.S. Department of Education. Specialized Training Program, University of Oregon, Eugene, OR 97403.

Hunt, R. (1993). Neurobiological patterns of aggression. *Journal of Emotional and Behavioral Problems, 2*(1), 14–20.

Hyman, I. A., & Lally, D. (1982). A study of staff development programs for improving school discipline. *The Urban Review, 14*(3), 181–196.

Institute of Medicine. (1989). *Research on children and adolescents with mental, behavioral and developmental disorders.* Washington, DC: National Academy Press.

Irvin, L. K., Walker, H. M., Noell, J., Singer, G. H. S., Irvin, A. B., Marquez, K., & Britz, B. (1992). Measuring children's social skills using microcomputer-based videodisc assessment. *Behavior Modification, 16*, 475–503.

Johnson, D. W., & Johnson, R. T. (1986). Mainstreaming and cooperative learning strategies. *Exceptional Children, 52*(6), 553–561.

Jones, V. (1979). *Adolescents with behavior problems.* Boston: Allyn & Bacon.

Jones, V. (1992). Integrating behavioral and insight-oriented treatment in school-based programs for seriously emotionally disturbed students. *Behavioral Disorders, 17*(3), 225–236.

Juel, C. (1988). *Learning to read and write: A longitudinal study of 54 children from first through fourth grade.* Paper presented at the Annual Conference of the American Educational Research Association, New Orleans.

Kameenui, E. J., & Darch, C. (in press). *Instructional classroom management.* White Plains, NY: Longman.

Kameenui, E. J., & Simmons, D. C. (1990). *Designing instructional strategies: The prevention and academic of learning problems.* Columbus, OH: Charles E. Merrill.

Kauffman, J. (1989). The regular education initiative as Reagan-Bush Education Policy: A trickle-down theory of education of the hard-to-teach. *Journal of Special Education, 23,* 256–278.

Kauffman, J. (1993). *Characteristics of emotional and behavioral disorders of children and youth.* New York: Macmillan.

Kauffman, J. (1994). Violent children and youth: A call for action. *Journal of Emotional and Behavioral Problems, 3*(1), 25–26.

Kazdin, A. (1977). Assessing the clinical or applied importance of behavior change through social validation. *Behavior Modification, 4,* 427–452.

Kazdin, A. (Ed.). (1985). *Treatment of antisocial behavior in children and adolescents.* Pacific Grove, CA: Brooks/Cole.

Kazdin, A. (1987). *Conduct disorders in childhood and adolescence.* London: Sage.

Kazdin, A. (1993). Treatment of conduct disorder: Progress and directions in psychotherapy research. *Development and Psychopathology, 5*(1/2), 277–310.

Kelley, M. (1990). *School-home notes: Promoting children's classroom success.* New York: Guilford Press.

Klein, M. (1994, May). *Gangs and gang violence.* Paper presented at the Council of State Governments Conference on School Violence, Westlake Village, CA.

Knitzer, J., Steinberg, Z., & Fleisch, B. (1990). *At the school house door: An examination of programs and policies for children with behavioral and emotional problems.* New York: Bank Street College of Education.

Kounin, J. (1970). *Discipline and group management in classrooms.* New York: Holt, Rinehart & Winston.

Kovacs, M., Paulauskas, S., Gatsonis, C., & Richards, C. (1988). Depressive disorders in childhood: A longitudinal study of comorbidity with and risk for conduct disorders. *Journal of Affective Disorders, 15,* 205–217.

Kutner, L. (1993, January). Young bullies often get worse. *Eugene Register Guard.*

Ladd, G. W. (1981). Effectiveness of a social learning method for enhancing children's social interaction and peer acceptance. *Child Development, 52,* 171–178.

Ladd, G., & Oden, S. (1979). The relationship between peer acceptance and children's ideas about helpfulness. *Child Development, 50,* 402–408.

Lasley, T. J., & Wayson, W. W. (1982). Characteristics of schools with good discipline. *Educational Leadership, 40*(3), 28–31.

Lee, J. (1993). *Facing the fire: Experiencing and expressing anger appropriately.* New York: Bantam Books.

Leitman, R., & Binns, K. (1993). *Violence in America's schools.* New York: Louis Harris and Associates.

Lieberman, C. (1994, May). *Television and violence.* Paper presented at the Council of State Governments Conference on School Violence, Westlake Village, CA.

Lloyd, J. W., Kauffman, J. M., Landrum, T. J., & Roe, D. L. (1991). Why do teachers refer pupils for special education? An analysis of referral records. *Exceptionality, 2,* 113–126.

Lochman, J., Burch, P., Curry, J., & Lampron, L. (1984). Treatment and generalization effects of cognitive-behavioral and goal setting interventions with aggressive boys. *Journal of Consulting and Clinical Psychology, 52*(5), 915–916.

Loeber, R. (1991). Antisocial behavior: More enduring than changeable? *Journal of the American Academy of Child and Adolescent Psychiatry, 30*(3), 393–397.

Loeber, R., & Dishion, T. J. (1983). Early predictors of male delinquency: A review. *Psychological Bulletin, 94,* 68–99.

Loeber, R., & Dishion, T. (1984). Boys who fight at home and school: Family conditions influencing cross setting consistency. *Journal of Consulting and Clinical Psychology, 52,* 759–768.

Loeber, R., & LeBlanc, M. (1990). Towards a developmental criminology. In M. Tonry & N. Morris (Eds.), *Crime and justice: A review of research* (Vol. 12, pp. 375–473). Chicago: University of Chicago Press.

Loeber, R., & Schmaling, K. B. (1985). Empirical evidence for overt and covert patterns of antisocial conduct problems: A meta-analysis. *Journal of Abnormal Child Psychology, 13,* 337–352.

Loeber, R., Wung, P., Keenan, K., Giroux, B., Stouthamer-Loeber, M., Van Kammen, W., & Maughan, B. (1993). Developmental pathways in disruptive child behavior. *Development and Psychopathology, 5*(1/2), 103–134.

Lombardi, T. P., Odel, K. S., & Novotny, D. E. (1990). Special education and students at risk: Findings from a national study. *Remedial and Special Education, 12,* 56–62.

Long, N. (Ed.). (1993). Rage and aggression [Special Issue]. *Journal of Emotional and Behavioral Problems, 2*(1).

Long, N., & Brendtro, L. (1992). Gangs, guns and kids [Special Issue]. *Journal of Emotional and Behavioral Problems, 1*(1).

Maag, J. W. (1989). Assessment in social skills training: Methodological and conceptual issues for research and practice. *Remedial and Special Education, 10*(4), 6–17.

Maddox, J. (1994). Bringing down the information wall. *National School Safety Center News Journal, 3,* 28–30.

Mager, R. (1968). *Developing attitudes toward learning.* Belmont, CA: Fearon.

Marriage, K., Fine, S., Moretti, M., & Haley, G. (1986). Relationship between depression and conduct disorder in children and adolescents. *Journal of the American Academy of Child Psychiatry, 25*(5), 687–691.

McFall, R. (1982). A review and reformulation of the concept of social skills. *Behavioral Assessment, 4*, 1–33.

McGinnis, E., & Goldstein, A. (1984). *Skillstreaming the elementary school child.* Champaign, IL: Research Press.

McKinney, J. D., Montague, M., & Hocutt, A. M. (1993). *A synthesis of the research literature on the assessment and identification of attention deficit disorder.* Coral Gables, FL: Univeristy of Miami.

Merrell, K. W. (1993). Using behavior rating scales to assess social skills and antisocial behavior in school settings: Development of the school social behavior scales. *School Psychology Review, 22*(1), 115–133.

Michelson, L., Kazdin, A., & Marchione, K. (1986). *Prevention of antisocial behavior in children.* Pittsburgh, PA: University of Pittsburgh School of Medicine, Western Psychiatric Institute and Clinic.

Miller, W., & Brown, J. (in press). Self-regulation as a conceptual basis for the prevention and treatment of addictive behaviors. In N. Heather, W. R. Mill, & J. Greeley (Eds.), *Self-control and addictive behaviors.* Elmsford, NY: Pergamon Press.

Mischel, W. (1969). *Personality assessment.* New York: Wiley.

Moreno, J. (1934). *Who shall survive? A new approach to the problem of human interrelations.* Washington, DC: Nervous and Mental Disease Publishing Co.

Morgan, D. P., & Jenson, W. R. (1988). *Teaching behaviorally disordered students: Preferred practices.* Columbus, OH: Charles E. Merrill.

Munthe, E. (1989). Bullying in Scandinavia. In E. Munthe & E. Roland (Eds.), *Bullying: An international perspective* (pp. 66–78). London: David Fulton.

National School Boards Association. (1993, January). Report of the National School Boards Association on Violence in Schools. *The Los Angeles Times.*

Neel, R., & Rutherford, R. (1981). Exclusion of the socially maladjusted from services under P.L. 94-142: Why? What should be done about it? In F. Wood (Ed.), *Perspectives for a new decade: Educators' responsibilities for seriously disturbed and behaviorally disordered children and youth* (pp. 32–41). (Monograph on severe behavior disorders.) Reston, VA: Council for Exceptional Children.

OERI. (1994). Office of Educational Research and Improvement Request for Proposals. Washington, DC: U.S. Office of Education.

Offord, D., Boyle, M., & Racine, Y. (1991). The epidemiology of antisocial behavior in childhood and adolescence. In D. J. Pepler & K. H. Rubin (Eds.), *The development and treatment of childhood aggression* (pp. 31–54). Hillsdale, NJ: Erlbaum.

Olweus, D. (1987). Bully/victim problems among school children. In J. P. Myklebust & R. Ommundsen (Eds.), *Psykologprofesjonen mot ar 2000.* Oslo: Universitetsforlaget.

Olweus, D. (1991). Bully/victim problems among school children: Basic facts and effects of a school-based intervention program. In D. Pepler & K. Rubin (Eds.), *The development and treatment of childhood aggression* (pp. 411–446). London: Lawrence Erlbaum.

O'Neil, R., Horner, R., Albin, R., Storey, K., & Sprague, J. (1990). *Functional analysis of problem behavior: A practical assessment guide.* Pacific Grove, CA: Brooks/Cole.

Oswald, L. K., Lignugaris/Kraft, B., & West, R. P. (1990). The effects of incidental teaching on the generalized use of social amenities at school by a mildly handicapped adolescent. *Education and Treatment of Children, 13*, 142–152.

Paine, S., Hops, H., Walker, H., Greenwood, C., Fleischman, D., & Guild, J. (1982). Repeated treatment effects: A study of maintaining behavior change in socially withdrawn children. *Behavior Therapy, 6*, 171–199.

Paine, S. C., Radicchi, J., Rosellini, L. C., Deutchman, L., & Darch, C. B. (1983). *Structuring your classroom for academic success.* Champaign, IL: Research Press.

Parker, J., & Asher, S. (1987). Peer relations and later personal adjustment: Are low accepted children at risk? *Psychological Bulletin, 102*, 357–389.

Patterson, G. R. (in press). Some characteristics of a developmental theory for early onset delinquency. In J. J. Haugaard & M. F. Lenzenweger (Eds.), *Frontiers of developmental psychopathology.* London: Oxford University Press.

Patterson, G. R. (1982). *Coercive family process: Vol. 3. A social learning approach.* Eugene, OR: Castalia Press.

Patterson, G. R. (1983). *Longitudinal investigation of antisocial boys and their families* [Research grant from the National Institute of Mental Health]. Eugene: Oregon Social Learning Center.

Patterson, G. (1988). Family process: Loops, levels, and linkages. In N. Bolger, A. Caspi, G. Downey, & M. Moorehouse (Eds.), *Persons in context: Developmental processes* (pp. 114–151). New York: Cambridge University Press.

Patterson, G. R., & Bank, L. (1989). Some amplifying mechanisms for pathologic processes in families. In M. R. Gunnar & E. Thelen (Eds.), *Systems and development: The Minnesota symposia on child psychology* (Vol. 22, pp. 167–209). Hillsdale, NJ: Erlbaum.

Patterson, G., & Bank, L. (1986). Bootstrapping your way in the nomological thicket. *Behavioral Assessment, 8*, 49–73.

Patterson, G., Chamberlain, P., & Reid, J. (1982). A comparative evaluation of parent training procedures. *Behavior Therapy, 13*, 638–650.

Patterson, G. R., DeBaryshe, B. D., & Ramsey, E. (1989). A developmental perspective on antisocial behavior. *American Psychologist, 44*, 329–335.

Patterson, G. R., Reid, J. B., & Dishion, T. J. (1992). *Antisocial boys: Vol. 4. A social interactional approach.* Eugene, OR: Castalia.

Pepler, D., & Rubin, D. (1991). *The development and treatment of childhood aggression.* Hillsdale, NJ: Erlbaum.

Perry, D. G., Perry, L. C., & Rasmussen, P. (1986). Cognitive social learning mediators of aggression. *Child Development, 57*, 700–711.

Pfiffner, L., & Barkley, R. (1990). Educational placement and classroom management. In R. A. Barkley (Ed.), *Attention-deficit hyperactivity disorder: A handbook for diagnosis and treatment,* New York: Guilford Press.

Pfiffner, L., & O'Leary, K. D. (in press). Psychological treatments: School-based. In J. L. Matson (Ed.), *Handbook of hyperactivity in children,* New York: Macmillan.

Pfiffner, L., & O'Leary, S. (1987). The efficacy of all-positive management as a function of the prior use of negative consequences. *Journal of Applied Behavior Analysis, 20*(3), 265–271.

Pfiffner, L., Rosen, L., & O'Leary, S. (1985). The efficacy of an all-positive approach to classroom management. *Journal of Applied Behavior Analysis, 18,* 257–261.

Phillips, E. L., Phillips, E. A., Fixsen, D. L., & Wolf, M. (1974). *The teaching-family handbook.* Lawrence, KS: University Printing Service.

Ramsey, E., Patterson, G., Bank, L., & Walker, H. M. (in press). From home to school to juvenile court: A social interactional model of delinquency. *Journal of Experimental Child Psychology.*

Ramsey, E., Patterson, G. R., & Walker, H. M. (1990). Generalization of the antisocial trait from home to school settings. *Journal of Applied Developmental Psychology, 11,* 209–223.

Ramsey, E., & Walker, H. M. (1988). Family management correlates of antisocial behavior among middle school boys. *Behavioral Disorders, 13*(3), 187–201.

Quay, H. (1986). Conduct disorders. In H. Quay & J. Werry (Eds.), *Psychopathological disorders of childhood* (pp. 35–72). New York: Wiley.

Reavis, H. K., Jenson, W. R., Kukic, S., & Morgan, D. (1993). *Utah's BEST Project: Behavioral and educational strategies for teachers.* Available from Ken Reavis, Utah State Office of Education, 250 East 500 South, Salt Lake City, UT 84111, (801) 538-7709.

Reid, J. (1990). *Prevention research in conduct disorders.* NIMH prevention center proposal, available from Oregon Social Learning Center, 207 East 5th Avenue, Suite 202, Eugene, OR 97401.

Reid, J. (1993). Prevention of conduct disorder before and after school entry: Relating interventions to developmental findings. *Development and Psychopathology, 5*(1/2), 243–262.

Reid, J., & Patterson, G. R. (1991). Early prevention and intervention with conduct problems: A social interactional model for the integration of research and practice. In G. Stoner, M. Shinn, & H. M. Walker (Eds.), *Interventions for achievement and behavior problems* (pp. 715–740). Silver Spring, MD: National Association of School Psychologists.

Repp, A., & Singh, N. (1990). *Perspectives on the use of nonaversive and aversive interventions for persons with developmental disabilities.* Sycamore, IL: Sycamore Publishing.

Rich, H., & Ross, S. (1989). Students' time on learning tasks in special education. *Exceptional Children, 55*(6), 508–515.

Richters, J., & Cicchetti, D. (1993). Toward a developmental perspective on conduct disorder. *Development and Psychopathology, 5*(1/2), 1–4.

Robins, L. N. (1978). Sturdy childhood predictors of adult antisocial behavior: Replications from longitudinal studies. *Psychological Medicine, 8*, 611–622.

Romer, D., & Heller, T. (1983). Social adaptation of mentally retarded adults in community settings: A social-ecological approach. *Applied Research in Mental Retardation, 4*, 303–314.

Rosen, L., O'Leary, S., Joyce, S., Conway, G., & Pfiffner, L. (1984). The importance of prudent negative consequences for maintaining the appropriate behavior of hyperactive students. *Journal of Abnormal Child Psychology, 12*, 581–604.

Rosenshine, B. (1979). Content, time, and direct instruction. In P. Peterson & H. Walberg (Eds.), *Research on teaching: Concepts, findings, and implications*. Berkeley, CA: McCutcheon.

Ross, A. (1980). *Psychological disorders of children: A behavioral approach to theory, research and therapy* (2nd ed.). New York: McGraw-Hill.

Roth, J. A. (1994, February). Understanding and preventing violence. *National Institute of Justice Research in Brief*. Washington, DC: U.S. Department of Justice, Office of Justice Programs, National Institute of Justice.

Ruhl, K. L., & Berlinghoff, D. H. (1992). Research on improving behavioral disordered students' academic performance: A review of literature. *Behavioral Disorders, 17*(3), 178–190.

Rutter, M. (1979). Protective factors in children's responses to stress and disadvantage. In M. Kent & J. Rolf (Eds.), *Primary prevention of psychopathology: Vol. 3. Social competence in children* (pp. 49–74). Hanover, NH: University Press of New England.

Sabornie, E., & Kauffman, J. (1985). Regular classroom sociometric status of behaviorally disordered adolescents. *Behavioral Disorders, 10*(3), 191–197.

Sabornie, E., Kauffman, J., & Cullinan, D. (1990). Extended sociometric status of adolescents with mild handicaps: A cross-categorical perspective. *Exceptionality, 1*(3), 197–207.

Safran, J. S., & Safran, S. P. (1985). A developmental view of children's behavioral tolerance. *Behavioral Disorders, 10*, 87–94.

Sampson, R. (1992). Family management and child development: Insights from social disorganization theory. In J. McCord (Ed.), *Facts, frameworks, and forecasts: Advances in criminological theory* (Vol. 3, pp. 63–93). New Brunswick, NJ: Transaction Press.

Sampson, R., & Groves, W. B. (1989). Community structure and crime: Testing social disorganization theory. *American Journal of Sociology, 94*, 774–802.

Sasso, G. M., Melloy, K., & Kavale, K. (1990). Generalization, maintenance, and behavioral covariation associated with social skills training through structured learning. *Behavioral Disorders, 16*(1), 9–22.

Schloss, P., Schloss, C., Wood, C., & Kiehl, W. (1986). A critical review of social skills research with behaviorally disordered students. *Behavioral Disorders, 12*(1), 1–14.

Schoen, S. (1986). Decreasing noncompliance in a severely multihandicapped child. *Psychology in the Schools, 23*, 88–94.

Schorr, L. (1988). *Within our reach: Breaking the cycle of disadvantage.* New York: Doubleday.

Schrumpf, F., Crawford, D., & Usadel, H. (1991). *Peer mediation: Conflict resolution in schools.* Champaign, IL: Research Press.

Schumaker, J., & Ellis, E. (1982). Social skills training of LD adolescents: A generalization study. *Learning Disabilities Quarterly, 5*, 409–414.

Severson, H., & Zoref, L. (1991). Prevention and early interventions for addictive behaviors: Health promotion in the schools. In. G. Stoner, M. Shinn, & H. M. Walker (Eds.), *Interventions for achievement and behavior problems* (pp. 539–557). Silver Springs, MD: National Association of School Psychologists.

Shapiro, E. (1989). *Academic skills problems: Direct assessment and intervention.* New York: Guilford Press.

Sheldon, J., Sherman, J., Schumaker, J., & Hazel, J. (1984). Developing a social skills curriculum for mildly handicapped adolescents and young adults: Some problems and approaches. In S. Braaten, R. B. Rutherford, Jr., & C. A. Kardash (Eds.), *Programming for adolescents with behavioral disorders* (Vol. 1, pp. 105–116). Reston, VA: Council for Children with Behavioral Disorders.

Shelly, L. (1985). American crime: An international anomaly? *Comparative Social Research, 8*, 81–95.

Shinn, M. (1989). *Curriculum-based measurement: Assessing special children.* New York: Guilford Press.

Shinn, M. R., Ramsey, E., Walker, H. M., Stieber, S., & O'Neill, R. E. (1987). Antisocial behavior in school settings: Initial differences in an at risk and normal population. *The Journal of Special Education, 21*(2), 69–84.

Shores, R., Gunter, P., & Jack, S. (1993). Classroom management strategies: Are they setting events for coercion? *Behavioral Disorders, 18*(2), 92–102.

Simcha-Fagan, O., Langner, T., Gersten, J., & Eisenberg, J. (1975). *Violent and antisocial behavior: A longitudinal study of urban youth.* (OCD-CB-480) Unpublished report of the Office of Child Development.

Slavin, R. (1984). Team assisted individualization: Cooperative learning and individualized instruction in the mainstreamed classroom. *Remedial and Special Education, 5*, 33–42.

Smith, M. A., & Misra, A. (1992). A comprehensive management system for students in regular classrooms. *The Elementary School Journal, 92*, 353–371.

Smylie, M. A. (1988). The enhancement function of staff development: Organizational and psychological antecedents to individual teacher change. *American Educational Research Journal, 25*, 1–30.

Sprick, R. (1985). *Discipline in the secondary classroom.* New York: The Center for Applied Research in Education.

Sprick, R. (1994). School-wide discipline policies: An instructional classroom management approach. In E. Kameenui & C. Darch (Eds.), *Instructional classroom management* (pp. 179–200). White Plains, NY: Longman.

Sprick, R., Sprick, M., & Garrison, M. (1992). *Foundations: Developing positive school-wide discipline policies.* Longmont, CO: Sopris West.

Steinhart, D. (1994, May). *What can state legislators do to curb youth violence?* Paper presented at the Council of State Governments Conference on School Violence, Westlake Village, CA.

Stephens, R. (1994). Preparing tomorrow's teachers. *School Safety, 3,* 1.

Stephens, R., Butterfield, G., & Arnette, J. (1994). *School crime and violence statistical review.* Available from National School Safety Center, Pepperdine University, Malibu, CA 90263.

Stephens, T. (1992). *Social skills in the classroom.* Odessa, FL: Psychological Associates Resources.

Stokes, T. F., & Osnes, P. G. (1986). Programming the generalization of children's social behavior. In P. S. Strain, M. Guralnick, & H. Walker (Eds.), *Children's social behavior: Development, assessment and modification* (pp. 407–443). New York: Academic Press.

Strain, P., Guralnick, M., & Walker, H. M. (Eds.). (1986). *Children's social behavior: Development, assessment, and modification.* New York: Academic Press.

Strayhorn, J., Strain, P. S., & Walker, H. M. (1993). The case for interaction skills training in the context of tutoring as a preventative mental health intervention in the schools. *Behavioral Disorders, 19*(1), 11–26.

Sugai, G., & Colvin, G. (1989). *Environmental explanations of behavior: Conducting a functional analysis.* Eugene: Behavior Associates.

Sugai, G., Colvin, G., & Scott, T. (1993). *Enhancing expected behavior* [Technical paper]. Eugene: University of Oregon, Project PREPARE, College of Education.

Sugai, G., & Fuller, M. (1991). A decision model for social skills curriculum analysis. *Remedial and Special Education, 12,* 33–42.

Sugai, G., Kameenui, E., & Colvin, G. (1990). *Project PREPARE: Promoting responsible, empirical and proactive alternatives in regular education for students with behavior disorders.* Grant proposal submitted to Special Projects Competition. Eugene: University of Oregon.

Sugai, G., Kameenui, E., & Colvin G. (1993). *Project PREPARE: Promoting responsible, empirical and proactive alternatives in regular education for students with behavior disorders.* Unpublished data. Eugene: University of Oregon, College of Education.

Sugai, G. M., & Tindal, G. A. (1993). *Effective school consultation: An interactive approach.* Pacific Grove, CA: Brooks/Cole.

Swick, K. L. (1985). *A proactive approach to discipline.* Washington, DC: National Education Association.

Thompson, T. (1991). People make a difference in school playground safety. *Executive Educator, 13*(8), 28–29.

Van Steenbergen, N. (1994). "If only we could . . ." *National School Safety Center News Journal, 3*, 20–22.

Wagner, M. (1989, April). *The national transition study: Results of a national, longitudinal study of transition from school to work for students with disabilities.* Paper presented at the Council for Exceptional Children's Annual Convention, San Francisco.

Wahler, R., & Dumas, J. E. (1986). "A chip off the old block": Some interpersonal characteristics of coercive children across generations. In P. Strain, M. Guralnick, & H. M. Walker (Eds.), *Children's social behavior: Development, assessment and modification* (pp. 49–91). New York: Academic Press.

Walker, H. M. (1986). The Assessments for Integration into Mainstream Settings (AIMS) assessment system: Rationale, instruments, procedures, and outcomes. *Journal of Clinical Child Psychology, 15*(1), 55–63.

Walker, H. M. (1988). Special education curriculum and instruction: Social skills. In T. Husen & N. Postlethwaite (Eds.), *International encyclopedia of education* (Supplementary Vol. 1, pp. 229–232). Oxford, England: Pergamon Books.

Walker, H. M., Block-Pedego, A., Todis, B., & Severson, H. (1991). *School archival records search (SARS): User's guide and technical manual.* Longmont, CO: Sopris West.

Walker, H. M., & Buckley, N. K. (1973, May). Teacher attention to appropriate and inappropriate classroom behavior. *Focus on Exceptional Children*, 5–12.

Walker, H. M., & Hops, H. (1993). *The RECESS program for aggressive children.* Seattle, WA: Educational Achievement Systems.

Walker, H. M., Hops, H., & Fiegenbaum, E. (1976). Deviant classroom behavior as a function of combinations of social and token reinforcement and cost contingency. *Behavior Therapy, 7*, 76–88.

Walker, H. M., Hops, H., & Greenwood, C. R. (1981). RECESS: Research and development of a behavior management package for remediating social aggression in the school setting. In P. Strain (Ed.), *The utilization of classroom peers as behavior change agents* (pp. 261–303). New York: Plenum.

Walker, H. M., Hops, H., & Greenwood, C. R. (1984). The CORBEH research and development model: Programmatic issues and strategies. In S. Paine, G. T. Bellamy, & B. Wilcox (Eds.), *Human services that work* (pp. 57–78). Baltimore, MD: Paul H. Brookes.

Walker, H., Hops, H., & Greenwood, C. (1993). *RECESS: A program for reducing negative-aggressive behavior.* Seattle, WA: Educational Achievement Systems.

Walker, H. M., Irvin, L. K., Noell, J., & Singer, G. H. S. (1992). A construct score approach to the assessment of social competence: Rationale, technological considerations, and anticipated outcomes. *Behavior Modification, 16*, 448–474.

Walker, H. M., & McConnell, S. (1993a). *The Walker-McConnell scale of social competence and school adjustment.* Eugene: Center on Human Development, College of Education, University of Oregon.

Walker, H. M., & McConnell, S. R. (1993b). *The Walker-McConnell scale of social competence and school adjustment* (rev. ed.). Eugene: University of Oregon, Center on Human Development.

Walker, H. M., McConnell, S. R., & Clarke, J. Y. (1985). Social skills training in school settings: A model for the social integration of handicapped children into less restrictive settings. In R. McMahon & R. D. Peters (Eds.), *Childhood disorders: Behavioral-developmental approaches* (pp. 140–168). New York: Brunner/Mazel.

Walker, H. M., McConnell, S., Holmes, D., Todis, B., Walker, J., & Golden, N. (1983). *The Walker social skills curriculum: The ACCEPTS program (a curriculum for children's effective peer and teacher skills).* Austin, TX: PRO-ED.

Walker, H. M., & Reid, J. (in press). Long-term follow-up of antisocial and at-risk boys: Stability, change and group differences over a decade. *Journal of Emotional and Behavioral Disorders.*

Walker, H. M., Schwarz, I. E., Nippold, M., Irvin, L. K., & Noell, J. (1994). Social skills in school-age children and youth: Issues and best practices in assessment and intervention. In M. Nippold (Ed.), *Topics in Language Disorders: Pragmatics and Social Skills in School Age Children and Adolescents, 14*(3), 70–82.

Walker, H. M., & Severson, H. H. (1990). *Systematic screening for behavior disorders (SSBD): User's guide and technical manual.* Longmont, CO: Sopris West.

Walker, H. M., Severson, H. H., & Feil, E. G. (1994). *The Early Screening Project: A proven child-find process.* Longmont, CO: Sopris West.

Walker, H. M., Shinn, M. R., O'Neill, R. E., & Ramsey, E. (1987). A longitudinal assessment of the development of antisocial behavior in boys: Rationale, methodology and first year results. *Remedial and Special Education, 8*(4), 7–16, 27.

Walker, H. M., Stieber, S., & Eisert, D. (1991). Teacher ratings of adolescent social skills: Psychometric characteristics and factorial replicability across age-grade ranges. *School Psychology Review, 20*(2), 301–314.

Walker, H. M., Stieber, S., & O'Neill, R. E. (1990). Middle school behavioral profiles of antisocial and at-risk control boys: Descriptive and predictive outcomes. *Exceptionality, 1*, 61–77.

Walker, H. M., Stieber, S., Ramsey, E., & O'Neill, R. E. (1990). School behavioral profiles of arrested versus nonarrested adolescents. *Exceptionality, 1*, 249–265.

Walker, H. M., Stieber, S., Ramsey, E., O'Neill, R. E., & Eisert, D. (1994). Psychosocial correlates of at-risk status among adolescent boys: Static and dynamic relationships. *Remedial and Special Education.*

Walker, H. M., & Sylwester, R. (1991). Where is school along the path to prison? *Educational Leadership, 49*(1), 14–16.

Walker, H., Todis, B., Holmes, D., & Horton, G. (1988). *The Walker social skills curriculum: The ACCESS program (adolescent curriculum for communication and effective social skills).* Austin, TX: PRO-ED.

Walker, H. M., & Walker, J. E. (1991). *Coping with noncompliance in the classroom: A positive approach for teachers.* Austin, TX: PRO-ED.

Wang, M. C., Reynolds, M. C., & Walberg, H. J. (1986). Rethinking special education. *Educational Leadership, 44,* 26–31.

Weaver, M. (1994). Gazing into a crystal ball. *National School Safety Center News Journal, 3,* 8–11.

West, D. J., & Farrington, D. P. (1977). *The delinquent way of life.* London: Heinemann.

White, O. R., & Haring, N. G. (1980). *Exceptional teaching* (2nd ed.). Columbus, OH: Charles E. Merrill.

Will, M. C. (1986). Educating children with learning disabilities: A shared responsibility. *Exceptional Children, 52,* 411–415.

Williams, S. L., Walker, H. M., Holmes, D., Todis, B., & Fabre, T. R. (1989). Social validation of adolescent social skills by teachers and students. *Remedial and Special Education, 10*(4), 18–27, 37.

Wilson, J., & Howell, J. (1993). *A comprehensive strategy for serious, violent, and chronic juvenile offenders.* Washington, DC: U.S. Department of Justice, Office of Juvenile Justice and Delinquency Prevention.

Witt, J., & Martens, B. (1983). Assesssing the acceptability of behavioral interventions. *Psychology in the Schools. 20,* 510–517.

Witt, J., & Robbins, J. (1985). Acceptability of reductive interventions for the control of inappropriate child behavior. *Journal of Abnormal Child Psychology, 13,* 59–67.

Wolf, M. M. (1978). Social validity: The case for subjective measurement or how applied behavior analysis is finding its heart. *Journal of Applied Behavior Analysis, 11,* 203–214.

Wong, K., Kauffman, J., & Lloyd, J. W. (1991). Choices for integration: Selecting teachers for mainstreamed students with emotional or behavioral disorders. *Intervention in School and Clinic, 27*(2), 108–115.

Young, K. R. (1993). The role of social skills training in the prevention and treatment of behavioral disorders. In B. Smith (Ed.), *Focus '93—Teaching students with learning and behavioral problems* (pp. 341–367). Victoria, British Columbia: Smith and Associates.

Zaragoza, N., Vaughn, S., & McIntosh, R. (1991). Social skills interventions and children with behavior problems: A review. *Behavioral Disorders, 16*(4), 260–275.

Zigler, E., Taussig, C., & Black, K. (1992). Early childhood intervention: A promising preventative for juvenile delinquency. *American Psychologist, 47*(8), 997–1006.

Zoccolillo, M. (1993). Gender and the development of conduct disorder. *Development and Psychopathology, 5*(1/2), 65–78.

NAME INDEX

Achenbach, T. M., 2, 17, 49
Adams, M., 35
Ager, C., 240, 241
Alberg, J., 55, 103, 261
Alberto, P. A., 164
Albin, R., 61, 260
Algozzine, R., 58, 166, 173
American Psychiatric Association, 4
American Psychological Association, 2, 37, 361, 367, 368
Andrews, D., 310
Arata, B., 437–438
Archer, A. L., 55, 104, 159
Arnette, J., 360
Asher, S., 2, 4, 5, 7, 218, 271

Bailey, D. P., 101, 136, 178
Bain, A., 245
Bank, L., 223, 401
Barkley, R., 64
Barton, E., 224
Bastien, J., 260
Behrmann, R., 56
Belding, M., 222
Bell, 372
Berlinghoff, D. H., 100
Besay, V., 214
Bierman, K. L., 247
Biglan, T., 42
Billingsley, F. F., 179, 180
Binns, K., 360
Black, D. D., 260
Black, K., 46
Block-Pedego, A., 221
Bostic, M., 359, 367
Boyle, M., 12
Brakke, N., 194, 218
Braun, D., 176
Brendtro, L., 25
Brophy, J., 13, 174, 178
Brown, J., 310
Brown, L. J., 260
Brown, M., 9
Buckley, N. K., 154
Bullis, M., 9, 44, 45, 55
Burch, P., 205
Butterfield, G., 360

California Commission on Teacher Credentialing, 358
Cangelosi, J. S., 154, 155, 158, 160, 166, 167
Canter, L., 273
Canter, M., 273
Cantrell, M., 25, 27
Capaldi, D., 17, 21, 22, 264
Carnine, D., 101
Carr, E. G., 179
Catalano, R. F., Jr., 46
Chamberlain, P., 46
Charles, C. M., 150
Chiles, J., 16
Cicchetti, D., 4, 5, 20, 188
Clapp, B., 269
Clarke, J. Y., 7
Clark, L., 288
Clements, B. S., 172
Cloninger, C., 154
Coie, J., 4, 9, 12, 194, 204, 205, 218, 222, 229, 362, 364
Cole, C., 240, 241
Colvin, G. T., 80, 100, 104, 123, 132, 134, 135, 155, 159, 161, 164, 172, 176, 178, 179, 325, 326
Conway, G., 413
Cotton, K., 122, 124, 147, 172, 326
Cox, G., 16
Crawford, D., 205
Crowe, T., 220, 361, 362, 372, 380, 381, 382
Cuban, L., 33
Cubbage, 380
Cullinan, D., 125, 219
Cummings, C., 166, 167, 172
Curry, J., 205
Curwin, R. L., 150

Danielson, L., 46
Darch, C. B., 155, 172, 222
Day, 63
Dear, J., 359, 360
DeBaryshe, B. D., 9
DeComo, R., 359
DeForest, D., 176
Dennis, R., 154

Denny, R., 63
Deutchman, L., 155
Dishion, T. J., 5, 39, 103, 160, 220, 264, 268, 271, 310, 392, 399
Dodge, K. A., 5, 7, 9, 18, 194, 200, 218, 219, 222, 223
Dougherty, B. S., 255, 424
Downs, J., 260
Doyle, W., 174
Drummond, T., 50
Duke, D. L., 123, 124
Dumas, J. E., 5, 19, 155, 271, 399
Dunlap, G., 260
DuPaul, G. J., 64, 223, 255
Durand, V. M., 179

Eckert, T., 223, 260
Edelman, S., 154
Eisenberg, J., 2
Eisert, D., 17, 393
Eller, A., 55, 103, 261
Elliott, S., 219, 224, 225, 230, 231
Ellis, E., 255
Emmer, E., 172
Engelmann, S., 101, 161, 179
Epstein, M. H., 125
Erhardt, D., 47
Escalante, J., 436–437
Evans, I. M., 179
Evertson, C. M., 13, 172

Fabre, T. R., 7, 203, 229
Farrar, D., 359
Farrington, D. P., 271
Farris, H., 245
Feil, E. G., 53
Fiegenbaum, E., 413, 422
Fine, S., 17
Finley, 380
Fisher, J., 24
Fixsen, D. L., 260
Fleisch, B., 100, 123
Foley, R. M., 125
Forehand, R., 301, 302
Forness, S., 4
Fowler, M., 4
Fowler, S. A., 255, 424, 425
Frame, C. L., 219, 222, 223
Friedman, 56
Fuller, M., 261
Furlong, M., 361, 362
Furman, W., 247

Gagnon, C., 190
Garmezy, N., 56
Garrison, M., 127
Gatsonis, C., 16, 64
Genaux, 56
Gerber, M. M., 49
Gershaw, N. J., 103
Gersten, J., 2
Gersten, R. G., 124, 222
Gettinger, M., 100, 123
Giangreco, M. F., 154
Gilfrey, J., 322–324
Gleason, M. M., 55, 104, 159
Golden, N., 103
Goldstein, A., 103
Good, T., 13
Goodlad, J. I., 154
Greenberg, S., 100
Greenwood, C. R., 9, 199, 208, 211, 212, 213, 220, 224, 225, 346, 396, 414
Gresham, F. M., 219, 224, 225, 227, 228, 230, 231, 252
Griesler, P., 268
Groves, W. B., 40
Guerra, N., 436
Gunter, P., 63, 413
Guralnick, M., 7
Guskey, T., 124, 326

Haley, G., 17
Han, S., 47
Hargreaves, J., 38–39, 429–435
Haring, N. G., 178
Hawkins, J. D., 46
Hazel, J., 229
Heller, T., 67
Henry, T., 345
Hersh, R. H., 7, 47, 64, 172, 218, 222
Hinshaw, S., 12, 47
Hocutt, A. M., 64
Hodgkinson, M., 154
Hollinger, J., 7, 16, 188, 220, 222, 223, 227, 240, 241, 244
Holmes, D., 7, 103, 203, 229
Hoover, J., 12, 189
Hops, H., 9, 42, 199, 208, 211, 212, 213, 220, 224, 345, 346, 396, 405, 413, 414, 422
Horne, A., 4
Horner, R. H., 60, 61, 63, 67, 179, 180, 260
Horton, G., 103
Howell, J., 362, 368, 369
Huber, A., 47
Hunt, R., 9, 10
Hyman, I. A., 125

Institute of Medicine, 3
Irvin, L. K., 194, 200, 236, 260

Jack, S., 63, 413
Jacobs, M., 4, 12
Jenson, W. R., 60, 65, 174, 298, 302, 414
Johnson, D. W., 247
Johnson, R. T., 247
Jones, V., 104, 123
Joyce, S., 413
Juel, C., 35
Juul, K., 12, 189

Kameenui, E. J., 123, 132, 134, 135, 172, 176, 325
Kauffman, J. M., 4, 48, 124, 154, 219, 358, 366
Kavale, K., 255
Kazdin, A., 2, 3, 4, 5, 18, 19, 23, 24, 39, 42, 46, 59, 60, 188, 268, 272, 399
Kelley, M., 276
Kiehl, W., 223
Kirby, K., 424
Klein, M., 27, 361

Klein, P., 103
Knitzer, J., 100, 123
Koegel, R. L., 260
Kohler, F., 424
Kounin, J., 123
Kovacs, M., 16, 64
Krehbiel, G., 229
Kukic, S., 60, 65
Kupersmidt, J., 9, 218
Kutner, L., 12

Ladd, G. W., 222, 224
Lally, D., 125
Lampron, L., 205
Landrum, T. J., 48
Langner, T., 2
Lasley, T. J., 125
LeBlanc, M., 50
Leitman, R., 360
Lenox, K., 439
Lewin, L., 42
Lieberman, C., 37, 38, 68, 362
Lignugaris-Kraft, B., 260
Likins, 56
Lloyd, J. W., 48, 124
Lochman, J., 204, 205
Loeber, R., 20, 21, 50, 268, 270, 271, 392
Lombardi, T. P., 270
Long, N., 21, 25

Maag, J. W., 224, 227, 229, 236
Maddox, J., 370
Marchione, K., 46
Marinucci, C., 372, 386
Marriage, K., 17
Marshall, D., 359, 360
Martens, B., 67
McClaskey, C., 9
McConnell, S. R., 7, 13, 103, 219, 224, 225, 237
McFall, R., 227
McGinnis, E., 103
McIntosh, R., 103, 240
McKinney, J. D., 64
McMahon, R., 301, 302
Melloy, K., 255
Mendler, A. N., 150
Merrell, K. W., 224
Meyer, L. H., 179
Michelson, L., 46
Miller, M., 16
Miller, W., 310
Mirigian, G., 436, 439
Mischel, W., 403
Misra, A., 160, 161, 173
Montague, M., 64
Moreno, J., 227
Moretti, M., 17
Morgan, D. P., 56, 60, 65, 174, 298, 302, 414
Munthe, E., 189

National Clearinghouse on Child Abuse and Neglect Information, 26
National School Boards Association, 22
National School Safety Center, 375
Neel, R., 221
Nelson, J., 150
Nelson, M., 63
Nippold, M., 260
Noell, J., 194, 260
North, B., 438
Novotny, D. E., 270
Nurcombe, B., 5, 20, 188

Odel, K. S., 270
Oden, S., 222
Office of Educational Research and Improvement (OER), 36
Offord, D., 12
O'Leary, K. D., 64, 413, 422
Olweus, D., 189, 190, 192
O'Neill, R. E., 12, 17, 61, 166, 192, 219, 323, 392, 393
Osnes, P. G., 255
Oswald, L. K., 260

Paine, S. C., 155, 255, 260, 424
Parker, J., 2, 4, 5, 7, 218, 271
Patching, W., 176
Patterson, G. R., 5, 7, 9, 11, 13, 16, 17, 18, 19, 20, 21, 22, 24, 25, 27, 39, 46, 50, 103, 160, 218, 220, 221, 222, 223, 264, 268, 269, 270, 271, 272, 298, 304, 399, 400, 401, 403
Paulauskas, S., 16, 64
Pepler, D., 188, 224, 229
Perry, D. G., 220
Perry, L. C., 220
Petry, C., 55, 103, 261
Pettit, G., 9
Pfiffner, L., 64, 413, 422
Phillips, E. A., 260
Phillips, E. L., 260

Quay, H., 2, 12, 404
Quesada, R., 437

Racine, Y., 12
Radicchi, J., 155
Ramsey, E., 9, 12, 17, 166, 192, 219, 323, 392, 393, 400, 401, 403
Rasmussen, P., 220
Reavis, H. K., 60, 65
Reid, J. B., 2, 4, 5, 9, 12, 17, 20, 27, 39, 42, 46, 103, 160, 220, 246, 264, 268, 269, 365, 399
Repp, A., 60
Reynolds, M. C., 154
Rhode, G., 60
Rich, H., 13
Richards, C., 16, 64
Richters, J., 4
Robbins, J., 67
Robins, L. N., 3, 7
Roe, D. L., 48
Romer, D., 67
Rosellini, L. C., 155
Rosen, L., 413, 422
Rosenshine, B., 13
Ross, A., 53
Ross, S., 13
Roth, J. A., 361, 362, 364
Rubin, D., 188, 224, 229

Ruhl, K. L., 100
Rutherford, R., 221
Rutter, M., 56

Sabornie, E., 219
Safran, J. S., 164
Safran, S. P., 164
Salazar, N., 377
Sampson, R., 40
Sanford, J. P., 172
Sasso, G. M., 255
Sayger, T., 4
Schattman, R., 154
Schloss, C., 223
Schloss, P., 223
Schmaling, K. B., 270
Schoen, S., 300
Schorr, L., 2, 23, 27, 28, 37, 56, 264
Schrumpf, F., 205
Schumaker, J., 229, 255
Schwarz, I. E., 260
Scott, K., 359, 360
Scott, T., 164
Semmel, M. I., 49
Severson, H. H., 53, 55, 56, 187, 221, 312
Shapiro, E., 159, 175
Sheldon, J., 229
Sheldon-Wildgen, J., 229
Shelly, L., 189
Sherman, J., 229
Sherman, R., 100
Shinn, M. R., 12, 159, 160, 166, 175, 192, 193, 219, 392, 393
Shores, R., 63, 413
Simcha-Fagan, O., 2
Simmons, D. C., 176
Singer, G. H. S., 194
Singh, N., 60
Skinner, M. L., 268
Slavin, R., 247
Smith, M. A., 160, 161, 173
Smith-Davis, J., 24
Smylie, M. A., 124, 326, 327
Sprafkin, R. P., 103
Sprague, J., 61
Sprick, M., 127
Sprick, R., 124, 127, 150, 172, 178
Steinberg, Z., 100, 123
Steinhart, D., 367
Stephens, R., 359, 360, 362
Stephens, T., 230
Stieber, S., 17, 192, 219, 323, 392, 393
Stokes, T. F., 255
Stoner, G., 64
Stoolmiller, M., 268
Storey, K., 61
Strain, P. S., 7, 47, 59, 241
Strayhorn, J., 59, 241
Sugai, G., 67, 101, 102, 123, 132, 134, 135, 136, 164, 172, 176, 178, 179, 261, 325, 326
Swick, K. L., 123
Sylwester, R., 12

Taussig, C., 46
Thompson, T., 190
Tindal, G. A., 102, 179
Todd, A., 67
Todd, N. M., 224
Todis, B., 7, 103, 203, 221, 229
Trinidad, R., 437
Troutman, A. C., 164
Twain, M., 34

Underwood, M., 204, 222
Usadel, H., 205

Van Steenbergen, N., 369, 370
Vaughn, S., 103, 240
VonCleve, E., 46

Wagner, M., 13, 389
Wahler, R., 5, 19, 155, 271, 399
Walberg, H. J., 154
Walker, H. M., 7, 9, 11, 12, 13, 14, 15, 17, 24, 44, 45, 47, 53, 55, 59, 60, 64, 103, 154, 166, 172, 187, 191, 192, 194, 199, 203, 205, 208, 211, 212, 213, 218, 219, 220, 221, 222, 224, 225, 227, 229, 230, 237, 241, 242, 253, 260, 262, 301, 302, 323, 345, 346, 365, 392, 393, 396, 400, 401, 403, 405, 413, 414, 422
Walker, J. E., 64, 103, 301, 302
Wang, M. C., 154
Wayson, W. W., 125
Weaver, M., 370
Wells, P., 260
West, D. J., 271
West, R. P., 260
White, O. R., 178
Will, M. C., 154
Williams, S. L., 7, 203, 229
Wilson, J., 362, 368, 369
Wilt, J., 176
Winokur, S., 372, 386
Witt, J., 67
Wolery, M. R., 101, 136, 178
Wolf, M. M., 59, 260
Wong, K., 124
Wood, C., 223
Woodward, J., 124
Worsham, M. E., 172

Young, K. R., 61, 260
Ysseldyke, J., 58, 173

Zaragoza, N., 103, 240, 244
Zigler, E., 46, 47
Zoccolillo, M., 17, 18
Zoref, L., 56, 312

SUBJECT INDEX

Absences, student, bullying and, 189
Abused children. *See* Child abuse/neglect
Academic-engaged time (AET), 161–162
Academic learning
  antisocial behavior and, 13–14, 63
  behavior-instruction approach and, 326
  special education referrals and, 48–49
  start-up activities for, 165
Acceleration phase
  behavioral characteristics of, 85–87
  intervention strategies for, 107–111
ACCEPTS program
  described, 253–255
  instructional sequence of, 242–244
  recess rating form, 254, 256–257, 258–259
ACCESS social-skills curriculum, 229, 253
Accommodation phase, 45–46
Accountability, 125
Achenbach Child Behavior Checklist/aggression subscale, 17, 49, 349, 394
Achievement tests, 12–13
Acting-out behavior
  behavior management form for, 93–94, 116–118
  empirical study on, 390–391
  example of, 77–78
  phases in cycle of, 80–89, 90–92
  strategies for managing, 98–115
The Acting Out Child (Walker), 60, 65, 66
Activating events, 361
Activity levels, 39
Adaptive behavior
  behavior-instruction plan and, 176, 177
  pre-correction procedures and, 176–182
  for specific social situations, 200–202
  steps for teaching, 172–175
Adaptive negative behavior, 193
Addictive behavior
  early intervention for, 56
  media violence and, 38
ADHD (attention-deficit hyperactive disorder), 10, 63–64
Adjustment profiles, 393–395
Adolescents
  conduct disorder in, 5, 7
  empirical study of delinquency in, 400–403
Adult praise, 65, 81
Adults, antisocial, 5
AET (academic-engaged time), 161–162
Affective aggression, defined, 10
Affective problems, 16–17, 64
Age-appropriate behavior, 218
Aggression Replacement Training: A Comprehensive Intervention for Aggressive Youth (Goldstein and Glick), 263
Aggressive behavior. *See also* Bullying; Violence
  anger management training and, 204–205
  bullying as, 189–193
  early signs of, 11–12
  empirical studies on, 390–391, 414–418
  media and, 37–38
  neurological injuries and, 39
  peer rejection and, 218–219, 222–223
  on playgrounds, 14–16, 188–189
  RECESS program and, 205–212
  resources for addressing, 213–214
  special education referrals and, 48–49
  types of, 9–10
Agitation phase
  behavioral characteristics of, 78, 84–85

Agitation phase *(continued)*
  intervention strategies for, 105–107
Alcohol abuse. *See* Substance abuse
Alienated America: Racial Division and Youth Violence, 383
"Alone" behavior, defined, 226
Alpha commands, 301
Amelioration phase, 45
America. *See* United States
American Psychiatric Association, 4
American Psychological Association, 2, 37, 361, 367, 368
Anger management, 203–205, 323
Answering machines, teacher-parent communications through, 278–279
Antisocial behavior. *See also* Behavior problems; Conduct disorder
  in adults, 5
  affective status and, 16–17
  attention-deficit hyperactive disorder and, 10, 63–64
  causes and origins of, 18–19, 24–28
  costs of, 23–24
  defined, 2
  developmental continuum of services/expectations for, 44–46
  developmental pathways to, 19–21
  early screening and identification of, 47–55
  empirical studies on, 387–428
  facts on, 6
  gender and, 17–18
  misinterpretation of social situations and, 219–220, 222
  noncompliance and, 296, 298–302
  peer rejection and, 194, 200–201, 218–219, 222–223
  prevalence of, 3–4
  school adjustment and, 7–8
  social-environmental factors and, 37–42
  sociometric assessments of, 218–219
Antisocial personality disorder, defined, 5
Arguing, 85
Arrest status, empirical studies on, 387–390
Assault, peak phase and, 87
Assessment
  of need for social-skills training, 224–226, 230–235
  of social-skills interventions, 236
Assessment plan, for acting-out behavior cycle, 93–95, 116–118
ASSET social-skills curriculum, 229
At-risk students
  classroom behavior of, 14
  long-term outcomes for, 17
  parenting practices and, 399–400
  playground behavior of, 15, 192–193
  school-linked services for, 36–37
  screening of, 47–49
  social-skills training for, 224–225
  teaching adaptive strategies to, 200
Attention, securing, 166
Attention-deficit hyperactive disorder (ADHD), 10, 63–64
Authority assumption, 75
Avoidance
  acceleration phase and, 86
  de-escalation phase and, 89
  student privileges and, 107
Awards, for positive behavior, 129–130

Behavior
  in agitation phase, 84–86
  encouraging positive, 319–322
Behavioral consultants
  intervention by, 316
  teacher support by, 104
Behavioral contracts, 288–293
Behavioral efficiency, 62–63
Behavioral expectations
  classroom structure and, 157–158
  communicating to students, 114
Behavioral expectations *(continued)*
  formal behavior-instruction plan for, 132–134
  guidelines for, 128
  procedures for teaching, 129–134
  prompting, 180
  setting high, 124
  specifying schoolwide, 125, 128–129, 172, 178
Behavioral rehearsals
  as anger-control strategy, 205
  conducting, 179
Behavior disorders, as disability, 154
Behavior form
  sample of, 110
  student completion of, 110, 113
Behavior-instruction plan
  application of, 176
  "Coming to Class Prepared," 330, 331–332
  example of, 177
  Project PREPARE and, 326, 329–330
  steps in, 132–134, 135
Behavior intervention plan, 181
Behavior management. *See also* Classroom management
  of acting-out behavior cycle, 98–115
  CLASS program and, 345–346
  common assumptions and practices for, 75–76
  as component of ACCEPTS program, 254
  by individual staff members, 136–139
  proactive approaches to, 123
  resources for, 60–61
  of serious school violations, 140, 142, 145–146
  through staff meetings, 139–140
  as war, 166
Behavior problems. *See also* Antisocial behavior
  academic engagement and, 161
  categories of, 330
  context modification and, 179
  defining and categorizing, 136

Behavior problems *(continued)*
early correction of, 166–167, 175
externalized vs. internalized, 53
identifying context and type of, 178
individual management of, 136–139
negative consequences and, 134–135
procedures for correcting, 134–146
procedures for record keeping, evaluation, and dissemination, 146–147
replacement behaviors for, 178–179
staff management of, 139–140, 332, 336–337, 339
Behavior-specific praise, 59, 65, 81
Behavior-teaching plan, 130, 132
Best-practice procedures
for evaluating social-skills interventions, 235–236
guidelines for, 61–67
for schoolwide discipline plan, 123–125
for social-skills training, 240, 260–261, 262
BEST project, 60
Beta commands, 301
Blaming others, 88
Boys, antisocial, 6, 17–18, 223
Brainstorming, 105, 279–282
Building Classroom Discipline: From Models to Practice (Charles), 150
Building-team approach. *See also* Schoolwide discipline plan
establishing, 147–148
Project PREPARE and, 326, 327–330
Bullies and Victims in Schools: A Guide to Understanding and Management (Besay), 214
Bullying. *See also* Aggressive behavior; Violence
interventions against, 190–192
RECESS program and, 205–212

Bullying *(continued)*
resources for use in addressing, 213–214
in school environment, 189–190
teasing as form of, 189, 197–198
Bully Proofing Your School, 214
Buros Mental Measurements Yearbook, 225
Busy hands, agitation phase and, 84

Calendars, teacher-parent communications through, 275, 276
California Commission on Teacher Credentialing, School Violence Advisory Panel, 359
Calmness, as intervention strategy, 108
Calm phase
behavioral characteristics of, 81–82
intervention strategies for, 98–103
Case studies on antisocial behavior. *See also* Empirical studies on antisocial behavior
child abuse/neglect, 352–354
encouraging positive behavior, 319–322
First Steps program, 347–352
increasing positive peer interactions, 314–315
Project PREPARE, 325–344
reducing high-risk life-style factors, 308–314
Second Step curriculum program, 263, 322–325
Castalia Publishing Company, 304
"Caught-in-the-Act" awards, 129–130
CBM (curriculum-based measurement), 159–160, 175
Censorship, media violence and, 68
Center for the Future of Children, 36
CH.A.D.D. Educator's Manual, 64

Changes in routine, as school-based trigger, 82
Checklist of operating procedures, 156–157
Child abuse/neglect
antisocial behavior and, 25–26
case study on, 352–354
facts about, 26
Judge Hargreaves on, 429–435
preventing, 302, 303
Children with Attention Deficit Disorders (CH.A.D.D.), 64
CLASS program
case study of, 349–350
described, 345–346
Homebase program and, 346–347
Classroom entry activity, 165
Classroom management. *See also* Behavior management
calm phase and, 98–103
as instructional vs. disciplinary exercise, 172
Project PREPARE and, 325–344
Classroom, regular
behavior of antisocial students in, 13–14
empirical studies on antisocial behavior in, 390–391, 396–399, 414–418
implementing universal social-skills program in, 252
teaching social skills in, 245–252
violence-prevention program, 322–325
Classroom, special education
empirical study on, 387–390
referral process and, 48–49
social problems and, 244–245
Classroom rules
classroom structure and, 157–158
consequences for noncompliance with, 164–165
implementing, 163–164
Classroom skills, teaching, 253
Classroom structure
defined, 155
implementing, 98–100

Classroom structure *(continued)*
operating procedures checklist and, 156–157
physical arrangement of classroom and, 155–156
teacher expectations and, 157–158
Collaboration, interdisciplinary, 125
Collegial commitment, 124
"Coming to Class Prepared" behavior-instruction plan, 330, 331–332
Commands
guidelines for giving, 302
noncompliance with, 300–302
Commitment practices, 326–327
Communications
administration and staff, 124
between teachers and parents, 273–279
Community
socialization process and, 39–42
violent crime and, 366–369
Community services
First Steps program and, 347
mental health services, 2
school support by, 104
Compliance. *See also* Noncompliance
fostering, 299–300, 301–302
partial, 85–86
teaching adaptive strategies for, 202, 203
Conduct disorder. *See also* Antisocial behavior
in adults, 5
affective problems and, 16–17
causes and origins of, 18–19, 24–28
developmental pathways to, 19–21
diagnostic classification of, 4
gender and, 17–18
prevalence of, 3–4
school adjustment and, 7–8
Conflict resolution strategies. *See also* Peer mediation
parenting and, 299
teaching, 203–205
violence prevention through, 369
Conflicts, as school-based trigger, 82
Confusion, de-escalation phase and, 88
Consequences
definitions of, 338–339
establishing, 109
for noncompliance with rules, 164–165
non-negotiability of, 114
office referral, 338–339
proactive vs. reactive, 142, 145
for violent crimes, 365
Context modification, 179
Contingent attention, 102
Contract, as outcome of office referral, 339
Control assumption, 75
Cool-down time, 113
Cooperation
acknowledging, 164
conflict resolution and, 205
facilitating, 59
interdisciplinary, 125
Cooperative learning, 235, 246–247
Coping skills, teaching, 253
Correction plan/procedures
deciding on, 175
for noncompliance with rules, 164–165, 180
Corrections
opportunistic teaching and, 260
as school-based trigger, 83
Cost contingency procedures. *See also* Positive reinforcement; Punishment
empirical studies on using, 404–418
as intervention strategy, 59, 66–67
Costs, of antisocial behavior, 23–24
Counseling
as intervention strategy, 310
as outcome of office referral, 339
as teacher support, 104
Covert antisocial behavior
defined, 6
development of, 20–21
CPTED (Crime Prevention Through Environmental Design), 380–382
Crime. *See also* Juvenile delinquency; Violence
school-crime assessment tool, 371–372
in schools, 360–361
Crisis intervention, 299
Crisis-prevention strategies, 109
Criterion problems, acceleration phase and, 85–86
Crying, acceleration phase and, 86
Curricular interventions
implementing, 103–104
social-skills training and, 245, 247
Curriculum-based measurement (CBM), 159–160, 175
Custodial ingenuity, 382

Daily schedule, 159
DARE (Drug Abuse Resistance Education), 56, 367, 377
Darting eyes, agitation phase and, 84
Data management
for pre-correction plans, 181
for schoolwide discipline plans, 125, 149
David and Lucile Packard Foundation, 36
Dead time, avoiding, 167
Debriefing
as intervention strategy, 111, 114
opportunistic teaching and, 260
in Playground Behavior Game, 250–251
student avoidance of, 89
De-escalation phase
behavioral characteristics of, 87–88
intervention strategies for, 113
Defensiveness, recovery phase and, 89
Defiance, acceleration phase and, 85

Delinquency. *See* Juvenile delinquency
Denial, de-escalation phase and, 88
Department of Education, U.S., 64, 261, 325
Depression, 16–17, 64
Destruction of property
  acceleration phase and, 87
  peak phase and, 87
Detachment, as intervention strategy, 108
Detention, 338
Developmental continuum of antisocial behavior, 44–46
Developmental pathways to antisocial behavior, 19–21
Deviant behavior, empirical study on, 392–393
Deviant peer groups. *See also* Gang affiliation
  formation of, 220
  juvenile delinquency and, 19, 25, 27
Diagnostic and Statistical Manual of Mental Disorders (DSM-III-R), 4
Direct observations, 236
Direct speech, 167
Direct teaching approach, 227
Disabled students, instructing, 154
Discipline plan, schoolwide. *See* Schoolwide discipline plan
Discipline problems. *See* Infractions; Violations
Discipline strategies
  as instructional instruments, 123
  for parents, 293–296, 299–300
Discipline with Dignity (Curwin and Mendler), 150
Disobedient antisocial behavior, 20–21
Dissemination plan, 147
Documentation
  of behavior problems, 109–111
  of social-skill acquisition, 236
Dropout rate, for antisocial students, 17, 64
Drug abuse. *See* Substance abuse
Drug Abuse Resistance Education (DARE), 56, 367, 377
Dysfunctional homes. *See also* Family circumstance; Parenting practices
  as nonschool-based trigger, 83

Early Screening Project (ESP), 53–55
Early starters, antisocial behavior of, 268
Economics
  of antisocial behavior, 23–24, 25
  of public school support, 34–35
Education, U.S. Department of, 64, 261, 325
Educational Achievement Systems, 214
Educational resources. *See* Resources, educational
Effective instruction, principles of, 58
Emotions, strategies for managing, 204–205
Empathy, teaching, 63, 323
Empirical studies on antisocial behavior, 387–428. *See also* Case studies on antisocial behavior
  acting-out/disruptive students, 390–391
  adjustment profiles of middle school boys, 393–395
  adolescent delinquency, 400–403
  arrested students, 387–390
  deviant behavior of middle school boys, 392–393
  in free-play settings, 418–422
  generalization of home and school behavior, 403–404
  increasing positive social interactions, 418–422
  maintaining behavioral gains, 422–424
  of middle school boys, 392–395
Empirical studies on antisocial behavior *(continued)*
  negative-aggressive students, 390–391, 414–418
  playground and classroom settings, 396–399
  poor parenting practices, 399–403
  positive and negative reinforcement procedures, 404–418
  RECESS program efficacy, 424–428
  in regular classrooms, 390–391, 396–399, 414–418
  response-cost interventions, 404–424
  special education students, 387–390
Encouragement
  importance of parental, 284, 287–293
  for positive behavior, 319–322
Enhancers, of school adjustment, 7
Entry routine, classroom, 165
Environment
  classroom, 155–156
  crime prevention and, 380–382
  need for positive, 125
  restoration of, 111, 113
Environment-program fit or match, 67
Error correction
  managing, 163
  as school-based trigger, 83
Escalating behavior chain
  avoiding escalating prompts in, 108
  recognizing pattern of, 78–80
  violence and, 370
Escapist behavior, acceleration phase and, 86
ESP (Early Screening Project), 53–55
Ethnic tensions, 372, 373
Eugene Register-Guard, 39
Evaluation
  of classroom discipline, 175

Evaluation *(continued)*
of schoolwide discipline plan, 146–147, 149
Exit paperwork, 109–110, 113
Exit routine, classroom, 168
Expectations. *See* Behavioral expectations
Explanation times and procedures, identifying, 173–174
Expulsion, school, 338
Externalized behavior problems
defined, 53
playground behavior and, 187–188
school-based support services and, 221
External support systems, resiliency and, 56

Fairness, student privileges and, 107
Family circumstance. *See also* Parenting practices
antisocial behavior and, 18–19, 20, 39–40, 155, 222, 268–272
case study on, 352–354
family-management techniques and, 299–300, 400–403
literacy and, 35–36
resiliency and, 56
Fast Track program, 373–374
Feedback system
in behavior-teaching plan, 132
for schoolwide discipline plans, 149
Feedback times and procedures, identifying, 175
First Steps program, 344–352
background of case study on, 347–349
CLASS program and, 345–346
community support services in, 347
described, 344–345
Homebase program and, 346–347
intervention strategies in, 345–346, 349–350
First Steps program *(continued)*
parent training module in, 346–347
results of interventions in, 350–351
summary analysis of, 351–352
Fit or match considerations, 67
Follow-through, consequences, 109
Formal methods
identifying problem behavior through, 178
for social-skills assessment, 231, 235
Forms, sample
ACCEPTS recess rating, 256–257, 258–259
assessment/behavior management, 93–95, 116–118
behavior-instruction plan, 177
determining social-skills deficits, 233, 234
office referral, 143–144, 333–334
point-reward chart/contract, 290–291
pre-correction checklist and plan, 182
problem-solving worksheet, 281–282
RECESS point record, 208, 209, 210
recording, 337
staff-meeting, 141, 340–341
student self-evaluation, 110
Free-play behavior. *See also* Playground behavior
of antisocial students, 186–189, 191–192
empirical study of, 418–422
generic social skills and, 202–203
peer-related adjustment and, 188–189
social-skills incentive system for, 248–252
Free-time activities, 156
Frequency ratings, 230, 231, 232
Full Inclusion Movement, 154
Functional analysis, 61
Functional replacements, 179
The Future of Children: School-Linked Services, 36

Gang affiliation
bullying and, 189–190
deviant peer groups and, 220
fact sheet on, 376–377
juvenile delinquency and, 19, 25, 27, 374–379
as modern tribalism, 375
as nonschool-based trigger, 83
prevention-intervention strategies for, 377–379
racial tensions and, 372
resources on, 383–384
social disorganization and, 40–41
violent behavior and, 22
Gang Assessment Tool, 374–375
Gangs in Schools (NSSC), 379
Gender differences, antisocial behavior and, 17–18
Generalization processes
empirical studies on, 403–404
social-skills training and, 246, 248
"Generals in the War on School Violence," 386, 436–439
Generic social-skills training, 202–203
as three-step process, 241–242
Generic strategies
defined, 61
for preventing/remediating negative playground behavior, 199–205
Girls, antisocial, 6, 17–18
Goal orientation, calm phase and, 82
Good news notes, teacher-parent communications through, 276, 278
Government institutions, media violence and, 69
Group-entry skill training, 204
Group involvement/withdrawal, agitation phase and, 84

Group reinforcement contingencies, 65
Group work, classroom arrangement and, 155–156
Guns
  availability of, 359
  in schools, 189, 379–380

Hands, containment of, agitation phase and, 85
Head injuries, aggressive behavior and, 39
Health awareness training, 56
Health problems, as nonschool-based trigger, 83
Helping Kids Handle Anger: Teaching Self-Control (Huggins), 263
High-risk life-style factors, reducing, 308–314
  background of case study on, 308–309
  intervention strategies for, 309–313
  results of interventions for, 313
  summary analysis of, 313–314
Homebase parent training program, 346–347
  content of lessons in, 348
Home behavioral contracts, 288–293
Home-discipline strategies, 293–296
  privilege removal, 295–296
  time-out, 293–294
  work chores, 296, 297
Home–school interventions, 282–284, 285–287. *See also* School-based interventions
  case study on, 319–322
  home behavioral contracts, 288–293
  home-discipline strategies, 293–296
  home–school cards, 283–284
  home–school contracts, 284, 287
Hormone levels, antisocial behavior and, 39
Hyperventilation, peak phase and, 87

IDEA (Individuals with Disabilities Act), 4, 309
Identification of antisocial behavior patterns, 47–49
Illegal behavior, defined, 136, 138, 330
Impairers, school adjustment, 7
Implementation recommendations, for intervention strategies, 64–67
Importance ratings, of social skills, 230, 231
Impulsive aggression, defined, 10
Impulsivity, 39
Incarceration
  of juveniles, 429–435
  prevention vs., 367
  violence and, 362, 364–365
Incentive-based approach
  for generalized social-skills program, 248–249
  performance deficits and, 227–228
Incentives, for home-school interventions, 285–287
Incompatible replacement behaviors, 179
Independent activities
  classroom arrangement and, 155
  as intervention strategy, 106, 113
Independent routines, establishing, 161
Individual reinforcement contingencies, 65
Individuals with Disabilities Act (IDEA), 4, 309
Informal methods
  identifying problem behavior through, 178
  for social-skills assessment, 231
Information delivery, 109
Information-sharing system, 380
Infractions. *See also* Violations
  minor, 136, 330, 332
  office referral, 138, 330, 332
  staff meetings for, 332, 336–337, 339
Injuries, playground, 190
In-school suspension/detention, 338
Institute of Medicine, 3
Instruction. *See also* Teaching practices
  as component of ACCEPTS program, 254
  intensive, 242
  interventions during, 163–168
  planned variation of, 160
  principles of effective, 58
  strategies for delivering, 158–163
Instructional objectives, 159
Instrumental aggression, defined, 10
Intensive instruction, 242
Interactions, teacher-student, 161
Internalized behavior problems
  defined, 53
  playground behavior and, 187–188
Intervention outcomes
  factors affecting, 42–44
  of social-skills interventions, 236
Intervention plan, for acting-out behavior cycle, 93–94, 116–118
Intervention strategies. *See also specific strategy*
  generic, 61–64
  implementation recommendations for, 64–67
  key target areas for, 55–57
  recommendations for, 59–61
  universal vs. selected, 57–59
Intimidation. *See also* Bullying
  acceleration phase and, 86
  intervention for, 386
Introductory letter, teacher-parent communications through, 274–275
Isolation, as intervention strategy, 113

Journal of Emotional and Behavioral Problems, 27
Juvenile delinquency. *See also* Aggressive behavior; Violence
conduct disorder and, 5, 7, 11, 17
deviant peer groups and, 19, 25, 27
early vs. late starters in, 21
Fast Track program and, 373–374
gang affiliation and, 19, 25, 27, 374–379
increases in, 362, 363–364
intervention approaches to, 364–374
parenting practices and, 271, 400–403
prevention of, 46–47, 367–369
resources on, 383–384
social disorganization and, 40–41
violent crime and, 359–361
Juvenile Justice and Delinquency Prevention, U.S. Office of, 383

Kindergartens
case study on behavior intervention for, 347–352
First Steps program and, 344–352

Letter of introduction, teacher-parent communications through, 274–275
Likert rating scales, 53, 225, 231, 232, 254
Limit testing, acceleration phase and, 85–86
Listening skills, 205
Literacy, reading opportunities and, 35–36
Long-term interventions, for peak-phase behavior, 112–113
Los Angeles Times, 27

Mainstreaming, 222
Maintenance processes
empirical studies on, 422–424
Maintenance processes *(continued)*
social-skills training and, 246, 248, 255
Major violations. *See* Violations
Managing Anger Skills Training (Eggert), 263
Mastery learning, 159
Mediation. *See* Peer mediation
Media violence
NCTV plan for, 68–69
violent behavior and, 37–38
Mental health, 58–59
Mental health services, 2
Middle school boys
adjustment profiles of, 393–395
deviant behavior of, 392–393
Minor infractions. *See* Infractions
Mission statement, 127
Modified behavior-teaching plan, 130, 132
Monitoring
parental, 299
of pre-correction plan, 181
Project PREPARE and, 329
of student performance, 159–160, 175
Movement activities, 106

NAME (National Association for Mediation), 369
National Centers for Disease Control, 358
National Clearinghouse on Child Abuse and Neglect Information, 26
National Coalition on Television Violence (NCTV), 37, 68–69
National Institute of Mental Health, 246, 373
National School Boards Association, 22
National School Safety Act of 1993, 190
National School Safety Center, 214, 370, 374, 375, 379, 380, 383
Nature-nurture controversy, 39
NCTV (National Coalition on Television Violence), 37, 68–69
Negative consequences
behavior management and, 134–135
establishing, 109
Negative social behavior, defined, 226
Negotiation skills, 205
Neighborhood factors, antisocial behavior and, 40–41
Neurological injuries, aggressive behavior and, 39
New Beginnings program, 36
Newsletters, teacher-parent communications through, 275, 277
New York Times, 359
Noncompliance. *See also* Compliance
acceleration phase and, 85
dealing with, 296, 298–302
defined, 300–301
Noncontingent attention, 102–103
Nonconversational language, agitation phase and, 84
Nonparticipant, in bullying behavior, 190
Nonschool-based triggers, 83
Normal behavior patterns, 187–188
Normative standards, teaching, 199
Northwest Media, Inc., 304
Notice board, 156
Nutritional deficiency, as nonschool-based trigger, 83

Observable replacement behaviors, 178
OERI (Office of Educational Research and Improvement), 36
Office conference, described, 338
Office of Juvenile Justice and Delinquency Prevention, U.S., 383
Office referral form
Project PREPARE, 330–331, 333–334
sample of, 143–144

Office-referral infractions
consequences for, 338–339
definitions for, 138, 335–336
Project PREPARE and, 330, 332–343
Office of Special Education Programs, U.S., 261, 325, 345, 346
Office of Technology Assessment, U.S., 383
Off-task behavior, acceleration phase and, 85
Off-task/on-task behavior, agitation phase and, 84
One-to-one instruction, 242
On-task behavior
calm phase and, 81
recovery phase and, 88–89
Operating procedures checklist, 156–157
Opportunistic teaching, 255, 260–261
Oregon Research Institute, 312
Oregon Social Learning Center, 304, 388
Outcome assessments, 236
Out-of-school suspension, 338
Over-aroused aggression, defined, 10
Overt antisocial behavior
defined, 6
development of, 20–21

Pacing, instructional, 160
Packard Foundation, 36
Paperwork, documentation and, 109–110
Parenting practices. *See also* Family circumstance
antisocial behavior and, 18–19, 20, 39, 218, 268–272
child abuse and, 302, 303
child encouragement and, 284, 287–293
child noncompliance and, 296, 298–302
Parenting practices *(continued)*
empirical studies on, 399–403
family-management techniques and, 299–300
Homebase training program and, 346–347, 348
home behavioral contracts and, 288–293
home-discipline strategies and, 293–296
home–school interventions and, 282–284, 285–287
juvenile delinquency and, 271, 400–403
prosocial behavior and, 268–269, 272
recommended resources on, 304
student achievement and, 269–273
teacher involvement in, 273–282
Parent telephone call/meeting, as outcome of office referral, 339
Parent training, First Steps program, 346–347
Partial compliance, acceleration phase and, 85–86
Peak phase
behavioral characteristics of, 87
intervention strategies for, 111–113
Peer groups
ACCEPTS program and, 255
deviant, 19, 25, 27, 220
do's and don'ts for entering, 196
entering, by antisocial students, 194, 200–201
generalized social-skills training in, 246–247, 248–252
involvement in social-skills interventions by, 244
rejection of antisocial students by, 218–219, 222–223, 244–245
Peer interactions, increasing positive, 314–319
background of case study on, 314–315
intervention strategies for, 315–317
Peer interactions *(continued)*
results of interventions for, 318
summary analysis of, 318–319
Peer mediation. *See also* Conflict resolution strategies
steps in, 205
violence prevention through, 369–370
Peer Mediation: Conflict Resolution in Schools (Schrumpf, Crawford, and Usadel), 263
Peer pressures, 312
Peer-related adjustment
aggression and, 9, 11
defined, 7
in free-play settings, 188–189, 191–193
survey on importance of, 229–230
teaching social skills for, 203
Peer tutoring
ACCEPTS program and, 255
facilitating positive mental health through, 59
social-skills training and, 193, 241
Performance deficits
ascertaining, 228
social-skills deficits and, 227–228
Perpetrator, of bullying behavior, 190
Perry Preschool Project, 47
Personality dispositions, resiliency and, 56
Person-environment fit or match, 67
Phone calls, teacher-parent communications through, 276–279
Physical arrangement, classroom, 155–156
Planned variation, 160
Playground behavior. *See also* Free-play behavior
ACCEPTS program and, 254
of antisocial students, 14–16, 186–189, 191–192
empirical study on, 396–399

Playground behavior *(continued)*
generalization training in social skills and, 246
peer-group entry and, 194
preventing/remediating negative, 199–205
RECESS program and, 205–212
social-skills incentive system for, 248–252
teasing and provocation as, 195–198
Playground Behavior Game, 246, 248–251
debriefing session, 250–251
materials needed for, 251
negative behavior in, 250
positive behavior in, 249–250
Point record form, RECESS program, 208, 209, 210
Point-recording form, ACCEPTS program, 254, 256–257, 258–259
Point-reward chart/contract, 289, 290–291
Police contact, as student consequence, 338
Positive behavior, encouraging, 319–322
background of case study on, 319–320
empirical study on, 418–422
intervention strategies for, 320–322
summary analysis of, 321–322
Positive Discipline (Nelson), 150
Positive mental health, facilitating, 58–59
Positive-play training
as intervention strategy, 204
Playground Behavior Game as, 248–251
Positive reinforcement. *See also* Cost contingency procedures; Rewards
for cooperative students, 164
for demonstrations of expected behavior, 134

Positive reinforcement *(continued)*
empirical studies on using, 404–418
home behavioral contracts and, 288–293
for increasing positive peer interactions, 316–317, 319
as instructional strategy, 163
as intervention strategy, 59
parenting practices and, 298, 299–300
schoolwide structures for, 129–130
teachers' preference for, 67
Positive temperament, resiliency and, 56
Poverty, literacy and, 35
Practice times and procedures, identifying, 174
Praise
calm phase and, 81
as intervention strategy, 65
Pre-correction, defined, 176
Pre-correction plan/procedures
application of, 181
behavior problems and, 104, 133–134
checklist for, 182
monitoring, 181
steps in, 176–182
Predatory aggression, defined, 10
Preferred activities, 106
Preschool children
ESP screening procedure and, 55
identifying antisocial behavior in, 47, 63
Pressure, as school-based trigger, 83
Prevention
behavior management through, 168
Fast Track program and, 373–374
incarceration vs., 367
Project PREPARE and, 325–344
universal interventions and, 57
of violence, 367–369
Prevention phase, 44–45

Principal, school, leadership role of, 123
Principles of effective instruction, 58
Prisons, educational funding vs., 34–35
Privileges
removal of, 295–296, 338
as rewards, 175
Proactive consequences, 142, 145
Proactive screening process, 48–49
Proactivity, behavior management and, 123, 168
Problem behavior. *See* Behavior problems
Problem-solving approach. *See also* Social problem solving
for antisocial behavior, 279–282
in parenting, 299
steps in, 280
for students, 114, 312–313
teaching skills for, 205, 247–248, 323
Problem-solving worksheet, 281–282
Procedures, identifying reinforcement, 174–175
Program-environment fit or match, 67
Project PREPARE, 325–344. *See also* Schoolwide discipline plan
background of case study on, 328
as intervention strategy, 328–339
office-referral behaviors, 335–336
office-referral form, 333–334
overview of, 325–328
recording form, 332, 337
results of intervention with, 339–343
summary analysis of, 343–344
Prompting
behavioral expectations, 180
opportunistic teaching and, 260
Prosocial behavior
defined, 2
parenting practices and, 268–269, 272

Providing attention, 101–103
Provocation
  acceleration phase and, 85
  do's and don'ts for responding to, 197, 201–202
  overview of responses to, 201
  responses to, by antisocial students, 195
  as school-based trigger, 82
Psychologists, teacher support by, 104
Public Attitude(s) Toward the Public Schools (Gallup Poll), 122
Public health campaign, on media violence, 69
Public schools
  community integration of, 39–32
  economics of, 34–35
  prevention/remediation of antisocial behavior by, 33–37
  public attitude toward, 122
  violence in, 25, 360–361, 370–372
"Pull-out" social-skills training programs
  ACCEPTS program and, 253–255
  problems with, 244–245
Punishment. *See also* Cost contingency procedures; Positive reinforcement
  behavior management and, 168
  as intervention technique, 60
  parenting practices and, 296
  teachers' concerns about, 67
Purpose statement, for school discipline plan, 127

Quality instruction, implementing, 100–101
Questioning, acceleration phase and, 85
Quiet-time areas, 156

Racial tensions, 372
Ratings system, for media violence, 68

RC procedures. *See* Response cost (RC) procedures
Reactive consequences
  behavior management and, 168
  proactive consequences vs., 142, 145
Reactive screening, 48–49
Reactivity, pre-correction vs., 176
Reading opportunities, literacy and, 35–36
Recess
  ACCEPTS program intervention and, 254–255
  behavior of antisocial students during, 188, 191
RECESS program, 205–212
  acquiring, 214
  components of, 205–206
  empirical studies on, 396, 404–405, 422, 424–428
  phases of, 206
  point record form, 208, 209, 210
  positive/negative response rates and, 211, 212
  referral graph, 206, 207
  rule-breaking rate and, 213
Recognition, for positive behavior, 130
Reconciliation, de-escalation phase and, 88
Recording form, Project PREPARE, 332, 337
Recovery phase
  behavioral characteristics of, 88–89
  intervention strategies for, 114
Reduce-and-replace strategy, 206
Referral graph, RECESS program, 206, 207
Referral process
  for mental health services, 2
  proactive screening and, 48–49
Regular Education Initiative, 154
Reinforcement. *See also* Cost contingency procedures; Positive reinforcement; Punishment
  contingencies for, 65, 174, 180

Reinforcement *(continued)*
  of home–school interventions, 285–287
Relationship building, 61, 310
Relationship skills training. *See* Social-skills training
Relaxation activities, 107
Relaxation training, 205
Remediation, Project PREPARE and, 325–344
Remediation phase, 44–45
Reminder times and procedures, identifying, 174
Remind procedure, 131–132
Replacement behaviors, specifying, 178–179
Reprogramming Environmental Contingencies for Effective Social Skills program. *See* RECESS program
Research Press Publishing Company, 304
Resiliency
  adverse family circumstances and, 272
  factors contributing to, 56–57
RESIST program, 56
A Resource Guide for Social Skills Instruction (Alberg, Perry, and Eller), 261
Resources, educational
  on aggressive behavior, 213–214
  on behavior management, 60–61
  on bullying, 214
  on gang affiliation, 383–384
  on juvenile delinquency, 383–384
  on parenting practices, 304
  on school safety, 383–384
  on social-skills training, 261, 263–264
  on teasing, 214
  on violence, 383–384
Respect, as intervention strategy, 108
Response cost (RC) procedures. *See also* Positive reinforcement; Punishment

Response cost (RC) procedures *(continued)*
  empirical studies on using, 404–418
  as intervention strategy, 59, 66–67
Responsiveness to directions/tasks, de-escalation phase and, 88
Review system
  for classroom discipline, 175
  for schoolwide discipline plans, 146–147, 149
Reward menu, 289
Rewards. *See also* Positive reinforcement
  generalized social-skills program and, 248–249
  home–school interventions and, 283–284, 285–287
  in Playground Behavior Game, 249–250
  teachers' use of, 175
"Rising Above Gangs and Drugs" program, 377, 379
Risky behavior. *See* High-risk life-style factors, reducing
Robert Wood Johnson Foundation, 36
Role-playing, 247
Rule-breaking rate, 213
Rule compliance, calm phase and, 81
Rules
  classroom structure and, 157–158
  consequences for noncompliance with, 164–165
  implementing classroom, 163–164
  schoolwide, 125

Safety, school. *See* School safety
San Francisco Examiner, 386
Scale of Social Competence and School Adjustment (SSCSA), 225
Scandinavia, studies of bullying in, 189
Schedule, daily, 159
School activities, resiliency and, 56–57
School adjustment, conduct disorder and, 7–8
School-based interventions. *See also* Home–school interventions
  defined, 32
  effective instruction and, 58
  facilitating positive mental health through, 58–59
  factors affecting outcomes of, 42–44
  Fast Track program and, 373–374
  First Steps program and, 345–346
  for gang problems, 377–379
  for preventing violence, 365–366, 369–374
  resiliency and, 56–57
  support services for, 221
  teachers' concerns about, 67
School-based triggers, 82–83
School-crime assessment tool, 371–372
School discipline manual
  developing/revising, 148
  Project PREPARE and, 329
School–home interventions. *See* Home–school interventions
School–home notes, teacher-parent communications through, 276
School-linked services
  for at-risk children, 36–37
  key target areas for, 55–56
School mission statement, 127
School safety
  concern about, 190
  increasing, 379–382
  resources on, 383–384
  violence and, 360–361
School Safety Checkbook (NSSC), 380
School Violence Advisory Panel of the California Commission on Teacher Credentialing, 359
Schoolwide discipline plan
  correcting problem behavior through, 134–146
Schoolwide discipline plan *(continued)*
  foundational phases in design of, 126–147
  implementation steps for, 147–149
  Project PREPARE as, 325–344
  research findings and best practices for, 123–125
  Second Step curriculum as, 322–325
  teaching behavioral expectations through, 128–134
  violence-prevention programs and, 322–325
Schoolwide positives
  example of, 131
  implementing, 129–130
Screening/identifying antisocial behavior patterns, 47–55
  with Achenbach Behavior Checklist, 49–50
  with ESP, 53–55
  guidelines for, 48
  on playgrounds, 187–188
  with Student Risk Screening Scale, 50–52
Second Step: A Violence Prevention Curriculum Committee for Children, 263, 322–325
  background of case study on, 322–323
  as intervention strategy, 323–324
  key features of, 325
  results of intervention with, 324
  summary analysis of, 325
Security systems, school, 190
Selected interventions. *See also* Universal interventions
  defined, 57
  determining, 235
  prevention/remediation of antisocial behavior through, 32
  social-skills training and, 253–255
  usefulness of, 57–59
Self-abuse, peak phase and, 87

Self-control building, 310
Self-esteem problems
  antisocial students and, 16–17, 221
  intervention for, 310
Self-management, as intervention strategy, 106–107
Self-related adjustment
  defined, 7
  survey on importance of, 229–230
  teaching social skills for, 203
Self-talk, as anger-control strategy, 205
Serious behavior, acceleration phase and, 87
"Seriously emotionally disturbed" label, 221, 222
Set Straight on Bullies, 214
Short-term interventions, for peak-phase behavior, 112
Situational risk factors, 361
Skill building, 310, 312
Sleep problems, as nonschool-based trigger, 83
Small-group instruction, 242
Social acceptability, of social-skills training, 230
Social-behavioral adjustments, for schoolchildren, 7–8
Social disorganization, 40–41
Social-environmental factors, 37–42
Social importance, of social-skills training, 229–230
Socialization process
  aggressive behavior and, 9, 11
  responsibility of schools for, 33–35
Socially responsible decision making, 63
Social maladjustment, defined, 4
Social problem solving. *See also* Problem-solving approach
  difficulties with, as trigger for acting out, 83
  establishing a plan for, 104, 114
Social problem solving *(continued)*
  social-skills training vs., 240–241
  teaching, 205, 247–248, 323
Social reinforcers, 175
Social significance, of social-skills training, 228–229
Social skills
  of antisocial students, 219–220
  approaches to teaching, 240–241
  definition and conceptualization of, 227–228
  documenting acquisition of, 236
  empirical study on improving, 418–422
  prompting, 260
  rating scales for, 225
Social-skills curricula/programs, 261, 263–264
Social-skills deficits
  ascertaining specific, 228
  determination form, 233, 234
  performance deficits and, 227–228
Social Skills Rating System (SSRS), 225, 230–231
Social-skills training
  ACCEPTS program and, 242–244, 253–255
  in anger management, 203–205
  best-practices guidelines for, 260–261, 262
  in calm phase of acting-out cycle, 103
  in conflict resolution, 205
  contextual factors mediating, 241–245
  cooperative learning and, 235, 246–247
  curricula for, 261, 263
  evaluating, 235–236, 261, 263
  in generic social skills, 202–203
  identifying students needing, 224–226
  as intervention strategy, 55–56, 59, 66
  on normative standards, 199
Social-skills training *(continued)*
  opportunistic teaching methods and, 257, 260
  peer rejection and, 223
  peer tutoring and, 193
  problems with "pull-out" programs for, 244–245
  resources for conducting, 261, 263–264
  selected approach to, 253–255
  social problem-solving strategies vs., 240–241
  for specific social situations, 200–202
  targeting skills for, 228–235
  teacher assessment of need for, 224–226, 230–235
  universal approach to, 245–252
  violence prevention through, 369
Social validity, 228–230
Social workers, teacher support by, 104
Societal problems
  antisocial behavior and, 39–42
  case study on, 352–354
  school-based interventions and, 33–37
  violence and, 359–362, 366–369
Sociometric assessments
  of antisocial students, 218–219
  of outcomes of social-skills intervention, 236
  social-skills training and, 224
The Solution Book (Sprick), 150
Space, providing, as intervention strategy, 106
Special education
  empirical study on, 387–390
  referral process and, 48–49
Special Education Programs, U.S. Office of, 261, 325, 345, 346
Spectrum, 383
Speech, direct, 167
"Sponge" activities, 167
SRSS (Student Risk Screening Scale), 50–52

SSBD (Systematic Screening for Behavior Disorders), 55, 187–188
SSCSA (Walker-McConnell Scale of Social Competence and School Adjustment), 225
SSRS (Social Skills Rating System), 225, 230–231
Staff development plan
  designing/implementing, 148
  Project PREPARE as, 326–327
Staff meeting form
  Project PREPARE, 340–341
  sample of, 141
Staff meetings
  behavior management through, 139–140, 338
  guidelines for conducting, 332, 336–337, 339
Stand and Deliver, 436
Standardized achievement tests, 12–13
Staring into space, agitation phase and, 84
Statement of purpose, for school discipline plan, 127
Stigmatization, 245
Storage materials, classroom arrangement and, 156
Strategies and Tactics for Effective Instruction (Algozzine and Ysseldyke), 58
Student contract, 284, 287
Student monitoring and review procedures, 175
Student Risk Screening Scale (SRSS), 50–52
Studies on antisocial behavior. *See* Case studies on antisocial behavior; Empirical studies on antisocial behavior
Study skills training, 55
Subdued behavior
  agitation phase and, 84
  recovery phase and, 89
Substance abuse
  child abuse and, 26
  drug use of antisocial boys and, 17
Substance abuse *(continued)*
  early intervention for, 56
  as nonschool-based trigger, 83
  violence and, 359–360, 361, 362
Successive interactions, recognizing, 80
Supervise procedure, 132
Suppression strategies, 362, 364–365
Survey, on adjustment types, 229–230
Suspension, school, 338
Syracuse University Family Development Research Project, 47
Systematic Screening for Behavior Disorders (SSBD), 55, 187–188

Tangibles, as rewards, 175
Tantrums, peak phase and, 87
Task responsiveness, 88
Teacher assessment, social-skills training and, 224–226, 230–235
Teacher-assistance team (TAT), 327, 328–330
Teacher expectations, planning, 157–158
Teacher proximity, 106
Teacher rankings/ratings
  evaluating social-skills interventions through, 236
  on need for social-skills training, 224–225
Teacher recognition, 106
Teacher-related adjustment
  defined, 7
  survey on importance of, 229–230
  teaching social skills for, 203
Teachers
  child-abuse prevention by, 302, 303
  concerns about school-based interventions, 67
  coping with noncompliance, 296, 298–302
Teachers *(continued)*
  home behavioral contracts and, 288–293
  home-discipline strategies and, 293–296
  home–school interventions by, 282–284, 285–287
  parental encouragement of students and, 284, 287–293
  positive attitude toward parents, 273–274
  problem-solving approach for, 279–282
  types of communications with parents, 274–279
Teacher's desk, classroom arrangement and, 156
Teacher-student interactions, 161
Teacher training, school discipline plan and, 124
Teaching practices. *See also* Instruction
  opportunistic, 255, 260–261
  strategies for, 158–163
Teams, disciplinary
  school building, 147–148
  for serious school violators, 145–146
Teasing. *See also* Aggressive behavior
  do's and don'ts for responding to, 197, 201–202
  as form of bullying, 189, 197–198
  overview of responses to, 201
  resources for use in addressing, 213–214
  responses to, by antisocial students, 195
Technology Assessment, U.S. Office of, 383
Telephone calls, teacher-parent communications through, 276–279
Television violence, NCTV plan for, 68–69
Temperament, antisocial behavior and, 39
Temporal proximity, violence and, 361

Threats, acceleration phase and, 86
Time, providing, as intervention strategy, 106
Time-out procedure
as home-discipline strategy, 293–294
as intervention strategy, 59, 66
Times and procedures, identifying instructional, 173–174, 175
Timing, of intervention strategies, 106
Token reinforcement procedures, empirical studies on using, 404–418
The Tough Kid Book (Rhode, Jenson, and Reavis), 60, 65, 66, 263
Tracking system, for schoolwide discipline plan, 146
Transitions, managing, 167
Tribalism, gang affiliation as, 375
Triggers phase
behavioral characteristics of, 82–83
intervention strategies for, 103–105
Triple A Routine, 312–313
Truancy, violent crime and, 359
Tutoring, as outcome of office referral, 338

Unemployment, crime and, 362
United States
educational spending in, 34
school violence in, 25, 360–361, 371–372
societal violence in, 25, 359–362
United States Children's Defense Fund, 25
Universal interventions. *See also* Selected interventions
classroom social-skills training and, 245–252
defined, 57
Universal interventions *(continued)*
establishing, 61
identifying selected interventions through, 235
prevention/remediation of antisocial behavior through, 32
Second Step curriculum and, 322–325
usefulness of, 57–59
USA Today, 25
U.S. Department of Education, 64, 261, 325
U.S. Office of Juvenile Justice and Delinquency Prevention, 383
U.S. Office of Special Education Programs, 261, 325, 345, 346
U.S. Office of Technology Assessment, 383
Utah's BEST Project: Behavioral and Educational Strategies for Teachers (Reavis, Jenson, Kukic, and Morgan), 60, 65, 66

Variation, planned, 160
Verbal abuse, acceleration phase and, 86
Victims
antisocial students as, 221
of bullying, 190
Violations. *See also* Infractions
major, 136, 138, 330
procedures for managing, 140, 142, 145–146
Violence. *See also* Aggressive behavior; Juvenile delinquency
in American society, 25, 359–362
antisocial behavior and, 22–23
assumptions and facts about, 360
causes of, 361
characteristics of, 359–361
curriculum for preventing, 322–325
Violence *(continued)*
Fast Track program and, 373–374
increases in juvenile, 362, 363–364
intervention approaches to, 364–374
media and, 37–38, 68–69
mediation and, 369–370
prevention strategies for, 367, 438
recommendations for reducing, 362, 364–374
resources on, 383–384
in schools, 25, 360–361, 371–372
societal factors associated with, 362
steps for reducing, 366
trends on, 361–362
war on school, 436–439
Violence and Youth: Psychology's Response (APA), 37
Violence-prevention program, 322–325

Walker-McConnell Scale of Social Competence and School Adjustment (SSCSA), 225
Weapons
availability of, 359
in schools, 189, 379–380
We Don't Have Bullies Here (Besay), 214
Whining, acceleration phase and, 86
Whole-class approach, to social-skills training, 245–252
Who's Who among American High School Students, 373
Withdrawal, de-escalation phase and, 88
Work chores, as home-discipline strategy, 296, 297

Yale Child Welfare Research Program, 47

CREDITS

This page constitutes an extension of the copyright page. We have made every effort to trace the ownership of all copyrighted material and to secure permission from copyright holders. In the event of any question arising as to the use of any material, we will be pleased to make the necessary corrections in future printings. Thanks are due to the following authors, publishers, and agents for permission to use the material indicated.

Chapter 1: 8, Figure 1.1 from "A Construct Source Approach to the Assessment of Social Competence: Rationale, Technological Considerations, and Anticipated Outcomes," by H. M. Walker, L. K. Irvin, J. Noell, and G. H. S. Singer, in *Behavior Modification, 16* (1992), 448–474. Reprinted by permission.

Chapter 2: 35, Table 2.1 from *Beginning to Read: Thinking and Learning about Print,* by M. J. Adams. Copyright © 1990 MIT Press, Cambridge, MA. Adapted by permission.

Chapter 8: 192, Table 8.2 from "Bully/Victim Problems among School Children: Basic Facts and Effects of a School-Based Intervention Program," by D. Olweus. In D. J. Pepler & K. H. Rubin (Eds.), *The Development of Childhood Aggression,* pp. 411–446. Copyright © 1991 Lawrence Erlbaum. Reprinted by permission. **209–213,** Forms 8.1 and 8.2, and Tables 8.8, 8.9, and 8.10 from *RECESS: A Program for Reducing Negative-Aggressive Behavior,* by H. Walker, H. Hops, and C. Greenwood. Copyright © 1993 by Educational Achievement Systems, Seattle, WA. Reprinted by permission.

Chapter 10: 243–244, 255–257, and 258–260, Box 10.1 and Forms 10.1 and 10.2 from *The Walker Social Skills Curriculum: The ACCEPTS Program (A Curriculum for Children's Effective Peer and Teacher Skills),* by H. M. Walker, S. McConnell, D. Holmes, B. Todis, J. Walker, and N. Golden. Copyright © 1983 by Pro-Ed, Austin, Texas. Reprinted by permission. **262,** Box 10.2 from "Social Skills in School-Age Children and Youth: Issues and Best Practices in Assessment and Intervention," by H. M. Walker, I. E. Schwarz, M. Nippold, L. K. Irvin, and J. Noell. In *Topics in Language Disorders: Pragmatics and Social Skills in School Age Children and Adolescents, 14*(3), 70–82. Copyright © 1994 by Aspen Publisher, Inc., Gaithersburg, MD. Reprinted by permission.

Chapter 13: 373, Table 13.1 from *Who's Who among American High School Students.* Copyright © 1993 Educational Communications, Inc., Los Angeles. Adapted by permission.

Appendix A: 401, Figure A.1 from "Family Management Correlates of Antisocial Behavior among Middle School Boys," by E. Ramsey and H. M. Walker. In *Behavioral Disorders, 13*(3), 1988, 187–201. Reprinted by permission. **426–428,** Figures A.10, A.11, and A.12 from "The Use of Peer Monitors to Reduce Negative Interactions during Recess," by B. S. Dougherty, S. A. Fowler, and S. C. Paine. In *Journal of Applied Behavior Analysis, 18,* 1985, 141–153. Reprinted by permission.

Appendix B: 429–435, from "Society Is Failing Its Children, Forsaking Its Future," by James Hargreaves. In Eugene *Register-Guard,* Sunday, April 10, 1994, page 1B. Reprinted by permission.

Appendix C: 436–439, from "Generals in the War on School Violence," by Carla Marinucci and Scott Winokur. In *The San Francisco Examiner,* Sunday, June 5, 1994, page B-1. Reprinted by permission.

PHOTO CREDITS

3, Elizabeth Crews; **16,** Myrleen Ferguson Cate/PhotoEdit; **28,** Tom McKitterick/ Impact Visuals; **34,** Jim West/Meese Photo Research; **41,** Amy Etra/PhotoEdit; **49,** Elizabeth Crews; **62,** Kathleen Olson; **79,** Elizabeth Crews; **86,** Kathleen Olson; **102,** Elizabeth Crews; **137,** Kathleen Olson; **158,** Elizabeth Crews; **173,** Gale Zucker; **186,** Elizabeth Crews; **219,** David Young-Wolff/PhotoEdit; **242,** Robert Finken; **270,** Charles Gupton/Uniphoto; **292,** Myrleen Ferguson Cate/PhotoEdit; **292,** Michael Newman/PhotoEdit; **292,** Tony Freeman/PhotoEdit; **292,** Myrleen Ferguson Cate/ PhotoEdit; **311,** David Grossman

TO THE OWNER OF THIS BOOK:

We hope that you have found *Antisocial Behavior in School: Strategies and Best Practices*, useful. So that this book can be improved in a future edition, would you take the time to complete this sheet and return it? Thank you.

School and address: ______________________________

Department: ______________________________

Instructor's name: ______________________________

1. What I like most about this book is: ______________________________

____

____

2. What I like least about this book is: ______________________________

____

____

3. My general reaction to this book is: ______________________________

____

4. The name of the course in which I used this book is: ______________________________

____

5. Were all of the chapters of the book assigned for you to read? ______________________________

If not, which ones weren't? ______________________________

6. In the space below, or on a separate sheet of paper, please write specific suggestions for improving this book and anything else you'd care to share about your experience in using the book.

____

____

____

____

____

Optional:

Your name: ______________________________ Date: ______________________________

May Brooks/Cole quote you, either in promotion for *Antisocial Behavior in School: Strategies and Best Practices*, or in future publishing ventures?

Yes: __________ No: __________

Sincerely,

Hill M. Walker
Geoff Colvin
Elizabeth Ramsey

FOLD HERE

NO POSTAGE NECESSARY IF MAILED IN THE UNITED STATES

BUSINESS REPLY MAIL

FIRST CLASS PERMIT NO. 358 PACIFIC GROVE, CA

POSTAGE WILL BE PAID BY ADDRESSEE

ATT: *Hill M. Walker, Geoff Colvin, and Elizabeth Ramsey*

Brooks/Cole Publishing Company
511 Forest Lodge Road
Pacific Grove, California 93950-9968

FOLD HERE

Brooks/Cole is dedicated to publishing quality publications for education in the special education field. If you are interested in learning more about our publications, please fill in your name and address and request our latest special education catalogue, using this prepaid mailer.

Name: ______________________________

Street Address: ______________________________

City, State, and Zip: ______________________________

FOLD HERE

BUSINESS REPLY MAIL

FIRST CLASS PERMIT NO. 358 PACIFIC GROVE, CA

POSTAGE WILL BE PAID BY ADDRESSEE

ATT: *Special Education Catalogue*

Brooks/Cole Publishing Company
511 Forest Lodge Road
Pacific Grove, California 93950-9968

FOLD HERE